ARCTIC INSTITUTE OF NORTH AMERICA

ANTHROPOLOGY OF THE NORTH:

TRANSLATIONS FROM RUSSIAN SOURCES

Editor: HENRY N. MICHAEL

ARCTIC INSTITUTE OF NORTH AMERICA

ANTHROPOLOGY OF THE NORTH:

TRANSLATIONS FROM RUSSIAN SOURCES/NO. 2

Studies in Siberian Ethnogenesis

Edited by H. N. MICHAEL

PUBLISHED FOR THE ARCTIC INSTITUTE OF NORTH AMERICA

BY UNIVERSITY OF TORONTO PRESS

ANTHROPOLOGY OF THE NORTH: TRANS-
LATIONS FROM RUSSIAN SOURCES is supported by National Science Foundation
grants 11411 and 18865

INTRODUCTION

THE SEVENTEEN ARTICLES contained in the second number of the series ANTHRO-POLOGY OF THE NORTH: TRANSLATIONS FROM RUSSIAN SOURCES have been published in the original language during the decade 1950–1960. They represent various facets of Soviet anthropology with a definite emphasis on the historical approach in solving questions of national origin. While this methodology is not too unusual, some of the sources employed are—records of the Siberian tax and fur-tribute collectors of the 17th to 19th centuries and, in the cases of the tribes of southern Siberia, Chinese chronicles. To be sure, the historical method is not the only one employed. The evidences of comparative linguistics, of physical anthropology, archaeology, material culture, and folklore are all brought into play.

These articles are direct translations rather than adaptations. While adaptations may result in smoother reading, they more often than not lose the "feel" of the original, and sometimes its accuracy.

In a complex undertaking such as this, the help of many was needed. Ten translators participated.* The technically difficult articles on the origins of the Koybals and Nganasans were translated by Mrs. Penelope Rainey and Mr. Gregory Jacoby respectively. Dr. and Mrs. Stephen P. Dunn ably translated Tretyakov's article on Oka-Volga place names and Dolgikh's *The Population of the Olenek and Upper Anabar River Basins.*

Dr. Schuyler Cammann of the University of Pennsylvania has read critically those articles that quote Chinese sources and contain Chinese terms and has adjusted the transliterations to conform to prevalent English usage. Dr. Lawrence Krader of the American University has helped with the Mongolian and Turkic terms that abound in the articles dealing with the ethnohistory of the peoples of southern Siberia. Dr. Krader has also offered fruitful suggestions concerning the translation of some of the more difficult passages from "Siberian" Russian. Mrs. Natalie Frenkley of the *Arctic Bibliography* staff has been of great help in the editorial processing of several of the articles.

In transliterating the place names the system recommended by the United States Board on Geographic Names was used with the exception that the trans-literation of the Russian "soft sign" with an apostrophe was omitted. In cases of well-established equivalents of place names in the English language, they were preferentially used: thus, *Moscow* rather than *Moskva*, *Tien-shan* rather than *Tyan-Shan*, and a few others.

Names of tribes and nations, both ancient and modern, presented especial difficulty. Where these names originated from Chinese sources, the Wade-Giles system was used. For instance, the collective name which when transliterated from Chinese into Russian is rendered as "Tele" becomes "T'ieh-lê." Names of some of the ancient peoples are well established in English and presented no particular problem. Thus, *Sogdian* rather than *Sogdiets* and *Bactrian* rather than

*Mr. Christopher Bird, Washington, D.C.; Dr. and Mrs. Stephen P. Dunn, New York; Mrs. Lyda Franzussoff, Washington, D.C.; Miss Carol-Joyce Howell, Philadelphia; Mr. Gregory Jacoby, Washington, D.C.; Mrs. Ludmila Krasovskaya, Washington, D.C.; Mrs. Julia Mants-vetov, Washington, D.C.; Mrs. Penelope Rainey, Valley Forge, Pennsylvania; Mrs. Lilian Volins, Washington, D.C.

Baktriets were selected. However, with other tribal names another type of difficulty arises, namely the question of what constitutes prevalent and/or best usage, i.e., it becomes more than just adherence to this or that transliteration system. Here selection was made on the basis of modern usage among the few English-writing specialists in the field of Siberian ethnology both in North America and in the United Kingdom: thus, *Koybal* rather than *Koibal*; *Buryat*, not *Buriat*; *Kirgiz*, not *Kirghiz*; *Nanay*, not *Nanai*; and so on.

The varied spellings of the names of some of the Siberian tribes by different Russian-writing authors should be pointed out. Thus, one author may prefer *Shologon* to *Sologon*, *Khatygyn* to *Khatygin*, *Khangalas* to *Kangalas*, and with another it will be *vice versa*. This compounds the difficulty of transliteration.

A few passages of ideological content have been omitted as being irrelevant to the subject. These passages usually contain quotations from the writings of J. V. Stalin on philology in connection with his denunciation of N. Ya. Marr's linguistic theories. The places of omission are indicated in the text. However, not all such passages have been omitted. In order to acquaint the reader with the "climate" prevalent in ethnological writings of the early 1950's, several such passages are presented in full.

February, 1962   HENRY N. MICHAEL

CONTENTS

GLOSSARY

alban—also *alba*; a tax or tribute paid by the dependent Mongol (see *kyshtym*)

amanat—a hostage; usually taken to secure a conquest or the payment of tribute

artel—Russian term designating "association for common work"

aymak—among the Mongols a generation, a tribe; later a small administrative unit, sometimes designated in Russian as a *volost*

bednyak—a poor peasant (see *srednyak* and *kulak*)

daruga—also *darga*; a captain-general of a league of banners under the Manchu imperial government

Gegen—a title bestowed since 1691 by the Manchu Emperor on a high Lama Buddhist reincarnation for worldly, political achievement

guberniya—in tsarist Russia a province, a large administrative district

Hutukhtu—a title bestowed on a high Lama Buddhist reincarnation for exceptional ecclesiastical merit

khosun—a hero of Tungus epic tales

kolkhoz—Russian abbreviation for collective farm or enterprise

kray—a very large administrative district usually subdivided into *oblasts*

kulak—a rich peasant

kyshtim, kyshtym—members of dependent tribes paying tax or tribute to another tribe

nasleg—among northern Siberian tribes originally an overnight camp; "clan" territory; a Yakut nomadic village of a dozen yurts; later a small administrative district

oblast—modern administrative district of large or intermediate size; may be part of a *kray*; subdivided into *rayons* and *soviets*

okrug—national territory of relatively small groups of native (non-Russian) peoples

prokolka—the spearing of wild deer at river crossings—central and northern Siberia

rayon—small administrative district, a subdivision of an *oblast*

sait—general term for Mongol aristocrat

Shanyu—an emperor of the Huns (Hsiu Nu)

shulenge—Kalmuck administrative office (tax collector)

soviet—council; administratively, a small territorial unit

srednyak—a peasant of intermediate means

taisha—a prince among the Mongols; usually leader of a tribe; among the Buryats a clan leader, a noble of low degree

ulus—village; community; later small administrative district; in tsarist Russia equivalent to a *volost*

uprava—administrative district, now obsolete

uyezd—small administrative district, now obsolete

volost—in tsarist Russia a small administrative district

yurt, yurta—a movable tent of nomads consisting of lattice work over which skins or felt was stretched

zaisan, saisan—among the Eleut Mongols a title designating higher nobility serving under a prince

zemlitsa—estate; grant of land; later a small administrative district

zveno—lit. "link," a small work unit of 6 to 12 people

STUDIES IN SIBERIAN ETHNOGENESIS

I. S. GURVICH

THE ETHNIC AFFILIATION OF THE POPULATION IN THE NORTHWEST OF THE YAKUT A.S.S.R.*

THE FORMATION OF NEW and larger ethnic groupings among the peoples of the North after the October revolution as a result of a drawing together of separate, formerly isolated, ethnographic groups is a problem hardly touched upon in our literature.

Often we come across entirely opposite tendencies, seeking to ignore new ethnic formations and to regard unified peoples as a series of independent ethnic groups. Thus, on ethnographic maps the population in the northwest of the Yakut A.S.S.R. (Olenek and Anabar river basins) appears as Evenk, while actually it is Yakut, albeit Yakut differing in economic and cultural traits from the Yakut population of the central regions of Yakutia. The correctness of assigning to the Evenks parts of the population of the lower Lena and lower Yana arouses considerable doubt.

The study of the processes of the consolidation of nationalities in the Siberian north stands as a formidable task before historians and ethnographers. In the present article we shall limit ourselves to an examination of the ways of formation of the Yakut people and the Yakut nation in northwest Yakutia—in the most remote, isolated, and inaccessible regions of the Yakut A.S.S.R. The study of the history of the population of the Olenek and Anabar river basins enables us to trace the evolvement of this northwestern group of Yakut reindeer-breeders.

In the 1620's and 1630's, about the time of the penetration of the Russian servitor gentry† and merchants into the Olenek and Anabar river basins, these regions, with the exception of the lower reaches of the Anabar basin, were populated by Tungus tribes. In the 1620's the Mangazeysk state officials were already collecting a fur tribute from the Tungus nomadizing in the upper reaches of the Olenek. In the tribute book of the Mangazeysk *uyezd* for the year 7132‡ (1623-4), the collection of tribute from the Azyan tribe of the Olenek Tungus is first referred to: "In the Pyandinsk winter quarters from new people from the Olenek river, the Achen clan, nine people paid five sables each."[1]

Yelisey Yurev (Buza) from Ustyug, the first to reach the mouth of the Olenek by sea, also discovered Tungus in the lower reaches of the Olenek. According to the report of Yurev's companion, the state official P. Lazarev, the detachment traveled up the Olenek as far as the Piripta river "and at the mouth of the Piripta river they caught a Tungus and from him took the sovereign's tribute of five "forties" [200] for the past year, 145 [i.e., 7145], and from the Olenek river they took this hostage to the Lena at the mouth of the Molodo river."[2]

*Translated from *Sovetskaya etnografiya*, 1950, no. 4, pp. 150–168.
†[*Sluzhilye lyudi* in the original.—Editor.]
‡[An archaic Russian system of noting years.—Translator.]

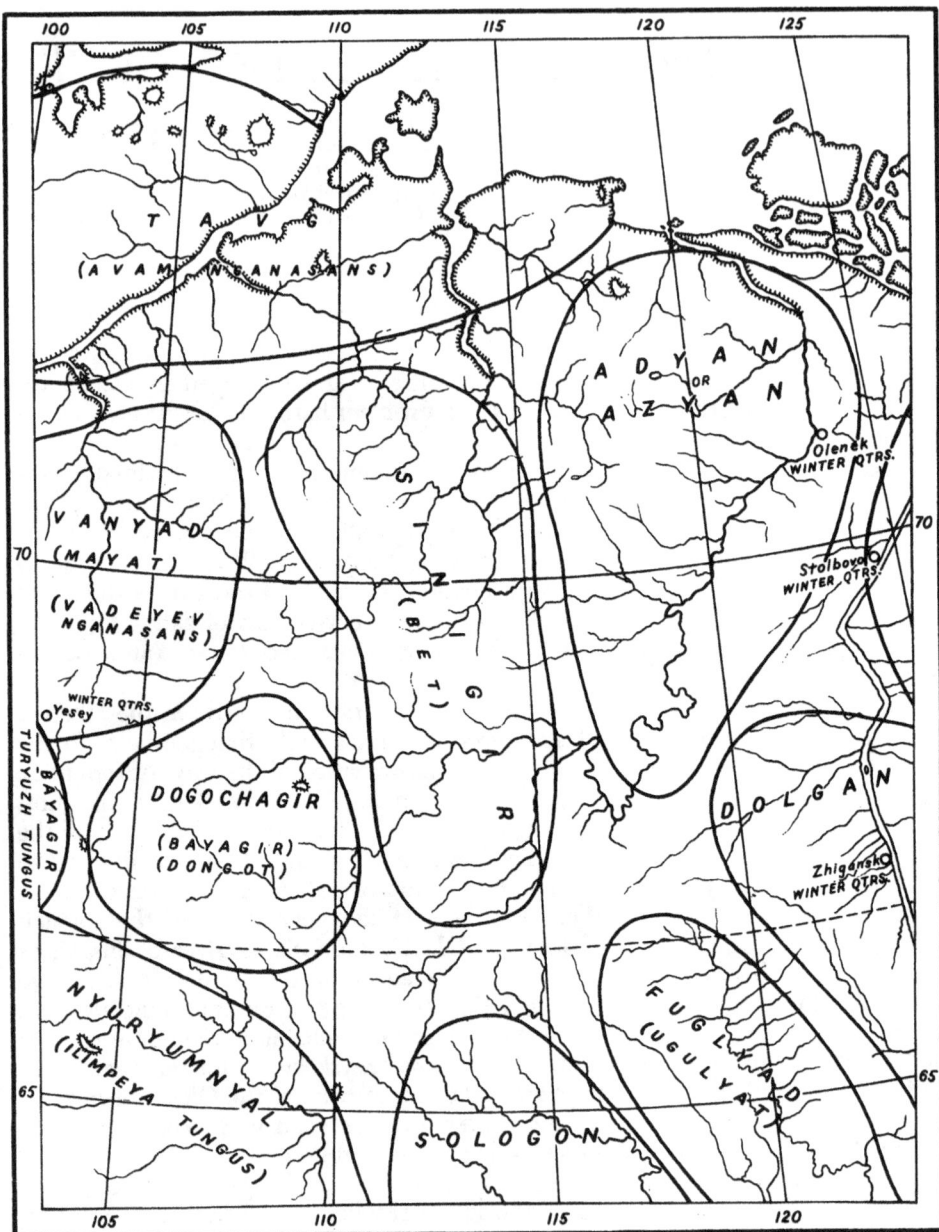

FIGURE 1. Distribution of tribes in the Anabar and Olenek river basins in the middle of the 17th century. (In parentheses are shown the names of the descendants of tribes and clans existing in the 17th century.)

One of the earliest references to the collection of tribute from the Olenek Tungus is found in the tribute book of the Yakutsk uyezd for the year 7148, i.e., for 1639–40: "The sovereign's tribute was collected by the Yeniseysk official Druzhinka Chistyakov and his men in the year 148 from the Tungus leader, Omnegin, the father, from Papyrok and his children and relations, 67 sables with tails, seven sables without tails and two Tungus sable coats."[3]

The population of the Olenek basin invariably is called Tungus also in other documents of the 1640's and 1650's—in tribute books, in the reports of the officials Ivan Rebrov, Kuzma Suzdelets, and Mikhail Telitsin, and in petitions of tribute-payers.

Tungus were also discovered on the Anabar by the forward party of the Mangazeya officials under the command of Vassili Sychev in 1644.[4] They inhabited the entire basin of the Anabar with the exception of its lower reaches. In these lower reaches and farther on, along the seacoast to the west, lived the ancestors of a part of the Avam Nganasans, the Tavgs. In 139 (1631) there were 80 adult Tavg males in the lower reaches of the Anabar. In the 1640's, perhaps under pressure of the Tungus, the Tavgs migrated west beyond the Khatanga.

The majority of the Olenek Tungus belonged to the Azyan tribe. In the middle of the 17th century this tribe evidently occupied all of the lower and middle course of the Olenek. The Azyans frequented the Lena, the upper reaches of the Olenek and Anabar, and reached Lake Yesey.

In 1639–40 three hostages were held at the Yesey winter quarters. Two of these belonged to the Vonyadyr tribe and one to the Azyan. In 1644 the Mangazeysk authorities took as hostages on the Anabar two people from the Azyan Tungus.[5] However, Lake Yesey and the Anabar were evidently alien territory to the Azyans. Members of the Azyan tribe considered the Olenek their basic area of habitation: "Yet, from time immemorial our home has been on the Olenek."[6] In 1667 "the tribute-paying Olenek Tungus of the Azyan clan, Katukanka and his people with all their clansmen" in their petition reported that hunters had settled

on the lower Olenek river at the mouth of the Pura in our old homeland in which places we, your orphans, Great Sovereign, hunt for your tribute . . . please, Great Sovereign, order the officer Vassily Ignatyev with his 10-man cossack detachment to go to them, to the hunters, on the Olenek river and tell them that they should not hunt sables in our home territories on the Pura and the Golimar [Kelimer] and lay waste to our hunting grounds.[7]

Another Tungus tribe, close to the Azyan, the Sinigir (Chinigir), or possibly Siligir, is more rarely referred to in documents. Data on the distribution of the Sinigir are most fragmentary. It was imparted in the instructions to governor Golovin: "and on those rivers, on the Chona and the Vilyuy, there live many of the Sinigir and Nanagir people."[8]

In 1644 two members of the Sinigir clan were being held hostage at the Yesey winter quarters. After the escape of the hostages in that same year the authorities seized new ones: six people from the Vonyadyr clan, one hostage from the "Mugal clan," and one from the "Sinigir clan." In 1647 the officials under the command of Yakov Semenov, who had been sent to the Anabar to relieve "Vassili Sychev and his men," wintering on the Kheta, made a long and difficult march to the Yesey winter quarters "to seek out the Sinigir hostage Lagon," and "brought back this Sinigir hostage Lagon to the Kheta in a healthy state on the 29th day of April." The officials, along with the Sinigir hostage, headed for the Anabar in search of the Tungus. "And in the Olenek range with the Tungus Lagon and on the rivers of the locality did Vassili Sychev with his men and Boris Lukyanov, all together, seek out the Tungus but did not find any."[9] Evidently, certain information was available to the Mangazeysk departmental headquarters to the effect that the Sinigir were nomadizing on the Anabar or its tributaries. This should explain the fact that the officials were given a Sinigir hostage from the Yesey winter quarters.

TABLE 1
Number of Tribute-Payers at the Olenek Winter Quarters from 1644 to 1712

Year	Tribute collected*	Number of tribute-payers	Number of tribute-payers appearing at the tribute collection
1644	324 sables, 25 in local tax	64	Not shown
1645	—	85	85
1646	494 sables, 24 in local tax	99	Not shown
1647	368 sables, 30 in local tax	74	Not shown
1648	475 sables, 27 in local tax	95	Not shown
1649	538 sables, 27 in local tax	110	Not shown
1650	453 sables, 21 in local tax	91	Not shown
1651	450 sables, 22 in local tax	90	Not shown
1653	451 sables, 22 in local tax	156	—
	Collected 233 sables	—	68
1654	93 sables	39	—
1655	66 sables, 1 in local tax	26 plus 14 departures	28
1657	84 sables	33 plus 12 departures	37
1662	112 sables	38 plus 4 arrivals	42
1665	113 sables	45 plus 1 arrival	42
1666	116 sables	42	?
1669	126 sables, 1 red fox	47	?
1673	97 sables	41	38
1678	101 sables, 3 red foxes	60	—
	Collected 74 sables, 7 red foxes		43
1679	93 sables, 8 red foxes	58	—
1681	94 sables, 9 red foxes	59	—
	Collected 50 sables, 1 silver fox, 12 red foxes	—	40
1682	93 sables, 31 red foxes	73	—
	Collected 44 sables, 7 silver foxes, 35 red foxes		48
1683	91 sables, 31 red foxes	92	—
1684	163 sables, 34 red foxes	180	—
1685	182 sables, 34 red foxes	180	—
1686	212 sables, 35 red foxes	167	—
	Collected 105 sables, 34 red foxes	—	102
1687	94 sables, 9 silver foxes, 53 red foxes	—	—
1688	201 sables, 38 red foxes	163	—
	Collected 94 sables, 7 silver foxes, 49 red foxes		104
1689	196 sables, 35 red foxes	158	—
1692	53 sables, 37 red foxes	69	—
	Collected 2 sables, 1 silver fox, 37 red foxes		35
1693	53 sables, 36 red foxes	68	—
1703	56 sables, 51 red foxes	88	—
	Collected 25 sables, 33 red foxes	—	57
1704	56 sables, 53 red foxes	90	—
1705	56 sables, 53 red foxes	90	—
	Collected 24 sables, 27 red foxes	—	52
1706	56 sables, 56 red foxes	93	—
	Collected 23 sables, 31 red foxes	—	54
1707	56 sables, 56 red foxes	93	—
1708	56 sables, 58 red foxes	95	—
	Collected ?	—	50
1710	59 sables, 60 red foxes	103	—
	Collected ?	—	115
1712	59 sables, 79 red foxes	119	—
	Collected 21 sables, 1 silver fox, 50 red foxes	—	126

*[The "sorok" or "bundle of forty" was converted by multiplication.—Translator.]

Note: The number collected is based on the factual collection for the year and on "lists of estimates."

The table was compiled from the tribute books of the Yakutsk uyezd, kept in the Central State Archive for Ancient Documents.

One should also connect the tribal Sinigir with one of the large tributaries of the upper Olenek, the Siligir river, with its tributaries, the Orto-Siligir, the Allara-Siligir, and others.

All these facts allow us to assume that the habitat of the Sinigir tribe was the region of the upper course of the Olenek and its tributaries, and possibly also the area of the upper sources of the Anabar, the Bolshaya Konamka, and Malaya Konamka rivers.

Data on the population of the Olenek and Anabar river basins appear in documents only after 1640. In 1644 the number of people paying tribute on the Olenek was not less than 64, since in addition to local tax* there were collected 8 lots of 40 sables each, i.e., 320 sables, as tribute.[10] In the 1640's there was collected from each tribute-payer on the Olenek five sables per year and a sixth for local tax.[11] Among the tribute-payers were also adolescents who paid a part-tax. Consequently, dividing the total amount of collected sables by the full-tax of five sables, we get a minimum figure of 64 for tribute-payers in 1644.

Documents on the tribute reflect only the number of tribute-payers, that is, of male adults or adolescents. Taking the number of tribute-payers, i.e., the adult male population, as 25 per cent of the total population and rounding off the number of tribute-payers to the higher round number—since, evidently, a part of the Tungus hid among their relatives from the tribute exaction—for the period 1645–52, one can propose the likely population figure of 600–700 persons of both sexes—130–160 tribute-payers (Table 1).

In 1652–3, as a result of a smallpox epidemic, there was a sharp reduction in the population on the Olenek. Out of 156 persons recorded on the rolls, 85 did not appear at the tribute exaction. As to the reason for their not appearing, the tribute book contains an entry that "those Tungus died of smallpox during the past year, 159, and henceforth those sables and the collection thereof are stricken from the lists."[12] During the next year, 1653, the epidemic continued; 54 additional payers died of smallpox. As a result of this and the defeat of the Olenek Tungus in 1653 by the Vonyadyr Tungus, there remained on the Olenek, according to the list, only 39 tribute-payers, i.e., 160–170 persons of both sexes.

During the following 25 years the number of tribute-payers on the Olenek oscillated between 38 and 45 persons. An idea of the number of tribute-payers on the Anabar is given in Table 2.

With 1678, the Olenek population increases. In 1678, 60 tribute-payers were recorded in the lists, and in 1682 there were 73.[13] In 1686 the number of tribute-payers reached a record figure for the 17th century: 163 persons of whom 102 appeared for the tribute exaction.[14]

The reasons for the population increase on the Olenek during the last decades of the 17th century are entirely clear. Beginning in 1678 not only the Tungus but "Yakuts and Tungus" were recorded in the tribute books. The population increase occurred because of the migration of Yakuts from the central Yakut areas. Seeking refuge from the tribute collections as early as the 1630's and 1640's, the Yakuts headed for the Vilyuy river basin and down the Lena to Zhigansk and Stolby. In the 1650's and 1660's these areas were already sufficiently populated and the stream of Yakut refugees pushed on farther, taking over "strange remote rivers"—the Olenek, Anabar, Yana (lower reaches), and Kolyma. The penetration of the Yakuts into the Olenek and Anabar basins was eased by the sharp drop in the Tungus population on those rivers, a consequence of the

*[*Pominka* is an old word for a "tithe" of the local authorities apart from the tribute paid to the Russian state.—Translator.]

TABLE 2

NUMBER OF ANABAR TUNGUS PAYING TRIBUTE FROM 1653 TO 1681

Year	Tribute collected, no. of sables	Number of tribute-payers according to data from the tribute collection	Number of tribute-payers according to documents
1653	64	22	—
1654	64	22	—
1655	42	16	—
1656	36	12	—
1658	33	11	—
1659	—	—	10
1661	—	—	10
1662	—	—	10
1664	—	—	7
1665	—	—	8
1666	24	8	—
1667	—	—	8
1668	—	—	8
1668–78	—	—	8
1679	—	—	7
1680	—	—	6
1681	—	—	6

Notes: The column entitled "Number of tribute-payers according to data from the tribute collection" has been filled only in those instances when the documents did not reveal data on the number of payers.

This table was compiled on the basis of B. O. Dolgikh's manuscript: Rodovoy i plemennoy sostav narodnostey severa sredney Sibiri (Clan and tribal composition among the peoples of the north of central Siberia).

epidemics referred to and of internecine conflicts. In 1640 even, at the mouth of the Molodo river where the Olenek Tungus were paying tribute, 23 Yakuts were also paying.[15]

In 1669, the Zhigansk administrator Petr Yaryshkin of the servitor gentry* reported to the Yakut governor Prince Ivan Boryatinsky:

In the past years the persons under the Zhigany [Zhigansk] administration have allowed tribute-paying Yakuts to go onto the Olenek river with wives and children in the amount of about 100 souls and more and in Zhigany with the Great Sovereign's tribute these did not appear, and other tribute-paying Yakuts, inciting tribute-paying Yakuts from Yakutia to flee, fled themselves over the mountains from the Olenek to the Central winter quarters on the Vilyuy because there are people on the Olenek with wives and children who are let go without an order by the Great Sovereign. And those Yakut and those wives and children will not be brought to Zhigany from the Olenek as formerly and the Great Sovereign's tribute will be very much underfulfilled.[16]

The migration of the Yakuts to the Olenek was not immediately reflected in the tribute books of the Olenek winter quarters. Only in the mid-1670's do Yakuts begin to be recorded as permanent tribute-payers on the Olenek.

To what social stratum these Yakut trans-migrants belonged can be deduced from a number of documents. Thus in the name-listing tribute book of the

*[Boyarskiy syn in the original.—Editor.]

Zhigansk winter quarters for 1640, one sees that all 72 of the Zhigansk Tungus paid three sables each, while the newly arrived Yakuts, who were generally at the bottom of the social stratum, paid a smaller tax.[17]

On the Olenek the newly come Yakuts paid one or two sables or one red fox, just like Tungus adolescents. Many "writs" sent to the Olenek to trace runaway bondsmen and debtors characterize quite adequately the make-up of the Yakut migrants. Thus, in 1682 the Zhigansk tribute-collector Zakhar Shikeyev reported on the capture of a runaway Yakut girl, Kuchineyka: "Fulfilling the order of the Great Sovereign and your commands, my governor, I sent on that same day, September 23, three cossacks for that runaway Yakut girl to the Olenek winter quarters to the official Artemi Krupetskiy, which girl those cossacks brought back to the Zhigansk winter quarters."[18]

The same Zakhar Shikeyev reported that another runaway girl, Tomotka, was found on the Olenek. In 1686 an official, Ivan Lytkin, was given an order "to seek in Zhigany and on the Olenek the runaway bondsman Sakharo Bultekeyev and his children Sylrysto and Kuter and his wife Namycheyka."[19] In the same year Andrey Amosov was given a "writ" to apprehend "in Zhigany or at the Olenek winter camp the runaway house-serfs of the cossack Maxim Mukhoplev and the Yakuts who incited them to run away."[20] The majority of the migrant Yakuts belonged to the "Suburban" Yakutsk *volosts*, the Kangalasy, Batulin, and other volosts.

The Olenek and Anabar regions, unfit for the horse- and cattle-breeding customary to the Yakuts, attracted the poorer of them by an abundance of wild reindeer and the possibility of hunting these at river crossings. In 1681 there was a famine on the Olenek as a result of a lack of wild reindeer (change in their migratory routes). Concerning this, the Zhigansk tribute-collector Zakhar Shikeyev reported:

And some Yakuts from the Olenek river went off to the Central Vilyuy winter quarters, others to the Anabar river, and still others came to Zhigany on the Krasnoye and others went off to unknown areas. And from the Olenek river many went to the Krasny Pesok [Red Sand] in Zhigany over the first snowy route with wives and children and many all but died from hunger and the townsman Isaak did die from hunger and the Yakuts left the Olenek because there was more starvation on the Olenek river, the Yakuts caught not a single animal on the Olenek in spring or fall.[21]

"Animals" (*kyyl*) is the name for wild reindeer on the Olenek even today. From an accounting of those tribute-paying Yakuts "departed" from the Olenek it appears that 17 Yakuts went to the Central Vilyuy winter quarters, and 10 Yakuts and three Russians went to the Anabar.[21]

After 1683, the population on the Olenek again increased, this time not only because of the arriving Yakuts but also because of the Yesey Tungus who "had defeated the officer Ilyushka Ryabov and his men" and resettled in Yakutsk uyezd.[22] Before 1686, these Tungus had paid tribute on the Olenek.

In the 1690's the population on the Olenek declined in comparison with the previous decade since the Yesey Tungus nomadized back into the area of the Mangazeysk uyezd. This decline was somewhat compensated by the flight to the Olenek and Anabar of the Zhigansk Yakuts and Tungus trying to get away from "pestilent infections," although the epidemic also affected the Olenek winter quarters. In 1693, the Zhigansk official Stepan Krivogoronitsin, reporting on deaths due to the epidemic, wrote, among other things: "And some alien Tungus and Yakuts fled the pestilent infections along tributary rivers . . . and I Stenka

[Stepan] sent two cossacks to find tribute-paying Tungus and Yakuts among these aliens on the Olenek and tributary rivers and I also sent two people to the Anabar river to look for tribute-paying Yakuts and Tungus."[23]

Thus, the last 30 years of the 17th century were characterized by a large flow of population into the Olenek basin, especially of the immigrant Yakut population. Indeed, the sources show quite specifically that at the end of the 17th century the Yakuts had become permanent residents of the Olenek and Anabar river basins. The spread of Yakuts into these basins was reflected in the *Atlas of Siberia* compiled in 1701 by Semyon Remezov. Under a conditional designation of the Olenek winter camp is written: "Yakuts live at the Olenek winter quarters. It takes five days and nights to go down river from the Olenek river at the mouth of the Lena to the sea, and many tribute-paying alien Tungus and Yakuts from various volosts live there."[24] Symbols for nomad camps are also indicated along the Anabar. Under them is the caption: "Yakuts live (on the) Anabar river."

To understand relations between ethnic groups in the 17th and 18th centuries in the Olenek and Anabar river basins we have to take into consideration the Russian settlers. With the first detachments of state officials to the Olenek and Anabar there also penetrated groups of Russian merchants and trappers. In 1637 with the small detachment of Yelisey Yurev (Buza) there came to the Olenek 40 men, trappers.[25] Some of them remained on the Olenek after the detachment of cossacks had gone on to the Lena. In 1643 the Olenek trappers submitted a petition pleading that officials be dispatched to them since they were suffering from attacks by the Tungus. In 1657–8 to the "inquiries" from Anabar was attached a signed petition of 41 trappers.[26]

The trappers lived in small groups of four to six people per winter camp. Some equipped themselves at their own expense but many were compelled to get all necessities, on most difficult terms, from usurers and merchants. Hunters lacking all means of acquiring equipment sought service with fur traders who sent out hunting expeditions for sables. In 1659, Mikhail Maximov was sent with 12 workers to the Olenek and with them were sent "stores of bread and other supplies worth a custom's price of 2325 rubles, 11 altyns* and 4 dengi.†"[27]

Unlike the state officials, the trappers went off for long periods to remote rivers, taking their wives with them, if they had them, or buying women on the way from the Yakuts or from the local population.

The trappers, especially the penurious group, did not hasten back to Yakutsk where they would have to pay their debts with servitude. In connection with this, as early as 1661 an order was given Mikhail Shadra, an official in the Zhigansk winter camp, by the Governor Golenishchev-Kutuzov:

For Mishka‡ . . . to go forth from Zhigany with a guide and his men by sledge taking the winter trail over the mountains on to the Olenek river because in this year, 169, at assembly in the fort of Yakutsk it became known to the Governor and Steward Ivan Fedorovich, the Great Golenishchev-Kutuzov, that there live on the Olenek river about 40 trappers or more for the past five or six years who are hunting sables on sable-hunting grounds and are not paying tithes on the sables of the Great Sovereign and are trading these sables among themselves without duties and tithes, buying and selling without paying head tax and duties.[28]

In 1660 an order was given to Khariton Belyai, an official, "to seek out in

*[Ancient Russian coin worth 3 kopeks.—Editor.]
†[Ancient "coppers"; ancient coin of lowest denomination.—Editor.]
‡[Diminutive for Mikhail.—Editor.]

Zhigany and on the Olenek" and to bring back to Yakutsk the trapper Yakov, known as Zyryanin, a debtor of the clerk Yermolin at the Yakutsk administration.[29]

The migration of Russians to the Olenek and the Anabar from Yakutsk increased particularly in the 1670's. In 1677 as a result of "lack of bread," townspeople in large numbers were permitted to go to Zhigany "to fend for themselves."[30] And although it was not permitted to let them go further, some of the poorer townsmen nevertheless went on to the Olenek (since in later orders of the Zhigansk administrator they were ordered to return immediately from the Olenek and Anabar). Orders for the return of townspeople from the Olenek were also given earlier than 1677.[31] Evidently to return the townsmen and trappers was not easy since in 1682 the Zhigansk administrator sent the cossack Kipriyan to the Anabar "to send back those tribute-payers and townsmen from the Anagar (Anabar) to Shigany or make sure that they send tribute and head tax from the Anabar each year on time in the fall without its having to be sent for."[32]

The Olenek and Anabar, by their remoteness, attracted fugitives and the malcontent. In 1684, Kuzma Mikhaylov, a "free-lancer" hired by the cossacks, fled to the Olenek;[33] in the same year some of the cossacks sent to the Kolyma appeared in the Olenek winter quarters.[34]

From settled fur-traders, fugitive townsmen, and children of cossacks a basic contingent of Russian "old-timer" population formed in northwestern Yakutia. The trappers, mostly people who had come from the Pomorye,* were familiar with the sea and life in the taiga and easily adapted to conditions in the northern regions of Yakutia. Surrounded by Tungus and Yakuts, they quickly became familiar with their language and intermarried with the local population. Evidently the more advanced Russian culture of that period penetrated to regions of the north both into the remote heartland and the periphery, principally through trappers who lived close to the natives.

Thus, at the end of the 17th century the permanent population in the Olenek and Anabar river basins consisted of aboriginal Tungus, Yakuts, and Russians.

Documents of the first quarter of the 18th century bear witness to significant migrations of Yakuts to the Olenek. In 1710, at the Olenek winter quarters, tribute was collected from 57 newly come Yakuts.[35] In 1712, 56 additional persons —"newly come 'suburban' tribute-paying Yakuts from various neighboring volosts" —arrived on the Olenek.[36] In the same year, tribute was collected at the Zhigansk winter quarters from 128 "newly come tribute-paying Yakuts."[37]

The stream of migrant Yakuts moved along the old route from Zhigansk. Many of the newly arrived Yakuts did not settle on the Olenek but either returned or moved on to the Mangazeysk uyezd. Thus, in 1712, of the 119 persons listed on the tribute lists of the Olenek winter quarters, 49 did not appear for the tribute exaction.

In the 1720's the number of Yakuts had already surpassed that of the Tungus in the Zhigansk and Olenek winter quarters. In 1721, of the 465 tribute-paying persons enumerated at the Olenek and Zhigansk winter camp,[38] only 115 belonged to the aboriginal population, and 350 were newcomers from various volosts of Yakutia.

With the decline of the sable industry on the Olenek at the end of the 17th and beginning of the 18th century, interest of the administration of Yakutia in the northwestern periphery of the Lena *kray* diminished. Perhaps it was for this very reason that the stream of Yakut settlers, seeking refuge from the onus of

*[The southern coast of the White sea.—Translator.]

tribute and taxes, increased still further. On the Olenek and Anabar the Yakut fugitives could hide, even though temporarily, from oppression by the administration and rich men of the *ulus*. Finding themselves in a northern environment, the Yakut livestock-breeders took on the Tungus way of life and were forced to get their subsistence from hunting wild reindeer and from fishing. The Russian settlers also integrated with the local population.

In 1735, Lt. Pronchishchev, a member of the Great Northern Expedition led by Captain V. Bering, found a small settlement at the mouth of the Olenek consisting of 20 families of Russian trappers. Up-river from the settlement, according to Pronchishchev, were the nomads' camps of the Tungus and Yakuts.[39] Isolated winter camps of Russian trappers, apparently established in the 17th century, still existed in the first half of the 18th century at the mouths of rivers and bays on the seacoast from the Olenek to the Khatanga. In 1736, Lt. Pronchishchev discovered a winter hut of a Russian trapper at the mouth of the Khatanga on the left bank. Evidently settled or half-settled Yakuts lived in a number of places, just like the Russian trappers. In 1739, the geodesist Chekin found half-settled Yakuts at the mouth of the Taymyra.[40] Valuable additions to the testimony of Pronchishchev are several entries in the diary of Kh. P. Laptev: "Here (at the mouth of the Olenek—Author) some 10 families of Russian trappers have lived in winter huts for a long time, who, having married native women, have become closely bound to the newly baptized Yakuts, and are like them in nature and customs."[41] Laptev found a similar population not only at the mouth of the Olenek but on the Khatanga as well.

The observations of participants in the Great Northern Expedition confirm the process, delineated by us from archival materials, of a blending of three ethnic components in the Olenek and Anabar basins. Especially interesting is the information provided by Laptev. Apparently in the 1840's the process of assimilation of the Russian old-time settlers by the Yakuts had already progressed very far. Also of great value are Laptev's reports that the entire population of the lower reaches [of these rivers] took part in the killing of reindeer fording the rivers. Thus the economic activity of the Tungus, Yakuts, and Russians with the decline of the sable industry in the 1730's and 1740's began to find a common level.

Our sources on the history of northwestern Yakutia in the second half of the 18th century are extremely meager. A few facts on the population of the lower reaches of the Lena and Olenek in the 1780's can be drawn from answers of the Zhigansk district officer Podchertkov to the Yakutsk commandant Marklovsky in connection with an order of the Irkutsk vice-regency to collect historical-ethnographic data on the population. From these answers it follows that Yakuts and Tungus who were united in three "village clans"[42] lived in the Zhigansk *okrug* in 1786. Declining to offer the description demanded, the Zhigansk district officer, among other things, reported: "the Yakuts of hereabouts inform me that, as far as they remember, when they were still in their early years, they had heard from older people that [their] ancestors, Yakuts from the vicinity of Yakutsk, had come here to Zhigansk and settled and this is why their speech, and faith and rites are similar to those of Yakuts from the areas around Yakutsk."[42] Thus, in the 1780's the migration from Yakutsk had not yet been erased from the memory of the Yakuts. The meager sources for the second half of the 18th century and the first half of the 19th century allow us to suppose that in the Olenek and Anabar basins the process of mixing of the Russian settled trappers with the Yakuts was continuing as well as that of the Yakuts with the Tungus.

While the immigrant population—Yakuts and Russians—was acquiring the Tungus way of life, skills and methods of a hunting economy worked out over centuries, the local population was adopting the Yakut language, Russian technology, and elements of Russian spiritual culture.

According to scattered data in the literature and information collected by us from on-the-spot interrogations it can be presumed that through the 19th century the areas of northeastern Yakutia continued to fill up with Yakuts from the central volosts and occasional Russian exiles (the lower reaches of the Olenek [were settled] during the first half of the 19th century).

The social composition of Yakut immigrants on the Olenek and Anabar in the 19th century, as far as our sources allow us to judge, was more varied than before the activity of the First Tribute Commission. The basic group of Yakut migrants, evidently, consisted of the Yakut poor, suffering from insults and oppression of the Yakut *toyens* [chieftains]; another group of migrants consisted of the Yakut merchant-elite.

After the introduction of levies in the 1770's, the Yakut trappers, encountering no opposition from the Russian administration, streamed into the Olenek and Anabar basins and farther on to the Khatanga river and Lake Yesey. Evidently, just as in later times, these Yakuts engaged also in hunting and in profitable activities as middlemen. R. K. Maak wrote:

At the start of the present century, when four uluses of the Vilyuysk okrug became one ulus (the Kangalas one), its leader was a rich Yakut, Akyda. Each year he traveled to the Olenek river where he carried on a profitable trade with the Tungus of Lake Zhessey (Yesey—Author), receiving from them sable, polar fox and other pelts in exchange for gunpowder, lead and Yakut ironware. Besides this, he was attracted to the Olenek river by the hunt for reindeer, especially in the autumn, at the time they forded the river.[43]

At the beginning of the 19th century the trade ties of the population of the Olenek and the Anabar with Zhigansk and of the upper reaches of the Olenek with Vilyuysk were markedly strengthened. According to Maak's reports at the beginning of the 19th century, the Vilyuysk Yakuts carried on a regular trade with the population of Lake Yesey, making trips there in winter on reindeer and in summer on horses. These ties were also kept later on.

During his trip on the Olenek in 1874, A. L. Chekanovskiy met Tungus from Lake Syurunga and a Yakut from the Konamka river on the middle course of the Olenek on their way to Vilyuysk for gunpowder and other purchases.[44] In his notes Chekanovskiy mentioned also that the Vilyuysk Yakuts go forth to trade on the Olenek. "A few of them," wrote Chekanovskiy about the Olenek Yakuts, "have close relations with their fellow tribesmen on the Vilyuy from whom they receive domesticated reindeer either to look after and to use or a certain quantity of goods for purposes of barter, goods in demand among the alien tribes on the Anabar river and farther to the northwest among the Dolgans."[45] Undoubtedly the links of trade and barter with Vilyuysk and Zhigansk furthered the Olenek and Anabar population's rapprochement with Yakut culture.

The information furnished by P. Khitrovo, A. L. Chekanovskiy, and partly by Maak indicates that by the second half of the 19th century, the population of the Olenek formed one linguistic, cultural, and economic unit. "In physiognomy, way of life, language and customs," P. Khitrovo wrote about the settlement of the Zhigansk ulus in the 1850's, "the local Russians and Tungus can be included with the Yakuts, since they have integrated with these latter in all respects."[46]

Chekanovskiy, reporting on the permanent residents of the Olenek, noted that they belonged partly to the Vilyuysk okrug and partly to the Verkhoyansk okrug. "On the Olenek they have their winter dwellings—Yakut yurts with a hearth. And then for the rest of the year they lead a nomadic life though not in a particularly large area. In origin they are Tungus, but their grandfathers had already acquired the language, customs and way of life of the Yakuts. They fish, and hunt wild reindeer, foxes and wood geese."[47] A part of the population not having winter huts and nomadizing over a wide area was classified by Chekanovskiy as "migrant" but even this group he did not identify with the Tungus. "The migrant population," wrote Chekanovskiy, "goes to the Olenek mainly by way of the Vilyuy valley. The Tungus of Lake Syurung and Lake Zhessey [Yesey] also visit the Olenek for hunting and fishing. But these natives come more rarely, their wanderings are limited to the upper reaches of the Olenek system and last no longer than a year."[48]

From the sources cited above, it follows that the population of the Olenek formed a kind of a unit differing within itself only in the extent and direction of its migrations. Undoubtedly, toward the second half of the 19th century, the three ethnic elements (Tungus, Yakut, and Russian) making up the population of the Olenek and Anabar basins integrated and a distinct group of northern Yakut reindeer-herders came into being.

From this it does not follow that in the second half of the 19th century no ethnic mixing took place in the basins of the Olenek and Anabar rivers and that the process of ethnogenesis was completed. As the descriptions of Chekanovskiy reveal, the upper reaches of the Olenek were often visited by Tungus from the basin of the Lower Tunguska, Yakuts from Vilyuysk, coming to trade and hunt, and Yakuts from the Lena.

In the second half of the 19th century the population of the upper reaches of the Olenek was included in the Upper Vilyuysk and Markhinsk uluses of the Vilyuysk okrug, while the population of the lower reaches belonged to the Zhigansk ulus of the Verkhoyansk okrug. According to P. Khitrovo, out of ten camps (*nasleg*) of the Zhigansk ulus, the following were considered Yakut: I and II Batulin, I, II, III, and IV Khatygyn, the Tumat, and the Kangalas. The Kubek (Kup) and the Elget (Ezhan) were regarded as Tungus. Members of the Tungus camps and the Tumat camp nomadized beyond the boundaries of the Olenek basin.

As distinguished from the Zhigansk ulus, in the Vilyuysk okrug the "Tungus clans" (with the exception of a number of camps of Tungus origin) were no more than Yakut camps uniting a nomadic reindeer-breeding population, called Tungus only to distinguish it from the Yakut cattle-breeders. This situation has already been noted in the literature. Thus, S. K. Patkanov wrote that "individual Yakut families, having entered into the structure of some Tungus-controlled clan or council, thus became Tungus, but in essence remained the same Yakuts they had been previously."[49] Klark, a Vilyuysk district officer, had noted already in 1861 that "among the Vilyuysk Tungus there exists a group which though called Tungus does not differ from the Yakuts in its dwellings, its customs, its habits, its clothing, or its language."[50]

Camps called Yakut in the Zhigansk ulus and the Turukhansk kray were called Tungus in the Vilyuysk okrug. According to data of the Tenth Inspection and Census in 1897, members of the Khatygyn, Chordu, and Betun camps, the "Yakutized" Tungus of the "Shelogon" [Sologon] and Ugulyat camps, and of others, were listed as Tungus in the Vilyuysk okrug. All of the population nomadizing around Lake Yesey and in the upper reaches of the Olenek (which belonged to the Vilyuysk okrug) was called "Yesey Tungus" in that area. However, in Yenisey *guberniya* it was called "Yesey Yakut." All travelers and explorers visiting these regions considered as Yakuts the residents of Lake Yesey and the upper reaches of the Olenek. The missionary M. Suslov, who visited Lake Yesey in 1884, reported that about 660 Yakuts were nomadizing around Lake Yesey.[51] "The Yesey Yakuts," wrote P. E. Ostrovskikh, who was on Lake Yesey in 1902, "belong to three camps the elders of which live in the Vilyuysk okrug, and have the names Chordu, Beti, and Khatykhyn."[52] "The living area of the Yesey Yakuts is mainly the entire middle and lower course of the Kotuy river and the lower reaches of the Mayero river with its tributaries and also the upper reaches of the Olenek and Anabar rivers,"[53] wrote the ethnographer V. N. Vasilyev, a member of the Khatanga Expedition. One should note that the population assigned to "Tungus clans" considered itself Yakut. This can be derived, for instance, from a document cited by Ostrovskikh: "Sukhochar, of the Ilimpey clan of the Tungus of Turukhansk kray, gave the present receipt to the Yakut V. S. Botul of the IInd Khatygyn Tungus clan in the same kray. . . ."[54]

Local tradition, incorrectly assigning the whole nomadic reindeer-breeding population to the Tungus (Evenk), affected not only the results of the 1897 census but also of the 1926–7 census. Although the economic census in 1926–7 gave no trustworthy information on the ethnic composition of the Olenek and the Anabar Yakuts, calling them Evenk, it gave necessary information on their numbers, the condition of their economy, and their distribution.[55] According to census data, the following camps existed on the territory of the future Olenek and Anabar *rayons* in 1926–7: Khatygyn (Osogostokh), 513 people of both sexes; Chordu, 218; Beti, 98; Ugulyat, 138; Sologon, 270; "Tundra" Yakuts,* 344; Kangalas and Khatygyn of the IIIrd Khatygyn camp, 359.[56] The camps, which were converted into administrative units in the 19th century, were not artificial formations and sometimes represented separate tribes in the past.[57] The Beti camp, according to B. O. Dolgikh, formed as a result of the "Yakutizing" of the local Sinigir tribe; the Ugulyat and Sologon camps, from "Yakutized" Tungus tribes who were known in the 17th century documents as the "Fuglyat and Sologon clans"; and the Khatygyn and Kangalas camps, by splinters of ancient Yakut tribes who moved north and increased in number.

In the Olenek and the Anabar basins remnants of the Brangat and Nakhra tribal splinter groups were also encountered. And here, too, came real Evenks— the Ilimpiyets and the Chapogirets from Krasnoyarsk kray. Besides these, the census included a small group of Yakuts from the central rayons who came to hunt and trade and a certain number of Yakuts and Russians—Soviet workers who came to carry out various tasks.

We have mentioned earlier that, in the census materials, the majority of the population—members of the Khatygyn (Osogostokh), Sologon, Ugulyat, Chordu, and other camps—were entered as Tungus (Evenk). However, locally it was possible to ascertain that members of all the principal clans referred to above, with the exception of the Ilimpiyets (Nyuryumnyal) and the Chapogirets, considered themselves real Yakuts, descendants of Yakuts who had come from southern regions of Yakutia. Questioning revealed that, in the determination of the nationality of a population, the census-takers were guided by traditional notions that counted all the population engaged in reindeer-herding as Tungus

*[*Zatundrennye yakuty* in the original, i.e., "Yakuts who have gone to the tundra."—Editor.]

and in cattle-husbandry as Yakut. Included in the latter category on the Olenek were only those individuals who had but recently engaged in cattle-husbandry, i.e., newly come Yakuts.

It should be noted that the Olenek and Anabar Yakuts themselves also understand their ascription to the Evenk (Tungus) to be but an expression of their

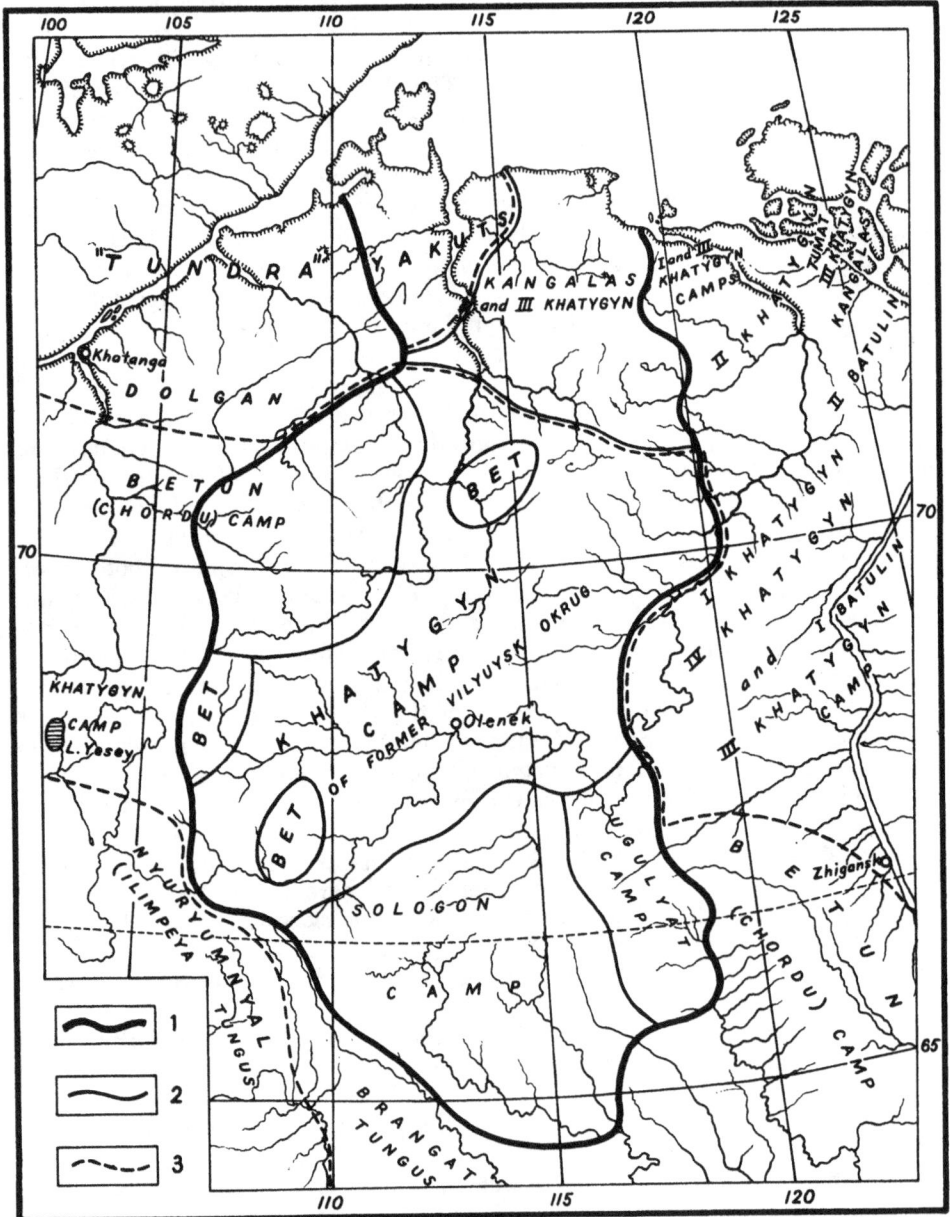

FIGURE 2. Map of the distribution of the population in the Olenek and Anabar basins in 1925–7: (1) boundaries of the Anabar and Olenek rayons of the Yakut A.S.S.R. in 1939; (2) boundaries between camps and former administrative clans; (3) boundaries between groups belonging, before the revolution, to various large administrative units (Vilyuysk okrug, Verkhoyansk okrug, Yenisey guberniya).

way of life and do not attach to this term any ethnic meaning in relation to themselves. The Evenks of Krasnoyarsk kray, as distinguished from the cattle-raising Yakuts, are looked upon by them as a completely different, unrelated people.

This situation has already been noted by A. A. Popov. "The word Tungus is often used not as the name of a people but as an attributive for reindeer-breeders in general. For this reason the Vilyuysk Yakuts who have cows and horses call the 'Tundra' reindeer-breeding Yakuts Tungus although these latter, when encountering the Dolgans, refer to themselves only as Yakuts."[58]

The Yakut national self-consciousness among the Olenek and Anabar Yakuts has found vivid expression in their genealogical traditions.

The founder of one of the branches of the Chordu clan is supposed to be the Yakut Kykhylov who migrated to a locality called Konora, near Zhigansk. He and his direct descendants were "princelings" (elders) of the Chordu camp. The genealogy of Kykhylov's great-grandson nicknamed Sekeney-uola, who died in the 1930's, is drawn in the following manner: Kykhylov–Samoyka–Sekeney–Nikolay (Seksney-uola). The Úryuney clan which entered into the composition of the Chordu camp, according to a member of this clan A. P. Grigoryev and other individuals, descended from a certain Úryuney-Yakut. With his brother, Úryuney was exiled from Yakutsk for misdemeanors of some kind. A. P. Grigoryev traces his genealogy in the following way: Úryuney–Grigori–Petr–A. P. Grigoryev (age 54).

The founder of the Ospëk clan, according to a member of that clan I. P. Semenov, was a Yakut by the name of Ospëk. Here is I. P. Semenov's genealogy: Ospëk–Chogurkan (not baptized)–Ignati (blind)–Vasili–Seman (Sookooki)–Semen (Adyaryksa)–Petr–I. P. Semenov (age 40). As told by the population, the Osogostokh clan descended from a Yakut woman who had arrived already pregnant on the Olenek.

Only the Beti clan is acknowledged, by local tradition, as Evenk-Yakut. Its founder is considered to be the shaman Mykal. Some consider him a Yakut; others place him among the Chapogirets.

In a similar way one can trace the descent of the Anabar and Lower Olenek clans: the Kangalas, II Khatygyn, Omoldon clan (Omoldottor), and the Edeter. The Kangalas clan on the Anabar (the Vinokurov), according to N. A. Vinokurov (age 82), was founded by his great-grandfather during the years of the Christianization of the Yakuts. Before migrating to the Anabar, the great-grandfather Vinokurov allegedly lived at the mouth of the Vilyuy and belonged to the Kangalas camp. The reason for his migration was a dispute with his kinsmen. As the distribution of the feathers of the totem bird ("as a god")–the *toyon-keter* (eagle)–Vinokurov's grandfather did not get any feathers–he was offered the down. Feeling insulted he migrated to the Anabar. Hearing that Kangalas people had settled on the Anabar, other individuals from this camp began to join them. N. A. Vinokurov's genealogy: Dugduur–Vasili–Afanasi–N. A. Vinokurov. Of course, the trustworthiness of these genealogical traditions is doubtful, but nevertheless they bear witness to a completely Yakut self-consciousness of the population of the Anabar and Olenek river basins.

It should be mentioned that the organizers of the Olenek cultural center, local Soviet and party workers, did not regard the population as Evenk. The ethnographer I. M. Suslov, sent on a mission by the Committee of the North to take charge of the establishment of the Olenek cultural center, noted in his book *Reka Olenek* (The Olenek River) that the population of the Olenek belonged to the nomadic Yakut reindeer-breeders. This was brought to light as well by the survey of the Olenek rayon carried out in 1934 by I. V. Vinokurov, commissioned by the Yakut Central Executive Committee. In the Olenek, Kirbey, and Dzhelindin camps (at first the Olenek rayon consisted of three camps), according to the data of the survey, the population consisted of Yakuts. Only 20 households of the Ilimpey clan belonged to the Evenks, and, of them, 10 went off to Krasnoyarsk kray when the Olenek rayon was organized.

The fact that the population of the northwestern rayons of Yakutia is Yakut was known not only on the Olenek but also in Vilyuysk. The secretary of the Olenek Rayon Party Committee, S. V. Danilov, who during the building of the cultural center was working as the secretary of the Vilyuysk Okrug Committee, reported to us in private conversation that he and the local party members did not support the proposals of the administration of the Committee of the North to organize a special national okrug on the territory of the northwestern rayons of Yakutia, because if one started to divide into national okrugs the territory where the Yakut-speaking population was engaged in reindeer-herding, then nothing would remain of the Yakut A.S.S.R. and Yakuts would figure as such only around the town of Yakutsk.

Who, then, are the Olenek and Anabar Yakuts? At the present time these reindeer-breeders are the northernmost segment of the Yakut people, having a number of different characteristics both in comparison with the basic mass of Yakuts of the central rayons of Yakutia and in comparison with the inhabitants of the two northern rayons of the Yakut A.S.S.R. where the Yakut population also disseminated.

The basic occupation of Olenek and Anabar Yakuts is reindeer-herding; after this, come hunting and fishing. In the Olenek and Anabar river basins there existed several types of reindeer-herding economies combining reindeer-husbandry with hunting and fishing in various ways conforming to separate natural zones.[59]

Reindeer-husbandry in the Olenek and Anabar basins is distinguished by a number of characteristic traits: reindeer-herding dogs are not used, unlike, in this respect, among the Dolgans and the Nganasans; there are various ways of packing reindeer for transport of goods; the reindeer on the far left is not used as the lead reindeer but the one on the far right as among the Evenks, the Dolgans, and the Yakuts of the central regions; the reindeer are milked and kept during the summer in wooded areas. With respect to their terminologies for reindeer-husbandry and hunting, the large number of terms borrowed from various Evenk dialects should be noted. Yet, the population speaks Yakut exclusively.

In the economic activities of the population before collectivization, hunting for large ungulates overshadowed trapping for furs. Methods for hunting wild reindeer and waterfowl among the Anabar and Olenek Yakuts are unknown to the Yakuts of the central regions. The complicated origin of the Olenek and Anabar Yakuts as a result of the crossing and interaction of three ethnic groups —the aboriginal Evenk population, the Yakut immigrants, and the Russian trappers—is reflected in their material and spiritual culture. The food of the Olenek and Anabar population, as of the Evenks and the Nganasans, conforms to their hunting economy. Basic foods were the meat of wild and domestic reindeer and fish. Nevertheless, a Yakut influence made itself felt in their diet, showing up in a liking for horsemeat and in the preparation of Yakut dishes. The basic type of dwelling of the Anabar and Olenek Yakuts was a conical nomadic tent of reindeer hide—the *tordokh.* As a winter dwelling, a specifically Yakut form of dwelling was used: the *yurt-balagan* and the log cabin adopted from Russian trappers. Permanent huts made of poles—*kholomo*—were also quite popular.

The hunting dress and footwear of the population on the Olenek and Anabar resemble, in the main, the Evenk national clothing. Only the breastplate is not used. Yakut influence was apparent mostly in the festive form of the costume—a fur coat with a turned-down collar, women's caps with high crown and clasp. Everyday clothing—shirts, dresses, and suits—have the Russian cut.

Yakut motifs predominate in the ornamental arts (wood carving) of the Olenek and Anabar Yakuts: spirals, curls, and crosses as distinguished from the realistic silhouetted designs of the Evenks.

An even more complicated intertwining of various forms of ethnic influence can be traced in the spiritual culture. Yakut and Evenk influences are discerned in the legal practices of the northern Yakuts, in inheritance customs which existed before the establishment of the Soviet regime.

In wedding ceremonies, basically the general Yakut forms are repeated: also there is evident a strong influence of Russian wedding rites. Archaic notions have been preserved in birth ceremonies concerning the woman. This group of rites links the Yakut reindeer-breeders closely to the Evenks, Nganasans, and Dolgans. Many original traits are disclosed in the oral traditions of the Olenek and Anabar Yakuts, in vivid epic tales of warriors—*khosuns*—and in other genres. The Yakut reindeer-breeders have retained a basic store of folklore from their kinsmen, the Yakut cattle-breeders, with the exception of epic tales, the *olonkho,* less popular in the north than in the central Yakut regions. One should point out that in many tales the traditional cattle-raising milieu is changed to a reindeer-herding one. The improvised songs of the northern Yakuts and the demonological traditions are close to Dolgan and Yukagir tales of this kind. Many works show a strong influence of Russian folklore.

In religious beliefs there is evident a complex intertwining of kindred Yakut and Evenk religious notions.

The original culture of Olenek and Anabar Yakuts, distinguished by a marked complexity, is nevertheless—and this should be particularly emphasized—an organic unit.

The group of northern Yakut reindeer-breeders, differing in its economic-cultural make-up from the Yakuts of the central regions, as was pointed out above, had already become a detached part of the Yakut people in the 19th century. The formation of this independent group of Yakuts over a long period of crossing and mutual influence of three ethnic components (the leading role of this process belonged to the Yakuts) was marked by the establishment of a broad ethnic community, resulting in the spread of the Yakut language and culture to the northwestern and northern regions of Yakutia. The ethnic unity also expressed itself in a Yakut self-awareness of the population of the northern tundra border regions. The unity of the northern Yakut reindeer-breeders was strengthened by territorial links and a political subordination to the same administrative centers. Nevertheless, the process of amalgamation of the northern Yakut reindeer-breeders with the bulk of Yakut cattle-breeders did not result, at the end of the 19th or the beginning of the 20th centuries, in their integration into a stable community or nation. The most important sign characterizing a nation was lacking—a commonness in economic life and economic solidarity.

What were the economic ties among the northern Yakuts and other groups of the Yakut people? Undoubtedly the northern Yakuts were linked to the general Russian market by a series of channels. The population of the northern regions was visited by merchants from Yakutsk and Vilyuysk fur-buyers and money-lenders who brought gunpowder, lead, arms, spirits, tea, tobacco, and other goods to the Olenek, Anabar, and lower Lena. It is known that at the end of the 19th century there was a significant differentiation in property among the Olenek and Anabar Yakuts. The camp elders and *kulaks* who owned herds of thousands of reindeer exploited the local population under the guise of mutual clan assistance. They also engaged in middleman trading, selling reindeer and furs bought or traded for tobacco, tea, and gunpowder. However, the bulk of the population was isolated by hundreds of *versts* of trackless swamp and forest both from the Yakuts of the central regions and from the nearest administrative centers. The horizons and interests of the northern Yakut reindeer-breeders were limited to their own group.

Actually the population carried on an economy based on a technology of the most primitive kind, barely adequate for their needs of food and clothing. Hunting for the fur trade was carried on only to a degree that would assure them the necessary quantity of ammunition, tea, and tobacco.

Owing to this low level of economic development the northern Yakuts could obviously have no strong economic ties with their neighbors. The integrative process of the northern groups of the Yakut people with the bulk of Yakuts was accomplished only in the Soviet era on a new political and economic basis. [. . .]

One of the first measures of the Soviet regime in overcoming the isolation of the Olenek and Anabar Yakuts from cultural centers was to render navigable the northern rivers—the main routes of communication in these trackless areas—i.e., the Olenek, Anabar, and Malaya Konamka. Large amounts of freight were sent to the north along postal routes. Air routes were established. Overcoming the isolation of the areas where the northern Yakuts lived was the premise for their further integration with the bulk of the Yakut people. Already during the introduction of collectivization, Yakuts—both Soviet [government] and Party workers—from the southern districts of the Yakut A.S.S.R. took an active part in carrying out the first cultural measures among the Yakut reindeer-herders.

The collectivization, the socialist construction, the basic reconstruction of the northern complex economy, and the converting of the fur industry from a secondary occupation into the leading branch of the economy sharply raised the income and well-being of the population. With the rise in production, close economic ties were established between the formerly isolated economy of the northern Yakuts, and the national economy of the Yakut A.S.S.R. This was reflected in the consciousness of the population. An awareness of national and governmental ties is replacing the narrow clan-tribal (camp) and territorial ethnic links. Yakuts of the central regions as well as Yakuts of the northern ones do not differentiate between their struggles to fulfill plans for fur production, plans for expansion of community animal-husbandry, and the general struggle of the whole Yakut Republic to fulfill the governmental plans.

A direct result of the socialist reconstruction of the hunting economy has been the expansion of economic ties between the northern and southern Yakuts. The collective farms of Olenek rayon have become nurseries of taiga reindeer for the southern rayons of Yakutia. Also spreading to the south is the experience gained by the northern Yakuts in reindeer-breeding and hunting. In a number of rayons occupied by northern Yakuts, where climatic conditions allow, cattle-husbandry and dairy farms are being organized, and the extensive experience accumulated in this field by Yakut cattle-breeders is penetrating into the area.

An exchange of cultural heritage accumulated by different groups of the Yakut people is also going on. The remarkable folklore (olonkho) of the Yakut cattle-breeders and the modern literary creations of Soviet Yakut writers, natives of the central rayons—Abaginski, Urastyrov, Ellyay, Suorun Omollon, Vasilyev-Borogonskiy, and others—are being read by the remotest reindeer-breeding groups of Yakuts. Tales, songs, and epic creations of the northern Yakuts are penetrating to regions where the Yakut cattle-breeders live.

The formation of a Yakut socialist culture also contributes to the enrichment of the Yakut literary language. Through books, newspapers, and magazines, the literary language becomes part of the daily vocabulary of the population, replacing local forms of speech. More than 30 newspapers and magazines in the Yakut language are being published in Yakutia. In recent years the works of Stalin have been published in this language, in an edition of over 700,000 copies. Important linguistic work is going on in Yakut schools, especially the northern ones, in order to develop a spoken literary language.

The general growth of culture and literacy is contributing to the unification of all groups of the Yakut people. An all-encompassing integration of every group of the Yakut people, the joining of the most northerly groups to the nucleus of the Yakut nation—the Yakuts of the central regions—to whom they are similar in culture, represents a process of consolidation of the Yakut socialist nation.

Notes and References

1. *Arkhiv AN SSSR* (Leningrad), Portfeli Millera (Archives of the U.S.S.R. Academy of Sciences, Leningrad, Miller Portfolios), sec. 21, op. 4, leaf 23.

2. *Ibidem*, leaf 92.

3. *TsGADA*, Sibirski prikaz (TsGADA, Siberian Dept.), book 145, leaf 152.

4. *Arkhiv AN SSSR*, Portfeli Millera, sec. 21, op. 4, leaf 226.

5. *Kolonialnaya politika Moskovskogo gosudarstva v Yakutii v XVII v.* (Colonial policies of the Moscow Government in Yakutia in the 17th century), Moscow–Leningrad, 1936, p. 19.

6. *Arkhiv Instituta istorii AN SSSR* (Leningrad), Yakutskiye akty (Archive of the Institute of History, U.S.S.R. Academy of Sciences, Leningrad, Yakut Acts), box 6, art. 5, leaf 3. (Cited below as: Yakutskiye akty—Yakut Acts.)

7. *TsGADA*, Fond Yakutskogo oblastnogo upravleniya (TsGADA, Records of the Yakut Oblast administration), op. 1, art. 235, leaf 92.

8. Yakutskiye akty, box 1, art. 1, leaf 1.

9. *Arkhiv AN SSSR*, Portfeli Millera, sec. 21, op. 4, leaf 235.

10. *TsGADA*, Sibirski prikaz, art. 257, leaf 253.

11. *Kolonialnaya politika . . .*, p. 19.

12. *TsGADA*, Sibirski prikaz, book 307, sheet 721.

13. *Ibidem*, book 688, leaf 482; book 712, leaf 817.

14. *Ibidem*, book 830, leaves 458–460.

15. *Ibidem*, book 150, leaf 193.

16. Yakutskiye akty, box 22 (205), art. 15, leaf 59.

17. *TsGADA*, Sibirski prikaz, book 145, leaves 155–160.

18. *Kolonialnaya politika . . .*, p. 121.

19. *Ibidem*, p. 216.

20. *Ibidem*, pp. 191–195.

21. Yakutskiye akty, box 33, art. 2, leaf 5 (part of the document is cited in Kolonialnaya politika . . .).

22. *Dopolneniya k "Aktam istoricheskim"* (Addenda to "Historical Acts"), vol. 11, St. Petersburg, 1869, p. 66. (Cited below as: *DAI.*)

23. Yakutskiye akty, box 44, art. 12, leaf 5.

24. *Chertezhnaya, kniga Sibiri 1701 g. S. Remezova,* Izd. Arkheologicheskoy komissii, 1882 (S. Remezov's Atlas of Siberia, 1701; published by the Archaeological Commission, 1882).

25. I. Fisher, *Sibirskaya istoriya s samogo otkrytiya Sibiri do zavoyevaniya sey zemli rossiyskim oruzhiyem* (The history of Siberia from its discovery to its conquest by Russian arms), St. Petersburg, 1779, p. 372.

26. Arkhiv AN SSSR, Portfeli Millera, sec. 21, op. 4, leaf 258.

27. *Kolonialnaya politika . . .,* p. 179.

28. TsGADA, Fond Yakutskogo oblastnogo upravleniya, op. 2, art. 50, leaf 127.

29. Yakutskiye akty, box 19, art. 19, leaf 36.

30. *Ibidem,* box 30, art. 4, leaves 4–49.

31. *DAI,* vol. 7, p. 138.

32. *Kolonialnaya politika . . .,* p. 121.

33. *DAI,* vol. 11, p. 124.

34. *DAI,* vol. 15, p. 62.

35. TsGADA, Sibirskiy prikaz, book 1533, leaf 50.

36. *Ibidem,* book 1564, leaf 91.

37. *Ibidem,* leaf 87.

38. TsGADA, Sibirskiy prikaz, book 980, leaves 161–184. (Account of the Olenek and Zhigansk winter quarters given jointly.)

39. *Zapiski Gidrograficheskogo departamenta Morskogo ministerstva* (Records of the Hydrographic Department of the Admiralty), part IX, St. Petersburg, 1851, p. 190.

40. *Ibidem,* p. 302.

41. L. S. Berg, Istoriya geograficheskogo oznakomleniya s yakutskim krayem (History of geographic study of the Yakutsk region), *Sbornik "Yakutiya",* Leningrad, 1927, p. 23.

42. A. P. Okladnikov, K istorii etnograficheskogo izucheniya Yakutii (History of ethnographic study in Yakutia), *Sbornik materialov po etnografii Yakutov,* Yakutsk, 1948, p. 25.

43. R. K. Maak, *Vilyuyski okrug Yakutskoy oblasti* (The Vilyuysk okrug of the Yakutsk oblast), vol. 2, pp. 103–104.

44. A. L. Chekanovskiy, Pismo k sekretaryu Russkogo geograficheskogo obshchestva (Letter to the Secretary of the Russian Geographic Society), *Izvestiya RGO,* vol. 11, 1875, p. 323

45. *Ibidem,* p. 332.

46. P. Khitrovo, Opisaniye Zhiganskogo ulusa (Description of the Zhigansk ulus), *Zapiski Sib. otdela RGO,* vol. 1, 1856, p. 66

47. Chekanovskiy, *op. cit.,* p. 332

48. *Ibidem,* p. 133.

49. K. Patkanov, *Opyt geografii i statistiki tungusskikh plemen Sibiri* (A study of the geography and statistics of the Tungus tribes of Siberia), part I, no. 2, St. Petersburg, 1906, p. 83.

50. Klark, Vilyuysk i ego okrug (Vilyuysk and its okrug), *Zapiski Sib. otdela RGO,* part VII, 1864, p. 129

51. M. Suslov, Putevoy zhurnal svyashchennika missionera Mikh. Suslova (Travel diary of the priest-missionary Mikhail Suslov), *Yeniseyskiye yeparkhialnye vedomosti,* 1884, nos. 19, 20, 21.

52. P. E. Ostrovskikh, Poyezdka na ozero Yesey (Journey to Lake Yesey), *Izvestiya krasnoyarskogo podotdela RGO,* vol. 1, no. 6, 1904, p. 27.

53. V. M. Vasilyev, Kratki ocherk inorodtsev severnogo Turukhanskogo kraya (A short sketch of the natives of northern Turukhansk *kray*), *Yezhegodnik Russk. antropologich. obshchestva,* 1905–7, no. 2, p. 58.

54. P. E. Ostrovskikh, O polozhenii zhenshchiny u inorodtsev Turukhanskogo kraya

(On the position of women among the natives of Turukhansk *kray*), *Izvestiya krasnoyarskogo podotdela RGO*, vol. 1, no. 5, 1904, p. 14.

55. I. S. Gurvich, Olenekskiye i anabarskiye yakuty (The Olenek and Anabar Yakuts), *Avtoreferat dissertatsii*, Moscow, 1949, p. 3.

56. B. O. Dolgikh, Sostav narodnostey severa sredney Sibiri (Ethnic composition of the peoples of the Central Siberian North), *Kratkiye soobshcheniya Instituta etnografii*, no. 5, 1949, p. 79. A part of the material, not readily available, was kindly provided by B. O. Dolgikh for our use.

57. B. O. Dolgikh, Plemya u narodov Sibiri (The concept of "tribe" among the peoples of Siberia), *Trudy II Vsesoyuznogo geograficheskogo sezda*, vol. 2, pp. 340–354.

58. A. A. Popov, Materialy po rodovomu stroyu dolgan (Contributions to the social structure of the Dolgans), *Sovetskaya etnografiya*, 1934, no. 6, p. 33.

59. For further details see: I. S. Gurvich, Olenekskiye i anabarskiye yakuty (The Olenek and Anabar Yakuts), *Avtoreferat dissertatsii*, Moscow, 1949, pp. 10–11.

B. O. DOLGIKH

THE POPULATION OF THE OLENEK AND UPPER ANABAR RIVER BASINS*

ONE OF THE MISUNDERSTANDINGS not yet cleared up in ethnography is the question of the ethnic affiliation of the nomadic reindeer-herding population of the northwestern part of the Yakut A.S.S.R. in the territory of the present Olenek *rayon* and also in part of the neighboring rayons.

Briefly, the question comes down to this: Although it was known quite early—at least from the second half of the 19th century—that this population speaks Yakut, the population was considered largely, and sometimes wholly, Tungus (that is, Evenk). It is so indicated in the majority of ethnographic maps, even the very latest, such as those of P. E. Terletskiy and Z. E. Chernyakov. This misunderstanding gave rise to a number of practical inconveniences; for example, literature and textbooks in the Evenk language were distributed in Olenek rayon and went unused, since the population did not know that language. The assignment of the entire population of Olenek rayon (which also included the headwaters of the Anabar) to the Evenks distorted the statistical data on the ethnic composition of the northwestern part of the Yakut A.S.S.R.

This misunderstanding was due to a number of causes. In the 17th century, when the Russians arrived in the Olenek basin, the Evenks (Tungus) actually lived there and on the upper Anabar and Popigay rivers. But as a result of epidemics in the mid-17th century, this population was very much reduced. At the same time, beginning with the middle of the 17th century, many Yakuts migrated from the central regions of Yakutia to the Olenek where they were found as early as the beginning of the 18th century in considerably greater numbers than the Evenks, whose remnants they assimilated. Thus, in the 17th century, there took place in this region a complete change in the ethnic composition of the population, but apparently a tradition persisted that the population of the Olenek was Evenk.

The second reason why the population of the Olenek region was considered Evenk (Tungus) until recently was the fact that, having settled on the Olenek, the Yakuts borrowed reindeer-breeding from their predecessors, the Evenks, and became reindeer-herding nomads, hunters, and fishermen, as the Evenks had been. These differences between the Olenek Yakuts and the main body of the Yakut people, who had adopted cattle- and horse-breeding under the influence of Russian culture and agriculture, and for the most part lived a settled life even before the revolution, reinforced the tradition of considering the reindeer-herding nomads of the Olenek as Evenk (Tungus).

The third reason why the population of the Olenek region was considered Evenk was the fact that in tsarist Russia it was officially recorded as Tungus although it spoke Yakut and was for the most part Yakut by origin. In this connection we must note that the tsarist administration, in classifying the reindeer-herding Yakuts of the northwest of the former Yakutsk *oblast* as Tungus, was not wholly consistent in its practice.

*Translated from *Sovetskaya etnografiya*, 1950, no. 4, pp. 169–173.

The population of northwestern Yakutia before the revolution fell into three large administrative units. A part of it made up the Zhigansk *ulus* of the Verkhoyansk *okrug*. Here it was considered Yakut, except for two clans—the Kyup and the Yezhan; these nomadized on the Lena and to the east of it, and were considered Tungus. They were actually "Yakutized" Tungus by origin. The remaining clan divisions (*naslegi*) of this ulus—the Ist and IInd Batulin, the Ist, IInd, IIIrd, and IVth Khatylin (Khatygyn), the Kangalas, and the Tumat—were considered Yakut, and the overwhelming majority of their members actually were Yakuts by origin, although they kept reindeer and followed a nomadic kind of life. They occupied the whole of the lower Lena from Zhigansk to the delta, the lower Olenek, the basin of the tributary to the Anabar, the Yuelga [Uele], and other tributary basins.

The other part of the population of northwestern Yakutia, particularly those people who wandered on the upper and middle Olenek and the upper Anabar as well as on the Kotuy and around Lake Yesey, was included in the Vilyuy okrug.[1] This population group belonged to the Khatygyn, Betu (also called Chordu), and Betil clan divisions (naslegi). The population of all three of these divisions spoke Yakut but was considered Tungus, although only the Betil—apparently derived from the Sinigir Tungus of the 17 century—could with any justification be considered Tungus in origin.

Thus, a population completely unified from an ethnic point of view was considered by the tsarist administration to be Yakut in one okrug and Tungus in another.

Finally, the lower Anabar was occupied by Yakuts of the Lower Tundra administration* (*uprava*) of Turukhansk *kray* in Yenisey *guberniya*. These Yakuts today form part of the population of the Taymyr National Okrug of Krasnoyarsk kray, and of the Anabar rayon of the Yakut A.S.S.R. Their ethnic affiliation is undisputed (although in part they appear to be descendants of Evenks assimilated by Tungus).

Thus, the lower Olenek and Anabar were (and are to this day) occupied by a population which belonged to the Zhigansk ulus and the Yenisey guberniya in the past, and which, although it practiced nomadic reindeer-herding, was Yakut and was recorded as Yakut.

On the other hand, the population of the upper Anabar and the upper and middle Olenek, which had the same way of life and spoke the Yakut language, but was located in Vilyuy okrug, was considered Tungus. Thus the question, properly speaking, comes down to this: whom should we consider to be the descendants of the Khatygin, Betu, and Betil clan divisions of the former Vilyuy okrug which made up the majority of the population of this region?

The numerical strength of these clans is shown by the data given in Table 1.

TABLE 1

Clan division	Census of 1859[2] (revised)	Census of 1897[3]	Census of 1926–7[4]
Khatygyn	470	880	1207
Betu	505	} 929	719
Betil	202		220
Total	1177	1809	2144

*[*Nizhne-zatundrennaya uprava* in the original.—Editor.]

These data are not entirely accurate. In 1859 the count of the Khatygyn clan was apparently not completed. For 1926–7 we have no data for part of the Betu clan division living around Lake Konor near Zhigansk (there were some 150–200 people).

In 1926–7, the descendants of the members of these clans lived partly in the Yakut A.S.S.R. and partly within the boundaries of Sibirsk kray.[5] The distribution of this population between the two regions is shown in Table 2. In the Sibirsk kray all members of these clans were registered as Yakuts by the census of 1926–7, while in the Yakut A.S.S.R. they were registered as Tungus.

TABLE 2

Clan division	Sibirsk kray	Yakut A.S.S.R.	Totals
Khatygyn	692	513	1205
Betu	501	218	719
Betil	122	98	220
Total	1315	829	2144

The Khatygyn and Betu divisions are made up of a number of clans: in the Khatygyn were the Botulu, Osogostokh, Yëspëkh, Maymaga, and Uoday clans; in the Betu were the Chordu, Batagay, Yuereney, and Këbëkh clans. In the census, members of one and the same clan were registered as Tungus in the Yakut A.S.S.R. and as Yakuts in the Sibirsk kray.

Moreover, there were cases where a father and his family were registered as Yakuts in Sibirsk kray, and his son, who had gone to visit his father-in-law on the Olenek, was registered as a Tungus. In another case, one son living on the Olenek in the Yakut A.S.S.R. was registered as a Tungus, while another on Lake Yesey in the Sibirsk kray was registered as a Yakut, and so on.

Above all it must be emphasized that the population of the middle and upper Olenek and the upper Anabar, and the population living in Krasnoyarsk kray in the region of Lake Yesey, on the Kotuy, Kotuykan, and Agynli rivers, between the Kotuy and Meymech (Medvezh) rivers, and on the Kheta river in the vicinity of the mouth of the Meymech, not only belonged to one division and clan in the past, but were ethnographically thoroughly unified—having the same language, way of life, dress, customs, etc. If one part is to be considered Yakut, so must the other; or, on the other hand, both must be regarded as Evenk (Tungus). For instance, to distinguish ethnographically the population of Lake Yesey (now part of the Evenk National Okrug, where it is correctly considered Yakut) from the population of the Olenek and Anabar is inconceivable. Either these people are all Yakuts or all Evenks. There can be no other solution.

During the period 1935–9 the author of these lines had occasion to make several visits to the region of Lake Yesey, the middle course of the Kotuy, and to the east of the Kotuy on the Arynli river near the Kirbey trading post. There is no doubt that the population there consists of Yakut reindeer-herding nomads, and there are no Evenks among them. No ethnographic difference can be found between the population of this region and that of the Olenek. At all times both individuals and whole families traveled from the Olenek into the Yesey region, and sometimes larger groups migrated. These constitute one ethnic group of Yakut reindeer-herders, connected by clan and personal ties, deriving from the very same clans, and considering themselves as one ethnic whole divided only by the boundary between the Yakut A.S.S.R. and Krasnoyarsk kray.

In this connection we may note that the original inhabitants of the Yesey and their fellow tribesmen and fellow clansmen of the Olenek considered themselves Yakuts (including the members of the Beti division, whose Evenk origin is remembered but who are not at all distinguished from the other Yakuts); everyone else considered them Yakuts. Incidentally, it is noteworthy that all the Yakuts in the Yesey, Kotuy, and Kheta regions migrated there in the past from the Olenek. They remember this very well.

But it is curious that the Yakuts from the Yesey and from the Olenek say that in Vilyuysk, where they sometimes happen to travel, they are considered Tungus and called "Dekhey Tongustar"—that is, "Yesey Tungus." This probably is the reason why the Olenek Yakuts were counted as Tungus within the boundaries of the Yakut A.S.S.R. Obviously, the old tradition, according to which the whole population of the middle and upper Olenek and Anabar was considered Evenk, was still strong and was reflected in the results of the 1926–7 census in the Olenek and Anabar basins.

The boundary between the Yakuts and the Evenks was quite clearly discernible when one happened to travel from the region of settlement of the reindeer-herding Yakuts (for example, from Lake Yesey or from Kirbey, or from other places) into the neighboring Evenk nomadic soviets [councils] of the Ilimpey rayon of the Evenk National Okrug (for example, the Chirindin). Here the population considers itself Evenk and speaks Evenk. It is also considered Evenk by the entire neighboring Yakut population of the Yesey and the Olenek. In this connection we must note that the Chirindin Evenks make no distinction between the Yakuts of the Yesey in their own National Okrug and the Olenek Yakuts of the Yakut A.S.S.R.—that is, those whom, as we have seen, the 1926–7 census considered as Tungus. The Evenks call both these groups "Yako," considering them a different people and finding the Olenek Yakuts no more Evenks than the Yesey. In clan composition, the Evenks were sharply distinguished from the Yakuts. The Evenks belonged to the following clans: Bayagir (with the subdivisions Katarel, Yaltakagir, Khavokigir), Ioldagir, Oëgir, Gurgugir, Ioligir, Kambagir, Khiragir, Khukochar, Yemidakil, Khutokogir, and Udygir. As we have already shown, the Yesey and Olenek Yakuts belong to different clans, all the names of which were, without exception, purely Yakut and not Evenk (see above).

Thus, it is entirely clear to us that the population of the Olenek and Anabar basins is Yakut, and distinguished from other Yakuts only by the economy and form of life but not by language (except for a number of dialectical peculiarities) or by ethnic affiliation. There is no justification for distinguishing ethnographically between the Olenek and Anabar Yakuts of the Yakut A.S.S.R. and the Yesey, Kirbey, and other Yakuts of Krasnoyarsk kray. Both represent one ethnic group, by origin as well as ethnographically, and regard themselves as one people.

There remains the question of the population of the Shologon and Ugulyat clans in the southern part of the present Olenek rayon, chiefly in the basins of the Markha and Tyung rivers. By origin these are Evenks, but as early as 1897 all of them spoke Yakut. Part of them carry on reindeer-breeding, and part, after the example of the Yakuts, cattle- and horse-breeding. The author has encountered some of these Shologons in Yesey and Kirbey. They call themselves Yakuts but at the same time remember their Evenk (Tungus) origin. They speak only Yakut. In order to resolve finally the question of their ethnic affiliation, it will be necessary to study it on the spot. Judging by what we know of them, the Ugulyats may be considered already fully amalgamated with the Yakuts, but the Shologons, although they have gone over to the Yakut language, retain consciousness of their Evenk origin.

Notes and References

1. The Kotuy and Lake Yesey rayon was in the territory of Yenisey guberniya, but the population of these localities was under the jurisdiction of Vilyuy okrug of the Yakutsk oblast.

2. *Pamyatnaya knizhka yakutskoy oblasti za 1863 g.* (Almanac for Yakutsk oblast, 1863), p. 68.

3. S. K. Patkanov, Opyt geografii i statistiki tungusskikh plemen (Sketch of the geography and statistics of the Tungus tribes), *Sibir*, part 1, no. 2, pp. 115–117, 124–126, 160.

4. B. O. Dolgikh, Rodovoy i plemennoy sostav narodnostey sredney Sibiri (Clan and tribal composition of the peoples of central Siberia), *Kratkiye soobshcheniya Instituta etnografii AN SSSR*, no. 5, 1949, p. 79. Some figures were inserted from I. S. Gurvich's data.

5. In 1926 and 1927 the Krasnoyarsk kray did not yet exist and all its territory was part of the Sibirsk kray (except for the area between the Khatanga and the Anabar which was then included in the Yakut A.S.S.R.).

I. M. SUSLOV

THE NATIONAL AFFILIATION OF THE PRESENT POPULATION OF NORTH-WESTERN YAKUTIA*

THE QUESTION RAISED in the pages of *Sovetskaya etnografiya* about the ethnic affiliation of the population of the basin of the Olenek and Anabar rivers is one of great practical and theoretical interest.[1] I consider it my obligation to share material which throws some light on this question.

In 1934 I was sent by the Committee of the North attached to the All-Soviet Central Institute of Culture to select a site and organize the construction of an Olenek cultural center. Construction was planned in the upper reaches of the Olenek, among the Tungus (Evenks). My attempts to obtain any kind of information about the population of the upper Olenek met with no success in either Yakutsk or Vilyuysk. All I succeeded in establishing was that in Vilyuysk the Olenek population is called "Yesey Tungus" or simply "Tungus." The sort of "Tungus" soon emerged on the way from Vilyuysk to the Olenek.

Our guide was one of the Olenek "Tungus," an old man of the Osogostokh clan, Christopher, nicknamed Yrygan. Along the way I noticed that although my Yakut companions called him a "Tungus," Yrygan knew no language but Yakut. Indeed, he called himself a Tungus, but my companions and coachmen, whom he had hired around Vilyuysk, he called Yakut.

During a conversation with Yrygan I conveyed to him my bewilderment about why he, a "Tungus," did not understand either the language or the customs of the Evenks from the Ilimpeysk rayon of the Evenk National Okrug, and I concluded that if Yrygan called himself a "Tungus," then he must also be an "Omuk," as all Tungus are called in Yakut terminology. This idea literally astounded the old man. "No!" he exclaimed with indignation, "I am not an Omuk, I am a Yakut." Yrygan added further that he was, at the same time, a Tungus, and by no means an "Omuk."

After this it was easy to guess that the nomadic Yakut engaged in reindeer-herding and, consequently, having an Evenk form of economy, called the semi-nomadic Yakut cattle-breeders by the Russian term "Tungus," but never applied to them the term "Evenk," much less "Omuk" (stranger, outlander). When I voiced this to Yrygan, he agreed with it completely.

When we questioned the population of the Olenek basin about their national affiliation we always ran into cases where the persons interrogated called themselves "Tungus" but did not identify themselves as Evenks. Members of the Osogostokh, Chordu, Shologon, Khatygyn, and other clans who replied that they were "Tungus" used this term in an economic sense only. They did not separate themselves from the Yakuts, protested against being identified with the "Omuk" (as the Evenks are designated on the Olenek), and stressed that they came from the cattle-breeding regions of Yakutia.

As it turned out, the genealogies of individuals from the local population

*Translated from *Sovetskaya etnografiya*, 1952, no. 2, pp. 69–72.

showed convincingly that this population is derived from the Yakuts and traces its ancestors to the Yakut regions. Meanwhile, in Vilyuysk, the entire population living along the Olenek and to the west of the Ugulyat settlement—for example, around Lake Eyaik—is considered Evenk at the present time.

I managed to visit the Eyaik group personally. There were 14 households (61 individuals of both sexes), with both cattle and reindeer. From the questioning of members of these households, it turned out that they belonged to the Shologon clan, but that they considered themselves Yakut, and only in census records were they classed as "Tungus." We did not succeed in finding other Evenks between the Vilyuy and Olenek, although my co-workers Efimov and Petrov traveled over this territory for the specific purpose of collecting statistical information and data on the nationality of the population. The Yakuts settled in the territory of the Markhinsk administrative *soviet* [council] turned out to be comparatively recent migrants from the basin of the Vilyuy river. Apparently some of them, with their livestock, were attempting to penetrate even farther west.

In this connection, it is not without interest that in looking for a site for the construction of a cultural center in the upper reaches of the Olenek, we discovered the ruins of a fodder-shed and peasant house. According to the local population, a Vilyuysk Yakut with cattle erstwhile lived there. Indeed, there are good meadowlands along the Olenek, and it is possible to keep horned cattle there.

The population of the Dzhelindin soviet proved to be partly Yesey Yakuts of the Osogostokh and Chordu clans, partly migrants of the Ugulyat and Shologon clans from Vilyuysk. Here, too, they did not consider themselves Evenks. In the Sukhana settlement, which was attached to the Zhigansk *rayon* in 1934, there were also no Evenks. The basic population of this settlement belonged to the Shologon and Osogostokh clans.

In the Kirbey settlement (basin of the Arga-Sala and its tributaries) the population also consisted of Yakuts who had migrated from Lake Yesey. The majority of the households of this group wintered near the Arga-Sala and its tributaries, the Dzhara and Kukuhunda. In summer, they nomadized to the mountains which form the watershed between the tributaries of the Khatanga —the Kotuykan and the Popigay.

The majority of the population in the upper reaches of the Olenek (Olenek settlement) also consisted of Yesey Yakuts.

According to legends told by old Yakut men, their ancestors were also Yakuts and they settled at Lake Yesey three hundred years ago (?). The Yesey Yakuts were divided into five patrilineal clans (*aga uukha*)—the Osogostokh, Ospëk, Botulu, Chordu, and Beti. The Osogostokh, Ospëk, and Botulu clans were governed by a "prince" (settlement headman) and two elders who had their residence at Lake Yesey. The Chordu and Beti clans had a "prince" and an elder each. The Chordu prince lived at Lake Konora, and the elder under him on Lake Yesey. The Beti prince resided at the Dzhelinda river (a tributary of the Anabar) and his elder at Lake Yesey. It is obvious from these data how scattered the Yesey Yakuts were. They nomadized in the upper Olenek, on the Anabar, the Khatanga tributaries, and some went even to the Lena.

In the territories of the Olenek, Kirbey, and Dzhelindin settlements of which the Olenek rayon was originally comprised, 15 households of Evenks were discovered in all. They came from the Ilimpey rayon for trade and comprised only 4.5 per cent of the total population.

Along the Markha river, six "Yakutized" Evenk households belonging to the Chapogir clan were discovered.

Thus our survey showed that the overwhelming majority (95%) of the population in the area of the future Olenek rayon was Yakut and that the cultural center was to be constructed not among Evenks, as had been assumed, but among Yakuts.

It should also be noted that population data of this sort were obtained as a result of a local census of the Department of the National Economic Census of the Yakut A.S.S.R., involving the Olenek, Kirbey, and Dzhelindin settlements. The census was taken at the beginning of 1934 by assistant Popov.

Thus only one ethnic group lived in the basin of the Olenek—i.e., Yakut—and not two—Evenk and Yakut—as P. E. Terletskiy presumed. Nevertheless, the toponymic evidence indicates that, in the past, the basin of the Olenek was occupied by Evenks. At present, most of the tributaries of the Olenek and Anabar have Yakut names, but Evenk names are also encountered: Bargydamat (i.e., "defiance"), Dzhelinda (Taymenya), Kukuhunda ("green"), Mainda, and others. According to Evenk beliefs, *main* is the invisible thread which goes from the head of a human being to the deity Khaboki. By the term *mainda* the Evenks designate long, narrow streams and rivers.

As the Olenek cultural center was to be converted later on into a center for a larger rayon, we carried out an investigation of the economy of the population and a survey of the territories attached to the reorganized rayon. Hence, a journey was undertaken to the settlements along the lower reaches of the Olenek and Anabar rivers.[2] The investigation showed that these were also populated by Yakuts. In the Anabar region we encountered the Khatygyn, Omoldon, and Khangalas clans, and small groups from the Emis, Edzhen, Barakh, Sedemi, and Bakhynay clans.

Thus, it was made clear that the population of the basins of the Olenek and Anabar rivers was one with respect to nationality. This fact was thoroughly emphasized by me in an account of the journey given to the administration of the Yakut A.S.S.R. and the R.S.F.S.R., in which the erroneous attribution, in ethnographic maps, of the Olenek population to the Evenks (Tungus) was pointed out. These results were obtained not as a result of a misinterpretation of the term "Tungus," as Terletskiy believes, but on the basis of a first-hand familiarity with the population and the clarification of its national affiliation.

The Yakut nationality of the population of the upper Olenek, erroneously assigned by Terletskiy to the Evenks, was clearly shown when northwestern Yakutia was being divided into districts. After my arrival on the Olenek as a member of the Committee of the North, many petitions were delivered from the Olenek, Anabar, Kirbey, Yesey, and Dzhelindin areas expressing the desire for their inclusion as part of Yakutia and for the inclusion of Lake Yesey in the newly formed rayon of the Yakut A.S.S.R. The petitions were motivated by the fact that the people around the Olenek, Kirbey, Dzhelinda, and Yesey did not know the Evenk language, and that they were connected by kinship and cultural ties with the Vilyuysk Yakuts. It should be noted that the question of the inclusion of this population into the composition of the Yakut A.S.S.R. was raised as early as 1928 in the pages of the magazine *Avtonomnaya Yakutiya* (Autonomous Yakutia). In an article "From the life of the Zhossey Tungus," it was stated: "The Zhossey Tungus have absolutely no desire to move from Turukhansk *kray*, nor do they want to be evicted therefrom, as they have their snares (traps) in the tundra of Turukhansk kray."[3]

As we know, during the redivision of districts, in view of the economic importance of Lake Yesey for the Evenk National Okrug, it was left within the limits of the latter, whereas a considerable number of the "Yesey Tungus" (in reality Yakuts), who were in no way distinguishable from the population of the upper Olenek and Anabar rivers, were entered into the composition of the Olenek rayon of the Yakut A.S.S.R.

In conclusion, I cannot fail to express my astonishment that Terletskiy, who has agreed to recognize the direct observations of ethnographers which indicate that the affiliation of the Yesey to the Evenks is erroneous, defends the infallibility of census forms with respect to the Olenek population which is in no way distinguished from the "Yesey Tungus," and that he repudiates all the testimony of eyewitnesses showing the affiliation of the Olenek population to be Yakut.

Notes and References

1. Cf., I. S. Gurvich, K voprosu ob etnicheskoy prinadlezhnosti naseleniya severo-zapada Yakutskoy ASSR (On the question of the ethnic affiliation of the population of the northwest of the Yakut A.S.S.R.), *Sovetskaya etnografiya*, 1950, no. 4; B. O. Dolgikh, K voprosu o naselenii basseyna Oleneka i verkhoviy Anabara (The population of the Olenek basin and the upper reaches of the Anabar), Sovetskaya etnografiya, 1950, no. 4; P. E. Terletskiy, Yeshche raz k voprosu ob etnicheskom sostave naseleniya severo-zapadnoy chasti Yakutskoy ASSR (More on the problem of the ethnic composition of the population in the northwestern part of the Yakut A.S.S.R.), *Sovetskaya etnografiya*, 1951, no. 1.

2. I. M. Suslov, *Reka Olenek* (The Olenek river), Leningrad, 1937, p. 167.

3. *Avtonomnaya Yakutiya*, 1928, no. 182.

I. S. GURVICH

À PROPOS THE ETHNIC AFFILIATION OF THE POPULATION OF THE OLENEK AND ANABAR RIVER BASINS*

QUESTIONS ABOUT THE ORIGIN and ethnic composition of the peoples of the Far North can be best solved only through the collective labor of scholars of various specialties. In this connection, we cannot but voice satisfaction that our notes and papers on the origin and ethnic affiliation of the population of northwest Yakutia—to be precise, the populations of the basins of the upper and middle courses of the Olenek and Anabar rivers—have aroused comment not only among ethnographers, but among others.

P. E. Terletskiy has approached the problem stated by us from a statistical point of view.[1] Unfortunately, it is difficult to agree with his conclusions about the national affiliation of the ethnic groups with which we are concerned. The practical importance of the question of the ethnic affiliation of the population of the Olenek and Anabar basins for cultural and economic undertakings is such that we cannot leave unanswered the principal remarks of Terletskiy à propos our paper "The question of the ethnic affiliation of the population in the northwest of the Yakut A.S.S.R."[2]

The principal objection of Terletskiy is directed against our assertion that in the Olenek and Anabar *rayons* there is a single ethnic group—the Yakut reindeer-herders. Assuming that the above is contradicted by census results, Terletskiy cited figures evidencing, in his opinion, the multinational make-up of the population. However, it is not difficult to see that the evidence has to do not with the territory surveyed in our paper but with a significantly larger district. This explains the number of Dolgans and Russians included in Terletskiy's table.

In our paper we dealt with the population of northwestern Yakutia within the boundaries of the present-day Olenek and Anabar rayons. This territory was delineated with a thick line on the schematic map appended to our paper. Apparently, Terletskiy somewhat broadened the territorial extent of our work. Of course, the correlation of national groups in the extensive territory covered by the tables of Terletskiy—the lower reaches of the Olenek river (Bulun rayon), the Khatanga river and its tributaries the Bludnaya, Zhdanikha, Rassokha, and Popigay—is rather different from that in the region considered in our work, and, as a consequence, the figures presented in the table cannot be at all useful for refuting the data we presented for a different, much smaller territory.

The fact that Terletskiy found 11 Russian families living in the lower reaches of the Olenek and Anabar indicates that by the Anabar rayon he actually means the territory of the Khatanga-Anabar rayon (which belonged to the Bulun *okrug* until 1931). Repeated examination of the primary sources (census household cards and lists of householders) showed that no Russian households were detected by the census on the Anabar.[3]

*Translated from *Sovetskaya etnografiya*, 1952, no. 2, pp. 73–85.

In Ust-Olenek (i.e., also within the boundaries of the territory surveyed by us), three Russian families engaged in fishing and hunting were encountered.[4] Of these, the family of a former convict, S. F. Ishchenko, numbering 7 persons and possessing 30 reindeer, cannot be included in the calculation, as it is not an "old-time" family.[5] Nor can the family of S. E. Grigorev, numbering 5 persons, who gave their native language as Russian, be assigned to the old residents of Ust-Olenek. In the confessional books of the Bulun church of the Ust-Olenek Christian community in the 1900's, and in the list of households of this community for 1916, neither Grigorev nor members of his family are mentioned.[6] A third family, that of G. E. Semennikov, numbering 5 persons, gave its native language as Yakut and its nationality as "Christian."[7] On the card a correction is inserted, obviously during the processing of the materials: over the word "Christian," written with another pencil, is the word "Russian." It should be noted that other members of Ust-Olenek, for instance the Cherepanovs, whom we know of from confessional entries, declared themselves Yakut.[8]

The remaining 8 Russian households belonging to "peasants who have taken to the tundra" were registered in the census in the former Khatanga-Anabar rayon but beyond the limits of the Olenek and Anabar basins. In Zhdanikha there resided the family of P. G. Portnyagin (5 persons); in Letov, there lived 5 families: the Portnyagins and Rudinskys (36 persons); on the Rossokha the family of N. Portnyagin (7 persons); and in Dalgdin a family numbering 8 persons.[9] Thus, the assertion of Terletskiy about the presence of Russian old-time inhabitants in the lower reaches of the Olenek and Anabar rivers, as well as his charge that we were ignorant of it, is based on a misunderstanding.

As far as the history of the Russian old-time residents of Ust-Olenek goes, it is not, according to documentary data, the same as Terletskiy depicts it. At the end of the 18th century, 46 males were counted in the town group of Ust-Olenek.[10] At the very end of the 18th century, townspeople engaged in fishing and hunting were listed in the census at their own request, as peasants, since by a special edict townspeople were forbidden to live beyond the limits of towns.[11] According to the data of the Tenth Revision (1858), the Ust-Olenek peasant community consisted of 62 persons of the male and female sex, including children.[12] In the 1860's the number of Ust-Olenek peasants, as reported by their headman, decreased sharply as a result of an "epidemic of smallpox and improper climatic conditions."[13] Only 10 adult males survived. In 1886, 15 males and 14 females, children included, were counted in Ust-Olenek. With regard to the condition of the Ust-Olenek peasants, it is stated in the report for this year: "Now they have become completely Yakutized, they have mixed with the local population, and only their blonde hair and blue eyes distinguish them and indicate their origin."[14]

We have already alluded [elsewhere] to the evidence of a participant in the Great Northern Expedition, Kh. P. Laptev, on the mixing of the Ust-Olenek old-time residents with the Yakuts, as well as to the observation of P. Khitrovo, who noted the same phenomenon in the middle of the 19th century.[15] In 1916, the Ust-Olenek community consisted of 9 families (16 males and 11 females), who spoke only Yakut.[16]

In connection with the problem of the territorial limits of our work, we should like to remark on Terletskiy's observation about the impossibility of separating the population of the Olenek and Anabar basins from the bulk of the population of northern Yakutia. Such an impression can, indeed, be created if only census materials are used as guides. On the other hand, during a personal visit to the

Olenek and Anabar Yakut reindeer-herders, the isolation of their territory and the marked differences in them from both the Evenks of the northwest and from the Yakut cattle-breeders of Vilyuy okrug became immediately apparent. The unity of this ethnic group has been noted repeatedly in the literature. During our work in the Olenek rayon of the Yakut A.S.S.R. from 1941 to 1946, we were able to convince ourselves personally of this by becoming closely acquainted with the population of this rayon, as well as of the Anabar rayon.

Our field material tells nothing about the Toguy, Zhokhut, Keltyat, Kyup, and Ezhan clans who nomadized far beyond the limits of the territory with which we are concerned. Terletskiy's reproach that we were not interested in their existence is therefore unjust, as is the assertion that "not only the Evenks of the rayons indicated, but also the Evenks of the remaining northern rayons of Yakutia, must, in the opinion of I. S. Gurvich, be considered as Yakut in nationality."[17] If one would sufficiently familiarize oneself with our paper, one would satisfy oneself that such an assertion is absent. Apparently, Terletskiy has interpreted in his own way the supposition advanced in our paper that the ethnic make-up of the population has not, by far, been correctly shown in all of the northern rayons of Yakutia, and that processes that took place in the Olenek and Anabar rayons also have their application in other rayons of northwestern Yakutia—for example, in the Zhigansk.

But let us turn to a more essential discrepancy. The basic position of Terletskiy is that there are two ethnic groups in the Olenek and Anabar basins: the Yakuts (the Osogostokh and Khatygyn clans and Yakuts who have taken to the tundra*) and the Evenks (the Beti, Ugulyat, and Shologon clans); these are supposedly clearly set apart by the census data of 1897 and 1926, but remain unobserved by ethnographers visiting the northwest of the Yakut A.S.S.R.

Terletskiy writes:

Concerning the population of the first three groups ("Tundra" Yakuts, Osogostokh and Khatygyn households), there is no doubt as to their Yakut origin and nationality. This is evidenced by the data of the 1926 census and by cartographic materials . . . . With respect to the Beti, Ugulyat, and Shologon clans, there is no doubt as to their Tungus origin . . . .

He maintains that

"Tundra" Yakuts, and the Osogostokh and Khatygyn clans, are pure Yakut in origin (according to the 1926 census they were entered as Yakut), and that the rest—the Beti, Ugulyat, and Shologon (as well as the Chordun), the so-called Yakutized Tungus— because of their Tungus origin undoubtedly a different group, declared themselves Evenks (Tungus) both in 1897 and in 1926.[18]

However, these categorical assertions of Terletskiy are flatly contradicted by the facts. In the 1926 census, members of the Osogostokh and Khatygyn clans, as well as of the Shologon, Beti, Chordu, and Ugulyat clans, were recorded as Tungus.

In order to avoid unsubstantiated statements, let us turn to the primary documents of the 1926 census—household lists of the former Vilyuy okrug—and cite a few examples, showing the card columns in the form of a table (Table 1). The given examples do not give evidence selected haphazardly. Of the 69 Osogostokh households registered in the census of the former Vilyuy okrug, 66 households

*[Henceforth "Tundra" Yakuts.—Editor.]

TABLE 1

Family, name, patronymic	Nation-ality	Native language	Age	No. of members of family	Places of nomadizing
		Khatygyn Clan[*]			
Nikolayev Ivan Konstantinovich	Tungus	Yakut	40	7	Tas-Dzhany, Olenek
Fedorov Konstantin Nikolayevich	"	"	70	6	Olenek, Dzhanyda
Vasilyev Prokopiy Vasilyevich	"	"	32	5	Arga-Sala, Dzyhanyda, Olenek
Vasilyev Vasiliy Semenovich	"	"	50	2	Olenek, Arga-Sala, tundra
Semenov Filipp Khristoforovich	"	"	30	9	"
Semenova Praskovya Petrovna	"	"	40	3	"
Semenov Vasiliy Tikhonovich	"	"	45	4	Kanavka river, Dzhanyda
Grigoryev Samson Dmitriyevich etc.	"	"	35	—	"
		Osogostokh Clan[†]			
Vasilyev Pavel Nikolayevich	Tungus	Yakut	30	2	Olenek
Pavlov Vasiliy Fedorovich	"	"	40	4	Udzha, Dzhanyda, Dogdokda
Tikhonov Nikolay Vasilyevich	"	"	57	2	Tas-Dzhany, Orto-Kirbey, Olenek
Khristoforov Moisey Nikolayevich	"	"	33	4	"
Pavlov Afanasiy Fedorovich	"	"	55	7	Billyakh, by the sea
Stepanov Innokentiy Dmitriyevich	"	"	60	8	Anabar, Billyakh
Chenkhokh (nickname) Prokopiy Dmitriyevich	"	"	30	5	By the sea, Dindya
Khristoforov Petr Khristoforovich	"	"	35	4	By the sea, Billir
Naumov Khristofor Vasilyevich	"	"	32	6	By the sea, Udzha Khatan
Naumov Innokentiy Konstantinovich	"	"	45	11	Udzha Khatan

[*]*TsGa YaASSR*, sec. 70-r, op. 32, d. 318, leaves 15–30.
[†]*Ibidem*, leaves 255–258, 265–270, 275–276, 281–282, 287–288, 291–294.

were recorded as Tungus, with Yakut being the native language. On three cards, the columns "Nationality" and "Native language" were not filled in.[19] Of the 17 households of the Khatygyn, 16 households were classified as Tungus with Yakut as the native language; on one card, the "Nationality" and "Native language" columns were not filled in.[20] All the Beti, Ugulyat, Shologon, and Chordu were also recorded as Tungus with Yakut being the native language. Thus, the main link in the evidence of Terletskiy, the data of the 1926 census, supplies no evidence of the presence of two ethnic groups in the region with which we are concerned.

As is known, all the investigators who have visited the basins of the upper and middle Olenek and the upper Anabar, and those who have gone to Lake Yesey and the Kotuy river, as well as those who have had some degree of contact with the native population of these regions, have noted the unity of the population in language, way of life, clothing, and customs. We have already alluded to the prerevolutionary literature on this point.[21]

Let us note some statements by Soviet ethnographers who have carried out practical work in the regions which interest us here. The ethnographer I. M. Suslov, exploring the Olenek basin, noted that along the middle course of the Olenek, in the Sukhana settlement, there were 50 Yakut seminomadic households in 1934.[22]

B. O. Dolgikh, after exploring in the northeast of Krasnoyarsk *kray*, wrote:

During the period 1935–9, the author of these lines had occasion to make several visits to the region of Lake Yesey, the middle course of the Kotuy, and to the east of the Kotuy on the Arynli river near the Kirbey trading post. There is no doubt that the population there consists of Yakut reindeer-herding nomads, and there are no Evenks among them. No ethnographic difference can be found between the population of this region and that of the Olenek . . . . [Both] constitute one ethnic group of Yakut reindeer-herders, connected by clan and personal ties, deriving from the very same clans, and considering themselves as one ethnic whole. . . . [23]

We refer, too, to our own observations, which coincide with those given above.[2]

Thus the ethnographic data, like the census materials, give evidence of the ethnographic unity of the population in the basins of the Olenek and Anabar rivers. However, even though the census data of the future Olenek and Anabar rayons did show the population to be Tungus, all observers unanimously pointed out that it appears to be Yakut. What is the reason for this discrepancy?

The principal reason for regarding the population of the Olenek rayon as Tungus (Evenk) lay in the fact that in the former Vilyuy okrug, apparently at the time when the reforms of Speranskiy were being applied, a tradition was established of designating all nomadic reindeer-herders, including the Yakut reindeer-herders, as Tungus (Evenk). In accordance with the "Regulations concerning the natives of Siberia," the Tungus (Evenks) were assigned to the category of "vagrants" (nomads) and were freed from a number of duties. They were permitted to roam about from district to district. The nomadic Yakut clans engaged in reindeer-herding were placed in the same category as the Tungus.

The difference between the economy of the Olenek and Anabar Yakuts (reindeer-herding, hunting, fishing) and the sedentary livestock-breeding economy of the rest of the Yakuts of the former Vilyuy okrug has been maintained and preserved by this tradition, and noted by most of the ethnographers visiting northwestern Yakutia.[24] Denying the influence of tradition on the results of the census, Terletskiy maintains that had it been operative, one would expect in the census totals no data on the Yakuts among the nomadic population. Because of this it is particularly necessary to become familiar with the household cards of the settlements referred to above, recorded in the territory of the Olenek and Anabar regions, to realize that it is chiefly women who were reckoned as Yakut, that is, migrants from the livestock-breeding regions. Let us cite a few examples.

Second Ugulyat settlement: Gerasimov Fedor—nationality, Tungus; native language, Yakut. His mother, Yevdokiya, is shown as a Yakut, and all the other members of the family are entered as Tungus.[25] The mother of Gerasimov Fedor, as we know, came from the former livestock-breeding Vilyuy okrug; this also explains why she was numbered with the Yakuts.

Shologon settlement: Borolo (nickname) Nikolay Lvovich—nationality, Tungus; native language, Yakut. Wife Tatyana, a Yakut.[26]

Second Ugulyat settlement: Sofronov Filipp Yegorovich—nationality, Tungus; native language, Yakut. Wife, Yakut; other five members of the family, Tungus.[27]

Chordu settlement: Khristoforov Nikolay Vasilyevich—nationality, Tungus; native language, Yakut. Wife Varvara, Yakut; other five members of the family, Tungus.[28]

Osogostokh clan: Davakay Afanasiy Federovich—nationality, Tungus; native language, Yakut. Wife Yevdokiya, Yakut; other members of the family, Tungus.[29]

In the Osogostokh clan, in the family of Semenov Alexey Petrovich, there was a hired worker, Nikolay, 32 years old, calling himself a Yakut. In columns 11 and 12 of the form he is an "unskilled workman," and "subsidiary." His yearly pay was two reindeer.[30]

In this way, in the territory of the present Olenek rayon, the census-takers recorded as Yakut only persons who had come from the southern livestock-breeding rayons.

TABLE 2

Clan, camp	Tungus		Yakut	
	Male	Female	Male	Female
Osogostokh	168	190	1	5
IInd Ugulyat	74	80	1	4
Chordu	52	50	—	1

Table 2 reflects the census correlation of Yakuts and Tungus in the clans under discussion, within the limits of the former Vilyuy okrug.[31] As the above examples show, the Yakuts mentioned in the census did not comprise families, and were interspersed in the composition of the "Tungus."

Thus, the tradition of counting the nomadic reindeer-herding population of the northwestern former Vilyuy okrug as Tungus was fully reflected in the census. However, as we have emphasized more than once, this does not mean that the Olenek and Anabar nomadic Yakuts identified themselves as Tungus-Evenks. In the presence of an obviously pronounced Yakut national consciousness, the majority of the nomadic Yakuts answered the question "What are you?" with "Tungus," as was accepted in the former Vilyuy okrug where they fell into the category of "Tungus clans." It should be noted that, in giving this answer, the nomadic Yakuts never identified themselves with the Evenks of Krasnoyarsk kray, regarding them as a completely alien, unrelated people.[32]

We shall reply in passing to Terletskiy's question about methods used to elicit national consciousness. From detailed questions as to what the population considered itself to be, and with whom it should be identified, it became clear from where it derived its ancestors. At the same time, genealogies were recorded; these have shown, in every respect, that the population considers its ancestors to be Yakut—migrants from the southern livestock-breeding rayons of Yakutia. Where there was doubt about national affiliation, the population protested sharply when we designated the Evenks of Turukhan kray as their fellow tribesmen and clansmen. In refuting this, most of our informants did, in fact, cite genealogies.

Thus, Terletskiy's division of the Olenek and Anabar camps into Yakut and Tungus ones is not justified by the census data or by the evidence of investigators. It remains to analyze the bases, developed by Terletskiy himself and used in affiliating the Osogostokh and Khatygyn clans to the Yakuts, and the Beti, Ugulyat, and others to the Evenks. "Their settling in the lower reaches of the Anabar and Olenek rivers and their economic characterization as tundra reindeer-herders does not raise doubts as to their Yakut nationality," writes Terletskiy in dealing with the national affiliation of the Khatygyn and Osogostokh. Such considerations were also the basis for assigning the Beti, Shologon, and Ugulyat clans to the Evenks. "Their settling in the taiga and forested tundra zone and their hunting type of economy underlines their Evenk nationality."

The unsubstantiated nature of these positions is obvious. Nationality is not determined by place of residence. It is well known that in the taiga and forested tundra there live not only Evenks, but also other national groups. Settlement in the lower reaches of the Olenek and Anabar rivers in itself cannot constitute a definition of Yakut national affiliation for the Khatygyn and Osogostokh.

At first sight, a more serious basis advanced by Terletskiy for assigning the Ugulyat, Shologon, Chordu, and Beti clans to the Evenks appears to be their Tungus origin. Actually, in the 17th century, as gleaned from archival sources, the territory of the basins of the Olenek and Anabar was peopled by Tungus tribes; but, over three centuries, there occurred in this region a complete change in the ethnic composition of the population, a complete supplanting of the Evenk language by the Yakut.[33] We should remind ourselves that the Tungus population in these river basins was sharply reduced in the 17th century as a result of epidemics, internecine wars, and famines. The remaining Tungus population became mixed with migrant Yakuts from livestock-breeding regions. To this, Terletskiy has not offered objections. In identifying origin (i.e., ethnic affiliation in the 17th and 18th centuries) with contemporary ethnic and national affiliation, Terletskiy, in our opinion, is in error when he regards it as something unchanged and ignores the immense changes that took place in its composition in the basins of the Olenek and Anabar in the past three hundred years.

At the present time it is more accurate not to speak of the Tungus origin of the Beti, Ugulyat, Shologon, and Chordu clans, since in these a complete inter-mixture of the Evenk population with the Yakut has taken place; the Yakuts, migrating from the central and Vilyuy regions, have prevailed over and assimilated the Evenk population—and even their clan names of Tungus origin.

Reference to economic characteristics, often cited by Terletskiy in determining nationality, cannot be useful. One can take as an example the Russians, who have long since been settled in a number of regions of the Far North and have been engaged in the same kind of economic activity (fishing, dog-keeping, hunting) as the indigenous population, but who still have retained their language and nationality.

Finally, as a basis for the presence of both Yakuts and Evenks in the basins of the upper and lower Olenek and the upper Anabar, Terletskiy has advanced "yet another very important circumstance which throws light on a certain stability of the two national groups in question." It seems that S. K. Patkanov, on the basis of census data for 1897, noted that "*the indigenous inhabitants of the northern regions of Yakutia—the Tungus, Lamuts, Yukagirs, and Dolgans—possess clan divisions.* And, contrariwise, with respect to the Yakut population, as a rule, *the absence of evidence of clan affiliation has been noted.*"[34] As Terletskiy showed, this is precisely what was confused by Patkanov. On the basis that the Yesey Yakuts were divided into clans, he assigned them to the Tungus. However, the Yesey Yakuts were regarded by Terletskiy as an exception, and he puts the word itself in quotes as an "error" of Patkanov, obviously assuming that the presence or absence of division into clans can serve as a basis for establishing the national affiliation of one or another group.

It would be unnecessary to examine this unfounded methodological position, if it were not for the conclusion of Terletskiy, based on it, that "in social relations, the two groups—the Tungus with a clan system and the Yakut represented by individual, separate families in the settlements, families which have severed ties with their clans—are quite different, taking their separate forms on the basis of nationality."[34] In rejecting the assertion about the presence of a clan system among the Tungus, long since refuted by Soviet science, one must not fall in with the position that the Yakuts referred to in Terletskiy's paper (with exception of the "Tundra" Yakuts) had lost their clan identity by the time the census was taken. As is known, the Khatygyn camp was divided into the Osogostokh, Maymaga, Botulu, and Ospëk clans. A most numerous clan was the Osogostokh, and so the Khatygyn camp was often designated as Osogostokh. To the contrary, the Beti settlement, purely Evenk in Terletskiy's opinion, was not divided into clans.

Terletskiy's position is not strengthened by the attempt to number the northern Yakuts as tradespeople and by this to separate them from the rest of the population. Historical documents of the 17th and 18th centuries show that the northern reaches of Yakutia were dominated, not by Yakut tradespeople, but by the indigent strata of the Yakut population, by fugitives escaping to the north from administrative* oppression and tribute requisitions.[35] The sources do not reveal data that would indicate that all the northern Yakuts were tradespeople. As far as the Yakut buyers of furs, particularly active in northern Yakutia in the 19th century, are concerned, they are not to be identified with the northern Yakut reindeer-herders. The fur-buying agents of commercial houses visited the north only for trading purposes. Most of the households in northern Yakutia were concerned not with trade, but with hunting and reindeer-herding, and found themselves irremediably in debt to these merchants.

Let us turn to the figures given by Terletskiy which, in his opinion, prove the existence of two ethnic groups in the Olenek and Anabar basins. As material for a statistical characterization of the population of the regions with which we are concerned, Terletskiy used the same census cards and lists that were used by B. O. Dolgikh, and that we also have had occasion to use. These data deal with 259 Olenek and Anabar households. Terletskiy divided the cards into two groups: Evenks, 128 households (in reality Beti, Chordu, IInd Ugulyat, and Shologon clans), and Yakuts, 131 households (Osogostokh and Khatygyn clans, and "Tundra" Yakuts). As we have seen, such a division is not justified by the actual data. It is no wonder that, as a result of a comparison of the economic indices for the two groups, Terletskiy obtained figures which are as uncharacteristic as the division itself. Having shown that most (80%) of the reindeer were owned by the group of "Yakuts" (the Osogostokh and Khatygyn clans and the "Tundra" Yakuts), and that in the group of "Evenks" (Beti and Chordu clans, and others) the number of reindeer was significantly smaller,[36] Terletskiy took this as confirmation of the presence of "two quite different groups." In reality, the figures given by him are only evidence that the bulk of the livestock was concentrated in the group of the tundra and forested tundra camps.

In the immense territory of the Olenek and Anabar region there were several types of reindeer-herding economies, corresponding to definite natural zones. In the lower reaches of the Anabar and Olenek rivers, in the open tundra, there lived reindeer-herders with a short breed of reindeer. In addition, in the lowlands a significant role in the economy was played by the hunting of wild deer, the raising of geese, and fishing. Reindeer-herders with the taiga-tundra breed settled in the winter in the forested tundra zone, nomadized in the spring to the pebbly barrens, and in the summer into the open tundra. Here, too, reindeer-herding was combined with wild deer hunting and fishing, but the role of fishing was much less important than in the first group.

In the taiga zone, immediately adjacent to the forested tundra, the main part of the economy consisted of hunting the large ungulates—wild deer and elk. Reindeer-herding (of the taiga breed) served as the basis for this activity. To

*[In the original, *toyon*, the Russian administrator of natives.—Editor.]

protect the reindeer against mosquitoes and midges, the herders nomadized to the pebbly barrens only in the summer months.

Finally, the hunters–reindeer-herders of the taiga zone (upper reaches of the Tyung, Markhya, and Markokya), who also kept reindeer of the forest breed but only in negligible quantity–nomadized up and down the course of these rivers in the summer. The husbandry of large herds (over a hundred head) in this zone in the summer was thought to be extremely onerous.

Thus, in the basins of the Olenek and Anabar rivers, several types of economic activities can be distinguished, differing according to the relative importance in each of hunting, reindeer-herding, and fishing. The predominance of reindeer in the tundra and forested tundra economies, noted by Terletskiy, is entirely natural, since the main part of the economy in these was reindeer-herding. However, Terletskiy derived quite a different conclusion from this: "In the Evenk system, reindeer [are used for] transportation . . . , it does not offer possibilities for the expansion of herds (?!), and the Tungus always had to turn to the Yakut reindeer-breeders for the replenishment of the livestock they used for transportation.[37]

If this proposition is analyzed, it follows that in the basins of the Olenek and Anabar rivers there were two groups, one of which depended on and, as a consequence, was exploited by the other. Or the members of the Beti, Chordu, Shologon, and IInd Ugulyat camps–"Evenks," according to Terletskiy–depended on and were exploited by the "Yakuts"–by the Osogostokh and Khatygyn clans, and also by the "Tundra" Yakuts.

In reality, the picture of the class relationships in the basins of the Olenek and Anabar rivers was quite different. It was not the "Tungus" (taiga camps) who depended on the "Yakuts" (tundra and forested tundra camps), but the whole population depended on the *kulak* households which exploited their fellow clansment and members of [to them] alien clans. There were such extortioners both among those whom Terletskiy assigned to the Yakuts and among those he assigned to the Evenks.

The reindeer stock was recorded by the census-takers from verbal statements; no count of the reindeer was made. This meant that the kulaks significantly understated the number in their herds. Nevertheless, all the census data enable us to detect the kulak households.

In the Osogostokh clan, the household of Kh. S. Vasilyev with 419 reindeer[38] stands out. In the annotations on his census card it is noted that among his dependents there were members of the Osogostokh clan–Khristofor Nikolayev ("Serse") with a family of 9 persons, Nikolay Titov with a family of 4, Khristina Samysar with a son, Akulina with a son, and a widow, Anna Vasilyeva. Of course, these "dependents" were also workers, serving the Vasilyev household. A member of the same clan, Kh. S. Soltos, had 255 reindeer. In an annotation on his card, it was indicated that among his dependents were, from the Osogostokh clan, Yevdokim Vasilyev with a family of 5 persons, and Konstantin Yegorov, with a family of 7.[39] I. D. Stepanov had 364 reindeer.[40] His household was served by Semen Khristoforov and family possessing 3 reindeer of their own[41] and Petr Khristoforov and family with 12 reindeer of their own.[42] (These are annotations on their cards.) In the household of Yefrem Stepanov (Chomo)[43] there were 245 reindeer. This household was served by two families numbering 12 persons in all.

In the Chordu clan, such exploiters were I. P. Filippova, nicknamed Kyupey, possessing, according to the census data, 690 reindeer.[44] Her household was served by four families. Khristoforova Praskovya had 316 reindeer,[45] and her household was served by a single family numbering 5 persons. E. V. Kokuy[46] had 284 reindeer. And there were others. Around them were grouped *bednyaks*, both fellow clansmen and members of alien clans, working as herdsmen.

Thus, the data do not suggest dependence of the "Evenks" on the "Yakuts," nor the dependence of one settlement on another, but the dependence of households with few or no reindeer on the big kulak ones. It should be noted, moreover, that economic units set up for nomadizing in the tundra were made up both of fellow clansmen and of members of alien clans.

In the mechanical assessment of household cards, Terletskiy reaches still another conclusion, evidencing (supposedly) the differences in the economy of the "Yakuts" and "Evenks." According to the census data, he writes, the Yakuts are hunters of the polar fox, and the Evenks (Tungus) are squirrel hunters.[47] Actually, there were polar fox in the region where most of the members of the Osogostokh and Khatygyn clans wintered; in the region of the taiga camps polar fox were rarely encountered, and the main object of fur trapping was the squirrel. Nevertheless, the use of the term "polar fox hunters" and "squirrel hunters" with respect to the population of the Olenek and Anabar rivers is not justified. Fur trapping in the regions under discussion was, until collectivization, only a secondary type of production. Pelts were secured for purchases of tobacco, tea, and hunting supplies from the merchants. As a matter of fact, the "squirrel hunters" secured, according to Terletskiy's data, an average of [only] 30 squirrels a year per family.[48] It is clear that they could not have existed on this. It is also difficult to imagine the existence of "the polar fox hunters." This is illustrated by Table 3, which was composed from household cards of the nomadic population in the former Vilyuy okrug and indicates the average number of polar foxes and squirrels secured per family in the various clans.[49]

TABLE 3

Clan or camp	Squirrels secured [per family]	Polar foxes secured [per family]
Osogostokh	2.1	2
Khatygyn	17.1	1.6
Chordu	2.6	3.7
Beti	5.8	4
Ugulyat	11.9	0.7
Shologon (nomadic)	29.3	—
Shologon (sedentary)	61.3	—

Note: Data on the Shologon were taken from analyzed materials of the census (*Sotsialisticheskaya Yakutia*, 1930, no. 3, p. 106). Data on the number of pelts secured by "Tundra" Yakuts, nomadizing near the Olenek and Anabar rivers, could not be discovered.

The actual basis of subsistence in the basins of the Olenek and Anabar rivers was the hunting of large ungulates, which fact, for some reason, Terletskiy did not find necessary to mention. The majority of the households in the region we have surveyed were engaged in hunting wild deer. On an average, the numbers secured per family were[50]: Osogostokh clan, 4.1 wild deer; Khatygyn, 6.7; Chordu, 5.9 and 3 elks; Beti, 7.6; Ugulyat, 2.1 and 0.2 elk.[51] Thus, the factual material indicates that the differences pointed out by Terletskiy in the economy of the groups separated by him are secondary, and tied in with residence in the different natural zones. More essential are the general features of the economy of this population. Reindeer-herding among the Olenek and Anabar Yakuts differed in a number of peculiarities: the absence in the economy of deer hounds, the use of the pack-load method of travel, the milch deer, etc. The hunting of large ungulates predominated over fur-trading and was, for the majority of households, the basic means of subsistence. Only the households with large herds subsisted by the slaughter of domesticated reindeer. The technique of reindeer-breeding (use of reindeer for transportation, different operations in reindeer-breeding), like the method of hunting wild deer, differed in the same way in the whole territory under examination.

Thus, it must be noted that all the proofs advanced by Terletskiy in favor of the presence of "two quite different groups" in the basins of the Olenek and Anabar rivers turn out to be groundless on close examination.

In conclusion, we may venture to broach the subject of the degree to which it is possible to utilize census data for determining the ethnic composition of the population of the Far North. Census data, as experience shows, usually give a realistic picture of the number and distribution of large nations, amounting to hundreds of thousands of persons. In these conditions, individual erroneous statements about national affiliation constitute an insignificant portion of a per cent and cancel out in the total sum.

An altogether different approach is needed in the case of census data on separate ethnic groups and peoples of the Far North, who may consist of a few hundred or a few thousand persons. Erroneous statements about national affiliation given by even a few families lead to distortion of the over-all census of such groups because of their small numbers.

With regard to the household census data of the circumpolar regions taken in 1926–7, it should be noted that quite a few errors crept into the resultant figures. The presence in the forms of a very large number of columns having to do with administrative and ethnic affiliation—okrug, administrative unit, *uprava* [judicial district], nationality of tribe, clan—made things very difficult both for the population and for the census-takers. Many of the population had no clear concept of their relationship with the population of neighboring regions and they were not prepared to answer questions pertaining to nationality and tribe. Let us illustrate this with concrete examples. In the Khatanga-Anabar region in the village of Popigay, the Dolgans answered the questions in the following way: Tuprin, Petr Parfenovich—nationality, Yakut; native language, Yakut;[52] clan, Sakha. Tuprin, Stepan Parfenovich—nationality, Yakut; native language, Yakut; clan, Dulgan.[53] Bolshakov, Miron Trifonovich—nationality, Yakut; native language, Yakut; clan, Dulgan.[54] Only a few individuals indicated their nationality as Dolgan. In the Bulun okrug on the Lena (in the village of Yebitem, for example), the following entries were found: Barbantski, I. Z.—nationality, Tungus; tribe, Yukagir; native language, Russian.[55] In the Kolyma district, in the cards of most Yakuts, the column "Tribe" was filled in with "Mongol"; the Russians entered their family name in the column "Clan."[56]

None of this is strange. We have already had occasion to note above that the members of the erstwhile Russian peasant communities, who had taken to the tundra, declared themselves, not as Russians, but as "Christians," and that all the nomadic Yakuts of the northwest of the former Vilyuy okrug, according to the census, were Tungus (Evenks). A survey of the census data for 1926–7 for the Vilyuy okrug indicated that they contain significant errors. According to the data of the Tenth Revision (1858), there were two Tungus clans in the Zhigansk ulus of the Bulun okrug–the Kyup and Ezhan–and eight Yakut–Ist and IInd Batulin; Ist, IInd, IIIrd and IVth Khatygyn; the Kangalas; and the Tumat. However, at the end of the 19th century, when the differences between the Tungus clans and the Yakuts were obliterated, owing to the fact that members of Tungus clans adopted the language of the Yakuts, the first and second, in differentiation from the Yakut livestock-breeders, were often called Tungus. Therefore, at the time of the 1926-7 census, in a number of places in the Bulun okrug, the Batulin, Khatygyn, and Kangalas were recorded as Tungus, while, at the same time, in some places the Kyup and Ezhan appeared among the Yakuts. Thus, in the fourth volume of census cards, members of the Kangalas, Ist Batulin, and IIIrd and IVth Khatygyn clans were designated as Tungus in the first 58 cards,[57] and in the following cards the members of these clans, as well as the members of the Kyup and Ezhan clans,[58] were designated as Yakuts. In the second volume of census cards for the Bulun okrug, the members of the Kyup, Tumat, Chordu, and Ezhan clans were assigned to the Yakuts in the first 44 cards,[59] and, in cards 45 to 78, the members of these same clans were designated as Yakut-speaking Tungus.

All these facts show that for the determination of the ethnic affiliation of the population of the Far North, census data may be enlisted only after a thorough critical analysis of each microregion and only after comparing them with objective evidence, i.e., the findings of ethnographers.

Notes and References

1. P. E. Terletskiy, Yeshche raz k voprosu ob etnicheskom sostave naseleniya severo-zapadnoy chasti Yakutskoy ASSR (More on the problem of the ethnic composition of the population in the northwestern part of the Yakut A.S.S.R.), *Sovetskaya etnografiya*, 1951, no. 1.

2. I. S. Gurvich, K voprosu ob etnicheskoy prinadlezhnosti naseleniya severozapada Yakutskoy ASSR (The question of the ethnic affiliation of the population in the north-west of the Yakut A.S.S.R.), *Sovetskaya etnografiya*, 1950, no. 4.

3. *Tsentr. gos. arkhiv Yakutskoy ASSR— TsGA YaASSR* (Central State Archives of the Yakut A.S.S.R.—Ts. G.A. Ya. A.S.S.R.), sec. 70-r, op. 32, documents 347, 397, 326.

4. *Ibidem*, d. 357, leaves 43–44, 113–114, 125–126.

5. According to a confessional book of the Bulun church dating from 1900, the Ishchenko family appeared among those attached to the Ust-Olenek Christian community (*TsGA YaASSR*, sec. 241, op. 2, d. 82, leaf 1).

6. *TsGA YaASSR*, sec. 108-i, d. 72, leaves 76–77.

7. *Ibidem*, sec. 70-r, op. 32, d. 357, leaves 125–126.

8. *Ibidem*, leaves 5–6

9. *Ibidem*, d. 326.

10. *Ibidem*, sec. 52, op. 1, d. 33, leaf 33.

11. *Ibidem*, d. 1, leaves 1–7.

12. *Ibidem*, d. 18, leaf 1.

13. *Ibidem*, leaf 8.

14. *TsGA YaASSR*, sec. 52, op. 1, d. 18, d. 33, leaf 33.

15. Gurvich, *op. cit.*, pp. 159, 161.

16. *TsGA YaASSR*, sec. 108, op. 1, d. 77, leaf 76.

17. Terletskiy, *op. cit.*, p. 92.

18. Terletskiy, *op. cit.*, p. 93

19. *TsGA YaASSR*, sec. 70-r, op. 32, d. 318, leaves 257–258, 293–294, 319–320.

20. *Ibidem*, leaves 23–24.

21. Gurvich, *op. cit.*, p. 161.

22. I. M. Suslov, *Reka Olenek* (The Olenek river), Leningrad, 1937, p. 111.

23. B. O. Dolgikh, K voprosu o naselenii basseyna Oleneka i verkhovev Anabary (On the question of the population of the Olenek and upper Anabar river basins), *Sovetskaya etnografiya*, 1950, no. 4, p. 172.

24. See: A. A. Popov, Materialy po rodovomu stroyu dolgan (Data on the clan system of the Dolgans), *Sovetskaya etnografiya*, 1934, no. 6, p. 133; Dolgikh, *op. cit.*, pp. 169–170; Klark, Vilyuyisk i ego okrug (Vilyuyisk and its environs), *Zap. R.G.O.*, Sib. otd., part XII, 1864, p. 133.

25. *TsGA YaASSR*, sec. 70-r, op. 32, d. 318, leaf 123.

26. *Ibidem*, leaf 209.

27. *Ibidem*, leaf 165.

28. *Ibidem*, leaf 233

29. *Ibidem*, leaf 273

30. *Ibidem*, leaves 237–238.

31. *Ibidem*, d. 254. Analysis based on form A-1.

32. It is interesting to note that in a number of census cards, several persons from the Beti and Khatygyn clans are recorded as Yakuts, apparently at their insistence. However, these depositions apparently gave rise to doubts in the processing of the cards, for on them "Yakut" was corrected to "Tungus." (*TsGA YaASSR*, sec. 70-r, op. 32, d. 318, leaves 15, 17, 43, 45, 83, 230, 243, 247, *et al.*)

33. Gurvich, *op. cit.*, pp. 150–161.

34. Terletskiy, *op. cit.*, p. 97. The italics are mine.

35. *Kolonialnaya politika Moskovskogo gosudarstva v Yakutii XVII v.* (Colonial politics of the Muscovite state in Yakutia in the 17th century), Leningrad, 1936, pp. 121, 193–195, 216.

36. Our data on the stocks of reindeer in the 259 Olenek and Anabar households referred to do not agree with those of Terletskiy. In all groups, according to the data in our possession, there were 10,545 reindeer. On the average, there were in the Khatygyn settlement (Khatygyn and Osogostokh clans) 46.4 per household; in the Chordu, 57.1; in the Beti, 26.6; in the Shologon, 13.7; in the Ugulyat, 20.3; and among the "Tundra" Yakuts, 63 reindeer.

37. Terletskiy, *op. cit.*, p. 94.

38. *TsGA YaASSR*, sec. 70-r, op. 32, d. 318, leaves 305–306.

39. *Ibidem*, leaves 259–260.

40. *Ibidem*, leaves 275–276.

41. *Ibidem*, leaves 289–290.

42. *Ibidem*, leaves 287–288.

43. *Ibidem*, leaves 309–310.

44. *Ibidem*, leaves 49–50.

45. *Ibidem*, leaves 237–238.

46. *Ibidem*, leaves 57–58.

47. Terletskiy, *op. cit.*, pp. 94–96.

48. *Ibidem*, p. 95.

49. *TsGA YaASSR*, leaves 16, 26, 34, 72.

50. *Ibidem*, d. 318.

51. According to data from the analysis of census materials on the Shologon clan, in one nomadic family of Shologon, 9.6 wild deer and 1.2 elk were secured in a year (*Sotsialisticheskaya Yakutia*, 1930, no. 3). Data on the number of wild deer secured by the "Tundra" Yakuts could not be found; according to the evidence of Solovyev, these Yakuts (of a Yakut settlement in the Khatanga-Anabar rayon) killed 2 deer each per family in a year. See: Solovyev, Olenovodstvo Khatangsko-Anabarskogo rayona (Reindeer herding in the Khatanga-Anabar rayon), *Sbornik po olenovodstvu, tundrovoy veterinarii i zootekhnike* (Collected papers on reindeer breeding, tundra veterinary medicine and zootechnology), Moscow, 1932, p. 177.

52. *TsGA YaASSR*, sec. 70-r, op. 32, d. 454, leaves 215–216.

53. *Ibidem*, leaves 183–184.

54. *Ibidem*, leaves 455, 307–308.
55. *Ibidem*, leaf 5.
56. *Ibidem*, d. 462, leaves 157–261.
57. *Ibidem*, d. 455.
58. *Ibidem*, d. 455, leaves 149, 157, 161, 165.
59. *Ibidem*, d. 456.

B. O. DOLGIKH

ON THE POPULATION OF THE OLENEK
AND ANABAR RIVER BASINS[*][†]

IN THE DISPUTE ABOUT the ethnic affiliation of the native population of the basins of the Olenek and Anabar rivers within the borders of the Olenek and Anabar *rayons* of the Yakut A.S.S.R., two opposing points of view have been developed. According to one, advanced principally by persons who have visited the locality, the population of these regions, since at least the middle of the 19th century, is Yakut. Those who hold the other point of view, based on statistical data in the literature of the 19th and early 20th centuries, consider the majority of the population of these regions to be Evenk (Tungus). The first viewpoint has already been set forth in the articles of I. S. Gurvich and by the author, the second in an article by P. E. Terletskiy.[1]

The principal argument in favor of regarding the population of the Olenek and Anabar as Evenk is reference to the results of the censuses for the years 1897 and 1926 in these regions. According to them the majority of the population here is indeed Evenk (Tungus). On the basis of the census data, in the opinion of Terletskiy, there is the "subjective (independent, personal) evidence of the population itself (from each of its individual members) about its national status as expression of its national consciousness." Terletskiy does not trust the data of Gurvich and other ethnographers, since, in his opinion, "the ethnographic method of investigation . . . gives, as a rule, only an approximate and general notion about ethnic composition."[2]

Although Terletskiy himself presents a further series of facts, whenever the census data were adjusted on the basis of an ethnographer's evidence, he considers in the matter of the ethnic affiliation of the Olenek and Anabar population that the statistics are correct and the observers in error.

Turning to the grounds for our point of view, we shall first of all indicate one important fact that can definitely throw light on the whole question. No one, including Terletskiy, denies that the indigenous population of the Olenek and Anabar, at least since the mid-19th century, speaks only the Yakut language.

The following circumstances must be discussed. Terletskiy, in his debatable paper, has greatly extended the territory in which the ethnic affiliation of the population is in dispute. He has included in his survey the population of the eastern part of the Taymyr National Okrug of Krasnoyarsk *kray*, in which there

[*]Translated from *Sovetskaya etnografiya*, 1952, no. 2, pp. 86–91.

[†]In opening the pages of *Sovetskaya etnografiya* to a discussion about the problem of the ethnic affiliation of the population of the northwest of the Yakut A.S.S.R. and in publishing a number of papers dedicated to this topic, the editorial board has proceeded from the belief that the solution of this problem is closely connected with the development of general principles for determining the ethnic affiliation of one or another group. This topic is of great interest for general theory.

The material presented in papers by I. M. Suslov, I. S. Gurvich, and B. O. Dolgikh in the current number offers persuasive evidence for the view that the indigenous population of the basins of the Olenek and Anabar rivers within the boundaries of the Yakut A.S.S.R. is Yakut.— Editors.

are also Dolgans, and "Yakutized" descendants of Russian peasants who have taken to the tundra. He also argues for his position by stating that Gurvich does not include in the population of the Olenek and Anabar the Evenks (Tungus) of the Tobuy, Zhokhut, Keltyat, Kyup, and Ezhan clans, and that he gives incomplete information on the Tungus of the Shologon, Ugulyat, Chordu, and Beti clans. Therefore, we are obliged to point out that the matter under discussion is the population of a quite definite territory, precisely delineated on the map published in Gurvich's paper.[3] Neither the Dolgans and the "Tundra" Yakuts, nor the descendants of the Tobuy, Zhokhut (more correctly Dzakhut, that is, Yakut), Keltyat, Kyup, and Ezhan (Zhigan) clans,[4] lived on this territory or live there now. Within the limits of Olenek and Anabar rayons the Shologon and Ugulyat live only in the southernmost part of Olenek rayon, and in exactly the number indicated by Gurvich. The rest of the descendants of these clans live even farther to the south or southeast, within the limits of the Vilyuy basin. Here also live, thoroughly mixed with the Yakuts, the descendants of the Tobuy, Zhokhut, and Keltyat clans mentioned above. As regards the Kyup and Ezhan, they are primarily concentrated in the Bulun rayon to the east of the Lena. Finally, the "Tungus" of the Chordu (Betu) and Beti clans are also given, in the data of Gurvich, in the number in which they were found in 1926 within the limits of the future Olenek and Anabar rayons. The larger number of these clan members lived and were recorded in 1926 within the limits of the Sibirsk kray as Yakuts of the Betu (Chordu) and Beti clans. These are a part of the same Yesey Yakuts whom Terletskiy mentions more than once. It is natural that, since a large number of the members of these clans (camps) were recorded as Yakut in Sibirsk kray, this substantially decreased the number of "Tungus" of the same clans (camps) registered in the Yakut A.S.S.R. I presented this in detail in the paper mentioned above.[5]

Thus, the positions of Terletskiy referred to above are based either on a misunderstanding or on an excessive broadening of the territory in which the ethnic affiliation of the population is in dispute.

It must be stated that over-all extension of the territorial limits of the dispute to the east, south, or northwest does not change the essence of the matter, or the basic conclusions. But as long as the original subject was the population of a defined territory, we, too, shall confine ourselves to it.

Among the clans (camps) whose descendants live in the Olenek and Anabar rayons of the Yakut A.S.S.R., there is no dispute, judging from Terletskiy's paper, about the ethnic affiliation of the clans (camps) of the Khatygyn (same as Osogostokh) of the former Vilyuy okrug, the Kangalas and the IIIrd Khatylin settlements of the former Verkhoyansk okrug,[6] and the "Tundra" Yakuts of the former Turukhansk kray (Yenisey guberniya). Nor is there any dispute about the Evenk origin of the Shologon, Ugulyat, and a part, at least, of the Beti; although, with respect to the latter, all is not clear, and the very name "Beti" is not encountered in the 17th century among the names of the Evenk clans in the basins of the Vilyuy, Olenek, and Anabar. At the present time, we repeat, the descendants of the Beti regard themselves as Yakuts, and they are also regarded as Yakuts by the surrounding population (the Yakuts and Chirindin and Ekondovsk Evenks).

Thus, in the matter of the ethnic affiliation of the population of the Olenek and Anabar rayons of the Yakut A.S.S.R., opinions differ only as to the origin and ethnic affiliation of members of a portion[7] of a single clan (camp) of Betu (Chordu), or, more precisely, 35 families in which there were 218 persons in

1926. In all, there were counted 1940 persons in the territory of the present-day Olenek and Anabar rayons in 1926.[8] Of these, 62.7% (1216 persons—Khatygyn and Osogostokh, Lower "Tundra" Yakuts, Kangalas, and Khatylin of the former Verkhoyansk okrug) are considered Yakuts even by Terletskiy; 26.1% (506 persons—Shologon, Ugulyat, and Beti) are probably primarily Evenk *in origin;* the remaining 11.2% consist of Olenek-Anabar Yakuts of the Betu (Chordu) camp, whose ethnic affiliation continues to be disputed. Terletskiy assigns them to the Tungus together with the Shologon, Ugulyat, and Beti, presents a series of average figures as if these were evidence of their economic unity, and points out that in comparison with the Yakuts, for these Tungus, "even the territory nomadized by them is different." He describes this territory as located to the south of that occupied by the Olenek and Anabar Yakuts. But it will suffice to look closely at the map mentioned above to see that the Betu (Chordu) live primarily far to the northwest, farther north than the majority of the Yakuts of the Khatygyn camp, which separates the Betu (Chordu) from the Shologon and Ugulyat.[9] The very name of the Betu settlement is the name of an ancient Yakut *volost*, located at the time of arrival of the Russians on the right bank of the Lena, above the Aldan estuary, where later on a Betu camp was also found. We have already mentioned that all the descendants in the Betu (Chordu) settlement in Krasnoyarsk kray (there were 501 of them in 1926) are considered, and consider themselves, Yakut.

Since the only thing that remains in dispute is the ethnic affiliation of that part of the composition of the Betu (Chordu) settlement which is within the limits of Olenek rayon, let us give more detailed consideration to this group. The proposition that those members of this "clan" (camp) who live within the limits of Krasnoyarsk kray are Yakuts is not disputed. As a rule, the composition of the settlements was ethnically homogeneous. Therefore, if a part of the population is indisputably Yakut, it would seem that the rest of it would also have to be considered Yakut. But Terletskiy does not agree with this. He ascribes to assimilation the circumstances that members of the very same clan divisions call themselves Yakuts within the limits of the Krasnoyarsk kray and "Tungus" in the Yakut A.S.S.R. Naturally the assumption that all 500 Betu (Chordu) were assimilated by the Yakut in the Krasnoyarsk territory, and that in the Yakut A.S.S.R. these same Betu, 218 of them, related to the first by various ancestral and kinship ties, remained Evenk, appears highly improbable. In reality, the Betu of Krasnoyarsk kray and the Betu of the Yakut A.S.S.R., who settled the so-called Kirbey[10] in the upper reaches of the Anabar, do not differ ethnographically.

As we have already mentioned, in 1926 there were within the limits of the Olenek and Anabar regions of the Yakut A.S.S.R. 35 families—218 individuals—of the Betu (Chordu) settlement altogether. We knew some of them personally, and we collected information about the ethnic and clan affiliations of others through third persons. In 1935 we gathered data on approximately half of the Betu (Chordu) of the Kirbey camp. All of them were considered, or considered themselves, Yakut. Thus, for one-half of the Olenek Betu (Chordu), it was possible to establish their ethnic affiliation. It is quite improbable that we just "accidentally" happened on Yakuts, and that the remaining half of the Olenek Betu (Chordu) all consisted of Evenks. Rather, the contrary can be assumed, that all of them were Yakuts, as their fellow clansmen told us and as is confirmed by Gurvich, who has been in contact with them and has studied them.

We happened to become rather closely acquainted with some of the members of the Betu camp affiliated with the Chordu clan and inhabitants of the Olenek region. Such, for example, was Dmitriy Stepanovich Chordu, in 1926 registered in the census as a "Tungus" of the Chordu clan under the name Dmitriy Stepanovich Khristoforov. We had occasion to talk with him quite a lot on ethnographic topics, in part on the origin of the local population, and on questions of the location of snares (traps) for the polar fox, and to become oriented on the whereabouts of other hunting grounds, belonging to or taken over by members of the Chordu clan living both in Krasnoyarsk kray and in the Yakut A.S.S.R. Beyond any doubt, he considered himself and the rest of his fellow clansmen in Kirbey in the Olenek region as Yakut reindeer-herders and not Evenks. Another Olenek Yakut, Samson Khristoforovich, from whom we have recorded many traditions and tales, also unreservedly regarded himself and his fellow clansmen on the Olenek and Anabar as Yakuts. He was married to an Evenk, Anna Lazarevna Emidak from Chirinda, from whom we also recorded some Evenk traditions and tales. No one in the place doubted that S. Kh. Chordu was a Yakut and his wife an Evenk.

We recorded a great many traditions, tales, and legends in 1938 from a third Olenek Yakut, Khristoforov Konstantin Fedorovich, also from the Chordu clan. He was a worldly wise person, who had lived both on the Vilyuy and on the "Lama" (i.e., on the Kheta—a tributary of the Khatanga) and had traveled all over the Olenek. We also talked with him especially about the origin of the Olenek Yakuts. In particular, he (like our other informants) related that the Olenek and Anabar Yakuts of the Chordu clan came from Lake Konor near Zhigansk, where their ancestors had migrated from central Yakutia. With respect to the Yakuts of the Betu (Chordu) camp within the limits of Krasnoyarsk kray, all of them, according to the statements of K. F. Chordu, were of the same original members of a Betu (Chordu) settlement on the Olenek and Anabar.

Other examples could be given. In any case, the assumption that the Betu (Chordu) camp was comprised of two different ethnic elements, of "Tungus" and Yakut, of which the "Tungus" of the Chordu clan would all be concentrated in the Yakut A.S.S.R., and the Yakut of the Chordu clan in Krasnoyarsk kray, appears to be altogether erroneous.

We do not wish to say that no admixture or assimilative processes took place here. To the contrary, sometimes the composition of the camps of northern Yakut reindeer-herders was very complex in derivation. In them, as we have already noted, descendants of Evenks and even descendants of Russians merged with the Yakuts. For example, there is reason for the claim that the Osogostokh clan, despite its purely Yakut name and the Yakut self-consciousness of its members, was derived from Evenks of the tribe Vanyadyr, who lived on Lake Yesey and in the region around it in the 17th century.

A large group of "Tundra" Yakuts, the so-called Sidim (Tyuprin or Tuprin, Chuprin), are also of Evenk origin, and probably kinsmen of some of the above-mentioned Yakut reindeer-herders of the Beti settlement of Tungus (Evenk) origin.

Other examples might be found also. Here the point is merely that peoples, like nations, consist of historically pooled communities of members of different races and tribes. The most important condition for the formation of a people, for the merging of their formative elements into a single whole, is the dominance of one of the languages of the merging tribes and ethnic groups. It is just this process that took place on the Anabar and Olenek.

Thus, the members of the Betu (Chordu) clan can, beyond any doubt, be assigned to the Yakuts. As matters stand, almost three-quarters of the population whose ethnic affiliation is in dispute can be considered Yakut, not only in language but also in their own recognition and, on the whole, in origin, and the remaining quarter "Yakutized" Evenks. If the question is about the distribution of Yakuts and Yakutized Evenks (Tungus) over the territory within the boundaries of the Anabar and Olenek rayons, then it can be shown that the Evenks by birth (the Shologon and Ugulyat) occupy, as has already been stated, the extreme south of the Olenek region, living in the basins of the tributaries to the Vilyuy —the Markha, Markoka, Tyung—and at the headwaters of a Lena tributary—the Muna. On the Olenek proper they were dominant only in the basin of the Silingir river and in a small area in the valley of the Olenek, where it forms a bend downstream from the mouth of the Silingir.

All considered, within the limits of the Olenek and Anabar rayons, the Yakuts come to 93.6% of the population, and if one also regards as Yakut the descendants of the Beti, then 100% of the indigenous population of these rayons proves to be Yakut.[11] The Beti are disseminated here among the Khatygyn (Osogostokh), in small groups and individual families. We have met a significant proportion of the adult males of the Beti clan (camp) who live or have lived in the Olenek rayon, or have gathered information about their clan or ethnic affiliation. As we have already pointed out, they regard themselves Yakuts and scarcely recall their Evenk origin. It must also be emphasized that these descendants of the Beti differ in no way from the descendants of the Betu (Chordu), or from the descendants of the Khatygyn (Osogostokh). The supposition that there are two distinct (Yakut and Evenk) ethnic groups on the Olenek and Anabar is based on an obvious misunderstanding.[12]

Since Terletskiy now regards the descendants of the former Khatygyn (Osogostokh) settlement as Yakuts, he thereby takes away his principal argument—that the censuses of 1897 and 1926 accurately determined the ethnic affiliation of the inhabitants of the Olenek and Anabar. The fact is that both the 1897 and the 1926 census counted the members of the Khatygyn (Osogostokh) camp of the Vilyuy basin district as "Tungus." Once Terletskiy acknowledges that these were Yakuts, he acknowledges, as a consequence, that the census was in error in determining the ethnic affiliation of these Yakuts. But if, in the 1926 census, there are errors with respect to 513 members of the former Khatygyn (Osogostokh) camp, then there might also be errors with respect to the 218 members of the former Betu settlement. The very same statistician visited and took the census of these peoples and others in the Olenek basin, within the boundaries of the present Olenek rayon.[13] Just as he designated the Khatygyn as "Tungus," so he also designated the Betu (Chordu) as "Tungus."

Terletskiy shows correctly that the self-awareness of the population is of decisive importance in determining their ethnic affiliation, and the point is, precisely, that all inhabitants of the Olenek and Anabar basins consider themselves Yakuts. We had the opportunity to talk with people from all the camps (except the Ugulyat) to which the population of the Olenek region had earlier belonged, with people who had been born and had grown up on the Olenek, who had in the past been headmen of these camps, and none of them had any doubt, with respect to either themselves or their fellow clansmen, that they were Yakuts. The members of the Beti camp were no exception. Only the Shologon said that they were "Tungus" by descent. Moreover, all of the Olenek Yakuts knew that they were called and "written" Tungus, and understood that this was tradition, but not reality.

Finally, Soviet ethnography and the practices of Soviet work in Siberia should take into account existing traditions about relationships of one group of the population to another. That there was and even is today, in the Yakut A.S.S.R., a tradition of calling the northern Yakut reindeer-herders "Tungus" is a fact. But what does this tradition signify? Is it a survival from the past or a sign of the direction taken by a past development, or of how it is proceeding today as the process of national consolidation in northern Yakutia goes on? Certainly, it is a survival from the past, a survival of artificial—we might even say of largely "departmental" armchair—origin, a survival throwing light on the history of the formation of the ethnic group of northern Yakut reindeer-herders, irregularly, one-sidedly, a survival which slurs over a completed process.

Should Soviet ethnography wait, while local statisticians and other subordinate workers of the Soviet apparatus cope with this confusion and these errors, and only then establish academically the changes that have taken place in the ethnic composition of the population? Or should we help these local workers by pointing out that they are incorrectly determining the ethnic affiliation of the population, that various traditions are operative here which give a false reflection of reality and to which, in the present case, it is necessary and possible to put a quick end? It seems to us that Soviet science should not only be based on practical experience, but should also assist practical affairs, point out the paths of practical activity, and in no case lag behind practice, only reporting the conclusions of the latter.

In the region with which we are concerned, historical development in the mid-19th century led to the formation of a new, distinctive ethnographic group of Yakut nationality. It seems to us that the task of Soviet ethnography is to furnish evidence of this, and not to obscure it.

Notes and References

1. I. S. Gurvich, K voprosu ob etnicheskoy prinadlezhnosti naseleniya severo-zapada Yakutskoy ASSR (The question of the ethnic affiliation of the population in the northwest of the Yakut A.S.S.R.), Sovetskaya etnografiya, 1950, no. 4; B. O. Dolgikh, K voprosu o naselenii basseyna rek Oleneka i verkhoviy Anabara (On the question of the population of the Olenek and upper Anabar river basins), ibidem; P. E. Terletskiy, Yeshche raz k voprosu ob etnicheskom sostave naseleniya severo-zapadnoy chasti Yakutskoy ASSR (More on the problem of the ethnic composition of the population in the northwestern part of the Yakut A.S.S.R.), Sovetskaya etnografiya, 1951, no. 1.

2. Terletskiy, op. cit., p. 88.

3. Gurvich, op. cit., p. 163.

4. We employ the word "clan" [rod] in referring to these groups (camps—naslegi) only because they are so designated in the literature. Actually, these "clans" were formed rather late and were themselves usually comprised of several clans.

5. Dolgikh, op. cit., pp. 170–171.

6. Terletskiy believes that the inclusion of these two camps in our work "obscures an already complicated problem." But the descendants of the members of these camps belong to the Anabar region, and live there between the Olenek and Anabar, some of them on the Anabar itself, so that they cannot be left out of the account. What complicates the problem is not this group of Yakuts, indisputable inhabitants of the region in which the population is in dispute, but reference to the faraway Keltyat, Tobuyets, and other groups who live beyond the borders of the Olenek and Anabar regions.

7. The greater number of the descendants of this settlement, as we know, are considered Yakuts within the boundaries of Krasnoyarsk kray, and there is no dispute about this.

8. Dolgikh, *op. cit.*, p. 163.

9. In another case Terletskiy confuses the Chordu clan in the lower reaches of the Olenek (*Sovetskaya etnografiya*, 1951, no. 1, p. 98). Hence he contradicts his own assertion (p. 94) that the Tungus (including the Chordu clan) live in the upper reaches and along the middle course of the Olenek.

10. Terletskiy erroneously points out that the Kirbey settlement is in the southern part of the Olenek region, whereas actually this is the most northwestern settlement of the region in question.

11. We are not considering several families of Ilimpey and Chapogir Evenks, who have moved to the territory of the present-day Olenek rayon. In 1926 there were five or six families in all.

12. There were differences between the Yakut reindeer-herders of the Olenek and Anabar and the Yakutized Evenks (the Shologon) living to the south of them. But these differences were not defined according to a policy separating a specifically Evenk economy, but according to one approximating the economy of the Shologon to the economy of the Vilyuy Yakut livestock-breeders. About 55% of the households of the Shologon in 1926 had horses and cattle, and some were already living a sedentary life. On the whole, the type of economy constituted was transitional from the nomadic economy of the Yakut reindeer-herders to the sedentary or semisedentary economy of the Yakut livestock-breeders of the Vilyuy.

13. In the Anabar region, there are very few descendants of the Vilyuy Khatygyn and Betu. The bulk of the population there is comprised of descendants of "Tundra" Yakuts of the former Yenisey guberniya and of Kangalas and Khatylin of the former Zhigansk ulus of the Verkhoyansk okrug.

A. P. OKLADNIKOV

ANCIENT PETROGLYPHS AND MODERN DECORATIVE ART IN THE AMUR REGION[*]

ABOUT SIXTY YEARS AGO, in 1902, B. Laufer, an outstanding sinologist and investigator of Far Eastern cultures and author of the first, and up to now only, general monograph on the art of the Amur peoples, wrote that "the history of the decorative art of the Amur tribes is shrouded in mystery, since no written records give any accounts of it." Comparing the materials of his own art collection with those of L. Schrenck made a half century earlier, Laufer wrote further that "The forms of this sphere of art have remained unaltered up to the present time, notwithstanding all political turbulence and change that have affected the Amur region in the meantime . . . the native art has been retained pure and intact," in spite of contact with the Russians. From this he was justified in inferring that their "artistic conceptions have taken deep root in the hearts of the people, and have acquired a high value in their intellectual world."[1]

Such stability in the art of the Amur tribes, and its deep roots in the aesthetic consciousness of the people, would seemingly indicate that some sort of a definite original core and local beginnings on Amur soil are to be expected. However, further in his work, Laufer develops opinions that change this general deduction basically. These opinions are connected to the problem of the origins of the art of the Amur tribes—to its sources. Here Laufer comes to the conclusion that the Amur tribes did not themselves create this rich and complex decorative art, but that, in the main, they borrowed it from without.

Having discovered in the art of the Amur tribes a number of elements of indisputably Chinese origin, he wrote that its "forms and conceptions are imbued . . . with a Chinese spirit" and that its basis rests "undeniably in China." In times immemorial, the Amur tribes, during contact with the Chinese, assimilated elements of Chinese art, at first simply as a bow to fashion, and then started developing it independently. As for the exact time of this contact and the first borrowing of elements of Chinese art, Laufer thinks that they coincide with the adoption of Chinese writing by the unlettered Amur tribes. Poor in culture, they nevertheless felt the need for a more developed ornamentation, which was acquired from these same Chinese. Since, according to him, the first native written language in the Amur appears in the era of the Jurchen kingdom, apparently it is also then that elements of Chinese art, Chinese ornaments, that subsequently underwent development on Amur soil, penetrated there.[2]

Laufer's opinions are, of course, interesting, above all as they represent the first, comprehensive effort to evaluate historically the art of the Amur peoples, to determine its characteristics, and to clarify its origins. Now, however, we are in possession of new factual data, which were lacking at that time and which permit us a broader and newer view of problems connected with the origin of art among the Amur tribes. These are archaeological data that allow us to look more deeply into the past of the Amur peoples, into the history of their art.

As I have had occasion to note many times,[3] the most ancient of the known examples of Amur art found in Neolithic sites bear an amazing general resem-

[*]Translated from *Sovetskaya etnografiya*, 1959, no. 2, pp. 38–46.

blance to the present-day decorative art of the Nivkhs (Gilyaks), Nanays, and Ulchans.* A characteristic design, such as an imitation basket-weave design, is found on sherds and on whole clay vessels extracted from Neolithic sod houses in the lower Amur valley, from Khabarovsk and lower—down to the ocean—and also in the Ussuri valley. This design has also been found in modern times quite a bit farther south, in the Maritime Province, in the region of Tetyukhe bay near the town of Ussuriysk, and in a Neolithic site near the village of Osinovka.[4] There can be no doubt that the Neolithic ornament in the form of weaving is the forerunner of the present-day design of the Amur peoples, although in form the latter is considerably more developed and more complex. In a number of cases, such ornaments retain their original simple forms to the present and do not differ essentially from their Neolithic prototypes. We see here the same rhombs, placed in a checkered design and separated from each other by plain stripes of the background. But this background itself is, in essence, the design, while the rhombs are simply the background. Such, for instance, is the ornament published by B. Laufer as an example of a Nanay ornament cut out of paper.[5]

Another type of ornamentation, just as typical of the Neolithic on the Amur, is the spiral. In the Maritime Province, the spiral design has been found on a vessel from a Neolithic site on Tetyukhe bay. On the Amur, this ornament is encountered only in sites that had a culture first revealed by excavation of a Neolithic sod house on Suchu island (Suchu 1). This ornament has also been found in the Neolithic of the Ussuri valley, near the village of Sheremetyevskoye. The spiral ornament, also analogous in principle to the Neolithic ones, is also common in the art of the Nanays, Ulchans, and the Nivkhs. In fact, it comprises the richest source of ornamentation of these peoples today, from which they evolve their designs and compose such popular motifs as figures of fish and cocks. Laufer rightfully brought attention to this in his definitive work.[6]

The coincidence between the art of the ancient Neolithic population of the Far East and the art of present-day Amur peoples can be observed not only in the two important elements of decorative art mentioned but in its general character. Unlike the decorative art of the forest hunting groups of East Siberia, primarily those Tungus groups neighboring on the peoples of the Amur—the Evens and Evenks—the Amur ornament has mostly a curvilinear ribbon-like character and not a straight-line, geometric one. This difference can also be detected in the Neolithic. The Neolithic ornaments of the forested Cis-Baykal of Yakutia, and the Trans-Baykal, have a strictly linear-geometric character; a curved line is altogether alien to them. The Neolithic ornamentation of the Amur stands out just as definitely by its curvilinear character, with a predominance of spirals and basket-weave design. To this should be added another important point that testifies to the presence of a definite genetic connection and of a succession of traditions linking the ancient and modern art of the Far East.

On cliffs on the right bank of the Amur, near the village of Sakachi-Alyan, and also in the Ussuri basin, unique pictographs have long been noted. These in no way resemble, either in substance or in style, any of the well-known pictographs of Siberia, Northern Europe, or Central Asia. These pictographs can be attributed to local provenience. The region wherein they spread is clearly delineated. They are found within strictly limited boundaries: the lower Amur (below Khabarovsk, at Sakachi-Alyan and the May encampment), the basin of the Ussuri (the village of Sheremetyevskoye, the Khor river), the Suiphun river [Sui-fên Ho] near the town of Ussuriysk (the ravine of the Medvezhi

*[Also known as Ulchi, Olchi, Ulchs.—Editor.]

depression). Therefore, we may call this provenience the Ussuri-Amur one. The pictographs on the cliffs of the Amur and Ussuri rivers are executed for the most part with one and the same persistently repetitive technique. They are cut into the cliffs with deep grooves. These grooves often run into one another and are not separated by a smooth space; sometimes, however, there is such a space.

The subject matter most common to these pictographs is an anthropomorphic drawing of very unique type. It is in the shape of the head of some kind of mythical being, spirit, or monster, or perhaps a mask resembling the dance masks of South Sea tribes or of the Tibetan cult theater [lama dancers] or of the Japanese "no" theater which depict just such spirits (Figs. 1 and 2).

A second group of pictorial representations on the cliffs of the Amur and Ussuri consists of drawings of elks or deer; a third, of snakes; a fourth, of birds (Fig. 5, items 2, 4, 6). There are also stylized representations of sailing boats with people in them.

In investigating the connections between ancient and modern art among the cliff representations of the Amur the anthropomorphic ones, the masks, were found to be particularly interesting. Among them are representations reminiscent of stylized heads of monkeys—with a wide upper part, huge round eye-sockets, and large round chins. In his time, Laufer definitely rejected the presence of anthropomorphic elements in the decorative art of the Amur peoples. He recognized only the zoomorphic and vegetal elements, primarily the stylized drawings of fish, cocks, dragons, as the characteristic elements of Amur ornamentation. For his time he was, of course, quite right. It is true that in the decorative art of the Nanays, Ulchans, and Nivkhs, there are no clearly anthropomorphic representations comparable with the precise drawings of cocks or fish. However, on examining examples of Amur art, one can see simian masks in them; these may not be exactly the same, but at least they are very similar, although they are highly stylized. Moreover, such figures are not the exception, but are the most widely used, and they are, in essence, the basic element of the rich decorative art of the Nanays and Ulchans.

Thus, in Plate XXV, item 1, in Laufer's book there is a complicated ornamental composition of double spiral lines and arcs. In its lower part, the simian mask so well known to us is clearly visible, with the wide and rounded upper part, inside which the huge eyes are indicated by a double spiral—just as in the petroglyphs. Lower, the wide simian nostrils are indicated, and lower still, the massive chin. From the sides of this muzzle protrude wide ears, also depicted by spirals. It was just like this that the ears were drawn in several of the petroglyphs. Particularly interesting are the two "outgrowths" rising out of the head like two rays. Straight lines are just as characteristic of the anthropomorphic masks represented in the petroglyphs. The outgrowths or "rays" crown them above and often fringe both sides (Fig. 4).

In tracing connections between the masks and analogous figures in the decorative art of the Nanays and Ulchans, it is interesting that aside from their general resemblance in contour, in several instances the entire representation of the mask in the petroglyph is made of concentric circles or spirals. Such is one of the masks on a cliff near the village of Sheremetyevskoye, which is represented by a seemingly continuous unwinding spiral-like band. This band begins at the right eye of the mask, encircles it and, by concentric circles, completely fills in the area of the mask. A second mask on the same cliff has two eyes, each of which is made of coils of spirals, the ends of which descend and fill in the oval of the face. From here, it is only a step to the spiral figures of the Nanay ornaments

FIGURE 1

FIGURE 2

mentioned earlier, to the simian, whimsical masks found in the—for them characteristic—complicated compositions as a permanent, integral part (Fig. 3).

Thus, the conclusion may be drawn that the strange anthropomorphic masks
of the Amur petroglyphs did not disappear without trace, but went into the
make-up of later decorative art as its basic subject matter.[7] It should be noted
that such masks are used in Amur decorative art in the same way as other figures,
such as, for instance, those of fish or birds. They served in their own way as a
sort of "building material," as details of complicated decorative compositions. But,
unlike the figures of fish and birds, they became part of the general ornamental
design and lost their independence to such an extent that they can be detected
only when compared with petroglyphs where these masks are still found in their
initial, separate forms.

Among the petroglyphs of the Ussuri and Amur valleys there are usually found,
together with the anthropomorphic masks, representations of deer with characteristic straight lines across the body. According to Laufer, after the cock and
dragon, the deer also plays an important part in the decorative art of the Amur

FIGURE 3.   1, 5: representations on the cliffs along the Ussuri river;
2–4, 6: Nanay ornaments (according to B. Laufer).

tribes. Among the examples that he published, there are figures of deer with exactly the same transverse bands as those in the petroglyphs. In the petroglyphs there are also figures of snakes, usually depicted by spirals and sometimes by wavy lines. They obviously correspond to the dragons (*mudur*) of the latest period of Nanay art, which are depicted in just this way.[8] Incidentally, the Nanays interpret a representation of a snake on one of the cliffs of Sakachi-Alyan as their customary image of a dragon.

As we have seen, among birds, the rooster predominates in present-day Nanay decorative art.[9] Nevertheless, in examining closely the examples of ornamentations published by Laufer, one can also find representations of waterfowl, such as geese, ducks, or swans, just as they are found in the petroglyphs. For instance, in the paper pattern published on page 45 of Laufer's book, there are such birds, and in some of them particularly, we can see a close agreement with the miniature figures of swimming waterfowl in the Sheremetyevskoye petroglyphs.[10]

Thus the basic subjects of the cliff representations are again repeated in modern ornamentation. These are: (1) simian spiral-like masks; (2) representations of deer with transverse lines on the body; (3) waterfowl; (4) snakes. All this, together with a wide application of spirals as the basic element and form-shaping method, connects the ancient cliff representations with the modern decorative art of the Amur peoples and is, consequently, evidence of a definite artistic tradition, uninterrupted for many centuries, and even, perhaps, for thousands of years (Fig. 5).

Laufer was undoubtedly right when he wrote that such important elements of Amur decorative art as the cock, the bat, and the fish are relatively late impor-

FIGURE 4. A: Nanay ornament (according to B. Laufer); B: anthropomorphic mask from a cliff along the Ussuri river.

tations from China. The cock, particularly, is alien to the hunting-fishing economy of the Amur tribes. Such a deduction is also confirmed by the petroglyphs, where we do not see any fish, cocks, or bats.

Among the relatively late importations that appear in the Amur region in the Middle Ages and are preserved to our times is the vegetal design in the form of

FIGURE 5. 1, 3, 5, 7: Nanay ornaments (according to B. Laufer); 2, 4, 6: representations on cliffs (2—Sakachi-Alyan; 4, 6—Ussuri river).

a "running spiral" or a wavy line with many symmetrically spaced spiral-like coils. Those who have investigated this motif propose that it is a stylized representation of grapevines with leaves and clusters. It spread widely during the classic and early Middle Ages from the Mediterranean to the Orient, to China and Japan, [arriving there] already in the T'ang period, which in the Maritime Province [Primorye][11] is the era of the P'o-hai empire and in Japan, the Nara period. Magnificent examples of it are also known from the Jurchen era of the "Primorye." Because of its curvilinearity, particularly the spirals, this motif became an integral part of the national decorative art of the Amur peoples. A "running spiral" of this kind is used as a favorite border of any drawing, and is the most widely used ornamental border in the women's national costume of the Nanays—a fishskin robe, which caused the Chinese to call them "the fish-skin Tatars" (*Yü-pi Ta-tzŭ*).[12]

It is very probable that these ornamental motifs, which have a definite symbolic meaning in China (which is what explains their popularity in Chinese daily life and folk art), were adopted by the Amur tribes at the time when they came into closest contact with China. The period of such contacts—economic, political, and cultural—begins when class differentiations appear in our Far East and the P'o-hai and Jurchen States were formed initially. It was then, we think, especially during the Jurchen period, that there began an intensified infiltration of these new motifs into the decorative art of the Amur tribes. And here the premises stated by Laufer retain their strength and convincingness.

But because of this, the aboriginal, basic stratum of Amur decorative art stands out all the more in contrast to elements obviously acquired from China. This stratum should be defined as Neolithic in its origin, its source of subject matter and style (in Laufer's wording, "its form"). The bases of this aboriginal, curvilinear-ribbon ornamentation are, as we have seen, the spiral and the basket-weave design, that is, elements by which one can define characteristics and peculiarities of the decorative art of the Far Eastern tribes for thousands of years, right up to the 19th and 20th centuries. One may suppose that in this aboriginal stratum there are several layers that reflect the complex cultural-ethnic relations and events of the past, including the very ancient past. Here, for instance, belong such characteristic motifs as the deer with transverse lines on its body or the deer with its head turned back.[13] Such motifs belong among the artistic elements so well known to scholars who study the history of the culture, beliefs, and arts of Siberia. They appear among the forest tribes of Siberia in the Bronze and early Iron Ages, in the Scythian era, and are evidence first of all of ties of these tribes with the inhabitants of the steppes of Asia and Europe, of contact of the forest cultures of northern Asia with the rich culture of the tribes of the steppes, spread over a vast territory from the Danube to the Yellow river.

We must, therefore, establish a chronology for the petroglyphs of the Amur and the Ussuri valleys, which are an intermediate link between the art of the Neolithic period and the decorative art of the 19th and 20th centuries. While studying the Sheremetyevskoye petroglyphs during the autumn of 1958, test trenches were dug inside the ancient fortified settlement on the top of the same cliff on which the representations were drawn. In them were found sherds of very archaic appearance, broken stone arrowheads, chips and miniature oddments of lead or bronze representing models of axes or adzes, which, evidently, were worn as charms. Judging by these finds, the settlement on the cliff above the petroglyphs existed in the transitory period between the Stone and Metal Ages, or, at the beginning of the Bronze Age in this area, i.e., the end of the second or the first half of the first millennium B.C. The same chronology should also be applied to the petroglyphs, which, in spite of their peculiarities, have remained to the present time interesting and enigmatical traces of the past of the Far Eastern tribes.

Thus, the antiquity of the art of the Far Eastern tribes mentioned above can be traced from the Neolithic to the Bronze Age, and thence to modern times.

The creative art of the Amur tribes is deeply rooted in their past and undoubtedly these roots are deeper than Laufer thought. The beginnings of the art of the Amur peoples go back to the very sources of their original culture, deep into Neolithic times. Thereafter, the art of these peoples experienced the deep progressive influence of Chinese art, creatively reworked, and as a result, there emerged the present-day rich and vivid art of the peoples of the Maritime Province.

Notes and References

1. B. Laufer, The decorative art of the Amur tribes, *Memoirs of the American Museum of Natural History*, vol. 7, 1902, p. 2.

2. *Ibidem*, pp. 2–4.

3. A. P. Okladnikov, K arkheologicheskim issledovaniyam v 1935 g. na Amure (The 1935 archaeological investigations on the Amur river), *Sovetskaya arkheologiya*, 1936, no. 1, p. 277; *Idem*, Neolit Sibiri i Dalnego Vostoka (The Neolithic of Siberia and the Far East), *Istoriya SSSR*, Moscow–Leningrad, 1939, pt. 1–2, pp. 72–80 (in print); *Idem*, Neoliticheskiye pamyatniki kak istochnik po etnogonii Sibiri i Dalnego Vostoka (Neolithic monuments as a source for the ethnic history of Siberia and the Far East), *Kratkiye soobshcheniya IIMK*, 1949, no. 9, p. 12; *Idem*, U istokov kultury narodov Dalnego Vostoka (At the culture sources of the peoples of the Far East), in *Po sledam drevnikh kultur; ot Volgi do Tikhogo okeana* (In the footsteps of ancient cultures; from the Volga to the Pacific), Moscow, 1954.

4. A. P. Okladnikov, Drevneyshiye kultury Primorya v svete issledovaniy 1953–1956 gg. (The oldest culture of the Maritime Province in the light of the 1953–6 investigations), in *Sbornik statey po istorii Dalnego Vostoka*, Moscow–Leningrad, 1958, p. 19, fig. 14, items 6, 9, 10.

5. Laufer, The decorative art . . . , fig. 20.

6. *Ibidem*, p. 78.

7. Therefore, it can not be stated as categorically as S. V. Ivanov did that G. Schurtz was completely in error in attempting to show that some elements of Ainu-Nivkh ornaments derived from representations of horned demon heads. See S. V. Ivanov, Ornament narodov Sibiri kak istoricheskiy istochnik (The ornament of the peoples of Siberia as a historic source), in *Tezisy dokladov na sessii Otdeleniya istoricheskikh nauk, posvyashchennoy itogam arkheologicheskikh i etnograficheskikh issledovaniy 1957 g.* (Theses of reports presented at the session of the Division of Historical Sciences, on results of archaeological and ethnographic investigations in 1957), Moscow, 1958, p. 16.

8. S. V. Ivanov, Materialy po izobrazitelnomu iskusstvu narodov Sibiri XIX—nachala XX v. (Data on the pictorial art of the peoples of Siberia in the 19th and early 20th centuries), *Trudy Instituta etnografii*, vol. 22, 1954.

9. It is true that Ivanov disagrees with Laufer and considers that most of the birds used in Nanay ornamentation are actually waterfowl and not cocks. However, how does he then explain the magnificent tail feathers typical of the cock? (Cf. Ivanov, Materialy po . . . , p. 223.)

10. *Ibidem*, especially figs. 97 and 98.

11. V. E. Larichev, Kitayskaya nadpis na bronzovom zerkdale iz Suchana, Primorye (Chinese inscription on a bronze mirror from Su-ch'ang, Maritime Province), *Epigrafika Vostoka*, 1958, no. 12, pp. 82–89.

12. Laufer, The decorative art . . . , Table VI, item 4; Table XI, item 4; figs. 12, 14, 18; Table XV, items 4, 5; Table XVI, item 14, letters *a*, *b*; Table XXI, item 1, letter *a*; Table XXV, item 6; Table XXVII, item 4.

13. Ivanov, Materialy po . . . , pp. 217–218.

A. V. SMOLYAK

CERTAIN QUESTIONS ON THE EARLY
HISTORY OF THE ETHNIC GROUPS
INHABITING THE AMUR RIVER VALLEY
AND THE MARITIME PROVINCE*

THE HISTORY OF the ethnic groups inhabiting our part of the Amur river valley and the Maritime Province has not yet been sufficiently studied. Questions concerning the early fates of these ethnic groups can not be easily clarified owing to the fact that they had no written language in the past and have left remains of material culture only.

Archaeological investigations of the Soviet Maritime Province are now being conducted rather intensively; however, the regions of the lower Amur river are as yet insufficiently explored archaeologically.[1] But even if all these archaeological sites were studied there would still remain the task of determining to what extent they represent the culture of the progenitors of the present inhabitants of this territory.

Interest in the past of our Maritime Province was already manifested in the 1860's and 1880's. In the periodicals of those decades there appeared repeatedly communications announcing the discovery of ruins of ancient fortresses, trenches, roads, and cities in the southern part of the Ussuri basin. The first systematic investigations in this region were carried out by the Archimandrite Palladiy [Palladius] (Kafarov). He was the first to link the uncovered remains of the ancient culture with the history of Manchuria and placed them in the epoch of the P'o-hai and Ch'in kingdoms mentioned in the Chinese chronicles.[2] Later the archaeologist F. Busse excavated remains of an earlier culture in the Maritime Province. He related these to the Ilu tribes, which also were mentioned in the Chinese chronicles.[3] In these chronicles it was written that in days of yore there lived in Manchuria the Sushêng tribes (from remote antiquity to the 3rd century B.C.), the Ilu (who appeared after the Sushêng and lived there until the 4th to 5th centuries A.D.), and the Mo-ho (from the 5th or 6th to the 8th or 9th centuries A.D.); that from the 9th to the beginning of the 10th century there existed in the territory of Manchuria the P'o-hai kingdom (which succumbed to the pressure of Khitan tribes) and from the beginning of the 12th to the 13th century the kingdom of Jurchen (Ch'in).

Busse's point of view was supported by many scholars. As a result, in the literature of the time, the Ilu tribes were considered as the inhabitants of the Maritime Province during the last centuries B.C. and the first centuries of our era. Once the Ilu were recognized as the ancient tribes of the Maritime Province, it seemed logical to write about the Sushêng and Mo-ho also as ethnic groups that had inhabited the Amur river valley and the Maritime Province.

In the voluminous literature on the Sushêng, the Ilu, the Mo-ho, the P'o-hai,

*Translated from *Sovetskaya etnografiya*, 1959, no. 1, pp. 29–37.

and the Jurchen, these tribes and ethnic groups have always been considered as the ancestors of the Manchus. The Manchus as well as the Chinese wrote about this. In the *Man-chou Yüan-liu-k'ao* the Ch'ien-lung emperor wrote that the Ch'in were the descendants of the Mo-ho inhabiting the former territory of the Sushêng and that the Ch'in are the ancestors of the Manchus.[4] Palladius advanced the point of view that, in accordance with Chinese data, the Sushêng are Jurchens and are the ancestors of the Manchus. On the basis of Chinese chronicles, other Russian orientalists maintained a similar point of view.[5]

Modern Chinese writers (Hua Shang, Pang Kêng-t'ang) are also of the opinion that the Sushêng, the Ilu, and the Mo-ho are the ancestors of the Jurchens.[6] Western European sinologists of the 19th century also shared this point of view.[7]

It is noteworthy, however, that Chinese and western European historians as well as Russian orientalists do not manifest any tendency to locate the Sushêng, the Ilu, and the Mo-ho necessarily on the lower course of the Amur or in the Maritime Province. Russian investigators who conducted archaeological work in these regions in a later period began to discuss this subject in their writings. The opinions of Busse were supported by A. V. Grebenshchikov,[8] A. N. Lipskiy,[9] N. A. Lipskaya,[10] and A. M. Zolotarev.[11] They considered these tribes the ancestors of the ethnic groups presently inhabiting the Amur river valley and the Maritime Province (the Nanays, Ulchi, Nivkhs, Orochi). But no attempt is made in any of their works to pose the question of the extent to which such an identification is justifiable.

Important contributions toward the clarification of the early stages of the history of the Maritime Province have been made by Soviet archaeologists. In his reports on the archaeological investigations in the Maritime Province, A. P. Okladnikov follows the tradition established in the literature; that is, he also speaks of the Ilu and the Mo-ho as the ancient inhabitants of the Amur river valley and the Maritime Province. In his very interesting work "Cultural Sources of Far Eastern Peoples" (1954), rich in new facts, he develops the thought that since remote antiquity the culture of the Ilu, Mo-ho, P'o-hai, and Jurchen tribes was developing both in the Amur river valley and in the Maritime Province. The Ilu tribes in the Maritime Province already knew agriculture, cattle breeding, and weaving. Their culture was inherited by the Mo-ho and P'o-hai. The Nanays, Ulchi, and Nivkhs are descendants of this ancient population.

The Mongols savagely destroyed the agriculture of the tribes inhabiting the Maritime Province, annihilating or carrying to captivity the bearers of this culture. . . . The blow of the Mongolian conquerors was so violent and devastating that the Maritime Province and the adjoining regions of the Far East have never recovered from it and remained desolate until the appearance, in the 17th century, of the Russians, who established the basis for a new, more advanced and incomparably higher culture. . . . Now the descendants of this ancient population who in the course of centuries had created a distinct and original culture—the Ulchi, Gilyaks, and Nanays—are as a united family of Soviet peoples building the new Socialist culture of the Far East.[12]

In the same work Okladnikov introduces the idea that the cultures of the P'o-hai and Jurchen states developed from the foundation laid by the Ilu and the Mo-ho tribes.[13]

We have noted earlier that the Sushêng, Ilu, Mo-ho, P'o-hai, and Jurchens are generally recognized in sinological literature as the ancestors of the Manchus. To assert that these tribes were the ancestors of the present-day peoples of the Amur river valley and the Maritime Province as well would mean to predetermine the origin of the latter. However, the ethnogenesis of the peoples of the Amur river valley and the Maritime Province has not as yet been fully elucidated and the period of their formation has not been established. On the basis of the available data, the origin of these peoples seems very complex. Into their composition have entered most diverse components. The problem of ethnogenesis is a subject for separate investigation. The author of this article wishes only to call attention to the fact that the question of the settling of the Sushêng, Ilu, and Mo-ho, as far as can be ascertained from the data available in the literature on the subject, is not yet fully clear.

According to Chinese sources, the Sushêng lived in Manchuria from antiquity until the 3rd century A.D. Their representatives visited China occasionally, bringing gifts of bows and arrows made from k'u wood, with stone arrow points. The data on the Sushêng, in the Chinese chronicles, are very scant. This is because of the lack of knowledge the Chinese chroniclers had of the remote regions of Manchuria[14] (though archaeological data indicate some contacts between the ancient inhabitants of the Maritime Province and the Chinese). In the Chinese writings of most recent times (18th to 20th centuries) there are attempts to determine, on the basis of ancient Chinese chronicles, the boundaries of the Sushêng settlement,[15] in spite of the fact that in antiquity there naturally existed no interest in the question. Efforts to determine the exact territory settled by the Sushêng, who had lived for a thousand years in country not sufficiently known to the Chinese, is a rather unrealistic undertaking. So much the more is the attempt to place the exact location of the Sushêng on the lower course of the Amur or in the Maritime Province. After all, this question did not interest the ancient Chinese writers, who knew little about such remote regions (although they had heard of the existence of the Amur river).

Evidently the Chinese use the name Sushêng to designate all the population of Manchuria, regardless of the ethnic origin of the different groups. It is possible that the name Sushêng had also been used to designate peoples living farther north.[16]

Much more information is to be found in the Chinese chronicles about the Ilu tribes, who lived in Manchuria, beginning with the last centuries B.C. According to these data the Ilu lived a settled life. They engaged in agriculture, swine breeding, and hunting, built mud huts, made good bows and arrows with stone arrowheads, and knew how to build vessels. Their neighbors suffered from their incursions.[17]

Concerning the area occupied by the Ilu settlement the Chinese chronicles state: "On the east it borders the Great Sea, in the south it is contiguous with Wu-chi. How far to the north—is not known."[18] The western boundary is also not determined. Thus the Ilu lived in regions washed in the east by the "Great Sea." The excavations recently carried out in the southern parts of the Soviet Maritime Province supplement substantially the information contained in the Chinese chronicles on the culture of the Ilu. Soviet archaeologists date this epoch of "shell heaps" to the period during which the Ilu tribes inhabited the Maritime Province.[19] The population of the Maritime Province of that epoch had a specialized culture of fishing and sea-mammal hunting, and built large seagoing vessels. The finding of stones for grinding grain and spinning whorls in this area, according to A. P. Okladnikov, serves as evidence of the existence of agriculture and weaving among the Ilu tribes living along the coast.[20]

The thesis about the advanced culture of the inhabitants of these regions is corroborated by a statement found in one of the Chinese chronicles little known in scientific literature that "the bases of Ilu economy were agriculture and cattle breeding. They cultivated the five [cereal] grains, bred cows and horses. In addition they liked swine breeding and engaged in sable hunting."[21] Okladnikov quotes these data from the Chinese chronicles without commentary, in spite of the discrepancy between them and the picture of Ilu culture established as the result of excavations carried out in the Maritime Province. In reality the "Ilu" of the Maritime Province were just sea-mammal hunters, and the few grinding stones that have been found there should be considered only as indirect evidence of agriculture.[22] The presence of grinders can not easily serve as sure evidence of the existence of agriculture. Neither does the presence of spinning whorls alone suffice to indicate weaving. The grinders could have been used for grinding the berries of the bird cherry or other plants. The Ilu could have used them for grinding grains of kao-liang [sorghum] and millet obtained from their southwestern neighbors. The whorls, with the assistance of a spindle, could well have been used for making yarn for nets.[23] No horse or cow bones have been found in the Maritime Province [excavations] although the breeding of these animals by the Ilu is claimed by the Chinese chronicles.

Okladnikov considers as evidence of the existence of agriculture among the Ilu the use of crescent-shaped stone knives with slots. Such knives were used in ancient China as sickles. But knives with slots, very similar to those used by the Ilu, were found in archaeological excavations on the Chukchi peninsula and yet no one considers this as evidence of the existence of agriculture there.

Reports in Chinese chronicles on agriculture practiced by the Ilu tribes cannot be applied to the population of the Maritime region. These data refer to populations of other localities. In the Chinese chronicles there is no mention of either the northern or the western boundaries of settlement of the Ilu tribes.

N. Ya. Bichurin wrote that the Ilu inhabited the eastern portion of Kirin Province.[24] But apparently the area populated by these tribes was wider. They inhabited also the western regions of this province as well as southern Manchuria. This follows from toponymic data. Some 60 to 80 *li* from Mukden is situated, as reported by Palladius, the village of Ilu, built on "the site of the ancient city of I-lu-hsien, so named in commemoration of the ancient people of Manchuria— the Ilu."[25] On the historical map constructed by Bichurin and appended to his book "Collection of Data . . ." the Ilu tribe is located in an area situated somewhat north of Mukden. In the geographic description of Manchuria, translated by V. P. Vasilyev from the Chinese, the place of the Ilu is mentioned as being located some 35 versts to the north of Mukden, where are to be found the ruins of the ancient city of Ilu.[26] In the *Historical atlas of China*, published in 1935,[27] the Ilu are located to the southwest and the southeast of Lake Khanka.

In all probability the Ilu tribes occupied a vast area, including the region of the present city of Mukden with its environs, the basin of the Sungari, a river flowing through the entire territory of Manchuria, and the land to the east of this river. Even more probable is the assumption that the Chinese used the name Ilu (as well as Sushêng) to designate not only a certain population group, but most of the population of Manchuria as well.[28]

It would be natural for such a vast territory to be inhabited by tribes of different levels of development. Alas, the information in the Chinese chronicles is of summary character and does not consider such differences. To carry over automatically all the cultural achievements of the Ilu of the central regions mentioned in the Chinese chronicles to the population of Maritime regions is not justified.

In the 3rd century A.D. in the Chinese historical sources the term *Wu-ki* appears in reference to tribes living in Manchuria. (Some writers connect *Wu-ki* with *Wu-chi*, or *Wo-chi*, which in translation means "forest people.") The majority of the sinologists of the 19th century agreed that the Wu-chi were Mo-ho forest tribes despite the fact that the name Mo-ho does not appear in the chronicles before the 5th to 6th centuries. In the Chinese chronicles it was stated that the Mo-ho engaged in agriculture, swine and horse breeding, hunting, fishing, and trading. (They sold furs, fishskins, fish glue and horses to Khitan tribes.[29]) In the winter the Mo-ho lived in semisubterranean huts with an entry at the top and in the summer, in tents.

The Mo-ho were, as stated in Chinese sources, divided into seven "stems." The most southern of these occupied the regions adjoining the Kao-li kingdom in the northern part of the Korean peninsula. Unfortunately the Chinese chronicles do not give definite data on the areas of settlement of all the Mo-ho tribes. It is only known that one group of Mo-ho lived along the Sungari (Sumo Mo-ho) as well as along the Amur (the Hei-Shui Mo-ho after the Chinese name for the Amur river—Hei-shui Ho, literally, the Black river).[30]

N. A. Lipskaya, A. N. Lipskiy, and A. M. Zolotarev, in their works, maintained that the Black River Mo-ho lived on the lower course of the Amur.[31] A. V. Grebenshchikov thought that all Mo-ho tribes were concentrated on the lands along the Sungari and the Amur rivers, extending to the very estuary of the latter.[32] This point of view is shared by other present-day historians.[33]

A. P. Okladnikov wrote that the Mo-ho tribes of the Maritime Province and the valleys of the Ussuri and Amur rivers engaged in agriculture and cattle breeding and made iron artifacts. They entered into direct communication with China and from 417 [A.D.] sent embassies to the Chinese court regularly. But most of the Mo-ho were independent of China and were feared by their neighbors.[34]

A careful examination of historical sources indicates no Mo-ho settlement on the lower Amur. The information about the Black river Mo-ho refers to a completely different region.

N. Ya. Bichurin writes that the Black River Mo-ho inhabited the Heilungchiang Province,[35] which was bordered on the north by the Amur and on the east by the Sungari. Moreover, he points out that "they occupied the right bank of the upper reaches of the Amur river. . . . They belonged to those Tungus tribes whose descendants live at present along both banks of the Naun under the tribal names of Solon and Daghor."[36] Grebenshchikov maintains that the name Hei-shui Mo-ho is derived from the Hei-shui, which the Chinese used to designate not the entire length of the Amur river, but only the middle course,[37] and that the mouth of the Bira river constituted the western boundary of the Mo-ho settlement on the Amur.

In the upper course of the Amur up to the mouth of the Zeya there have been uncovered numerous archaeological remains—ruins of fortresses, trenches, ramparts. The archaeologist G. S. Novikov-Daurskiy considers them Mo-ho.[38] It is precisely here and not on the lower part of the river that modern Chinese historians place the Black River Mo-ho—the ancestors of the Jurchen.[39]

The Black River Mo-ho lived along the Amur river and also farther west, west of the junction of the Zeya. This is confirmed by toponymic data. The name Mo-ho has been preserved to the present in a small place situated near the junction of the Shilka and the Argun.[40] The Mo-ho river originates in the spurs of the Khingan mountains—the Russian name of the river is Zheltuga [Yellow]— and it flows into the Amur.[41]

On the map appended to the book "P'o-hai" by Z. N. Matveyev, the Black River Mo-ho are placed in the region of the upper and middle Amur.[42]

Thus we have no irrefutable data that prove that the Black River Mo-ho lived on the lower course of the Amur, whereas sufficient evidence is available on their settlement along the middle and the upper courses of this river. Also there is no basis for the statement that the Amur River Mo-ho were the strongest of all Mo-ho tribes. To the contrary, this area was the periphery of Mo-ho settlement and the Amur Mo-ho were remote from the events taking place in the more southerly regions of Manchuria.

The numerous mentions in the Chinese chronicles of the relations of the Mo-ho to China refer to groups living considerably to the south of the Amur. In these chronicles it is repeatedly stated that the Korean domain of Kao-li was bordered by Mo-ho tribes.[43] It was these southern groups who entered into dealings with China and the Kao-li state. In the wars of the two, the Mo-ho allied themselves at times with China, at times with Kao-li. In the 7th century the Mo-ho became definitely the allies of Kao-li. In all battles, in the forefront always was the strong Mo-ho cavalry, numbering several tens of thousands. The Chinese chronicles *Pei-shih*, *Sui-shu*, and *T'ang-shu* contain extensive information on this subject.[44]

Mo-ho notables sometimes ruled over Korean lands. Thus in the 7th century the Mo-ho obtained a part of the Po-chi domain, situated in southern Manchuria.[45] The father of the founder of the state of P'o-hai was a Mo-ho from the upper part of the Sungari river and had possessions in Kao-li.[46] Between the Mo-ho and the Koreans there apparently was no sharp geographic boundary such as that established later between Manchuria and Korea. We think that some groups of Koreans, because of close relationships, fused with the southern Manchu. In turn, groups of Manchu entered into the composition of the northern Koreans.

Thus the Mo-ho tribes occupied a wide territory stretching from the upper and middle courses of the Amur river in the north to the boundaries of Korea in the south. The population of this territory was not heterogeneous in ethnic composition or in cultural development.

In "Essays on the History of the U.S.S.R." it is stated: "In language the Mo-ho belonged to the Tungus-Manchu group." The descendants of the Mo-ho from the lower Amur and Ussuri basins "are the Nanays (Golds), who live at present along the Ussuri and Amur rivers, near Khabarovsk."[47] In our opinion such an assumption is untenable, as there are practically no data on the Mo-ho language, and no special studies on this subject have been made.

There are no bases for considering the Mo-ho as ancestors of the Nanays, since the Amur Mo-ho lived on the upper and middle course of the Amur, whereas the Nanays at present live on the Ussuri and the lower Amur river.[48] Moreover, the ethnic composition of the Nanays is very complex, as it includes tribes of different origins.[49] Further, by merely stating that the Nanays are descendants of the Mo-ho, we solve nothing. The name Mo-ho is a collective name, used to designate the population of the extensive territory of Manchuria with its heterogeneity in ethnic composition and cultural development. Their neighbors to the west were the Shih-wei tribes, which, according to Chinese chronicles, were also thoroughly uneven in culture. It is difficult to say anything about their ethnic origin. The ethnic origin of the Khitans (also western neighbors of the Mo-ho), about whom more information has been preserved in historical sources, is not fully clear at the present.

68 A. V. Smolyak

Were the Mo-ho, Ilu, and Sushêng Tungus? This is a very complex question and it exceeds the limits of the present study. There are many theories of their origin. One may assume that the authors of the "Essays on the History of the U.S.S.R." consider the Mo-ho as Tungus-Manchu. The historians of the 19th and the beginning of the 20th century (Gorskiy, Bichurin, Matveyev, and others) considered the entire population of Manchuria as Tungus, and Bichurin even included the Koreans among the southern Tungus.[50] However, some fifty years after the appearance of Bichurin's theory, who considered the Tungus as the aborigines of Manchuria, P. Schmidt promulgated a new theory of the existence in Manchuria of a pre-Tungus population.[51] The author of the present article does not propose to solve the problem of the origin of the Mo-ho, Ilu, and Sushêng. However, he thinks that it cannot be solved as simply as in Bichurin's time. The history of the Mo-ho people is unknown to us and the meager and summary data available in Chinese chronicles contribute very little toward an essential nature of this people. What did the various Mo-ho groups represent in way of ethnic composition and culture? What was the nature of their relationships? How did they develop in the course of several centuries, and what was the late history of the individual groups? The Chinese chronicles certainly give no answer to any of these questions.

As far as the history of the Mo-ho during the 8th to 10th centuries is concerned, it is generally assumed that during this period they all entered into the P'o-hai state. However, there are certain data indicating that some groups of Mo-ho remained outside this state.[52] The history of these separate Mo-ho groups (especially the southern ones) during the 8th to 10th centuries and later remains completely obscure.

The early history of the ethnic groups of the Soviet Far East and Manchuria, closely interrelated already in most remote times, has not as yet been sufficiently studied. Such a study could throw light upon the complex problems of ethnogenesis. An important contribution to the solution of ethnogenetic and historical problems of the groups in our Amur river region and the Maritime Province, as in the vast territory of Manchuria, must be made by archaeologists. To achieve this it is necessary to carry out on a large scale combined archaeologic, ethnographic, and linguistic studies.

In conclusion we wish to call attention to the fact that the lower part of the Amur river and the Ussuri region are often considered by historians, archaeologists, and ethnographers as one territorial unit. This is not entirely correct. If we speak of the past of the Ussuri region, we must consider both the P'o-hai (8th to 10th centuries A.D.) and the Ch'in (11th to 12th centuries A.D.) states, the peripheries of which were the southern districts of the Ussuri region. As far as the population of the remote territory of the lower Amur is concerned, it did not constitute a contiguous part of either of the states mentioned. All we see on the lower Amur are remains of semisubterranean dwellings, fragments of ceramics, and primitive implements. The remains of higher culture seen there belong to the early 15th century, when on the Tyr rock a stele had been erected in commemoration of the march of the Chinese to the lower Amur. (As we know this march also failed to establish close relations between the Chinese and the local population.) Thus, the population of the lower part of the Amur river and of the northern part of the Maritime Province developed relatively independently of the population of the more southern districts, although we should not neglect to take into account the influence of these higher southern cultures and civilizations on it.

Notes and References

1. Archaeological explorations were carried out here by A. P. Okladnikov in 1935, but the rich materials then collected have not been fully published. The findings of this expedition are mentioned in only three short articles by A. P. Okladnikov: K arkheologicheskim issledovaniyam 1935 na Amure (The 1935 archaeological explorations on the Amur river), *Sovetskaya arkheologiya*, 1936, no. 1; Drevneye poseleniye v padi Bolshoy Dural na Amure (The ancient settlement in the Bolshoy Dural Hollow on the Amur river), *Sovetskaya arkheologiya*, 1951, no. 15; and Neoliticheskiye pamyatniki kak istochniki po etnogonii Sibiri i Dalnego Vostoka (Neolithic remains as sources in the ethnogeny of Siberia and the Far East), *Kratkiye soobshcheniya IIMK*, no. 9, 1941.

2. Palladiy [Palladius], Etnograficheskaya ekspeditsiya v Yuzhno-Ussuriskiy Kray (An ethnographic expedition into the southern Ussuri region), *Izv. Russkogo Geograficheskogo Ob-va (RGO)*, vol. 7, no. 2, 1871.

3. F. Busse, Ostatki drevnostey v dolinakh rek Lefu, Daubikhe, Ulakhe (Ancient remains in the valleys of the Lefu, Daubikhe, and Ulakhe rivers), *Zapiski Ob-va izucheniya Amurskogo Kraya*, Vladivostok, 1888.

4. See: Terrien de Lacouperie, The Djurtchen of Manchuria, *Journal of the Royal Asiatic Society*, n.s., vol. 31, London, 1889, p. 436. These data are also cited in the chronicles of the 12th and 13th centuries (see: "Ch'in-shih," A. Malyavkin's translation, Harbin, 1942).

5. Palladiy [Palladius], Dorozhnye zametki na puti ot Pekina do Blagoveshchenska cherez Manchzhuriyu v 1870 g. (Traveler's notes on a journey from Peking to Blagoveshchensk through Manchuria in 1870), *Zapiski RGO po obshchey geografii*, vol. 4, 1871, p. 387; A. Gorskiy, Nachalo i pervye dela manchzhurskogo doma (The beginnings and the initial actions of the House of Manchu), *Trudy chlenov Rossiyskoy dukhovnoy missii v Pekine*, vol. 1, Peking, 1885, p. 4; N. Ya. Bichurin, Sobraniye svedeniy o narodakh, obitavshikh v Sredney Azii v drevniye vremena (A collection of data on the peoples living in Central Asia in the remote past), vols. 1–3, Moscow–Leningrad, 1950–3; vol. 2, p. 8; V. P. Vasilyev, Istoriya i drevnosti vostochnoy chasti Sredney Azii ot X do XIII veka (The history and antiquities of eastern Central Asia from the 10th to the 13th centuries), *Trudy Vostochnogo Otdela Russkogo Arkheologicheskogo Ob-va*, part IV, no. 1, 1858, pp. 30–31, 196–197.

6. Hua Shang and Pang Kêng-t'ang, O razlozhenii rodovogo stroya i obrazovaniya gosudarstva u Chzhurchzheney (On the disintegration of the social structure and administration of the Jurchen state), *Pênshihchê*, 1956, no. 6 (in Chinese).

7. See: Terrien de Lacouperie, *op. cit.*, pp. 432–434, 440; E. Parker, The Manchus, *Transactions of the Asiatic Society of Japan*, vol. 15, Yokohama, 1887; H. E. James, *The long white mountain*, London, 1888, chap. II.

8. A. V. Grebenshchikov, *Manchzhury, ikh yazyk i pismennost* (The Manchus, their spoken and written languages), Vladivostok, 1912, pp. 1–7.

9. A. N. Lipskiy wrote that the Mo-ho group (Hei-Shui-Pu) lived along the lower course of the Amur from the mouth of the Sungari to the ocean; in the 4th to 10th centuries the Hei-Shui tribe—very likely, the present-day Golds—was on a low cultural level. The name of this tribe was derived from the name of the lower course of the Amur—Hei-Shui. See his article: Kratkiy obzor manchzhuro-tungusskikh plemen basseyna Amura (A short survey of the Manchu-Tungus tribes of the Amur basin), in the collection, I tuzemnyy sezd Dalne-Vostochnoy oblasti (The First Convention of the Natives of the Far Eastern Region), Khabarovsk, 1925, p. VII.

10. See: *Narody Sibiri* (The peoples of Siberia), Moscow–Leningrad, 1956, chapter on "The Nanays"—an historical sketch.

11. A. M. Zolotarev, K voprosu o genezise klassoobrazovaniya u Gilyakov (On the origin of class formation among the Gilyaks), *Za industrializatsiyu Sovetskogo Vostoka*, 1933, no. 3, In another study he was more cautious and wrote: "Sushêng, Ilu, Mo-ho are collective names for several ancient tribes, considered as the ancestors of the Tungus-Manchus. Most likely the Neolithic population of the Amur basin was included

70 A. V. Smolyak

in those peoples who were collectively designated in the Chinese chronicles under these names."—See: A. M. Zolotarev, *Rodovoy stroy i religiya ulchey* (Social structure and religion of the Ulchi), Khabarovsk, 1939, p. 7.

12. A. P. Okladnikov, *U istokov kultury narodov Dalnego Vostoka* (Cultural sources of Far Eastern Peoples), Collection: *Po sledam drevnikh kultur* (Traces of early cultures), Moscow, 1954, pp. 259–260.

13. *Ibidem*, p. 258.

14. D. N. Pozdneyev doubts, in general, the very existence of the Sushêng: "The existence of the Sushêng is subject to doubt in view of the absence of evidence"; see his: *Opisaniye Manchzhurii* (A description of Manchuria), vol. I, St. Petersburg, 1897, p. 7.

15. An attempt has been made, in particular by Hu Wei, the author of the book *Yü-kung chui-chih* (1693–1714); see: Bichurin, *Sobraniye svedeniy* . . . , vol. 1, 1950, p. xxv.

16. In the *Ta-Ming I-t'ung-chih*, published in 1461 in Peking, it is stated that among the products of the country of the Sushêng are "whale pupils" and "walrus tusks." Cited from the Russian unpublished translation of N. V. Kyuner; p. 105 in the Chinese original.

17. Bichurin, *Sobraniye svedeniy* . . . , vol. 2, pp. 23–24.

18. *Ibidem*, p. 23.

19. *Ocherki istorii SSSR. Pervobytno-obshchinnyy stroy i drevneyshiye gosudarstva na territorii SSSR* (Essays on the history of the U.S.S.R. The aboriginal social structure and the most ancient states in the territory of the U.S.S.R.), edited by P. N. Tretyakov and A. L. Mongayt, Moscow, 1956, pp. 409–410. (The author of the section "The tribes of Siberia and the Far East" is A. P. Okladnikov.)

20. *Ibidem*, pp. 409–410.

21. *Ibidem*, p. 410.

22. Okladnikov, *U istokov kultury* . . . , p. 251.

23. Many northern nationalities of Siberia and of the Far East made their nets from nettle fibers spun into threads by means of a spindle; hand spindles were known even to Yukagirs. But no data are available that would indicate the existence, in the past, of weaving among these ethnic groups.

24. Bichurin, *Sobraniye svedeniy* . . . , vol. 2, p. 24.

25. Palladiy, *Dorozhnye zametki* . . . , p. 373.

26. V. P. Vasilyev, *Opisaniye Manchzhurii* (A description of Manchuria), *Zapiski RGO*, vol. 12, 1857, p. 63.

27. Albert Hermann, *Historical and commercial atlas of China*, Cambridge, Mass., U.S.A., 1935, maps 27 and 31.

28. Opinions on this point expressed by P. N. Menshikov, P. N. Smolnikov, and A. I. Chirikov are confirmatory, i.e., that the region of Ilu occupation included "the entire eastern portion of Heilungchiang and Kirin provinces and later also the Ussuri region." See: *Severnaya Manchzhuriya* (Northern Manchuria), vol. 2, The Heilungchiang Province, Harbin, 1919, p. 417; the border line between the Heilungchiang and Kirim provinces was the Sungari river.

29. V. P. Vasilyev, *Istoriya i drevnosti* . . . , p. 27.

30. A. V. Grebenshchikov, *Dalniy Vostok* (The Far East), a historical essay in *Severnaya Aziya*, 1926, nos. 5–6, p. 100. See also his: *Manchzhury, ikh yazyk i pismennost* (The Manchus, their spoken and written languages), Vladivostok, 1912, pp. 3–4.

31. N. A. Lipskaya, *op. cit.*; A. M. Zolotarev, *Iz istorii narodov Amura* (From the history of the Amur river peoples), *Istoricheskiy Zhurnal*, 1937, no. 7; A. N. Lipskiy, *op. cit.* p. VII.

32. Grebenshchikov, *Dalniy Vostok*, p. 115.

33. See: *Ocherki istorii SSSR*, Period feodalizma (Essays on the History of the U.S.S.R., the feudal period), part 1, Moscow, 1953, p. 746.

34. Okladnikov, *U istokov kultury* . . . , p. 257. In the section dealing with the ancient

tribes of the Far East in *Vsemirnaya istoriya* (World history), vol. 2, Moscow, 1956, pp. 719–720, it is stated that the Ilu and the Mo-ho lived in the maritime regions as well as along the Amur river; they engaged in agriculture, cattle breeding, fishing, and hunting; the Mo-ho traded with the Chinese and the Koreans. The author of the section places all seven Mo-ho tribes on the Amur, pointing out only that in the lower parts of the Amur river and on the Ussuri river there lived the least culturally advanced Mo-ho tribes.

35. Bichurin, *Sobraniye svedeniy* . . . , vol. 2, p. 8.

36. *Ibidem*, vol. 1, p. 380.

37. Grebenshchikov, *Dalniy Vostok*, p. 105. The Chinese divided the course of the Amur river in accordance with the color of its water. The Sungari river brings into the Amur turbid, clayey water and at the point of its inflow into the Amur the water of the latter becomes light colored, distinctly different from the purely "black" water of the Amur in its upper and middle course. This feature is mentioned in all geographic descriptions of Manchuria.

38. G. S. Novikov-Daurskiy, *Priamurye v drevnosti* (The Amur region in antiquity), *Zapiski Amurskogo Oblastnogo Muzeya Krayevedeniya i Obshchestva Krayevedeniya*, vol. 2, Blagoveshchensk, 1953. A. P. Okladnikov is of the opinion that it is fully justifiable to ascribe these monuments to the Mo-ho tribes; see his review of the cited work of G. S. Novikov-Daurskiy in *Sovetskaya arkheologiya*, 1955, no. 22.

39. Hua Shang and Pang Kêng-T'ang, *op. cit.*

40. Pozdneyev, *Opisaniye Manchzhurii*, vol. ɪ, map.

41. Hsü Chiung-Liang, *Ocherki Khey-lun-tszyanya* (Essays on Heilungchiang), Translated from the Chinese and published as a supplement to the periodical "Life on the Eastern Border," book ɪ, Chita, 1896, p. 18.

42. Z. N. Matveyev, Bokhai (P'o-hai), *Trudy Dalnevostochnogo Gosudarstvennogo Universiteta*, ser. 6, no. 7, Vladivostok, 1929.

43. Bichurin, *Sobraniye svedeniy* . . . , vol. 2, pp. 91, 98, *et al.*

44. *Ibidem*, vol. 2, pp. 69–72, 83, 85, 92, 104–105, 111–112, 118, 129; vol. 3, p. 218.

45. *Ibidem*, vol. 2, p. 129.

46. *Ibidem*, p. 136.

47. *Ocherki po istorii SSSR*, Period feodalizma, p. 746; see also: A. N. Lipskiy, *op. cit.*, p. vɪɪ.

48. It may be admitted that some Mo-ho groups from the middle course of the Amur could have moved to its lower part. However, evidence on this point is lacking.

49. In their ethnic composition they include, for instance, a number of Evenk tribes as well as some remains of the pre-Evenk aboriginal population.

50. Bichurin, *Sobraniye svedeniy* . . . , vol. 2, p. 7.

51. P. Schmidt expounded his views in numerous articles published in *Acta Universitatis Latviensis* (see: P. Schmidt, The language of the Negidals, no. 5, 1923; The language of Olchas, no. 8, 1923; The language of Orochs, no. 17, 1928). In Lopatin's *Goldy* (The Golds), Vladivostok, 1922, a communication of Schmidt states his views on this question. Schmidt's theory on the Paleo-Asiatics in Manchuria was supported by S. M. Shirokogoroff (*Social organization of the Northern Tungus*, Shanghai, 1929, pp. 142–146). But if Schmidt considered the population of Manchuria as Paleo-Asiatic until the 10th century A.D., then Shirokogoroff does not give a definite answer about the origin of the Sushêng, i.e., whether they were Tungus or Paleo-Asiatics. The contemporary Chinese ethnographer Ling Ch'un-shêng (in his *The Gold tribe on the lower Sungari river*, Nanking, vols. I and II, 1934, Introduction), following P. Schmidt and S. Shirokogoroff, acknowledges the existence of a pre-Tungus population of Manchuria, but he leaves unanswered the question as to whether the Sushêng are Paleo-Asiatics or Tungus. This question requires additional extensive and intensive study. We wish to call attention to the following interesting fact: all Chinese sources, when mentioning the Sushêng, relate that they made arrows out of *k'u* wood. The available information on the language of the Sushêng is extremely scant, but this term is used in the same meaning by the present-day Nivkhs—a Paleo-Asiatic group living along the lower

course of the Amur and on the island of Sakhalin. We think that this coincidence is not accidental. It is true that the Nivkhs call the arrows *ku* and not the wood from which they are made, but such a distinction seems to us unessential.

52. The Black River Mo-ho lived beyond the boundaries of the P'o-hai domain. In southern Manchuria there also lived groups of Mo-ho that had not been incorporated into the P'o-hai domain. In a Chinese chronicle there is an interesting statement that the lands of Po-chi were divided among the P'o-hai, Mo-ho, and Hsinlo. See: Bichurin, *Sobraniye svedeniy* . . . , vol. 2, p. 129. The P'o-hai and Hsinlo had some type of state structure, but nothing is known in this respect about the southern Mo-ho. In the beginning of the 8th century the P'o-hai and the Mo-ho joined forces and devastated the town of Tin-chen in southern Manchuria (*ibidem*, p. 133).

B. O. DOLGIKH

CONTRIBUTIONS TO THE HISTORY

OF THE BURYAT PEOPLE*

WHEN THE RUSSIANS ARRIVED in eastern Siberia during the period 1630–40, the ancestors of the modern Buryats were a group of tribes and clans speaking dialects of the Mongolic language group although, with a very few exceptions, they were not considered to be Mongols.

Apparently, the remote ancestors of the tribes and clans from which the Buryat nation ultimately arose did not all speak languages of the Mongolic group. Probably the Mongolic dialects of some of these tribes formed as a result of the ascendancy of languages of the Mongolic group over the Turkic and perhaps Tungus dialects of these tribes and clans, at different times, prior to the arrival of the Russians in the Cis-Baykal region. The presence in the make-up of the Buryat tribes and clans of a certain number of clans of Mongol origin indicates one of the ways in which the Mongolic language penetrated into the ancestry of the Buryats. But this process of "Mongolization" of the ancestors of the Buryat was not completed. . . . The dialects of the ancestral tribes of the Buryats had not fused at the time when the Russians arrived and had not been completely engulfed by a strictly Mongolic language, and these tribes never became members of a Mongol group. The arrival of the Russians, and the fact that the ancestors of the Buryats came to constitute a population of the Russian state, guided their ethnic development in another direction, in the direction of the formation of an independent, new people, although one cognate by language to the Mongols.

In the past, the ideas of the Buryats about their origin were involved to a significant degree in a framework which had not yet freed itself of a patriarchal ideology. The ancestor of all Buryats was considered to be the mythical dark-gray bull *Bukha-noyon-baabay.* The ancestors of individual tribes which later formed the Buryat people were alleged to be the sons of this mythical ancestor, and the sons of the ancestors of the tribes were the founders of the clans.

This arrangement was indicative, and when in the second half of the 19th century their genealogies were recorded, the Buryats were aware of themselves as a unified people. Thus the process of formation of a people was reflected in their consciousness. But these genealogies certainly cannot be considered as evidence explaining the origin of the Buryat people. The main thing that can be extracted from them is that the names of clans and tribes, some not always correct, are indications of the origin of, or of the greater or lesser interrelationship between, some of these clans, and give information on some mythologic and zoolatrous ideas that were peculiar to the ancestors of the Buryats. The idea that peoples, and even nations, derive from certain specific ancestors through the development of families into clans, clans into tribes, and tribes into a nation unified by a state, has been adduced by believers in that doctrine of scientific consensus explaining the origin of nations. It can be assumed that the formation of national bonds did not signify the development of, but as a rule, the breakup

*Translated from *Sovetskaya etnografiya*, 1953, no. 1, pp. 38–63.

of clan-tribal ties, and thus inevitably it led to the destruction of the latter. However, in order to determine the component elements out of which the Buryat people were formed, it is necessary to study the clan-tribal composition of the ancestors of the Buryats as found by the Russians in the middle of the 17th century. At the same time, we should ascertain what the distribution of the ancestral Buryat tribes was, and determine their numbers. In studying the origin of the Buryats, it is also very important to trace the migrations of their ancestors. The process of formation of the Buryat people from a number of tribes was complicated and conflicting. Side by side with the unification of tribes into a people also occurred the separation of parts of some of these tribes who chose another historical road for themselves.

It must also be kept in mind that at the end of the 17th and at the beginning of the 18th century, to the basic tribes and clans from which the Buryat people were formed, some new ones deriving from Mongolia were apparently added. But these new elements did not exert substantial influence on the large, basic groups of the clan-tribal structure of the Buryats and only supplemented it with a number of new, small clan divisions.

In the Buryat linguistic literature, there has been no complete, systematic characterization of the ancestral tribes and clans of the Buryats who were found by the Russians in the Cis-Baykal and Trans-Baykal regions. In particular, there have not been complete data on the settlements and numbers of these groups; this created an opportunity for the projection of various insufficiently founded assumptions.

Usually, an attempt has been made to squeeze the clan-tribal composition of the Buryats into a scheme with a triple division: the Bulagat, Ekherit, and Khorinets.

Until recently it has also been assumed that the most complete information on the clan and tribal composition of the Buryat ancestors was contained in the confused summary of B. B. Bambayev.[1] In this summary, the Ekherit clan Shono (Chenorut) was assigned to the Bulagat, and the Bulagat clans Babay, Sharalday, Abaganat, and Boyan (Buyan) to the Ekherit. There are similar gross errors with respect to other Ekherit and Bulagat clans. For example, for some reason, to the list of branches of the "indigenous Ekherit-Bulagat clans," the author has assigned the Tutur and Ocheul. But, concerning these, it is easy to recognize in them the designations of the Tutur and Ocheul Evenks, and so on.

More recent achievements in the field of Buryat studies were reflected in "The History of the Buryat-Mongol Autonomous Soviet Socialist Republic," the first volume of which was published in 1951. In this work a generally accurate characterization is given of the tribes ancestral to the Buryat people who were encountered by the Russians in the 17th century to both the west and east of Lake Baykal. But the problem of the Buryat ancestral tribes is stated without the necessary details and without proper reasoning. Moreover, there are a number of inaccuracies in this work; it fails to reflect many essential questions connected with the ethnic elements, tribes, and clans that make up the Buryat people.

The author of the present paper does not wish to undertake the task of settling the problem of the formation of the Buryat people. The complete solution of this problem will be possible only as a result of a comprehensive study of the history of the Buryat-Mongols during the second half of the 17th century, as well as during the 18th and 19th. Besides special historical and ethnographic research, much work by linguists will be required, concerning both the study of Buryat dialects and the history of the Buryat literary language and its dissemination among the masses. Our aim is to point out the component elements (tribes and clans) of the Buryats as they existed at the time of the arrival of the Russians in eastern Siberia, and the historical events that influenced the entry of certain of these tribal and clan groups into the composition of the Buryat people. Questions of origin of those ancestral tribes and clans of the Buryats found by the Russians in the 17th century along both sides of the Baykal will not be raised in the present paper.

In the second half of the 17th century, when the Russians firmly organized the whole territory settled by them, the ancestors of the Buryats were assigned to the following administrative units:

1. In the Krasnoyarsk *uyezd*—to the Udinsk fortress in the complex of the "Brotherly Udinsk Estate."

2. In the Yenisey *uyezd*—to the Bratsk and Teno fortresses.

3. In the Ilim *uyezd*—to the Verkholensk fortress and to the Idinsk fortress built somewhat later (1672). In 1686, both these fortresses, with the Buryats assigned to them, were transferred to the Irkutsk *uyezd*.

4. In the Irkutsk *uyezd*—to the Irkutsk and Selenginsk fortresses. In the region of the Selenginsk fortress there were also tribes of the Tabunut, standing somewhat apart in their relations to the Russians and to other groups ancestral to the Buryats.

5. In the Nerchinsk *uyezd*—to the Itantsin fortress (winter quarters).

We shall examine separately the tribal and clan composition of the ancestors of the Buryats in each of these regions. We should first state that we use the terms "Buryat" and "Buryatization" conditionally, since a single Buryat people did not yet exist in the 17th century. We call "Buryat" those ancestral tribes and clans of the Buryats who spoke comparatively closely related dialects of the Mongolic language group, and, by the term "Buryatization," we mean the influence of these tribes on other neighboring tribes, which was accompanied by the transition of some of the latter to dialects of the Mongolic language group.

TABLE 1

No.	Ulus (clan)	Number of tribute-paying people	Tribute rate		
			Sables	Foxes	Other
1	Ashekhabat Prince Dyuchki	26	53	3	6
2	Ashekhabat (new emigrants)	43	66	4	7
2	Sharait	17	73	—	3
3	Turalit	14	57	—	2
4	Karagas	29	140	—	—
5	Manzhir	21	99	—	1
6	Kangat	10	54	—	—
7	Eudin	43	218	—	—
8	Kubalit	4	7	1	—
9	Korchin (Mangaly)	33	116	3	2
10	Bayberin	7	31	—	2
11	Ulegot	12	45	—	2
12	Shurtos	29	99	4	2
13	Iya Korchun	19	25	2	4
14	Kochemar	10	31	1	1
15	Karmagin	13	29	1	—
16	Karanot	19	33	3	2
	Total	349	1176	22	34

In Table 1, data are given on the clan composition, numbers, and tax rate of the "fur-tribute-paying people" of the Brotherly Udinsk Estate of the Krasnoyarsk uyezd in 1690.[2] Among the clans (*ulus*) of the Brotherly Udinsk Estate enumerated there, the only Buryat ones in the 17th century were the Ashekhabat, Sharait, and perhaps the Turalit. The Karagas, Manzhir, Kangat, Eudin, and Kubalit clans were ancestral to the modern Tofalar (Karagas). The clans of Mangal, Bayberin, Ulegot, Shurtos, and Iya Korchun represented the eastern periphery of the Kotts. The Kochemar, Karmagin, and Karanot (Kharanut) uluses were Evenk (Tungus). All the clans of the Udinsk Estate felt, to some degree, the influence of the Buryats, and, later, some of the non-Buryat clans became Buryat.

In Table 2 are given data showing the change in the number of inhabitants of the Udinsk Estate and testifying to its rapid increase. The reduction in numbers between 1712 and 1735 is explained by the emigration of Buryats and "Buryat-ized" Karanot (Kharanut) Evenks to the Trans-Baykal region, on the ceding to Russia, by the Burinsk (Kyakhta) agreement of 1727, of land along the Selenga above the mouth of the Chikoy, in the region of the modern towns of Kyakhta and Troitskosavsk. Also, in accordance with this agreement, a part of the ancestors of the Tofalar came within the borders of China, and therefore their numbers also diminished.

The very large increase in the number of Buryats between 1658 and 1671 occurred as a consequence of the return, in 1667-8, of a part of the Ashekhabat from beyond the border.[3] The Ashekhabat of the Udinsk Estate retired beyond the border, in all likelihood, after the rebellion of 1656. This rebellion was inspired by the ruling leaders of the Ashekhabat, defending their "right" to the exploitation of the *kyshtym* [dependent tribes], and it was not supported by the rest of the population of the Udinsk Estate. The rebellious Ashekhabat therefore chiefly fell upon their former kyshtym, and, as the sources state, "these thieves, the Udinsk Ashekhabat princelings . . . beat up these Udinsk tribute-paying people and took them as prisoners with them."[4]

Data on the distribution of clans in the Udinsk Estate are quoted from the manuscript of G. F. Müller. This information concerns the beginning of the 1730's.[5] However, it may be assumed that approximately such a distribution existed in the 17th century, since the various data encountered in the archives dating from this period do not contradict the data given in Müller's manuscript, which data we have also transferred to the attached map.

With regard to the western limits of Buryat distribution, the following should be kept in mind: In 1631, a detachment of the Yeniseysk official Mikhail Shorin

TABLE 2

Years	Number of tribute-paying people					Source
	Buryats	Ancestors of Tofalars	Kotts	Evenks	Total	
1658	31	65	81	29	206	Sec. 214, book 384, leaves 72 ob., 76
1671	79	89	72	28	268	Sec. 214, book 543, leaves 233 ob., 237
1677	91	100	83	33	307	Sec. 214, book 643, leaves 182–210
1690	100	107	100	42	349	Sec. 214, book 958, leaves 428–457
1700	119	131	105	48	403	Sec. 214, book 1241, leaves 24–34
1701	129	133	111	48	421	Sec. 214, book 1241, leaves 64–73
1712	154	147	139	68	508	Sec. 214, book 1577, leaves 11–14
1735	115	89	110	32	346	Sec. 21, op. 4, no. 27, leaves 11–17

came upon the "Brotherly people of Korendey and their companions" at the Chun (Uda) river. In 1633 the Krasnoyarsk ataman Zlobin came upon a group of Buryats consisting of nine yurts headed by Uchek; this at the Biryus river, that is, within the eastern limits of the "Kansk Kott Estate." Obviously, Uchek was wandering in the region of the modern settlement of Tayshet, where today the highway and railroad cross the Biryus (Ona), and where there are (and, obviously, were in the past) the most important stretches of meadow on the Biryus suitable for cattle-breeding. Zlobin also reached the "brotherly" princeling Korondoy (compare with Korendey *supra*) on the Osh (Uda?) river. But when this Korondoy or Korendey was sought in the following year, 1634, it turned out that he was wandering "among the distant uluses on the Oka river and there, too, he died."[6]

These reports also delimit accurately the sojourn of the Buryats on the Biryus and Uda to the first half of the 17th century. Other information from the first quarter of the 17th century, usually cited in apocryphal form as "brothers and mothers," at the best, shows that the ancestral clan aristocracy of the western Buryats raided the tribes occupying the region of the modern towns of Krasnoyarsk and Kansk.[7]

On the Biryus and Uda, the ancestors of the Buryats found themselves on alien soil, on the land of their own kyshtym. In the Biryus basin and the lower courses of its tributaries, the Tumanshet and Tagul, there were three *volosts* of Kotts—the Pelengut, Agash, and Ingolot—in which the population numbered 200–300 persons. On the Uda river, as noted above, there also lived the Kotts of the Korchun,[8] Bayberin, and Ulegot clans (uluses).

Thus the Buryats Uchek on the Biryus and Korondoy (Korendey) on the Uda, together with their people, constituted only a small part of the ancestors of the Buryats, nomadizing among the Kotts, probably carrying on barter with them, and perhaps collecting *alban* (tax) from them. It was not by chance that, after the appearance of the Russians on the Uda river, Korondoy wandered to the Oka river, where the western Ashekhabat lived, i.e., he returned to his ancestral clan territory.

A Krasnoyarsk official of the servitor gentry, Sebastian Samsonov, calls the Kotts of the Ingolot volost on the Biryus "the brotherly kyshtym."[9] But farther west of the Biryus, in the Kan basin, the Kotts were the kyshtym of the Kirgiz, or more precisely, of the Tubins. The Tubin Kirgiz princelings with their peoples also nomadized at times among their kyshtym, the Kansk Kotts, just as the Ashekhabat Buryat princelings wandered among their Kott kyshtym on the Uda and even the Biryus. Such was the well-known Tubin princeling Soyt, who gave much trouble to the Russian officials before they dislodged him from the Kansk lands of the Kotts[10]

G. D. Sanzheyev, in his study of the Lower Uda Buryats in 1929, noted the following clans: Kkhotômut, Tümêshe, Sharät, Külmêngge, Mânzhiräk, Turalak, and Kkhorshong.[11] Thus, at the beginning of the 18th, as at the beginning of the 20th century, there were no Ashekhabat among the Lower Uda Buryats.

According to the data of the 1897 census, the western Ashekhabat lived for the most part in the basin of the Oka river, chiefly on the Kimiltey and Kharik rivers (the village of Karymskoye and others), that is, in the same places where their ancestors lived at the beginning of the 18th century. In 1897, the western Kharanut lived mainly in the basin of the Zima river.[12]

Thus, the largest Buryat group in the Krasnoyarsk uyezd was the Ashekhabat, who lived on the Oka river near the eastern border of this uyezd. On the Uda

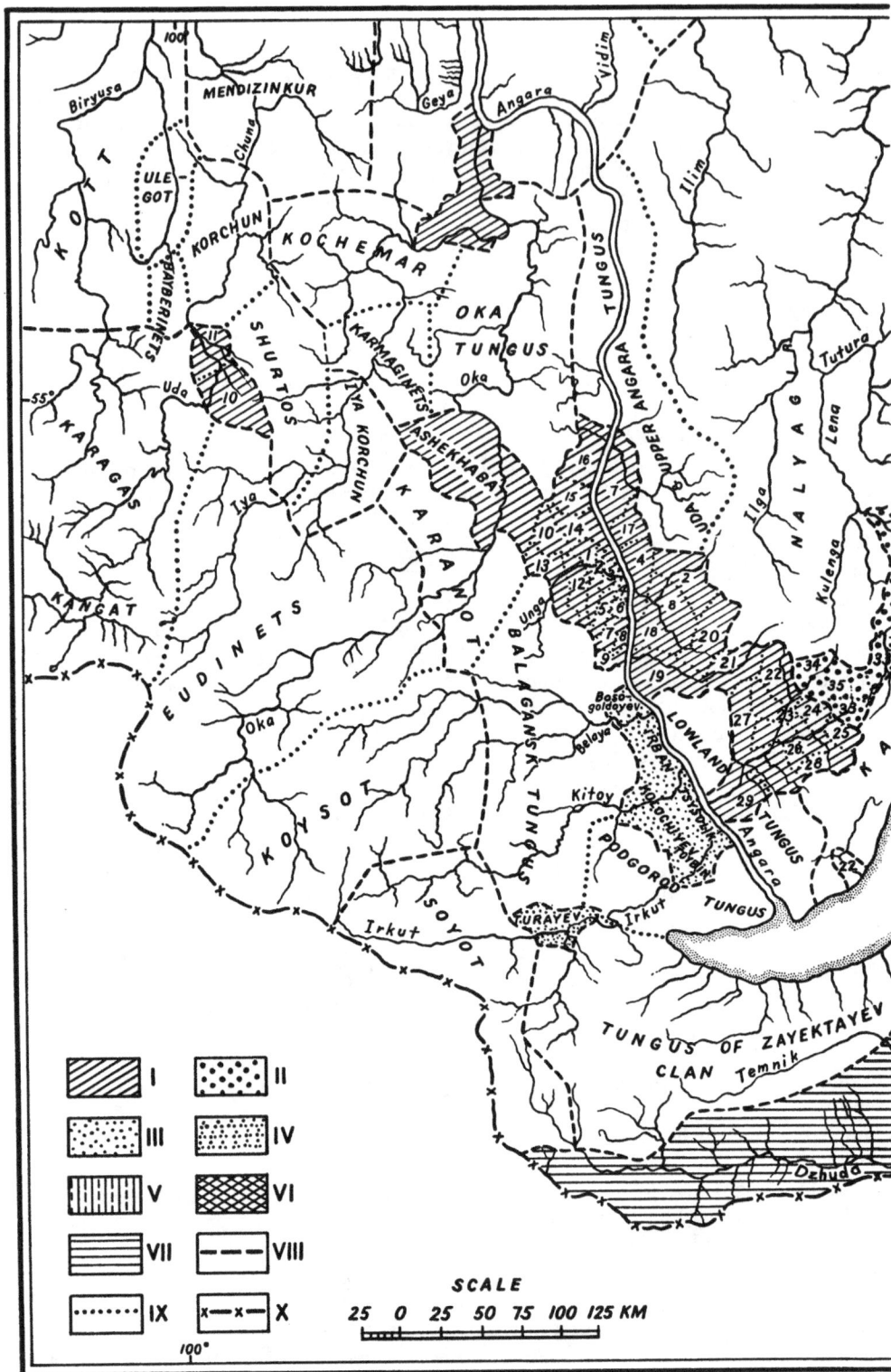

Distribution of the tribes that formed the Buryat people in the first half of the 17th century: I, Bulagat; II, Ekherit; III, Khongodor; IV, Khorin; V, Tabunut; VI, Atagan and Sartol; VII, Mongols; VIII, territorial boundaries of the distribution of ethnic groups and tribes; IX, territorial boundaries of clans within the limits of an ethnic group or tribe; X, boundary with China according to the treaty of 1727.

Note: There are no data on the distribution of the Khorin and Tabunut. The location of the Solengut and Khoguy clans is shown as a guide.

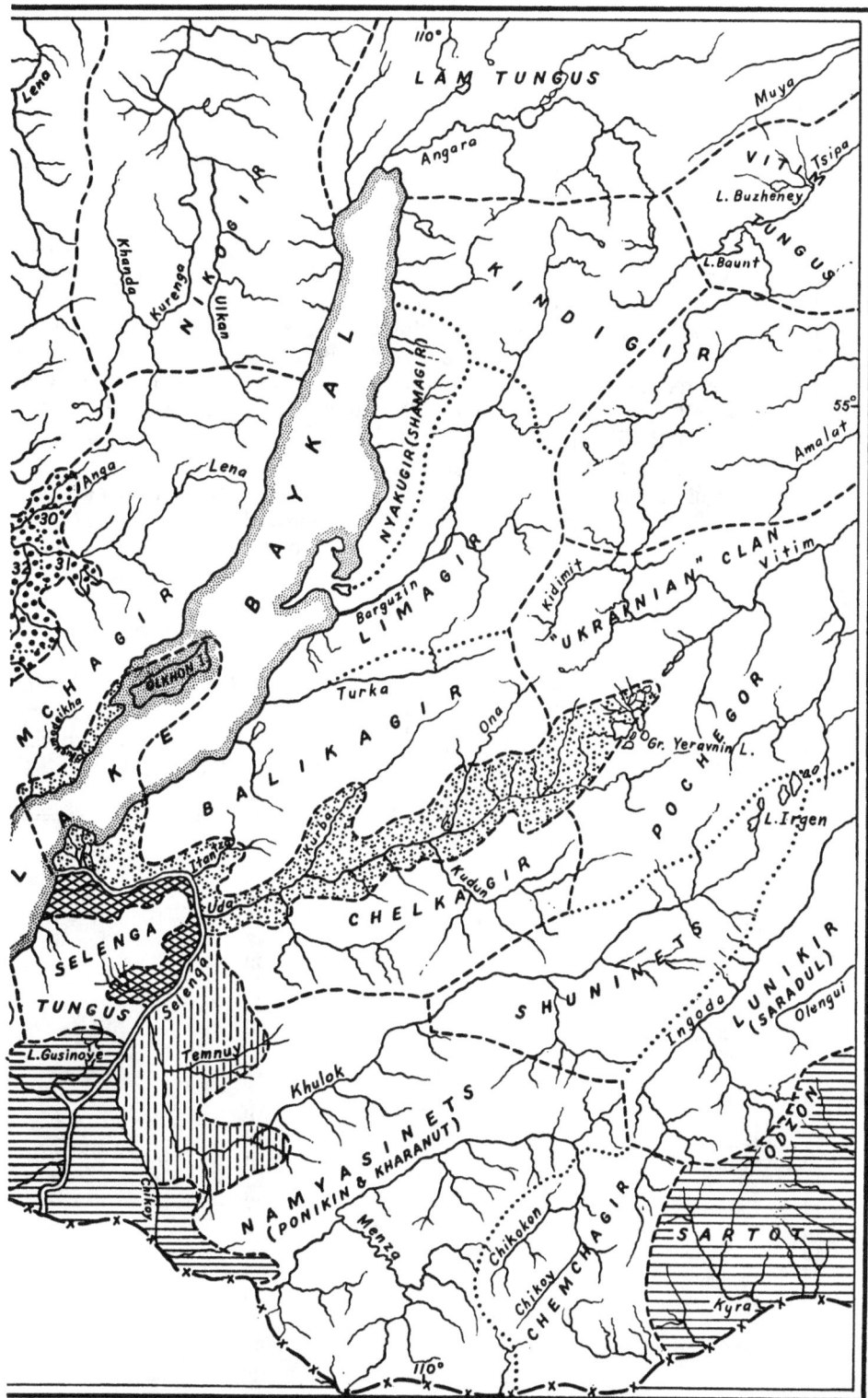

Clans designated on the map by numerals. Bulagat tribes: 1, Solengut; 2, Ongoy; 3, Olzoy; 4, Onkhotoy; 5, Ikisat; 6, Khoguy; 7, Noet; 8, Kholtubay; 9, Sharanut; 10, Sharait; 11, Turalit; 12, Bolot; 13, Kulemet; 14, Muruy; 15, Zungar; 16, Bykot; 17, Boroy; 18, Irkid; 19, Gotel; 20, Engut; 21, Sharalday; 22, Ashekhabat; 23, Kharanut; 24, Bulagat; 25, Kurumchin; 26, Abaganat; 27, Buyan; 28, Algut; 29, Kurkut. Ekherit tribes: 30, Khengelder; 31, Bur; 32, Chenorut; 33, Abyzay; 34, Olzon; 35, Bayenday.

river there lived only two small Buryat or "Buryatized" clans—the Sharait and Turalit (Agalit).

To the west, the permanent camps of the Buryats did not extend farther than the Uda river. In their military expeditions, the Buryat clan aristocracy perhaps got as far as the Yenisey. For trade, probably, and for the collection of alban, the Buryat princelings nomadized along the middle course of the Biryus. But on the Uda and also on the Biryus, and to the west of the latter, they were in territory settled for the most part by the Kotts.

In the Yeniseysk uyezd, those Buryats living along the lower reaches of the Oka and its tributary, the Iya, were attached to the Bratsk fortress. This group of Buryats represented an islet of a Mongolic-speaking, cattle-raising population surrounded on all sides by the Evenks. Dominant among the Buryats of the Bratsk fortress was the Ikinat clan, as S. A. Tokarev[13] convincingly demonstrated —only he calls the Ikinat a tribe and not a clan.

The number of Lower Oka Buryats is rather difficult to determine, although they were the first Buryats to come into contact with the Russians. In 1669, the Lower Oka Buryats consisted of two uluses, which contained 25 tribute-paying people in all; in 1702 there were also two uluses, in whcih there were 45 tribute-paying people, and the whole population probably numbered about 250 persons. In the first half of the 17th century they probably comprised some 400 persons.[14]

Like the Ashekhabat of the middle Oka, the Ikinat of the lower reaches of that river headed a group of clans of their kyshtym, who consisted exclusively of Evenks. From these clans around the Ikinat new tribes arose, although this

TABLE 3

No.	Clan	Number of tribute-paying people	Sables	Foxes	Wolverines
1	Muru	32	33	5	—
2	Ongo	42	43	5	3
3	Bykot (Karanit)	29	42	1	—
4	Kulemet	39	45	3	—
5	Olzo	13	18	3	—
6	Sharait	6	6	—	—
7	Bolot	12	13	1	—
8	Solegut	11	11	3	—
9	Khanit	3	5	—	—
10	Ikinat	15	19	2	1
11	Ongoto	16	19	1	—
12	Sharanut	7	8	—	—
13	Khuguy	22	21	3	2
14	Irkidey	5	7	—	—
15	Khotol	3	3	—	—
16	Kholtubay	21	22	2	1
17	Zyungar	9	11	—	—
18	Noet	10	13	—	—
19	Engut	5	4	—	1
20	"Mungal [Mongolian] emigrants"	11	7	3	1
	Total, Buryat	311	349	32	9
21	Borondoy	12	47	1	2
22	Karanut	9	41	—	1
	Total	332	437	33	12

TABLE 4

Year	Number of tribute-paying people	Source
1669	141	Sec. 212, book 527, leaves 252 ob., 256
1689	332	Sec. 214, book 941, leaves 59 ob., 75
1696	476	Sec. 214, book 1099, leaf 281
1699	570	Sec. 214, book 1229, leaf 682
1701	570	Sec. 214, book 1259, leaf 159 ob.
1702	584	Sec. 214, book 1345, leaf 232
1735	664	Sec. 199, no. 481, copybook 7, leaf 6 ob.

process was far from complete. But individual Tungus clans living alongside the Ikinat fused with them toward the end of the 17th century. Such were the uluses of the Zanoko and Nagata mentioned among the tribute-paying peoples of the Bratsk fortress at the end of the 17th century.

The Buryats who paid tribute in the Balagansk fortress comprised the western part of the principal mass of the tribes of the Bulagat or "the great brotherly peoples," as they were called in Russian documents of the 17th century. In Table 3 data are given on the number, clan composition, and tribute rate of the Balagansk fur-tribute-paying peoples in 1689;[15] and Table 4 shows the change in the number of tribute-paying people attached to the Balagansk fortress during the 17th century.

It is important to establish the number of Bulagats in 1658, before the brutality and extortion of the bailiff Ivan Pokhabov eventually compelled them to retire to Mongolia.

The growth in the number of tribute-paying people of the Balagansk fortress over the period from 1669 to 1699 was due not only to natural increase, but also to the gradual return of the Balagansk Bulagat from Mongolia.

In 1658 (or more accurately, in the winter of 1657–8) before the flight of the Bulagat, a tribute of 7 measures of "forty" (each containing 37 sable and 7 fox pelts) was collected in the Balagansk fortress. Such a tribute rate corresponds to a maximum of 300–320 tribute-paying persons, i.e., roughly the same number as there were in the Balagansk fortress in 1689 (*vide supra*). It is possible, however, that in the first years after the subjection of the Balagansk Bulagat, their registration was to some degree imprecise. Therefore, it is perhaps proper to use later information and to reckon with 570 tribute-paying people as the initial quantity. On this basis it can be assumed that the Balagansk Bulagat numbered 2850 persons in the 17th century.

In 1699, the Sharanut clan nomadized to the Alar and there joined the Khongodor. The Irkidey, Khotol, and Engut clans were parts of corresponding clans of the Ilimsk uyezd, and subsequently formed the special Idinsk department.

At the beginning of the 19th century, the Solegut, Khanit, and Khugu clans ceased to exist as independent units. Their extinction can not be assumed, since, according to ethnographic data, the Khogoy (cf. Khuguyev) and Khonyut (cf. Khanit) clans were in existence at the beginning of the 20th century.[16] Apparently, they merged with other clans.

The remaining 12 principal clans of the Balagansk Bulagat formed, in the beginning of the 19th century, the Balagansk department. Six of these clans—the Muru, Bykot, Kulemet, Olzo, Bolot, and Zyungar—were assigned to the Balagansk department as whole clans, and portions of the rest of the clans were entered into other administrative units. Thus, four clans—the Ongo, Ongoto, Kholtuba, and Noet—were in part assigned to the Idinsk department, the Sharait clan to the "Brotherly Udinsk Estate" of the Krasnoyarsk uyezd, and the Ikinat clan to the authority of the Bratsk fortress. The Evenks, who paid tribute in the Balagansk fortress, remained as separate clans even at the beginning of the 19th century and later, but they were already counted as Buryats; to be numbered among the Evenks was not profitable—they paid a tribute four times as large as the Buryats.

The Balagansk Bulagats were settled in the basin of the Unga river and along the entire left bank of the Angara from the mouth of the Uda to the mouth of the Ida.

By using the 17th century sources indicated and the data on land use from the first half of the 19th century,[17] we have attempted to reconstruct the distribution of Bulagat clans, including the Balagansk, at the time of the arrival of the Russians. Wherever migrations occurred, the distribution of clans is approximately indicated, on the basis of 17th century data.

In 1686, the majority of the ancestors of the Cis-Baykal Buryats were to be found within the authority of the Verkholensk [Upper Lena] fortress of the Ilimsk uyezd. Some of these Buryats paid tribute directly in Verkholensk; some, beginning in 1679, to the Idinsk fortress, founded in 1672. In 1681 all the tribute-paying Buryats under the authority of these fortresses numbered 1158 persons, and they paid the tribute of 1192 sables. Of these tribute-paying people, 639 were Bulagat, 507 Ekherit, and 12 were kyshtym. Of the latter, the majority were probably of Tungus origin.

In Table 5 are given data showing the change in the number of "the brotherly people" paying tribute in the Verkholensk and Idinsk fortresses. Clarification is required for the information concerning the number of Ekherit and Bulagat in 1735. The increase in the number of Ekherit over the Bulagat is due to the fact that in the period 1701–35, when the expulsion of the Cis-Baykal Buryats to the Trans-Baykal occurred, fewer of the Ekherit were evicted. Moreover, the Ekherit who were evicted to the island of Olkhon and to Kudara in 1735 continued to be accounted for in the Verkholensk fortress, whereas the evicted Bulagat had already been transferred by this time to the authority of the Selenginsk fortress.

The over-all increase in the number of tribute-paying people in the Verkholensk fortress, as well as in the Udinsk Estate and in the Balagansk department, can be attributed to three causes: (1) natural increase, (2) more accurate bookkeeping, and (3) the influx of Buryats from beyond the border. On the whole, the increase in the number of ancestors of the western Buryat-Mongols did not exceed the limits of possible normal natural increase. This supposition is also supported by official documents. For example, in 1672, among the Ekherit and

TABLE 5

Year	No. of tribute-paying people			Source
	Ekherit	Bulagat	Total	
1672	452	558	1010	Sec. 214, book 627, leaves 32–60
1677	497	588	1035	Sec. 214, book 627, leaves 628–642
1681	507	651	1158	Sec. 214, book 696, leaves 310–316
1696	652	846	1498	Sec. 214, book 1141, leaves 172–198
1701	728	940	1668	Sec. 214, book 1316, leaves 153–168
1735	1238	1052	2290	Sec. 199, no. 481, copybook 7, leaf 6 ob.

Upper Lena Bulagat the number of the younger males aged 6 to 18 years exceeded 500 persons.[18] Again in 1691, in the Verkholensk jurisdiction, 142 persons were found to be youths and Buryats from "over the ridge."* Further, in the assessment of defaulting tribute-paying people, 44 youths were "found" and, over and above this, 114 more youths were discovered from whom the tribute for 1691 could not be collected and who were registered for tribute collection in 1692.[19]

Such a large number of minors of the male sex can be found only in conditions of rather great natural increase. And, indeed, in 1699 the Verkholensk bailiff Afanasy Beyton, one of the heroes of the defense of Albazin, complained that he was short of material valuables for "wages" (i.e., presents) to Buryats who had discharged their tribute obligations; he wrote that "in various clans of the brotherly people, over the years youths reaching tribute age are increasing. And, in the past year 206 (1698), in the brotherly clans there were 33 youths newly found." Thus the rapid natural increase of the Buryat population at the end of the 17th century did not escape the attention of the Russian administration.

The influx of immigrants had little effect on the numbers and clan composition of the Bulagats and Ekherits. The immigrants were few, and a considerable portion of these were not immigrants, but reimmigrants who on some occasion had left the Cis-Baykal region for one reason or another and gone to Mongolia, but later returned to their homeland.

The Verkholensk Buryats were settled in three principal groups.

One group was comprised of Bulagats occupying the basins of the Ida, Osa, and, in part, of the Uda rivers. Later on, these Buryats formed the Idinsk department, from which the Molkinsk, Uleysk, Bilchirsk, Ukyrsk, and Bokhansk departments were already detached in the 19th century.

Another group of Bulagats occupied the basin of the Kuda river. Later on, this group formed the Kudinsk department, from which the Kapsalsk department was subsequently detached.

A third group consisted of Ekherits who lived in the northern part of the basin of the Kuda river, along the Manzurka river, and in the upper reaches of the Lena, in the region of its confluence with the Anga, Manzurka, and Kulenga. They formed the Verkholensk department, and, after their expulsion to Olkhon and to the Barguzin and Kudarin steppes beyond Lake Baykal, they formed the Olkhonsk, Barguzinsk, and Kudarinsk departments as well.

Some information on the residence of separate Bulagat and Ekherit clans is found in 17th century sources. This information is usually given incidentally, in the course of a description of one or another event, particularly in accounts of criminal and civil actions. Thus, in 1698, the Buryats of the "Khenkheldur clan," 34 persons in all, considered as their "ancestral land" (reinforcing this by recollections of old allotments) the territory "along both sides of the Anga river," upstream "as far as the Ocheul lakes, and along the lower side as far as Rassokha." The Khengelder complained that on this land of theirs, the "brotherly men of the Toanats (i.e., the Chenorut) clan, Nudgey Togloyev and companions" had begun to wander, and because of this they had "quarrels over the years."[20]

In 1697, the whole Buyanov clan "of 100 persons" designated as their "ancestral lands" the territory along the Kue river (i.e., the Kuyada) and along the "Kaptsala," i.e., the same land the Buryats of this clan held at the end of the 19th century, when they formed the Kapsalsk department.[21]

Quite a few such data, affording direct or indirect insight concerning the

*[*Zakhrebetnik* perhaps best translated here as "stranger."—Editor.]

TABLE 6

CLAN-TRIBAL STRUCTURE OF THE BULAGATS AND EKHERITS OF THE ILIMSK UYEZD

1672–7			No. of tribute-paying people		1681			No. of tribute-paying people	Departmental affiliation at beginning of 19th century
Name of "hundred"	Name of clan	Name of prince	1672	1677	Name of "hundred"	Name of clan	Name of clan leader	people	
Bulagat of Bagun	—	Bagun	134	132	Sosoya of Bagun	Ongoy	Sosoy Bagunov	52	Idinsk
						Koltubay	Kiladay Ashakhayev	20	
						Onkotoy	Tolokchin Tarchiyev	22	
						Baray	Akshay Barayev	22	
						Noyets	Shulenge Mukuyev	23	
						Yrkidey	Odulay Tyrgeyev	15	
	Kotel	Kangay	37	37		Kotel	Zebaka Bultugudayev	49	
		Temirey	21	26		Engutets	Khogday Tabunov	16	
Bulagat of Tabu	—	Tabuy of Kaurtay	216	224	Bushkhay and Noyenk	Sharalday	Bulguy Bukhureyev	18	Kudinsk
						Bulagat (Kugurdey)	Bushkhay Nomokhonov	32	
						Bulagat* (Babay)	Noyen Toromov	46	
						Kurumchin	Kiney Muushayev	36	
						Karamut	Elbenkuy Khulbeyev	44	
						Buyanov	Bukunay Bulzuyev	72	
—	Alguts	—	17	17	—	Algut	Zatisha Ilbulayev	48	Kitoy
—	Sipugats	Monko	62	67	—	Asipugat	Monkhoy Borekhoyev	76	
—	—	Imakhan of Akchey	48	53	—	Abaganat	Kutzuy	57	
—	—	Mokhan	23	32	—	Kurkut	Nokhodoy Mokhonov	21	
Ekherit	Obyzay	Kucha of the Ongo	111	125	Olgyn	Obyzay	Olgyn Tsorokov	51	Verkholensk, Olkhonsk, and Barguzinsk
						Obyzay	Olongo Boordayev	85	
—	—	Butukhey of Cheule	120	133	Botukey	Chernorutf	Botukey Tsoulov	73	
						Chernorut	Abuk Chentukeyev	67	
						Dorgiyevshin	Bychiy Momin	12	
						"Zakhrebetnik"	—	6	
—	—	Bura	120	127	Abakhay	Burovshchina	Abakhay Burindayev	50	
						Khynkydyrt	Irbaday Korogonov	75	
—	—	Dorgiy	101	112	Butunay	Olzon	Butunay Mokhoborov	43	
						Bayendayevshchina	Khebyney Kokoyev	48	

*Also Botoy. In 1735, the Kugurdey (also Kourtay) and Babay clans were united with the Kurumchin and adopted their name. In the 19th century, the Kugurdey and Babay clans were under the name of Babay.

†The Chenorut and Khengelder were still called Kharbatov(?).

residence of one or another clan of the Verkholensk Buryats, have been preserved. By comparing this information with later, more accurate sources, and particularly with materials on land use,[22] and with materials from the 1897 census (published by S. K. Patkanov[23]), which also contains information on the distribution of clans and whole departments, we have succeeded in plotting on the map the principal Buryat and Ekherit clans of the Verkholensk department of the Ilimsk district.[24]

A peculiarity of the clan-tribal structure of the Bulagat and Ekherit of the Ilimsk uyezd was the occurrence among them, in addition to the division into tribes and clans, of the *sotnya* ["hundred"] and the *pyatidesyatnya* ["fifty"]. The "hundreds" included several clans of a single tribe[25]; the "fifties" were apparently made up of subdivisions of clans. But among the Bulagat there were clans that did not enter into the formation of a hundred. With the Ekherit, the hundreds were comprised of four principal clans: Chenorut, Khengelder, Olzon, and Abyza. As for the Burovshchina clan, it was a subdivision of the Khengelder (Khengeldur, Khynkydyr) clan, and the clan Bayendayevshchina was a subdivision of the Olzon clan.

In Table 6, the clan-tribal structure is given, and the division of the Ekherit, and also of the Kudinsk and Idinsk Bulagat, into "hundreds" is indicated. The "fifties" are not indicated in this table, since comprehensive data on all of the clans comprising them are not available. As the table shows, part of the Gotel was called the Engut clan. It is known that their other part comprised the Bumal clan. A portion of the Gotel of the Engut clan went to Mongolia. This apparently explains the decrease in the number of Gotel of the Engut clan from 1677 to 1681. At the end of the 1680's, these Engut returned to Russia again.

In the Irkutsk uyezd, some of the "brotherly people" were within the authority of the Irkutsk fortress. In Table 7 are presented data showing the number, clan composition, and tax rate of the Irkutsk Buryats for 1682.[26] Table 8 indicates data on the change in the number of Buryats paying tribute in the Irkutsk fortress.

TABLE 7

No.	Clan (ulus)	Number of tribute-paying people	Sable rate
1	Toybin (Sagan)	30	42
2	Irban	35	46
3	Bosogoldoy (on the Tayturka)	16	23
4	Kolochiy	36	36
5	Emigrants of the Komkodor clan living in the Torsk steppe	27	34
	Total, Khongodors	144	181
6	Tsysolik	14	15
7	Turay (clan emigrants)	48	73
	Total, Khongodors with clans affiliated to them	206	267
8	Abaganat (on the Kuda)	36	39
9	Kurkut	10	13
	Total, Bulagats	46	51
10	Ekherits of the Olzon clan	15	22
	Total	267	340

TABLE 8

Year	Number of tribute-paying people				Source
	Khongodor	Bulagat	Ekherit	Total	
1669	93	45	12	150	Sec. 214, book 527, leaves 257–262
1681	206	46	15	267	Sec. 214, book 941, leaves 453–465
1682	212	48	16	276	Sec. 214, book 768, leaves 542–561
1693	210	109	18	337	Sec. 214, book 1034, leaves 270–289
1694	217	104	18	339	Sec. 214, book 1034, leaves 270–289
1695	274	113	17	404	Sec. 214, book 1034, leaves 270–289
1696	320	133	27	480	Sec. 214, book 1141, leaves 133–165
1700	362	162	35	554	Sec. 214, book 1316, leaves 134–147
1701	365	206	36	607	Sec. 214, book 1316, leaves 134–147
1735	571	211	48	830*	Sec. 199, no. 481, copybook 7, leaves 22–25

*Not counting 65 "buryatized" Soyots (Tuvins).

The major part of the Buryat population, coming under the authority of the Irkutsk fortress, consisted of the Khongodor tribe and the Turay (Terte) and "Tsysolik" (Sheshelok) clans contiguous to it. The Khongodors, with the clans contiguous to them, lived on the left bank of the Angara only. Often the Khongodors were regarded as a Bulagat clan. However, it is difficult to conceive of a populous tribe, consisting of several clans (uluses) and speaking its own dialect, as of a clan. The Alar pronunciation of the Buryat language is no different from the dialect of the Khongodors that has been preserved to this day.

The opinion prevails that the Khongodors made their appearance in the Cis-Baykal region only in the late 17th century, as a result of the wars of Bushukhtu khan. This opinion is certainly incorrect. S. A. Tokarev presents quite convincing material, which shows that the Khongodors were living in the Cis-Baykal region in the 1640's and 1650's.[27] The legend of the arrival of the Khongodors in the time of the Galdan Bushukhtu khan is probably connected with the fact that several groups of Khongodor left for Mongolia in the middle of the 17th century and then returned at the time when a detachment of Galdans was moving through Mongolia.

The Khongodors were also called Rosnut (Rusnut, Urusurnat, et al.)[28] and sometimes Khabarnut. The designation Khongodor was used chiefly in the Irkutsk uyezd, and Rosnut in the Yeniseysk (in the Balagansk).

The distribution of the Khongodors in the 17th century is shown on the map.

The migration of the Khongodors to Alar took place in 1699. Together with the Khongodors, the Sharanut clan of the Balagansk department also went to Alar. The descendants of this clan are living to this day among the Alar Khongodors.

On the Irkut [river], into the composition of the Tunkin Buryats entered chiefly those Khongodors who lived there after the establishment of the Tunkinsk fortress in the Torsk steppe. Thus the division of the Khongodors into Alar and Tunkin goes back to the end of the 17th century.

In the 17th century, the Turay (Tertey) clan and the Tsysolik (Sheshelok clan) are always mentioned together with the Khongodors but neither at this nor at any other time are they called Khongodor, nor does the oral tradition of the Buryats consider them Khongodor. The locale of the Tertey (Turay) clan was the Torsk steppe. Sometimes the Tertey also nomadized in the lower reaches of the Irkut.[29]

The Tsysolik are recorded mostly in the Irkutsk region and on the Kitoy [river] among the Khongodors. On the right bank of the Angara in the Irkutsk authority of the 17th century, there was a group of Tungus called the "Podgorod" ["Below-the-town"], as well as various small groups of Bulagats and Ekherits. The overwhelming majority of the Buryats of these tribes were registered, as we know, in the Ilimsk and Yeniseysk uyezds; they paid tribute in Verkholensk (and from 1679 on, also in Idinsk) and in Balagansk. In 1672, the Ilimsk officials were still laying claims on the Bulagats and Ekherits who paid tribute in Irkutsk, maintaining that in past years these "brotherly tribute-paying people had for many summers paid tribute in the Ilimsk uyezd in the Verkholensk fortress and (live together) with their brothers and tribesmen in the same uluses here. (And in) past years tribute has been taken willfully from these people in Irkutsk."[30] Despite the protests of Ilimsk, these groups of Bulagats and Ekherits remained within the authority of the Irkutsk fortress, and thus the Abaganat and Kurkut clans of the Bulagats, and the Olzon clan of the Ekherits, were divided among different uyezds.

The Kurkuts of the Irkutsk uyezd apparently nomadized close to the fortress itself and in the lower reaches of the Kuda river, together with their kinsmen who paid tribute to Verkholensk. At the end of the 17th century, the Irkutsk Kurkuts were also seen in the lower reaches of the Irkut. The Abaganats and Olzons of the Irkutsk uyezd also nomadized, together with their kinsmen of the Verkholensk jurisdiction, in the Kuda basin.

In 1735, the following clan-tribal groups of Buryats paid tribute in the Irkutsk (and Tunkinsk) fortresses: Khongodor proper, 465 tribute-paying people; Tsysolik, 48; Tertey, 58; Bulagat (Abaganat clan), 46; Kurkut, 57; Buyana, 31; Ashekhabat, 21; Kharanut, 21; Babay, 20; Algut, 3; Gotel, 1; Ekherit (Chenorut clan), 29; Abyzay, 9; Bayenday, 4; Olzon, 6. Besides these, we have conditionally numbered among the Bulagats 9 of the Zongor clan and 2 other persons.

The decrease in the numbers in the Algut, Ashekhabat, and Olzon clans from 1701 to 1735 is explained by their expulsion to the Selenga. The attachment to Irkutsk of some new Bulagat and Ekherit families in 1735 was due to the growing importance of Irkutsk as the administrative and economic center of eastern Siberia. The increase in the number of Khongodors, apart from natural increase, is also explained by the influx from beyond the border. At the end of the 17th

TABLE 9

	Number of tribute-paying people								
Year	Atagan	Sartol	Khatagin	Uzon	Tabunut	Bulagat	Ekherit	Total	Source
1681°	16	35	—	—	—	—	—	51	Sec. 214, book 941, leaves 490–493 ob.
1683°	24	35	—	—	—	—	—	59	Sec. 214, book 768, leaf 585
1721†	205	128	—	—	356	127	7	823	Sec. 214, book 1619, leaves 1–12
1735‡	405	239	80	21	710	642	147	2244	Sec. 199, art. 481, copybook 7, leaves 49–60

°The Atagan rate was 16 sables, the Sartol rate 36 sables.
†The number of Tabunut—ancestors of the three Tabunut clans—we have determined as 180 tribute-paying people. In the Tabunut Tsongol clan there were 160 tribute-paying people, making a total, therefore, of 356 Tabunut tribute-paying people.
‡The data on the Khatagin were calculated by us. Among the Tabunut, there were 360 tribute-paying people in the Tsongol clan, 247 in the three Tabunut clans, and 103 tribute-paying people in the Podgorod clan.

century, many "Mungal emigrants" are noted among the Khongodors.[31] All these emigrants from Mongolia were assimilated by the Khongodors and fused with them.[32]

Selenginsk, in contrast to the other fortresses of Siberia in the 17th century, was important principally as a military frontier post. However, the absence of a permanent, large contingent of tribute-paying people within the Selenginsk authority in the 17th century does not mean that there was no indigenous population around it. To the contrary, Selenginsk environs were inhabited by a large tribe of Tabunuts, who came under Russian subjugation only at the end of the 17th century and the beginning of the 18th, but were an important component part of the Buryat nation.

Statistical data on the Selenginsk Buryats are given in Table 9. The Buryat population that came under the authority of the Selenginsk fortress consisted of three groups: (1) four separate clans—Atagan, Sartol, Khatagin, and Uzon; (2) a tribal grouping of Tabunuts; (3) Bulagats and Ekherits—emigrants from the Cis-Baykal. Of the first group, only the Atagans and Sartols paid tribute in the 17th century. In the period 1688–92, the Khatagins were apparently Russian subjects also, but later they went to Mongolia, from where they finally returned in 1732. The Uzons came into Russia between 1720 and 1732. Most of them entered the Nerchinsk uyezd, where they were considered "Tungus"; a smaller portion went to the Irkutsk uyezd, where they entered into the composition of the Selenginsk Buryats. These four clans apparently represent northern groups of Mongols of diverse origins.

In the 17th century, the Tabunuts had not been under Russian subjugation for long, although in 1646, in the person of Turukhay-Tabun, they had probably already entered into friendly relations with the Russian cossacks dispatched by the ataman Vasily Kolesnikov to the Selenga river. In 1647, the official Ivan Pokhabov also visited Turukhay-Tabun. Later on, the assumption was made that the Russians had encountered the chief of the Khorins in the person of Turukhay-Tabun. However, the Khorins did not nomadize at all where Turukhay-Tabun was encountered. In 1893, the leaders of the Khorins wanted to take advantage of the similarity of the name Turukhay to the patronymic Turakin as the basis for their political and property claims. The Khorin "ancestral version" that the Khorin *shulenge*, Badan Turakin, was a son of Turukhay-Tabun has been repeated since then by all investigators studying the history of the Buryats. But even though Turukhay-Tabun was not related in any way to the Khorins, it is quite probable that he was the chief of the Tabunuts and that his title gave the name to the tribe that he led.

Let us introduce several of the principal points of Tabunut history at the end of the 17th century. In the years 1660–70, the Tabunuts threatened the Tungus in the region of the Yeravnin lakes, the upper reaches of the Uda river, and in the environs of the Irgensk fortress.[33]

In 1674, a Nerchinsk official, traveling to the Tabunuts for negotiations, reported that

they reached the ulus of the Tabunut princeling Ketayzha. But they (the Tabunuts) did not let them through the Uchuroy khan, and told them that they did not serve Uchuroy khan and that before they had not been under his command. And these Tabunut people live apart, under the command of the Tabunut princelings Irkem and Ketayzha. And the lands on which they nomadize and . . . from which their tribute is gathered, the tribute-paying people of the Telenbinsk (i.e., Nerchinsk) uyezd say, again and again, is their land.[34]

In 1682, a truce was concluded between the Selenginsk officials and the nearby Mongol feudal lords. At the conclusion of the agreement, the Mongols "were ordered by the officials to swear to the interpreter Taras that the Kukanovshchin Mongols would not attack them while they were in assembly or on the march and that the Mongols would not go to war against or massacre them. . . . But the Kukanovshchin did not swear allegiance for the Tabunuts, since, they said, this people live by themselves and not under our *taisha*."[35]

On September 16, 1688, F. A. Golovin defeated, beyond the Great Khilok, the Tabunut taisha Seren Sekulai who rebelled against the Russians in alliance with the Mongol feudal lords. On October 1, 1688, 1200 yurtas of the Tabunuts asked to be received into Russian overlordship. Golovin received their proposal and permitted them to nomadize between Selenginsk and Udinsk,[36] probably their former pastures. In the beginning of 1689, a formal agreement was concluded with the Tabunuts (with Sain Okin Tarkhan Batur and others) concerning their transfer to Russian overlordship.[37]

On March 28, 1691, there appeared in Selenginsk a Mongol, Dambo Gychyul, a retainer of the Dalai Hutukhtu (Undur Gegen), who declared that he had some orders from Hutukhtu for the Russian subjects, the "Bargut and Tabunut peoples."[38] The purpose of the mission of Dambo Gychyul was clarified in the same year. At the end of October, 1691, the Tabunut taisha Seren Sekulai left for Mongolia,[39] with 800 of his people, despite the strong attempts of the Selenginsk bailiff Demyan Mnogogreshny to restrain them. Somewhat later, in the same year, the Tabunuts of Okin-*zaisan* also retired into Mongolia.[40]

In November 1695, Okin-zaisan, taking advantage of the fact that the Mongol feudal lords had been crushed by the Dzungarian Bushukhtu khan, came back to Selenginsk "90 persons on foot," and they were permitted to nomadize along the right bank of the Selenga below Selenginsk.[41] This group of Tabunuts later formed the Tsongol clan.[42]

In 1721, 727 more Tabunuts, having pushed through the Mongol guards, fled to Russia.[43] From these Tabunuts, the First, Second, and Third Tabunut clans were later formed, as well as a part of the Podgorod clan of the Selenginsk Buryats.[44]

On the number of Tabunuts we have the following data. In 1674, in the region of the Yeravnin lakes, two or three thousand Tabunuts were nomadizing (counting women and children). In 1688, there were 1200 yurts of Tabunuts in the Khilok region, the population of which must have comprised about 6000 persons. In 1691, approximately 1000 Tabunuts were regarded as Russian subjects; moreover, a certain number of them were found beyond the limits of Russian possessions. Thus the total number of Tabunuts was probably around 6000 persons. In 1735, there were approximately 3500 Tabunuts in Russia. It can, therefore, be assumed that from about 2000 to 3000 Tabunuts had been detained in Mongolia by their feudal masters. The distribution of the Tabunuts is indicated on the map.

In the opinion of S. A. Tokarev, the designation Tabunut was derived from the Mongol title *tabunang* ("princely son-in-law"). It is highly probable that by way of marriage to the taishas, heads of tribes, attempts were made to bring the Tabunuts under the influence of some powerful feudal lord, most probably Tsetsen khan. The descendants of the Tabunuts consider their ancient clan name to be Bata.[45] Actually, the Batot clan entered into the composition of all three administrative Tabunut clans and also into the composition of the Tsongol clan.[46] Ya. S. Smolev also reports that the Tabunuts derived from the Tabolyn tribe.[47]

It can be conjectured that a transposition of letters occurred here: in place of "Batalyn" or "Batulin," Smolev had recorded "Tabolyn." From the 1640's to 1680, the tribal name of Batulin or Baturin, together with the name Khorin, is always mentioned in the Cis-Baykal and Trans-Baykal regions. The Tsongol pronunciation of the Selenginsk Buryats probably goes back to the tribal dialect of the Batulin (Tabunut).

Unlike among other ancestors of the Buryats, there were, among the Tabunuts in the 17th century, not only a number of zaisans, but also taishas and a whole category of persons of distinction (*sait*). In the case of the Bulagat, Ekherit, and Khongodor, only clan shulenges are mentioned, and among the Khorins there were the shulenges, *darugas*, and zaisans. Thus the Tabunuts came under a stronger influence of feudal Mongolia than the other ancestral tribes of the Buryats. In 1735, the following Bulagat and Ekherit clans were in the Selenginsk region:

Bulagat:

Ashekhabat	271 tribute-paying people
Alaguy	47
Kharanut	45
Kharanut	155
Bumal-Gotol	73
Babay and Kurunchin	51

Ekherit:

Olzon	65 tribute-paying people
Chenorut	82

Before the arrival of the Russians, there were no Bulagats or Ekherits on the Selenga. They migrated there at the beginning of the 18th century. Only the Ashekhabats appeared at the very end of the 17th century. In 1692–6 the Ashekhabats, having crossed to the eastern shore of Lake Baykal, nomadized along the Itantse, the lower reaches of the Uda, and along the Kurba, and later, around 1707, they moved to Selenginsk.[48]

The rapid increase in the number of all these emigrants from the western shore of Lake Baykal in the period 1721–35 is noteworthy. Apart from natural increase, a large role in this increase in the number of Selenginsk Buryats was obviously played by the influx of immigrants, partly from the Cis-Baykal region,[49] also from the Krasnoyarsk uyezd,[50] and partly from Mongolia.[51] It should be noted, however, that after the agreement of 1727, the border was closed, and thereafter the Buryat population of Transbaykalia increased only through natural causes and immigration from the Cis-Baykal region.

All in all, it can be assumed that the number of the Atagan, Sartol, Khatagin, and Uzon clans approximately reflected the specific proportion of the Mongol element in the composition of the 17th century Selenginsk Buryats; the number of the Tsongol, the three Tabunut, and the Podgorod clans reflected the Mongol proportion of the Tabunuts, and the number of the Bulagat and Ekherit clans that of the Bulagats and Ekherits—all this referring to the composition of the Buryat population in Transbaykalia.

In the Nerchinsk uyezd, within the authority of the Itantsinsk winter quarters, the Khorin tribes comprised one of the important segments of the Buryat people. The history of the Khorins in the 17th century, on the basis of Russian sources, may be divided into two periods. The first lasts until the beginning of the 1650's, when the Khorins, who by then entered into the composition of the Russian state, in part and at times paid tribute in the Barguzinsk fortress. There are very few data on this period. It ended with the departure of the Khorins across the Ingoda and Onon into eastern Mongolia. The second period in the history of the Khorins begins with the return of the first groups into Russia in 1674, after which the majority of them entered into the composition of the population in the Nerchinsk uyezd.

A detailed summary of studies on the first historical period of the Khorins was assembled by S. A. Tokarev.[52]

"The Khorins and Batulins" are reported on the western shore of Lake Baykal and on the island of Olkhon in 1642, 1643, and 1645. They were separated from the Verkholensk Ekherit and Bulagat by the Onotskiy range, in which the reindeer-herding Tungus nomadized.

Another large portion of the territory of the Khorins was found to the east of Lake Baykal. In fact, as early as 1641 the Russians had information that "on the other side of the Lama there live the brotherly horse-people."[53] In 1645, the *ataman* Vasily Kolesnikov, in the Kudarinsk steppe near the mouth of the Selenga river, actually reached "the great brotherly people," living ". . . together with the Mongol people."[54] These "brotherly people" on the eastern side of Lake Baykal could have lived only on the right bank of the Selenga, since the Mongols nomadized on the left bank.[55] "The brotherly people" living to the east of Lake Baykal could have been only the Khorins. The Tabunuts, Sartols, and Atagans were not considered Buryats ("brotherly people") in the 1640's. It is known, too, that later the Khorins claimed this territory along the right bank of the lower reaches of the Selenga, especially on the Kudarinsk steppe, as their "ancestral land."

The fact that part of the Khorins paid tribute in the Barguzinsk fortress in the first half of the 17th century is explained in connection with their exodus from Mongolia in 1675.[56] Spafary also refers to this (calling the Khorins, the Bargut).[57] Accurate information on the departure of the Khorins into Mongolia in the middle of the 17th century is not available. In 1656 and 1658 the Khorins (then called Bargut) were found in the region of the confluence of the Onon and Ingoda and to the east or southeast of it. It can, therefore, be assumed that the departure of the Khorins from Lake Baykal into eastern Mongolia took place in 1651 or 1652. Probably the murder, in 1650, of the Russian envoy Yerofey Zabolotskiy was the principal reason that induced the Khorin zaisans and shulenges to flee from Russian territory.[58]

In the 17th century, as has been mentioned above, the Khorins were also called the Bargut. In Russian documents, the Khorins, in contrast to all other ancestors of the Buryats, were called "the Nerchinsk brotherly people." In the first half of the 17th century they were known under the double name of "Khorins and Batulins."

After their departure for eastern Mongolia, the Khorins again appeared in the environs of Nerchinsk in 1667, and for three years they paid tribute, but afterwards they were taken away again by the Mongol feudal lords. In 1674, the Khorins, headed by the shulenge Zerbo, returned once more to the vicinity of Nerchinsk, but in 1675, in consequence of threats from the Mongol feudal lords, they had to leave again. In the same year, however, more than a thousand Khorins, led by Abakhay and Turakhay, came once again to Nerchinsk and accepted Russian overlordship.[59] In 1679, these Khorins were already in the Kudarinsk steppe, and the Itantsinsk winter quarters were established on the Selenga for the collection of their tribute.

On March 15, 1680, new groups of Khorins under the leadership of the daruga Artsakhay and the shulenges Bodoroy, Bortzoy, Olyukey, Zerbo, and others reached the Nerchinsk region from eastern Mongolia. In the same year, some of these Khorins crossed the Uda and went to Lake Baykal[60]; others remained in the steppes around the Yeravnin lakes.

In 1682, four shulenges of the Khorins at the Yeravnin lakes turned traitor and went with their clans numbering 400 persons to Mongolia. The rest of them headed by Zerbo were sent to the Barguzinsk steppe where they nomadized until 1683.

In 1683, the Khorins were living along the Itantse at Lake Baykal about the estuary of the Selenga, on the western shore of Lake Baykal near the Bolshaya and Malaya Buguldeyka rivers, and on the island of Olkhon.[61] All of these territories were regarded by the Khorins as their "ancestral" lands.

In 1685, the movement of the Khorins from the western shore of Lake Baykal and from Olkhon to the eastern shore of Lake Baykal begins to be noticeable. The cause was their collision with the "Verkholensk brotherly people," i.e., with the Ekherits and Bulagats.[62]

In 1689, a large group of "brotherly and Onkots people" once again left Mongolia for the vicinity of Nerchinsk. In the same year, however, at the time of the negotiations taking place in Nerchinsk between the representatives of Russia and China, these new immigrants went off to Mongolia.[63] On November 3, 1690, the Khorin shulenges Bakbay and Kolboy, who had run away the previous year, again came to the vicinity of Nerchinsk. These "emigrants and their children, brothers and tribesmen, married and single" numbered 343 persons.[64] These Khorins, or at least some of them, including the shulenge Kolboy, were the same who had run away from the region of the Yeravnin lakes in 1682. Toward the middle of 1691 they were already in the region of the Itantsinsk winter quarters.

For this same year, 1691, there are data on the number and clan composition of the Khorins (not including new emigrants).[65]

1.	Clan of shulenge Ulukey and his son Bambakhay[66]	24 married persons
2.	Clan of shulenge Urtugur and his brother Kondokhoy	19
3.	Clan of shulenge Badan Turakin (Galzut)	21
4.	Clan of shulenge Kuytugur	13
5.	Clan of shulenge Zerbay (i.e., Zerbo)	48
6.	Clan of shulenge Sagday (Bodongut)	15
7.	Clan of shulenge Bodoroy (Kharganat)	76
8.	Clan of shulenge Bortsoy	10
9.	Clan of shulenge Artsakhay and his son Neltuy	42
10.	Clan of shulenge Orol and Zamalay (Khuday)	46
11.	Clan of shulenge Kolkontsok (Kobdut)	35
	Total	349 married persons

In 1691, three "newly baptized" serfs, two men and one woman, escaped the Selenginsk "chief of fifty," Anton Berezovsky. They were killed and robbed by the Ulyukiyev clan of the Khorins. The chief offender was hanged and "head money" was adjudged to Berezovsky—150 horses and large horned cattle. Clans whose members had not taken part in this murder but who were nevertheless required to pay a portion of the "head money" (which was apportioned among all the Khorins) were very displeased with this judgment.[67]

Just at this time there also appeared among the Tabunuts and "Barguts" (i.e., Khorins), the above-mentioned emissary of the Mongol spiritual (and, probably secular) feudal lords, Dambo Gychyul. For a short time after the arrival of Dambo Gychyul, the Khorins remained loyal to their agreements with the Russians. Three hundred of the Khorins even accompanied the Selenginsk cossacks in pursuit of the escaping Tabunuts.[70] But all the shulengs— Zerbo, Kutugur, Neltuy, and Orol, with Zamalay—on July 15, 1692, proceeded to leave for Mongolia.[69] The shulengs who had lived with them on the Uda— Bodoroy, Bortsoy, and Sagday—remained loyal to the Russians and were besieged by the traitors. Having learned what took place on the Uda, the clans that had been nomadizing by Lake Baykal—the Ulyukey, Urtugur, Turakin, and Kolkont-sok—dispatched 80 persons, led by Badan Turakin, to pursue the fugitives. But on reaching the Kudun river, none of them were able to overtake them. Bodoroy, Bortsoy, and Sagday succeeded in escaping the siege by themselves and in getting away from the Uda "from the Great steppe" over the mountains to the Ona and Kurba rivers.

Some time later, there "ran away" from the traitors "the brotherly muzhiks of Neltuy of the Omeyko clan, of Badanov of the Urtu clan, and Basytayko with comrades from 15 yurtas. And they turned away from the Great Khilok and they were reached, in time, by the Yeravnin Tungus Balturik with 8 companions and there was a battle between Zerbo and them. And of Zerbo's people . . . 7 persons were killed, even Zamalay, the shulenge, was killed . . . many were wounded."[70] Thus, the rank and file of the Khorins detached themselves from the shulengs at the first opportunity and, aided by the timely arrival of the Evenks, made war on the traitors.

In 1703, the Khorins presented their celebrated petition to Peter I. In it they were already claiming a rather large territory in Transbaykalia, evidently, because of their actual settlement there at the time. The principal object of this petition was the return of the Khorins from Irkutsk uyezd (where they were sent in 1693) back to Nerchinsk. This request "for their aliens" was granted by Peter I. Judging by this petition, some of the Mongols of the taisha Bintukhay and of others had also become a component part of the Khorins.

The Khorins who went off to Mongolia in 1692 were living in the princedom of San-beyse on the Uldza river in 1726. In 1730, 1732, and 1734, these Khorins, among other subjects of the Mongol feudal lords, attempted to return to Russia.[71] They belonged to the Khoatsay, Galuzut, and Kubdut clans, and in especially large numbers to the Khuday. But all of them were deported to Mongolia again. The Russian government, not wishing to complicate relations with China, adhered strictly to the clauses of the treaty, which prohibited the reception of deserters.

After this, as they were not received in Russia, these Khorins (the Khuday, Galzut, Khoatsay, Khalbin, and Ulyat clans and others) moved to Khulunbuir (Barga), where they were included in the Manchurian military organization under the designation "the new Bargut."[72]

The first complete list of Khorin clans remaining in Russia dates from the year 1735. It was probably composed somewhat earlier, but F. Müller obtained it in 1735 as the very latest data on this group of Buryats.[73] The data contained in this list are given in Table 10.

Of these clans, the first ten, numbering 1553 tribute-paying people, were regarded as the Khorins proper. The Guchit clan was Evenk, which paid tribute in the Kuchidsk fortress earlier and was registered in the Itantsinsk winter quarters at the beginning of the 18th century. The Zheltuts and Mungal clans— a few yurtas of Nerchinsk Tungus of the Zheltot clan and some Mongols—were also assigned to the Itantsinsk fortress.

The Khuday, Khalbin, Galzut, and, apparently, the Khaotsay clans were

TABLE 10

No.	Clan	Number of tribute-paying people
1	Khalkhut (Galzot)	163
2	Khargana (Karaganat)	320
3	Botongut (Botongut)	99
4	Kubdut (Kubdut)	258
5	Koatsey (Koatsay)	240
6	Batonay (Batanat)	84
7	Charait (Sharait)	144
8	Khuday (Kuday)	177
9	Tsakhan (Tsaganarut)	99
10	Khalbin (Kalbin)	79
11	Guchit (Guchit)	79
12	Zheltut and Mungal	9
	Total	1641

divided, as has already been mentioned, between the Khorins who remained in Russia and those who had gone to Khulunbuir.

The earliest data on the number of Khorins within the borders of Russia go back to 1712. At that time there were 598 tax-paying Khorins, 285 were not assessed, and 10 were "newly baptized," i.e., 894 persons in all. The tax consisted of one sable per year. The "non-assessed" persons paid one sable for every three persons per year.[74] However, the Khorins seldom paid with sables; they met their obligations chiefly with foxes and livestock, and, in the early 18th century, with money.

By estimating the payment of tribute for a series of years, and keeping in mind that only married Khorins paid tribute up to 1712, we have attempted to determine their number. According to our calculation, the Khorins in Russia, including women and children, numbered 3,500 persons in 1687, 4,000 in 1692, 4,300 in 1700, 6,000 in 1712, and 8,200 in 1735.

In 1690, about 1700 Khorins came with Kolbo, and in 1692 some 1300 persons left with Zerbo. In 1730–5, the total number of Khorins was probably around 13,000, about 8,000 of whom were in Russia and about 5,000 in China.

It can be estimated that the number of Khorins in the 1640's, when they first encountered the Russians, came to 6,000–7,000 persons.

The ancient territory of the Khorins can be visualized in the form of a long belt of territory reaching from the island of Olkhon and the Bolshaya and Malaya Buguldeyka rivers on the west, along the lower reaches of the right bank of the Selenga river (including the Kudarinsk steppe and the steppe along the Itantse river), up to the mouth of the Uda and upstream of the latter, and then farther into the region of the Yeravnin lakes as far as Lake Korgo (Khorga).[75]

As early as 1735, however, the Khorins occupied the whole basin of the Uda, had crossed to the lower reaches of the Khilok to the Tugnuy, and were even nomadizing along the Ingoda. They occupied the region of the Yeravnin lakes completely, and later they also settled the Aginsk steppe. Gradually, a considerable portion of the Khorins turned up in the Aginsk steppes. In 1839 the Aginsk Khorins were separated, for administrative purposes, from their tribesmen and formed a separate steppe council.

Thus formed a large and distinctive group of the Buryat nation—the Aginsk Buryats.

TABLE 11

Territory	Bulagat	Ekherit	Khongo-dor	Khorin	Tabunut	Mongols	Total
Uda and Oka rivers, middle course	100	—	—	—	—	—	100
Lower reaches of the Oka	100	—	—	—	—	—	100
Angara and Unda	600	—	—	—	—	—	600
Osa and Ida	300	—	—	—	—	—	300
Upper Lena and Kuda	500	700	—	—	—	—	1200
Belaya, Kitoy, Irkut	—	—	350	—	—	—	350
Island of Olkhon; Buguldeyka, Itantsa, and Uda rivers; Yeravnin lakes; Kudarinsk steppe	—	—	—	1200	—	—	1200
Lower reaches of Khilok and Chikoy	—	—	—	—	1000	—	1000
Left bank of lower reaches of Selenga	—	—	—	—	—	150	150
Total	1600	700	350	1200	1000	150	5000
Percentage	32.0	14.0	7.0	24.0	20.0	3.0	100.0

Having shown the component elements out of which the Buryat people had formed, we shall now consider the change in their numbers and proportion. In Table 11 are given data showing the ancestors of the Buryats before the arrival of the Russians, i.e., in the 1630's to the 1640's. In this connection, the later data cited in the description of separate tribes were used after some corrections. This table shows the number of adult males—the future tribute-paying people.

The over-all number of Buryat ancestors, counting women and children, came to around 25,000 persons at the time of the arrival of the Russians.

By 1735, the different incursions and expulsions of the ancestors of the modern Buryats across the border between Russia and China had, in the main, ceased. By this time there are more accurate data on all portions of the Buryat-Mongol people, with the exception of the Buryats of the Bratsk fortress living in the lower reaches of the Oka and Iya rivers. For the latter, the data for the year 1702 may be accepted. This group of Buryats was numerically small and later merged with the Russians.

The data in Table 12 reflect the tribal composition of the Buryats in 1735.[76] The over-all number of Buryats in 1735 amounted to about 40,000 persons.

TABLE 12

Fort	Bulagat	Ekherit	Khongo-dor	Khorin	Tabunut	Mongols	Others	Total
Udinsk Estate	115	—	—	—	—	—	142*	257
Bratsk	45	—	—	—	—	—	6†	51
Balagansk	634	—	—	—	—	—	30†	664
Idinsk	552	—	—	—	—	—	—	552
Verkholensk	500	1238	—	—	—	—	—	1738
Irkutsk	211	48	571	—	—	—	65‡	895
Selenginsk	642	147	—	—	710	745	12†	2256
Itantsinsk	—	—	—	1553	—	—	88§	1641
Total	2699	1433	571	1553	710	745	343	8054
Percentage	33.5	17.9	7.1	19.1	8.9	9.2	4.3	100.0

*Kotts and Evenks.   †Evenks.   ‡Tuvins.   §Mostly Evenks.

By 1823, the Buryats already numbered 156,943 persons,[77] not counting the Buryat cossacks, who numbered approximately 10,000 persons. Thus, from the beginning of the 18th century to the beginning of the 19th century, the number of Buryats increased more than fourfold.

During the 18th century, and especially in the 19th, the process of fusion of all the tribal groups enumerated above into a single people went forward. This process was facilitated by the fact that all these tribes spoke cognate dialects of the Mongolic language group. But there were other reasons as well that were conducive to the merging of all of these tribes into a single people and to their differentiation from other Mongolic-speaking peoples and tribes.

One of the principal reasons why a group of Mongolic-speaking tribes formed a new Buryat nation and did not become, for instance, a part of a Mongol nation, was, as we have already indicated, the fact that all these ancestral tribes of the Buryats entered into the structure of the Russian state. This circumstance sharply differentiated them from the Mongols proper as well as from kindred tribes of Buryats who remained subject to the Manchu dynasty of Mongolia and Barga. The Bulagats, Ekherits, Khorins, Khongodors, and Tabunuts, and also the rest of the Mongol clans within the borders of Russia, began to recognize themselves as a single ethnic whole in contradistinction to the peoples and tribes of Mongolia and Barga. Also, very significant was the fact that the economic and socio-political system of Russia, despite all the negative aspects of a feudal, serf-owning order and of the tsarist autocratic regime, was, on the whole, far more progressive in comparison with the extremely backward economic and socio-political system of feudal, fragmented Mongolia with its primitive, nomadic way of life.

In joining the Russian state, the ancestors of the Buryats were linked in economic and socio-political life with the various classes of the Russian people, in particular with the numerous and industrious Russian peasantry. These ties gave a definite imprint to the economy, culture, and way of life of the tribes who became Russian subjects. This detached the tribes more and more from their kinsmen remaining in feudal-theocratic Mongolia, and led to mutual understanding. As already noted, even in the 18th century, clans of quite different affiliation were already merging in the basin of the Selenga. Later on this process was intensified and began to involve other groups of Buryats as well.

Only in becoming a part of Russia did all the tribes of the ancestors of the Buryats acquire a common name, which did not exist among them before. At first, the Russians lumped them under the name of "brotherly people," and later "Buryats," which latter came to supplant the old tribal names. The consciousness of belonging to different tribes began to be replaced by the consciousness of belonging to a single people.

Thus, the formation of a single Buryat people from separate and often mutually hostile tribes is connected, to a significant degree, with the fact that the ancestors of the Buryats came to form part of the Russian state, and with the influence of the Russian people and of Russian culture. Not by accident did the ethnographic boundary between the Buryat and Mongol peoples ultimately coincide with the frontier between Russia and Mongolia. In addition, the formation of the Buryat people was facilitated and to a considerable extent prepared by the closeness of the dialects of the tribes who made up the Buryat people, and by the common features in their culture.

Therefore, the history of the Buryats after their ancestors became a part of the Russian state must be considered in close relationship with the history of Russia as a whole and of eastern Siberia in particular. The problem of the formation of the Buryat people is one of the problems of the history of eastern Siberia after it came to be a part of the Russian state. Starting on its historical journey with a group of small tribes, whose over-all number scarcely amounted to 25,000 persons, by 1823, in less than 200 years, the Buryats nevertheless expanded to form a numerous people of more than 150,000. This completely disproves the false assertions of the bourgeois nationalists that the Buryats, after entering Russia, died (in excess) and diminished in number.

Certainly, tsarist Russia was not the promised land for the peoples who inhabited it. The ruling classes of tsarist Russia skinned "seven hides" off the workers of their country. The working Buryats underwent cruel national suppression. Under the conditions of the colonial regime created by the tsarist government for the peoples of Siberia, the Buryats remained, right up to the October revolution, a backward people on the outskirts of tsarist Russia. Nevertheless, in adopting the Russian methods of economy and coming under the influence of the Russian peasants, the Buryats turned to a more cultured and, in part, more settled way of life. Also, the arrival of the Russians resulted in the cessation of bloody intertribal and interclan clashes, and created conditions for an increase in numbers to almost the same degree to which the Russian peasants increased through natural causes on settling in Siberia. Land-pressure and landlord ownership, that scourge of the agricultural population of European Russia constituting insuperable obstacles to the development of the economy and culture of the vast masses of the people, were almost unknown in eastern Siberia.

Hushing up the fact that the Buryats in Russia increased in number was a great omission on the part of historians and ethnographers interested in the Buryats earlier. Had the ancestors of the Buryats not entered into the Russian state, they would probably have remained just such a backward, numerically small ethnographic group as were, for example, up to very recent times, the Bargut of Khulunbuir (Barga). The inclusion of the Buryat ancestors in the population of Russia was a condition for their new, more progressive development, which in other circumstances, before the October socialist revolution, would have been impossible for these tribes.

Notes and References

1. We give an account of this material as it was cited in the work of A. P. Okladnikov, *Ocherki iz istorii zapadnykh buryat-mongolov* (Sketches from the history of the western Buryat-Mongols), Leningrad, 1937, p. 271.

2. Sec. 214, book 958, leaves 428–457. (For the citations of the archival sources, the following abbreviations have been adopted: Sec. 214 = *Tsentralny gos. arkhiv drevnikh aktov* (TsGADA), section no. 214, Siberian Department; sec. 1121 = *TsGADA*, section no. 1121, Irkutsk Departmental Office; sec. 1142 = *TsGADA*, section no. 1142, Nerchinsk Departmental Office; sec. 199 = *TsGADA*, section no. 199, Müller Portfolio; sec. 21, op. 4 = *Arkhiv AN SSSR*, no. 21, Müller Portfolio, entry 4; *DAI = Dopolneniya k aktam istoricheskim*.)

3. Only in 1667 did the Krasnoyarsk cossacks bring out fur-tribute-paying people of the Ashekhabat clan who crossed from Mongolia in the vicinity of Irkutsk (sec. 21, book 23, leaf 175).

4. S. A. Tokarev, *Rasseleniye buryatskikh plemen v XVII veke* (The distribution of Buryat tribes in the 17th century), *Zap. Bur.-Mong. in-ta yazyka, literatury i istorii*, no. 1, 1939, p. 112.

5. Sec. 199, no. 526, part II, copybook 9, leaf 28.

6. Tokarev, *op. cit.*, pp. 101–102.

7. G. F. Müller, *Istoriya Sibiri* (History of Siberia), vol. ɪ, Moscow, 1937, p. 422; vol. ɪɪ, Moscow–Leningrad, 1941, pp. 227, 251 ("Bogasars," "Bagazars"—these were the Basagars, a clan group in the Chulym basin, which later entered into the composition of the Kyzylets); pp. 257–258, 289, 346.

8. G. F. Müller calls the Korchun *aymak* (in the Buryat language) the Lower Udinsk Estate of the Kochun ulus (*TsGADA*, secs. 199, 526, part ɪɪ, copybook 9, leaf 28). The term "Kochun" is obviously a self-designation. According to Castren, in the Kott language *Kotyuan* signifies Kott (plural); see: M. A. Castren, *Jenisei-ostjakischen und Kottischen Sprachlehre*, St. Petersburg, 1858, p. 206. The Buryats altered this self-designation of the Kott to Korchun, probably by analogy with the Mongolic *kharachu*, i.e., a person of subjugated, tributary clans. See: B. Ya. Vladimirtsov, *Obshchestvenny stroy mongolov* (Social structure of the Mongols), Leningrad, 1934, pp. 118, 189,

9. Müller, *Istoriya Sibiri*, vol. ɪɪ, p. 540.

10. *Ibidem*, pp. 352, 353, 362, 363.

11. G. D. Sanzheyev, *Foneticheskiye osobennosti govora nizhneudinskikh buryat* (Phonetic peculiarities of the dialect of the Lower Uda Buryats), Leningrad, 1930, p. 10; Sanzheyev here expresses the opinion that the sound "K" (Ḱ, Kkh) in the Lower Uda dialect of the Buryat language was adopted as a result of Turkic influence. In this connection it is important to point out that the sound "kkh" (q) is very characteristic of the Ket language. It is no accident that the Kott-derived designations of the Lower Uda Buryat clans Kkhotomut and Kkhorshong begin with just this letter.

12. S. K. Patkanov, *Statisticheskiye dannye, pokazyvayushchiye plemennoy sostav naseleniya Sibiri, yazyk i rody inorodtsev* (Statistical data showing the tribal composition of the population of Siberia, language and alien clans), vol. ɪɪɪ, St. Petersburg, 1912, pp. 470–471, 495.

13. Tokarev, *op. cit.*, pp. 108–109.

14. A. P. Okladnikov proposes that on the arrival of the Russians, more than one thousand Buryats lived on the Oka, not counting their kyshtym. See: *Ocherki iz istorii zapadnykh buryat-mongolov*, p. 44. It will be closer to the truth to assume that the Lower Oka Buryats, together with their Evenk kyshtim, numbered more than one thousand (see below).

15. Sec. 214, book 941, leaves 69 ob., 75.

16. Okladnikov, *op. cit.*, p. 271.

17. *Materialy po issledovaniyu zemlepolzovaniya i khozyaystvennogo byta selskogo naseleniya Irkutskoy i Eniseyskoy gubernii* (Materials for the study of land utilization and economic life of the rural population of the Irkutsk and Yeniseysk provinces), vol. ɪɪ, part 3, Moscow, 1890.

18. Sec. 214, book 627, leaves 32–59. Besides the youths, a certain number of persons from "over the ridge" were revealed, but in general, there were not many of the latter.

19. Sec. 1121, art. 222, leaf 69.

20. Sec. 1121, art. 452, leaf 14.

21. Sec. 1121, art. 398, leaf 4.

22. *Materialy po issledovaniyu . . .*, vol. ɪɪ, part 3. The maps of land utilization appended to this volume are of great interest.

23. Patkanov, *Statisticheskiye dannye. . . .*

24. One should bear in mind, however, that owing to the nomadic way of life, individual Buryats and entire clans could be found far from those places that were their native residences. For example, it is noted of the Gotel and Engut clans in the tax book for 1672: . . . "and of these fraternal princelings of the Kotel clan, Kangay and Temirey, 58 persons of their ulus people, and of their children, brothers, and tribesmen, are not registered this year, because they do not appear in the census for the year 180, having wandered from the upper Lena farther away to Lake Baykal for the fishing. But they will be registered as they come from Lake Baykal with the tribute for the year 181." (Sec. 214, book 627, leaves 59, 59 ob.) Some of the Kudin Ashekhabat ("Asipugat")

also spent the summer on the Baykal, chiefly in the region of the estuary of the Goloust-naya river, where they ultimately settled. The Algui and some of the Kudin Kharanut also went to Baykal and later settled there.

25. Sec. 1121, art. 452, leaf 69.

26. Sec. 214, book 941, leaves 453–465.

27. Tokarev, *op. cit.*, pp. 110–111.

28. Sec. 214, art. 419, leaf 222.

29. A small group of them, headed by one Bazigiday, often nomadized in the region of the Kultuksk winter camp among the Evenks (Tungus) of the Zayektayev clan. The descendants of this group later came to be officially considered as Tungus and entered, along with the Tungus of the Zayektayev and Tzingidin clans, into the composition of the Armak Tungus council. Bazigiday was married to a Tungus widow and owned the hunting territory of the deceased Tungus. Thus he paid a tribute of six sables a year— one sable for himself and five at the "Tungus rate" as the heir to the property and land of the deceased Tungus. Such a large rate was never paid by any of the Buryats.

30. Sec. 214, book 627, leaf 60.

31. In a document dated 1690, the shuleng Bakhuk Irbanov was directed, in view of the great number of these emigrants, not to relax his vigilance toward them. See: *Buryatskiye skazki i poverya* (Buryat tales and superstitions), Irkutsk, 1889, p. 137.

32. From these groups assimilated later, many of the non-Khongodor clans among the Alar Buryats apparently derive—the Khotogoy, Khakhta, Sartul, Bodorkhon, Dartul, Dolongut, and others.

33. Sec. 21, op. 4, no. 28, leaf 196; no. 23, leaf 172 ob.; sec. 214, art. 1659, part II, leaves 289, 307–308.

34. Sec. 214, art. 1659, part II, leaves 307–311; sec. 1142, art. 1, leaves 1–4.

35. Sec. 1121, art. 23, leaf 64.

36. N. Bantysh-Kamensky, *Diplomaticheskoye sobraniye del mezhdu Rossiyskim i Kitayskim gosudarstvami s 1619 po 1792 god* (Collection of diplomatic transactions between the Russian and Chinese states from 1619 to 1792), Kazan, 1882, p. 58.

37. Sec. 21, op. 4, no. 28, leaf 97.

38. Sec. 1121, art. 213, leaves 25–31.

39. Sec. 1121, art. 261, leaves 18–27; sec. 21, op. 4, no. 48, leaf 120.

40. Sec. 21, op. 4, no. 28, leaves 119–120, 131–132; sec. 1121, art. 441, leaves 56–57.

41. Sec. 21, op. 4, no. 28, leaves 131–132; sec. 1121, art. 441, leaves 56–57, art. 88, leaves 65–66.

42. This was documented by E. M. Zalkind in his: Iz istorii zapadnogo Zabaykalya v kontse XVII—nachale XVIII v. (From the history of western Transbaykalia in the late 17th and early 18th century), *Uchenye zapiski LGU*, seriya vostokovedcheskikh nauk, vol. 1, Leningrad, 1949, p. 219. The Tabunut of Okin-zaysan were first called the Tsongolov clan in 1729 (see: Bantysh-Kamensky, *op. cit.*, p. 147).

43. Bantysh-Kamensky, *op. cit.*, p. 96.

44. Not all of the Tabunut were accepted. Those who came earlier, but did not become Russian subjects after the agreement of 1689, were sent back to Mongolia.

45. Ya. S. Smolev, Tri tabunutskikh roda Seleginskikh buryat (Three Tabunut clans of the Selenginsk Buryats), *Trudy Troitskosavsko-Kykhtinskogo otdeleniya Priamurskogo otdela Russkogo geograficheskogo obshchestva*, vol. 1, no. 3, 1898, Moscow, 1900, p. 82.

46. Legends of the Buryat as recorded by various collectors, *Zap. Vost.-Sib. otdela RGO po etnografii*, vol. 1, no. 2, Irkutsk, 1890, p. 119; Yu. D. Talko-Grintsevich, *Materialy k antropologii i etnografii Tsentralnoy Azii*, no. 1, Leningrad, 1926, p. 61.

47. Smolev, *op. cit.*, p. 79.

48. Sec. 1121, art. 144, leaves 60–69; art. 319, leaf 27; See also *Materialy vyso-chayshe uchrezhdennoy pod predsedatelstvom stats-sekretarya Kulomzina komissii dlya, issledovaniya zemlevladeniya i zemlepolzovaniya v Zabaykalskoy oblasti* (Materials of the High Commission established under the chairmanship of the State Secretary Kulomzin for the investigation of land ownership and land tenure in the Transbaykal *oblast*), St. Petersburg, 1897, vol. 5, Supplement, p. 19. In the 1730's it was believed

in Selenginsk that the Ashekhabat had been paying tribute since 1703 (sec. 199, no. 484, copybook 7, leaf 63 ob.).

49. Sec. 199, no. 481, copybook 7, leaf 64.

50. Sec. 21, op. 4, no. 27, leaf 10 ob.

51. See the data on the clan composition of the Selenginsk Buryat-Mongols in the collection: Skazaniya buryat, zapisannye raznymi sobiratelyami (Legends of the Buryat as recorded by various collectors), *Zap. vost.-Sib. otdel. RGO po etnografii*, vol. 1, part 2, Irkutsk, 1890, pp. 118–120; and in the work of Yu. D. Talko-Grintsevich, *Materialy k antropologii i etnografii Tsentralnoy Azii* (Materials on the physical anthropology and ethnography of Central Asia), part 1, Leningrad, pp. 60–62.

52. Tokarev, *op. cit.*, pp. 118–123.

53. *DAI*, vol. 2, p. 248.

54. *Ibidem*, vol. 2, p. 23.

55. *Ibidem*, p. 248.

56. Sec. 214, book 1659, part ı, leaf 371; sec. 1142, art. 4, leaf 32.

57. *Puteshestviye cherez Sibir ot Tobolska do Nerchinska i granits Kitaya russkogo poslannika Nikolaya Spafariya v 1675 g.* (Journey across Siberia in 1675), St. Petersburg, 1882, p. 149. See also: Stateyny spisok posolstva Nikolaya Spafariya v Kitay 1675–1678 gg. (Outline of the embassy of Nikolay Spafary to China, 1675–1678), *Vestnik arkheologii i istorii*, vol. 17, St. Petersburg, 1906, p. 171.

58. In 1653, evidently on the basis of very early intelligence, it was shown that "the tribute-paying people of the Barguzinsk and Angara fortresses nomadize along the shores of Lake Baykal, travelling from the Angara river to the Barguzinsk fortress on the right [south] side, and wandering on the left side of the same Lake Baykal are the brotherly hostile muzhiks, those who massacred the ambassador, the Tobolsk official, one Yarofey Zabolotskiy and his companions, and not the people who pay tribute in the Verkholensk fortress" (sec. 21, op. 4, no. 28, leaf 170). In reality, by 1653, the Khorins had already moved from Baykal to the east. "The hostile brotherly muzhiks" on the western shore of Lake Baykal prior to 1653 could only be the Khorins.

59. Sec. 214, art. 1659, part ı, leaves 89, 371–376; sec. 21, op. 4, no. 23, leaf 355; sec. 1142, art. 4, leaves 1, 32–33.

60. Sec. 1142, art. 11, leaves 26, 29; sec. 1105, art. 1, leaves 10–11.

61. Sec. 1121, art. 43, leaves 144–145; art. 71, leaves 32, 34–35; sec. 1142, art. 34, leaves 1–2, 4, 8; art. 19, leaves 29, 31. See also: Tokarev, *op. cit.*, p. 121; sec. 214, art. 355, leaves 169–170; sec. 1142, art. 15, leaves 1–2; art. 21, leaf 6; *DAI*, vol. 11, p. 73, and others.

62. Sec. 1142, art. 18, leaf 57; art. 21, leaves 19–20.

63. Sec. 214, book 782, leaves 315, 345 ob.; art. 12–14, leaf 294; sec. 1142, art. 33, leaves 8–9.

64. Sec. 1142, art. 36, leaves 3–18.

65. Sec. 1142, art. 37, leaves 1–63.

66. In this clan, the shulenge was still Kunek Mongultsok.

67. Sec. 1142, art. 38, leaves 1–9.

68. Sec. 21, op. 4, art. 28, leaf 119 ob.

69. Sec. 214, art. 1214, leaves 167–169.

70. Sec. 1142, art. 42, leaves 8–9.

71. Sec. 199, no. 481, copybook 7, leaves 65–66 ob.

72. A. Baranov, *Barga*, Harbin, 1912, pp. 30 ff.

73. Sec. 199, no. 526, part ıı, copybook 2, leaf 66 ob.; no. 481, copybook 7, leaves 96–97.

74. Sec. 214, book 1520, leaves 6–14 ob.; see also sec. 214, book 782, leaf 117; sec. 1142, art. 21, leaf 19.

75. We have examined this question in greater detail in the paper: Plemena i rody Zabaykalya i Yuzhnogo Pribaykalya v XVII veke (Tribes and clans of Transbaykalia and southern Cis-Baykalia in the 17th century), *Kratkiye soobshcheniya Instituta etnografii*, no. 16, 1952.

76. The years cited here and above are conditional since these data, as already noted, were obtained by G. F. Müller in 1735, and the actual counting was made somewhat earlier.

77. *Irkutskiy obl. arkhiv, f. Glavnogo upravleniya Vost. Sibiri, delo o privedenii v ispolneniye Ustava inorodtsev. Vedomosti o chisle inorodtsev, obitayushchikh v Irkutskoy gubernii* (Irkutsk regional Archive, Section of the Central Administration of Eastern Siberia, instructions on the administration and duties of the Bureau for Aliens. Register of the number of aliens living in Irkutsk province).

S. A. TOKAREV

ON THE ORIGIN OF THE
BURYAT NATION*

1. THE FOLLOWING PUBLICATIONS deal with the origin of the Buryats: Chapter 4 of the recently published first volume of the "History of the Buryat-Mongol A.S.S.R.,"[1] by G. N. Rumyantsev; a paper by the same author read at a special conference on questions of Buryat-Mongol history, October 30, 1952; and finally, an article by B. O. Dolgikh "Findings concerning the history of formation of the Buryat people."[2] The viewpoints of Rumyantsev, as well as Dolgikh, deserve serious consideration. Unlike the old, mostly bourgeois authors who wrote on the origin of the Buryats, the new Soviet scholars try to adhere to a strictly historical point of view. . . . However, the views of Rumyantsev and Dolgikh differ considerably. The first tries to summarize everything of value concerning the origin of the Buryats compiled both by the old and by modern scientists. Dolgikh, on the other hand, does not consider the problem in its entirety, but cites detailed and precise data on clan and tribe compositions of the Buryat population in the 17th century, the time of arrival of the Russians in the Cis-Baykal region, and on the number and distribution of separate clan and tribal groups. From these data he draws a very significant conclusion concerning the problem of Buryat ethnogenesis: In the 17th century—in the opinion of Dolgikh—Buryat tribes did not yet form one single people. As yet they did not have the concept of national unity; they did not even have a common name. The formation of the Buryat people took place, according to Dolgikh, only after Buryat tribes became part of the Russian state. Only then did the name "Buryat" appear, as well as "the realization of belonging to one people."[3]

This last thought, apparently the basic idea of Dolgikh's article, appears to be rather controversial. Debatable too are some personal assertions of the author. In spite of the great value of the material—entirely new to science and skillfully summarized by the author—the article needs, I think, significant corrections.

2. The early history of the Cis-Baykal region has by now been relatively well explored owing to the intensive work of several generations of archaeologists. In the course of the last few years especially, much has been done in this field by Professor A. P. Okladnikov who has summarized all previous works and, on the basis of his own extensive research, has built a thoroughly substantiated pattern of periodicity for the cultural history of the Cis-Baykal region from the end of the Paleolithic Age to the appearance of written records.[4] However, despite his works, which deal mainly with the Neolithic and the early metal ages, the later stages of development of human culture in the Cis-Baykal region, namely the Iron Age, remain practically unexplored.

As for the ethnic history of the region in question, assumptions can only be drawn on the basis of existing archaeological research. Quite plausible is the hypothesis of Okladnikov, strengthened by archaeological data and those of comparative ethnography, that the Neolithic cultures of the northern Cis-Baykal region of the third and second millennia B.C. are tied to the ethnogenetic process

*Translated from Sovetskaya etnografiya, 1953, no. 2, pp. 37–52.

of the Evenks.[5] It is quite probable that the broad expansion of the Evenks and of their culture started in the Cis-Baykal region. This movement expanded fan-wise toward the northwest, north, northeast, and east, and accounts for the present spread of the Evenks (and related Evens) over the enormous area from the basin of the Ob river to the Pacific ocean and from the Arctic ocean to Manchuria.

In the last centuries B.C., iron metallurgy spread widely in the Cis-Baykal region. Possibly this was connected with the submission of the peoples of the Cis-Baykal region to the "tribal union" of the Huns, who had surrounded them-selves with many heterolingual tribes and peoples from eastern Manchuria to the Cis-Aral region. Although the ethnic composition of the Hun tribal union is not altogether clear, it is quite probable that Turkic elements played an important role in it.[6] To this period of Hun supremacy, i.e., the beginning of our era, the "Turkization" of the population of the Cis-Baykal region should probably be assigned.

In a very convincing way Okladnikov has developed a theory, now accepted by all Soviet investigators, that the culture of the "Kurumchinsk blacksmiths" characteristic of the Cis-Baykal region in the first millennium A.D. is assignable to the Kurykans, a people mentioned in the Orkhon inscriptions of the 8th cen-tury. In Chinese sources this people is known as Ku-li-kan [Guligans]. It was a powerful and large nation that had diplomatic relations with China in the 7th century. The Kurykans practiced cattle-breeding and hunting, but were familiar with agriculture as well. The discovery of several inscriptions in the Orkhon script leave no doubt that the Kurykans were a Turkic-speaking people.[7]

By the 6th century A.D. Turkic languages had spread very widely through Central Asia and southern Siberia. Turkic runiform inscriptions have been found in various places in Mongolia, in Tuva, in the Altay Mountains, in the Khakas-Minusinsk *kray*, and in the Cis-Baykal region. Up to the beginning of the 10th century A.D., Turkic-speaking peoples were leaders in the fields of politics and culture: they took turns in heading the large intertribal unions. From the middle of the 6th to the middle of the 8th century it was the Orkhon-Yenisey Turks ("tugyu" [T'u-chüeh in Chinese]), from the middle of the 8th to the middle of the 9th century the Uygurs, and from the middle of the 9th to the beginning of the 10th century, the Kyrgyz (Khakas).

Thus from the 7th to the 10th century A.D. the Cis-Baykal region, particularly its western part, was populated by Turkic-speaking tribes. Yet, in the begin-ning of the 17th century, the Russians, arriving in the Cis-Baykal region, found Mongolian-speaking Buryats. Apparently the "Mongolization" of the population of this region must have taken place in the interval between the 10th and 17th centuries. When, in what manner, and why did it occur? When and from where did the Mongolian language appear and how did it gain pre-eminence? This is one of the basic and least clear questions concerning the problem of the origin of the Buryats.

3. For a long time science held to the opinion that "Mongols" were the aboriginal population of Central Asia, that during the history of its governments it was only the names of the ruling clans that successively changed while the ethnic aspect of all these states was and continued to be the same, i.e., they were all Mongol. This point of view, already mentioned casually in the 18th century (Deguignes, Pallas), has been most fully and logically developed by N. Ya. Bichurin [later Iakinf, i.e., "Hyacinth"]. He expressed this opinion very clearly in one of his early

works, "Notes on Mongolia" (1828),[8] and held to it unswervingly to the end of his life. In his last large volume, he wrote:

From times immemorial Mongolians lived intermingled with the Chinese in the northern regions of China. . . . In Central Asia there has always been a system of independent administration, i.e., the state was divided into small principalities, which in their turn sometimes united, at other times split and formed new states. Moreover, the Mongolian nation took its name after that of the ruling house. Thus, one and the same people called themselves Huns under the ruling house of the Huns and Dulgasets under the Dulga (Tukyue [T'u-chüeh]); under Mongol rule they were known as Mongolians and will continue to call themselves so until some other people subjugates them and imparts to them its own, different national name.[9]

This point of view, although it represented, to a certain extent, a healthy reaction against theories of unrestrained migration favored by foreign scientists, obviously suffered at the same time from the absence of historical method. The factual unsoundness of this theory of an aboriginal Mongolian population in Central Asia has been revealed by the discovery of the purely Turkic script of the Uygurs and Orkhon-Yeniseyan Turks—the Tugyu (whom Bichurin also considered to be Mongols—"dulga"). Yet the problem of the antiquity of the Mongolian languages in Central Asia and of their origin in general remains unsolved. Apparently the presence (and, even more, the prevalence) of Mongolian elements in the language or languages of the Huns still remains unproved[10]; the Mongolism of the Hsien-pi and Jurchen is not proved. Only in the case of the Khitans are there reasons for asserting with greater certitude that they were a Mongolian-speaking people.[11] The Khitans are known from Chinese sources of the Nan Wei dynasty, approximately from the end of the 5th century.[12] Their original area of occupancy lay, according to these sources, in southwestern Manchuria, which, to be sure, hardly agrees with speculation about their aboriginal Mongolism. They are mentioned in Orkhon records under the name "Khitai" [Qytai]. The Turks waged wars against them in A.D. 722 and 734.[13] Later, having formed a powerful tribal union, the Khitans subjugated northern China forming the Liao dynasty and their nomadic bands occupied Central Asia after driving out the Kirgiz—Khakas at the beginning of the 10th century. Then, as is usually assumed by historians,[14] the rule of Turkic-speaking peoples in Central Asia ended forever and the rule passed to Mongolian-speaking people. The Khitans were succeeded (in the 12th century) by reputedly Mongolian-speaking Tatars, Keraits, Naimans, and, in the 13th century, by the Mongols proper.

Actually, the Mongols, who later gave their name to the greatest, though short-lived, empire, and in scientific terminology to a whole family of languages and even to one of the three basic human races, were, apparently, only a small tribe in the beginning. The name "Mongol" is mentioned for the first time in the chronicles of the T'ang dynasty in the form "Mêng-u," and in the chronicle of the Liao dynasty as "Men-ku-li." They are described as nomadic hunters and cattle-breeders, with meat and sour milk as their staple food. Their land lay four thousand li from "Shang-ch'ing" ("The Northern Capital").[15] This last statement probably does not contradict information given in Mongolian legends, which refer to the basins of the rivers Onon and Kerulen as the original areas of habitation for the Mongols.

The unification and strengthening of Mongolian tribes under Temuchin (Genghis Khan) as well as their subjugation of neighboring and related tribes, the Merkits, Taijuts, Tatars, Keraits, and Naimans, resulted in wide diffusion of the term "Mongol" and included a number of linguistically related peoples who, previously, did not call themselves Mongols. No doubt, this was accompanied by linguistic assimilation and Mongolization of many other tribes of non-Mongolian origin. Rashid-ed-din, an outstanding historian of the beginning of the 14th century, noted and expressed this very well. He wrote:

At the present time, because of the prosperity of the Mongols under Genghis Khan and his kin, who are Mongols, (various) Turkic tribes,[16] such as the Jalairs, Tatars, Oirats, Onguts, Keraits, Naimans, Tanguts and others, who all had their own names and special appellations, are now for purposes of self-glorification (also) calling themselves Mongols, though in the past they did not recognize this name. Thus their present descendants imagine they have belonged to the Mongol family since times immemorial and so call themselves (by this name). However, this is not so, for in ancient times the Mongols were (only) one tribe among a complex of Turkic steppe tribes. Since Genghis Khan and his clan came from the Mongol people and from them many branches were formed, particularly in the time of Alan-Goa, approximately 300 years ago, there arose a prolific branch whose people are called Nirun and who have become respected and exalted. All these have become known as Mongols, although at that time there were other tribes not called Mongol. As their appearance, stature, name, language, customs, and manners were akin to each other, even though in the past they did have slight differences in language and customs, now it has come to pass that the peoples of Cathay and the Jurchen[17] are called Mongols, (as well as) the Nangyas, Uygurs, Kipchaks, Turkmens, Karluks, Kalach, and all those who have been taken prisoner and also those of Tadzhik nationality who grew up among the Mongols. And this conglomeration of peoples considers it proper for their own aggrandizement and dignity to call themselves Mongols.[18]

The phenomenon described here by Rashid-ed-din was very complex. Three aspects or three consecutive stages that developed differently during various periods and in different parts of the Mongol empire may be distinguished. First, an ethnic consolidation of true Mongol tribes and peoples and the spread of the original tribal name "Mongol" to a group of tribes and peoples related to them by language and origin. Second, a linguistic assimilation and Mongolization of certain tribes and peoples of non-Mongolian origin. Third, the use of the name "Mongol" as a purely political term to designate different peoples who had become part of the Mongol empire but had in no way become assimilated with the Mongols either in language or in culture.

Of these three stages the last can be most easily traced. Among the peoples enumerated by Rashid-ed-din there is a clearly noticeable group that had never been and had never become Mongolian but had only temporarily adopted this purely political designation. These were the Kipchaks, Turkmens, Uygurs, and other Turkic-speaking peoples of the western part of the empire; in the east they were, for instance, the Tanguts (Tibetans).

It is far more difficult to delimit the first two stages, although they are of the greatest interest for our immediate topic. It would be extremely important to learn which of the tribes and nations known to us (at present or from historical sources) as Mongolian speaking—the Jalairs, Tatars, Oirats, Keraits, and others —had always spoken Mongolian and which were Mongolized in the course of the Mongol expansion of the 13th century A.D.[19]

Here we return again to our basic topic. When and how did the population of the Cis-Baykal region become Mongolized? Had this occurred already before the rise of the Mongol empire of Genghis Khan, the inclusion of the Cis-Baykal tribes being only part of a political consolidation of previously established ethnical and cultural ties? Or did the Mongolization of these tribes result from their assimilation by the Mongol empire, in which case such Mongolization did not necessarily occur at once, but could have taken place gradually in the course of several centuries of Mongol rule?

Different views have been expressed in the literature. A. P. Okladnikov believes, on the basis of archaeological data, that the Mongolization of the population of the Cis-Baykal region occurred in the main during the 10th and 11th centuries. He deduces this from the appearance in the Cis-Baykal region (on the upper Lena river) of a new type of burial ("Segenut burial mound"), different from the earlier Kurykan type.[20] In Okladnikov's opinion a displacement of population might have taken place at that time as a result of the formation of the Khitan (Liao) empire. However, this suggestion seems to lack reliable substantiation. I do not want to start a discussion (not being an archaeologist, I do not consider myself competent in this respect) concerning the correctness of the chronological dating of the "Segenut" burial mound, or of the question as to whether it is possible to make conclusions regarding the change of a culture for an entire country on the basis of a single site. (Okladnikov does not mention any others and, apparently, there are none.) Yet, one has the right to doubt a deduction implying a change of language solely on the basis of a change in the form of culture. We must remember that the concepts "Turkic" and "Mongolian" refer exclusively to language. Right now, we are interested in the temporal displacement, in the Cis-Baykal region, of the Turkic language (of the Kurykans of the 7th to 10th centuries) by the Mongolian tongue (of the 17th century Buryats). As for the appearance of a new type of archaeological remains of the 10th and 11th centuries similar to those of Mongolia, this may show at the most a cultural influence on part of Mongolia but not a change in language. Analogous phenomena are found (at a later date) in Tuva: the Tuvins, having been for a long time under the rule of Mongol princes, were subjected to the cultural influence of the Mongols to a high degree but remained Turkic speaking. Only a few local groups of the Tuvins, namely the Darkhats on Kosogol lake and the Urianghaians of the Mongolian Altay (from the basin of the Black Irtysh and the upper reaches of the Urungu river), became Mongolized in their language as well; at that, the Urianghaians underwent this process quite recently, about the middle of the 19th century.[21]

According to another view often found in the literature, that of N. N. Kozmin, the penetration of Mongolian elements into the Cis-Baykal region (and the formation of the Mongol core of the Buryat nation) took place primarily in the first half of the 14th century and was connected not so much to Mongol conquests as to the termination of these conquests when the sources of enrichment through pillaging were cut off for the Mongol soldiers.[22] The arbitrariness and artificiality of such an "explanation" are perfectly obvious, but the dating itself cannot be rejected offhand.

Thus, up to the present no sufficient proof has been presented for a convincing solution of the question concerning the time of the Mongolization of the population of the Cis-Baykal region or, what amounts to the same thing, the time of the formation of a Mongolian-speaking core of the Buryat nation. For the time being this question must be left open. At the present state of knowledge the most probable assumption seems to be that it was just the Mongol conquest at the time of Genghis Khan, followed by mass movements of Central Asian tribes extending also to the Cis-Baykal region, that resulted in the Mongolization of the population. In other words, it can be presumed that the beginning of the formation of the Mongolian-speaking core of the Buryat people dates from the first decades of the 13th century.

4. It is necessary to emphasize that Mongol elements coming from the south, from the steppes of Mongolia, formed only one of the components of the Buryat people. This people is a mixed one, and purely local, aboriginal elements are undoubtedly also present in its composition. This can be seen best in the case of the Western Buryats, among whom it may be presumed that the aboriginal element was apparently connected to the Kurykans and prevailed; in the [subsequent] clash of the languages, however, the Mongolian of the newcomers triumphed over the Turkic of the aboriginals.

The physical type of the Western Buryats is closest to one prevalent among the Yakuts. Having established this, the Soviet physical anthropologists M. G. Levin and G. F. Debets[23] explain it quite correctly by the presence of one and the same Kurykan element in the composition of both the Yakuts and the Buryats. Incidentally, this fact could probably also explain the existence of many coincidences in given cultural traits of the Yakuts and the Buryats, similar religious beliefs, and so on. This may also be the most natural explanation for the presence of noticeable Mongolian elements in the Turkic language of the Yakuts. Inversely, there can be found in the Buryat language many words of Turkic origin, mainly in that area of terminology dealing with agriculture and sedentary cattle-breeding.[24]

It may be supposed that the contact of the Turkic-speaking population of the western Cis-Baykal region (presumably the Kurykans) with Mongolian-speaking newcomers lasted over a sufficiently long period of time. Having already been subjected to considerable Mongolian influence, yet retaining their Turkic language, the Kurykans gradually began to move northward to the middle Lena river region, forming there an essential component of the Yakut people. As for the remainder of the Kurykans, they were completely Mongolized and eventually became the Western Buryats.

The existence of a powerful aboriginal stratum in the Western Buryat population is corroborated by some very significant facts. It has been repeatedly noted, for example, that the Buryat legends about tribal ancestors in most cases are linked precisely to the Cis-Baykal region. The legends of Khoridae and Buridae, forefathers of the Buryats, and the legends of Ekherit and Bulagat, born of two shaman women, and the tales about *Bukha-noyon-baabay*, the mythical ancestor of all Buryats—all are connected with this area, as are others.[25] It must be noted, however, that other Buryat legends, those of genealogical character, do speak about a migration of the ancestors "from beyond the Baykal."[26] Both kinds of legends apparently reflect a historical reality: the presence of aboriginal and foreign elements in the composition of the Buryats.

The aboriginal stratum in Buryat culture is reflected in certain legends about "the era of *zegete-aba*" (battue hunts), when a supposedly unique military hunting system formed the basis of their social structure, M. N. Khangalov, a famous Buryat collector and folklorist, after a comprehensive study of the "zegete-aba" legends, linked them to the forest zone, even now inhabited by the northern (i.e., western) Buryats, and to the era of a predominantly hunting economy, which was later supplanted by cattle-breeding.[27] M. N. Bogdanov, though refusing to pin-point the geographical area of the zegete-aba legends, nevertheless was of the opinion that they dated back to a period preceding the Mongolian empire of Genghis Khan.[28]

Even in the 17th century, at the time of the arrival of the Russians, the economic organization of the Western Buryats was, in many ways, a continuation of an old tradition rooted in the seminomadic "Kurumchin" culture of the 1st millennium, although characteristics of a steppe cattle-breeding economy were also prominent. By that time hunting had lost its past significance. "We, your bondsmen," said the Ilim Buryats in 1683, "do not hunt any animals, live amid barren steppes and near us, your bondsmen, there are no black forests."[29] "We, your bondsmen, are steppe people," said the Buryats of the Verkholensk region in 1682–3, "live in the steppe in nomad's camps and do not know, Great Lords, how to catch sables and foxes for your tax."[30] "By ourselves, we, your bondsmen, cannot catch sables and other animals for your tax," complained the Balagansk Buryats in 1695, "because we, your bondsmen, are alien horsemen."[31] This was one reason, among others, why the Buryats repeatedly asked the tsarist administration to collect taxes from them not in furs, as was customary, but in cattle. This request was not granted, although the tsarist government, taking into consideration the insufficient development of hunting among the Buryats, did assess them with a considerably lower fur tax than, for instance, the Tungus hunters. Usually, the Buryats paid as their tax share one, rarely two sable pelts per person, while the Tungus customarily paid five each.[32]

However, for individual Buryat groups, hunting remained of great importance. In 1701, the same Verkholensk Buryats complained about Russian soldier settlers and peasants who, allegedly, "took from us all our hunting grounds and game stockades and traps and from these traps and stockades we get animals with fur for your tax, Great Lord, and these stockades and traps provide us with food in plenty, as we do not till the soil."[33]

Some Buryat clans dwelling near Lake Baykal made a living mainly from fishing. Thus, in 1685, the Korinsk and Batulinsk *shulenges* reported that "there are among them some people from across the mountains, who have no cattle, live near the Baykal sea, and feed themselves with fish."[34]

Of great significance is the presence of agriculture among the Western Buryats in the 17th century. Tilling of the soil was obviously a heritage of the Kurumchin era, as it represented an economy alien to the Mongolian peoples of the steppe. Even before the first contacts between the Russians and the Buryats, rumors already reached Yeniseysk that the Buryats were "soil-tilling people."[35] In 1641, the Ekherit princeling, Kurzhum, reported to the Russians that "the brotherly people on the Angara river sow millet."[36] Of the Ekherits, who lived on the Anga river, it was also said that "they grow millet grain," and this too was noted of the Buryats from Olkhon island.[37] After the well-known flight of Angara Buryats to Mongolia in 1658, the Russians saw on the abandoned lands "carts and grates and sacks left behind, and millet sown along the Unga river."[38]

For the majority of Buryats animal-breeding was of prime importance. However, it differed greatly from the steppe variety of horse-breeding in Mongolia. With them the number of horned cattle predominated. In one complaint of the Verkholensk Buryats we find a report that in 1690 a Buryat, Badzhidag, lost 60 cows, 40 horses, and 50 sheep as a result of the requisition of his pasture land.[39] Around 1700, a proposal was drafted to collect the tax from the Verkholensk Buryats in cattle instead of pelts. The tax was to be payable in the form of three-year-old and six- to seven-year-old bulls. In the opinion of the Irkutsk officials such a tax "would not be a burden to the Buryats, because they have plenty of cattle."[40] As is well known, horned cattle do not usually take first place in the herds of purely nomadic steppe people.

In addition to winter pasturing of stock, common among steppe peoples, the Buryats were also familiar with the preparation of feed for winter use. Already in 1635, soldiers stationed on the Yenisey, in choosing a fort site at the confluence of the Angara and the Oka rivers, "saw a suitable place at the mouth of the Oka river . . . near the brotherly yurts and summer pastures and hay meadows."[41] In 1684 a Balagansk Buryat complained that Ilim peasants seized his "hay meadows" along the Uda river.[42] Among the eleven court cases involving Buryats of the Verkholensk region in the year 1699 that have come down to us, three cases deal in one way or another with meadows or mowed hay.[43] In a petition of these same Verkholensk Buryats in 1701 we find a complaint against peasants who seized 600 haycocks and then again 100 more.[44] There are numerous similar references pointing to a Buryat hay-procuring economy.

Thus, even in their economy, the Buryats, particularly the Western Buryats, differed from the Mongols as a specific ethnic group as far back as the 17th century. This proves once more that the Buryats are a people of mixed origin and not simply a Mongol branch as was believed by Buryat bourgeois-nationalistic scholars, who, therefore, introduced the artificial definition "Buryat-Mongols," instead of the self-appellation "Buryats."[45]

5. When then, did the Buryat people emerge in their present ethnic composition? Did they exist already before the arrival of the Russians in the Cis-Baykal region (in the beginning of the 17th century) or did they develop only after they became a part of the Russian realm? Most scholars hold to the first opinion. The point of view that the Buryat people formed ethnically only in the period following their annexation by Russia, previously mentioned only in passing,[46] is expounded more thoroughly in a recent paper by Dolgikh. To us the first opinion seems correct.

Indeed, only one point has been made in favor of a late formation of the Buryat people, a point also advanced by Dolgikh: before the appearance of the Russians, Buryat tribes allegedly had no collective name; consequently, there was no concept of national unity; "Buryat" as a collective name became common only in Russian times. Obviously this view cannot stand up to critical analysis.

In the 17th century the Russians called the Buryats "brothers" or "brotherly people." Where did this name come from? It has been established long ago that it is a distortion of "pyrat," as the Buryats were called by the Turkic-speaking peoples on the Yenisey river, and "pyrat" is, in its turn, a distortion of the autonym "Buryat," already mentioned in Mongol sources of the 13th century. The "Secret History of the Mongols" the most reliable record of the history of Mongol tribes dating from A.D. 1240 tells of a campaign in the "year of the hare" (A.D. 1207) by Jochi, [Choch'in], one of Genghis Khan's military commanders, against "forest peoples" and his subjugation of the "Oirats, Buryats, Barkhuns, Ursuts, Khabkhanas, Khankhas and Tubas."[47] Apparently, the territory west of Lake Baykal is meant here, for Jochi, continuing his campaign, subjugated later the Yenisey Kirgiz and some peoples of the Altay region.[48]

A well-known reference to the "Oirat-Buryats" made by the Ordos historian Sanang-Setsen must also be taken into account. Of course, this reference can not be dated to the year 1189 (the year of the alleged subjugation of the "Oirat-Buryats" by Temuchin) as has been done in the past.[49] It can only be dated to the time of Sanang-Setsen's writing (1662) or shortly before. Sanang-Setsen wrote his version of history according to Mongol legends and written records and, obviously, in no way depended on Russian sources. Therefore, the term "Buryat" existed among the Mongols of the 17th century and was not borrowed from the Russians.

Of course, we cannot assert that in the "Secret History of the Mongols" the name "Buryat" applied to the entire people. In those times it could well have been used to denote an individual tribe, in no way distinguished from a number of others. However, at the time of Sanang-Setsen the term "Buryat" (even in the combination "Oirat-Buryat") could mean only the whole people; there was no individual "Buryat" tribe in the 17th century, otherwise we would have known about it from Russian sources.[50]

Numerous attempts have been made in the literature to find an etymological explanation of the ethnonym "Buryat," to link it at least to other known ethnonyms: the tribal names "Bulagat" and "Bargut."[51] Further, an attempt was made to connect the name "Bargut" with the well-known "Bayyrku" of the Orkhon inscriptions.[52] It is the task of linguists to determine whether such comparisons are philologically permissible. There is nothing improbable, historically, in the assumption that the ethnonym "Buryat" or its possible prototype "Bayyrku" belonged to some Turkic-speaking tribe or nation and was introduced only at a later date into the family of Mongolian ethnic names.

Completely arbitrary and unfounded is the supposition (of the same Baradin[53]) that originally, i.e., before the arrival of the Russians, the Bulagats alone (or the Bulagats and Ekherits) among all Buryat tribes considered themselves Buryats and that this name spread only later to other tribes. In a somewhat different way, this supposition was recently repeated by G. N. Rumyantsev, who held that, for instance, the Khorins (as well as the Tabunuts) "did not consider themselves Buryats and did not use that name" at that time.[54] As far as the Tabunuts are concerned, this supposition is quite correct. The Tabunuts, however, are a group of different origin, which will be dealt with later. In all documents of the 17th century, the Khorins are invariably called "brotherly people," and there is no reason to doubt that they considered themselves Buryats.

Contrary to such views, at the time of Russian arrival, all Buryats were fully conscious of belonging to one and the same people. In the records of administrative personnel there were no entries concerning specific tribal groups; all of them are usually called "brotherly people." Apparently, the Russian officials did not attempt to differentiate them from the Tungus, Mongols, and other peoples. In their rather numerous petitions, the Buryats, regardless of tribe, clan, or administrative region, always called themselves by a common ethnic name (manifestly "Buryat"), which in Russian documents was translated as "brotherly people," or "brotherly muzhiks (peasants)."

6. Although they comprised one nation, the Buryats, nevertheless, were fragmented into separate tribes in the 17th century, tribes that were completely independent of each other and often at war. Until recently, the literature reflected the opinion that there were only three such tribes: the Bulagats, Ekherits, and Khorins. The first two lived west and the third east of Lake Baykal. This opinion rested upon ethnogenic and genealogic legends of the Buryats recorded at the end of the 19th century. It is, however, very far from certitude. In 1939 the author of the present article already tried to show, on the basis of documented

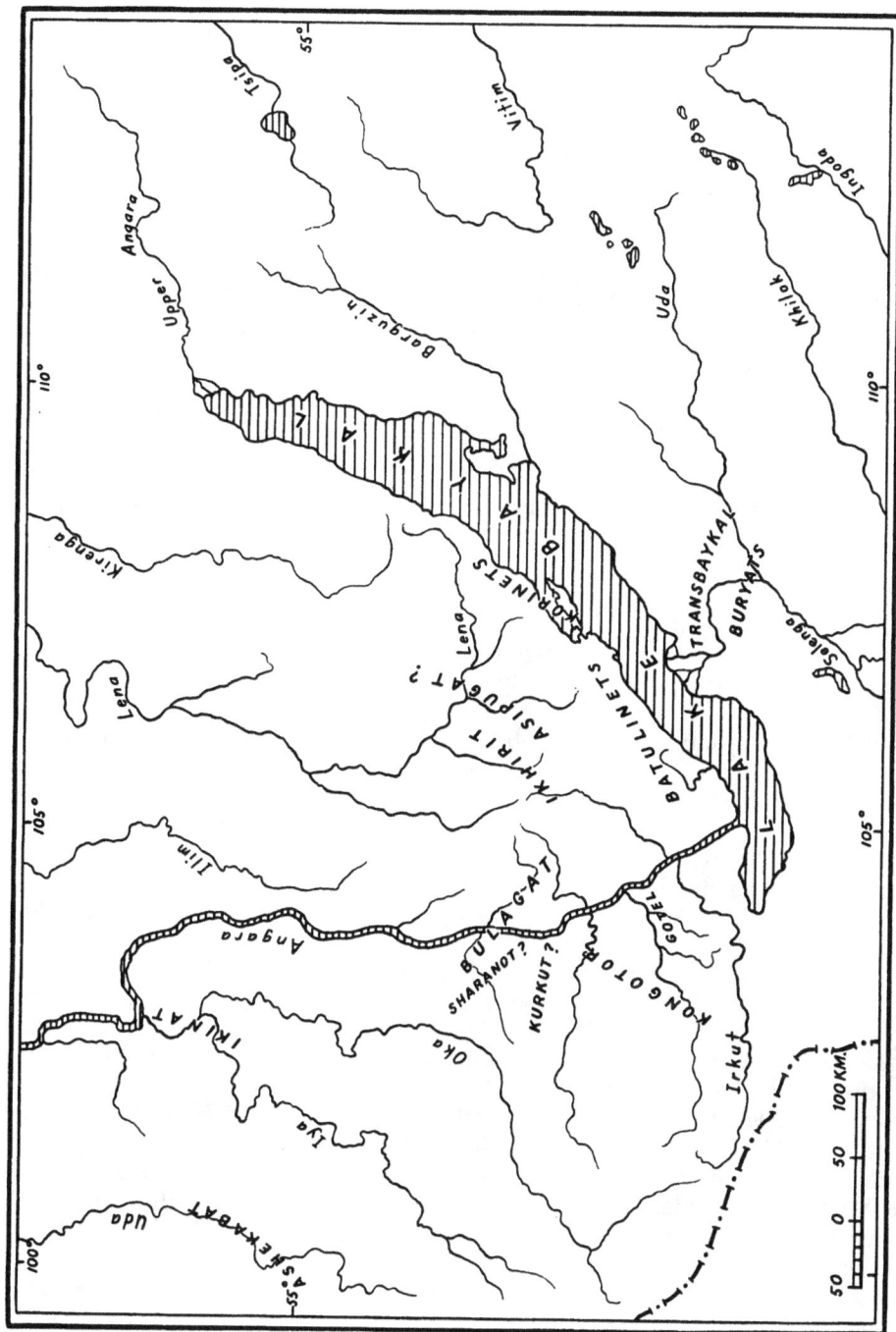

FIGURE 1. Distribution of Buryat clans in the 17th century.

sources of the 17th century, that: first, at that time, there existed more than three —possibly as many as ten—Buryat tribes; and second, that all these tribes, including the Khorins and related Batulins, lived west of Lake Baykal up to the arrival of the Russians. The Khorins and Batulins settled in the Trans-Baykal region only toward the end of the 17th century after prolonged wandering. Before Russian penetration, the Buryats, too, lived in the Trans-Baykal region next to the Mongols. However, these Trans-Baykal Buryats, like the Mongols, had already lost their tribal divisions by that time.[55] In his most recent article, Dolgikh introduces a number of new definitions on the grouping of Buryat tribes in the 17th century as well as in later times. He also adds a great deal of extremely valuable information, including some rather convincing statistical data. It seems to me, however, that the picture drawn by him is in need of some modification.

The views of Dolgikh on three specific problems of Buryat studies arouse objections (I am disregarding here the more general question concerning the time of formation of the Buryat people, dealt with previously): the problem of the Ikinats, Khorins, and Tabunuts. The first of these questions is of no particular significance,[56] but the questions concerning the Khorins and the Tabunuts are quite important, as their interpretation affects the choice of approach to the basic questions of the given problem, that is, the Buryat population of the Trans-Baykal region in the 17th century and its origin.

In disagreement with me, Dolgikh assumes that before the arrival of the Russians the Khorins (apparently together with the Batulins) lived not only on the western, Verkholensk side of Lake Baykal and on Olkhon island, but also beyond Lake Baykal, on the right bank of the Selenga, and further, that there "the greater part of the Khorin territory" was located.[57] What reasons are there for such a statement? Dolgikh does not dispute the fact that there is not a single source mentioning the presence of the Khorins beyond Lake Baykal before the 1670's (when they actually did move there). Nevertheless, he presumes that the Buryats living beyond Lake Baykal "could have been only the Khorins."[58] This argument is, however, absolutely unconvincing. Apparently, Dolgikh, even though he does not share the belief in the traditional theory about the "tripartite division" of the Buryats (their division into three tribes only), unwittingly follows this theory in the above case: Since there were only three Buryat tribes, and since there were neither Bulagats nor Ekherits in the Trans-Baykal region up to the middle of the 17th century,[59] then none of the Buryats but the Khorins could have lived there!

Only a single argument could be cited in support of Dolgikh's view (Dolgikh mentioned it in an oral discussion of the problem): There was not enough room on the Verkholensk side of Lake Baykal and Olkhon island for a tribe as large as the Khorins (particularly together with the Batulins), and therefore they had to occupy the wide and open spaces on the east side of Lake Baykal along the Selenga river. However, even this argument cannot be considered convincing. At that time Olkhon island was densely populated. "Many brotherly people live on that island, and they have all kinds of cattle in quantity and their cereal crop is millet," states the *Rospisaniye rek* ("Description of rivers") of 1640–1.[60] If on Olkhon island there were arable lands, meadows, and grazing pastures, and also a long-established and developed fishing economy, it could well support a large population. Incidentally, there were 834 people on Olkhon island according to the census of 1897,[61] while the entire non-Russian population of the Kutula district including Olkhon island and the adjacent littoral of Lake Baykal numbered 2,644. However, the tribal territory of the Khorins (and Batulins) could have included, at least partially, the land later under the jurisdiction of the Bayandayev, Olzonov, and Khogotov minority administrations, which in 1897 had a population of 7,579.[62] Thus in 1897 over 10,000 people (almost exclusively Buryats) lived in the territory (to the west of Lake Baykal and on Olkhon island) that belonged, if only in part, to the Khorins and Batulins in the first half of the 17th century. Supposing that, in the 17th century, only half as many people lived in the same territory as in the 19th, this territory should almost satisfy the statistical calculations of Dolgikh that set the number of the Khorins in the middle of the 17th century at six to seven thousand.

Incidentally, the greater part of the territory on the Verkholensk side of Lake Baykal, where, we think, the Khorins and the Batulins might have lived, appears on Dolgikh's maps as inhabited by the Kamchagir-Tungus.[63] The reasons for such a demarcation of the Buryat and Tungus ethnic territories are not clear. In more recent times (in the late 19th century) there were hardly any Tungus within the boundaries of the four above-mentioned administrative districts. The Tungus actually did migrate into the area of the Verkholensk fort, but there is no evidence that the administrative area of Verkholensk fort was separated from the shore of Lake Baykal, especially from the Khorin camps, by an uninterrupted stretch of Tungus camping sites as appears on the maps of Dolgikh.

7. As for the Tabunuts, I have tried to clarify the origin of this distinct Buryat group in the previously mentioned article of 1939. The facts show that the Tabunuts were not an aboriginal and differentiated tribal group of the Buryats. Originally, i.e., since the 1660's when the Tabunuts are first mentioned in documents, they do not appear as an ethnic entity, but as a purely political one, as subjects of the princeling Turukay Tabun. He was a Mongol, to wit a very close relative (son-in-law or brother-in-law) of Tsetsen khan, one of the most powerful feudal rulers of Mongolia. The bulk of his subjects probably consisted both of Buryats and of Mongols. In documents dated prior to the 1690's, the Tabunuts are never called Buryats but are usually counted as Mongols. Only since the last years of the 17th century, after many reverses, did the ethnic composition of the Tabunuts become predominantly Buryat. In 1698, for instance, a petition was filed by "the tax-paying brotherly and Tabunut peoples of zaisan Batur Okin, and shulenges with the people of their uluses."[64] There are, therefore, no reasons whatever for considering the Tabunuts as an independent Buryat tribe and for allotting to them on a map, as did Dolgikh, considerable territory along the Selenga and Khilka rivers. In his presentation of Tabunut history, Dolgikh shows inconsistencies. He admits that this group received its name from Turukay Tabun[65]; he also admits that Russian 17th century sources do not number them among Buryats[66]; yet he considers them as a separate, specifically Buryat, tribal group and, using rather weak criteria, he suggests that the Tabunuts are a part of the Batulins who had broken away from the Khorins.[67] Should we even agree with this last assumption, the Tabunuts still would not have any right to a separate place on the ethnic map of the Trans-Baykal region, as it appeared at the time of Russian penetration. At that time, as we already know, both the Batulins and the Khorins lived west of Lake Baykal, and they left only in the 1640's.

Dolgikh also cites several other tribal names of Mongol-speaking groups connected with the Trans-Baykal region; there are the four clans of Atagan, Sartol, Khatagin, and Uzon, assigned to the Selenga fort. Yet, according to his own admission, these are actually Mongol (i.e., not Buryat) clans, and he does not enter them on his maps.

8. What Buryat tribes are left that could be linked to the Trans-Baykal region as their initial ethnic territory? There are none. There is no doubt that Buryats lived—and even in considerable numbers—beyond Lake Baykal, particularly along the Selenga river. Already in 1645 a Russian military party under the command of Vasily Kolesnikov, advancing for the first time beyond Lake Baykal, came to "brotherly lands, to the Kutora steppe at the mouth of the Selenga river, to the numerous brotherly people . . . adjacent to the Mungal [Mongol] people."[68] There are also other reports about Trans-Baykal Buryats. However, there is not a single tribal name that could be attached to them. As I have already mentioned,[69] this is no mere coincidence. Having been connected with feudal Mongolia since ancient times, the Trans-Baykal Buryats, like the Mongols themselves, had probably long ago lost their tribal divisions. Among them class and feudal-serf relationships were more strongly developed. The existence of greater class distinctions among the Trans-Baykal Buryats than among the Cis-Baykal tribes was repeatedly noted even in later times, in the 18th and 19th centuries. It is not surprising that lamaism, a reflection of a feudal-serf organization, gained strength in the Trans-Baykal region, while the Western Buryats held until recently to the archaic beliefs of shamanism, closely linked to clan-tribal traditions. The clan-tribal structure, already extinct in the Trans-Baykal region by the time of Russian penetration, reappeared there again with the migration of the Khorins, Batulins, and others from Western Buryatia.

9. Thus, by the time of Russian penetration in the early 17th century, the Buryats already presented a fully formed national entity. Geographically they were divided into two parts, unequal in development. The Trans-Baykal Buryats, connected since ancient times with neighboring feudal Mongolia, had already lost their tribal divisions and probably formed administrative-political, feudal groupings only. The Cis-Baykal Buryats, though part of the same people, nevertheless retained the more archaic division into tribes.

The origin of individual Buryat tribes and clans, the component parts of the Buryat people, has often been described and will not be referred to here. There is no doubt that many of these tribal and clan groups were of a very ancient origin, older by far than the Buryat nation. Investigators have repeatedly pointed to the similarity between the names of some Buryat tribes and clans and the names of tribes and peoples mentioned by Rashid-ed-din, in the "Secret History," and even in the Orkhon-Yenisey inscriptions. There is nothing improbable in assuming that individual tribal names will be found to be of even greater age.

An objection raised occasionally against the thesis that the Buryats had become a fully formed national group as early as the 17th century is the following argument: a national group is a kind of ethnic entity, developing only in conjunction with the appearance of class society. However, prior to the arrival of the Russians, the Buryats had not yet completed the transition from a primitive-communal organization to a class society. This objection, however, is based on an abstract and schematic understanding of the historic, and specifically the ethnogenetic, process. The facts have it that national groups existed and still exist at the level of primitive-communal organization.[70] Without leaving Siberia proper, we can draw on a great number of facts of this nature. In the 17th century a primitive-communal organization was still in existence among the

Itelmens, Koryaks, Chukchis, Gilyaks (Nivkhs), Tungus (Evenks), and Kets, not to mention others. Yet, these were quite indisputably national groups (and not tribes), each with its language, defined territory, customs, and culture, even though no common autonym has been discovered for some of them (Chukchi, Koryaks). With respect to their level of social structure, all these national groups were clearly inferior to the Buryats. Beyond the borders of Siberia there are also numerous examples of this kind: the Eskimos, Aleuts, Tlingits, Salish, Navahos, Apaches, and other groups of North America; the Araucanians of South America; the Bataks, Minahassa, Karens, Shans, and several others in southeast Asia. There is no reason why all these ethnic groups should not be considered as separate peoples (national groups), although until recent times there still prevailed some stage of a primitive-communal organization.

To be sure, in the 17th century, the formative process of the Buryat people was far from complete. In the late 17th, 18th, and even the 19th centuries, this national group continued to absorb various linguistically alien elements that came from Mongolia, the Tungus, and others, all of which were assimilated by adoption of the Buryat language and culture. The Buryat tribal groups gradually merged, consolidated, and mixed among themselves. Dolgikh is quite right in his opinion that paramount in this unification and consolidation of the Buryat people was the fact that they became part of the Russian state and thus separated themselves from Mongolian-speaking groups across the border, in Mongolia and Manchuria. These foreign, Mongolian-speaking groups remained in a state of feudal fragmentation until recently, while the Buryats in Russia, with her more progressive socio-economic structure and centralized administrative apparatus, found themselves in conditions more favorable to ethnic consolidation.

Nevertheless, in Russia too, until recently, there existed considerable isolation among certain component groups of the Buryat people. The Eastern and Western Buryats, in particular, were divided, to a considerable degree, geographically as well as by their economy, administration, language, and culture. The final unification of the Buryat people, their consolidation into a socialist nation, came only with the Soviet regime . . ., which created the Buryat-Mongol A.S.S.R., and ensured optimal possibilities for the cultural development of the people.

Notes and References

1. *Istoriya Buryat-Mongolskoy ASSR* (History of the Buryat-Mongol A.S.S.R.), Ulan-Ude, 1951.

2. B. O. Dolgikh, Nekotorye dannye istorii obrazovaniya buryatskogo naroda (Some data concerning the history of formation of the Buryat people), *Sovetskaya etnografiya,* 1953, no. 1.

3. *Ibidem,* p. 53; see also p. 31.

4. See: A. P. Okladnikov, Neolit i bronzovy vek Pribaykalya (The Neolithic and Bronze Age of the Cis-Baykal region), *Materialy i issledovaniya po arkheologii SSSR,* 1950, no. 18; and his other works.

5. A. P. Okladnikov, Neoliticheskiye nakhodki v nizovyakh Angary (Neolithic finds in the lower reaches of the Angara river), *Vestnik drevney istorii,* 1939, no. 1, pp. 181–186; *Ibidem,* Epokha pervobytno-obshchinnogo stroya na territorii Buryat-Mongolii (The era of primitive-communal organization in the territory of Buryat-Mongolia), *Istoriya Buryat-Mongolskoy ASSR,* vol. 1, p. 34.

6. K. Inostrantsev, *Khunnu i gunny* (The Khunnu [Hsiung-hu] and the Huns), second enlarged edition, Leningrad, 1926.

7. It is somewhat strange that Rumyantsev considers them a "Mongolian group of

tribes" even though subjected to Turkic influence. See: G. N. Rumyantsev, *K voprosu o proiskhozhdenii buryat-mongolskogo naroda* (On the origin of the Buryat-Mongol people) theses, Soveshchaniye po osnovnym voprosam istorii Buryat-Mongolii pri Institute istorii AN SSSR, 27/10 1952 g. (Conference on the basic problems of the history of Buryat-Mongolia at the Institute of History of the Academy of Sciences, U.S.S.R., October 27, 1952), Theses of reports, Ulan-Ude, 1952, p. 26. It is difficult to imagine what proofs could be found in favor of the Mongolism of the Kurykans.

8. Iakinf, *Zapiski o Mongolii* (Notes on Mongolia), St. Petersburg, 1828, pp. 1–2.

9. N. Ya. Bichurin (Iakinf), *Sobraniye svedeniy o narodakh, obitavshikh v Sredney Azii v drevniye vremena* (Collection of data on nations which inhabited Central Asia in ancient times), Moscow–Leningrad, 1950, vol. 1, pp. 8–10.

10. See: K. Shiratori, Sinologische Beiträge zur Geschichte der Türk-Völker. 2. Über die Sprache der Hiungnu und der Thungu-Stämme, *Izvestiya Akademii Nauk SSSR*, vol. 17, no. 2, Sept. 1902; K. Inostrantsev, *Khunnu i gunny*.

11. Shiratori, *op. cit.*; E. M. Zalkind, Kidane i ikh etnicheskiye svyazi (The Khitans and their ethnic relationships), *Sovetskaya etnografiya*, 1948, no. 1.

12. Kovalevskiy, Kidan, *Zhurnal Ministerstva narodnogo prosveshcheniya*, sec. 2, part 24, 1839; Bichurin, *op. cit.*, vol. 1, p. 362.

13. W. Radloff, *Die alttürkischen Inschriften der Mongolei*, 3-te Lief., 1895, p. 428.

14. See: V. V. Bartold, *Istoriya turetsko-mongolskikh narodov* (History of the Turko-Mongolian peoples), Tashkent, 1928, pp. 9–10 *et al.*

15. W. Schott, Älteste Nachrichten von Mongolen und Tataren, Berlin, 1846, pp. 13–17.

16. Rashid-ed-din used the term "Turks" in a broad sense to include all nomadic steppe peoples of Asia who were predominantly Turkic-Mongolian.

17. That is, of China and Manchuria.

18. Rashid-ed-din, *Sbornik letopisey* (Collection of chronicles), vol. 1, book 1, Moscow–Leningrad, 1952, pp. 102–103; see also p. 77.

19. The attention of historians should be drawn to a considerable gap in the study of the ethnic history of Central Asia, to wit, the 10th to 12th centuries. When and how did the Mongolian steppes, which in the beginning of the 10th century were still ruled by Turkic-speaking peoples, become occupied by the Mongolian nomads who appear there as masters in the 12th century? Did all these peoples, the Naimans, Keraits, Merkits, Tatars, and others, actually speak Mongolian tongues at that time? Up to now, all these extremely important questions have been almost entirely disregarded by historians. (See: V. P. Vasilev, Istoriya i drevnosti vostochnoy chasti Sredney Azii ot 10 do 13 v. (The history and antiquities of the eastern part of Central Asia from the 10th to the 13th centuries), *Zapiski imp. arkheol. ob-va*, vol. 13, St. Petersburg, 1859.)

20. *Istoriya Yakutii* (History of Yakutia), vol. 1, Yakutsk, 1949, pp. 329–331; *Istoriya Buryat-Mongolskoy ASSR*, vol. 1, p. 82. V. I. Sosnovskiy related the beginning of the Mongolization of the Cis-Baykal region approximately to the same period in his: *K voprosu ob obrazovanii buryatskoy narodnosti* (Formation of the Buryat nation), Verkhneudinsk, 1929. He based this opinion, however, on other sources, i.e., on folkloristic data and on the study of historic ethnonyms. He considered the Khorinets to be the oldest of Buryat tribes and dated their penetration into the Cis-Baykal region to the early 10th century. The proofs presented by Sosnovskiy are, however, not particularly convincing.

21. G. E. Grumm-Grzhimaylo, *Zapadnaya Mongoliya i Uryankhayskiy kray* (Western Mongolia and Uryankhaysk kray), vol. 3, part 1, 1926, pp. 19, 20–21, 174–175.

22. M. N. Bogdanov, *Ocherki istorii buryat-mongolskogo naroda* (Essays on the history of the Buryat-Mongols), Verkhneudinsk, 1926, pp. 25–27. The chapter "K voprosu o vremeni pereseleniya buryat v Pribaykalye" (The time of Buryat migration to the Cis-Baykal region) is written by N. N. Kozmin.

23. M. G. Levin, Drevniye pereseleniya cheloveka v Severnoy Azii po dannym antropologii (Ancient migrations of man in Northern Asia according to physical anthropological data), in *Proiskhozhdeniye cheloveka i drevneye rasseleniye chelovechestva*

(Origin of man and world distribution of mankind in antiquity), Akademiya Nauk SSSR, *Trudy Instituta etnografii*, vol. 16, Moscow, 1951, pp. 492–493; G. F. Debets, Antropologicheskiye issledovaniya v Kamchatskoy oblasti (Physical anthropological research in Kamchatka province), *Trudy Instituta etnografii*, vol. 17, Moscow, 1951, pp. 80–81.

24. *Istoriya Buryat-Mongolskoy ASSR*, vol. 1, pp. 80–81.

25. Bogdanov, *op. cit.* pp. 1–4; B. B. Bambayev, *K voprosu o proiskhozhdenii buryat-mongolskogo naroda* (On the origin of the Buryat-Mongols), Verkhneudinsk, 1929, p. 7; P. T. Kuaptayev, *Kratkiy ocherk istorii buryat-mongolskogo naroda* (Short outline of the history of the Buryat-Mongols), Ulan-Ude, 1942, pp. 9–10.

26. T. A. Zemlyanitskiy, *Rodoslovnye buryat* (Buryat genealogies); the manuscript is kept in the library of the Society for the Study of Eastern Siberia, Irkutsk.

27. D. A. Klements and M. N. Khangalov, Obshchestvennye okhoty u severnykh buryat (Communal hunting among northern Buryats), *Materialy po etnografii Rossii*, vol. 1, St. Petersburg, 1910, pp. 136, 148 *et al.*

28. Bogdanov, *op. cit.* p. 15.

29. *TsGADA* (Tsentralny gosudarstvenny arkhiv drevnikh aktov), Sib. prikaz, art. no. 913, leaf 421.

30. *Ibidem*, leaf 244.

31. *Ibidem*, art. 1150, leaf 471.

32. *Ibidem*, art. 402, leaf 103; book 941, leaves 389–433, *et al.*

33. *Ibidem*, book 1292, leaf 53 verso.

34. *Ibidem*, art. 355, leaf 170. Incidentally, until very recently the Mongols did not eat fish.

35. *Ibidem*, art. 12, leaf 108.

36. *DAI* (Dopolneniya k aktam istoricheskim), vol. 2, p. 251.

37. *Ibidem*, pp. 247, 248.

38. *TsGADA*, Sib. prikaz, art. 589, leaf 83.

39. *Ibidem*, book 1292, leaf 54 verso.

40. *Ibidem*, leaves 59 verso, 60.

41. *Ibidem*, art. 53, leaf 19.

42. *Ibidem*, art. 913, leaf 183.

43. *LOII* (Leningradskoye otdeleniye Instituta Istorii AN SSSR) (The Leningrad section of the Institute of History of the Academy of Sciences, U.S.S.R.), paper 231, no. 4, leaves 1, 16, and the last leaf.

44. *TsGADA*, Sib. prikaz, book 1292, leaves 53, 54.

45. See: B. B. Baradin, Buryat mongoly, Kratkiy istoricheskiy ocherk oformleniya buryat-mongolskoy narodnosti (The Buryat-Mongols, a concise historical outline of the formation of the Buryat-Mongol nation), *Buryatiyevedeniye*, 1927, nos. 3 and 4.

46. See: Baradin, *op. cit.* pp. 46–47, 61; V. I. Sosnovskiy, *op. cit.* pp. 1–2.

47. S. A. Kozin, Sokrovennoye skazaniye . . . (Secret History . . .), *Mongolskaya khronika 1240 goda* (Mongolian chronicle of 1240), vol. 1, Moscow–Leningrad, 1941, p. 174.

48. Until now this undisputable reference to the Buryats of as early as the 13th century has not attracted the due attention of scholars, probably because this chronicle was known only through its incomplete translation by Palladiy Kafarov until the recent publication of the "Secret History of the Mongols" by S. A. Kozin. In the translation the pertinent paragraph reads: "When Jochi reached Shikhshit, the Oira, Tubas and all other clans bowed to him" (*Trudy chlenov Rossiyskoy dukhovnoy missii v Pekine*, vol. 4, St. Petersburg, 1866, p. 131). Only in the footnote did the translator add a different reading; "Oira, Buliya (Buriya), Barkhun, Ursu, Khakhanas, Kankhas and Tuba (Tubas)" (*ibidem*, p. 234).

49. Sanang-Setsen, *Geschichte der Ost-Mongolen.* Translated from the Mongolian by I. J. Schmidt, 1829, p. 75.

50. A very strange wording is used to describe the formation of the Buryat nation in a book repeatedly referred to, *Istoriya Buryat-Mongolskoy ASSR*, vol. 1, noting quite

correctly that at the time of Russian penetration (early 17th century) the Buryat tribes "did not present a unified political entity, as they had not yet developed their own political system." The author draws the following conclusion: "This was, therefore, a national group only in the ethnographic and not in the political sense of the word, as it lacked a common administration and solid political ties" (p. 84). Every nation, however, is always a national group "in ethnographic sense only." What the author has in mind with the phrase "nation in the political sense of the word" is hard to fathom.

51. Baradin, *op. cit.*, p. 45.

52. *Istoriya Buryat-Mongolskoy ASSR*, vol. 1, p. 80.

53. Baradin, *op. cit.*, pp. 45–46.

54. Rumyantsev, Theses, p. 27.

55. S. A. Tokarev, Rasseleniye buryatskikh plemen v 17 veke (Distribution of Buryat tribes in the 17th century), *Zapiski Buryat-Mongolskogo gos-naucho-issled-instituta yazyka, lit. i istorii*, no. 1, 1939.

56. The data collected by me as a proof of the independent position of the Buryat-Ikinats on the lower reaches of the Oka river have been acknowledged as "convincing" by B. O. Dolgikh. However, he does not see them as a separate tribe, but considers them only as a clan (*Sovetskaya etnografiya*, 1953, no. 1, p. 44). He in no way substantiates this claim, except for a listing of the Ikinat clan in the table of "clans" who paid taxes at the Balagansk fort in 1689 (p. 45). It is known, though, that a great many independent tribes were called "clans" in the phraseology of 17th century documents. The inclusion of the Ikinats in the taxation domain of Balagansk fort at the end of the 17th century certainly does not disprove that, at the time of Russian penetration, the Ikinats were an absolutely independent tribe unconnected with either the Bulagats or any other Buryat tribes.

57. Dolgikh, *op. cit.*, p. 47.

58. *Ibidem*, pp. 47, 48.

59. *Ibidem*, p. 46.

60. *DAI*, vol. 2, p. 248.

61. S. Patkanov, *Statisticheskiye dannye, pokazyvayushchiye plemennoy sostav naseleniya Sibiri* . . . (Statistical data showing the tribal composition of the population of Siberia . . .), vol. 3, St. Petersburg, 1912, pp. 512–513.

62. Patkanov, *op. cit.*, pp. 502–503.

63. See the maps in *Istoriya Buryat-Mongolskoy ASSR*, vol. 1, pp. 80–81; also *Kratkiye soobshcheniya Instituta etnografii*, vⅢ, 1949, p. 36, and xvⅡ, 1952, p. 38.

64. *TsGADA*, Sib. prikaz, art. 1397, leaf 185; a similar document is kept in the Irkutsk museum, which states the case even more clearly: "tax-paying brotherly Tabunut people" (without the conjunction "and").

65. Dolgikh, *op. cit.*, p. 52.

66. *Kratkiye soobshcheniya Instituta etnografii*, xvⅢ, 1952, p. 37.

67. *Ibidem*, p. 39.

68. *DAI*, vol. 3, p. 109.

69. Tokarev, *op. cit.*, p. 129.

70. The board of editors does not share the author's opinion that "national groups existed and still exist at the level of primitive-communal organization."—Editor's note, *Sovetskaya etnografiya*.

A. BERNSHTAM

ON THE ORIGIN OF THE

KIRGIZ PEOPLE*†

UNDER THE CONDITIONS EXISTING in Central Asia, ethnic and cultural communities became established sooner and lasted longer in the regions of settled agricultural economy than in the regions of cattle breeding. In other words, among the settled population of Central Asia, specifically among the Tadzhiks, the elements of national culture had formed earlier than among the nomads. By no means does this suggest that the nomads developed according to some special historical laws. The question concerns only the particular way, tempo, and time of formation of ethnic characteristics.

In reference to the first millennium B.C., we can talk about ethnic names of the ancestors of the present peoples. Yet, we can not say anything positive about their ethnic affiliations. The Sarmatians-Alans of the first centuries A.D. do not yet represent the Turkmens, the ancient Yenisey Kirgiz of the 3rd century B.C. are not yet the Tien-shan Kirgiz, and the Bactrians of the end of the first millennium B.C. are not yet the Tadzhiks. In 1943, at a session on the ethnogenesis of peoples of Central Asia, S. P. Tolstov said:

In the presence of the long-established historical and territorial communities which served as a basis for the consolidation of the present-day peoples of Central Asia out of the heterogeneous, aboriginal and alien elements, none of these peoples descended directly from any ethnic group of antiquity. On the contrary, the ancient local and alien peoples became absorbed in various proportions into the structure of several, sometimes of all the peoples of Central Asia and partially even of the peoples beyond its borders.[1]

At the present stage of our knowledge of history we cannot yet determine who constituted the principal ethnic nucleus in the formation of any particular people of Central Asia. The Saka [Sacae], the Bactrians, the Sogdians, and the Tocharians played, no doubt, an important role in the formation of the Tadzhik people; yet it is not clear which of these tribes and nationalities was the carrier of the ancient Tadzhik language. Excepting the Bactrians, whose language is unknown, all the other ethnic groups spoke North Iranian languages. The Tadzhik language, however, belongs to a West Iranian (or according to another terminology, a South Iranian) branch. It is quite clear that the culture of Sogdiana was of enormous significance in the formation of Uzbek culture. The Sogdians, however, were Iranian-speaking people and therefore could not become "transformed" into the Turkic-speaking Uzbeks and apparently must have been "Turkicized" (in language) by other Turkic-speaking tribes, most probably by one of the tribes of the West Turkic khanate and especially by the Karluks. However, we should not equate the tribes of the West Turkic khanate (the Karluks) with the Uzbeks, because it is known that many tribes of the West

*Translated from Sovetskaya etnografiya, 1955, no. 2, pp. 16–26.
†[The omitted initial paragraphs of this article review the theories of N. Ya. Marr on the origins of nations and the author's objection to them.—Editor.]

Turkic khanate—for instance the confederation of Dulu [Tulu] tribes—entered into the composition of the Kazakh Dulats. The details of this process are as yet unknown. In trying to understand it, we see a bare outline, and what is known compels us to shy away from attempts to identify the present nationalities directly with any of the ancient ones. We should not forget the different ways in which culture forms and the unique ways in which language develops. And the latter is the most important index of ethnic affiliation.

Various Turkic tribes, most often of southern Siberian (Altayan) or Central Asiatic origin and particularly those from Semirechye, intermixed with the Kushan and Sogdian tribes of Central Asiatic mesopotamia [i.e., the interfluve between the Oxus and Jaxartes] and formed the basis of the Uzbek people already during the time of the West Turkic khanate of the 6th to 8th centuries. Such intermingling increased even more during the period of the Karakhanids, on whose territory the Uzbek people formed, and continued to absorb other tribes up to the 16th century.

The Turkmens underwent a process similar to that of the Uzbeks almost contemporaneously. In their formation a decisive part was played by the Oghuz, who united a group of local Sarmatian-Alan and Ephthalite (Hun) tribes.

The Kazakhs and the Kirgiz constitute probably the most recent formations. Although they had ancestors in antiquity and an early governmental structure, their formative process was disrupted by Mongolian incursions and was subsequently slowed by weak agricultural development and a number of specific historical factors. One such impeding factor was their displacement beyond the boundaries of the Yenisey and southern Siberia and their long subjugation to various other peoples.

All peoples of Central Asia, the Kazakhs and Kirgiz in particular, arose historically from different tribes, nationalities, and races. The written records concerning the Kirgiz, for example, note the difference in their physical characteristics only in the course of one millennium. I refer to the descriptions of the Chien-kun at the turn of our era by the Chinese, and of the Kirgiz in the 11th century in the work of Gardizi. The intermixtures are particularly striking among nomadic peoples and are recorded not only in written documents but primarily in the ethnonymics of these tribes. Disregarding all possible reconstructions of tribal names from the Chinese transcription, we can point out that ethnonymics reflect many common tribal names among the Kirgiz on the one hand and the Kazakhs, Uzbeks, and Turkmens on the other, for instance, T'ieh-lê, Tulu, Kangli, Kongrat, Mongol, Jalair, and Khitai. This indicates a certain commonness in ethnic structure, a division of a number of ancient tribes, and the entry of their parts into various ethnic formations. The ethnographic kinship revealed by many manifestations of the national culture of these peoples is not accidental; the commonness of subjects in the folklore is a direct result of the commonness of their historical development.

The peculiarity of Kirgiz ethnogenesis lies in its having taken place in two areas—along the banks of the Yenisey and in the Tien-shan. The Yenisey branch is of greater age. The developmental process of the Kirgiz tribes on the Yenisey led them, during the era of the establishment of the class pattern, to the creation of their own state and to the formation of specific cultural traits, e.g., the Kirgiz, runiform writing in the so-called literary language of the Orkhon Turks.[2] The political and economic isolation of the Yenisey Kirgiz and the unique path of their historical development encouraged the expansion of their economy and the appearance of distinctive features in their way of life. An important part in it was played by the rise of agriculture as a subsidiary branch of their economy, as well as of urban settlements and well-developed trades, especially metallurgy.

The Yenisey Kirgiz developed also their economic contacts with the neighboring regions, as can be clearly discerned from the data in written sources and from remains of the material culture. There is the well-known statement of the T'ang dynastic history *T'ang-shu* for the 7th to 8th century that the Kirgiz "have always been on friendly terms with the Dashi [Ta shih] (Arabs of Central Asia), Tufan (Tibet), and Gelolu [Ko-lo-lo] (Karluks of the Semirechye)."[3] And further: "Not more than twenty camels used to come from the Dashi with patterned silk fabrics; but when it was impossible to pack everything, the material was distributed among twenty-four camels. Such caravans were sent once every three years."[3]

Economic contacts were also realized as a result of military operations, which often ended in military and political alliances. This is told, for instance, in a story about Bassbeg, a Kirgiz leader, on a stele with runes set up in honor of Kyul-Tegin [Kül Tegin]. The stele reads that the Turks "bestowed on him the title of khan and gave him (in marriage) my (Kyul Tegin's) younger sister, the princess."[4] Military campaigns of the Yenisey Kirgiz led them south into the steppes of Mongolia and to the frontiers of China as well as west—to the Altay and the Semirechye. A direct result of these campaigns was, first, the absorption of alien tribal elements, primarily those of the Altay, and the consequent appearance of some cultural patterns of a non-Kirgiz origin. Second, it led to the adoption by the Kirgiz of some cultural traits from China and Central Asia, which can be traced very easily through their art. As examples of the first instance, there is the spoken *zhe*-sounding Kirgiz language, which is different from the *yo*-language of written records. The existence in Kirgiz folklore of the "Manas" epic brings to mind [connections to] the Altay territory, the birthplace of Zhakyp, the father of Manas. Finally, let us recall the statement of the T'ang-shu chronicle that the Kirgiz state "spread east of Kulikan (the Kurykan of the Cis-Baykal region—Author), south to Tibet, southwest to Ke-lo-lu (i.e., the Semirechye—Author)."[5] As an example of the second instance, let us mention such outstanding objects of art as bronze platelets [sewn] on saddlecloth from the Kopensk Chaatas, in which the archaeologists S. V. Kiselev and L. A. Evtyukhova convincingly traced Near Eastern as well as Chinese motifs.[6]

Quite inevitably some of the distinctive cultural traits were lost during the military campaigns and in the process of intermingling with other cultures. This represented a great danger from the point of view of the Turkish khans. In this connection the remarkable words of the Kyul-Tegin and Bilge-Khan texts which they addressed to their troops may be recalled:

Chinese people, who (now) give (us) without any constraint (to us) so much gold, silver, grain and silk, always had sweet words and "soft" gifts; with enticing words and luxurious gifts they attracted the faraway (living) people very strongly, (while these) settling next (to the Chinese) assimilated the local 'education.'

(However, the truly) good and wise people and great warriors they could not budge; and even if any (of the Turks) fell prey to this temptation they (the Chinese and their followers) never (again) let them go to their families, their people, or their country. By letting them tempt you with their words and luxurious gifts, you Turkish people (even within my recollection) have perished in great numbers. Oh, Turkish people (this was) your downfall; when you, Turkish people, wanted to settle to the right (in the south) not only in Chugay wilderness but in the Tunsk valley as well. This was your downfall, (because) there the 'educated' people enticed you by saying 'Who lives far gives poor gifts; who lives near gives good gifts,' with these words they (strongly) enticed you (to settle with the Chinese). And so you, people, who had no true wisdom, listened to such words and coming close (to the Chinese borders) perished (there) in great numbers.

Thus, oh Turkish people, when you go to that land you put yourself in great danger; however, when you live in Utuken land (Khangay), and send only the caravans (for gifts) and remain in Utuken wilderness where there are no riches but also no oppression (on the part of the Chinese), you can live and support your eternal tribal union.[7]

This topic is not new. It is characteristic that already in the time of the Huns [Hsiung-nu] in the 2nd century B.C. Chung-Hsing-y'uen, an adviser to the *Shanyu* Laoshang Tsê-yü warned him with the following words against becoming assimilated to the Chinese culture:

The number of the Huns cannot be compared with the population of a single Chinese province, but their strength lies in the excellence of their clothing and food for which they do not depend on China. However, at present, *Shanyu*, you are changing the customs and you like Chinese things. If China would use only one-tenth of their possessions, every single Hun would be on the side of the house of the khan. When you receive from China silk and cotton fabrics, tear the clothes made of them by running among thorny plants and show in this way that you prefer cheese and milk.[8]

Apparently, even in the 2nd century B.C., in a milieu analogous to that of the Kirgiz, the problem of preserving ethnic characteristics, customs, and way of life had been present. These texts disclose the meaning of autonomy for national unity.

The significance of military campaigns undertaken by the Yenisey Kirgiz is by no means exhausted with the above-mentioned economic circumstances. These campaigns resulted in the penetration of part of the Kirgiz into the Tien-shan, a penetration that became considerably stronger in the 8th to 10th centuries when finally the Tien-shan branch of the Kirgiz became entrenched. Let us review the basic data concerning the migration of the Yenisey Kirgiz to the Tien-shan.[9] The appearance of the Yenisey Kirgiz in the Tien-shan is connected with the uprising of the *Shanyu* Chih-chih in 49–47 B.C., at which time the first groups of Kirgiz settled in the northern slopes of the Tien-shan (the Talas valley). At the beginning of the 3rd century A.D. the Chinese source (Wei-liao) mentions the existence of the western branch of the Chien-kun (Kirgiz) in the Semirechye region. In the 7th century, Pi-ts'ê Tunge Gin, the leader of the Kirgiz living on the Yenisey, was genealogically and by marriage related to the representatives of the Tyurgesh and Karluk nobility of Semirechye. To this period also belong the Semirechye finds of Yenisey Kirgiz runes and objects of material culture (e.g., the Kochkor hoard, harness ornaments, clothing, and arms) greatly similar to those of the Yenisey. There are quite definite indications in such sources as "Hudud-al-Alam" and the work of Istakhri of the presence of the Kirgiz in the Tien-shan in the 10th century; "Hudud-al-Alam" mentions also the "city of a Kirgiz khan" to the north of the Tien-shan.[10] These sources note the gradual accumulation of the Kirgiz tribes in the Tien-shan; yet, this does not form a basis for assuming the predominance of these tribes in that region in ethnic, cultural, or political respects, particularly in the pre-Mongol period.

Analysis of epic plots, language, ornaments, and artifacts of the Tien-shan in that period, as well as of modern Kirgiz ethnography, reflects most clearly

Altayan plots and analogies, indicating the movement of the Kirgiz across the Altay and the steppes of Mongolia. Aside from the above-cited archaeological and written facts, the plots are particularly well represented in the epos "Manas." In this respect Kirgiz ethnonymics also reveal important data, as has been pointed out by Aristov.[11] In the period from the 6th to the 10th centuries they infiltrated the Tien-shan region under the leadership of "good princes"; however, they did not establish their own state there. The Yenisey Kirgiz who migrated to the Tien-shan intermixed on the way with the tribes of the Altay and Central Asia, infiltrated the ethnically alien environment, and became culturally and politically dependent on the local ethnic and state formations of the Tien-shan. In antiquity these were the Wu-sun, later the Western Turks, Tyurgesh [Türgesh], Karluks, and, above all, the Sogdians. These were also the Uygurs, Yagma, Kara Khitai, and other ethnic groupings.

It is precisely in this environment and its cultural contacts—primarily with the tribes and peoples of Central Asia and the oases of eastern Turkestan—that the history of the Tien-shan Kirgiz developed in the pre-Mongol period. The Kirgiz tribal minority, having come from the Yenisey, found itself inevitably under the influence of the indigenous majority of the Tien-shan tribes and peoples, part of whom stood above them both economically and culturally. Naturally, the Kirgiz became most closely related with the nomadic population of the country.

Archaeological research in Semirechye and the Tien-shan reveals the following significant ethnic and cultural developments in that territory beginning from the second millennium B.C. and, specifically, from the Saka [Shaka] period.[12] First, the structure of the local ethnic base, which we shall call the Saka-Wu-sun, and which is represented by burial sites in ground pits under a cromlech-like covering structure. Second, a systematic and continuous interrelationship between the Tien-shan tribes and the cultural environment of southern Siberia that is documented in particular by the stone[-lined] graves, by burials under a layer of logs, and by two-chamber graves. Contacts with southern Siberia are traceable from the 2nd millennium B.C. to the 10th century A.D. Third, from the beginning of our era, the appearance of ethnic components in Central Asia represented by the Catacomb culture of Tien-shan, the distribution of these tribes coinciding basically with the present distribution of the Kirgiz. In the Catacomb culture, we find very many traits indicating its kinship with the Kirgiz. The origin of the Catacomb culture of Central Asia is rather complex. The bearers of this culture, probably the tribes of a Hunnic union, were subjected to strong influence from Sarmatian-Alan and other tribes of Central Asia and Kazakhstan. The later the date of the catacombs of the period from the 3rd to the 5th centuries A.D., the fewer the elements of Central Asiatic origin, and the more numerous the traits of Sarmatian-Alan culture. From the middle of the 1st millennium A.D., there is notably rapid development of settled agriculture and crafts, which is primarily connected with the penetration into this region of the Sogdians from Central Asian mesopotamia [the area between the Syr and Amu Daryas].

Because of the absence of many means of production and particularly of agriculture, the nomadic tribes procured the lacking consumer goods by barter or wars with the settled population and thus became acquainted with the cultural patterns of the latter. The influence of Sogdian craftmanship manifested itself most clearly in building and ceramics. Side by side with Sogdian influence in the western Tien-shan, there also appears an equally active influence of the Fergana, as indicated by building techniques and the contents of the cultural layers in the sites of ancient Tien-shan towns, such as Chaldivar on the Mana-keldy river, Tokuz-Taru, the Shirdabek fortress, and Koshoi-Kurgan and others.

The second important circumstance that shaped the ethnogenesis of the Tien-shan Kirgiz was the political sovereignty of the Tien-shan states over the Kirgiz, i.e., the khanate of the Western Turks in the 6th to 8th centuries, the Karluk state in the 8th to 10th centuries, the Karakhanid state in the 11th to 12th centuries, and the Kara Khitai state in the 12th century. We have no indications whatever that these were Kirgiz states. To the contrary, there is every reason to believe that the Kirgiz were subordinated to these political entities. These states broke up the Kirgiz tribes with the result that other ethnic elements entered into the composition of the ancient Kirgiz—as well as the Uzbeks and Kazakh. And, by the 13th century, this process had not yet been completed. Let us recall such ethnic names of the pre-Mongol period as Ku-Su-Geshu, Nu-shih-pi Wu-sun, and Tieh-le; or those of the post-Mongol period, such as Mongodo, Mongush, Kipchak, Naiman, and Argyn.[13]

This indicates that the process of formation of the Kirgiz nationality continued in the post-Mongol period as well, that more and more new ethnic groups were becoming components of Kirgiz tribes, and that these groups brought new elements to the future national culture of the Kirgiz. This is the reason why the material culture, art, and folklore of the Kirgiz are preserved side by side with ancient Kirgiz motifs and also those elements of culture that became Kirgiz only later. The Kirgiz culture, taken in all its multiformity, shows which ethnic layers became part of the Kirgiz people already prior to the 16th century, when they began to play a political role in the Tien-shan.

The mass movement of the Yenisey Kirgiz to the Tien-shan in the 9th and 10th centuries was of particularly great importance for the formative process of the Kirgiz people. It is precisely in the 10th century that western authors begin to single out a Kirgiz group in the Tien-shan that ultimately became sovereign again in the post-Mongol period. As nomads wandering in the mountain valleys of the Tien-shan, they withstood the blow of the Mongol conquest more easily than the settled urban population. On this territory they absorbed various Turkic tribes, such as the Sogdians, the Iranian-speaking population of this region, which was distributed in the Karluk Semirechye already in the 11th century; and the Fergana [valley] began to be "Turkicized" from the middle of the 7th century —as reported in Chinese written sources and epigraphic material. It is seen that the ethnic composition of the Tien-shan was already becoming more or less homogeneous in the 6th to 8th centuries A.D., and particularly from the 11th to 12th centuries on. Therefore, there entered into the composition of the Tien-shan Kirgiz Iranian-speaking tribes that had already been "Turkicized," for instance, the Sogdians.

Such are, in our opinion, the basic stages of the ethnic history of the Tien-shan Kirgiz. They differ greatly from those of the ethnic history of the Yenisey Kirgiz. The socio-economic and political history of the Tien-shan Kirgiz also took a course different from that of the Yenisey.

The movement of the Kirgiz to the Tien-shan was a gradual one. Historic sources clearly separate two main stages of this movement: the 1st century B.C. and the 8th to 10th centuries A.D. It can be projected that the third stage of the migration took place under the Kara Khitai and Mongols, when the basic ethnic composition of the Tien-shan Kirgiz took final shape. Such gradual settlement of the Kirgiz in the Tien-shan could not lead, naturally, to any radical changes in the socio-economic conditions already existing there. Since archaeological results characterize the Kirgiz tribes mainly as belonging within a rural "nomadic district," it is quite unlikely that their economic and social structure represents a leading pattern in the historical development of the Tien-shan. I think it possible to periodize the history of the Tien-shan Kirgiz on the basis of the periodization of the historical process in the Tien-shan and in Semirechye. I tried repeatedly to formulate this periodization in my historical-archaeological works. The period prior to the 18th century falls roughly into the following principal stages.

The first stage deals with the Tien-shan Kirgiz within the structure of the Saka-Wu-sun and the Hun tribal unions in the Tien-shan and Semirechye and possibly the Fergana and Alay ranges. These Kirgiz formed a nomadic and democratic militant periphery of the states of Central Asia, in the first place of the Fergana [valley], the Tashkent oasis, partially Sogdiana, and the middle Syr Darya. Only in this aspect should we examine the role of the ancestors of the Kirgiz in the "Hellenistic" and Kushan periods of Central Asiatic "antiquity."

The second stage takes place in the 5th to 6th centuries A.D., when agricultural settlements form in the Semirechye on the Chu and Talas rivers. In relation to these, the ancient Kirgiz as well as other nomadic tribes of the Tien-shan retain the role of a nomadizing periphery.

The third stage is the feudal period. In the West Turkic khanate, the Tyurgesh, and particularly in the Karluk state of the 8th to 10th centuries, a process of drawing of the Kirgiz tribes into the stream of feudal development takes place. This process is intensified as a result of the penetration from the Yenisey of new groups of Kirgiz with unquestionably better developed social structure than that of the Tien-shan Kirgiz. Reference to the city of a Kirgiz khan ("Kyrgyz khan"),[14] the strengthening of territorial and communal bounds, and the formation of separate groups of southern and northern Kirgiz give reason to presume a stabilization of certain traits characteristic of a new ethnic category—nationality. This stabilization was based on the development of feudal relations. The low level of development of these relations allows a designation of the 9th to 10th centuries as the early feudal period in the history of the Tien-shan Kirgiz and as the first stage in the formation of a Kirgiz nationality. In this period the formations of states among the neighboring peoples became an obstacle to independent development of the same among the Kirgiz and to their territorial consolidation. The Sinkiang, Fergana, and Tien-shan branches of the Kirgiz remained separated, as did the Yenisey branch. In their way stood the feudal fragmentation of the Kara Khitai and the Karakhanid states, in which the Kirgiz continued to remain as subordinates. This constitutes the fourth stage of their history.[15]

If in the 15th and 16th centuries the Kirgiz, fighting vigorously for their independence, earned from their oppressors the nickname "the wild lions of Mogulistan" (as reported to us by Muhammed Khaidar), then it was the state of Mogulistan and the Kalmuks ruling over the Tien-shan and the Cis-Fergana Kirgiz that constituted an obstacle that prevented their development into a united people. The isolation of the Kirgiz from agricultural settlements, their economic exhaustion, and the political oppression delayed both the breakdown of the patriarchal system and the development of a feudal one, and thus created a stabilization of semipatriarchal and semifeudal relations. This constituted the fifth stage.

In the sixth stage, migrations of the Kirgiz from the Tien-shan to Sinkiang in the 16th century, from the Tien-shan to Fergana in the 17th, the breaking up of their territorial unity, the endless dismemberments of Kirgiz tribes, and the entries of their parts into various states (the Kokand, Khitai, and Kazakh khanates) led to additional intermixture, rupture of the growing ethnic unity, and disturbance of the processes that create economic and cultural homogeneity. The period preceding the annexation of the Kirgiz by Russia in the middle of the 19th century, particularly the 16th to 18th centuries, is a period of the struggle of the Kirgiz for their independence under the conditions of a patriarchal and feudal fragmentation. This period is delineated quite clearly by sources beginning with the Tarikhi-Rashidi (16th century) and ending with the Chinese records of the *Hsi-yü T'u-shih* or the *Hsi-yü Wên-chien-lu* (18th century).

The Chinese sources of the 18th century indicate the fragmentation of the Kirgiz. They not only note their division into the western and eastern groups (corresponding apparently to their division into the Adygene and Tagay groups) but also an intertribal division with stable military and democratic traditions. The *Hsi-yü Wên-chien-lu* reports:

their sovereigns (*chün*) are called *pi*. Some *pi* have from ten to twenty *amans* (auls), while others have up to thirty amans and persons who are called their slaves (*k'u-lang*). Although all of them are called the Burut, they have more than one *pi*. The sovereign (*chün*) has his own land and his subjects (*ming*). They are all equal and [economically] dissimilar from each other (*pu-hsiang*). When a *pi* dies, another takes his place, his son or his brother, and no other person can take it.[16]

Evidently the last sentence characterizes the hereditary right of succession only within the limits of a tribe or a clan, because in large social groups the power of the leader was not hereditary. In this connection I refer to another passage in the *Hsi-yü T'u-shih*. It reads: "All these leaders (*t'ou*) are independent of each other. Every year they select a person, an elder (*chang*), who provides general administration and to whom everything is subordinated. The leader (*t'ou*) who becomes an elder (*chang*) is called Mamuk Kuli. He is only the head of the tribe (*pu*) temporarily."[16]

The cited facts show clearly, particularly if we take into consideration the widely known data extracted by V. V. Bartold* from Iranian and Turkic literature, that in the 18th century the Kirgiz had not yet emerged from semipatriarchal, semifeudal relations. This patriarchal-feudal fragmentation, preserved in the Kirgiz tribes of the post-Mongol period, was a decisive factor impeding the final formation of Kirgiz national culture. Fragmentation, which such public figures as Ormonkhan have tried to overcome already in the 19th century, was also a factor determining the intermixture of the Kirgiz with other tribes in the course of two thousand years, the instability of their ethnic structures, and the possibility of penetration into their milieu of alien ethnic and cultural elements. This then constituted the uniqueness of the ethnic characteristics of the Tien-shan Kirgiz, a uniqueness that can be explained by the peculiarities of their historical development.

I have attempted to characterize in a general way the most important eras in the ancient history and ethnogenesis of the Kirgiz people, eras that explain, it seems to me, the peculiarities in the development of their Tien-shan branch.

There is no doubt that the Yenisey Kirgiz constituted the main core in the formation of the present-day Tien-shan Kirgiz. The number of the Tien-shan Kirgiz grew not only because of the immigration of the Yenisey Kirgiz and the natural increase of population, but also to a great extent because of the assimi-

*[Barthold.]

lation by the Kirgiz of the nomadic and part of the settled population of the Tien-shan. Many things become clearer in the history of the Tien-shan Kirgiz in the light of the Marxist concept of the formation of peoples from various tribes, nationalities, and races. It is characteristic that our present knowledge about the racial structure of the Tien-shan and Pamir-Altay population, i.e., of the region of Kirgiz distribution, indicates a great variety of racial types. Even more diverse is the cultural development of the Tien-shan and the Semirechye. Thus, in the Semirechye there exist various written records—Sogdian, Syrian, Arabic, runiform-Turkic, Chinese, Uygur, Sanskrit, etc. In the remains of material culture, the traits of the heterogenous origin of the artistic traditions and handicrafts, particularly in building, painting, sculpture, as well as in metallurgy and pottery, are sufficiently clearly discernible.

If the nomadic culture of the aborigines of the Tien-shan and Semirechye was formed out of local elements interacting with those of Central Asia and southern Siberia, then the culture of settlements, particularly urban ones, was formed as a result of the interaction of the local nomadic and settled Central Asian cultures, such as those of Sogdiana and the Syr Darya area. Manifestations of the local nomadic culture can be traced particularly clearly from the Bronze Age to the 10th century A.D., and of sedentary Central Asian from the 5th to the 10th centuries A.D. After the 10th century, this diversity of cultural interactions becomes greatly reduced, and the differences among the ethno-cultural elements of Tien-shan become less clear. This gives us grounds for assuming that from this time on, first among the nomadic population, traits typical of Kirgiz culture begin to form. However, even the 10th century does not yet represent the century of the final formation of the Kirgiz culture and of the Kirgiz tribes in the Tien-shan.

Does all this mean that the peoples of the Tien-shan and their culture have to be regarded as absolutely alien to Kirgiz culture? In my opinion, no. Since it was this environment where the Kirgiz tribes became solidified, since the ethnic groups of the Saka, Wu-sun, the tribes of the Hunnic Union, Karluks, etc., with their cultures, languages, and customs constituted this environment and the components from which the Kirgiz people were being formed, then their history was to a certain extent the history of the Tien-shan Kirgiz. This is what gives historians grounds for analyzing the Kirgiz ornament, the Kirgiz folklore, and the Kirgiz ethnonyms, for reconstructing these items of the Kirgiz people side by side with their ancient, basic, ethnic core. However, in defining the remains of the ancient Tien-shan as those of the Saka, Wu-sun, Huns, Sogdians, etc., we cannot call them Kirgiz because at that time the Tien-shan Kirgiz culture proper had not yet been formed, and the Saka, Wu-sun, Huns, and Sogdians were part of the structure of other peoples as well. Without calling their culture a Kirgiz one, we can still rightfully call all these phenomena a cultural heritage of the Kirgiz people. The Tien-shan Kirgiz culture proper—prior to the formation of the Kirgiz nationality—should be considered the culture of the Yenisey Kirgiz groups in the Tien-shan; and this culture is clearly identified from the, so far, few records of the early Middle Ages.

It is impossible to learn the history of the formation of the Kirgiz people if we isolate it from the social environment in which they lived and the contacts that they developed. Taking into consideration the particularly wide movements of the Kirgiz tribes, their frequent fragmentation and intermixture, one has to admit that they had especially strong possibilities for such contacts.

The recording of the whole diversity of definitive facts that influenced the formation of the Kirgiz people is a necessary prerequisite for the reconstruction of historical truth.

Notes and References

1. A. Bernshtam, *Drevneyshiye tyurkskiye elementy v etnogeneze Sredney Azii* (The earliest Turkic elements in the ethnogenesis of Central Asia); Sbornik *Sovetskaya etnografiya*, nos. 6–7, Moscow–Leningrad, 1947, p. 304.

2. S. Malov, *Yeniseyskaya pismennost tyurkov* (The Yenisey writing of the Turks), Moscow–Leningrad, 1952.

3. N. Ya. Bichurin, *Sobraniye svedeniy o narodakh, obitavshikh v Sredney Azii v drevniye vremena* (Collection of information on the peoples inhabiting Central Asia in ancient times), vol. 1, Moscow–Leningrad, 1950, p. 355.

4. *Zapiski Vostochnogo otdela Russkogo arkheologicheskogo obshchestva* (referred to hereafter as ZVO), vol. 12, nos. 2–3, p. 69; cf. S. Malov, *Pamyatniki drevnetyurkskoy pismennosti* (Records of ancient Turkic writing), Moscow–Leningrad, 1951, p. 58.

5. See: Bichurin, *op. cit.*, vol. 1, p. 354.

6. See: S. V. Kiselev, *Drevnyaya istoriya Yuzhnoy Sibiri* (The ancient history of Southern Siberia), Moscow, 1951.

7. ZVO, vol. 12, no. 203, pp. 61–62; cf. Malov, *Pamyatniki drevnetyurkskoy pismennosti*, pp. 34–35.

8. Bichurin, *op. cit.*, vol. 1, pp. 57–58.

9. See: A. Bernshtam, *Arkheologicheskiy ocherk Severnoy Kirgizii* (An archaeological essay on Northern Kirgizia), Frunze, 1941.

10. V. Bartold, *Khudud-al-Alem* (Hudud-al-Alam), Leningrad, 1930; V. Minorsky, *Hudud al Alam*, London, 1937. Indexes.

11. N. Aristov, *Zametki ob etnicheskom sostave tyurkskikh plemen i narodnostey i svedeniya ob ikh chislennosti* (Notes on the ethnic composition of Turkic tribes and nationalities and data on their numbers), *Zhivaya starina*, nos. 3–4, 1896.

12. See my: *Pamyatniki stariny Tallasskoy doliny* (Remains of antiquity in the Talas valley), Alma-Ata, 1941; *Arkheologicheskiy ocherk Severnoy Kirgizii* (An archaeological essay on Northern Kirgizia), Frunze, 1941; Osnovnye etapy istorii kultury Semirechya i Tyan-Shanya (Basic stages in the cultural history of Semirechye and the Tien-shan), Sbornik *Sovetskaya arkheologiya*, vol. 11, Leningrad, 1949; Chuyskaya Dolina (The Chu valley), MIA, no. 14, Moscow–Leningrad, 1950.

13. See: Aristov, *op. cit.*

14. Bartold, *Khudud-al-Alem*, folio 18b.

15. The Sinkiang group of the Kirgiz has not been studied at all, although there were some Kirgiz in Sinkiang and in Cis-Tibet [i.e., Cis-Tibet as viewed from the territory of the Soviet Union] already prior to the 10th century. See the published Tibetan documents of F. W. Thomas in *Journal of the Royal Asiatic Society*, January, 1927, p. 55; October, 1927, p. 817; 1928, p. 96. These data are particularly important for the history of the southern Kirgiz.

16. A. Bernshtam, Istochniki po istorii kirgizov 18 veka (Sources for the history of the Kirgiz in the 18th century), *Voprosy istorii*, 1946, nos. 11–12, p. 128.

G. F. DEBETS

THE ORIGIN OF THE KIRGIZ PEOPLE IN THE LIGHT OF PHYSICAL ANTHROPOLOGICAL FINDINGS*

1. THE PRESENT ARTICLE serves as an introduction and, to a certain extent, as a conclusion to the published results of the work of physical anthropologists connected with the Kirgiz Joint Archaeological-Ethnographical Expedition of 1953.

The theoretical basis for the utilization of physical anthropological data as a historical source in connection with problems of ethnogenesis was presented in a special article. Essentially, the basic premises of this article are quite elementary:

1. "Language and culture may spread regardless of physical types but physical types never spread without culture and language."

2. Phenomena of change and mixture of physical types observed by anthropologists "represent only a reflection of physical peculiarities due to migrations and mixtures of tribes, peoples, and nations."

3. "Therefore, in cases where anthropological data indicate diffusion of this or that physical type, historians and archaeologists, ethnographers and linguists are faced with the problem of ascertaining the historical conditions that produced this diffusion and the historical-cultural and linguistic phenomena that were connected with it."[1]

Notwithstanding the simplicity and elementariness of these obvious propositions, some representatives of the humanities, when studying problems of the origin of peoples, sometimes prefer not to deal with data of physical anthropology and proceed from an essentially correct but erroneously interpreted proposition that there is no direct connection between the physical and the linguistic divisions of humanity. It is certainly true that establishment or, more often, invention of such connections serves as a basis for all kinds of falsifications about race. However, the struggle against racism in this field should not result in a negation of the role and the meaning of physical anthropological findings but in an exposition and rebuttal of non-scientific attempts to represent historical process as a result of physical phenomena when precisely the opposite takes place.

The main task here, as in other questions and in other fields of knowledge, consists in ascertaining the real meaning of the process itself. However, since racist falsifications of this process do exist, the opposition to them represents a necessary, although not a principal link of scientific investigation.

The Kirgiz language is a member of the Turkic language family. Therefore, the problems of ethnogenesis of the Kirgiz people have direct bearing on the problems of formation of the Turkic language community. As is well known, the history of a language is inseparable from the history of the people. This becomes

*Translated from *Trudy kirgizskoy ekspeditsii*, vol. 1, 1956, pp. 3–17.

particularly clear in the study of processes of diffusion and interchange of languages, the reasons for which do not depend on the characteristics of the language itself but are determined by historical circumstances. As the latter determine at the same time the physical composition of peoples, the anthropologist should certainly keep in mind these historical circumstances and take into consideration all attempts to falsify them.

People who speak languages of the Turkic family are diffused, as is known, over an enormous area from the Okhotsk to the Black sea, and from the Kama basin to the Persian gulf. Physically they are very diverse but, if we limit ourselves to the basic classification of major races, that is, races of the first order, all diverse types of Turkic peoples may be entered under two types: Mongoloid and Europoid. For example, in the east, the Yakuts[2] lack—or at least it has not been established that they have—an admixture of Europoid types (leaving out their [later] mixing with the Russians); in the west, the Kumyks[3] lack—or at least it is not established that they have—an admixture of the Mongoloid type. No less great are the differences in culture. It is hardly possible to find anything common, except attitudes that are general to any culture, in the ethnographic characterization of the Dolgans and Azerbaijans or the Chuvash and Sary-Uygurs. With all the diversity of physical type and culture of Turkic-speaking peoples, there is no doubt that the Turkic languages have a common origin. There is also no doubt that they could not have been formed simultaneously in the whole, enormous area occupied by them now, in the midst of peoples so different in physical type and culture. The area of the initial formation of the Turkic languages must have been considerably smaller than the area occupied by them now; the people who spoke the earliest Turkic language must have been much more homogeneous culturally and physically.

The general concept about the origin of Turkic peoples, or to be more correct, about the history of diffusion of Turkic languages, was already formulated in the 19th century. In reference to countries where monuments of ancient written language exist (Turkey, Azerbaijan, Turkmenia, Uzbekistan), it was established with certitude that Turkic languages appeared there less than fifteen hundred years ago and appeared, moreover, in the place of languages (mainly Iranian) so remote from them that there can be no possibility of direct continuity among them. These countries should therefore be excluded as areas of the earliest formation of Turkic languages. The majority of the ancient population inhabiting the southern steppes undoubtedly spoke Iranian languages. This southern Russian steppe also should be excluded as an area in which the Turkic languages were initially formed. It is known, however, that at the beginning of the 2nd millennium A.D. Turkic languages were widely diffused in the southern steppes. Archaeological data give many indications that allow us to state that during the Iron Age, particularly in its later part, there appear many objects of eastern origin in the cultural remains of the population of these steppes. Palaeontological data indicate with even greater certainty that at that time there appeared Mongoloid peoples of Central Asian origin in southern Russian steppes whose area of origin lay between the Mongolian Altay and the Great Khingans. It would be very natural to suggest that all these events are interconnected, that the eastern elements in the culture were brought in by people who migrated from Central Asia, spoke Turkic languages, and were characterized by the Mongoloid physical type. Passing to Kazakhstan, it should be first noted that archaeological and palaeoanthropological data, when used as sources for the ancient history of the peoples of this country, disclose a far-reaching analogy with the archaeological and palaeoanthropological data of the population of southern Russia steppes. We do not mean here the resemblance of manifestations but the unity of the process, and, because of this, it is most likely that Kazakhstan also was not the area of origin for the Turkic languages. Consequently, we should exclude also the area of the middle Volga and the Kama regions, which thus appear to be cut off from the "Turkic area." The suggestion that the Turkic languages were formed initially in the Kama river region is an example of a useless hypothesis.

In the east, Yakutia should certainly be excluded as an area of origin for the Turkic languages. Here, although there are no literary remains of pre-Turkic languages and therefore no indisputable indicators of language, the memory of the southern origin of the nucleus of the Yakut people is so clearly preserved in the folklore that there is no cause to doubt its historical trustworthiness, the more so since it is solidly supported by ethnographical and anthropological data.

Thus, there remains only Central Asia. Comparative linguistics, above all, testify in favor of the opinion that Central Asia was the area of origin of the earliest Turkic language. No doubts arise regarding the kinship of the Turkic and Mongolic languages, and to look anywhere else for a place where this kinship was formed except in Central Asia, and, broadly speaking, outside the limits of the present-day Mongolian Peoples Republic, is hardly possible without new, useless hypotheses. From there, from Central Asia, the Turkic languages spread westward and northward.

However fragmentary the data on the physical characteristics of the ancient peoples of the steppe belt of the U.S.S.R. are at present, they nevertheless draw for us a picture of the gradual increase of the proportion of Mongoloid elements in the physical make-up of these peoples. Chronologically, the testimony of physical anthropology is related to two great historical stages: "the Hun-Sarmatian period" (1st centuries B.C. and A.D.), and the "time of the later nomads" (the end of the 1st and beginning of the 2nd millennium A.D.).

To the first stage are related Mongoloid skulls discovered in the burials of the Tashtyk culture,[4] in the uplands of the Altay mountains,[5] and apparently in eastern Kazakhstan where, as V. V. Ginzburg states,[6] on the basis of up-to-now not extensive materials, skulls from burials dated to the 1st centuries B.C. are characterized by Mongoloid traits that are lacking, or at any rate not so sharply pronounced, in more ancient skulls. To the same period are related the writings of ancient authors about the physical type of the Huns who then invaded Europe,[7] writings that have been repeatedly scrutinized by anthropologists. However, all these indicate comparatively slight traces of Mongoloid admixture. In the Altay-Sayan uplands, in Kazakhstan, as well as in the steppes of southern Russia, various types of the Europoid race were the basis of the composition of the population. Strictly speaking, if we stay within the realm of anthropological facts, we cannot even state categorically that Mongoloid elements found in the composition of ancient peoples during "Hun-Sarmatian times" in the regions just enumerated have an undoubted Central Asiatic origin. If historical data could supply us with a basis, it could be supposed that the Mongoloids of "Hun-Sarmatian times" penetrated into the belt of steppes not from Central Asia, but, for example, from the forest belt of western Siberia or of the middle Volga region.

Anthropological evidence of mass migrations from Central Asia of peoples of Mongoloid type pertains to the "time of the later nomads." This evidence is clearly shown in the physical type of peoples of the later part of the Iron Age dwelling in the Minusinsk basin and the Altay uplands, and in the nomads of the Volga region and the Ukraine.[8] Undoubtedly (although we do not have published data as yet), the features of the Central Asian Mongoloid type were no less clearly manifested, at that time, in the peoples of Kazakhstan.[9] Finally, to the same period should also be dated the penetration into the middle Lena region of the Angara-Lena physical type, also a member of the Central Asian group.

With reference to the "time of the later nomads," there are many reasons for believing that the migrations, fixed in time by anthropological data, were migrations of peoples speaking Turkic languages. In regard to the "Hun-Sarmatian period," an analogous hypothesis is probable and useful as it explains much, but it still remains a hypothesis only.

However, if all Mongoloid peoples migrating from Central Asia spoke Turkic or Mongol languages, it does not follow that all peoples diffusing Turkic languages were characterized by Mongoloid traits. The transition to Turkic languages of the ancestors of the Kumyks, Azerbaijans, or Turks was not followed by the migration of any significant numbers of representatives of the Mongoloid race.

[Two omitted paragraphs deal with the Turkish nationalistic concept "Gyunesh-dil" and the linguistic theories of Marr. Both are rejected by the author.]

The theory of formation of the earliest Turkic language among Central Asiatic nomads in whose physical type Mongoloid traits predominated, while not rejected, did not interest the well-known Turkologist S. Ye. Malov.[10] He asserts that the Turks were living mainly where they live now even in the five centuries B.C., and that in the Volga region, long before that time, two groups of Turkic languages were already formed: the Bulgar and the Mishar. This conclusion was based on the considerable differences among the eastern Turkic languages, for the formation of which a considerable time was required. Malov's profound knowledge and great merit in regard to the Turkic languages are completely obvious. However, I believe that an anthropologist, even when he does not know one Turkic language and has no knowledge of the methods of linguistics, can be allowed to ask a question: What are the methods for determining a chronological scale for the formation of this or that degree of linguistic differentiation? It is possible though, and completely admissible, to rely in this respect on the intuition of an authoritative investigator, as long as exact methods are not yet worked out. But even if the differentiation between the eastern and the western Turkic languages did actually require no less than three thousand years, can it be admitted that the differentiation took place in Central Asia only? Some Turkologists (I say, the majority) do think so: For example, N. A. Baskakov,[11] who also differentiates strongly between the eastern and the western Turkic languages, but dates this division to the time of the disintegration of the Hun union and the consolidation of the established differences to the time of the dissolution of the Turkic khanate. As is known, both of these events took place in Asia.

We permit ourselves to assert that the theory of the Central Asiatic origin of the Turks which became so widespread that it is even difficult to name its first originators without a special historiographic investigation, remains unshaken in its basic tenets.[12] The facts briefly summarized above, as well as many similar facts forming its basis, were not disproved essentially by any critics of this theory. They are so obvious that conclusions about the Pamir or Mediterranean or any other origin of the Turkic languages can be arrived at only by suppressing them. The same applies to the assertion that it is impossible, at present, to determine the place of origin of the Turks, as proposed by S. Ye. Malov. The Central Asian theory should constitute the basis of all specific investigations dealing with the history of the entry of separate peoples into the body of the Turkic language community, including the Kirgiz people.

The first investigators of the physical composition of Central Asiatic peoples have already established that it contained two basic elements: (*a*) a very ancient, Europoid element whose formation is of great antiquity, with Central Asia as the territory of formation, and (*b*) a more recent, Mongoloid element which spread from the east, out of the Central Asiatic steppes. Two language families were no less clearly brought to light: the Iranian and Turkic. And, finally, in the culture of Central Asiatic peoples, there were established long ago in addition to ancient elements of local provenience, cultural influences of Central Asiatic nomads. Further investigations introduced a number of essential data of greater exactitude into this general scheme. The most important of these is the conclusion that in the interrelation of the two basic elements the interaction of cultures and mixing of physical types predominated rather than a contest between them, as depicted by the first investigators. With the best of intentions, the followers of Marr's theory attempted, in the name of strengthening the brotherhood of nations but relying on erroneous mechanical premises, to discover the same profound mutual interactions in the languages too. The discussion of 1950 aided in the correction of errors made in this field.

Physical anthropologists have ascertained long ago that Mongoloid traits are expressed in the Kirgiz more clearly than in the Uzbeks. Results of the anthropological section of the Kirgiz Joint Expedition established that the Kirgiz differ in this respect also from the Kazakhs, although to a lesser extent than from the Uzbeks. A. I. Yarkho[13] found that the Fergana Kirgiz have a greater admixture of Europoid elements than the Tien-shan Kirgiz. The works of the expedition's physical anthropological section also confirmed this, and additionally found that the Kirgiz of the Chu and Talas valleys resemble more closely the Fergana valley Kirgiz than those of the Tien-shan. However, it does not follow that the role of the Europoid element should be exaggerated in the make-up of the physical type of the Chu, Talas, and Fergana valley Kirgiz. Although their distinctions from the mountain groups of Kirgiz are completely real, nevertheless all of the Kirgiz, not excluding the Fergana ones or representatives of the Ichkilik groups, still differ from the Kazakhs and even more so from the Uzbeks by a greater prominence of Mongoloid characteristics.[14]

Let us now return to the questions of methodology. Archaeologists and ethnographers should keep in mind the indisputable condition that among the ancestors of the present-day Kirgiz there were many more inhabitants of Central Asiatic steppes than ancient inhabitants of Kirgizia, related to the modern Tadzhiks and to the basic nucleus of the Central Asiatic Uzbeks. This fact, established on the basis of anthropological data as well as on all other "anthropological" facts, has a real historical basis and merits a real historical explanation. At the same time it would certainly be inadmissible to utilize this conclusion mechanically in the determination of the specific position and meaning of the cultural elements of local and Central Asiatic origin in the formation of the culture of the Kirgiz people. In calling on anthropologists and ethnographers to take into consideration the results of physical anthropological investigations, we do not counsel them to forget about archaeological or ethnographic materials. The essence of ethnogenetic investigation, as well as the very nature of ethnogenetic phenomena, is not in contest and submission but in mutual help and interaction.

2. Having established the strong dominance of Mongoloid elements in the formation of the physical type of the Kirgiz, we shall not limit by this our participation

in working out the problem of Kirgiz origins. The next problem is the question of the time of Mongoloid penetration into Kirgizia and, certainly, a more detailed characterization of the physical make-up of the newcomers from central Asia. The point is that the Turkic nomads arriving from the east may have already had an admixture of Europoid elements. There is no doubt that the ancient population of Sinkiang belonged to the Europoid race. Unfortunately the composition of the ancient population of western Mongolia is unknown to us. But in the Altay-Sayan highlands the most ancient population was clearly Europoid. What was the type of the Yenisey "Kyrgyz"? Whatever the solution of the problem of their relationship to the Tien-shan Kirgiz, we can not leave this question without attention. In the article of V. P. Alekseyev skulls are described (unfortunately still too few) that could be attributed to the Yenisey "Kyrgyz." They certainly differ from the ancient Europoids of the Altay-Sayan region. The dominant type of the Yenisey "Kyrgyz" was Mongoloid. But there is an indisputable admixture of Europoid elements in their composition. The specific position of this admixture is approximately the same as with the modern Kirgiz. This fact cannot be left without attention in evaluating the role of immigrant and local elements in the formation of the Kirgiz people. It indicates that even that small part of Europoid admixture that is established in the physical type of the modern Kirgiz may have, to a considerable extent, the same eastern origin (in relation to the territory of Kirgizia) as the basic Mongoloid type. Ancestors of the Kirgiz arriving from Central Asia were perhaps already mixed.

Unfortunately, palaeoanthropological materials obtained in 1953 have not yet been closely studied. Our review is limited, therefore, to data contained in the works of V. V. Ginzburg, which are based on the study of materials collected by the expeditions of A. N. Bernshtam.

As yet, palaeoanthropological data on the Saka and Wu-suns are not numerous. Investigations of Ginzburg[15] indicate that skulls from Saka burials in the Pamir (as determined by Bernshtam) differ noticeably from skulls attributed by the same author to the Saka of Tien-shan and the Altay. Among the Pamir Saka there is no indication of Mongoloid admixture. In outward looks the Pamir Saka resemble most the Afghans or northern Indians. During the Saka [Shaka] period, the type of population in the mountain valleys of Tien-shan differed, according to Ginzburg's data, essentially from the inhabitants of the Pamir.[16] Not mentioning the completely different form of the brain case (the difference in the cephalic index amounts to 10 units: 72 in the Pamir and 82 in Kirgizia), The Saka skulls of Tien-shan and Altay, particularly the female ones, are distinguished by a somewhat flatter face. True, this characteristic is not expressed with sufficient sharpness to permit a categorical assertion that there is a Mongoloid admixture in the physical type of the Kirgiz Saka. In his description of individual skulls, Ginzburg points out a possible Mongoloid admixture in only one skull and even this one is from rather late times. At that, the Kirgiz Saka are distinguished from the Pamir ones also by the form of the face, which in the Tien-shan and Altay Saka was not only somewhat flatter, but also considerably wider. The malar diameter of male skulls differs by 9 mm and the difference in the width of the face was thus the same as between modern Russians and Kirgiz. As the Pamir Saka had at the same time a higher face, their "face oval" was thus much more elongated. The difference in the facial index amounted to 6 units, i.e., it was large enough to be noted even before it was measured.

Skulls from burials excavated in different parts of Kirgizia are related to just the turn of the Christian era and to the first centuries A.D. They are ascribed to the Wu-suns and generally resemble the skulls of Tien-shan Saka. But the facial part of these skulls is even flatter, so much so that there is no doubt about the Mongoloid admixture.

Skulls from graves that Bernshtam considered to be those of the Huns are of particular interest. As a rule, these skulls are artificially deformed.

In the archaeological and anthropological literature of recent years an assertion was often reiterated that the Mongoloid type appeared in Central Asia first with the migration of the Huns. So far as we know this assertion was published first in the account of Bernshtam, evidently based on preliminary conclusions reached by Leningrad anthropologists. The "historical importance of the graves . . . ," wrote Bernshtam, "is very important . . . as the graves represent the most ancient central Asian Mongoloid type."[17] In the same account he presents a definition of the skeletons found in the principal burial of one of the mounds (no. 10), in both the catacomb and the corridor (dromos) leading to it. "In the catacomb itself," he wrote, "were two Mongoloid skeletons with deformed skulls; the skeletons at the entrance belonged to Europoids, obviously slaves from the local population of the Pamir-Fergana race."[18]

All this is unfortunately incorrect and is not repeated in the article of Ginzburg and Ye. V. Zhirov that describes the palaeoanthropological materials from the Kenkol burials.[19]

The figures in Table 1 clearly indicate that there are no real differences between the bodies buried in "the dromos" and in the catacomb in the degree of horizontal profile of the face. However, in the archaeological works of Bernshtam, the period of the Kenkol burials continues to be characterized as "the epoch . . . of the introduction of Mongoloid features into the Europoid substratum of the local population." The Europoid slaves, the Wu-suns, also continue to be mentioned.[20] Unfortunately, the contrasting of Wu-suns with "Huns"—because the former lack Mongoloid admixture and the latter have it—has again appeared in the works of Ginzburg. These were published after his own article describing the skeletons of the Kenkol burials written in co-authorship with Zhirov was published. In it nothing is said about the strengthening of the Mongoloid element in the Huns as compared with the Wu-suns, and the two peoples are not compared at all.

TABLE 1

COMPARISON OF THE HORIZONTAL PROFILE OF SKULL FACES FROM THE CATACOMBS AND THE
ENTRANCE CORRIDOR (DROMOS) OF KURGAN NO. 10 OF THE KENKOL BURIAL PLACE
(EXCAVATIONS OF 1939)

Placement of burials and sex	Naso-malar angle	Zygo-maxillary angle	Dacryon height	Simotic height	Angle of nasal prominence
Catacomb, man	141°	129°	13.3	4.4	26°
Catacomb, woman	133°	132°	13.9	4.0	26°
Corridor (dromos), 1st man	140°	139°	12.3	2.8	26°
Corridor (dromos), 2nd man	140°	132°	11.1	3.2	25°
Average of the entire series:					
Men	139.6°	130.1°	11.5	3.4	25.7°
Women	138.9°	128.4°	11.1	3.3	24.0°

In a summarizing article, dedicated to the basic problems of ethnic anthropology of Central Asia, Ginzburg proposes that "Mongoloid traits appear for the first time on the territory of Central Asia in the Kenkol and other Hun burial places."[21] Analogous opinions are expressed also in later works.[22]

An objective comparison of various series of ancient skulls from Kirgiz territory indicates that with the available data there is not sufficient basis for the conclusion that the admixture of Mongoloid elements is greater among the "Huns" than among the Wu-suns. The physical type of the Kirgiz "Huns" certainly included a Mongoloid element, but in approximately the same proportion as in the Usuns or even to a somewhat less extent. However, because of the insufficient number of observations, this latter could hardly be insisted upon (Table 2).

Thus, from a number of arguments in favor of the conclusion that the Kenkol burial place belongs to the Huns, palaeoanthropological data should be excluded. It does not follow from this that the palaeoanthropological data disprove Bernshtam's hypothesis. It is certainly possible that the Huns, after their arrival in Kirgizia, assimilated a large number of other peoples who were Europoid in physical type and non-Turkic in language. Available data do not contradict this hypothesis, but they do not confirm it.

Hence, palaeoanthropological materials from Kirgizia lead to the conclusion that an admixture of Mongoloid elements is found in the composition of the

TABLE 2

CRANIOMETRIC DATA ON THE HORIZONTAL PROFILE OF THE FACE IN THE ANCIENT POPULATION OF KIRGIZIA AND PAMIR AS COMPARED WITH THE REPRESENTATIVES OF VARIOUS PRESENT-DAY PHYSICAL TYPES

Ethnic groups	Sex	Naso-malar angle		Zygo-maxillary angle		Dacryon height		Simotic height		Angle of nose prominence	
Pamir Saka	M.	137.8°	(7)	123.9°	(8)	14.5	(8)	4.5	(9)	34.7°	(8)
	F.	137.6°	(3)	128.0°	(4)	12.6	(3)	3.6	(3)	30.7°	(4)
Kirgiz Saka	M.	143.6°	(6)	130.9°	(8)	13.0	(5)	4.2	(6)	31.0°	(4)
	F.	150.4°	(6)	129.7°	(4)	11.2	(3)	3.1	(4)	23.0°	(3)
Kirgiz Wu-suns	M.	143.1°	(8)	131.0°	(9)	12.3	(8)	3.4	(9)	26.0°	(11)
	F.	151.5°	(3)	137.5°	(4)	8.4	(3)	2.6	(3)	19.0°	(4)
Kirgiz Huns	M.	141.1°	(21)	130.7°	(21)	12.0	(22)	3.8	(22)	27.6°	(19)
	F.	140.3°	(14)	131.4°	(14)	10.5	(15)	2.9	(15)	22.9°	(13)
Kirgiz Turks (?) (5–8 cent.)	M.	145.9°	(10)	137.1°	(10)	10.7	(8)	2.7	(8)	22.4°	(7)
	F.	143.7°	(5)	131.9°	(5)	11.1	(6)	2.7	(6)	21.0°	(6)
Sogdians (?) of the Chu valley (11–12 cent.)	M.	139.2°	(9)	129.3°	(9)	11.8	(10)	4.9	(11)	29.7°	(3)
	F.	143.1°	(6)	130.6°	(5)	10.1	(5)	3.2	(6)	22.8°	(4)
"Nestorians" of Chu valley (13–14 cent.)	M.	142.4°	(10)	130.9°	(10)	11.6	(8)	4.0	(9)	29.6°	(8)
	F.	141.3°	(10)	125.2°	(11)	10.4	(9)	3.6	(9)	26.9°	(9)
Abkhazians	M.	138.7°	(33)	125.9°	(30)	13.0	(30)	4.8	(33)	31.1°	(28)
	F.	136.6°	(12)	123.2°	(11)	11.4	(13)	3.9	(11)	27.7°	(10)
Tashkent Uzbeks	M.	140.7°	(43)	130.4°	(42)	11.3	(44)	3.3	(44)	24.4°	(39)
	F.	143.5°	(13)	129.8°	(13)	10.0	(13)	2.7	(13)	23.9°	(9)
Western Buryats	M.	145.8°	(36)	141.4°	(36)	8.9	(35)	2.7	(36)	18.2°	(32)
	F.	145.1°	(27)	138.6°	(27)	8.0	(28)	2.4	(27)	18.4°	(24)
Tungus	M.	149.1°	(28)	141.6°	(28)	8.7	(28)	2.4	(28)	18.7°	(22)
	F.	149.9°	(27)	142.6°	(27)	7.6	(27)	1.8	(28)	14.4°	(21)

ancient population at least since Usun times. The heavy predominance of Mongoloid features characteristic of the modern Kirgiz came about later. Radical changes in the physical type of the ancient population of Kirgizia should be placed, according to Bernshtam's dating, in the 5th to 8th centuries A.D. These changes thus coincide with the formation of the Turkic khanate. The palaeoanthropological materials of this time are not numerous but very expressive. The flattening of face and nose is on the average not less than in the skulls of modern Kazakhs, although Ginzburg notes, with firm support, indications of variations in the structure of individual skulls. Mongoloid traits are also clearly expressed in several ancient skulls from the vicinity of Lop-nor in Sinkiang. These were obtained by S. Ye. Malov from burials that, in his opinion, belonged to an ancient, settled people.[23]

Yet, the settled population of the valleys of Kirgizia was characterized for a long time to come by preservation of characteristics of the ancient Europoid type —it continued to exist side by side with the Mongoloid aliens from Central Asia.

The skulls from graves in the Krasnorechensk site in the Chu valley,[24] dated to the 11th to 12th centuries, sharply differ from those of present-day Kirgiz graves. The same can be said about an even later series from a Nestorian cemetery of the 13th to 14th centuries. It is supposed that in this cemetery representatives of a Turkic people were buried. Inscriptions on the gravestones give sufficient grounds for this supposition. But in the physical type no more Mongoloid traits were observed than in the Wu-suns.[25] Recent additional investigations of the horizontal profile of these skulls confirmed this conclusion. If the Nestorians of the Chu valley were the ancestors of the present-day Kirgiz population of Frunze oblast, they were not the only ones by far and, numerically, by far not the dominating ones. It is doubtful whether their descendants represent even a tenth of the modern Solto tribe—the principal inhabitants of this area in our time.

In order to achieve maximum efficiency in the utilization of anthropological materials as a historical source, results of somatological investigations should be compared with palaeoanthropological ones. Such an undertaking encounters, however, a number of methodological difficulties. Palaeoanthropological skull measurements are difficult to compare exactly with those of the living. In the case of absolute dimensions a comparison does not present particular difficulties, as the average thickness of tegument generally can be determined with sufficient exactitude. But in those cases where traits are utilized for the delimitation of Europoid and Mongoloid types, direct comparison is either most difficult or simply impossible. An indirect approach must be employed.

For effective comparison of somatological materials with palaeoanthropological ones a craniological study of the present-day population is necessary. Provided the craniological series is closely related to the populace subjected to a somatological investigation, it then represents a "bridge," with the help of which a comparison of live observations and those on ancient skulls can be carried out.

Unfortunately, at present we do not have at our disposal a sufficiently representative series (i.e., one including the 19th century) of modern Kirgiz skulls. Some specimens, obtained in 1953 by the L. R. Kyzlasov archaeological expedition from a cemetery below Tokmak, can not be utilized with assurance for comparisons because of their insufficient number. We had to effect a comparison in a "roundabout fashion."

Differences between the Fergana Tadzhiks, investigated by the anthropological team of the Kirgiz Joint Expedition in 1953, and the Alar Buryats, investigated

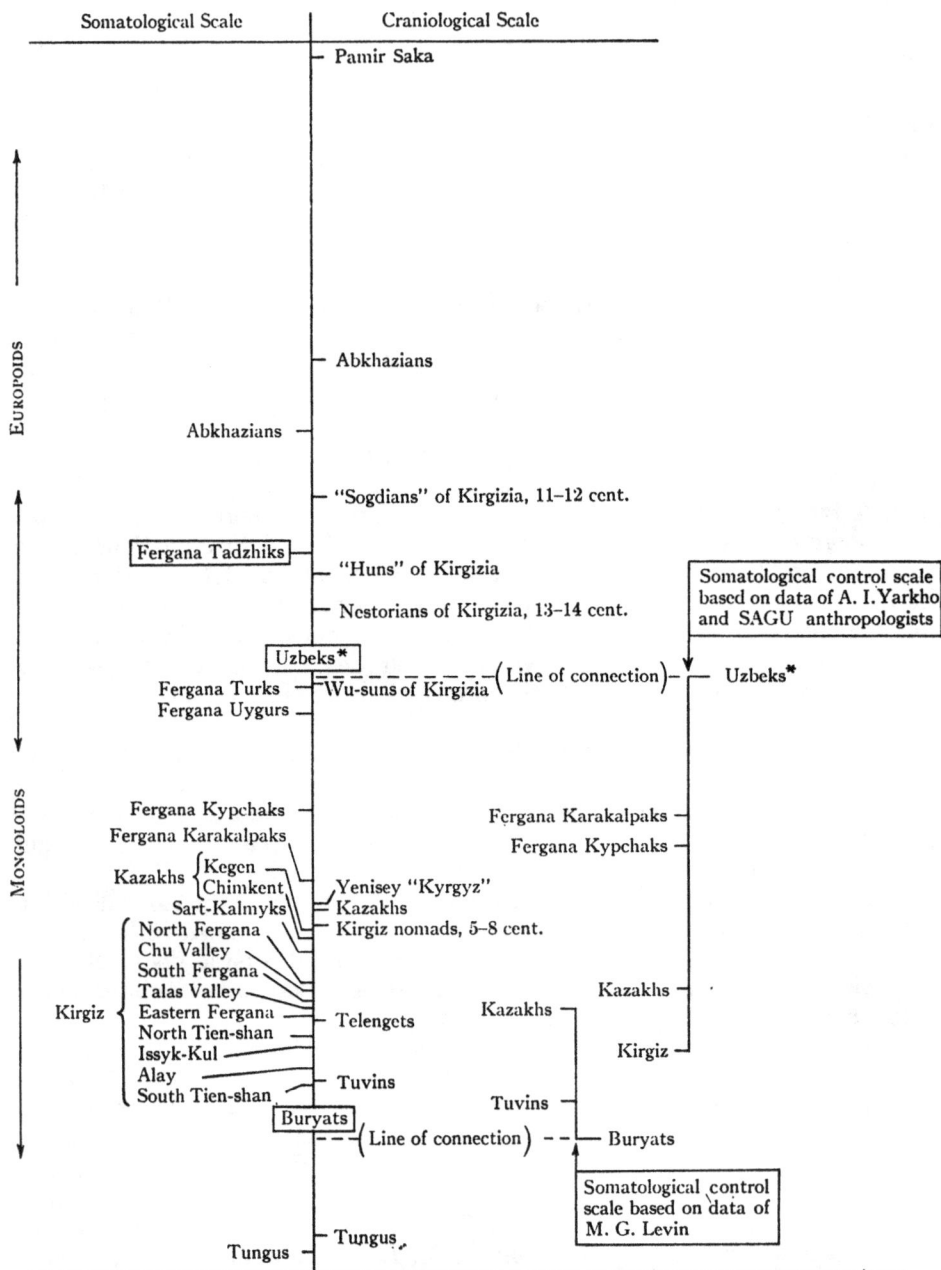

FIGURE 1.   Distribution of ancient and present-day groups of the population of Kirgizia and other regions on the basis of the degree of Mongoloid and Europoid traits.

*Clanless.

by the author in 1948,[26] were used as a qualitative scale for somatological comparisons. The differences were determined on the basis of those traits that indicated maximum diversity between the two groups. (See the article of I. M. Zolotareva in reference 31.) These traits were: beard growth, extent of chest hair, frequency of epicanthic fold, development of fold in the proximal section of eyelid, horizontal profile of face, prominence of cheekbone, height of nose bridge, transverse profile of the *dorsum nasi,* and the upper lip profile. The growth of eyebrows was not utilized, as there were serious doubts about the possibility of comparing determinations of 1948 and 1953. The index of 100 was taken as the difference between Buryats and Tadzhiks. On this basis, the difference of each group compared with the Buryats and Tadzhiks was determined (Fig. 1).

A number of western Buryat[26] and Uzbek skulls from Tashkent[27] were used as a scale for the craniological comparisons. Both series can be attributed with a sufficient degree of probability to populations within the same clan divisions as the somatologically investigated Buryats and clanless Fergana Uzbeks. Therefore, these series were utilized as basic material for the comparison of somatological and palaeoanthropological observations. The difference between the two series of skulls on the bases of naso-malar and zygo-maxillary angles, dacryon and simotic heights, and angle of protrusion of nose bones, was indexed as 100. Later, the position of the skull series being compared was determined on the basis of this standard. For control purposes, the position of the Tungus on the craniological and somatological scale was calculated. The coincidence was found to be almost complete. Further, for control of the extent of the diversity of the Buryat and Tuvinian skulls, the difference between Buryats and Tuvinian cattle-breeders was determined in accordance with live measurements taken by M. G. Levin.[28]

Buryats, investigated by the author and Levin, are conditionally regarded as one population in order to evade the influence of subjectivity in the determinations. It was found that the Tuvinians differ approximately equally from the Buryats on the basis of both the craniological data of the author and the somatological data of Levin. It is possible to go even further and to compare, using the accepted standards, the somatological and craniological observations on peoples even more remote from Central Asia. Figure 1 includes data on the Abkhaz investigated craniologically by M. G. Abdushelishvili[29] and somatologically by the same investigator with the direct participation of the author.[30] The coincidence in this case was also found to be completely satisfactory. Our data were finally compared with the data of other investigators of the physical make-up of middle Asiatic peoples. Uzbeks from Fergana valley within the same clan division were investigated by A. I. Yarkho and L. V. Oshanin and his pupils, and were compared with Uzbeks investigated by us.[31] Proceeding with this parallelism, the positions of other ethnic groups were determined, with almost complete coincidence of data. It should be noted, however, that such results were obtained only by summation [combination] of divergences in the data of Yarkho and Oshanin. If the data of each author are used separately, the results will be found to be somewhat different. The Kirgiz, investigated by Oshanin, were found to be even more Mongoloid than the Buryats. According to Yarkho, the Kirgiz definitely occupy an intermediate position with the Altayans and Tuvinians on one side and the Uzbeks on the other. This position should be taken into consideration in organizing future investigations that provide for direct comparison of the Kirgiz with peoples of Central Asia and southern Siberia. Notwithstanding, the data of both investigators give similar results in a comparison of Kirgiz and Kazakhs. From a study of Yarkho's data, as well as those of Oshanin and ours, the same conclusion is reached: Mongoloid features are more clearly expressed in the Kirgiz than in the Kazakhs.

The stated method for comparing craniological and somatological data (which method permits an evaluation of the degree of expressiveness of Mongoloid and Europoid features) thus produces completely satisfactory results.

Figure 1 gives an idea only of the morphological correlation of the groups compared, without taking into account their chronological position. In order to obtain a more complete idea of the time dimension, a second diagram was prepared (Fig. 2) where both morphological and chronological factors were taken into consideration. The proportion of Mongoloid elements in the composition of each group is determined on the same basis as in Figure 1. As a standard,

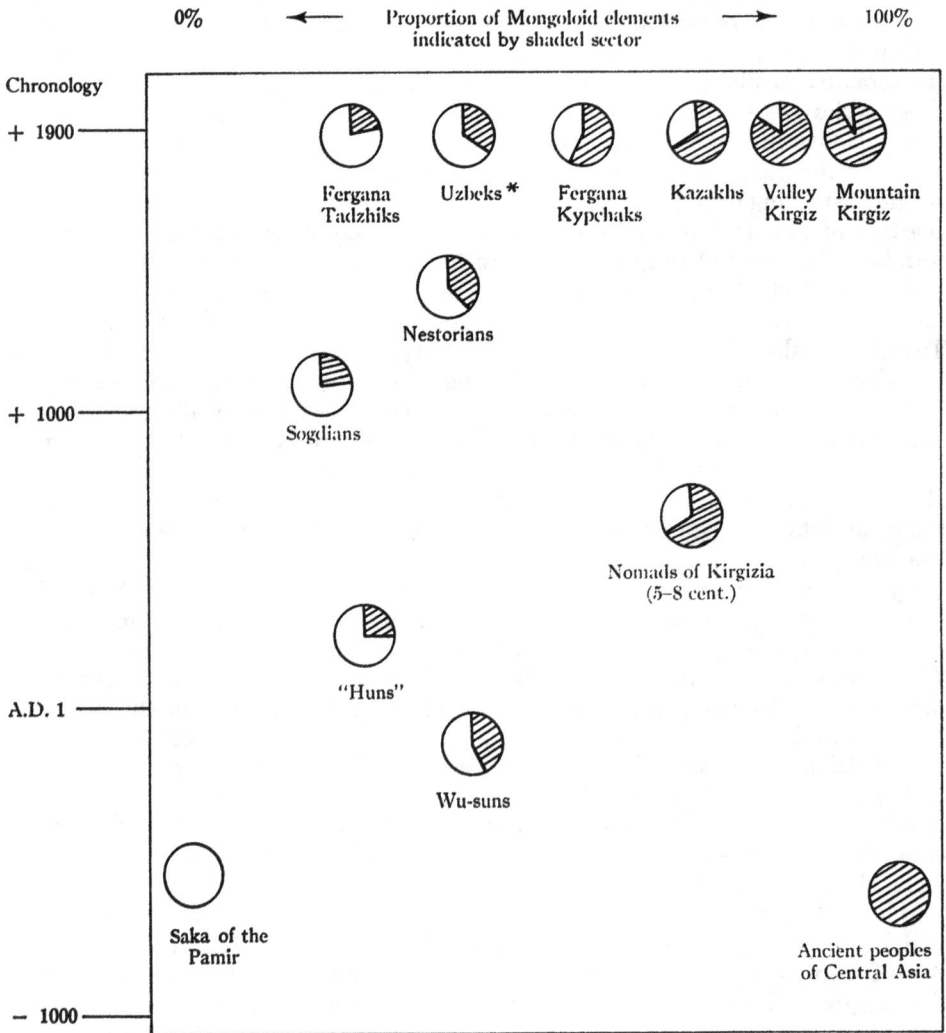

FIGURE 2. Diagram of the approximate proportion of Europoid and Mongoloid elements in the composition of the ancient and present-day populations of Kirgizia and adjoining regions.

*Clanless.

two groups contrasting in their morphological indicators were used: the Tungus and the Abkhaz. The proportion of Mongoloid elements is presumed to be 100 per cent in the first and 0 per cent in the second.

A comparison of palaeoanthropological and somatological data allows a number of conclusions, which we recommend to the attention of linguists, ethnographers, archaeologists, and historians who are working on the problem of the origin of the Kirgiz people.

1. The conclusion arrived at by the first investigators of the physical composition of Central Asiatic peoples, namely, that two basic elements participated in it, Central Asiatic Mongoloid and local Europoid, is, generally speaking, correct and should form the basis for further constructive works.

2. The most ancient of the physical types of Kirgizia known to us—the type of the Saka period—was characterized by the predominance of Europoid features. The conclusion of V. V. Ginzburg about the presence of "Andronovo" type traits, peculiar to the majority of skulls found in Kirgizia and belonging to that period, is well founded.

3. During the Saka period of Kirgizia, Mongoloid admixture was very insignificant but its existence may be admitted on the basis of a comparison of skulls of this period from Kirgizia with skulls of the same period found in the Pamir.

4. Admixture of Mongoloid elements becomes more noticeable in the Wu-sun period. Physiognomically the Wu-suns of Kirgizia resembled present-day clanless Uzbeks or Fergana Tadzhiks, that is, the Europoid features were still decidedly predominant in them.

5. The type of people who were responsible for Kenkol and other burials of that type, and who were distinguished by the custom of intentional skull deformation, was similar in facial structure to the Wu-suns. Notwithstanding repeated assertions to the contrary, the Mongoloid traits in these skulls were no more pronounced than in Wu-sun skulls. Physiognomically the Kenkol people, as other "Huns" and the Wu-suns as well, resembled present-day clanless Uzbeks or Fergana Tadzhiks.

6. Thus, the physical anthropological data do not establish sufficient grounds for ascribing to the Huns burial places with deformed skulls.

7. The Mongoloid admixture becomes more pronounced after the 5th century A.D. At that time Kirgizia was inhabited by people resembling the present-day Kazakhs. It should be noted that the Mongoloid traits were still less pronounced than in the Buryats or, particularly, in the Tungus.

8. Close to the above-mentioned type (basically Mongoloid, but with undoubted Europoid admixture) were the skulls of nomads from the later part of the Iron Age, found in Minusinsk *kray*. There are grounds for suspecting that these skulls belonged, at least for the most part, to the Yenisey "Kyrgyz." Physiognomically they also resemble most the present-day Kazakhs.

9. Thus, the Europoid admixture in the Yenisey "Kyrgyz" was no less pronounced than in the Tien-shan Kirgiz.

10. Consequently, it is very probable that some admixture of Europoid elements, which undoubtedly exists in the Kirgiz, already existed, at least partially, in the composition of those Central Asian nomads who participated in the formation of the Kirgiz people.

11. The ancient Europoid type continued to exist in Kirgizia for a long time after the mass migration of peoples from Central Asia. These peoples were characterized by Mongoloid traits. Even in the beginning of the second millennium A.D. people resembling present-day Tadzhiks lived in the Chu valley.

12. The overwhelming majority of the physical ancestors of the modern Kirgiz sprang from Central Asia.

13. Small differences in the physical type of the valley Kirgiz which differentiate them from the mountain Kirgiz allow the suggestion that the ancient Europoid population of these valleys entered, even if to a slight degree, into the composition of the Kirgiz people.

14. In order to bring greater exactitude to our ideas on the ethnogenesis of the Kirgiz people, it is first necessary to organize the following: (a) a collection of craniological materials of 19th and 20th century Kirgiz; (b) the organization of interdisciplinary investigations in the territory situated between the Tien-shan and Minusinsk basin, territory within the limits of the Chinese and Mongolian People's Republics and the Tuva Autonomous Oblast of the R.S.F.S.R.; (c) the collection of additional archaeological and palaeoanthropological materials on the Yenisey "Kyrgyz"; (d) the execution of a systematic comparative study of archaeological, ethnographic, and linguistic materials already collected, and their publication and comprehensive critical analysis in the press.

Notes and References

1. G. F. Debets, M. G. Levin, and T. A. Trofimova, Antropologicheskiy material kak istoricheskiy istochnik izucheniya voprosov etnogeneza (Physical anthropological material as a historical source for the study of ethnogenesis), Sovetskaya etnografiya, 1952, no. 1).

2. M. G. Levin, Antropologicheskiy tip Yakutov (Physical anthropology of the Yakuts), Kratkiye soobshcheniya Instituta etnografii, no. 3, 1947.

3. N. N. Miklashevskaya, Nekotorye materialy po antropologii narodov Dagestana (Selected materials on the physical anthropology of Dagestan), Kratkiye soobshcheniya Instituta etnografii, no. 19, 1953.

4. V. P. Alekseyev, Materialy po paleoantropologii naseleniya Minusinskoy Kotlovinv vremeni Tashtykskoy kultury (Palaeoanthropology of the population of the Minusinsk basin during the Tashtyk period), Kratkiye soobshcheniya Instituta etnografii, no. 20, 1954.

5. G. F. Debets, Paleoantropologiya SSSR (Palaeoanthropology of the U.S.S.R.), Moscow, 1948, pp. 136–145.

6. V. V. Ginzburg, Materialy po antropologii vostochnogo Kazakhstana (Materials on the physical anthropology of eastern Kazakhstan), Kratkiye soobshcheniya Instituta etnografii, no. 14, 1952.

7. D. N. Anuchin, Ob antropologicheskom tipe gunnov (On the physical type of the Huns), Trudy etnograf. otd. Obshchestva lyubiteley yestestvoznaniya, antropologii i etnografii (OLEAE), vol. 7, Moscow, 1886.

8. See: Debets, Paleoantropologiya SSSR, pp. 203–211, 214–225, 251–265.

9. See: G. F. Debets, Antropologicheskiye issledovaniya v Kamchatskoy oblasti (Anthropological investigations in the Kamchatka oblast), Moscow, 1951, p. 81.

10. S. Ye. Malov, Drevniye i novye tyurkskiye yazyki (Ancient and new Turkic languages), Izvestiya AN SSSR, otdel literatury i yazyka, vol. 11, no. 2, 1952.

11. N. A. Baskakov, Klassifikatsiya Tyurkskikh yazykov v svyazi s istoricheskov periodizatsiyey ikh razvitiya i formirovaniya (Classification of Turkic languages on the basis of the historical periodization of their development and formation), Trudy Instituta yazykoznaniya, vol. 1, 1952.

12. For a specialist this will not present any difficulty. Summarizing works on this subject are not known to me.

13. A. I. Yarkho, Kirgizy (The Kirgiz), in the collection Za industrializatsiyu Sovetskogo Vostoka, Moscow, Izdaniye Tsentralnogo byuro prosveshcheniya, 1934.

14. Bases for these conclusions are given in articles of N. N. Miklashevskaya and I. M. Zolotareva published in the collection cited in ref. 13.

15. V. V. Ginzburg, Materialy k paleoantropologii vostochnykh rayonov Sredney Azii (Materials on the palaeoanthropology of the eastern regions of Central Asia), *Kratkiye soobshcheniya Instituta etnografii*, no. 11, 1950.

16. V. V. Ginzburg, Drevneye naseleniye tsentralnogo Tyan-Shanya po antropolo- gicheskim dannym (The ancient population of the central Tien-shan on the basis of physical anthropological data), Sredneaziatskiy etnograficheskiy sbornik (Central Asiatic ethnographic collection), vol. I, *Trudy Instituta etnografii*, n.s., vol. xxI, 1954.

17. A. N. Bernshtam, Arkheologicheskiye raboty v Semirechye (Archaeological works in the Semirechye), *Kratkiye soobshcheniya Instituta istorii materialnoy kultury (IIMK)*, v, 1940, p. 46.

18. Bernshtam, *op. cit.*, p. 45.

19. See: V. V. Ginzburg and Ye. V. Zhirov, Antropologicheskiye materialy iz Kenkol- skogo katakombnogo mogilnika v doline reki Galas Kirgizskoy SSR (Anthropological materials from the Kenkol catacomb burials in the Galas valley, Kirgiz S.S.R.), *Sbornik muzeya antropologii i etnografii*, x, Leningrad, 1949.

20. A. N. Bernshtam, Osnovnye etapy istorii kultury Semirechya i Tyan-Shanya (Basic stages in the history of the Semirechye and Tien-shan cultures), *Sovetskaya arkheologiya*, 1949, vol. xI, pp. 359–360.

21. V. V. Ginzburg, Drevniye i sovremennye antropologicheskiye tipy Sredney Azii (Ancient and present-day physical types of Central Asia), in Proiskhozhdeniye chelo- veka i drevneye naseleniye chelovechestva (Origin of man and ancient populations), *Trudy Instituta etnografii*, n.s., vol. xvI, 1951, p. 382.

22. Ginzburg, Drevneye naseleniye tsentralnogo Tyan-Shanya . . . , p. 381.

23. A. N. Yuzefovich, Drevniye cherepa iz okrestnostey ozera Lobnor (Ancient skulls from the environs of Lop-nor), *Sbornik muzeya antropologii i etnografii*, x, 1949.

24. V. V. Ginzburg and V. Ya. Zezenkova, Cherepa iz mogilnika karakhanidskogo vremeni na Krasnorechenskom gorodishche v Chuyskoy doline (Skulls from the Karakhanid period burial place in the Krasnorechensk site in the Chu valley), *Kratkiye soobshcheniya Instituta etnografii*, no. xvII, 1952.

25. G. F. Debets, *Paleoantropologiya SSSR*, pp. 282–284.

26. G. F. Debets, *Antropologicheskiye issledovaniya v Kamchatskoy oblasti* (An- thropological investigations in Kamchatka oblast).

27. B. V. Firshteyn, Materialy k kraniologii uzbekov Tashkenta (Craniological materials of Tashkent Uzbeks), *Kratkiye soobshcheniya Instituta etnografii*, no. xIII, 1951.

28. M. G. Levin, K antropologii yuzhnoy Sibiri (Contributions to the physical anthro- pology of southern Siberia), *Kratkiye soobshcheniya Instituta etnografii*, no. xx, 1954.

29. Unpublished materials.

30. A. N. Natishvili *et al.*, Materialy ekspeditsii 1950 goda po antropologii sovremen- nogo naseleniya Gruzinskoy SSR (The 1950 expedition for the study of the physical anthropology of the present-day population of the Georgian S.S.R.) *Trudy In-ta eksperim. morfologii AN Gruz. SSR*, vol. iv, 1953.

31. A. I. Yarkho, Antropologicheskiy sostav Turetskikh narodnostey Sredney Azii (Anthropological composition of the Turkish peoples of Central Asia), *Antropologiche- skiy zhurnal*, 1933, no. 3. Part of the data on these groups was taken from the archives of the Institut antropologii MGU [Moscow State University]. See also: Idem, *Altaye- Sayanskiye Tyurki* (The Altay-Sayan Turks), Abakan, 1947; L. V. Oshanin and V. Ya. Zezenkova, *Voprosy etnogeneza narodov Sredney Azii v svete dannykh antropologii* (The ethnogenesis of Central Asian peoples in the light of physical anthropological data), Tashkent, 1953.

L. P. POTAPOV

THE ORIGINS AND ETHNIC COMPOSITION

OF THE KOYBALS[*]

THE QUESTION OF the ethnic origin and composition of the Koybals [Koibals] is part of the broader and more general problem of the origin and formation of the modern Khalka people. During our study of the origins of the modern Khalkas, we gathered and analyzed substantial historical material which allowed us, fairly accurately and many-sidedly, to throw light on the origins and ethnic composition of the Koybals. In prerevolutionary as well as modern historical-ethnographic literature, the Koybals habitually are presumed to be one of the Khalka tribes. N. Kostrov, one of the first investigators who devoted a special article to the Koybals, called them "a small tribe of nomadic foreigners [i.e., non-Russians] living in the Minusinsk okrug of Yenisey guberniya."[1] S. A. Tokarev also calls the Koybals "a Khakass tribe" and even finds blood kin organizations among them—the seoks.[2] However, there is no factual evidence for such a classification. On the contrary, the facts indicate that the Koybals constitute a small ethnic group formed comparatively recently, of complex origin, composed of diverse ethnic elements, and, finally, one that can certainly not be called a tribe.

The Koybals are first mentioned in Russian historical documents of the middle 17th century as "the Koybal ulus of the Tubin territory (zemlitsa) in Krasnoyarsk kray." The ulus was named for the Mator chieftain "Koybal," who at that time headed the so-called "stone" Mators. Russian officials first came in contact with the Mators in 1609 on the right bank of the Yenisey when the Mators together with the Tubans became Russian subjects and brought tribute in furs.[3] These new tax-paying volosts were situated "beyond the Kirgiz."[4] The Mators were fairly numerous for the 17th century among the local groups of people, who were characterized by the most varied descent and the most scattered ethnic elements. According to B. O. Dolgikh's calculations, they numbered about five hundred. As to their economy, they were divided between horse-riding cattle herders and trappers-hunters, living in the mountain forests. The latter were called the "stone" Mators, and lived along the upper reaches of the Kazyr and Amyl rivers, the Oya, and in places in the Kan river basin. They were living in the same regions in the 18th century, where they were found by E. Pesterev. The Mator herders led a nomadic existence in the Amyl valley, along the Tuba (or Up) river, and along the right bank of the Yenisey.

In the 17th century the Mators were grouped in the following uluses in the "Tubin territory":

1. The Koybal ulus, which according to the tax records included the largest group of Mators. The "stone" Mators are mentioned in 1685 as "kishtym to the Kirgiz, that is, taxpayers dependent on the Yenisey Kirgiz.[5] In 1690 the "stone" Mators were headed by the two sons of Koybal, Seren and Tebyuga, and their ulus was already called Turochakov (Taradzhakov) or Mador.

[*]Translated from Sovetskaya etnografiya, 1956, no. 3, pp. 35–51.

2. Shyshelek ulus, called after the chieftain Shishlek, paying tax in Krasnoyarsk while Andrey Dubenskiy was first governor of that city (1628–9).

3. Bugach ulus, called after the Tubin chieftain Bugach.

4. Karnaskham ulus.[6]

One must not confuse the Mators with the Mads or Matsk volost of the 17th century, as G. Müller did in the 18th century, and S. A. Tokarev in our own times.[7] The Mators spoke one of the Samoyed languages or dialects. After the death of Koybal the name of the Koybal ulus of the Mators disappears in the 17th century, and it only reappears in the 18th.

"Koybal Territory" in the 18th Century

In the 18th century documents known to us, the existence of the Koybal territory is established for the year 1711. In that year the Krasnoyarsk mounted cossack Grigori Begunov was sent in search of runaway taxed natives attached to the Abakan fort of the Krasnoyarsk Judiciary, who had escaped from Koybal to Mungal territory.[8] According to the tax records of 1718 there were 16 uluses in the Koybal territory, and in them there were 292 taxpayers.[9] In the historical documents there are no entries indicating when and how the Koybal territory took shape. There is no doubt, however, that it appeared after 1704, after the migration of the Yenisey Kirgiz into Dzungaria. It is established in the documents that "Ivan Zlobin with his men" was sent from Krasnoyarsk in 1704 to the Yenisey Kirgiz to collect tribute. At that time the Kirgiz had already been taken into Dzungaria, and Zlobin naturally did not find them in their usual nomadic encampments. Therefore, on returning to Krasnoyarsk, he related in his report: "None of the Kirgiz chieftains came out, but seven persons of the Tubins who had been left behind previously appeared." But Zlobin with his men visited some areas along the right bank of the Yenisey on this trip, with the result that, according to the above-mentioned report, they "in their zeal to secure payment of the tax to the Great Sovereign, searched for the various uluses of the Kirgiz and Tubin kishtym." In this document Zlobin enumerates these "various uluses" with a record of how much tax came from each. In this inventory are contained the following 16 uluses: Malyy Baykatovskiy, Kon, Sharodanov, Tatarov, Arshupov, Bolshoy Baykatovskiy, Urchin, Syskoy, Aska, Kaydynov, Ingara, Kaydynov [sic], Bugachev, Ship, Urgunov, and the remaining Tubins.[10] These were the same 16 uluses that, united into a special territory, were given the name Koybal. This is not hard to confirm if one compares the list of the uluses in the Koybal country made by G. Müller in Krasnoyarsk in 1735 with the list of Zlobin.[11] According to Müller's records:

the Koybal territory in the upper reaches of the Yenisey between the Abakan and Sayan forts is composed of the following uluses: (1) Maloy Baykotovskiy, 22 people; (2) Bolshoy Baykotovskiy 36 p.; (3) Tarachakov, 24 p.; (4) Arshupov, 10 p.; (5) Urchin, 5 p.; (6) Ingara, 11 p.; (7) Karnatskoy, 11 p.; (8) Kol, 7 p.; (9) Syskoy, 8 p.; (10) Aska, 3 p.; (11) Yardchi (Yerdchi) or Dzherchi, 10 p.; (12 Urgunov, 15 p.; (13) Bugachev, 11 p.; (14) remaining Tubins, 6 p.[12]

Thus it is clear that the Koybal territory was delimited by administrative fiat, by uniting the remaining former kishtym of the departed Kirgiz and Tubins. One should go into Müller's information about the uluses of the Koybal territory more thoroughly as he not only lists the names of the uluses, but also gives valuable data about their distribution and language. The first eight uluses of Müller's report, that is, Malyy Baykotovskiy, Bolshoy Baykotovskiy, Tarachakov, Arshupov, Urchin, Ingara, Karnatskoy, and Kol, are uluses that include a large part of the population of the Koybal territory. They were found along the Tuba river and on Lake Tazik-kol, the latter being situated some ten miles to the south of the Tuba river. The Syskoy ulus was in the headwaters of the Sid river, after which it was named, "as in local speech this river is called Si." The uluses Aska, Yardchi, Urgunov, and Bugachev were on the river Oye or Oe. The remaining Tubins (or the Tubin ulus), who according to Müller represented "the remnants of the Kirgiz who did so much damage in the Krasnoyarsk uyezd," had as their home the Abakan valley.

From the writings of Müller it is clear that, at that time, part of the Koybals were already living in the so-called Koybal steppe, which lies in the triangle between the Abakan river, the Yenisey, and the Item mountain range which forms the northern foothills of the Sayans. As for Müller's information on the Koybal language, the essentials are contained in the following remarks: The population of the Tarachakov ulus, he writes, speak in their own language and not in the Tatar (that is, Turkic), and "are called the Motors and Koybals after the names of their ancestors, the two brothers Koybal and Modor." Müller then notes that the populations of the Malyy and Bolshoy Baykotovskiy, the Urchin, Syskoy, Kol, Arshupov, and Ingara uluses speak the Kott language (that is, were at that time Ket speaking). The inhabitants of the Karnatskiy, Aska, Dzerchi, Urgunov, and Bugachev uluses spoke the Kamasin language (that is, were Samoyed speaking). Thus it is now established that the whole Koybal territory, shortly after its formation, was diverse in tongues and spoke Ket and Samoyed dialects, but not Turkic, with the possible exception of the "remaining" Tubans, who probably spoke Turkic if Müller took them for the remains of the Yenisey Kirgiz. This new evidence of the scientific literature, of a scholar who was occupied specifically with the study of questions of origins, language, culture, and economy of Siberian peoples, finally solves the problem of the mixed origin of the Koybals on the basis of the Samoyed-speaking and Ket-speaking ethnic components, with the preponderance of the latter as shown by the fact that the majority of the population was in the uluses listed as Ket speaking.

Somewhat later P. Pallas published a list of the uluses in the Koybal territory on the basis of data collected in the early 1770's. In this list are the very same uluses that the records of Zlobin and Müller contain, in some cases written with slight differences in transcription. The total number is one less than Müller's. This is explained by the fact that Pallas lists the Urgen ulus together with the Bugudzhi (Müller's Urgunov and Bugachev uluses).[13] According to Pallas the number of taxpayers in Koybal territory was already 239, but the total population was 400 persons. Pallas lists the uluses in the following order:

Between the Abakan and Yenisey were the uluses Tarachak, with 22 persons, Bolshoy Baygatol (36 p.), Karnat (32 p.), Urgen together with the Bugudzhi *aymak** or ulus (about 30 p.), Arshupov (23 p.). To the uluses of the Koybal territory on the eastern bank of the Yenisey belonged: the Syskov (15 p.), Askasov (8 p.), Kolskiy (16 p.), Angarov (31 p.); the Tubans and, included with them, the Mators (29 p); the Abugachev (16 p.), Archinskoy (25 p.), Maly Baygatol (42 p.).[14]

In addition there were 65 people living in this region who were associated with the Bolshoy Baygatol ulus.[13]

Müller and Pallas omit only four of the uluses listed by Zlobin. Of these, the Kaydynov ulus appeared as part of the Yarin territory.[15] But there are two uluses listed by Müller and Pallas that are absent in Zlobin's list, namely Tarachak and Karnatskoy. The first of these was inhabited by descendants of the 17th century "stone" Mators, formed into the Turochakov or Taradzhakov ulus, headed by the two sons of Koybal. The second was made up of descendants of a part of the population of the Karanat ulus, which had become part of the Udin territory of the Krasnoyarsk *uyezd* in the 17th century.

The data noted above, in particular those collected by Müller, make it possible to put on solid ground the ethnic composition of the Koybal territory in the 18th century. As almost all these uluses formed part of various territories in the 17th century, these same data bear significantly on the ethnic composition of several uluses of the 17th century tax-paying population. The Koybal ethnic conglomerate, which gave its name to the Koybal territory, consequently consisted of the remains of tribes that had, in the 17th century, formed into the uluses corresponding to the Tubin, Kashin, Kamasin, and Udin territories of that century. The Tarachak ulus consisted of descendants of the Turochak ulus of the 17th century Tubin territory, headed by the sons of the Mator chief Koybal. The 17th century Mators were also incorporated in the Kamasin territory. The populations of the Kol, Bolshoy, and Malyy Baykotov uluses were descended from the people of the uluses that were included under the very same names in the same 17th century Tubin territory. We find the Urgen and Bugachev uluses in the Kamasin territory of the 17th century. The Archi ulus was [occupied by] descendants of the Yargashina or Shalba ulus of the 17th century Kashin territory. The Karnat ulus made up part of the Udin territory in the 17th century.[16]

In the 18th century the population of the Koybal territory was strongly influenced by the Turkic-speaking Kachins, Sagay and Beltirs, and mixed with them. In the course of the 18th century the Kachin Turkic language became predominant here, and the Koybal uluses were already Turkic speaking by the beginning of the 19th century, although remains of Samoyed and Ket dialects were still preserved into the 19th century.

D. Messershmidt, who regarded the Koybals as kishtym Tatars, gives evidence of the mixture of the Koybals (as we shall now generally term the population of this territory) with the Beltirs and the Sagays in the 18th century. In that traveller's unpublished diary it is stated that:

As for the kyshtym Tatars, they lived in the forests, and their chief submitted to the Arinets and at the same time to the Russians. He is said to have been called 'Koybal' and for this reason part of these Tatars are called the 'koybal-kyshtym Tatars,' and are divided into various uluses, volosts or tribes, some of whom left with the Kirgiz, but many have remained here to the present. The chief tribe among them was the Beltir, living on the river Uybat, and paying tax in Kuznetsk. To this tribe were joined the uluses Bogochi, Modur or Modor, and also Kuramat, Yus-Sagaye and Baykotove. They are now living along the Uybat and Abakan rivers, and also along the Yenisey at Ust-Abakan.[17]

From this interesting communication, for which Messerschmidt acquired data by questioning the local population, we learn that a part of the Beltirs was living on the river Uybat at the beginning of the 18th century, that the Mators had already joined the Koybals at the very start of the 18th century, and that the Mator chief Koybal (as Müller also noted) had given his name to the ulus, and subsequently to the whole territory, and that this was known to the local people. In this connection we might once more emphasize how important and trustworthy local traditional legends are, for the origin of the ethnonym "Koybal" from the chief's name can not be doubted; it has been demonstrated in the documentary sources mentioned above.

The absorption of the Samoyed and Ket dialects by the Turkic language in all the uluses of the Koybal territory took place gradually and it was not until the 19th century that the Turkic language was fully dominant. Pallas found out that at the time of his trip in the early 1770's the Koybals and Mators, as well as the Karagas and Kamasins, had not entirely lost the Samoyed language. He wrote:

The Koybals with whom I became acquainted on this trip are a people entirely distinct from all the pagan Tatar-speaking people described up to this point; they differ not so much in their present dwellings and dress as in their appearance, speech, and consequently, origin. Their faces are for the most part similar to the Tungus, round and flat, but at the same time quite bearded. . . . Their speech closely resembles the Samoyed, and although a great deal of Tatar dialect is mixed with it, one can still easily distinguish the remains of the Samoyed apparent in the Koybal horde, in the Karagas, Kaymash and Motors living on the eastern side of the Yenisey and in the Soyots wandering in the mountains beyond the Russian border, so that it is altogether likely that all these are what is left of one people driven asunder and away from their own former dwellings towards the present northern Samoyed area. To prove the similarity of their languages it will suffice to cite those dialects that may be compared with the Mator, the closest of all to the Soyot (not known to me), as is uniformly affirmed by both the Mators and Koybals who trade with the Soyots along the frontier.[18]

Georgi, who found that the Koybals in appearance resembled the Samoyeds more closely than the Tatars, also claims that "Their language is a Samoyed dialect mixed with many Tatar words."[19] G. Spasskiy, who visited the Koybals at the very beginning of the 19th century, confirmed that even at that time the Koybals

are distinct in language and appearance from the neighboring peoples, in this resembling the inhabitants of distant Siberia, such as the Samoyeds and Ostyaks. Although a considerable number of Tatar words are found in their speech, it is easy to see that these words did not originally belong to them but have been adopted either because they express objects that were unknown to the Koybals before they came to know the Tatars, or because they were easy to pronounce. The Koybals of the Kol ulus have a somewhat peculiar speech, unlike either the Koybal or the Tatar.[20]

Spasskiy, as is known, compiled dictionaries of the Koybal and Mator languages at the time of his trip. We have found them in the manuscript files of the Leningrad public library. The dictionaries clearly support the opinions of Pallas, of Spasskiy himself, and of others that the Turkic language replaced the Samoyed and Ket dialects among the Koybals.

The diverse origins and varied ethnic composition of the Koybals is reflected in their culture and economy. Pallas called attention to some traits of the Koybal culture similar to those of the Samoyed-speaking Kamasins: "Formerly they particularly resembled the Kaymash rather than the neighboring Tatars in the action and dress of their *volkhvi* (shamans—Author)."[21] This referred to the shaman's costume with a breastpiece, innumerable iron pendants, and a cap ending in iron reindeer horns, as well as to the shaman's drum. Religious traditions are the most lasting and conservative. They continued to exist among the

Koybals, bearing witness to the former common ground of their culture with that of the Kamasins. In the report of the Krasnoyarsk officer Kyrill Khudonogov "The settlement of the Koybal territory" (compiled in 1737), the following is said about the life and culture of the Koybals: "They are people [living] opposite the Kan territory." This signifies that the Koybals were not distinct in their way of life and economy from the Kotts, who are described as taiga hunters in a similar document of those times. On the other hand, there were herders and farmers among the Koybals, since they inhabited not only the mountain-taiga areas, but also the steppes. According to I. Fisher, "the Koybals live along the Abakan and Tuba rivers, also in the taiga."[22] From this we may conclude that part of the population ascribed to the Koybal territory lived in steppe areas. This information is fully supported by Müller's fragmentary remarks about some aspects of Koybal culture and economy. He notes that one finds dwellings of felt as well as birch bark among the Koybals since there are those among them who are strongly interested in cattle raising. In another place Müller compares the Koybal type of cattle raising with that of the Barabinsk Tatars, noting the preponderance among the Koybal herds of horses and large horned cattle, and the insignificant numbers of sheep.[23] E. Pesterev corroborates the same in some detail; he says that the Koybals nomadize along the right bank of the Abakan, and along the lower Biya, Dabat, and Ut. Formerly these nomads had fine herds, many were rich, but then smallpox killed off a great many, and lack of hay brought about loss of cattle. Their horses were small but hardy. These nomads do a little farming, but the most energetic farmer among them does not cultivate more than half a *desyatina* of land [desyatina = 2.7 acres]. They store hay only for the sheep. As for the horses and cattle, they graze all winter on the steppe, as there is little snow there. The Koybal hunt along the course of the three Kebesh, the Oe, Amyl, Kandant, and Shedat and their tributaries, which are all right tributaries of the Yenisey. The sables here are not good. All the Koybals are Christians.[24] Pallas also writes of Koybal herders, farmers, and hunters. Here are some isolated quotations from his description of the occupations and economy of the Koybals, on the basis of his own observation. The Koybals

are not very rich in herds, but by good hunting and careful farming they live comfortably and there are those among them who have up to one hundred horses. . . . They use a Russian (wooden) plow, which they call in their own language *saban*; [they] sow more grain than they need and sell the surplus to the neighboring Tatars. From this, and from all that they do, it is easy to see that they are altogether alien to the Tatar character. . . . Many of them have wooden houses for the winter, and of those who live in yurts, some keep chickens.[25]

Pallas informs us that the Koybals gathered and harvested wild buckwheat growing in the large fields where they lived along the right bank of the Yenisey. The seeds they roasted in cast-iron bowls and ground in wooden mortars. With the groats they cooked a porridge with milk. They gathered wild flax and nettles in great quantities and made cord from these. The Koybals lived in a sedentary fashion. In the summer they moved from their wooden houses to yurts, although some of them lived in yurts in the winter also. The yurts were of the Kachin type. Koybal clothing was a mixture of Kachin and Russian. Many of the unbaptized men wore a pigtail; some wore a headdress of Mongol type. Georgi characterizes the Koybals as herders and notes their possession not only of sheep but also of camels. At the same time he emphasizes the Koybal fondness for hunting.[26]

As was mentioned above, some Mators, descendants of the 17th century Mators, were also present in the Koybal territory of the 18th century. In the 18th century they had split into several groups. One of these lived along the upper reaches of the Kan river and comprised the Tatar ulus of the Kamasin territory in which there were 12 taxpayers. Referring to this ulus, Müller commented as follows: "Of these the majority are Modors, whom the Kamans call *Modor-sang*, and the Tatars *Modorlar*." In addition, Müller noted that the inhabitants of the Tagin ulus in the Kan territory (called by the Kamans *Nigisang* and by the Tatars *Takalar*) who lived along the upper Kan "have a common language with the Modors, distinct from the Kamashin language."[27] A second group of Mators [also] was a part of the Koybal territory. In 1735, Müller related that the population of the Tarachakov ulus in the Koybal territory called themselves Mator and spoke their own language, but not Tatar (that is, not Turkic). Along with several other uluses of the Koybal territory, Tarachakov ulus was found along the river Tuba at this time. These Mators were descendants of the population of the Tarachakov ulus of the Tubin territory in the 17th century. The Mators probably appeared on the lower Tuba as a result of their removal from the mountains beyond the Sayan ridge; the Russian authorities wished to remove the tax-paying population as far as possible from the border to be established between Russia and China, so that they would pay taxes to Russia. As a matter of fact when this border was drawn in 1727, the majority of the Mators turned out to be Chinese subjects all the same and were included among the Soyots, ancestors of the present-day Todzhin Tuvins. Thus, in the 18th century the most numerous group of Mators was located beyond the Sayans; however, in the Koybal territory there was still a small group of the population that called itself "Motors." They lived in the mountains near the Shedat outpost on the river Karatuz, which flows into the Amyl (one of the rivers that forms the Tuba). It is unknown so far to what ulus this third group of Mators belonged in 1735 when Müller was in the Krasnoyarsk uyezd. It is most likely that it belonged to the Tarachakov ulus, since it was the population of this ulus in the Koybal territory about which Müller wrote that it called itself "Motor." However, by the time of Pallas the picture is different. Here, 37 years after Müller's visit, the Tarachakov ulus is found together with some other uluses between the Abakan and Yenisey, that is, on the west side of the Yenisey. Part of this ulus, however, probably remained in the Tuba-Amyl basin as formerly, and continued to call itself "Mator"; it was about these that Pallas wrote: "Sie nennen ihren Aimak selbst Mator."[28] But, judging by Pallas, the Mators now belonged to the Tubin ulus, since in his inventory of the uluses in Koybal territory he writes: "die Tubinzen, worunter itzt die Motoren mit inbegriffen sind, von 29."[29]

In 1760 there were 30 tax-paying Mators. Soon after this they were decimated by smallpox, and in 1772, at the time of Pallas' visit, there were only 10 families. Eighteenth century investigators judged the Koybals, together with the part of them situated in Tuva, by their economy, language, and religious belief to be "the remains of a Samoyed tribe."[30] According to Pallas' description:

in behavior and dress they do not greatly differ from the Kaybals, poor, with few herds of cattle, they live by hunting and working for the rich Kashin Tatars; they do not farm, but gather *sarana* [martagon, day lily], which they dry and mix, powdered, with any kind of food. It has been thirty years since they have been baptized; formerly they placed their dead between three planks in the trees. They cover their yurts with birch bark, and for warmth in winter they fill them with hay. The doors face east.[31]

E. Pesterev, visiting them in 1773–4 near the Shedat guardhouse, wrote that:

they eat day lilies, adder's tongue, and peonies. They have no agriculture but they buy a little flour and groats from the Russians, which they take with them when hunting. They hunt along the Amyl river and its tributaries, and like the Kandins (that is, Kaydins—Author), they use birch-bark boats. They have few horses and cattle, are very poor, but do not complain of their fate. They pay tax in money to the Krasnoyarsk collectors.[32]

Pesterev also notes here that "the Motors have no domestic (domesticated—Author) reindeer." In 1806, G. Spasskiy visited the Mators, and he was the first to compile a dictionary of the Koybal and Mator languages. Spasskiy found two very old Mators who knew their language very well. "These dictionaries," wrote Spasskiy, "entirely uphold the resemblance between these languages and the Samoyed."[33] ". . . They nomadize along the upper Karatus rivulet and near the Shadat outpost. Their ulus consists of only 20 very poor yurts. A few of them work for the Kachins. The Mators have almost abandoned their natural tongue. . . . They are small in stature, with faces pale and emaciated; but this may be due to their slovenliness and poor diet."[34]

At the beginning of the 19th century the uluses became consolidated. The Koybal territory consisted then not of 14 or 15 uluses, as was the case in Pallas' time, but of 6. The population was not 400 (according to Georgi, 415), but 528, [composed as follows:] Bolshoy Baykotovskiy (138 people), Malyy Baykotovskiy (88), Kol (138), Tarazhakov (95), Abugachev (95), Arshi (60).* These figures are from the Fifth Survey of 1794. From this it is evident that the Koybal uluses had become larger. For instance in the Kol ulus there were 138 persons, instead of 16. The following uluses had ceased to exist officially: Karnat, Urgen, Bugud-zhi, Arshupov, Syskov, Askasov, Angarov, and Tubin. They were distributed among the remaining uluses, as is evident from the fact that, in 1847, M. A. Castren put down their names as "tribal" names (e.g., Ingara, Ingen, Begedi, Toda, Karnat). More will be said about these later.

The Koybal Steppe Duma† in the 19th Century

The new administrative organization was strengthened by the reforms of 1822,[35] when the Koybal Steppe Administration was established. It consisted of seven uluses. In addition to the consolidated uluses referred to above (data of the Fifth Survey), the Kandykov ulus was included, which previous to the reform had belonged to the Yarin territory. Thus the structure of the Koybal Steppe Duma at the time of its organization was as shown in Table 1. The settlement of Uty on the left bank of the Yenisey was the administrative center.

Under the new administrative division, the Mators living near the Shedat outpost were registered with the Kachin Steppe Duma, whose administrative center was near the mouth of the Abakan in the foothills of the Izykh.[36] This change was brought about because the "Shedat Mators" lived considerably closer (about 100 km) to the center of the Kachin Duma than to the Koybal. It has not yet been established into which ulus of the Kachin Duma this group of Mators was incorporated. It is known that, with the development of gold mining in the Amyl basin, the village of Karatuz developed in the locality of the Shedat

* [Figures add to 614, not 528.—Editor.]
† [In this case, a council-governed territory.—Editor.]

TABLE 1

Tribal government or ulus	Number of persons		Tribute in rubles
	Herders and hunters	Nomadic farmers	
Tarazhakov	142	—	194
Kol	52	—	101
Abugachayev	85	—	155
Malo-Baykotov	89	—	184
Bolshe-Baykotov	129	—	213
Kandykov	52	—	81
Arsha	45	—	142
Totals	594	—	1070

outpost in the early 1830's and became the administrative center of this gold-mining region. Subsequently the Mators settled in this Karatuz region on the river Kunduluk, where they founded a settlement in 1832, which received the name "Matorskoye," and gradually became Russianized. This is why Castren did not find any Mators at the Shedat outpost on his trip in 1847 in the Karatuz and Amyl territory.

According to the data of 1827, the population of this Duma consisted of 1292 persons of both sexes, of whom by far the greater majority were counted officially as Christians (only 200 persons of both sexes were counted as shamanistic). At that time most of the population lived in yurts, which numbered 256. The main occupations of the people were cattle herding and hunting. In seven uluses of the Duma the following animals were listed: 701 horses, 1122 cows, 3553 sheep.[37] In the first official statistics at our disposal, agriculture is not reported although it already existed among the Koybals. The boundaries of the Koybal Duma were defined as follows:

Along the left bank of the Yenisey beginning at the Shushenskoye volost from Ozna-chennoye village downstream to the juncture of the tributary Abakan, flowing from the same [volost?—Editor], then along the right bank of the Abakan river from its mouth . . . and as far as its juncture with a channel connecting the Abakan with this same Yenisey; the adjacent meadows belong to the Koybal aliens.[38]

Thus it is established that the Koybal Steppe Duma kept the former structure of administrative clans or uluses whose ethnic origin we have just clarified. It should be added that the study of the tribal structure of the Koybals made by traveling scholars in the 19th century fully confirms our conclusions made on the basis of historic and ethnographic materials. M. A. Castren,[39] visiting the Koybals as well as a number of other groups living in the Minusinsk basin in the middle of the 19th century for ethnographic and linguistic studies, noted that the Koybals considered themselves the earliest inhabitants of the country. He identified among them a number of tribes that he understood were related by blood, and he took their names for tribal autonyms originating among blood-related tribes. In Castren's notes we find the following tribes: Bolshoy and Maly Baygado (Bay), Kang, Taradzhak, Toda, Mador, Kel, Ingara, Bëgëdy, Irgen, Arshy, Keyek, and Kaydeng. But it is easy to see that Castren wrote down as authentic tribal names what were really only the names of the 17th and 18th century uluses out of which the Koybal territory had been organized—and later the Koybal Steppe Duma. It may be that in fairly old and stable names of uluses there might be preserved tribal or even family names, as in Mador or Mator, Toda or Chota, Baygodo Bögödzhi. However, as we noted above, the Russian names of tax-paying uluses recorded in the official documents, and above all in the tax records, do not by far correspond with the authentic autonyms of this or that tribal-family group. In the given case, for example, the tribal name Kang may simply serve as the name of the Kan territory, to which the ancestors of this tribe were attached in the 17th century. The name Kaydeng is apparently synonymous with the term Kaydyn, which is derived from the Kott chieftain Khaytyn, or Khayton, and so on.

Castren thought that the majority of the Koybals were of Samoyed origin, but some tribes, the Baygoda and Kaydeng, were Yenisey-Ostyak. Actually most of the Koybals came from a Ket-speaking population related to the Kotts, as Müller ascertained soon after the organization of the Koybal territory. On the basis of ethnographic and linguistic data, Castren came to the conclusion that the Koybals had a common origin and close ethnic ties with the Karagas and the Soyot-Tuvins, and also that all these groups were of Samoyed origin ethnically.[40] This conclusion is only correct in a general sense. A more detailed study of the Koybals, Karagas, and Tuvins reveals their more complex origin, without, however, contradicting the fact that the Samoyed-speaking ethnic elements in their composition appear to be the basic ones.

The organization of the Koybal Steppe Duma with the same ulus structure that for a century had been characteristic also of the Koybal territory helped form and develop the geographical, linguistic, and cultural community of the Koybals. The foundations for this community had already been laid among the 18th century Koybals under the influence of their change to a sedentary way of life, a common administrative control, and the side-by-side living and intermixing of uluses of different origins. Even then the territory populated by the Koybals had been defined, their numbers grew, new settlements sprang up and were developed, and general characteristics of their economy, community, and household living were formulated. At that time also the Turkic language became predominant, gradually replacing the Samoyed and Ket dialects. During the 19th century the process of consolidation of the Koybals progressed, especially after the administrative reforms of 1822. Also, in the 19th century the Koybals were drawn into another and more general process of consolidating the population of the Minusinsk basin. They developed a common language, culture, and life with the Kachins, Beltirs, and Sagays. This process had actually begun in the 18th century, when the Kachin felt yurt already existed among the Koybals as affirmed by Müller and Pallas, and their clothing, in the words of Pallas, was a mixture of Kachin and Russian. As among the Kachin, some men wore a pigtail and Mongolian headdress. In the course of the 19th century the cultural and economic development of the Koybals proceeded in two directions. The Koybals most readily adopted from the Russian peasants who lived with them or near them elements of their economy and household living. But in general all that differentiated the Koybals from their Russian neighbors was the same as that which differentiated the Kachins, Beltirs, and Sagays.

The establishment of a common language, culture, and economy among the Koybals, Kachins, and Sagays was assisted by the fact that the Koybal Steppe Duma was abolished in 1858.[41] Its administrative tribes or uluses were divided between the Sagay (or, as it was officially called, the Duma of United Tribes of Diverse Origins) and the Kachin Steppe Dumas. Five tribes—the Tarazhak, Bolshe-Baykotov, Abugachiyev, Kol, and Arshi—were combined into one Koybal tribe and assigned to the Duma of United Tribes of Diverse Origins (the Sagay), but the Kandykov and Malo-Baykotovskiy tribes, geographically distant from the others (since they had been resettled along the Tuba and Salba), were united into a Salbino-Koybal tribe, which was assigned to the geographically much closer Kachin Duma.

In the light of the historical facts cited above we have a basis for the claim that the Koybals, like the Sagays,[42] were not a tribe. They were a numerically small ethnic conglomerate created through administrative manipulations from diverse tribal and linguistic elements. However, as a result of the adaptation of a sedentary life and of living in common with others, this conglomerate gradually acquired a common language, culture, and economy, first under the strong influence of the Kachins and later of the Sagays. Subsequently, and particularly in the 19th century, the Koybals were involved in the general process of consolidation of the Khalka peoples, who were also formed of ethnic elements quite diverse in language and origin, on the basis of the Kachin Turkic language. The consolidation of the Khalka people proceeded under the strong and beneficial influence of Russian national culture, and its essential character was formed by the time of the October revolution.

Below is appended a dictionary of the Koybal language, compiled by Spasskiy.[43]

Supplement

Dictionary of the Koybal language collected in 1806 by Grigory Spasskiy, Member of the St. Petersburg Society of Amateurs of Science, Language, and the Arts*

B

Baba, zhenshchina	woman	ne
Baran	ram	kucha*
Bezdetny	childless	assizet
Bezzuby	toothless	timazet
Bezpamyatny	without memory	sagaiset
Bezrogi	hornless	amnyzech
Bereza	birch	kuyu
Beresta	birch bark	so
Bich, plet	whip	kamdzhi*
Bleyu	bleat	sederla
Bliznetsy, dvoyni	twins	ikere
Blokhi	fleas	kazaptyuk
Bludodeyaniye	adultery, prostitution	sero
Bludny syn, vyblyadok	prodigal son	suras*
Bluzhu v tayge	I wander in the forest	dzhyurzulyam
Blyudo	dish	tabak*
Beru	I take	ilyam
Blyuyu	I guard, I keep	sederbam
Bober	beaver	sade
Bogaty	rich	bay*
Bogateyu, bogat delayus	I grow rich	baimnagam*
Bog	god	kudai
Bodlivy	inclined to butt, to gore	syuskyu
Boloto	bog	sas*
Bolny	ill	inzide
Bolshi	big	urga
Boroda	beard	sagal
Borozda	furrow, trench	ade
Boryusya	I struggle	dzhyabdollam
Bosy	barefoot	dzhyalam*
Boyusya	I fear	pymlyam
Branyusya	I quarrel	kudollam
Brat bolshi	big brother	kagam

*[For explanation of diacritical marks see note on p. 166. Also, at this point the reader is referred to entry 43 in the "Notes and References" on p. 168.—Editor.]

Brat maly	little brother	pabim
Brezhu	I talk deliriously (nonsense)	dzhyudrim
Bratya	brothers	pidibe
Brov	brow	kumuske*
Brosayu	I throw	bablam
Bryukho	belly	nany
beremennaya zhenshchina	pregnant woman	nanezbe
Buzhu	I awake	sudurlyam
Byk	bull	buga*
Byu rukami	I beat with my hands	toblam
Begayu	I run	ityrlyam
Bely	white	syry
Belka	squirrel	tyzyp

V

Valyayu	I knead	tyrdylyam
Varyu	I cook	pădlam
Vash	your	se
Vedu	I lead	pogonla
Vezde	everywhere	ibre
Vezu k sebe	I bring	lyatygam
Vezu ot sebya	I take away	kunaldygam
Verevka	rope, cord	konye, uru
Verchu	I turn around	paidlyam
Versha, morda	creel, muzzle	kȳr*
Verkhova loshad	saddle horse	dzhalan*
Verkh	upper part, top	nygnan
Veslo	oar	iski
Vesna	spring (season)	byudyun
Vecher	evening	nyude
Vznuzdyvayu	I bridle	pydla
Vizhu	I see	kubam
Vizhdu	I yell, scream	nrarlam
Vino	wine	arga*
Vinopitsa, pianitsa	wine drinker, drunkard	izryl
Vintovka	rifle	multyk
Vikhr	whirlwind	kuyun
Vishu	I hang	adlya
Vmeste	together	obri
Vnuk	grandchild	asen asen
Voda	water	bū
Vodovorot	whirlpool	kailgak
Vozvrashchayu, otdayu nazad	I return, give back	pyudyumlya
Vozdykhayu	I sigh	tynarem
Volk	wolf	măkně
Voldyr, vered	blister, abscess	koch
Volna, val	wave, roll	shalga*
Volos	hair	abde
Volshebnik, sheman	magician, shaman	tarbe
Von	out, away	ubda
Voruyu	I steal	dzhyapdolla
Vor	thief	tole
Vorona	crow	bare
Voron	raven	kule
Vorochayu	I turn, roll	parla
Vorchu	I grumble	nardla
Vostok	east	bla
Vot	here, there	de
Vosh	louse	uně
Voyu, plachu	I howl, weep	dzheorla
Vperedi	in front of, before	dzhyardygandy
Vse	all	bar

Vstayu	I get up	ublam
Vstrechayu	I meet	udurbde
Vtykayu, tychu	I thrust in(to)	nublya
Vchera	yesterday	talyn
Vverkh podnimayu	I lift up	mnellyam
Vybivayu, vyshibayu	I beat or knock out	sabyĭ obdem
Vyvikhivayu sostav	I dislocate a joint	dzhyu-duk-dube
Vyvorachivayu	I turn (inside) out	pyuryuldle
Vygonyayu	I drive out	mangorla
Vydra	otter	tpyat
Vyigryvayu	I win	utarbam
Vykapyvayu	I dig out	tyllyaplya
Vynimayu	I take out	sabyllyailya
Vydirayu	I tear out	itchily̆am
Vezu	I take along, transport	kunadlagam
Vypryagayu	I unharness	ubdllam
Vysoki	high	pritse
Vychishchayu	I clean	ardyrlam
Vyu	I twist, wind	taymydlyam
Vetv, suk	branch, twig	mu
Veter	wind	byrsy̆
Veter poludenny	south wind	tusbyarsy
Veter zapadny	west wind	arakbyarsy
Veter severny	north wind	takarbyarsy*
Veter gorny	mountain wind	myyanbyarsy
Veter protivny	contrary (cross) wind	kayanbersy*
Veshu	I weigh	adlyam
Vy	you (pl.)	s(y)e
Veyu	I blow	aksubla
Vyazhu	I tie	sarla

G

Galka	jackdaw	tan
Gvozd	nail	bozuk*
Gde	where	kudegan*
Gde nibud	somewhere	kydenynda
Glazhu	I smoothe	sibapidbam
Glaz	eye	sima
Glina	clay	se
Glozhu kost	I gnaw a bone	tugulam
Glotayu	I swallow	pinzillya
Glotok	a swallow, mouthful	pooldola
Gluboki	deep	pudu
Glupy	stupid	alykh*
Glukhi	deaf	usker*
Gnida	nit	tārš
Gnily	putrid, rotten	pysva
Gniyu	I rot, decay	tyaplyaganda-ga
Gnoy	pus, matter	te
Gnevayusya, serzhusya	I am angry	korolya
Gnezdo	nest	pide
Govoryu	I talk	nyurblyam
God	year	pe
Godovy	annual	opsube
Golik	besom, broom	pudyul
Golova	head	ulu
Golodny	hungry	piola
Golos	voice	kuryu
Goly	naked	tyrzet
Golenishche	bootleg	trey*
Gonyayusya	I chase	mingorla
Gora	mountain	myya
Gorki	bitter	namzyde

Gorlo	throat	agman
Gorodba	fence, enclosure	chikden*
Gorst	handful	pam
Gorshok	pot	kudesh*
Goryu	I burn	amolam
Goryachi	hot	dzhibde
Gospodin	lord, master	kŏň
Gospodinova zhena	master's wife, mistress	minzech
Gost	guest	alzhe*
Gotovlyu	I prepare	belechrem
Gotovy	ready	bilen*
Grabli	rake	tarbosh
Grad	hail	tebei*
Greben	comb	typsen
Grebu veslom	I row with an oar	tukblā ām
Grib, gubka	mushroom, sponge	mishke
Griva	mane	kundu
Grom	thunder	kayan
Grudi, titki	breast, teat	nyuyu
Grud sosu	I suckle	nyuyu nemerlya
Gryzu	I gnaw	blalam
Greyu	I warm, heat	ayumlya
Gryaz	mud	balgash*
Guba	lip	monda
Gulyayu	I take a walk	edaylyam
Gusty	thick, dense	nalgo
Gus	goose	tāzy
Gushcha	thicket	nalgot
Gremlyu	I roar, make noise	kuremdlya

D

Da, tak	yes, just so	yaa dyrget
Davlyusya	I choke	suktulyam
Davno	long ago	kondzhyugan
Daleko	far	kunga
Dan, yasak	tax, tribute	alban melya
Darom vozmi	take it for nothing	ttrogit
Dayu	I give	melyam
Dver	door	ai
Dvor	courtyard	kazhi*
Den	day	dzhyala
Dengi	money	akcha*
Derevnya	village (countryside)	tirra
Derevo	tree	pa
Derzhu	I hold, keep	dzhyabolam
Deru	I tear, whip	nyngylyam
Deshevo	cheap	syumka
Diki	wild	imnik
Dyra, skvazhina	hole, chink	si
Dlya chevo	for what	mola
Dobry	good	dzhyakshi*
Dozhd	rain	suruno
Dolgi	long	numo
Domovy	household (adj.)	matzibe
Dom, yurta	house, yurt	mach
Doroga	road	ade
Dorogo	dear, expensive	sede
Doska	board	tchyardy*
Dostayu	I obtain	ilya*
Dayu	I give	urdem
Dremlyu	I doze	konoldam
Drovni, sani	sledge, sled	shor*
Drozhu	I tremble	kaldyrlya

Drug	friend	naydzhi*
Dumayu	I think	tenlya
Duyu	I blow	tublya
Dym	smoke	syunë
Dyshu	I breathe	tynarlam*
Devitsa, devushka	girl	kobdo
Delayu	I do, make	palem
Delyu	I divide, share	taarlam
Deti	children	a se
Detorodny ud muzheski	genitalia, male	kĭ
Detorodny ud zhenski	genitalia, female	pe
Dolzhnik	debtor	aly*
Dogonyayu	I overtake	bidibyam

E

Esli	if	igábe
Eshche	still, yet	bazy*
El	fir, spruce	sy

ZH

Zhavoronok	lark	karachagay*
Zhadny	greedy	kadzhyalu*
Zhazhda, pit khochu	thirsty, I wish to drink	byubyuttam
Zhaluyusya	I complain	namanyzlem
Zharenoye myaso	roast or fried meat	dzhyapsy no uya
Zharki	hot	dzhibide
Zharyu	I cook (without water), i.e. fry, roast, grill, broil	dzhyapsylam
Zhvachka	cud, or chewing cud	kepsenerbe
Zhgu	I burn	nyandlya
Zheleza	gland	bilchargay
Zhelty	yellow	segey
Zhelch	gall, bile	poda
Zhelezo	iron	baze
Zhenikh	suitor, bridegroom	izit
Zhenskoe plate	women's dress	kep
Zherebey brosayu	I draw lots	synaăm
Zherebenok	foal	kulun*
Zhivu	I live	bibëm
Zhidki	liquid	suuk*
Zhila	vein	tan
Zhirny	fat, greasy	kobў
Zhir	fat, grease	syl
Zhnu	I reap	pўdlam
Zhovany	chewed (adj.)	todadobe
Zheltok	yolk	os*
Zhuravl	crane	kurerok
Zhuyu	I chew	todólam

Z

Zabluzhdayus	I lose my way	dzhyurzalem
Zabyvayu	I forget	numilem
Zavtra	tomorrow	karan
Zagashayu	I extinguish, put out	kubdrem
Zagibayu	I fold, bend	munublyam
Zadni	back, rear	byudnyan
Zadnitsa	rump	kuten*
Zdes	here	dugun
Zayats	hare	kozan*
Zazhigayu	I set on fire	nandlya
Zazhimayu	I press, grip	takh chydzhyable
Zaikayus, zaika	I stammer, stammerer	tyldfik
Zakalayu, kolyu	I stab, puncture	budem

Zakisayet	it turns sour	namzyble
Zakryvayu	I close	khaylyam
Zakutyvayu	I muffle up	surlem
Zapirayu	I lock	takhtym
Zapryagayu	I harness	kulerda*
Zastavlyayu	I compel	yudyulyam
Zatayu	I conceal, keep secret	pegǎndyba
Zatykayu	I stop up	tikhchem
Zakhozhdenye	setting (of the sun)	uzlagandaga
Zayezzhayu	I stop by (for)	tokchogam
Zbirayu	I gather, take	opla
Zvezda	star	kynzygey
Zver	animal	kona
Zdirayu	I quarrel	kyrle
Zdravstvuy	hello, how are you?	izen*
Zeleny	green	kok*
Zemletryaseniye	earthquake	dzhyumangylde
Zemlya	earth	dzhya
Zemlyak	fellow countryman	obdzhë
Zerkalo	mirror	korndas*
Zzhimayu	I press, grip	kazadzhyablam
Zima	winter	kǎ
Zimnik	winterer (one spending the winter)	kystag*
Zloy	wicked	kazyr*
Zmeya	snake	nǎnzy
Znakomlyus	I make the acquaintance of	tymdrobyam
Znayu	I know	tymnemym
Zrachek v glazu	pupil in the eye	pyuchtiyé
Zoloto	gold	altyn*
Zub	tooth	tyme
Zybka	cradle	dzhyapsy
Zevayu	I yawn	amoylyam̌
Zyabnu	I feel cold	kronlá
Zyat	son- or brother-in-law	manmem

I

Igla	needle	neme
Igrayu	I play	serla
Idu	I go	kandagam
Izvest	lime	se
Ikra u nogi	calf (of the leg)	my̌ga
Ikra u ryby	roe, caviar	turme
Imya	name	nym
Istok	source (as of river)	niurdy
Ishchu	I seek	pilya

K

Kadka	tub, vat	saban*
Kazhetsya	it seems	idymla
Kakoy	what kind of	kadoch
Kamen	stone	pi
Kachayu	I swing, shake	orda
Kashitsa	gruel	myya
Kashel	cough	kǔtla
Kedr	cedar tree	sany
Kidayu	I throw	bablam
Kiplyu	I boil	minzile
Kislo	sourly	namzyde
Kishka	gut	badë
Kladenye	castrated, gelded	akhta
Kladu chto	I place something	pallya
Klanyayusya	I bow, salute	numanuzlya

Kley	glue	nime
Kogda	when	kamen
Kobyla	mare	syuima
Kobolka [kobylka]	filly	sibisku
Kozha	hide	kuba
Koza	nanny goat	podo
Kozel	billy goat	muno
Kozlenok	kid	neka
Kokushka [kukushka]	cuckoo	cega
koloda	log, trough	niŭtme
Kolos	ear (of rye), spike	ulut
Koleno	knee	syne
Komar	mosquito, gnat	niny̆un
Konets	end	nerde
Kono [Kon?]	[?] [horse]	ine
Kopayu	I dig	tyllya
Kopeytso u strely	shaft of arrow	ne
Konchu	I shall finish	kamnylla
Kopyto	hoof	kuda
Kora	bark, rind	pere
Koren	root	myna
Kormlyu	I feed, nourish	obydla
Korova	cow	tyuzey
Kosa na golove	braid, pigtail	kydzhade*
Kost	bone	le
Kosy	slanting	kairsima
Kochka	hillock	bakty
Kochuyu	I nomadize	suylya
Kray	border, edge	tobde
Krapiva	nettle	kalagay
Krasny	red	kŭme
Krivy	crooked	pildysima
Krik	cry	kuryu
Krovlya, kryshka	roof	kăibĕ
Krov	blood	kam
Króyu	I cover	kaylya
Kroyu	I cut out	py̆tla
Krutoye mesto	steep, (tight) place	pyallë
Krylo	wing	koder
Kryuk	hook	byda
Kto	who	sem
Kuda	where, whither	kudyr
Kusayu	I bite	talbla
Kulik	grouse	su
Kuritsa	hen	takak
Kuryu	I smoke	khamnylla

L

Ladon	palm of hand	pyam
Lastochka ptichka	swallow	karachagay
Last	ton (measure)	mŏdla
Lgu	I tell a lie	saya
Led	ice	boy
Lezhu	I lie, repose	bipbam
Letayu	I fly	nargolyam
Lisitsa	fox	mingay
List na dereve	leaf (tree)	dzhaba
Lodka	boat	ane
Lomayu	I break	byldyla
Los, sokhaty	moose	ka
Lug	meadow	koy
Luk, koim strelyayut	bow, for shooting	ine
Lysy	bald	kaldzhen

Lyu	I pour	kamnyla
Lenivy	lazy	bagylzech
Lesny, tayezhny	forested, of the taiga	dzhilyamy
Leto	summer	tăgá
Lyagushka	frog	tamne

M

Mazhu	I smear, grease	dzhyupla
Maly	small	udzhyuga
Malchik	boy	ese
Marayu	I soil	sigarmdla
Maral syn	reindeer fawn, m.	maymi
Mat	mother	yam
Medved	bear	mayna
Melyu	I grind, mill	neplem
Merznu	I freeze	konbam
Mertvy	dead	kubĕ
Migayu	I wink	kafla
Mladenets	infant	tchyaazasy
Mnogo	much	yugo
Mogila	tomb	sorach dzhyudzhĕ
Mogu	I can	pale
Mozg	brain	kŭyu
Moy	my	măn
Mokry	wet	dzhĕrpĕ
Molniya	lightning	syusagaralcha
Moloko	milk	syut*
Molchu	I keep silent	tyzarlam
Molyusya	I pray	namanyzdlyat
More	sea	dalay*
Moroz	frost	syste
Mocha	urine, water	kynze
Mochu	I wet	dzhyutpem
Moyu	I wash	byzla
Muzh	husband, man	byuze
Muravey	ant	kaduma
Muka	flour	surusari
Mel	chalk	turzuga
Mesyats	moon	kyio
My	we	me
Myaso	meat	uya
Myagki	soft	nĕmor

N

Navznich	backward	kutde
Nagibayusya	I bow down	meden
Naduvayu	I swell, inflate	pyūblya
Nadevayu	I put on, clothe	serlya
Nazyvayu	I name	nimilyam
Nakhozhu	I find	kulam
Nakladyvayu	I lay on	pallyam
Na koleni stanovitsya	to kneel	sintle tlyanuam
Nalivayu	I pour	kamnylam
Nasiluyu zhenshchinu	I do violence to a woman	dzhyabem
Nasmekhayus	I laugh at	bastirlyam
Nastupayu	I step on	tonla
Natyagivayu	I stretch	neblya
Nauchayusya	I learn	tuzlya
Nachalnik	leader, chief	kon
Nash	our	me
Nebo	sky	num
Nĕbo vo rtu	palate (in the mouth)	nyani

Nevesta	bride	izech-kuza
Nevestka	daughter-, sister-in-law	meim
Nedavno	recently	tatagan
Ne znayu	I do not know	abychymnem
Ne mogu	I cannot	iñzlya
Neprovorny	slow	aby
Nitki iz zhil†	sinew thread	ta symdakh
Novy	new	tobla
Nogot	nail	koda
Nozhik	knife	tagay
Nozhny	sheath	señ
Nozdri	nostrils	aich
Nos	nose	püya
Nochuyu	I spend the night	salem
Noch	night	pë
Noshu	I carry, wear	minzizyam
Nemy	dumb	sekazet
Net	no	năga

O

Oba	both	obry
Obmachivayu	I soak	dzhochpendlya
Obnimayu	I embrace	kamyrla
Obrubayu	I prune	bolkhla
Obuvayu	I shoe	serdya
Obuzdyvayu	I bridle	anadlam
Obuchayu	I teach	tuzullyam
Obyavlyayu	I proclaim	ninallyam
Obeshchayu	I promise	drimelyam
Ovtsa	sheep	ular
Ovchina	sheepskin	kuba
Oglyadyvayutsya	to look around, scan	pyuittokhulam
Ognivo	flint	pida
Ogon	fire	syu
Ozero	lake	tō
Okrovovlyayu	I make bloody	kandzhyubla
Olen	reindeer	sume
On	he	de
Opasayusya	I guard against, fear	pymlyam
Opuskayusya	I sink down, drop	uzlyam
Opukhol	swelling, tumor	bazyrbe
Opushka	fur trimming	tobdot
Orel	eagle	nek
Orekh	nut	sana
Osa	wasp	kop
Osen	autumn	ire
Ostavlyayu	I leave (somebody, something)	pelyabidbam
Ostayusya	I remain	pinamgo i gam
Ostrov	island	noro
Ostry	sharp	potme
Otvoryayu	I open, set open	ayakharlam
Otets	father	abam*
Otkryvayu	I open, disclose	karla
Otkuda	whence	kudega
Otnimayu	I take away (off)	dzhyablaygam
Otstayu	I drop behind	koëgam
Otkhozhu	I go off	uplagandagam
Okhayu	I groan	kunulyam

†Sinew thread is prepared as follows: they take the sinew of wild or domestic animals, dry it, break it up, and lastly divide it into tiny parts, twist it, and use it.

P

Padayu	I fall	uzarem
Pazukha	bosom	mugma
Pepel	ashes	symo
Perevozhu	I transfer	kanalla
Perepravlayus	I get across	beÿlya
Pero	feather	khodyar
Pesok	sand	prya
Pechen	liver	mëtt
Plachu	I weep	dëorlam
Pletu	I weave, braid	kurlyam
Plecho	shoulder	bat
Plyvu	I swim	milya
Plyuyu	I spit	suzlam̆
Podkradyvayus	I steal to, sneak up	manaplam
Pokazyvayu	I show	perdlam
Polnoch	midnight	pindzhyar
Polovina	half	peldoy
Pologoye mesto, nekrutoye	a sloping place, not steep	pelle
Pomnyu	I remember	tenlyam
Ponuzhayu	I force, compel	meninlyam
Posle	after (in time)	pisnyanda
Postelya	beds	sokhtoch
Posylayu	I send	otlyam
Potlivy	subject to sweating	nŭgó
Potop	flood	bië
Pot	sweat	nogo
Pyu chto	I drink something	ninlya
Poyu kogo vodoyu	I give someone water	byumulya
Poyas	belt	dzhe
Prazdnik	holiday, feast	urgadzhyala
Prezhde	before (time)	dzhirdygandy
Privyazyvayu	I tie	surlam
Prizhigayu yednut†	I brand (a child) with a spot	tyunyaglyam
Primechayu	I notice	tymneleymam
Promyshlyayu	I earn my living	samaylyam
Protoka	tributary stream	nagm̆a
Proch	away	pereno
Proshu	I ask	korlam
Puzhayusya	I am frightened	kumleyam
Puzyr	blister, bladder	pyar
Pulya	bullet	ne
Pup	navel	san
Pushchayu strelu	I shoot an arrow	panydlya
Pushchayu dym iz rotu	I let smoke out of the mouth	obdolem
Pyu	I drink	bitlya

R

Razuyusya	I take off my shoes	angallem
Razdayu	I distribute	suylam
Razgonyayu	I drive apart	mangorlam
Razdelyu	I shall divide	taarlam
Raznimayu	I separate	bozlaim
Rana	wound	merg
Razsvetayet	it gets light	tlyalymlya
Rastoplyayu	I stoke	nygnylyam
Rvet menya	I vomit	sse erla
Rebro	rib	kott
Revu	I howl	kurymlyam

†*Yedna* is a spot branded on the chests of nomads of both sexes, young children 2 to 3 years old, so that saliva should not run out of their mouths and they should have no pain in the mouth; this is on the chest, but they [also] burn in tattoos on the body.

Remen	strap (leather)	minya
Rzhet	it neighs	inarla
Rov, yama	ditch, pit	tchyutellya
Roga	horns	amna
Rosa	dew	dzhibda
Rossomaga	glutton	mugne
Rot	mouth	aň
Rublyu	I chop, fell	bodem
Rugayu	I scold	kudolla
Ruka	hand, arm	oda
Ruka pravaya	right hand	mana
Ruka levaya	left hand	sola
Ryba	fish	kola
Rys	lynx	nogamayna
Reka	river	meanlay

S

Sazha	soot	kuya*
Sazhayu	I seat, set	amnaleybam
Salo	fat, grease	sel
Sam	self	maň
Sapogi, pimy	boots	pema
Svat	matchmaker, father-in-law	myno
Svakha	matchmaker	mynogne
Sverbit	to itch	khodalla
Svishchu	I whistle	sundulyam
Svoy	my, his	men
Svezhi	fresh	tobda
Svechu	I make light	dzhyalokbla
Svyazyvayu, vyazhu	I tie	sarlam
Segodnya	today	tepmnan
Sedlo	saddle	konzan
Serdity	angry	kurola
Serdtse	heart	sey
Serga	earring	kogoy
Sizhu	I sit	amnam
Skoblyu	I scrape	tandlam
Skorlupa	shell	sana
Skoro	soon	byuze
Skochu	I jump	sumelya
Sladko	sweet	nemyde
Slezy	tears	kyil
Slyuna	saliva	suzo
Slovo	word	tano
Slyshu	I hear	nyunybam
Sleg	joist, truss	ade
Smert	death	kube
Smerkayetsya	it grows dark	nyude
Smeyu	I dare	bisterlyam
Snimayu	I take off	ilyam
Sneg	snow	syra
Sobaka	dog	myan
Sobirayu	I collect	oplam
Sobol	sable	syle
Solntse	sun	kuya
Sosna	pine tree	dzhë
Spina	back	byagal
Sporyu	I quarrel	dzhektyrlam
Splyu	I sleep	konollam
Ssoryusya	I quarrel	kodolla
Starik	old man	bëziya
Starukha	old woman	nemyka
Step	steppe	karat

Stoyu gde	I stand (somewhere)	nugam
Strigu	I cut, shear	pedlyam
Strela, pulya	arrow, bullet	ne
Strelyayu	I shoot	chidlem
Stupa	mortar	siste
Stydlivy	shameful	sarlyan
Sukhi	dry	koturbe
Syn	son	ne
Semya	family	urgulok
Seno	hay	no
Syuda	here, hither	so

T

Tam	there	tygan
Tashchu	I drag, pull	ustyulyam
Tverdy	firm, hard	kaskak
Tvoy	thy	tan
Temno	dark	tolo
Teplo	warm	aë
Teryayu	I lose	dzhyurdym
Test	father-in-law	imet
Techet	it flows	meanla
Teterya	heath hen	dzhiyu
Titka	teat	nyuyu
Tovarishch	comrade, companion	pelya
Tolkayu	I shove	myudyudlya, companion
Tolsty	fat	dzhiryam
Tolko	only	tychok
Tonki	thin	todam
Tonu	I drown, sink	byunyuzlyam
Topayu	I stamp	balababdel
Topol	poplar	pine
Topchu	I trample	tonbla
Trova [trava]	grass	not
Trut	tinder	pyadmya
Tucha	cloud	tў
Telo	body	uya
Ty	thou	tan

U

Ubivayu	I kill	kudlam
Ugol	corner	dzhët
Uzda	bridle	agnet
Umirayu	I am dying	kulyagandam
Ustal	(I am) tired	ubdem
Uste	mouth	tagat
Ukho	ear	ku
Ukha	fish soup	mi

KH

Khvatayu	I seize	tchyablam
Khvory	sickly	izdz
Khvost	tail	tyĭma
Khlebayu	I sip	bĭkhlya
Khozhu	I go, walk	nungam tonlam
Khorëk	polecat	kuzen
Khudy	bad	bilya

TS

Tsar	tsar	kan
Tsvet	color	naregot
Tselyusya	I aim	panargadlal
Tsel	target	syri
V tsel popadayu	I hit the mark	uglyutchyudlya
Tsena	price	ulu

CH

Chad	smoke	syunë
Chashka	cup	toë
Chelovek	man	kuza
Cheren u nozha	haft of a knife	pog
Cherny	black	sagar
Cherpayu	I scoop up, ladle	supblaan
Chishchu	I cleanse	arymdlam
Chuzhi	foreign, of another	kuzan

SH

Shag	step	azybla
Shapka	cap	yuzyu
Sherst	wool	tar
Sheya	neck	baygǎ
Shtany	trousers	pakma
Shutka	joke	sero
Shuba	fur coat	proga
Shyu	I sew	sodlyam

SHCH

| Shcheka | cheek | ógoy |

YE

| Yedu | I ride | kandagam |
| Yem | I eat | amlam |

YA

Ya	I	mon
Yazyk	tongue	seka
Yaytso	egg	muny
Yastreb	hawk	pi yǎ
Yashcheritsa	lizard	tanza

1—unem	11—bedop	21—sydybetop
2—sēda	12—bepsyda	22—sydybesyda, etc.
3—nagor	13—betnagor	30—nagorb
4—tade	14—betade[44]	31—nagorbetop, etc.
5—sumula	15—betmuntut	40—karak*
6—muktut	16—betmutut	41—karakop, etc.
7—ssefgbe	17—betsseygbe	50—ilikh*
8—syitaře	18—besyntade	60—alton,* etc.
9—tagos*	19—betogos	
10—beř	20—sydybet	

Notes: For accurate pronunciation of the words used in the Dictionary:

(1) ′ This sign indicates that the letter over which it is written should be pronounced in the nose, for example *igábe* (if), as this is the way it is spoken.

(2) ˘ This sign, and particularly over a letter that it is not put over in Russian, means that that letter should either be pronounced very shortly, or in the throat, for example: *pўdpam* (I harvest).

(3) ‒ This sign indicates that the letter under it should be pronounced in a prolonged manner, for example: *pābim* (little brother).

(4) * This sign indicates that the word after which it is placed either is still in use among the nomads of the upper Yenisey and has been adopted from them into the Koybal language, or is derived from the language of nomads. The words in use by nomads are included because the Russian words of one meaning were written first and, therefore, the closeness of the nomad tongue to the Tatar can be judged from these words.

In addition the Latin letter "g" has been used though there is no such letter in the Russian language. This accuracy of pronunciation in the words seemed necessary in this language, which has no written form and is very subject to change, so that it could be compared with other languages of Asiatic peoples.

Notes and References

1. N. Kostrov, Koybaly (The Koybals), *Zapiski Sibirskogo Otdela RGO*, book vi, Irkutsk, 1863, p. 109; cf. E. K. Yakovlev, *Etnograficheskiy obzor inorodcheskogo naseleniya doliny Yuzhnogo Yeniseya* (Ethnographic survey of the native population of the southern Yenisey valley), Minusinsk, 1900; W. Radloff, *Aus Sibirien*, vol. 1, Leipzig, 1884, p. 206.

2. S. A. Tokarev, Perezhitki rodovykh otnosheniy u Khakasov v XIX v. (Survivals of tribal relations among the Khalkas in the 19th century), Sibirskiy etnograficheskiy sbornik I, *Trudy Instituta etnografii AN SSSR*, vol. 18, Moscow–Leningrad, 1952, pp. 108–110. See also: N. Kozmin, *Khakasy* (The Khalkas), Irkutsk, 1925, p. 18; *Sibirskaya sovetskaya entsiklopediya*, vol. 11, p. 797.

3. See: G. Müller, *Istoriya Sibiri* (History of Siberia), vol. i, Moscow–Leningrad, 1937, document 65, p. 423

4. *Ibidem*, p. 430.

5. *Dopolneniya k Aktam istoricheskim* (Addenda to Historical Acts), vol. 11, St. Petersburg, 1869, p. 162.

6. For more detail see my: *Kratkiye ocherki istorii i etnografii Khakasov* (Short essays on the history and ethnography of the Khalkas), Abakan, 1952.

7. Tokarev, *op. cit.*, p. 113. For the difference between Mator and Mad see reference 6.

8. See: V. Radlov, *Sibirskiye drevnosti* (Siberian antiquities), vol. i, no. iii, St. Petersburg, 1894, p. 78.

9. *Arkhiv AN SSSR* (Archive of the U.S.S.R. Academy of Sciences), sec. 21, op. 4, no. 20, leaf 236.

10. See: *Pamyatniki sibirskoy istorii* (Monuments of Siberian history), book i, St. Petersburg, 1882, pp. 233–236.

11. G. Müller, Description of the Krasnoyarsk district of the Yenisey province in its present situation in 1735 (manuscript in the German language), *Tsentr. gos. arkhiv drevnikh aktov (TsGADA)*, sec. 199, d. 9, portfolio 526, part ii, leaves 1–32 ob.

12. *Ibidem*, leaf 27.

13. P. Pallas, *Reise durch verschiedene Provinzen des russischen Reichs*, part iii, St. Petersburg, 1776, p. 376.

14. Gmelin recalls the Baykoton (Baykotov) ulus in the Koybal territory whose members lived north of the Lukaz factory. See: Gmelin, *Reise durch Sibirien . . .* , part iii, Göttingen, 1752, p. 325.

15. There was a Tatarov ulus in the 17th to 18th centuries in the Kamasin territory on the upper Kana. It is possible that the tax-paying Tatarov ulus found by Zlobin did not become part of the newly formed Koybal territory because it was already assigned to the Kamasin territory.

16. For all the uluses listed see my: *Kratkiye ocherki . . .* , pp. 77–89.

17. D. Messershmidt, Zhurnal puteshestviya iz Tobolska, stolitsy Sibiri, cherez Taru, Tomsk i dalshe po Sibirskomu tsarstvu (Journal of a trip from Tobolsk, capital of Siberia, through Tara, Tomsk, and further through the Siberian tsardom), Original manuscript in the German language in the Archive of the Academy of Sciences of the U.S.S.R., *Arkhiv Instituta etnografii*, sec. K-1, d. 13, case 1, p. 145.

18. P. Pallas, *Puteshestviye po raznym provintsiyam Rossiyskogo gosudarstva* (Voyage through different provinces of the Russian empire), St. Petersburg, 1788, part iii, pp. 523–524. On pp. 524–526 Pallas introduces illustrative comparative lexicological material of Samoyed, Koybal, Mator, and Karagas words.

19. I. G. Georgi, *Opisaniye vsekh v Rossiyskom gosudarstve obitayushchikh narodov . . .* (Description of all the peoples living in the Russian empire . . .), vol. iii, St. Petersburg, 1799, p. 13.

20. See: *Sibirskiy vestnik*, St. Petersburg, 1819, part v, p. 58.

21. P. Pallas, *Puteshestviye . . .* , iii, p. 526.

22. See the manuscript of I. Fisher in German, but under the title: "Geographica et historica discriptio itineris et regionum Tomas inter et Ircutum oppida interia centium," *Arkhiv AN SSSR*, sec. 21, op. 5, no. 52, leaf 18. I am indebted to A. I. Andreyev for calling my attention to this manuscript.

23. G. Müller, Description of Siberian peoples (in the German language), *TsGADA*, no. 763/1386, part ɪ, leaves 93 ob., 117.

24. Notes on contacts with peoples living along the Chinese border, made by Egor Pesterev in 1772 to 1781, *Novye yezhemesyachnye sochineniya*, no. ʟxxxɪɪ, 1793, pp. 12–13.

25. Pallas, *Puteshestviye . . .*, part ɪɪɪ, p. 527. The word "saban" shows that the Koybals took the name from the Kachins.

26. Georgi, *op. cit.*, vol. ɪɪɪ, pp. 13–14.

27. G. Müller, Description of . . . , *TsGADA*, sec. 199, d. 9, portf. 526, part ɪɪ, leaf 27.

28. Pallas, *Reise . . .*, part ɪɪɪ, p. 378.

29. *Ibidem*, p. 376.

30. Georgi, *op. cit.*, vol. ɪɪɪ, p. 16.

31. Pallas, *Puteshestviye . . .*, part ɪɪɪ, pp. 529–530.

32. E. Pesterev, *op. cit.*, *Novye yezhemesyachnye sochineniya*, no. ʟxxɪx, pp. 71–72, 81–82.

33. G. Spasskiy, *Slovar yazyka Koybalskogo . . .* (Dictionary of the Koybal language . . .), p. 59. See, at the end of this article, Spasskiy's dictionary of the Koybal language.

34. *Ibidem*, pp. 59–60.

35. This reform, whose author was M. Speranskiy, is known in the legislation of tsarist Russia as "Code of regulations for the governing of natives."

36. A. P. Stepanov, *Yeniseyskaya guberniya* (The Yenisey guberniya), St. Petersburg, 1835, part ɪɪ, p. 50.

37. *Abakanskiy gosudarstvennyy oblastnoy arkhiv* (Archive of the Abakan administrative oblast), sec. 2, report 49 for 1827.

38. *Abakanskiy gosudarstvennyy oblastnoy arkhiv*, sec. 2, report 115, leaf 35.

39. M. A. Castren, *Reiseberichte und Briefe aus den Jahren 1845–1849*, p. 322 *et al.*; *idem*, Puteshestviye v Sibir (Travels in Siberia), *Magazin zemlevedeniya i puteshestviy*, Moscow, 1869, vol. vɪ, pp. 375, 392, 397

40. Castren, Puteshestviye . . . , pp. 375, 429 *et al.*

41. This duma was abolished by the chief administrator of the Minusinsk region against the wishes of the Koybals. The administrative center of this duma was the village Uty on a tributary of the Abakan of the same name, some seven versts from the settlement of Bei.

42. See my: Etnicheskiy sostav sagaytsev (The ethnic composition of the Sagays), *Sovetskaya etnografiya*, 1947, no. 3.

43. The Koybal dictionary, compiled by Spasskiy, is deposited, with the dictionary of the Motor language, in the State Public Library named after Saltykov-Shchedrin, in the section of F. Adelung. In publishing the dictionary, we have fully preserved the original orthography. [Not fully applicable to the translation, although an attempt has been made to preserve the different spellings of the early 19th century.—Editor.]

44. An error of the copyist of Spasskiy's dictionary. Should be "betsumula."

L. P. POTAPOV

THE ORIGIN OF THE ALTAYANS[*]

IN CONNECTION WITH the short outline of the political history of the Altay tribes, it is necessary to examine their ethnic origin.

In the ethnography of Siberian peoples, the ethnogenesis of Turkic-speaking Altay tribes is one of the most difficult and least developed problems. Although the Altay region has long attracted the attention of scientists, only two have touched upon its history—V. V. Radlov and N. A. Aristov—and at that not specifically but only in passing.[1] Radlov held that the Altay region was the most ancient homeland of Turkic tribes. He assumed that the study of Turkic-speaking Altay tribes, to which he devoted a number of years, would shed light on the question of the origin of Turkic tribes in general and on their way of life in ancient times. The other investigator, Aristov, also considered the Altay as the place of origin of Turkic tribes in general. In examining the origin and ethnic composition of all Turkic tribes and national groups, he also considered the south Siberian Turkic tribes, among them the southern as well as the northern Altayans. Aristov suggested that the southern Altayans were descendants of the Kao-ch'ê tribes, identified in Chinese sources also by the term T'ieh-lê. Concerning the northern Altayans, he supported Radlov's opinion that they were Turkicized Yenisey Ostyaks (Kets) and Samoyeds.

It follows, therefore, that the present attempt to elucidate specifically the origin of the Altayans is essentially the first of its kind. I am undertaking it despite Radlov's pessimistic statement that "it will hardly ever be possible to solve the question of the origin of Siberia's ancient inhabitants."[2]

In order to resolve questions on Altayan origins, it is expedient to follow separate lines of research on two large groups (separated by geographical positions): the southern and the northern. There exists between them a sharp difference in language, culture, and mode of life, as well as in physical type. To the southern group belong the Altayans proper, the Telengits, the Teles; to the northern one the Shors, the Chelkans, the Kumandins, and the Tubalars, although among the latter there occur some elements characteristic of the language, culture, and mode of life of the southern Altayans. This can be explained by the geographic location of the Tubalars, who are situated along the border between the northern and southern Altayans, which contributed to the emergence of cultural-historical ties and the intermingling of the Tubalars and southern Altayans.

It is a matter of general knowledge that in the linguistic classification of Turkic languages the southern Altayans belong to the group which also includes the Kirgiz, Kazakhs, a part of the Uzbeks (those having settled on the territory of present-day Uzbekistan in connection with the collapse of the Juchi ulus in the beginning of the 16th century under Shaibani Khan, and, prior to the revolution, often called nomadic Uzbeks), the Bashkirs, the Tobol and Barabinsk Tatars, and others. This group of Turkic languages is called the northwestern or Kipchak group, because of the fact that present-day Turkic-speaking peoples who speak the languages and dialects of that group are connected, by linguistic

[*]Translated from Ocherki po istorii altaytsev, chapter v, pp. 133–162. Second edition, Moscow, 1953.

derivation, with the Turkic-speaking tribes and peoples belonging to the political union led by the Kipchaks—the Polovets of Russian chronicles and the Comans of Byzantine literary sources. The northern Altayans, according to the basic classification, belong to the other, the so-called northeastern group of Turkic languages, which is also called Uygur [Uighur] after its chief language.

The difference in the form of economy, culture, and way of life between the southern and northern groups of Altayans is very great. The ethnographic peculiarities of the southern and northern Altayans were formed on different material bases and under different geographical conditions (within the area of the Altay upland). The peculiarities of the culture and mode of life of the southern Altayans developed, as we have seen [in previous chapters], on the basis of nomadic and seminomadic cattle-herding, whereas those of the northern Altayans developed over a period of many centuries on the basis of hunting on foot, taiga fishing, hoe tilling, and collecting of wild edible plants. A marked difference between the northern and southern Altayans is seen in the shape, construction, and materials used for housing and clothing, in the character and manner of food preparation, in the means of transportation, in the folklore, in the fine arts, in morals and customs, in rituals and cults.[3]

Finally, there is also no doubt as to the great physical difference between the southern and northern groups of Altayans. The southern Altayans, as well as the Tuvinians, Buryats, Mongols, and Yakuts, are classified by Soviet anthropologists as the most Mongoloid, so-called Central Asian group of the Siberian population. Among the northern Altayans, the basic Mongoloid traits are much less pronounced, and Europoid traits are present. Together with a number of Ugor [Ugrian] and Samodiy [Samoyed] nationals these people belong to the Ural group.[4] Thus by measurable and descriptive traits the northern Altayans, particularly the Shors and Kumandins, manifest a common physical type not with the southern Altayans, but rather with the Ugrians of the Ob region, the Khants [Ostyaks] and Mansi [Voguls]. Therefore, a separate examination of the question of the origin and ethnic composition of the southern and northern Altayans is a prime necessity and not something motivated by the convenience of scientific analysis.

The earliest data on the physical type of the most ancient inhabitants of the Altay upland are provided by palaeoanthropological materials from the oldest burial sites. These indicate that during the 2nd and 1st millennia B.C. the Altay was peopled by inhabitants of Europoid appearance, sharply differing from the Mongoloid physical type of present-day southern Altayans. In physical type and interrelated culture these most ancient inhabitants were kindred to the inhabitants of the Minusinsk basin and apparently belonged to that group of tribes that in Chinese sources were called the Ting-ling [Dinlin]. The well-known basic work of S. V. Kiselev, *Drevnyaya istoriya yuzhnoy Sibiri* (Ancient history of southern Siberia), on the basis of extensive archaeological materials, including those of physical palaeoanthropology, treats very fully the questions of the physical type and character of Ting-ling culture.

The penetration of the Mongoloid physical type into the Altay upland dates to the middle of the 1st millennium B.C. Apparently it was intensified during the time of the Huns. There is every reason to believe that the Mongoloid population that penetrated into the Altay through Tuva and northwestern Mongolia, as evidenced by the archaeological record, was preponderantly Turkic speaking; this becomes indisputable by the 4th century A.D. Palaeoanthropological materials make it possible to follow fully the mixing of the Mongoloid arrivals with the

Ting-ling tribes. This intermingling of Mongoloid tribes with the local Ting-ling naturally was not restricted to physical intermingling. To the contrary, it manifested itself to a larger degree in respect to culture and language. There is no doubt that already in the first centuries of our era the Turkic languages prevailed in the Altay. Additionally, the analysis of archaeological remains in the Altay, dating to the last centuries of the 1st millennium B.C. and the first centuries A.D., indicates for that period the presence of cultural ties and contacts of the Altay tribes with the nomadic population of Central Asia, apparently with the Massagetae (the Yüeh-chih of Chinese sources) and tribes inhabiting the steppes of present-day western Siberia, Semirechye, and the southern Ural region.[5] It is necessary to suppose a mixing of the two groups, which, of course, influenced the ethnic composition of the Altay population, making it more complex. Therefore, even the oldest data on the ethnic composition of the early Altayans bear witness to their complex and heterogeneous origin and do not support the assumption of ethnic purity of the Altay Turks, as they do not support Radlov's assumption that the Altay was the original homeland of the Turks, since, in agreement with the data of physical anthropology, the Mongoloid Turks replaced the local Ting-ling tribes only gradually.

Domination of the Mongoloid type in the Altay upland is established only in the first centuries A.D., which fully conforms to the evidence of Chinese chronicles on the presence of Turkic-speaking tribes in the Altay (the T'ieh-lê, T'u-chüeh [Tugyu], Kipchak, etc.). The ethnic composition of the Altay upland population becomes known in the 6th century with the establishment of a Turkic khanate. The origin of the latter is related to the Turkic-speaking Altay tribes, which, according to Chinese chronicles, belonged to two large groups: the T'ieh-lê and the T'u-chüeh.[6] Both these terms represent the collective names for groups of Altay tribes. Of these, the T'u-chüeh, as mentioned [in a previous chapter], founded a new military-administrative union with T'umen as its first khan.

The military-administrative and political center of the Turkic khanate was moved to Mongolia soon thereafter. The narrow mountain valleys and steppes of the Altay provided poor winter pastures and could not feed the large herds of the numerous nomad nobles of the Turkic khanate. The spacious Mongolian steppes were more suitable for that. Probably this is also the reason why the location of the governing and ruling aristocratic upper caste of the large but usually provisional military administrative nomad unions in east central Asia (both before and after the Turkic khanate) was found mainly in Mongolia.

The Turkic-speaking tribes of the Altay and its adjacent regions, constituting the nucleus of the Turkic khanate, did not represent a single nationality. They showed a variegated ethnic composition, which was, in addition, temporary and rather unstable. The ethnic composition of the Altay Turks could not be stable under the prevailing historical conditions, primarily because of the absence of an economic community, and a firm ruling power, and of their nomadic way of life. Although they were unified by a common political rule of Turkic khans, the tribes of the Altay and the surrounding regions belonging to the "Türk" union in essence had their individual way of life. They spoke their own language and dialects, though these were related to each other, and had their own ethnic designations. Furthermore, they differed in some customs and religious rites. Finally, they were often at odds, making armed raids against each other for the purpose of taking war booty and prisoners. Mutual armed attacks of the T'ieh-lê and T'u-chüeh tribes are mentioned repeatedly in Chinese sources. The organization of campaigns and raids for the purpose of looting and taking prisoners formed the basic policy of the Turkic khanate's nomadic aristocracy, as well as that of other similar military-administrative nomadic societies.[7] Under these conditions, in different parts of the Turkic khanate, there constantly rose and fell (depending on the success or failure of the organizers) provisional small and large groups of different tribes and families, reflecting the desire of the nomadic upper caste to seize wealth and power. But this also led to the constant splitting and parting, mixing and mingling of various tribes and families (or their groupings). The rise and disintegration of such temporary family-tribal societies was expedited by the simplicity of the production and the economic life of the nomads.

Turning to the ethnic composition of the Altayans in the period of the Turkic khanate, it is necessary, first of all, to keep in mind the Ting-ling ethnic element. The Ting-ling (this name, from Chinese chronicles, is applied for the pre-Turkic population of the Altay) in time were assimilated fully into the Turkic-speaking Altay tribes, losing their own, and acquiring a Turkic language. To the Altay-Turkic community—Mongoloid in appearance—the Ting-ling brought, however, the traits of their Europoid physical type. These features appear up to the present time in individual Altayans and Khalkhas, among whom fair-haired and light-eyed types are found. Thus, the Ting-ling ethnic component among the Altayans can be determined not only through historical, but also through physical anthropological data.

There can also be no doubt of the mixing of the Turkic-speaking Altay nomads with Mongols. This is indicated, for instance, by the ancient Turkic language in the Yenisey-Orkhon inscriptions, in which Paul Pelliot uncovered some Mongol lexical elements (in the titles and the names of the Turkic ruling aristocracy). It is also expressed in grammar, for instance, in the use of the Mongol plural.[8]

On the ethnic composition of the Altay Turkic-speaking population and its surrounding regions, there is documented information, first of all, in the Yenisey-Orkhon rock inscriptions with their early Turkic language, and, further, in Chinese dynastic chronicles. In the inscriptions mentioned such ethnonyms as the following are encountered: *Türk, Oguz [Oghuz], Kipchak, Karluk, Kirgiz (Kyrgyz), Toles, [Tölös], Tardush, Türgesh, Uygur, Chik, Az,* and others.[9] Chinese chronicles cite names of individual tribes and clans belonging to the T'ieh-lê union and others.[10] The majority of the ethnonyms enumerated are preserved in the clan-tribal names of modern Altayans, representing the most important proof of their historic-genetic ties with the Turkic-speaking Altay population of the 6th to 8th centuries.

The term "Türk" appears in Orkhon inscriptions as a name for a political union, which, in the ethnic sense, represents a complicated conglomerate.[11] In Chinese sources these names are represented by the term "T'u-chüeh" and their locality of habitation is given as the southern Altay as early as the first half of the 5th century. In the genealogical legend of T'u-chüeh origin, recorded in the chronicles, the kindred origin of T'u-chüeh tribes is emphasized. This legend was adroitly interpreted by N. A. Aristov, who connected it with ethnonyms and toponyms of modern Altayans.[12] This legend also reflects some specific traits of social and familial relationships (features of the matriarchate and minorate), religious beliefs and rites (totemism, magic influence on the weather). Of the latter, particularly interesting is the reference to the ability of the elder brother —ancestors of the T'u-chüeh born of a she-wolf—to summon winds and rains. It is well known to ethnographers that before the revolution the southern Altayans had a special category of sorcerers (*yadach*) who were supposed to be able to bring on any kind of weather with the help of the "Yada-tash" [Yada-stone].[13] Historically, the cultural kinship of present-day Altayans and the Turkic Tu-chüeh is particularly well established by archaeological and ethnographical materials. The Chinese [T'ang dynastic] chronicle *T'ang shu* contains a description of the T'u-chüeh way of life, which is quoted here for reasons of comparison.

T'u-chüeh customs: They let their hair down, wear the left flap of the robe over the right one, live in felt tents and yurts, move from place to place looking for adequate grass and water, are engaged in cattle breeding and hunt animals, eat meat, drink kumiss, wear fur and wool clothing. As weapons they have: horn bows with whistling arrows, cuirass, spears, sabers and broadswords. Standards with a wolf head in gold. . . . They skilfully shoot arrows from horseback. They have no written (Chinese—Author) language. The number of people, horses, tributes, and cattle they add up by making notches on sticks. . . . The body of a deceased is laid out in a tent. The sons, grandchildren, and relatives of both sexes slaughter horses and sheep, and, spreading these in front of the tent, offer them in sacrifice. Then, on an appointed day, they take the riding horse of the deceased and belongings that he had used, burn them together with the corpse, gather the ashes and bury them at a different time of the year. . . .

There follows the description of a wealthy man's funeral, and the custom of placing an "engraved likeness of the deceased" near the grave together with a number of stones corresponding to the number of enemies slain by him is pointed out.

Generally, if he killed one man, one stone is set up. In other cases the number of stones reaches a hundred and even a thousand. After the sheep and the horses are sacrificed, all their heads are hung on posts. . . . Upon the death of a man's father, elder brothers, or paternal uncle, that man marries his stepmother, sister-in-law, or aunt. . . . The letters of their alphabet resemble the letters of the Khu people. . . . They drink mare kumiss and keep drinking until they are dead drunk. They sing songs facing each other. They worship spirits and believe in sorcerers. . . .[14]

Materials obtained by archaeologists from excavations of burials of the Turkic period recreate the same picture of the mode of life of the nomadic Altay T'u-chüeh as do the chronicles. Apart from cattle breeding, which was the main occupation of the Altay T'u-chüeh (as confirmed by the bone remains of horses, sheep, goats, camels, and yaks), they were familiar with the hunt (there are articles made from the antlers of the Siberian stag, elk, and mountain goat, scraps of fur clothing, and skins of fur animals) and partly with agriculture (finds of hand millstones). The use of agriculture by the Altay T'u-chüeh is also confirmed by remains of irrigation canals. S. V. Kiselev also discovered traces of iron-ore smelting in southern Altay.[15] During the investigation of Altay burial sites of this period, archaeologists also discovered a burial with cremation. Finally, archaeological materials corroborate the report of the Chinese chronicle on the custom of placing stone images of the dead man and stones at the grave of a rich man, and the presence of the arms enumerated above: bows, whistling arrows, sabers, and others.

The T'u-chüeh way of life as depicted in the Chinese chronicle is substantiated to an even greater extent by the ethnographical materials from southern Altay, dating from the end of the 19th and the beginning of the 20th centuries. The southern Altayans wore long fur coats closed with the left flap over the right, and lived in felt yurts, but they wore their hair in a pigtail. They also herded cattle on summer and winter pastures and hunted wild animals. In the interior regions of Altay whistling arrows were used by them for hunting until the time of the revolution. Figures on the number of heads of cattle, amount of debts, etc., they expressed by carving notches in small wooden boards (*kere agash*). The southern Altayans fed themselves on meat and kumiss. They became drunk on home-brewed spirits and, while entertaining guests, knelt on one knee facing each other and sang songs. The custom of marrying widows of elder brothers [the levirate] was also widely practised by them.

Kinship terminology customary to the southern Altayans was also preserved in the Orkhon-Yenisey cliff inscriptions. To such terms belong, for instance, *ātā* (father), ana (pronounced in Altayan *ānā*—mother), *ini* and *achi* (younger brother, brother's son), *apa* and *sinil* (the older and younger sister and others), *kālin* (sister-in-law).

Even more amazing is the preservation among the southern Altayans, up to the beginning of the 20th century, of elements of religious shamanistic cults. First, there is the sacrificial offering of sheep and horses including the custom of exhibiting the head and skin of the sacrificed animal. The gods of the Turkic tribes mentioned in Orkhon inscriptions—Koku Tengri (blue heaven) and Yer-Su (earth and water)—were worshipped by the southern Altayans under the same names up to the time of the revolution.

Let us examine the material pertaining to the Tölö group. The term T'ieh-lê is known from Chinese sources since the 5th century; it replaced the term Kao-ch'ê. In the Wei dynastic chronicle *Wei-shu*, the names of 12 clans comprising the Kao-ch'ê–T'ieh-lê ancestors are mentioned: (1) Li-fu-li, (2) T'u-lu, (3) I-chan, (4) Ta-lien, (5) K'u-ho, (6) Ta-pu-kan, (7) A-lun, (8) Mo-yün, (9) Ssû-fên, (10) Fu-fo-lo, (11) Ch'i-yüan, (12) Yu-shu-pei. The term T'ieh-lê, apparently, stood for all nomadic cattle-herding tribes, i.e., it denoted the nomadic way of life. This, probably, explains the information in the Sui dynastic *Sui-shu* chronicle that T'ieh-lê clans number more than 8,000 and are settled on a huge territory —from Manchuria to the Caspian Sea.[16] The Chinese sources differentiate between the burial rites of the T'u-chüeh and the T'ieh-lê. They mention that the T'ieh-lê buried their dead in the ground, whereas the T'u-chüeh cremated them. This difference is also confirmed by our archaeologists, who investigated Altayan burial sites of the period under consideration.

The history of the T'ang dynasty (618–907 A.D.) contains additional information on the Kao-ch'ê, i.e., T'ieh-lê, generations of which the following are mentioned: (1) Hsieh-yen-t'o, (2) Pa-yeh-ku, (3) P'u-ku, (4) T'ung-lo, (5) Hun, (6) Ch'i-pi-yü, (7) To-lan-ko, (8) A-tieh, (9) Ko-lo-lo,* (10) Pa-hsi-mi,† (11) Tu-po, (12) Ku-li-kan, (13) Pai-hsi, (14) Hsi-chieh.

T'ieh-lê and T'u-chüeh unions were rarely permanent. For reasons examined above, their composition was fluid and changed frequently. Only the commonness of their cultural and living conditions as recorded by Chinese chronicles and confirmed by archaeological data is beyond doubt. However, there were some differences in language, judging by the languages of various modern Turkic-speaking peoples and tribes whose origin is connected with the Turkic khanate. The differences are restricted to the framework of kindred Turkic languages.

The above-mentioned material concerning the historical cultural relationship of the present-day southern Altayans and the T'u-chüeh and T'ieh-lê tribes of Chinese sources makes it most important and necessary to examine the T'u-chüeh and T'ieh-lê ethnonyms for comparison with the clan and tribal names of present-day Altayans. Chinese sources contain ethnonyms only for the T'ieh-lê tribes

*[In the Chinese source, Yuan-ho is given.—Editor.]

†[In the Chinese source, Ssu-chieh is given.—Editor.]

and not for the T'u-chüeh. However, this gap is closed by the Orkhon-Yenisey inscriptions in which the names of tribes and clans belonging to the Turkic union are quite well represented. They contain also those which, according to Chinese sources, belong to the T'ieh-lê tribes. In the cliff inscriptions mentioned, the following ethnonyms are found: Türk, Oghuz or Toghuz-oghuz, Tölös, Kipchak, Tyurgesh, Karluk, Tardush, Uygur, Kirgiz, Bayirku, Kurykan, Tongra, Basmali, and others. Some of these are known also from Chinese chronicles, where they are included in the T'ieh-lê tribes. Thus, for instance: Ko-lo-lu (Karluk), Hsi-yang-t'o (Sir-Tardush),[17] Ku-li-kan (Kurykan),[18] T'ung-lo (Tongra),[19] Pai-yeh-ku (Bayirku),[20] Pa-hsi-mi (Basmali).[21]

The word "Türk," as mentioned above, was a political name for a military-administrative union, representing, in an ethnic sense, a rather colorful conglomerate. V. V. Bartold believed the ethnographic name for the tribes that formed the basis of the Turkic khanate was "Oghuz," and was subdivided into the Tardush and Toles.[21] This opinion is not confirmed by factual material. The nine Oghuz tribes comprised only a part of the above-mentioned conglomerate, which encompassed also many other tribes and families, mentioned in the cliff inscriptions under their ethnic names. Thus, the term "Toghuz-oghuz" belongs to a separate union of tribes, related among themselves, but differing in language from other Turkic-speaking tribes, for instance the Kipchaks. The term "Oghuz" acquired a wider meaning only later, particularly in the writings of eastern authors, as evidenced by political history. We know that the nine Oghuz tribes, which along with, for instance, the Kipchaks, the Karluks, and others formed an important part of the Turkic khanate, completed their westward movement with the fall of that khanate. There, in the 9th century they mixed with descendants of the turkicized Ephthalite-Kidarits[22] and founded a new basis for the union of Turkic-speaking tribes with the lower part of the Oxus river (Syr Darya) as its center. Because of their political importance, the Oghuz gained great renown, which is reflected in the works of eastern authors. The latter give the name of Oghuz or Ghuz not only to the population included in the sphere of influence of this new military-administrative society, but also to the territory of the Aral and Caspian steppes, calling the latter the "steppes of the Ghuz"[23] in the 10th century and, later, when the rule of the Ghuz was replaced by the rule of Kipchaks, the "Kipchak steppe" (Dasht-i-Kipchak).[24]

The ethnonym *Oghuz* is not encountered among the clan-tribal names of the Altayans. This is quite natural, considering that the Oghuz wandered off westward. The absence of the Oghuz element in the ethnic composition of the southern Altayans is most conclusively demonstrated in the evidence of language. The language of the southern Altayans with its dialects belongs to the Kipchak group of Turkic languages, which is very different from the Oghuz group represented by present-day Turkmen, Azerbaijan, and Turkish languages.[25] The language of the Yenisey-Orkhon inscriptions, with which mainly the nomadic nobility was conversant, belongs to the Oghuz group of Turkic languages.[26] Its phonetic and morphologic characteristics remain in the present-day Turkmen, Azerbaijan, and other languages. However, the vocabularies of the Oghuz and Kipchak languages have words in common. This is explained both by the affinity of these languages and also by the fact that the Oghuz and Kipchak tribes experienced a common history within the Turkic khanate. Of the ethnonyms mentioned in the Orkhon-Yenisey inscriptions and Chinese chronicles those having the widest circulation among the present-day southern Altayans are *T'ieh-lê* (*Tölös*) and *Kipchak*. The majority of tribal names of the southern

Altayans—Telengit, Tölös, Teleut—have as their basis the ethnonym *Tölö*. It has been acknowledged long ago that the names "Telengit" and "Teleut" were a transformation of the ancient ethnonym *Tölö* in the grammatical form of the Mongolian plural.[27] In this respect the only doubt was raised by the ethnonym Tölös authenticated in the Yenisey-Orkhon inscriptions. V. Radlov, V. Thomsen, F. Hirth, E. Chavannes, and others expressed themselves in favor of identifying the ethnonym *Tölös* with the *T'ieh-lê* of Chinese chronicles.[28] However, this was doubted by V. Bartold [W. Barthold], who was supported by P. Melioranskiy.[29] At present this question is fully resolved, since it has been established by Turkologists that the affix *z* (*s*) is the indicator of the plural form in early Turkic languages and in particular in the language of the Orkhon rock inscriptions.[30] Thus, the ethnonym *Tölös* manifests a grammatical form of the Turkic plural of *Tölö*. Consequently, the Tölös of the southern Altayans, similar to their kin, the Telengits and Teleuts, have preserved in their autonym a strong indication of affinity to their distant historical ancestors, to the Tölö union, the Tölös of the Orkhon-Yenisey inscriptions, the Mongol legends, etc., part of whom inhabited the Altay and its surrounding regions already in the 6th and 7th centuries A.D. It may be added that one of the autonyms of the present-day southern Altayans—Telegit—is recorded in the afore-mentioned Chinese sources by the term "To-lan-kê" as a name of the Tölö tribes. This has attracted the attention of a number of scholars.[31] Among the southern Altayans, a large part of the population is connected with the ethnonym *Tölös*. Apart from the fact that quite a large group of southern Altayans inhabiting the Chulyshman and Bashkaus river basins calls itself Teles, the presence of the Tölös clan among the Telengits and the Altayans proper should be noted. According to 1897 data, the Tölös clan alone, not counting the Chulyshman Tölös, numbered 1,799 persons of both sexes, which comprised 7.9% of the entire population of southern Altay. Furthermore, the Orgonchi and Tittas clans must be counted as Tölös. These were considered to be related to the Tölös to such a degree that marriage among them was forbidden.[32] All this points to the connection of a large part of the present-day southern Altayans with the ethnonym *Tölö*, and this serves as an important indication of their origin from the Turkic-speaking Altayan population of the 6th to 7th centuries A.D. which the Chinese sources affiliate with Tölö tribes.

A less important indication of the antiquity of the ethnic base of the southern Altayans is the ethnonym *Kipchak*, widely prevalent among them. At the present time it is possible to raise with confidence the question of the Kipchak origin of the southern Altayans, and of the existence of Altay Kipchaks. This is first of all confirmed by their present-day language, which belongs, as mentioned, to the Kipchak group of Turkic languages. Linguistic materials must be considered the most important source and proof in solving the question of the origin of the southern Altayans, because, as Stalin has pointed out, "the elements of contemporary languages originated in the deep past, before the epoch of slavery."[33] Of course, in doing so, it is necessary to proceed on the solid base of the history of the Altayans because in the process of historical development tribes and peoples with different languages and different ethnic origin may blend. We know, for instance, that some groups of present-day Khalkhas spoke, as late as the 17th century, languages belonging to the Samoyed- or Ket-speaking tribal group and then, as a result of linguistic mixing, became a strictly Turkic-speaking group. It would not be correct, of course, to attribute the origin of the Khalkha group to this or that ancient Turkic tribe or people on the basis of their present-day Turkic language. In this connection Stalin's substantiation is to the point: "A language and the way of its development may be comprehended only if its study is inseparably linked to the history of the society, to the *history of the people* to whom the language under study belongs and who are the creator and user of that language."[84] (Emphasis mine—Author.) And, taken factually, the history of the southern Altayans proves that the Altay mountains, at least from the 6th century onward and up to our time, were settled by Turkic-speaking tribes. Consequently, we can well assume that elements of the present-day language of southern Altay were formed in very ancient times and may go back to the period under review.

This is also confirmed by certain parallels with Kirgiz data. The fact is that the southern Altayans and the Kirgiz, now separated by vast distances, appear to have much in common, as they belong to the same grouping by language and common ethnonyms, for instance by such clan-tribal names as Kipchak, Teles, and Munduz.[35] These parallels reflect, of course, a former community of some ethnic elements between the southern Altayans and Kirgiz, confirmed also by lexicology. Probably these common features go back to the time of the existence of large unions of Tölö tribes, for they have a number of ethnonyms in common, such as, *Tele* (Teles), *Munduz*, (cf., the Teleut clan *Munduz*). The Kipchak language of the Altayans emerged in ancient times and was linked with the Altay territory. The latter proposition can be proved by the fact that historical sources, at a very early period, mention the ethnonym *Kipchak* as being connected with the Altay. The term "Kypchak" is mentioned in the text of a Chinese chronicle reporting on the conquests of the Hun *shanyu* [emperor] Mo-tun in the 3rd century B.C. Among the tribes living to the north of the Huns, Ting-ling, Kirgiz, and others conquered by Mo-tun, there were tribes with the name of Yüeh-chih (*Chüeh-shê*)[36]—a name which, as A. N. Bernshtam has noted, in the ancient Chinese pronunciation of the hieroglyphs according to B. Karlgren, sounded like *kiychak*, and probably stood for the already existing name "Kipchak."[37]

It is also possible to assume that the Kipchaks were settled in the Altay and regions close to it, because Kipchaks are mentioned along with the Basmali and Bo-ma [Po-ma] (apparently Selkups and Ostyaks), as well as the Kirgiz, among tribes who from the year 641 became dependents of the west Turkic khan Tulu (died in 653), who lived, as correctly stated in Chinese sources, to the northeast of the western Turkic tribes.[38] A century later, the Kipchaks are mentioned in an inscribed stone monument found by Ramstedt on the Selenga river. It states that the Turkic Kipchaks ruled over the Uygurs[39] for 50 years and, apparently, played an important part in the eastern khanate, under the rule of the Orkhon Turkic tribes, whose Altayan origin is indubitable. When the center of the khanate was shifted from the Altay to the Orkhon, the Turkic-speaking population did not leave the Altay. To Orkhon moved mostly the Turkic nomadic aristocracy and its ruling families, who possessed very large flocks. Naturally, part of the rank and file nomadic population, dependent on them, moved also. At the same time, there is reason to believe that only part of the Kipchaks appeared in Orkhon, that the Altay did not become deserted, and that a Kipchak population remained settled there. Proof of this, quite apart from the fact that the Kipchak language continued to be spoken in the Altay, is provided by several archaeological monuments, and, in particular, burial sites with stone statues near them, characteristic of the Kipchak burial rites of the middle of the 13th century. They depict a man holding a cup in his hand. [William of] Rubruck, having observed this ritual, writes that the Kipchaks make a large mound over the deceased "and erected a statue in his honor, facing east and holding a bowl in its hand in front of the navel."[40] L. A. Evtyukhova, who had investigated similar stone statues of the Altay upland, convincingly dates them to the 7th to 10th centuries and correctly attributes them, both in the Altay and in Mongolia, to the Orkhon Turkic tribes of Altay origin.[41] I suggest that these stone statues be considered works of the Kipchaks, since later, in the 13th century, in the Dasht-i-Kipchak, such statues were erected, as shown by [William of] Rubruck, by none other than Kipchaks. Furthermore, it should be kept in mind that the Kipchaks were an important part in the composition of the Orkhon Turks.

In this connection let us note another detail. [William of] Rubruck reported that Kipchaks carried small bags (*kaptargak*) into which they put all kinds of trivia. In the Kipchak stone statues of the Altay, such bags are shown suspended from the belt. Similar bags—leather satchels of semicircular shape—were worn until recently by Altayan hunters and were also called *kaptarga*. I brought back a bag of this type as part of the ethnographic collection gathered by me for the State Museum of Ethnography in Leningrad.

In the Minusinsk basin, statues such as those described above are exceedingly rare. Other stone statues of an earlier type are characteristic for this region.[42] In this connection it is interesting to note that the language of the Turkic-speaking population of the Minusinsk basin belongs not to the Kipchak group but to a different one, provisionally named Uygur. Altay Kipchaks, apparently, did not populate the Minusinsk basin, but Yenisey Kirgiz lived there since ancient times.

I do not insist at all that the above-mentioned stone statues of the Altay, Tuva, and Mongolia belong solely to the Kipchaks. We know very well that the custom of erecting them existed also among the Turkic tribes of the Orkhon, who cannot be fully identified with the Kipchaks. The latter formed a large part of the Orkhon Turks and probably belonged to the Tölö tribal group, since the modern Telengit, Teleut, Teles, and the group of Altayans proper speak a language of Kipchak origin. To a direct genetic link between present-day southern Altayans and the ancient and medieval Kipchaks points also the presence of the clan (*seok*) Kipchak among the southern Altayans. This clan is found literally among all southern Altayans—Teles and Telengit as well as Teleut and Altayans proper. Consequently, it becomes generic for all southern Altayans. Furthermore, before the revolution, the Kipchak clan was one of the most populous.

Table 1 lists the numerically most important clans of the southern Altay. It was prepared on the basis of the 1897 census conducted among the Altayans under the direction of S. P. Shvetsov.[43]

The Mundus clan was considered to be related by blood to the Kipchak clan. This blood relationship was underlined by prohibition of marriage between these clans; it is also mentioned in a legend of Mundus origin. According to this legend, the founder of the Mundus *seok* was born to a girl of the Kipchak clan who had conceived a son as a result of having eaten three hailstones (*mus*). The Mundus clan, particularly prevalent among the Teleut, is known, as stated previously, as one of the clan-tribal subdivisions of the modern Kirgiz. The clan-tribal subdivision Mundus, being common to both the southern Altayans and the Kirgiz, reflects the historical common heritage of the ancestral ethnic elements of these peoples. This is also confirmed by the nature of their language, which belongs to the general Kipchak group.

The data in Table 1 show that among the southern Altayans the Kipchaks (including the Mundus) comprise 15.5%. Also, ethnographic data indicate that

TABLE 1

	Name of *seok* (clan)	Size of population	
		Absolute	% in relation to total
1.	Todom	2982	13.1
2.	Kipchak	2117	9.3
3.	Mundus	1417	6.2
4.	Irkit	2015	8.9
5.	Mayman (Naiman)	1912	8.4
6.	Kobek	1604	7.0
7.	Toles	1799	7.9
8.	Tonzhoan	1106	4.8
9.	Kergil	1100	4.8
10.	Sagal	934	4.1
11.	Soyen, Sayan (Tuvin)	728	3.2
12.	Almat	660	2.9
13.	Chapty	558	2.4
14.	Ochy	528	2.3
15.	Various: Koobolu, Sary, Olyup, Myurkut, Purut, Tumat, Baylagas, and others	3306	14.5
	Total	22766	100

the Kipchak clan was in close tribal relationship with the Todosh clan since they had a *kudalyshka* relationship, i.e., a relationship based on once mandatory (later preferential) marriage. Thus these clans were *kuda* to each other, i.e., in-laws. This merits special attention as it conforms fully to a similar ancient custom that existed among the Kipchak-Polovets, who were in an "in-law" relationship with the Pecheneg. The Ipatyevsk chronicle, in relating the campaigns of the Russian princes in 1187–92, mentions the kinship of the Pecheneg and Polovets who called each other "in-law" and refused to fight each other.[44] On this basis it is reasonable to assign to the Kipchak clan all those Altayan clans that were in a kudalyshka relationship with them. Thus the content of the Kipchak tribal element among the southern Altayans increases to 28.6% and, taking into account the *kudalyshka* relationship between the clans Todosh and Chapty, to 31.5%.

Another fact that also points to the antiquity of Kipchak elements among the southern Altayans is that from among these clans, the southern Altayans had *zaisan* "ancestors" in their blood line, the so-called *uktu-jaizan*, whose names were ancient and inherited. This was noted already by Radlov, who reported the presence among the southern Altayans of zaisan descendants by blood from the clans of Kipchak, Mundus, Todosh, and Irkit. Besides all this, some traits of culture and mode of life were preserved by present-day southern Altayans up to the revolution, particularly in the area of religious cults, which were characteristic of medieval Kipchaks and are known from descriptions by western European travelers who visited the Kipchak steppes in the 13th century. Marco Polo describes the deity "Natigay," for instance, in the following manner: "He is in every house; they make him from felt and cloth and keep him in their houses; they also make the wife of that god and his sons. . . . From time to time during meals they will suddenly daub the mouths of the god, his wife, and sons with a juicy morsel."[45] Such deities in the shape of little felt dolls had a wide circulation among the Altay Telengits and Teleuts before the revolution. They were kept in every yurt, and fed exactly in the way described by Marco Polo. Furthermore, present-day Telengit called this deity Natigay (as recorded by G. N. Potanin during his journey through the Chuya river valley,[46] i.e., by the same term that was heard by Marco Polo). The Teleut sewed this deity from sackcloth, stuffing the dolls with rags, felt, or wool. With the Teleut the deity had already lost its name and was called by the generic term *emegender* ("old woman's ancestors").

In connection with the above, let us note some peculiarities of Kipchak burial rites as reported by [William of] Rubruck. To his already quoted report that the Kipchaks built a mound over the deceased "and erect a statue for him facing east and holding a cup in its hand in front of the navel," let us add his additional words: "I have seen a recently deceased one, near whom they (the Kipchaks— Author) hung from tall poles 16 horsehides, four on each side of the cardinal directions."[47] An analogous ritual during funerals was retained by the southern Altayans up to the end of the 19th century and was called *koylogo*. The horse chosen to accompany the deceased to the world beyond was called *koylo at*.[48] All this points to the present-day southern Altayans' being, in their ethnic origin, descendants of the ancient and medieval Kipchaks of the Altay.

Notice should also be taken of the ethnonym *türgesh*, which may indicate the presence, amid the Altayans, of descendants of the ancient Türgesh who played an important role in the western Turkic khanate. The Türgesh were part of the T'u-chüeh and lived, in the 7th to 8th centuries, principally to the west of the Irtysh in the immediate vicinity of the Western Altay mountains.[49] In the 7th century the Türgesh were part of the union of Tulu tribes roaming the Semi-rechye territory.[49] Tulu, as noted above, is mentioned in a Chinese chronicle in a list of T'ieh-lê generations. The ethnonym *türgesh* was preserved among the Tubalars as a clan (*seok*) name (Radlov considered it a tribe)[50] and also in the name of the Kergesh volost mentioned in Russian historical documents of the 17th to 20th centuries. A. V. Adrianov correctly noted that the Tubalar-Tirgesh (according to Adrianov, Kergesh) belong, in ethnographic traits, to the southern Altayans.[51] The men wore their hair braided into a short pigtail, and the women a sleeveless outer gown (*chegedek*), both particularly characteristic for the southern Altayans.[52] To this we should add the dairy products they produced; the manner of preparation and the terminology are characteristic for the nomadic southern Altayans. Thus the Tubalars of the Türgesh clan are clearly of southern Altay origin and have not yet lost the peculiarities of their ancient mode of life linked with the culture of southern Altay tribes. It is noted in Russian documents of the 17th century[53] that the "Tirkhesh" formerly paid tribute to the Teles, i.e., they were "*kishtym* to the Teles people."

Aside from the ancient ethnonyms of the Turkic-speaking Sayan-Altay highland tribes already analyzed, the following ethnonyms are encountered among present-day Altayans: *Kyrgyz*, indicative of the participation of the Yenisey Kirgiz in the ethnogenesis of the Altayans, *dubo* and *aba*, mentioned in the assemblage of T'ieh-lê generations in Chinese chronicles, and others. The last two ethnonyms should be examined in connection with the ethnogenesis of the northern Altayans.

In reference to the above, it should be realized that the archaeological, physical, ethnographic, historical (the written sources), and linguistic materials all concur in linking the present-day southern Altayans in their ethnic origin to the Turkic-speaking population that was predominant in the Altay and its neighboring regions in the 6th to 8th centuries.[54] This population appears in Chinese sources under the collective names of "T'ieh-lê" and "T'u-chüeh." In the composition of both groups were Kipchak tribes whose language prevailed and was preserved during the process of mingling of various Turkic languages and dialects over the many centuries of southern Altay history. Historically, ancient Kipchak (in language) tribes were the early ancestors of the southern Altayans. The period of the Turkic khanate may be considered as the earliest ethnogenetic phase of the present-day southern Altayans. These ancient ethnic elements continued to prevail in the Altay also in subsequent historical periods and have survived to our time. This, naturally, does not mean that the ethnic composition of Altay Turkic-speaking tribes remained constant during the more than one thousand years. On the contrary, the ethnic composition of the Altayans was exposed to changes in connection with known historical events that took place in the eastern part of Central Asia, but it retained, nevertheless, its Kipchak foundation.

The influence of Mongolian tribes must be recognized as an essential factor in the ethnic history of Altay tribes of that time. This was particularly evident in the 11th to 13th centuries when the Altayans came under Naiman rule, and again during the empire of Genghis Khan and his descendants. The Altay at that time continued to be inhabited by a Turkic-speaking population. Kipchak tribes, a part of which is known to eastern authors under the name Kimak, are mentioned already by Ibn-Khordadbekh [Cordoba?], the Arab geographer of the first half of the 9th century. According to the Gardizi manuscript (written in the first half of the 11th century) the Kimaks "live in the forests, ravines and steppes, all own cattle and sheep herds; camels they do not have . . . in the summer they nourish themselves with milk from mares, which they call kumiss; for the winter they prepare dried meat of sheep, horses, cows, each according to his means. The Kimaks hunt for sable and ermine."[55] The Kipchaks constitute the western branch of the Kimaks. In the works of eastern writers the Kimak-Kipchak tribes are depicted as inhabiting the Irtysh valley and the western Siberian steppes. Doubtless, they also lived in the Altay mountains, particularly in the western part, where they hunted for sable and ermine for which these mountains were still famous even in very recent times. The southern Altay Kipchak tribes, for instance the Altayans proper, who nomadized in the western Altay as late as the 18th century, also continued to leave for the winter with their herds for the left bank of the Irtysh where they grazed their cattle and hunted for roe deer. The Teleuts nomadized the steppes of the Irtysh region and the Ob in the late 16th and even in the 17th century. To the western Siberian steppes the Kipchak tribes could have come only from the Altay, as Semirechye, after the fall of the Turkic khanate, was first in the hands of the Türgesh and then, beginning with the second half of the 8th century, of the Karluks, who are also regarded as emigrants from the Altay. The Aral and Caspian steppes were under the Oghuz hegemony. A part of the Kipchaks could have been on the Irtysh since toward the end of the 5th century (as the Chinese chronicles report for the year 492) a part of the T'ieh-lê tribes wandered away from the Selenga to the Irtysh.[56]

Having spread their rule to the Altay, the Naimans nomadized close to the upper reaches of the Irtysh. Their influence apparently extended also to the southwestern Altay as the Teles and Telengit became vassals of the Mongols much later, under Genghis Khan, when the Mongol influence on the Altayans was particularly strong.[57]

The intermingling of the Altayans with the Mongol-speaking Naimans is attested to by the presence, among the Altayans, of the populous Naiman clan (with its various subdivisions). When the mixing of the Naimans and the Altayans occurred, the Turkic language prevailed and the Naimans were dissolved into the Turkic-speaking Altay environment, retaining only the names of some clan subdivisions of the Altayans. The "Secret history of the Mongols" contains a rather definite statement concerning the mingling of the Altayans and the Mongols. It mentions that in the beginning of the 13th century, by order of Genghis Khan, the Teles and Telengit were incorporated with the population of a realm under the authority of the military leader Khorchi [Horchi?]. This population included the Mongol clans Baarinets, Adarkinets, Chinosets, and the forest population (Mongol-speaking people among them) who inhabited the Sayan-Altay highlands.[58] In the process of admixing, the Teles, Telengit, and Teleut preserved their Turkic language, and they still speak it today. During this process, a considerable number of Mongol words penetrated into the Turkic language of the Altayans. They are preserved in its vocabulary to the present and have enriched the content of that language.

The Mongols who had entered into the composition of the Altayans brought with them some specific traits of their nomadic ways. For instance, the Mongol name for the drink made of fermented milk—*chigen* [yogurt]—and its method of preparation from boiled milk gained such wide use among the Altayans that the name *ayran* current among Turkic peoples was displaced, as was even their method of preparing it from raw milk (as is the custom with many Turkic-speaking nomads). Or, note the ancient [and modern] Mongol way of killing sheep by slitting the belly, reaching into the chest cavity, and pulling out [and squeezing] the heart instead of cutting the throat as the Altayans did, and so on. The acceptance of particulars of the Mongol way of life by the Altayans shows itself also in the clothing, prose and poetry, national calendar, religious beliefs, and others. These, like the linguistic data, serve as impressive proof of the blending of Mongol ethnic elements into the Altayan medium as a result of fragmentation and dissemination of some Mongol tribes.

An important phase in the ethnogenesis of the southern Altayans, with which the origin of their nearest historical ancestors is directly connected, is the ethnogenetic process that took place from the 11th through the 15th centuries in the wide steppes from the Altay to the Crimea and even the Danube. Its result was the formation of such peoples as the present-day Kazakhs, Uzbeks, Siberian Tatars, and others. As is known, during this period, the west Siberian steppes, Kazakhstan, the north Aral and Caspian regions, the south Russian steppes including the northern shores of the Black Sea, the Crimea, and the Danube, were within the sphere of many nomadic Turkic-speaking tribes. Of these, the strongest for a time were the unions of Turkic tribes in the steppes of the Aral and Caspian regions, under Pecheng leadership (10th to 12th centuries), and particularly of the Kipchaks in the south Russian steppes. Known from Hun and Turkic times in the Altay and later on the Irtysh, the Kipchaks advanced as a short-lived but powerful political unit in the 12th and the beginning of the 13th century. As mentioned earlier, the large areas of steppe, where the rule of the Kipchaks prevailed, were called Dasht-i-Kipchak in eastern sources. The temporary union of the Turkic-speaking nomads under Kipchak hegemony helped create a common mode of life and culture for these tribes, who shared approximately the same stage of socio-economic development.

The Mongol state of Genghis Khan put an end to the political rule of the Kipchaks. In the third decade of the 13th century the Mongols became the political masters of Dasht-i-Kipchak. With the creation of Juchi ulus the process of Turkic ethnogenesis was complicated by new Mongol influence. However, basically it was still formed by combinations of various Turkic-speaking tribes making up the majority of the Dasht-i-Kipchak population, although in conjunction with others, principally Mongol, tribes. The rank-and-file Mongol nomads were dissolved into the Turkic-speaking Kipchaks not in the Altay alone.

For this we have direct proof from Moslem authors. Al-Omari, a 14th century Arab historian, reports the following on [the Western] Juchi ulus or the Golden Horde:

In ancient times this state was the land of the Kipchaks. But when the Tatars (i.e., Mongols—Author) took over, the Kipchaks became their vassals. Then they (the Tatars) mixed and became related with them (the Kipchaks) and the land gained over their (the Tatar's) natural and racial qualities and they all became like Kipchaks, as if from the same clan, because the Mongols (and the Tatars) settled on Kipchak land, entered into marriages with them and remained there to live on their (Kipchak) soil.[59]

The Turkic linguistic substratum of the mentioned process reveals itself also in the fact that even the literary language in Juchi ulus was a Turkic language containing Kipchak elements, not to mention dialects of the nomad tribes populating the steppes where the Kipchak elements prevailed. The official charters of the khans of the Golden Horde were written in the Turkic literary language and some even in "local Kipchak language" (e.g., the Charter of Toktamish Khan of 1393).[60]

The southern tribes of the Altay, who belonged to the Eastern Juchi ulus (the White Horde), represented the eastern edge of Kipchak tribal dissemination and shared the cultural and domestic mode of life with the neighboring Kipchak tribes of the White Horde.

After the death of the khan Batu (1256), in the process of political fragmentation of Juchi ulus, there apparently emerged new combinations of Turkic-speaking Kipchak tribes who, mingling with Mongols, exerted a great influence on the ethnic composition of such present-day peoples as the Kazakhs, Uzbeks, Karakalpaks, Bashkirs, and others, and a large part of the southern Altayans (including the Teleuts). All this explains the well-known fact that we encounter in the clan-tribal composition of the Kazakhs, Kirgiz, Karakalpaks, formerly nomadic Uzbeks, Bashkirs, southern Altayans, and other people who lived at a great distance from one another over a number of centuries, the same clan-tribal names, such as Kipchak, Naiman, and Merkit. This also clarifies the fact that the epic art of the period of the Golden Horde (for instance the legends of Kara-Batye, Edig, Toktamish) was preserved until recently in the Crimea and among the Noghays of the northern Caucasus, among the Kazakhs and among various groups of Siberian Tatars, and also among southern Altayans and other Turkic-speaking peoples.[61]

Aside from epic poetry another proof of a common way of life of the southern Altayans and several of the peoples enumerated for the Juchi ulus period is a homogenous cultural and domestic mode of life that can be traced through ethnographic materials to the present time. Suffice it to say that the portable yurts (*kerege*) of the southern Altayans are identical with those of the Kazakhs, Kirgiz, Uzbeks, and others not only in material and construction but also in the terms used for separate parts (the lattice foundation walls, the roof sticks, the wooden ring for the smoke hole, etc.). This identity in terms also applies to men's clothing. Let us compare the expression for the Altay robe—*chokpen*—with the Kazakh *shokpen,* or the term for a sheepskin coat (*ton*), a fur coat with the fur on the outside (*yargak*), and so on. A particularly close agreement is observed in the method of preparation of meat and dairy products and the terminology involved. The *kurut* of the Altayans—a cheese made from sour milk—is known under the same name to the Kazakhs, Kirgiz, Bashkirs, and others. The same can be said for cream from boiled milk (*kaymak*), for sour milk (*ayran*) for which the Altayans also retain the Mongol *chegen* (meaning "kumiss" [?] in Mongolian), and so on. Even the name of the vessel for keeping sour milk—*saba*—is equally known in the Altay, to the Kazakhs, Kirgiz, and others. Or let us consider a simple tool, such as the serrated stick for beating and currying hides. We find that this tool, bearing the same name (*idrek*) among the Altayans and the Pamir Kirgiz, is produced by either people and is so identical in shape that two such tools, when placed next to each other, can not be told apart. These astonishing "coincidences" could also be continued in regard to national ornaments, national calendars, national musical instruments, terminology of the kinship system, a number of national customs and pre-Moslem beliefs of the Kazakhs, Kirgiz, nomadic Uzbeks, southern Altayans, and others.

From all that has been presented, the following deductions can be made: The historical ancestors of the present-day southern Altayans were the Kipchak, Turkic-speaking tribes. This applies to those who lived in the Altay from ancient times as well as to those who got there as a result of the collapse of the Juchiya ulus and in particular of its eastern part—the White Horde. A great displacement of Turkic-speaking tribes there (the movement of the Uzbek tribes to Central Asia where they mingled with local Turkic and Iranian-speaking populations) is a well-documented historical fact. In the Altay these later Kipchak elements, as pointed out previously, mixed not only with descendants of other ancient Turkic-speaking Altayan tribes of the Turkic khanate era (the Teles, Türgesh, and others), but also with western Mongols.

With the collapse of the Golden Horde, the historical and ethnic development of the Altayans proceeded under the strong influence of western Mongols or Oirats. This is due to the fact that from the end of the 15th and the beginning of the 16th centuries, the Altay mountains became the sphere of political influence of west Mongolian or Oirat khans. West Mongolian tribes extended their nomadic activities even to the Altay uplands. However, even then they disintegrated in part and became assimilated with the southern Altayans through intermarriage. During this interbreeding the Turkic language of the southern Altayans again prevailed. Proof of this process is the presence among present-day southern Altayans of the clans (*seok*) Choros, Terbet, Tumat, and others. The ethnonyms quoted are well-known among the western Mongols or Oirats, among whom they were names of separate large tribes or of tribal and clan unions. The influence of the western Mongols continued until the middle of the 18th century when their Dzungarian state collapsed.

Thus on the basis of everything mentioned above, it can be deduced that the ethnic origin of the southern Altayans came about as a result of a drawn-out and complicated historical process, as a result of division and separation, mingling and interbreeding of various, preponderantly Turkic-speaking tribes whose language was Kipchak. Consequently, they are descendants of ancient Altay and medieval Kipchak tribes in whose formation Mongol ethnic elements played repeatedly an important part. With all this, with all the multilingual crossings, the Turkic language of the southern Altayans, which had originated very long ago on the basis of Kipchak dialects, prevailed. The southern Altayans are related by reason of ethnic origin to a number of Turkic-speaking nationalities of our country and primarily to the Kazakhs, Kirgiz, part of the Uzbeks, the Siberian Tatars, and others.

The origin of the northern group of Altayans has a different history. First of all, the language of the northern group in the above-mentioned classification of

Turkic languages belongs to the northeastern group, which is also called the Uygur since its phonetic peculiarities are similar to those of the language of an ancient Turkic-speaking nation—the Uygurs. This similarity can also be traced in the vocabulary. In the dialect of the northern Altayans, for instance, the words dog (*aday*) and cart (*kanga*) bear Uygur names. At the same time, the southern Altayans had different names for them (dog—*ut*; cart—*abra* or *arba*), names that are in use among Turkic tribes and peoples linked by their origin with the Kipchak group. By linguistic analysis, to this same northeastern group also belong a number of the Khalka dialects. Even in prerevolutionary times, the attention of linguists (e.g., Korsh, Radlov) was attracted to some of the phonetic peculiarities of the northern Altayan language, which were explained as links with the eastern Finnish or Ugrian languages. Soviet investigators have established that these peculiarities are characteristic of Ugrian-Samoyed languages such as those of the Nenets, Selkup, and also of the Khanty [Ostyak] and Mansi [Voguls].

The indication of some common bonds between the languages of the northern Altayans and those of the Ugrian and Samoyed peoples of western Siberia is in accord with physical-anthropological data. Essential physical differences between the inhabitants of the southern and northern Altay become apparent already in the period of the 6th to 10th centuries during which time they acquired the characteristics that they possess today. Distinguished by less-pronounced Mongoloid characters of their basic physical traits, the northern Altayans, especially the already mentioned Shors and Kumandins, display a homogeneity of physical type, in terms of measurable and describable traits, with the Ob Ugrians—the Khanty and the Mansi. Homogeneity also reveals itself strongly in ethnographic materials. Of particular interest in this respect is their clothing. As the research of N. F. Prytkovaya has shown, the open outer garment worn by northern Altayan men and women (i.e., among the Shors, Chelkans, Kumandins) is identical in cut with that of the Surgut Khanty clothing (the Khanty of the middle or lower reaches of the Ob) and with the clothing of the so-called Tomsk Tatars. This similarity is also noted in the material, which is homemade linen. A comparison of ornaments reveals the same analogies. S. V. Ivanov, who investigated this, came to the conclusion that the rectilinear geometric ornament, characteristic of the woven and knitted goods of the Shors and Kumandins, is also widespread among the southern Khanty who live along the Irtysh, Salym, and Konda rivers, and among the southern Mansi and Narym Selkups. In the classification of ornaments of Siberian peoples, Ivanov classifies the ornamentation of the southern Khanty and Mansi and that of the Kumandins and Shors as a single type. This comparison of elements common to the national cultures of the northern Altayans, particularly the Shors, and the Khanty and Mansi, can be extended also to other examples. One of these is agreement in the type of sledges on which hunters on skis pull a load of food supplies and hunting gear. The Shors, like the Khanty and Mansi, have a hearth (*chuval*) of the same type, with a clay-coated chimney made of poles. As a utility building, erected in the taiga in the hunting regions as well as near the home, these peoples construct small sheds on high poles for the protection of food products and in particular of meats.

In their shamanistic cults, the Khanty and the Kumandins have notably similar wooden idols with pointed heads.[62] During some of the public shamanistic performances, the Kumandins as well as the northern Shors used a birchbark mask (*kocho-kan*) worn by individual participants. This is typical also of the Khanty and Mansi public performances in which such a mask played an important part. Also, it is known that the Mansi and the Khanty, in observing a ritual to mark the slaying of a bear, made a wooden phallus.[63] Elements of a phallic ritual during bear hunting were also observed by the Shors who used a switch instead of a wooden phallus.[64] The making of a wooden phallus was practiced until recently by the Shors living in Khakasia in the Tashtyn and Matur uplands. In the 18th century they had moved there from the Mras-Su river.[65] The visualization and portrayal of ancestral spirits in the form of winged people, so typical to the Khanty and Mansi, finds a complete analogy in the pictures of certain shaman spirits drawn on the drums of the Shors. Such analogies are not unique.

Ethnographic material and toponymic data permit the establishment of traces of homogeneity between the Shors and Ket-speaking inhabitants of the Yenisey basin, that is, with the Kets or so-called Yenisey Ostyaks, and with the Kotts of the 17th and 18th centuries who were later assimilated by Turkic-speaking tribes of the Minusinsk basin. Thus, Radlov noted that in northern Altay, mostly in the region settled by the Shors, the river names end in *zas*, *sas* (Anzas, Pyzas, and others). In his opinion these came from the Yenisey-Ostyak language (Ket).[66] Later Radlov, proceeding on the basis of toponymic data, formulated the hypothesis that the Shors were Turkified (in language) Yenisey-Ostyaks who, having lost their native language, retained the toponymics of that language.[67] If we dismiss the obvious exaggeration of this hypothesis, namely the presentation of the origin of the Shors in an oversimplified way (while it is undoubtedly more complicated), the uniformity of some Ket and Shor ethnic elements is something that can not be doubted. Thus, until quite recently, the Kets worshipped the benevolent deity "mother-Tom," who, they believed, lived far to the south in a stone house. In this notion there is preserved the memory of the past life, of part of the Kets, in the stony mountains along the upper reaches of the Tom, where the Shors preserve to this day the Ket toponymy. A number of peculiarities of Ket and Shor domestic life, rituals, and customs reflect even in our time the common character of their historical life and, apparently, ethnic origin. Let us keep in mind that in the 17th century both, in spite of the distance separating them, were famous for their "blacksmithing," i.e., their ability to make iron products. Consequently, the *volosts* they inhabited on the Tom and Yenisey bore the identical names, "the blacksmith's" [*kuznetskiye*]. In the life of both, hunting was of primary importance. Some details of Kott hunting customs described by Georgi in the 18th century bear an astonishing resemblance to those of the present-day Shors. Thus, for instance, Georgi reports on the Kott custom of sleeping during the hunting season "near the fire in pairs so that they lie with their heads in opposite directions, and one having the other's legs under his arms."[68] This is exactly the way in which present-day Shors sleep while hunting in the taiga, particularly those whose ancestors moved from the Mras-Su river valley to the Abakan basin, where they became known in ethnographic literature as the "Sagay." Before the revolution both had similar rituals of burying deceased small children, wrapped in birch bark, in a tree. In the shamanistic beliefs of both peoples, the birch plays an important role as the favorite tree of benevolent spirits, and so on. The shaman's drum of the Shors and the Kumandins has a great similarity to that of the Kets. E. D. Prokofeva, after determining this in her special investigation, classified the Shor, Kumandin, and Ket drums as one common type.

Finally, as direct proof of the dissemination of Ket ethnic elements in the Altay we have the Altayan clan Ara whose members are descendants of the 17th century Arins who had nomadized in the Yenisey basin.

The south Samoyed ethnic element must be regarded as one of the most important ethnic components of the northern Altayans. Data on this can be found in written historical as well as ethnographic materials. Let us examine first the historical material concerned with the ethnonymy of the northern Altayans. In it we will not find that astonishing similarity of clan-tribal designations that we observed in comparing them with present-day ethnonyms of the southern Altayans. However, even here there are rare genetic links in evidence. Eminently, one concerns the ethnonym Tuba, which is a general designation of a part of the northern Altayans—the Tubalars. This ethnonym is known from Chinese chronicle sources in the form *Tu-po* and appears in the Wei dynasty annalistic chronicle as one of the designations of the Kao-ch'ê T'ieh-lê generations. In the annals of the T'ang dynasty, this generation is considered to belong to the Türk (T'u-chüeh) of whom the "skiing T'u-chüeh" were the eastern neighbors of the Khalka-Kirgiz. Let us quote the passage in precise translation:

All of the rivers flow northeastward. Having passed through this domain they join and, to the north, flow into the sea (i.e., into Lake Kosogol, as Iakinf remarks). In the east they (the travelers) reach three settlements of the Chüeh Mu-ma (*mu-ma* literally means "wooden horses," i.e., skis) or skiing T'u-chüeh: they are called Tu-po, Mi-li-ke and Ê-chih. Their elders are all Hsia-chin (Gyegin [?] in Iakinf's transcription). The houses are covered with birch bark. Many good horses. Usually they travel on wooden horses (*mu-ma*, i.e., skis), running on the ice. Legs are propped up by wooden planks: leaning on a crooked wood (stick) under the armpit makes for an immediate powerful spurt of a hundred paces.[69]

The same chronicle preserved a short but expressive description of the Tu-po:

They were divided into three *aymaks*, each being ruled by its chief. They did not know the year's seasons (did not have a calendar); they lived in grass huts, did not practice cattle herding or tillage. Day lilies (*sarana*) are abundant there; they gathered the roots and made porridge out of them. They caught fish, fowl, and animals and used them for food. They clothed themselves in sable and deer skins; but the poor made clothing out of bird feathers. At weddings the rich gave horses as presents and the poor deer skins and sarana roots. The dead were put into coffins and placed on mountains or tied into trees. In escorting the deceased, they produced weeping sounds in the same way as the T'u-chüeh. There were no punishments, no fines. Having stolen something, a man paid double for the stolen object.[70]

It is apparent from this description that the ethnonym *Tupo* referred to hunters in the taiga who were dependents of the Türk (T'u-chüeh). Later, the ethnonym *Tupo—Tuba*—is found in "The secret history of the Mongols" (*Yüan-chao pi-shih* of the 13th century), in an account of the subjugation in 1207 by Juchi, the son of Genghis Khan, of the forest people inhabiting the Sayan-Altay upland. It is applied to one of these peoples.[71] This ethnonym remained in the clan-tribal names of Sayan-Altay upland peoples to our time. It is typical that present-day Sayan-Altay tribes and nationalities among whom the ethnonym *Tupo* was preserved (the Tofalar-Karagas, the Tubalar-Altayans), before the revolution, also belonged in culture and economy to the taiga hunting tribes whose ethnic origins were linked to the southern Samoyeds. This is so, because some of them were Samoyed speaking or retained remnants of that language as late as the 17th and 18th centuries. Tuba and Samoyed kinship was already pointed out by Georgi.[72] Later this view was stated and substantiated by M. A. Castren and V. V. Radlov.[73] In our time, the connection of the ethnonym *Tuba—(Tupo)* to the south Samoyed tribes was confirmed by G. N. Prokofiyev.[74] The ethnonym *Mi-li-ke*, [mentioned earlier], by which one of the *Tupo* generations is called in Chinese chronicles, should perhaps be compared to the name "Milisy." The latter designation was used in 17th century Russian historical sources as a name for one group of Chulyma Tatars, who later were called "Melets Tatars." Melets Tatars were one of the components of the Turkic-speaking population along the Chulyma river. There, the Baygul clan was also known to reside. G. E. Grum-Grzhimaylo proposed that they (together with the Kamasins, i.e., the south Samoyed clan Bayga) were descendants of the generation Bayegu [Pa-yeh-ku] of the Chinese historians or of the Bayirku mentioned in the Orkhon inscriptions.[75] In Chinese chronicles the Pa-yeh-ku appear together with the Tu-po among a number of T'ieh-lê generations and it was said of them: "They loved the hunt passionately; they were but little interested in tillage. They hunted reindeer over the ice on skis. Their customs most resembled those of the T'ieh-lê, there was a small difference of speech."[76] Thus, the members of the Bayegu clan also belonged, by culture and mode of life, to those forest tribes and peoples of the Sayan-Altay uplands who by origin, like the Tupo, were apparently connected with Samoyed ethnic elements but were dependants of Turkic-speaking T'ieh-lê and T'u-chüeh tribes and were subjected to Turkization. This is indicated also in the vocabulary of present-day Samoyed languages, where *bay* and *bayga* are among the ethnonyms of Samoyed clans and tribes (e.g., the Turukhan, Karasin Samoyeds, and Kamasins).

Thus the possession by the northern Altayans of some of the above-mentioned ethnonyms, especially the ethnonym *Tuba*, is witness that the southern Samoyed tribes took part in the ethnogenesis of the northern Altayans. This is indicated not only by the distribution of the *Tuba-Dubo* [Tu-po] ethnonym but also by additional data. Let us refer to separate ethnographic parallels, for instance, between the Shors, Chelkans, Kumandins, and Selkups. It is known that before the revolution a special type of hearth, the so-called *chuval*, was shared by these peoples. The Selkups made the *chuval* from an old boat (dugout).[77] The Shors and Chelkans also formerly made the chuval from a dugout as indicated by its designation *kebe* or *kebege* (literally: boat). The Shors and Chelkans call the chimney of such a hearth *sugen*, which means fishing gear woven from switches (fishing basket, creel). Indeed, the chimney is woven from switches in the fashion of a creel and is then coated with clay. It is possible that if a boat was used for the stack of the hearth, old creels may have been used for the chimney. Selkup and Kumandin legends offer proof that birch-bark boats were known to them in the past. The chief meaning of this is that they reflect the important part fishing played in the economic life of the Chelkans and Selkups in the past. This can not be called typical of the indigenous Turkic-speaking nomadic cattle herders, if the premise is applied that the Shors and Chelkans are descendant from early Turkic nomads of the Altay as was established for the southern Altayans. But this is well in accord with the economic conditions of the taiga hunting tribes from the Sayan-Altay uplands, linked in origin to the Samoyeds among whom taiga fishing was part of the over-all economy.

Further, the family name Karalkin is encountered among the Kumandins. This name is common even among the Selkups living along the Tym and Ob. It originated, as G. P. Prokofiyev demonstrated, from the designation of the Zhuravl* (*karal-kup*) clan in the process of the breakdown of the clan system

*[Crane.—Editor.]

among Selkups and the consequent transformation of clan and tribal names to family names.[78] The existence among the northern Altayans (the Kumandins and Tubalars) of the family or sib Chotu or Chota should be noted.[79] This sib is common for the Koybals, Karagas-Tofalars, and some of the northeastern Tuvins (Tocharians) whose southern Samoyed origin has been fully established. A legend links the appearance of the Choty clan (*seok*) among the Kumandins to the arrival on the Biyu of three brothers who were the forefathers of that clan among the Kumandins and Tubalars of Komdosh *volost*. The Choty [clan] was also found among the Shors. Several Shor legends relate that in the distant past a people by the name of Chot lived on the Mras-Su river near the present-day ulus Sosnovaya Gora [Pine Mountain]. The legend indicates that the major part of this people died out from some illness and that the survivors joined the Shors—the inhabitants of Sosnovaya Gora. This, of course, refers to the same Chotu or Chota sibs of Samoyed origin that became part of the present-day Shors.[80]

In this connection some Kumandin hunting legends that mention the milking of reindeer, even though this is attributed to Kumandin mountain spirits, assume a special meaning.[81] This may be taken as a recollection that some of the Kumandins, linked by origin to the southern Samoyeds, kept reindeer in the distant past. The reindeer were used for riding and their milk for food, as is still done by the Tofalar-Karagas and Tuvin-Tocharians and as was also practiced by the Koybals in the 18th century. The presence of the Toon clan among the Kumandins, as well as the Shor name *toon-kizhi* for them, are also indicative of the carrying on of reindeer herding in the past among some of them. *Toon* means "reindeer" and *toon-kizhi* may mean "reindeer herders"—the same as the term *todzhi*, the name of the northeastern reindeer-herding Tuvins.[82] The Tuvins of northern Altay could not retain reindeer herding because of the natural conditions of this region, which make it devoid of feeding lands for reindeer.

Aside from these data on the penetration of southern Samoyed ethnic elements into the Altay region, one can refer also to the existence of the Modor clan among the Altayans. Inhabitants belonging to this clan should be recognized as the descendants of the Samoyed-speaking Mators who, in the 17th century, lived in the Tubin *zemlitsa* of Krasnoyarsk *kray*, which later, in the 18th century, became the Tubin *aymak* or ulus. However, so far it has not been determined when and under what circumstances a part of the Mators, as well as a part of the formerly Ket-speaking Arins, appeared in the Altay. It is known only that in the middle of the 17th century there appeared in the Altay the Tocharians (the "Tochi" of Russian documents) who nomadized along the Katun river together with other Tuvin tribes, the Sayans and Mingats.[83]

Let us consider yet another ancient ethnonym among the Kumandins. It is mentioned in "The secret history of the Mongols" as the name of one of the forest peoples who together with the Tubas submitted to Genghis Khan's son, Juchi.[84] The reference is to the name for the Kumandin clan (seok) Tas (pl. Tastar). The tribute book of the Tomsk *uyezd* for the year 1690 records that part of the Tastars were to be found in the upper reaches of the Tom "in flight from the Kirgiz robbers." The Tastar volost paid its tribute in beaver and sable pelts. The legend about the origin of that clan relates that the Tastars were fishermen (*balik chylar*) in the past. They joined the Tuvins (*Soyots*) and Upper Kumandins (*Öre kumandy*). The latter they regarded as blood relatives and therefore marriage between them and the Öre kumandy clan was not permitted.[85] The common traits of the Tastars and Upper Kumandins stand out also in the similarities of their economic life, as captured in the legends. Thus, according to legends of the Upper Kumandins, they practiced fishing and built boats of birch bark (*tos kebe*). Both clans then were linked in economic activity and some elements of material culture that were characteristic of forest tribes of Samoyed and Ket origin who inhabited the Sayan-Altay uplands.

The most important source for detecting the Turkic ethnic element in the composition of present-day northern Altayans is their language. As noted previously, it does not belong to the Kipchak group of Turkic languages, which is characteristic of the southern Altayans, but to the Uygur group linked in origin to the ancient Uygurs, whose domination in the 8th century in the eastern part of Central Asia replaced the political rule of the Turkic khanates. Linguistic data openly indicate that ancient Uygur Turkic-speaking peoples participated in the ethnogenesis of the northern Altayans and assimilated the small, multilingual tribes and clans (Uygur, Samoyed, Ket) in the Sayan-Altay uplands. At the same time, there are data that confirm that the Türk (T'u-chüeh) also took part in the ethnogenesis of the northern Altayans. In this connection the ethnonym *So*, the name of one of the Kumandin clans, is of great interest.

The legend concerning the origin of the Türk (T'u-chüeh), recorded in Chinese chronicles and successfully interpreted by Aristov, has been mentioned *supra* in considering the origin of the southern Altayans. It takes on even greater meaning if the ethnonym *So* is taken into account. The legend traces the origin of the Türk (T'u-chüeh) from the So tribe that lived north of the Huns, probably in the northern Altay region, inasmuch as the southern Altay was part of Hun territory. Investigators acknowledge that the Kumandin clan (*seok*) So is genetically linked by name as well as by location with the So tribes mentioned in the legend. To this may be added that the area of occupancy by tribes and clans with the ethnonym *So* can be extended beyond the limits of the Kumandin clan So, perhaps to include the Yakuts. In any case the clan or sib Soo or Sogo, as late as the 17th century, was part of the population of Kachin *zemlitsa* on the Yenisey belonging to the Toylar *aymak*. There are also other transcriptions of the ethnonym *so—Soko, Soky, Sokho*, and so on. In the tribute books after 1664, the Toylar aymak is called Kubanov ulus. This seok was preserved among the Kachins into the 20th century within the administrative system of the Kubanov clan. It is quite possible that the Kumandin volost, mentioned in Russian historical documents of the first half of the 17th century as belonging to the Kondosh volosts, i.e., volosts situated in the Kondosh river basin, was related to the Kubanov ulus by composition of its population.[86] Thus, one of the most ancient ethnonyms of a Turkic-speaking population of the first centuries A.D., recorded in Chinese chronicles, was preserved through the medium of legends in the clan and tribal names of present-day Kumandins and Khalkas.

The ethnonym *Kibi* is also of note. Ki-pi is referred to in Chinese sources as the name of one of the T'ieh-lê generations. Grum-Grzhimaylo links it with the name of the Shor *seok* Kibi or Kivi.[87] The ethnonym *Kibi* (*Kivi*) was preserved in the name for the Kivin volost among the Shors and Sagays and is mentioned in Russian historical documents of the 17th century.[88] Finally, there is the name for the Kao-ch'ê generation—A-pa—mentioned in the chronicles of the Sui dynasty (581–618 A.D.). However, in the opinion of N. V. Kyuner, Bichurin's translation confuses the term A-pa, assigning it to a khan A-po rather than to a T'ieh-lê generation.[89] Chavannes mentions this ethnonym as one for a T'ieh-lê generation in the year 603 A.D.[90] The name Aba is known from Russian historical documents of the beginning of the 17th century as a name for a volost and a generation of "Blacksmith Tatars," ancestors of the present-day northern Shors. Among the latter, the ethnonym *Aba* is taken by all investigators as a *seok* name. Members of the Russian "academic" expedition of the 18th century, Gmelin, and particularly Georgi, give a comparatively detailed description of the culture and economy of the Abins and stress their full resemblance to the Teleuts "in respect to appearance, spiritual qualities, internal organization, morals, language, calculation of time, and rites."[91] Apparently, in the 16th century the Abins still entered into the composition of the Teleuts, as in the 7th century they were a part of the Tölö. Although in the beginning of the 17th century the Abins were described as hunters and metallurgists, they were also cattle herders because, as Georgi notes, their "cattle herding fully resembles that of the Teleuts." This means that in the 18th century the Abins still knew nomadic cattle herding in contrast to the ancestors of the southern Shors who only engaged in hunting, fishing in taiga [rivers], and root gathering. In connection with this, the folklore of the northern Shors includes epics which reflect the life, culture, and economy of cattle-herding nomads, at a time when only short stories, hunting tales, and legends are characteristic of the culture and economy of taiga-dwelling foot hunters. As previously noted, the existence of a Shor epic identical with one of the southern Altayans is explained by the participation of the Teleuts in the ethnogenesis of the northern Shor, i.e., of ancient nomadic cattle-herders, whose origin is linked to Turkic-speaking Altay tribes of the 6th to 8th centuries.[92]

Thus several separate ancient ethnic elements enter into the composition of the northern Altayans. In the 6th to 8th centuries they served to unify the Turkic-speaking tribes of the sprawling Sayan-Altay region and are known in Chinese chronicles as T'ieh-lê and T'u-chüeh. Therefore it is quite natural that among some of the most conservative elements in the prerevolutionary life of the northern Altayans there were preserved remnants of shaman beliefs of the Altay or Orkhon Turkic tribes of the 6th to 8th centuries A.D. The cult of a female goddess is typical of this. Among the northern Altayans and some of the Shors the goddess is the patroness of the children Umay or May-Ene. Her name and cult are known from the Orkhon inscriptions. Indeed, as demonstrated by the preceding account, these ancient ethnic elements, although they do not determine the ethnic composition of the northern Altayans, can not be ignored in clarifying the problem of the ethnogenesis of the group of Altayans.

In summing up these remarks on the ethnic composition of the northern Altayans, it can be ascertained that they came into being as a result of a complex and protracted process of fragmentation and dispersion, mingling and inter-breeding of different Turkic, Ugrian, Samoyed, and Ket ethnic elements, primarily in the taiga regions of the Sayan-Altay uplands. Cultural peculiarities of the northern Altayans that evolved on the basis of foot hunting, taiga fishing, hoe cultivation, and the gathering of wild edible plants distinguish them sharply from the southern Altayans. At the same time, many cultural traits of the northern Altayans show an astonishing resemblance to those of a number of other Siberian peoples—linguistically Ugrian, Samoyed, and Ket—now separated from the northern Altayans by many hundreds and even thousands of kilometers. Such a resemblance can not be accidental. It points to common ethnic elements for these people in the past and to a common historical development. Indeed, in the 17th century the territories of the Ugrian and Turkic tribes of western Siberia were contiguous.

The process of breaking up and mingling of the above-mentioned ethnic groups was accomplished by the crossing of different languages and dialects, as a result of which some languages achieved predominance while others were gradually subjected to complete assimilation. The victor in this process was the Turkic language of the northern Altayans, which arose from the basis of the ancient Uighur language. The Turkization of these various ethnic groups in the Sayan-Altay uplands began in remote antiquity. It dates at least from the period of the Turkic khanates and their political heirs—the Uygur khanates and the khanates of the Yenisey Kirgiz. This is clearly brought out by the vocabulary and some peculiarities of grammatical structure in the language of the northern Altayans. It should be emphasized that at a later time these small Turkic-speaking tribes and clans were also subjected to Mongol influence, particularly to that of the Oirat or western Mongol (Dzungarian) khanates.

The process of Turkization of small tribes of the Sayan-Altay uplands who spoke different languages, particularly of the Samoyed-speaking and Ket-speaking Mators, Kamasins, Kotts, Assans, Arins, and others, was drawn out into later times, the 17th and 18th centuries, occurring under the influence of the most recent ancestors of the present-day Khalkas in whose composition the Yenisey Kirgiz played an important role.

Thus, it is evident that the present-day southern and northern Altayans are first, of different, and second, of complex, ethnic origin. Their designation as Altayan was used in the literature because they lived in the Altay. Before the revolution only one small group of southern Altayans, inhabiting the Katun, Charysh, and Peshchanaya river basins, called itself Altayan (Altay-Kizhi). However, today the name Altayan has been widely and firmly accepted and the recognition of the Altayans by [the establishment of] the Gorno-Altay Autonomous Oblast was done independently of their autonyms before the revolution.

Notes and References

1. V. Radlov, *Obraztsy narodnoy literatury tyurkskikh plemen* (Examples of the national literature of Turkic tribes), 1st edition, St. Petersburg, 1866; W. Radloff; *Aus Sibirien*, vols. 1 and 2; N. A. Aristov: Zametki ob etnicheskom sostave tyurkskikh plemen i narodnostey (Notes on the ethnic composition of Turkic tribes and nationalities), *Zhivaya starina*, nos. 3–4, 1896.

2. W. Radloff, *Aus Sibirien*, vol. 2, p. 143.

3. These differences are pointed out in a number of my works. See, for instance, the monograph *Razlozheniye rodovogo stroya u plemen severnogo Altaya* (Disintegration of the clan system among the tribes of northern Altay) and also the present work.

4. G. F. Debets, *Antropologicheskiye issledovaniya v Kamchatskoy oblasti* (Anthropological researches in the Kamchatka region), Moscow, 1951, pp. 71, 119.

5. See: S. V. Kiselev, *Drevnyaya istoriya yuzhnoy Sibiri* (Ancient history of southern Siberia).

6. The term T'ieh-lê also refers to the nomadic tribes living far from the borders of the Altay.

7. The reasons that engendered such a policy are disclosed and investigated in Kiselev's *Drevnyaya istoriya yuzhnoy Sibiri*, p. 505.

8. P. Pelliot, L'origine des Tou-kiue, nom chinois des turks. *T'oung Pao*, vol. 16, 1915, pp. 687–689.

9. See: W. Radloff, *Die alttürkischen Inschriften der Mongolei*, 3rd edition, St. Petersburg, 1895, pp. 424–428.

10. N. Y. Bichurin (Iakinf), *Sobraniye svedeniy* . . . (Collected information . . .), vol. 1.

11. V. V. Bartold, Ocherk istorii turkmenskogo naroda (Historical sketch of the Turkmen people), *Turkmeniya*, vol. 1, Leningrad, 1929, pp. 9–10.

12. N. A. Aristov, Zametki ob . . . , *Zhivaya starina*, nos. 3–4, 1896, p. 5.

13. The superstition about "Yada-tash" was very widespread among present-day Turkic-speaking tribes and peoples. See: S. E. Malov, Shamanskiy kamen "yada" u tyurkov zapadnogo Kitaya (The shaman stone "Yada" of Turkic tribes in western China), *Sovetskaya etnografiya*, no. 1, 1947. A detailed survey of the material on this problem is represented by the work of F. Adrian, Über den Wetterzauber der Altaier, *Correspondenzblatt der deutchen Gesellschaft für Anthropologie, Ethnologie und Urgeschichte*, no. 8, 1893.

14. Bichurin (Iakinf), *Sobraniye svedeniy* . . . , vol. 1, pp. 229–231.

15. Kiselev, *op. cit.*, p. 516.

16. D. Pozdneev, Istoricheskiy ocherk Uygurov (A historical sketch of the Uygurs), pp. 37–41.

17. F. Hirth, Nachwort zur Inschrift des Tonjukuk, in W. Radloff, *Die alttürkischen Inschriften der Mongolei*, 2nd edition, 1899, pp. 56, 129, 133, 140. This identification was also accepted by E. Chavannes in his *Documents sur les Tou-kiue (turcs) occidenteaux*, pp. 94, 95, 105.

18. Hirth, *op. cit.*, p. 133.

19. V. Thomsen, Inscriptions de l'Orkhon, *Mém. soc. finno-ougrienne*, vol. 5, 1896, p. 178.

20. *Ibidem*, p. 123; E. Chavannes, *Documents sur les Tou-kiue (turcs) occidenteaux*, p. 86.

21. W. Bartold, Die historische Bedeutung der alttürkischen Inschriften, in W. Radloff, *Die alttürkischen Inschriften der Mongolei*, neue Folge, 1897, p. 8. See also Radloff's *Ocherk istorii turkmenskogo naroda* (Historical sketch of the Turkmen people), pp. 9–10, and his Ocherk istorii Semirechya (A sketch of Semirechye history), in *Pamyatnaya knizhka Semirechenskogo oblastnogo statisticheskogo komiteta za 1898 g.*, vol. 2, Verny, 1898, pp. 87–88 and others.

22. S. P. Tolstov, Goroda Guzov (Cities of the Ghuz), *Sovetskaya etnografiya*, no. 3, 1947, p. 100.

23. V. Bartold, Novy trud o nasobtsakh (New researches on the Nasobets), *Russk. istor. zhurnal*, book 7, Petrograd, 1921, p. 142.

24. In his research mentioned above, S. P. Tolstov reached the following conclusion: "The descendants of the Ephthalite-Kidarits "Turkified" in the 6th and 7th centuries are known in the 8th to 11th centuries under the collective name Oghuz—both in their old territory, where the Hun political tradition continues to hold out most steadily, and on the southern and eastern edges of the Ephthalite domain (Toghuz-Oghuz) is the name subsequently given to the Uygurs in East Turkestan."

25. Because of this, the Polovets-Kipchaks and the Oghuz cannot be considered one nation as thought by Marquart (J. Marquart, *Über das Volkstum der Komanen*, Berlin, 1914, p. 29).

26. S. E. Malov, *Pamyatniki drevnetyurkskoy pismennosti* (Monuments of ancient Turkic writing), p. 7.

27. Aristov, Zametki ob . . . , *Zhivaya starina*, 1896, nos. 3–4, p. 341.

28. Radloff, *Aus Sibirien*, vol. 1, p. 126; V. Thomsen, Inscriptions de l'Orkhon, *Mém. soc. finno-ougrienne*, vol. 5, 1896, p. 146; F. Hirth, Nachwort zur Inschrift des Tonjukuk, p. 133; E. Chavannes, *Documents sur les Tou-kiue (turcs) occidenteaux*, p. 14; L. Cahun, *Introduction à l'histoire de l'Asie*, Paris, 1896, p. 101.

29. Bartold, Die historische Bedeutung . . . , p. 9; P. M. Melioranskiy, Pamyatnik v chest Kyul-Tegina (Monument in honor of Kyul-Tegin), *Zapiski vost. otd. Russk. arkheol. obshch.*, vol. 12, nos. 2–3, 1899, p. 109.

30. A. N. Kononov, *Grammatika turetskogo yazyka* (A grammar of the Turkic

194   *L. P. Potapov*

language), Leningrad, 1941, p. 95 (contains also references bearing on this problem); *idem., Grammatika Uzbekskogo yazyka* (A grammar of the Uzbek language), Tashkent, 1948, p. 36–37; S. E. Malov, *Pamyatniki drevnetyurkskoy pismennosti*, pp. 50–52.

31. W. Radloff, *K voprosu ob Uygurakh* (Questions concerning the Uygurs), p. 89–90; G. Schlegel, Die chinesische Inschrift auf dem uigurischen Denkmal in Kara-Balgassun, *Mém. soc. finno-ougrienne*, vol. 9, Helsingfors, 1896, p. 1; Aristov, Zametki ob . . . , *Zhivaya starina*, nos. 3–4, 1896, p. 301 and others.

32. S. A. Tokarev, *Dokapitalisticheskiye perezhitki v Oyrotii* (Precapitalistic survivals in Oirotia), pp. 20, 22.

33. Stalin, *Marksizm i voprosy yazykoznaniya*, p. 26.

34. *Ibidem*, p. 22.

35. Mundus—the name of one of the most ancient and most widespread clans among the Teleuts.

36. Bichurin (Iakinf), *Sobraniye svedeniy* . . . , vol. 1, p. 50.

37. A. N. Bernshtam, Drevneyshiye tyurkskiye elementy v etnogeneze Sredney Azii (The earliest Turkic elements in the ethnogenesis of Central Asia), *Sovetskaya etnografiya*, nos. 6–7, 1947, p. 154; B. Karlgren, *Analytic dictionary of Chinese and Sino-Japanese*, Paris, 1923 (Cited in A. N. Bernshtam, *op. cit.*, p. 154).

38. Chavannes, *Documents sur les Tou-kiue (turcs) occidenteaux*, pp. 28–29.

39. G. Ramstedt, Perevod nadpisi "Selenginskogo kamnya" (Translation of the inscription on the "Selenga Stone"), *Trudy Troitsko-Savsko-Kyakhtinsk. odt. Priamursk. otdela Russk. Geograf. Obshch.*, vol. 15, no. 1, 1912, p. 40.

40. V. Rubruk [William of Rubruck], *Puteshestviye v vostochnye strany*, Perevod A. Maleina (A journey to eastern countries, Translated by A. Malein), St. Petersburg, 1911, p. 80. Nizami reported even before Rubruck on the erection of a stone woman in Juchi ulus by the Kipchaks or Polovets—in V. Bartold, *Otchet o poyezdke v Srednyuyu Aziyu s nauchnoy tselyu v 1893–1894 gg.* (Account of a journey to Central Asia for scientific purposes in 1893–4), St. Petersburg, 1897.

41. L. A. Yeftyukhova, Kamennye izvayaniya severnogo Altaya (Stone sculptures of northern Altay), *Trudy Gos. Istor. Muzeya*, no. 16, Moscow, 1941.

42. M. P. Gryaznov and E. Shneyder, Drevniye izvayaniya Minusinskikh stepev (Ancient sculptures in the Minusinsk steppes), *Materialy po etnografii*, vol. 4, no. 2, 1929.

43. S. P. Shvetsov, Kochevniki Biyskogo uyezda (The nomads of the Biysk uyezd), in: *Gorny Altay i ego naseleniye* (Gorno-Altay and its inhabitants), vol. 1, no. 1, pp. 8–23. Also Appendix 5, A table showing the division of the Altayans by clan, *dyuchina*, and volost. The number of the combined southern Altayans concentrated in seven Altay *dyuchins* and two Chuy volosts added up to 23,797 persons of both sexes. The clan affiliation of 1,031 of this number has not been defined. Therefore, I calculated the clan membership in percentage figures proceeding from the total number of southern Altayans who had indicated their clan, i.e., 22,766 persons.

44. Ipatevskaya letopis (The Ipatevsk chronicle), *Poln. sobr. russk. letopisey*, vol. 2, St. Petersburg, 1843, pp. 134, 141.

45. Marco Polo, *Puteshestviye* (Travels), Leningrad, 1940, pp. 63, 117.

46. G. N. Potanin, *Ocherki Severo-zapadnoy Mongolii* (Essays on northwestern Mongolia), vol. 4, p. 97.

47. Rubruk, *Puteshestviye v vostochnye strany*, p. 80.

48. Compare the Mongolian *khoylga* as a name for the custom of burying a horse with the deceased, as told in the 17th century by Sanang Setsen. (See, Sanang Setsen, *Geschichte der Ost-Mongolen* [translated from the Mongolian language by J. Schmidt], St. Petersburg, 1829, p. 235.) Among the Yakuts *khoyluga* is the animal which is killed at the funeral repast; among the Khalkas (Kachins, Sagays, Beltirs) it is *koylaga*.

49. Radloff, *Die alttürkischen Inschriften der Mongolei*, 3rd edition, p. 427; Aristov, Zametki ob . . . , *Zhivaya starina*, 1896, nos. 3–4, p. 301.

50. Radloff, *Aus Sibirien*, vol. 1, p. 213.

51. A. V. Adrianov, Puteshestviye na Altay i za Sayany v 1881 g. (Journey to the Altay and Sayan in 1881), *Zapiski Russk. Geograf. Obshch. po obshch. etnografii,* vol. 11, St. Petersburg, 1886, p. 294.

52. The custom of wearing the hair braided in queues is mentioned in Chinese sources on the Sayan-Biysk tribes of the 3rd and 4th centuries. These, in the ethnic sense, represent a conglomerate of Mongol, Turkic, and Ting-ling elements. See: Bichurin (Iakinf), *Sobraniye svedeniy* . . . , vol. 1, pp. 167, 208–209. There is also information on the wearing of braids among the Ting-ling. See E. Chavannes, Les pays d'Occident d'après le Wei-Liao, *T'oung Pao,* ser. 2, vol. 6, 1805, p. 524. This is confirmed by the fact that their distant progeny, the Yenisey Ostyak-Kets, kept this custom until the revolution.

53. Tokarev, *Dokapitalisticheskiye perezhitki v Oyrotii,* p. 86

54. Unfortunately I could not present lexical materials here indicating the connection of the vocabulary of the Orkhon-Yenisey inscriptions with the present-day Altay language. This can be easily verified, however, by perusal of the dictionary appended to the work of S. E. Malov, *Pamyatniki drevnetyurkskoy pismennosti,* and the well-known dictionaries of the Altay language of V. Verbitsky and N. Baskakov and T. Toshchakova.

55. V. Bartold, *Otchet o poyezdke v Srednyuyu Aziyu s nauchnoy tselyu v 1893–1894 gg.* (Account of a journey to Central Asia for scientific purposes in 1893–4), St. Petersburg, 1899, p. 107.

56. Bichurin (Iakinf), *Sobraniye svedeniy* . . . , vol. 1, p. 195.

57. S. A. Kozin, *Sokrovennoye skazaniye* . . . (Secret history . . .), p. 161.

58. *Ibidem,* pp. 161, 174, 175.

59. V. Tizengauzen, *Sbornik materialov, otnosyashchikhsya k istorii Zolotoy Ordy* (Collection of materials pertaining to the history of the Golden Horde), vol. 1, St. Petersburg, 1884, p. 235 of the Russian translation.

60. B. D. Grekov and A. Yu. Yakubovskiy, *Zolotaya Orda i yeye padeniye* (The Golden Horde and its downfall), Moscow–Leningrad, 1950, p. 66.

61. See my article: Geroicheskiy epos Altaytsev (The heroic epos of the Altayans), *Sovetskaya etnografiya,* no. 1, 1949.

62. Radloff, *Aus Sibirien,* vol. 1, p. 332.

63. K. Patkanov, *Die Irtisch-Ostjaken und ihre Volkspoesie,* vol. 1, 1897, p. 130.

64. N. Drenkova, Bear worship among Turkish tribes of Siberia, *Proc. of the 23rd Intern. Congress of Americanists,* 1928, p. 437.

65. According to P. I. Karalkin.

66. W. Radloff, *Phonetik der nördlichen Türksprachen,* Leipzig, 1882, p. 66.

67. Radloff, *Aus Sibirien,* vol. 1, pp. 188–189.

68. L. Georgi, *Opisaniye vsekh obitayushchikh v Rossiyskom gosudarstve narodov* (Description of all peoples inhabiting the Russian domain), part 3, p. 27.

69. N. V. Kyuner, Novye kitayskiye materialy po etnografii kyrgyzov (khakasov) VII–VIII vekov n.e., (New Chinese materials on the ethnography of the Kirgiz-Khalka of the 7th and 8th centuries A.D.), *Zap. Khakassk. Nauchno-issled. inst.,* no. 2, Abakan, 1951, p. 14. Compare with: Bichurin (Iakinf), *Sobraniye svedeniy* . . . , vol. 1, p. 354.

70. Bichurin (Iakinf), *Sobraniye Svedeniy* . . . , vol. 1, p. 348.

71. Kozin, *Sokrovennoye skazaniye* . . . , p. 175.

72. I. Georgi, *Opisaniye vsekh* . . . , part 3, p. 17.

73. A. Castren, Reiseberichte und Briefe aus den Jahren 1845–1849. *Nordische Reisen und Forschungen,* vol. 2, St. Petersburg, 1856, p. 351; Radloff, *Aus Sibirien,* vol. 1, pp. 191, 212, 213.

74. G. N. Prokofiyev, Etnogoniya narodnostey Ob-Yeniseyskogo basseyna (Ethnogeny of the peoples of the Ob-Yenisey basin), *Sovetskaya etnografiya,* 1940, no. 3, pp. 69–70.

75. G. E. Grum-Grzhimaylo, *Zapadnaya Mongoliya i Uryankhayskiy kray* (Western Mongolia and the Uryankhaysk kray), vol. 2, Leningrad, 1926, p. 250.

76. Bichurin (Iakinf), *Sobraniye svedeniy* . . . , vol. 1, p. 344.

77. E. D. Prokofeva, Drevniye zhilishcha na rekakh Tym i Ket (Ancient dwellings on the rivers Tym and Ket), *Sovetskaya etnografiya*, 1947, no. 2, p. 200.

78. Prokofiyev, Etnogoniya narodnostey . . . , *Sovetskaya etnografiya*, 1940, no. 3, p. 74.

79. The name of this clan is pronounced also *Choty, Ioty*, and among the Tubalars *Duuty*. See: Slovar Oyrotsko-Russkogo yazyka N. Baskakova i T. Toshchakovoy (Dictionary of the Oirot-Russian language by N. Baskakov and T. Toshchakova), 1945, p. 216.

80. Cf. Shor legends of wars with the Chot or Shot peoples who used to approach the Shors through the upper reaches of the Mras-Su river, *Shorskiy folklor* (Shor folklore), p. 309.

81. N. P. Dyrenkova, Okhotnichi legendy kumandintsev (Kumandin hunting legends), *Sbornik muzeya antropol. i etnogr.*, AN SSSR, vol. 11, 1949, pp. 121, 123, 125.

82. V. Radlov, Etnograficheskiy obzor Tyurkskikh plemen Sibiri i Mongolii (Ethnographic survey of Turkic tribes in Siberia and Mongolia), Irkutsk, 1929, p. 25; see translator's notes.

83. Additions to *Akty istoricheskiye*, vol. 3, p. 319; G. Miller, *Istoriya Sibiri* (History of Siberia), vol. 2, p. 534.

84. Kozin, *Sokrovennoye skazaniye* . . . , p. 175.

85. Traditions recorded by P. I. Karalkin.

86. L. P. Potapov, Etnicheskiy sostav Sagaytsev (The ethnic composition of the Sagays), *Sovetskaya etnografiya*, 1947, no. 3.

87. Grum-Grzhimaylo, *Zapadnaya Mongoliya* . . . , vol. 2, p. 248.

88. Potapov, Etnicheskiy sostav Sagaytsev, *Sovetskaya etnografiya*, 1947, no. 3, pp. 110–111.

89. Bichurin (Iakinf), *Sobraniye svedeniy* . . . , vol. 1, p. 238.

90. Chavannes, *Documents sur les Tou-kiue (turcs) occidenteaux*, p. 50 (with reference to the Suishu and St. Julian chronicle).

91. A. Gmelin, *Reise durch Sibirien von dem Jahre 1733 bis 1743*, vol. 1; Georgi, *Opisaniye vsekh* . . . , vol. 2, p. 162.

92. See my review of "Shorskiy folklor" (Shor folklore) in *Sovetskaya etnografiya*, 1948, no. 3.

P. N. TRETYAKOV

VOLGA-OKA PLACE NAMES AND SOME PROBLEMS OF THE ETHNOGENESIS OF THE FINNO-UGRIC PEOPLES OF THE VOLGA REGION*

1. AT THE END OF 1955, in the journal *Voprosy yazykoznaniya* (Problems of Linguistics), no. 6, there was published an article by B. A. Serebrennikov, "Volga-Oka place names in the territory of the European U.S.S.R.," which was of great interest for the study of the ethnogenesis of the Finno-Ugrian peoples of the Volga region. The essential feature of Serebrennikov's article was its attempt to reconsider radically the traditional concepts of the Finno-Ugric origin of the basic pre-Slavic stratum of place names in the Volga-Oka interfluve.

Until the present time, it was usually held that on the basis of toponymic data, particularly river names, there existed at one time in the northern part of the European U.S.S.R. two great ethnic regions: the ancient Baltic (Letto-Lithuanian) region, including the upper Dnieper, Neman, and Dvina regions, and the region of the Volga, the North, and the Urals, where the original stratum of place names, it was thought, was Finno-Ugric. The boundary between these regions passes somewhat to the west of Moscow; the upper Oka, according to toponymic data, is situated in the Baltic ethnic region. It was thought that just here, on the Dnieper-Volga watershed, close contact took place over a long period between the Balts and the Finno-Ugrians—contact which was later disturbed by Slavic colonization.

The Baltic (Letto-Lithuanian) character of the original stratum of place names of the upper Dnieper and its periphery is not subject to any doubt whatever. To this stratum belong such river names as Luchesa, Istra, Lemna, Upa, Zhizdra, Zhuzhala, Nara, Sozh, Verpeta, and hundreds of others. It is entirely clear that the Slavic newcomers not only found a Baltic population in the upper Dnieper region but also lived and mixed with it for a long time and took over from it the names of almost all the rivers and lakes. The stratum of Slavic-Russian place names in the upper Dnieper region is quite insignificant. It includes chiefly the names of small rivulets and brooks on the watersheds, in places occupied until recent times by large forested tracts.

Judging by B. A. Serebrennikov's article, a completely different picture obtains in the region of the Volga-Oka interfluve, which is usually included within the boundaries of ancient Finno-Ugrian territory. It is found that the original stratum of ancient place names ("hydronymics") in this region, of which the "riverine" suffixes -*ma*, -*ga*, -*sha* are especially characteristic (Klyazma, Andoma, Kudma, Vichuga, Shuga, Shoksha, Tesha, and others), cannot be explained by analysis with modern Finno-Ugric languages of the Volga. All of the numerous attempts by investigators to compare the names of the majority of the rivers of the Volga-Oka region with different modern Finno-Ugric languages were unsuccessful. The

*Translated from *Sovetskaya etnografiya*, 1958, no. 4, pp. 9–17.

Volga-Oka place names are equally foreign to the Slavic-Russian language and to the Mordvin, Mari, Udmurt, and other Finno-Ugric languages. They are also very different from the Baltic (Letto-Lithuanian) place names. Undoubtedly another, non-Baltic, language is involved here.

Reviewing this question, Serebrennikov mentions the opinions about the Volga-Oka place names expressed by a number of investigators. Among these figures the well-known ethnographer of the Volga region, I. N. Smirnov, who has shown in his time that the place names of the Mari and Udmurt territories do not correspond to the Mari, Udmurt, or other Finno-Ugric languages.[1] The article also refers to the opinion of Academician A. I. Sobolevskiy, who considered the Volga-Oka place names as Indo-European and perhaps Scythian.[2]

The area of Volga-Oka place names, in Serebrennikov's opinion, includes the following: the western part of Smolensk *oblast,* and the oblasts of Moscow, Ivanovo, Gorki, Yaroslav, Kostroma, Ryazan (and also Vladimir—Author), Kirov, Vologda, and Archangelsk, the Mordvin and Mari [autonomous] republics, and part of the Udmurt [autonomous] republic. Separate small islands of these place names occur in Karelia, the Komi republic, and the northwestern oblasts of the R.S.F.S.R. Serebrennikov attempts to compare the distribution of Volga-Oka place names in the northern regions with the hypothesis of A. Ya. Bryusov and M. E. Foss on the migration of Neolithic tribes from the Oka basin to the north, up to the territory of southern Karelia, which took place in the 3rd and at the beginning of the 2nd millennia B.C.[3] In the Ural region, on the Kama, and within the boundaries of the Bashkir, Chuvash, and Tatar republics, place names of a Volga-Oka character are found very rarely, as exceptions. The original ancient stratum of place names in these places is Finno-Ugric.

We shall not comment here on the comparison made by Serebrennikov between the areal distribution of Volga-Oka place names and the hypothesis of Bryusov and Foss concerning the migration to the north of the Neolithic tribes of the Oka. This comparison deserves the most serious attention of the specialists concerned, who should carry out a detailed comparative study of two maps, the one showing place names and the other Neolithic sites. If these maps coincide, it will be a great gain to both sides—to Serebrennikov and to the archaeologists concerned with the Neolithic cultures of northern European Russia. But it seems to us that in the long run a still more important matter for the clarification of questions of ethnogenesis would be an attempt to compare the toponymic map with that showing the archaeological sites belonging to a population from which the immigrant Slavic-Russian population might have taken over the Volga-Oka place names. Serebrennikov, who only touches on the post-Neolithic history of the Finno-Ugrians,[4] makes no such comparison, which in our opinion constitutes a significant deficiency of his article; we shall attempt to supply this comparison in the course of a certainly very preliminary formulation of the question.

2. Basically, the territory in which the Volga-Oka place names are distributed was occupied, beginning with the early Middle Ages, by a Russian population in one part and by Finno-Ugrian tribes and peoples of the Volga in the other, eastern, part. Regarding this, we may assume that both the Russian population and the Finno-Ugrian population known in the Middle Ages stood in the same relation to the Volga-Oka place names: in both parts of the territory, the Volga-Oka names constitute the original ancient toponymic stratum immediately preceding the Slavic-Russian stratum in the more westerly districts and the Mordvin, Merian, and Murom stratum in the eastern. Individual names of a Finno-Ugric

character that occur in the western portions of the Volga-Oka interfluve occupied by a Russian population do not change the general picture. These names are so few that they literally drown among the multitude of names belonging to the Volga-Oka category. Serebrennikov can hardly be right when he doubts that the carriers of the Volga-Oka place names came in contact with the Slavs.

The situation is different in those districts where the Slavs, moving eastward, occupied the lands of Finno-Ugrian tribes—Merians, Muroms, and Vesians. The stratum of Finno-Ugric place names, as is known, is very prominent here, in the Kostroma, Yaroslav, Ivanovo, and Gorki oblasts.

Proceeding from this and from what has been said above, we may draw the following tentative conclusions: (1) at one time the Volga-Oka interfluve and its periphery was occupied by the originators and carriers of the Volga-Oka place names—unknown tribes apparently not belonging to any of the groups of Finno-Ugrian tribes that persisted until historical times; (2) the Finno-Ugrians—ancestors of the Merians, Muroms, and Mordvins—inhabited originally the more easterly of these districts, while the Balts inhabited the more westerly, that is the Neman, Dvina, and upper Dnieper regions; (3) in the course of later migrations, the eastern part of the territory of the carriers of the Volga-Oka place names was occupied by Merians, Muroms, Mordvins, Mari, and Udmurts, and the western part by Slavs; (4) the Finno-Ugrian tribes of the Volga region listed above never occupied the western part of the territory that is marked by Volga-Oka place names; (5) the Slavs, moving northward, encountered not two but three other ethnic groups—the Balts, who were akin to them, the Volga Finns, and the carriers of the Volga-Oka place names.

Let us now try to compare these conclusions, drawn on the basis of place names, with the historical and archaeological data. In order to make clear to which archaeological period the carriers of the Volga-Oka place names (who transmitted the names of rivers and lakes directly to the Slavic newcomers) should be connected, we shall begin our review by determining the time at which the Slavs arrived in the upper Dnieper.

In the course of archaeological work of the past years it has become increasingly obvious that the appearance of the Slavs in the region of the upper Dnieper was connected with the appearance on the middle Dnieper of the carriers of the so-called Zarubinets culture; this took place during the first half of the 1st millennium A.D. In the middle of the 1st millennium A.D., the Slavic element in the upper Dnieper and its periphery achieved dominance, which found expression in the development of individual Slavic tribal cultures—the Krivich, Slovene (Novgorod Slovene), Vyatich, and others.[5] The first half and the middle of the 1st millennium A.D. were thus the time when the Slavic-Russian population assimilated Baltic (Letto-Lithuanian) place names in the upper Dnieper and Volga-Oka place names in the more easterly districts.

Judging by the archaeological data, how many ethnic groups were there in the areas of the upper Dnieper and the Volga-Oka interfluve at the time of the arrival there of the Slavs, the carriers of the Zarubinets culture? Was there among them a group that we may relate to the carriers of the Volga-Oka place names?

Yes, it seems that there was such a group. We refer to the ancient population of the Volga-Oka interfluve, the archaeological remains of which, from the middle of the 1st millennium B.C. to the middle of the 1st millennium A.D., are archaeologically known as the Dyakovo fortified sites [gorodishche], first studied by A. A. Spitsyn in 1903.[6]

The fortified sites of the forested zone of the European U.S.S.R., which seemed earlier to be homogeneous, actually fall into a number of local groups, doubtless corresponding to the ancient ethnic divisions of the population. One of these groups was the Dyakovo group just mentioned; another included the fortified sites of the upper Dnieper, which in turn have a number of subdivisions; a third was the group of Ananino fortified sites in the Kama and Vetluga regions; the fourth was the group of so-called fortified town sites on the right bank of the Volga, south of the Oka. All of these have been very inadequately studied, but on the basis of materials relating to them one can nonetheless form some concept of the chief groupings of the forested zone of the European U.S.S.R. on the eve of the first arrival there of the Slavs.

About twenty years ago I began to work on archaeological maps showing the cultures of the middle and second half of the 1st millennium B.C. and published the first versions of such maps in 1940 and 1941.[7] The most important deficiency of these first versions was that the sites of the upper Oka, at that time still extremely poorly known, were identified with the Volga-Oka (Dyakovo) sites.

Later this deficiency was corrected.[8] It is now well known that the boundary between the Dyakovo fortified sites, with net-impressed pottery, and those of the upper Dnieper group, does not pass exactly along the watershed between the upper Dnieper and upper Volga systems, but somewhat to the east, separating the region of the upper Oka, with its tributaries the Ugra and the Zhizdra (within which Baltic place names are heavily represented), from the Volga-Oka basin. The western boundary of the Dyakovo fortified sites, both in the region of the watershed between the upper Dnieper and the upper Volga and on the upper Oka, coincides exactly with the boundary dividing Baltic from Volga-Oka place names.

The northern boundary of the distribution of Dyakovo fortified sites is very poorly known. They included the banks of the upper Volga and its tributaries, and are found in the region of the Valday hills. Net-impressed pottery resembling the Dyakovo type is also known in places farther to the northwest, right up to southern Karelia and the southeastern Baltic, but its relation to the Dyakovo culture has not yet been established. It would be very interesting to compare the archaeological map showing the sites with net-impressed pottery with a toponymic map, keeping in mind Serebrennikov's assertion that Volga-Oka place names are known in the northwest. But this is a matter for the future.

The southern boundary of the Dyakovo fortified sites coincides generally with the course of the Oka, which also roughly corresponds to the boundary of the Volga-Oka place names. To the east, the boundary of the Dyakovo culture crosses to the left bank of the Volga, reaching the headwaters of the Kostroma and the Galich and Chukhloma lakes. On the Kama and Vyatka, within the borders of the Komi republic and in other eastern districts where Volga-Oka place names do not occur, Dyakovo fortified sites are not found. In these regions there was an entirely different population, represented by the Ananino and Pyanobor cultures on the Kama, Vyatka, and Vetluga, and related cultures in the more northerly regions.[9] On the right bank of the Volga, south of the Oka, is found the fortified town site culture distinguishable from the Dyakovo by a number of characteristics. The basic region of the "town" culture also falls outside the limits of distribution of the Volga-Oka place names. Both cultures—the Ananino and the "town"—are commonly regarded as Finno-Ugrian.

Thus, developing the thought expressed by B. A. Serebrennikov about Volga-Oka place names, we advance the proposal that the originators of these place names may have been tribes of Dyakovo culture—large, settled populations living for centuries in the same places, which could not but facilitate the development of specific place names. This supposition does not at all contradict Serebrennikov's attempt to connect the Volga-Oka place names with the Neolithic tribes of the Oka, who in the past had migrated to the north. B. S. Zhukov in his time showed that the Dyakovo culture, with its net-impressed pottery, developed on the basis of local Neolithic (and Neolithoid, during the Bronze Age) culture.[10] We may add that the Dyakovo culture originated among the Volga-Oka population, apparently as a result of the spread of cattle breeding, agriculture, and metals, which could not but be reflected in the aspect of the culture. Consequently, tribes of the Dyakovo culture and Neolithic tribes of the Oka may both equally have been the originators and carriers of the Volga-Oka place names.

3. How is it possible to connect our conclusion with the concept, traditional in archaeological literature, that the Dyakovo culture was a Finno-Ugrian culture? It is quite obvious that it is not possible to reconcile the one with the other. Either our supposition, based on Serebrennikov's opinion, is basically mistaken, or else the Dyakovo culture was not actually Finno-Ugrian.

The idea that the Dyakovo fortified sites belonged to a Finno-Ugrian population was first expressed by A. A. Spitsyn.[11] Later this idea was apparently never called to task, unless we count the attempt to regard the Dyakovo tribes as stadial predecessors of both Finno-Ugrians and Slavs; such attempts, proceeding from the concepts of N. Ya. Marr, were made, in his time, particularly by the present author. In a recently published article "On the question of the ethnic composition of the population of the Volga-Oka interfluve in the 1st millennium A.D.," I considered the population of the Dyakovo fortified sites as Finno-Ugrian, subjected in the western districts to assimilation by the Slavs, even before the Merian, Murom, and Oka Mordvin tribes were assimilated.[12] In A. P. Smirnov's opinion, this article "brings clarity to a confused problem and in large measure solves it correctly. . . . Tretyakov's basic conclusion as to the Finno-Ugrian affiliation of the culture of the Dyakovo fortified sites as a whole . . . is no doubt correct."[13] But is this actually the case, and have not both the present author and Smirnov been too hasty in considering the problem already solved when it is still under investigation from all sides?

But what, strictly speaking, is the basis of the opinion that considers the Dyakovo culture as Finno-Ugrian—closely related to the culture of the tribes of the Volga, Kama, and Ural regions? Are there undisputed archaeological data showing that there existed a genetic connection between the Dyakovo culture and the one that replaced it in the eastern regions—the ancient culture of the Volga Finno-Ugrians known to archaeologists: the Merian, Murom, and Mordvin tribes, who lived on the middle Oka in former times? It must be admitted that such archaeological confirmation is not at our disposal.

Spitsyn, attempting to determine to whom the Dyakovo fortified sites belonged, started from the premise that they were sacrificial places, such as the ancient pagan cairns* known among the Finno-Ugrian peoples of the Volga, or like the ossuaries of the Kama area; on this basis he ascribed the Dyakovo fortified sites to the Finno-Ugrians.[14] However, the excavations later carried out on a number of Dyakovo sites did not confirm this idea: they were not the sites of a cult, but ordinary dwelling sites. Thereupon Spitsyn's argument collapsed, but his conclusion remained.

Another argument for Finno-Ugrian affiliation of the tribes of the Dyakovo

*[In Russian "keremet," a word of Chuvash origin.—Editor.]

period was the finding, at the fortified sites, of individual objects characteristic of ancient Merian, Murom, and Mordvin burial grounds. But, as V. A. Gorodtsov has correctly pointed out, the number of these finds is very small, and they date from a later time, when the Finno-Ugrian tribes—the Merians, Muroms, and Mordvins—had already been formed in the Volga region and on the Oka.[15]

For the majority of students, the main argument in favor of the Finno-Ugrian affiliation of Dyakovo culture has always been the place name data of the Volga-Oka interfluve, which were considered indisputably Finno-Ugric. But Serebrennikov's article now refutes this argument.

The numerous burial grounds and settlements in the Volga region and on the Oka were indisputably Finno-Ugrian, going back in a few places to the first centuries and in others to the middle of the 1st millennium A.D.; they formed several local groups corresponding to ancient individual tribes known from the *First Chronicle*—the Mordvins on the middle Oka, the Murom at the city of Murom, and the Merians on the territory of the present Yaroslav, Ivanovo, and Kostroma oblasts. The culture of these tribes in all its elements is so closely and inseparably bound to the ancient culture of the Volga peoples, known from ethnographic data, that there is no room here for doubt.

None of the archaeologists studying Finno-Ugrian antiquities has succeeded, however, in showing that the genetic predecessor of the culture of the Volga Finno-Ugrian tribes, known from numerous burial grounds and separate settlements, comprised the population of the Dyakovo fortified sites with net-impressed pottery. As has already been pointed out, indisputably Finno-Ugrian antiquities are distributed only along the eastern edge of that territory which the ancient Dyakovo fortified sites occupied in the preceding period. Between the cultures of these fortified sites and the Merian, Mordvin, and other Volga tribes, there is a significant difference. And it is not by chance that one of the great specialists in the field of Finno-Ugrian antiquities of the Volga region, P. P. Yefimenko, expressed in the 1920's the opinion that the population of the ancient Dyakovo fortified sites and that of the Ryazan-Oka (Mordvin) burial grounds had nothing in common.[16] Later, in 1937, not speaking so categorically, he nonetheless pointed to a number of factors that indicate a considerable gap between the culture of the Dyakovo fortified sites with net-impressed pottery and that of the Finno-Ugrian burial grounds, settlements, and fortified sites that replaced it.[17] The attempts of other students—in the first instance A. P. Smirnov, and also partly the present author—to dispute Yefimenko's views[18] were based not so much on the strict verification of factual data as on the prevalence at one time in our archaeology of "autochthonic" tendencies. It must be admitted that the question of the link between the culture of the Dyakovo fortified sites with net-impressed pottery and that of the Finno-Ugrian tribes of the Volga region, known from the chronicles, is not at all decided, and it is very possible that its resolution will be found by way of denial of direct genetic connection between these two cultures.

The process went otherwise in the western regions of the territory over which the Dyakovo fortified sites were distributed, and where the culture of the Volga tribes known from the chronicles was not found. Here the culture of the ancient fortified sites with net-impressed pottery was transformed step by step into Late Dyakovo (first half and middle of the 1st millennium A.D.),[19] in which burial grounds were not known, and which differed significantly in a number of other characteristics from the culture of the Merian, Murom, and Mordvin tribes.

Thus, it is quite possible that the Merian, Murom, and Mordvin tribes in the territory of the present Kostroma, Yaroslav, Ivanovo, Vladimir, and, in part,

Ryazan oblasts were not an autochthonous population but a population pushing forward into the territory of the Dyakovo culture in the first centuries A.D. In this connection, there is no doubt that in the course of this advance, cultural exchange took place and possibly also processes of assimilation.

Whence could the Finno-Ugrian—Merian, Murom, and Mordvin—tribes have pushed into the region of the Volga-Oka interfluve? Taking into account the numerous finds of metalware in the burial grounds, we may consider that the most ancient burial grounds in the western Volga region (Koshibeyev, Sergach, Shatrishchen, and others) contain a number of objects of the Pyanobor type in the graves dated to the first centuries A.D. This takes us into that region of the eastern Volga and Volga-Kama where there existed an ancient tradition of interment in burial grounds, deriving from the Bronze Age (Turbino, Ananino, and Pyanobor burial grounds), and where the sources of many cultural phenomena characteristic of the ancient culture of all the Finno-Ugrian peoples on the Volga and Ural regions—especially in the field of costume and decoration—are found. Even in the event that our position is shown to be erroneous, and someone succeeds in proving the autochthonous nature of the Merians and Muroms, and of the Mordvin tribes on the middle course of the Oka, it remains beyond question that the Ananino and Pyanobor cultures were the cradle of the Volga-Oka Finno-Ugrian tribes—that just there, in the Volga-Kama region, lay the most important center for the formation of the culture of the Volga Finno-Ugrians.

Yefimenko, in his time, pointed out the important role of the Volga-Kama in the formation of the culture of the ancient Mordvin-Murom tribes in the Oka river country (from the materials of the Koshibeyev burial ground and others near it), considering that a population from the Kama region had arrived on the Oka and mixed with the local population.[20] Smirnov, supposing that there is not sufficient evidence to derive the Koshibeyev people from the Kama region, none-theless recognizes that the presence of a number of Pyanobor objects in burial grounds of Koshibeyev type indicates the close interrelationship of right-bank and left-bank Volga tribes, and the special influence of the Pyanobor people in this regard.[21] E. I. Goryunova introduced into her work a number of ideas about the ties of the ancient population of the present-day Kostroma, Yaroslav, Ivanovo, and Vladimir oblasts with the population of the Kama and Ural regions, using in particular some of the present author's observations.[22] It is impossible, how-ever, to agree with Goryunova when she attempts to identify the Dyakovo culture with the culture of the Merian tribes.

4. We wish to emphasize once again that everything set forth above is by no means a hypothesis or a point of view of the author, but only some thoughts evoked by Serebrennikov's article on Volga-Oka place names—a source almost neglected among us, one that has not drawn the attention of scholars. Never-theless, this source undoubtedly indicates much.

First of all, the Volga-Oka place names put specialists in Finno-Ugrian archaeology and ancient history on guard against the creation of a simplified, straight-line ethnogenetic scheme—which would view the Finno-Ugrian tribes as a population holding unbroken sway from ancient times over the eastern European North. It is known that Finno-Ugric languages differ very markedly from one another. The Finno-Ugric linguistic family is in this regard incom-parably more variegated than the majority of other linguistic families of the Old World. In the opinion of linguists, this variegation of the Finno-Ugric languages cannot be explained as the result of long-past linguistic "cleavages." Rather, it arose as a consequence of repeated hybridization of the Finno-Ugric languages with other ancient languages, which have not survived to the present time— this at the expense of the role of the linguistic substratum, during the movement of Finno-Ugrian tribes. Consequently, other tribal groups must also have lived in the northern zone of the European U.S.S.R., where the history of the Finno-Ugrian tribes ran its course. One of these groups, possibly, was the ancient carrier of the Dyakovo—and of the Volga-Oka place names. Serebrennikov supposes that the Finno-Ugrians who appeared in the western Volga region "assimilated a part of the Volga-Oka population. As a consequence of this assimilation, new Finno-Ugrian peoples came into being, which continue to exist even now."[23] Here the linguist Serebrennikov has arrived at the same conclusion that was expressed by the archaeologist Yefimenko in 1926, when he said that the tribe that established the burial ground at Koshibeyev and others close to it arrived from the Kama and mixed with the local population.

In our literature on the archaeology and ancient history of the Finno-Ugrians, one tradition has been established against which we must struggle. Any hypothesis and any fact concerning the ethnogenesis of, let us say, the Scythians or the eastern Slavs or the Thracians, usually has to contend at once with a volley of captious criticism. Proofs are demanded of the author of the hypothesis, which by no means always exist. As regards the Finno-Ugrian problem, there is relative tranquillity. It is considered axiomatic that the Finno-Ugrians lived from ancient times in the wooded northern zone, that the ethnogenetic processes ran their course here autochthonously, and that here there is, properly speaking, nothing to dispute. This is certainly far from being the case. The ancient history of the Finno-Ugrian tribes was also extremely complex, abounding in migrations, assimilations, etc.

In conclusion, returning to the question of the Volga-Oka place names, it is to be desired that Serebrennikov and the other linguists concerned with Eastern European subjects come closer to the solution of the question of the ethnic affiliation of the carriers of the Volga-Oka place names. Serebrennikov strongly doubts that they belong to the ranks of the Finno-Ugrian tribes. A. I. Sobolevskiy connected them with the Indo-Europeans, tentatively mentioning the Scythians. But many other linguists have attempted to look upon the language of the Volga-Oka place names as some kind of extinct Finno-Ugric or related language. In any case, this was a language mixed since time immemorial with the ancient Finno-Ugric speech.

It is necessary, however, to bear in mind one more circumstance concerning the ancient inhabitants of the Volga-Oka interfluve to which Kh. A. Moora has recently turned his attention. In a number of his works, he has declared that the formation of the Baltic (Letto-Lithuanian) tribes took place with the active participation of the "Corded Ware" (or "Battle Axe") tribes, coming into the southeastern Baltic regions, whose Indo-European origin is now recognized by the great majority of archaeologists.[24] In his latest work, Moora went still further. He expressed the opinion that the tribes of the Fatyanovo culture, who arrived in the upper Volga region and the Volga-Oka interfluve from the Dnieper region at the end of the 3rd and the beginning of the 2nd millennium B.C., also belonged to the ancient Balts.[25]

This proposition is very much disputed. It is difficult to conceive that under the conditions of that period a homogeneous ethnic group occupied the huge territory of eastern Europe. The "Corded Ware" and "Battle Axe" tribes, who occupied a vast region in northern and eastern Europe, were evidently the ancestors of a whole group of Indo-European tribes, including in their number, besides the ancestors of the Balts, also those of the Slavs, the Germans, and undoubtedly many other ethnic groups that have not survived to the present time.

The aggregate of archaeological data show that the Fatyanovo tribes in the upper Volga region and the Volga-Oka interfluve were the "vanquished" ethnic group, which melted into the local population. From this it obviously follows that in the post-Fatyanovo period, the 1st millennium B.C. and later, some Indo-European elements may have entered into the place names of the Volga-Oka population.

An approach to the solution of all these highly complex problems is possible only through the close collaboration of linguists and archaeologists.

Notes and References

1. I. N. Smirnov, *Votyaki, istoriko-etnograficheskiy ocherk* (The Votyaks: A historical-ethnographic sketch), Kazan, 1890, pp. 33–34.

2. A. I. Sobolevskiy, Nazvaniya rek i ozer Russkogo Severa (The names of rivers and lakes of the Russian North), *Izv. Otdeleniya russkogo yazyka i slovesnosti Akademii nauk*, vol. 32, 1927, pp. 2–16.

3. A. Ya. Bryusov, *Ocherki o istorii plemen evropeyskoy chasti SSSR v neoliticheskuyu epokhu* (Outlines of the history of the tribes of the European U.S.S.R. in the Neolithic period), Moscow, 1952; Idem, *Istoriya drevney Karelii* (History of Ancient Karelia), Moscow, 1940; M. E. Foss, Drevneyshaya istoriya severa evropeyskoy chasti SSSR, (The ancient history of the North of the European U.S.S.R.), *Materialy i issledovaniya po arkheologii SSSR (MIA)*, no. 29, Moscow, 1952.

4. B. A. Serebrennikov, Volgo-Okskaya toponimika na territorii evropeyskoy chasti SSSR, (Volga-Oka place names in the territory of the European part of the U.S.S.R.), *Voprosy yazykoznaniya*, 1955, no. 6, p. 30.

5. P. N. Tretyakov, *Vostochnoslavyanskiye plemena* (The East-Slavic tribes), Moscow, 1953, pp. 116 ff.

6. A. A. Spitsyn, Gorodishcha dyakova tipa (Fortified sites of the Dyakovo type), *Zap. Otdela russkoy i slavyanskoy arkheologii Russk. Arkheolog. Ob-va.*, vol. 5, no. 1, St. Petersburg, 1903.

7. P. N. Tretyakov, Nekotorye voprosy etnogonii vostochnogo slavyanstva (Some questions of the ethnogeny of the eastern Slavs), *Kratkiye soobshcheniya IIMK*, vol. 5, 1940, pp. 12–14; idem, Severnye vostochnoslavyanskiye plemena (Northern east-Slavic tribes), *MIA*, no. 15, 1941, pp. 13 ff.

8. P. N. Tretyakov, *Vostochnoslavyanskiye plemena*, Moscow, 1953, pp. 44, 94; idem, *Ocherki istorii SSSR: Pervobytno-obshchinny stroy i drevneyshiye gosudarstva na territorii SSSR* (Outlines of the history of the U.S.S.R. The primitive-communal structure and the ancient states in the territory of the U.S.S.R.), Moscow, 1956, pp. 373 ff.

9. A. V. Zbruyeva, Istoriya naseleniya Prikamya v ananinskuyu epokhu (History of the population of the Kama region in the Ananino period), *MIA*, no. 30, 1952, pp. 15, 19 ff.

10. B. S. Zhukov, Teoriya khronologicheskikh i territorialnykh modifikatsiy neoliticheskikh kultur (The theory of chronological and territorial modifications of Neolithic cultures), *Etnografiya*, 1929, no. 1.

11. Spitsyn, *op. cit.*, pp. 113–114.

12. P. N. Tretyakov, K voprosu ob etnicheskom sostave naseleniya Volgo-Okskogo mezhdurechya v I tysyacheletii n.e. (On the question of the ethnic composition of the population of the Volga-Oka interfluve in the 1st millennium A.D.), *Sovetskaya arkheologiya*, 1957, no. 2, pp. 64–77.

13. A. P. Smirnov, Nekotorye spornye voprosy finno-ugorskoy arkheologii (Some

disputed questions of Finno-Ugrian archaeology), *Sovetskaya arkheologiya*, 1957, no. 3, pp. 28–29.

14. Spitsyn, *op. cit.*, pp. 113–114.

15. V. A. Gorodtsov, Starsheye Kashirskoye gorodishche (An old fortified site at Kashirsk), *Izv. Gos. Akademii istorii materialnoy kultury*, no. 85, Moscow–Leningrad, 1934, p. 46.

16. P. P. Yefimenko, Ryazanskiye mogilniki (The Ryazan burial grounds), *Materialy po etnografii*, vol. 3, no. 1, Leningrad, 1926, pp. 63–64.

17. P. P. Yefimenko, K istorii zapadnogo Povolzhya v pervom tysyacheletii n.e. po arkheologicheskim istochnikam (On the history of the western Volga region in the 1st millennium A.D. according to archaeological sources), *Sovetskaya arkheologiya*, no. 2, 1937, pp. 44–45.

18. A. P. Smirnov, *Ocherki drevney i srednevekovoy istorii narodov srednego Povolzhya i Prikamya* (Outlines of the ancient and medieval history of the peoples of the middle Volga and Kama regions), *MIA*, no. 28, Moscow, 1952, pp. 42–61.

19. As an example, one may point to the three upper Volga fortified sites studied by O. N. Bader—the Ivankovskoye, Sannikovo, and Pekunovo. See: Bader, Drevniye gorodishcha na verkhney Volge (Ancient fortified sites on the upper Volga), *MIA*, no. 13, Moscow–Leningrad, 1950.

20. Yefimenko, Ryazanskiye mogilniki, pp. 83–84.

21. Smirnov, *Ocherki drevney* . . . , pp. 137–138.

22. E. I. Goryunova, K voprosu o kulturnykh i etnicheskikh svyazakh naseleniya verkhnego Povolzhya i zapadnogo Priuralya v I tysyacheletii n.e. (On the question of the cultural and ethnic connections of the population of the upper Volga and western Ural regions in the 1st millennium A.D.), *Uch. zap. Mariyskogo nauchno-issled. in-ta yazyka, literatury i istorii*, vol. 6, Yoshkar-Ola, 1954.

23. Serebrennikov, *op. cit.*, p. 31.

24. Kh. A. Moora, Voprosy slozheniya estonskogo naroda i nekotorykh sosednikh narodov v svete dannykh arkheologii (Problems of the development of the Estonian people and some neighboring peoples in the light of archaeological data), *Voprosy etnicheskoy istorii estonskogo naroda*, Tallinn, 1956, pp. 67–75.

25. Kh. A. Moora, O drevney territorii rasseleniya baltiyskikh plemen (On the ancient territory of settlement of the Baltic tribes), *Sovetskaya arkheologiya*, 1958, no. 2.

N. N. CHEBOKSAROV

QUESTIONS CONCERNING THE ORIGINS OF THE FINNO-UGRIAN LANGUAGE GROUP[*][†]

1. The problem of the origin of the Finno-Ugrians undoubtedly occupies an important position among problems of the ethnic history of the Soviet peoples and of their neighbors, particularly the Hungarians and Finns. This problem has been the center of attention for investigators of different nationalities—Russian, Hungarian, Finnish, Estonian, and others—during the course of development of such branches of science as linguistics, ethnography, archaeology, ethnic anthropology, and historical geography. Ever since the end of the 18th century there has been a continued ideological struggle around the basic questions of Finno-Ugrian ethnogenesis, based on one or another concept of general linguistic or historical character.

One of the first historians interested in these questions was V. N. Tatishchev, who in paying tribute to Herodotus which was customary during that period, had the whole family of Finnish peoples descending from the Sarmatians, and attempted to make the ancient ethnic population groups of eastern Europe correspond with the modern. Thus, for example, Tatishchev identifies Herodotus' Arimaspi with the Udmurts, known in some medieval chronicles as "Aryan."[1] The great 18th century leading figure of Russian science M. V. Lomonosov likewise took the keenest interest in the problem of the origin of the Finno-Ugrians whom he quite rightly identified with the "Chuds" of the manuscripts. "Considerable numbers of the Chuds," wrote Lomonosov, "united with Slovenian tribes and have a part in the formation of the Russian people."[2] This gifted Russian scientist considered the ancient Finnish culture to be original in character and sufficiently advanced. "When one judges the varied races that comprise Russia," he emphasized, "no one can consider them as discrediting."[3] Many ethnogenetic theories of Lomonosov, especially his ideas about close cultural and historic ties between the Finns and the eastern Slavs, have retained their value up to modern times. Especially noteworthy is the profound patriotism that runs through all his "Ancient Russian History," particularly through the first three chapters, devoted to the questions of ethnogenesis, under the highly significant titles: "Ancient Inhabitants of Russia," "The Greatness and the Races of the Slovene People," "On the Antiquity of the Slovene People." Observations on the Finno-Ugrian tribes are concentrated for the most part in the first of these chapters.

Within the limits of an article intended for a periodical it is neither possible nor necessary to pause in any detail over the different conceptions of Finno-Ugrian origin proposed by Russian and foreign scientists of the 19th and 20th centuries. I shall merely point out that since the 1820's Finnish and Hungarian linguists have worked hard on the problem of the origin of the Finno-Ugrian language group. Undoubtedly, A. Castren played an important role in the development of Finno-Ugrian comparative linguistics. He set forth a definitive

[*]Translated from *Sovetskaya etnografiya*, 1952, no. 1, pp. 36–50.
[†]Read at a conference on the methodology of ethnogenetic research, November 2, 1951.

theory of Ural-Altay ethnogenesis for the Finno-Ugrians that locates their area of origin to the east of the Urals in close proximity to the area of formation of the Samoyeds, who form with the Finno-Ugrians part of the Uralian linguistic family.[4] Later Castren's theories were for the most part revised, and in traditional "Finno-Ugrian studies" they were supplanted by other theories whose authors looked for an "aboriginal fatherland" for this race in eastern Europe. The Hungarian investigator B. Munkácsi, for example, considered that this aboriginal fatherland "lay among the well-watered valleys in the forest to the north of the Caucasus,"[5] while at the same time Munkácsi's compatriot József Szinnyei favored the opinion that it lay somewhere along the middle course of the Volga.[5] The greatest fault with all such fabrications lay in [the projection] that they regard the ethnogenesis of the Finno-Ugrians as though it took place unconnected with the history of neighboring peoples (in particular, the Slavs), and actually as though it led to a series of linguistic subdivisions and migrations into an empty area where supposedly no one had lived before the appearance of the Finno-Ugrians. These tribes, therefore, were represented as the sole original inhabitants of the entire woodland zone of western Siberia and eastern Europe from the Ob-Yenisey watershed to the Baltic sea. The distribution of the Finno-Ugrians over this enormous territory was depicted almost exclusively on the basis of linguistic materials without sufficiently taking into account the archaeological, physical anthropological, or ethnographic evidence, and sometimes even in direct contradiction to it.

. . . In the works of many Finnish linguists and ethnographers of this period—U. Sirelius, T. Itkonen, H. Paasonen, E. Setelys, I. Wichmann, and others—the idea is presented of the existence not only of a Finno-Ugrian language family (which undoubtedly exists) but also of a specific Finno-Ugrian culture supposedly peculiar to all peoples of this family from the Lapps to the Hungarians and from the Estonians to the Khanty.[6] At the same time, ignoring the facts, the Finnish scientists attempt to pass over in silence or to suppress the great similarity between the Finno-Ugrian and the eastern Slavic peoples, which is so conspicuous in nearly all elements of their material and spiritual culture. The scientists of bourgeois Estonia followed their Finnish colleagues. Thus, for example, in the major work of I. Manninen, "The Material Culture of Estonia," a great deal of space is devoted to the ethnographic similarities between the Estonians and other Finno-Ugrians, and also between the Estonians and the peoples of western Europe; there is, in the book, almost no comparison of the culture of the Estonians with that of the neighboring Russians.[7] . . .

2.   Soviet scientists representing various linguistic and historical disciplines have been keenly interested in questions of Finno-Ugrian origin during the whole course of Soviet scientific development from the time of the October revolution to the present. In working over these questions, however, as in other problems of ethnogenesis, many errors were made, usually connected with the influence of the "new teaching" about language of Academician N. Ya. Marr and his disciples. Marr wrote a great deal about different languages of the Finno-Ugrian group, but produced no complete theory of their origin. Indeed, he could scarcely have produced such a theory, considering the unsoundness and contradiction of his premises concerning "a single world process of glottalization," his characterization of language by superimposed classes, the "stages" of development resulting from "explosions" caused by racial crossing, the necessity of a "Japhetic" step in the development of all world languages. In accordance with

these mistaken theories Marr, as we know, asserted that "prehistoric tribes therefore, all similarly Japhetic in speech, are represented in the Russians of the Kostroma district, as well as in the Finns, and in the Turks along the Volga, who prehistorically formed their original Ural-Altaic descent, along with the Finns, from Japhetic stock, presumably much earlier than the Indo-Europeans formed theirs from the same prehistoric ethnic environment."[8] In this way it was understood that the Finno-Ugrian speaking people, along with all other peoples of eastern Europe and western Siberia (and indeed of the whole world) originated through a transformation of the aboriginal Japhetic tribes in the area which they first inhabited. When, where, and why this sudden transformation occurred, Marr was unable to explain. To establish its feasibility he had recourse to the notorious "analysis by four elements" consisting of a sort of pseudo-scientific linguistic gymnastics. . . .

[In three omitted paragraphs, the author points out his erroneous adherence to Marr's theories in his earlier publications.]

The basic aim of the present article is to show how solidly based physical anthropological materials may be used in the study of Finno-Ugrian ethnogenesis. In setting himself such a task, however, the author must immediately make the reservation that it is far from his mind to give conclusive answers to all questions that may arise in this connection. This would be utterly impossible, since neither physical anthropology nor ethnography, either separately or together, can decide definitively all problems connected with Finno-Ugrian origins. One must remember that the very concept "Finno-Ugrian" is primarily a linguistic one, not ethnographic and certainly not physical anthropological. The cultural-material as well as the racial differences between modern peoples of the Finno-Ugrian language group are so great that if we did not know of the linguistic relation of these peoples it would never occur to us to study them as an entity, as an ethnic unit all of whose members are distantly interrelated. What is there indeed in common between the Khanty [Ostyaks] and the Estonians, or between the Magyars and the Lapps, aside from some similarity of language? Who would think of comparing the cultures of these peoples, geographically dispersed, living under thoroughly different natural and historical conditions, if comparative linguistics had not shown their membership in one linguistic family? Thus problems of the origin of peoples of the Finno-Ugrian language group should be defined as a linguistic problem or, speaking more accurately, a historical-linguistic one, since it is a question of the history of the formation of a group of languages bound by real genetic relationship. However, in deciding this historic-linguistic problem there should be used, in addition to the linguistic evidence, ethnographic and physical-anthropological data that open up to the investigator the cultural peculiarities and racial composition of the people who created the Finno-Ugrian tongue. It is certainly true that "language and the laws of its development can be understood only when they are studied in direct connection with the history of the society, of the people, to whom the language belongs and who are the creators and carriers of that language."[9]

3. It is when working on problems connected with the early periods of Finno-Ugrian ethnogenesis that the best use can be made of ethnological data, in particular when they concern the period of the original distribution of these languages over the broad forest belt of western Siberia and northeastern Europe. It may be said with confidence that in the clarification of the process of occupation of this territory by people of the postglacial period, the leading role, together

with the archaeological materials, will be played by the findings concerning the composition of the early population of this part of the *oikoumene*. The most recent work of Soviet anthropologists makes it more and more certain that this population was not racially homogeneous in the 4th to 3rd millennium B.C., but was composed of representatives of two great races, the Europoid and Mongoloid, which were gradually blending. Thus, for example, among the skeletons from the Early Neolithic burials on Yuzhny Oleniy Ostrov [South Reindeer Island] on Lake Onega, together with the preponderant Europoid racial type, morphologically close to the Crô-Magnon, are found a few individuals characterized by specifically Mongoloid traits. In describing this series, E. V. Zhirov expressed the very probable theory that "the physical peculiarities of the South Reindeer Island people are the result of cross-breeding between the tall, rather broad-faced, Khamekonkhen Europoids, that is, Crô-Magnons, with the sparser Mongoloid population."[10] Mixed Europoid-Mongoloid types are conspicuous also among the skulls from burials of the 2nd millennium B.C. excavated by A. Ya. Bryusov in the locality of Karavaikha near Lake Vozhe in Vologda oblast.[11] Some of these skulls show traits resembling the modern Lapp forms, which also characteristically combine Europoid and Mongoloid traits (together with a very specific general morphological aspect). Apparently close to the Lapp type of face are isolated skulls of the Neolithic period from Yazykov (Kalinin *oblast*) and Volosov (Murom *rayon*).[12] Similar observations were made on skulls from Rinnekalno in Latvia, which possibly belong to the pre-metal period.[13] Very recently M. M. Gerasimov has reconstructed the face on a woman's skull from the Early Neolithic Shighir site in the trans-Ural; the Lapp, or more accurately, transitional Europoid-Mongoloid cast of this face is very apparent.[14]

Thus we may consider as firmly established the presence of Mongoloid elements in the Neolithic population of the northern forests of eastern Europe and trans-Uralia. In the remote past these elements were mingled over this area with the heavy Europoid type of Crô-Magnon aspect, clearly expressed for example in the well-known Ladoga skulls,[15] or among the skeletal remains of different Estonian sites belonging to the 2nd millennium B.C.[16] It is unlikely that the Mongoloid and Europoid types belonging to the two major races could have developed simultaneously within the limits of the same geographical area. Considering that the forest of north Europe was first populated in compartively late times (in the Mesolithic and Early Neolithic) one must conclude that both the Mongoloids and the Europoids, fully developed, penetrated here along different routes. It is clear that the Mongoloids could spread only from the east, from beyond the Urals, where all evidence points to Central Asia as the area of their formation. This route is also indicated for them by the finding of a child's skull with clearly defined Mongoloid characteristics in the Upper Paleolithic site of Afontova Gora II, near Krasnoyarsk.[17] It is difficult to say how far the Mongoloids penetrated to the west but some palaeoanthropological evidence in eastern Germany indicates that the earliest waves of migrations from Asia may have reached Central Europe.[18] The routes of penetration of the Europoids into the northern forests appear to have been shorter; they apparently start along the northern shores of the Black Sea, where Crô-Magnon types are traced, according to palaeoanthropological evidence, at least from Mesolithic times.[19] It is also possible that the mixing of Mongoloids and Europoids took place as early as the Neolithic, if not earlier, not only in eastern Europe but also in western Siberia, where Europoid types were able to concentrate in the southern steppes, while the Mongoloid centered in the northern forests.[20] The probability of such an occurrence seems to be supported by the transitional morphological type of the Shigir skull, which bears witness to early inter-racial mixture in trans-Uralia.

Almost all conclusions drawn from palaeoanthropological evidence about the original routes of migration into the forest belt of eastern Europe are well reaffirmed by the most recent work of Soviet archaeologists. A. Ya. Bryusov writes, for example:

Contrary to the hypothesis of a possible settlement of this zone from the west, a study of the material leads one to the conclusion that the population of the area moved in from the east, apparently from the central Urals. A chronological investigation of sites in the Urals reveals that the oldest culture levels of the Shigir peat-bog should be dated to the 5th to 4th millennium B.C. or perhaps earlier. In the 3rd to the 2nd millennium B.C. a new population wave appears in the north of the European part of the Soviet Union, stemming principally from the region between the Volga and Oka rivers. This is confirmed by many northern sites of the period, which contain an inventory typical of the Volga-Oka Neolithic culture.[21]

As we see, the eastern settlers of our northern forests belonged, from a racial point of view, to the Mongoloids or in any case included Mongoloid elements. The tribes that spread to the north from the area between the Volga and Oka were, anthropologically speaking, diverse; a considerable part of their composition was contributed by the Europoid types apparently originally associated with the area directly north of the Black Sea.[22] Of course, we have not at our disposal any direct evidence bearing on the languages of this earliest population of northeast Europe and western Siberia. . . . However, it is perfectly logical to assume that the languages of the first settlers in the northern forests, which were only occupied in the 4th to 2nd millennium B.C., belonged to the great language families that still exist today. . . . [Passage referring to Marr's and Stalin's linguistic theories omitted.]

Taking all these considerations into account, it is natural to propose that the groups of peoples who penetrated from the east into the northern European part of the Soviet Union and who were preponderantly Mongoloid in physical type were the carriers of languages related to those of the most recent west Siberian peoples, languages that may have belonged, at least in part, to the Ural (Finno-Ugrian–Samoyed) group. At the same time the languages of the peoples moving up from the south, preponderantly Europoid in type, may have belonged to the Indo-European family, whose existence as early as the 3rd to 2nd millennium B.C. can scarcely be doubted.[23] Similar populational movements, undoubtedly accompanied by the crossing of languages and the drowning out of the weaker by the stronger ones, also occurred later in eastern Europe. Again palaeoanthropological evidence, this time from the Bronze and Iron Ages, convincingly bears witness to these populational movements. Thus, for example, in the middle of the 2nd millennium B.C. tribes of nomadic pastoralists from the south penetrated into the central Volga area. These were, anthropologically speaking, comparatively narrow-faced Europoids of eastern Mediterranean type.[24] In the period of the Ananino culture (7th to 2nd centuries B.C.), a new wave of Mongoloid elements spread through the Cis-Kama [river] region, one connected with the migration from beyond the Urals of some tribes that very probably belonged to the Finno-Ugrian linguistic family.[25] Medieval series of skulls, whose ethnic ascriptions can in most cases be trusted, show the complexity of the Finno-Ugrian peoples of that period. Among these, three basic groups of physical types stand out: the transitional Mongoloid-Europoid, concentrated for the most part in the Volga-

Kama region and only occasionally found in the easternmost part of the Baltic, along the Gulf of Finland; the broad-faced Europoid, spread over the wide area from the Baltic Sea to the middle Volga (in general to the west and partly to the south of the first group); the narrow-faced Europoid, gravitating for the most part to the south of the Volga-Oka district.[26] Representative of the first group are, for example, the skulls from the 9th century Polom burials (Kirov *oblast*).[27] Characteristic of the second group are the Izhora skulls from the 13th to 14th century burial near Gatchina,[28] and of the third group, the skulls from the Finnish burials of the 8th to 10th century along the Tsna river.[29] The data on all these craniological series make possible comparisons with materials from the present-day population of the corresponding regions of European Russia.

Data on the physical composition of a modern population should be used with great caution in connection with questions of ethnogenesis as in many cases this composition has been finally developed only in the last two or three centuries and reflects significantly only very recent historical processes that have no direct connection with the origin of separate peoples, much less with their large groups speaking related languages. Thus, for example, an anthropological study of the Kolva Nenets living in Ust-Usa *rayon* of the Komi A.S.S.R. shows that they are a typically mixed group in which were combined darker Mongoloid and lighter Europoid elements. Hence it might be possible to draw conclusions about the time of racial intermixture in the basin of the lower Pechora and of its great importance in the history of the physical type of the Nenets people. This hypothesis, however, falls to pieces as soon as the investigator begins to acquaint himself with the history of the formation of the Kolva Nenets. It appears that they were only formed into an ethnic unit in the 1830's when a village was founded by orthodox missionaries on the Kolva river, with a population made up of young women from Izhma and Nenets men who moved in from the Bolshezemelskaya [Great Land] tundra.[30] But it would be a mistake to think that the evidence of ethnology concerning a modern population could never be used to solve ethnogenetic problems. On the contrary, such a use is entirely possible and even essential, if only the investigator retains historical perspective and always tries to establish a solidly based chronology and geographic location for the formative process of this or that anthropological type. It is from this point of view that we should approach an analysis of the modern physical type of the Finno-Ugrian language group.

The most recent works on the ethnic anthropology of eastern Europe and western Siberia, for the most part by Soviet authors, show clearly that at least three groups are represented in the composition of these people. The first of these, frequently designated in scientific literature as "Uralic,"[31] for many reasons occupies an intermediate position between the Mongoloids and Europoids. Characteristic traits of this group include: soft, but straight, usually black or dark-red hair, sparse by European standards, tertiary hair cover; eyes of hazel or mixed color; a somewhat flattened, often low [-profiled] face; strongly developed folds of the upper eyelid, sporadic epicanthus; nasal bridge of medium height, curved nasal ridge and a tendency to prominence of the lips. Traits specific for the Uralic group show up most clearly among the Finno-Ugrians in the majority of Khanty and Mansi [Ostyaks and Voguls].[32] In a less distinctive form these traits can be traced among the Udmurts and Mari,[33] and also in isolated groups of the Mordvins[34] and Komi, along the upper reaches of the Kama, on the Inva, Sysola, and upper Mezen.[35] Among the members of the Uralic group there are both comparatively long-headed and comparatively short-headed variants; to the latter belong, in particular, the so-called "Laponoid" type, extremely short in stature and flat-faced, characteristic of the Saams (Lapps), but found also among their neighbors, the northern Karelians.[36] Out of the bounds of the Finno-Ugrian language family different types of the Uralic group are widely spread among the Nenets and Selkups,[37] the Tobolsk and Barabinsk Tatars,[38] the Shors, Altayans, and Khalkhas,[39] and also among the Bashkirs,[40] the Volga Tatars,[41] and the Chuvash.[42] "Laponoid" and the closely related "sub-Lapanoid" elements have penetrated into the make-up of the Russian population of the northern European part of the U.S.S.R.[43]

The second group of physical types usual among peoples of the Finno-Ugrian language family is the "White Sea–Baltic."[44] It belongs to the general Europoid race but discloses some traits that indicate a small admixture of early Mongoloid.[45] The characteristic trait complex for this group includes: straight or slightly wavy hair, light brown or blond in color; fairly developed tertiary hair cover; light eyes; a relatively small face of an average profile in horizontal cross-section; quite clearly defined folds of the upper eyelid; nasal bridge of medium height; concave or straight nasal ridge. The different types of this group, both short-headed and long-headed, are especially widely distributed among the Baltic-Finnish peoples: Estonians,[46] Livonians,[47] Veps,[48] Karelians,[49] Finns-Suomi,[50] as well as among the Udorsk, Izhma, and the Vychegda Komi,[51] and the Lukoyanov Mordvins-Erzi.[52] To a great extent the White Sea–Baltic complex of traits is also present among the Letts, Lithuanians,[53] Poles, White Russians, and northern Great Russians.[54] Thus the White Sea–Baltic group fully justifies its name, as the types of which it is composed actually do gravitate to the shores of the White and Baltic Seas.

In my proposed classification I have called the third group of types that play an important role in the composition of peoples of the Finno-Ugrian family, the "Atlanto–Black Sea" group.[55] This group, like the preceding one, belongs to the general Europoid race and occupies an intermediate position from the point of view of pigmentation between its basic subdivisions: the Indo-Mediterranean brunettes and the north European (Baltic) blondes.[56] For all the Atlanto–Black Sea types the following traits are characteristic: dark, quite often broadly wavy or straight hair; considerable development of tertiary hair cover; eyes hazel or of a mixed color; narrow and usually long face strongly profiled in horizontal cross-section; slightly developed fold of the upper eyelid; high or medium-high nasal bridge, straight or slightly arched nasal ridge. Geographically the Atlanto-Black Sea types fall into two subdivisions: the western or Atlantic, and the eastern or Black Sea (also called "Pontic"). In the present work we are chiefly interested in the latter subdivision, which has elements markedly conspicuous in several of the Finno-Ugrian groups: the Ivdel Mansi of the Sverdlovsk and Molotov [Perm] *oblasts*,[57] the Inva Komi-Permyaks,[58] the Izhersk Udmurts,[59] and in particular the Narovchat Mordvins–Moksha.[60] The specific features of the Atlanto–Black Sea types among all the above-mentioned groups are combined with mesocephaly or slight brachycephaly. Analogous combinations of physical traits can be seen also in many groups of the southern Great Russians[60] and the Volga Tatars,[61] as well as in some peoples of the Balkan peninsula and of the northwestern Caucasus, as, for example, the Plovdiv Bulgars[62] or the Adyge.[63] More short-headed variants of the same trait complex, known in anthropological literature as "Alpine" and "Dinaric," play an important role in the racial make-up of the Hungarians and the neighboring peoples of Central Europe, who speak Slavic and Germanic languages.[64] All Atlanto–Black Sea physical types have an obvious tendency to gravitate southward to the Mediterranean and Black Sea basins.

To what realistic exposition of the ethnogenetic process do these materials on the ethnic anthropology of peoples speaking the Finno-Ugrian language lead? An analysis of this material leads us first of all to the conclusion that the Finno-Ugrians have been fundamentally and for a very long time a racial mixture, so that racial unity is out of the question for them even in the very remote past. If, however, one is to accept, along with most modern Soviet linguists, the hypothesis that all Finno-Ugrian languages developed from one root, an ancient basic tongue,[65] then it will be necessary to admit the existence in some historical period of a unified ethnic society creating this basic tongue. It is hard to imagine that such a society, occupying of course a very definite, geographically limited area, could be physically as diverse as the modern peoples of the Finno-Ugrian family. It is more likely that this society incorporated only one of the three groups of physical types described in the preceding pages. But precisely which one? It can scarcely be the Atlanto–Black Sea group, as it is clearly not characteristic of the peoples of the Finno-Ugrian family and is concentrated only in the southern limits of their area of distribution. The principal area of this complex of traits lies in those parts of the Black Sea shore and of western Europe where there obviously were no early Finno-Ugrians. It would be difficult to imagine that the ancient Finno-Ugrians originally belonged to the Atlanto–Black Sea group and later "changed" their physical type almost entirely to the Uralic or White Sea–Baltic one. As regards the two other groups, the White Sea–Baltic and the Uralic, the "advantage"—as far as our problem is concerned—seems to lie with the second, since the first, though widely distributed among the Finno-Ugrians (or, more accurately, among the Finns) is no less commonly present in the make-up of other east- and central-European peoples—the Slavs, Balts (Letto-Lithuanians), and Germans. The origin of this group as a whole is tied to the shores of the White Sea and the Baltic, which could scarcely have been the area of formation for the Finno-Ugrian language family. The Uralic group, however, though it does not seem as specifically Finno-Ugrian, is yet more characteristic either of them or of the peoples genetically related to them (the Selkups, the Nenets, in part the Shors, Altayans, and Khalkhas). The types of the Uralic group took form presumably in Cis-Uralia and western Siberia, that is, as it happens, just where many linguists are looking for the area of formation of the Finno-Ugrian languages.

The theory of a "Ural" base, anthropologically speaking, for the Finno-Ugrians has already been proposed by V. V. Bunak.[66] One must emphasize, however, that the definition of a "racial prototype" scarcely fits the Uralic group, which we can see is in no respect a primary race, but a whole conglomeration of close physical-anthropological complexes, formed during the process of fusion of the Mongoloids and Europoids. This fusion, which had apparently begun already at the end of the Paleolithic Age, undoubtedly preceded the establishment of the Finno-Ugrians as an ethnic unit, as this unit from the very start must have combined those Mongoloid and Europoid racial elements that, in the course of time, were to become more and more closely interwoven. Since the archaeological material points to the settlement of the northern European U.S.S.R. from the east only in the Mesolithic or early Neolithic times, one may presume that the mixture of the two major races originally took place beyond the Urals, where also lay the formative area of the oldest Finno-Ugrian ethnic society. It is quite justifiable to ask whether this society may not be connected with the Shigir culture, which probably belonged to a group already complex physically. The fact that among the Finno-Ugrians the same Uralic physical types are present as are found among the Nenets, Selkups, Siberian Tatars, Shors, and some of the Altayans and Khalkhas seems to point to deep ethnogenetic ties between all these peoples. This leads to the thought that in the past they spoke closely related tongues, which subsequently partly disappeared. Thus materials of physical anthropology bring us face to face with a whole series of vital problems in the ethnic history of the Finno-Ugrians and other peoples of western Siberia and the Altay-Sayan highlands.

A comparative analysis of the physical components of the Finno-Ugrians and their neighbors in eastern Europe presents equally interesting ethnogenetic problems. With what ethnic groups, one asks, were the widely-spread White Sea–Baltic types originally connected and where and when did these groups form? It would seem absurd to propose that these types penetrated to the Finno-Ugrians during their period of contact with the Slavs, Balts (Letto-Lithuanians), or Germans in medieval times, as such a hypothesis would lead to the ridiculous conclusion that whole groups of the population, speaking Indo-European languages, changed over very recently to the Finnish tongue. For instance, could it be admitted that the forefathers of the Estonians, Karelians, or Veps, who belong physically to the White Sea–Baltic group, had originally been Indo-Europeans! It is a more likely supposition that the formation of the White Sea–Baltic types in eastern Europe and the diffusion there of the Finno-Ugrian language from the east occurred at the same time, in the dawn of the Neolithic Age, when people were first occupying the vast areas of northern forest that had comparatively recently been freed of ice. The oldest Finno-Ugrian groups emigrating from beyond the Urals, who were already mixed, as they moved westwards, absorbed more and more Europoid elements that had seeped in to the forest belt from the south. What tongues these Europeans spoke we have no way of knowing, as their languages were apparently absorbed by the more numerous Finno-Ugrians. One should in any case not ignore the hypothesis of the many Finno-Ugrian linguistic specialists who assert that the ancestors of the Baltic-Finnish people (and also of the Lapps) originally spoke languages not belonging to the Finno-Ugrian group, and that they only later acquired the Finno-Ugrian language, introducing into it several distinctive phonetic peculiarities.[67] It is highly probable, therefore, that long before the Slavic tribes started to move into the northern part of eastern Europe, the Finno-Ugrians already had incorporated into their group thoroughly depigmented White Sea–Baltic types, which were no less widely spread among them than were the Uralic types. There is reason for the legend that arose among the much darker Russians about the "light-eyed magician" who disappeared into the ground.

The history of the penetration of the Atlanto–Black Sea types into the Finno-Ugrian group is undoubtedly quite different. One can really speak here of the penetration of the Finno-Ugrian milieu by tribes that were originally associated with the Aral-Caspian or the Black Sea steppes. These areas are known to have been settled, up to the early years A.D., by different Iranian-speaking tribes, which belonged, anthropologically speaking, to the relatively depigmented Europoid Pontic type. After all, it is not by chance that the most distinct, dark components of the Atlanto–Black Sea type are best expressed among the Mordvins-Mokshi, the most southerly ethnic group of the Finno-Ugrians. To explain the concrete reasons for, and the routes of, penetration of these elements to the different peoples of the Finno-Ugrian family, one should employ not only physical-anthropological but also historical-ethnographic data. The author intends to devote his next article dealing with Finno-Ugrian ethnogenesis to the analysis of such data.

Notes and References

1. V. N. Tatishchev, *Istoriya rossiyskaya* (Russian history), book 1, part 1, 1768, p. 14.

2. M. V. Lomonosov, *Drevnyaya rossiyskaya istoriya* (Ancient Russian history, St. Petersburg, 1786, p. 7.

3. *Ibidem*, p. 9.

4. The numerous works of Castren published in a twelve-volume edition under the editorship of A. Shifner; M. A. Castren, *Nordische Reisen und Forschungen*, St. Petersburg, 1853–62.

5. Quotation from V. N. Chernetsov's thesis, K voprosu o meste i vremeni formirovaniya finnougorskoy etnicheskoy gruppy (On the place and time of the formation of the Finno-Ugrian ethnic group), Subjects of reports and addresses of associates of the Institute for the History of Material Culture, Academy of Sciences of the U.S.S.R., prepared for the conference on the methodology of ethnogenetic research, Moscow, 1951, p. 24.

6. See, for example: U. T. Sirelius, *Suomen kansanomaista Kulttuuria*, vols. I and II, Helsinki, 1919–21; T. Itkonen, *Suomen sukuiset kansat*, Helsinki, 1921, as well as the collection *Suomen Suku* (The Finnish race), vols. I and II, Helsinki, 1926. All of the authors noted above participated in this work.

7. I. Manninen, *Die Sachkultur Estlands*, vols. I and II, 1931–33.

8. N. Ya. Marr, Privolzhskiye i sosedniye s nimi narodnosti v Yafeticheskom osveshchenii ikh plemennykh nazvaniy (The Volga tribes and their neighbors: the Japhetic interpretation of their tribal names), *Izbrannye raboty* (Selected works), vol. v, p. 306.

9. Stalin, *Marksizm i voprosy yazykoznaniya* (Marxism and questions of linguistics), p. 22.

10. E. V. Zhirov, Zametki a skeletakh iz neoliticheskogo mogilnika Yuzhnogo Olenyeva ostrova (Notes on the skeletons from the Neolithic burial place on South Reindeer Island), *Kratkiye soobshcheniya IIMK*, no. 6, 1940, pp. 51–54.

11. See: M. M. Gerasimov, *Osnovy vosstanovleniya litsa po cherepu* (Principles of facial reconstruction from the skull), Moscow, 1949, pp. 88–89.

12. O. N. Bader, Arkheologicheskiye raboty u der. Yazykovo i na oz. Skorbezh letom 1935 g. v svyazi s voprosom o drevnem laponoidnom komponente v antropologicheskom tipe naseleniya Vostochnoy Yevropy (Archaeological work at Yazykovo village and on Lake Skorbezh in the summer of 1935 in connection with the question of the ancient Laponoid element in the physical type of the population of eastern Europe), *Antropol. zhurn.*, 1936, no. 2, pp. 257–262; G. F. Debets, *Paleoantropologiya SSSR* (Palaeoanthropology of the U.S.S.R.), Moscow–Leningrad, 1948, p. 87.

13. R. Virchov, Archeologische Reise nach Livland, *Ztschr. f. Ethnologie*, Verhandl. d. Berlin, Gesellschaft f. Anthrop., Ethnolog. u. Urgeschichte, 1877; Debets, *Paleoantropologiya SSSR*, p. 95.

14. Oral communication of M. M. Gerasimov.

15. A. P. Bogdanov, Chelovek kamennogo veka (Stone Age man), in A. A. Inostrantsev, *Doistoricheskiy chelovek kamennogo veka poberezhya Ladozhnogo ozera* (Prehistoric Stone Age man on the shores of Lake Ladoga), St. Petersburg, 1882; Debets, *Paleoantropologiya SSSR*, pp. 89–90.

16. J. Aul, *Étude anthropologique des ossements humaines néolitique de Sope et d'Ardu*, Tartu, 1935 (reprint); Debets, *Paleoantropologiya SSSR*, pp. 90–92.

17. G. F. Debets, Fragment lobnoy kosti cheloveka iz kulturnogo sloya stoyanki Afontova gora II pod Krasnoyarskom (Fragment of the frontal bone of a man from the

culture level of the site Afontova gora II near Krasnoyarsk), *Byull. komissii po izu-cheniyu chetvertichnogo perioda,* 1946, no. 8, pp. 73–76.

18. N. N. Cheboksarov, Mongoloidnye elementy v naselenii Tsentralnoy Yevropy, (Mongoloid elements in the population of Central Europe), *Uchenye zapiski Mosk. gos. un-ta,* vol. 63, 1941, pp. 249–252. (Concerning the Mongoloid skulls of the Mesolithic period from the shores of Pritzerbe lake in Mecklenburg.)

19. Debets, *Paleoantropologiya SSSR,* pp. 43–45. (Skeletons of the Mesolithic period from the Crimea.)

20. *Ibidem,* map on p. 294.

21. A. Ya. Bryusov, Zaseleniye severa Yevropeyskoy chasti SSSR v neoliticheskuyu epokhu (Settlement in the north of the European part of the U.S.S.R. in the Neolithic period); subjects of reports and presentations of the associates of IIMK AN SSSR prepared for the conference on methodology in ethnogenetic research, Moscow, 1951, p. 23.

22. For example, the two skulls from the Volodarsk Neolithic site in Gorkovo oblast appear to be Europoid in type; see: T. A. Trofimova, Antropologicheskiye materialy k voprosu o proiskhozhdenii chuvashey (Anthropological materials bearing on the origin of the Chuvash), *Sovetskaya etnografiya,* 1950, no. 3, p. 56.

23. B. V. Gornung, K postanovke voprosa ob istoricheskoy obshchnosti indoyevro-peyskikh yazykov (On the formulation of the question of the historic unity of Indo-European languages), *Izv. AN SSSR Ord. Literatury i Yazyka,* vol. 9, no. 5, 1950, pp. 337–350; *idem,* O nekotorykh voprosakh, svyazannykh s obrazovaniyem i razvitiyem indo-yevropeyskoy semyi yazykov (Some questions connected with the formation and spread of the Indo-European languages). Subjects of reports of the scientific associates of the Institute of Linguistics for a combined session of the Institute of Ethnography, the Institute of the History of Material Culture, the Institute of History, and the Institute of Linguistics of the AN SSSR, Moscow, 1951.

24. Trofimova, Antropologicheskiye materialy . . . , pp. 57–61.

25. T. A. Trofimova, Antropologicheskiy tip naseleniya ananinskoy kultury v Priuralye (The physical type of the population of the Ananino culture in the Cis-Ural area), *Kratkiye soobshcheniya IIMK,* no. 9, 1940, pp. 42–47.

26. Debets, *Paleoantropologiya SSSR,* pp. 214–248; V. V. Sedov, Antropologicheskiye tipy naseleniya severo-zapadnykh zemel Velikogo Novgoroda (Physical types in the population of the northwest lands of Veliki Novgorod), manuscript, 1951; N. N. Cheboksarov, Ilmenskiye poozery (The environs of Lake Ilmen), *Trudy Instituta etnografii,* n.s., vol. 1, Moscow–Leningrad, 1947, pp. 264–267.

27. Debets, *Paleoantropologiya SSSR,* pp. 215–267.

28. E. V. Zhirov, Drevniye izhorskiye cherepa (Ancient skulls from Izhora), *Sovet-skaya arkheologiya,* no. 2, 1937, pp. 151–160.

29. Debets, *Paleoantropologiya SSSR,* pp. 229–230 (see also figs. 94–95).

30. Cheboksarov, Etnogenez komi po dannym antropologii, *Sovetskaya etnografiya,* 1946, no. 2, p. 72.

31. This term was first proposed by V. V. Bunak in his article: Antropologicheskiy tip cheremis (The physical type of the Cheremis), *Russk. antropol. zhurn.,* vol. 13, nos. 3–4, 1924, pp. 137–177. In my work: Osnovnye printsipy antropologicheskikh klassifi-katsiy (Basic principles of anthropological classifications), there is separated a specific Uralic group of types, occupying an intermediate position between the Europoids and Mongoloids; see the collection: Proiskhozhdeniye cheloveka i drevneye rasseleniye chelo-vechestva (Origins of man and the ancient distribution of mankind), *Trudy In-ta etno-grafii,* n.s., vol. 16, Moscow–Leningrad, 1951.

32. S. I. Rudenko, Antropologicheskoye issledovaniye inorodtsev severo-zapadnoy Sibiri (Physical anthropological investigation of the native population of northwestern Siberia), *Zapiski Akademii Nauk po fiz-mat. otd.,* vol. 33, no. 3, St. Petersburg, 1914; T. A. Trofimova and N. N. Cheboksarov, Antropologicheskoye izucheniye mansi (A physical-anthropological study of the Mansiets), *Kratkiye soobshcheniya IIMK,* no. 9, 1940, pp. 28–37.

33. Bunak, Antropologicheskiy tip cheremis; P. I. Zenkevich, Kharakteristika vostochnykh finnov (Characteristics of the eastern Finns), *Uchenye zapiski Mosk. gos. un-ta*, no. 63, 1941.

34. V. V. Bunak, Antropologicheskiy tip mordvy (The physical type of the Mordvins), *Russk. antropol. zhurn.*, vol. 13, nos. 3–4, 1924, pp. 178–210.

35. N. N. Cheboksarov, Etnogenez komi po dannym antropologii (Ethnogenesis of the Komi on the basis of physical anthropological data), *Sovetskaya etnografiya*, 1946, no. 2, see summary table, pp. 74–75.

36. D. A. Zolotarev, *Kolskiye lopari* (The Kola Lapps), Leningrad, 1927; *idem*, *Karely SSSR* (The Karelians of the U.S.S.R.), Leningrad, 1930; G. F. Debets, "Neprivetlivye" i "radushnye" ("unfriendly" and "friendly"), *Antropol. zhurn.*, 1933, nos. 1–2, p. 237.

37. Rudenko, *op. cit.*; S. A. Shluger, Antropologicheskoye issledovaniye nentsev (Physical anthropological investigation of the Nenets), *Kratkiye soobshcheniya o nauchnykh rabotakh In-ta i Muzeya antropologii MGU*, Moscow, 1941, pp. 23–26; G. F. Debets, Selkupy; antropologicheskiy ocherk (The Selkups, a physical anthropological sketch), *Trudy In-ta etnografii*, n.s., vol. 2, Moscow–Leningrad, 1947, pp. 103–145.

38. T. A. Trofimova, Tobolskiye i barabinskiye tatary (The Tobolsk and Barabinsk Tatars), *Trudy In-ta etnografii*, n.s., vol. 1, Moscow–Leningrad, 1947, pp. 194–215.

39. A. I. Yarkho, *Altaye-sayanskiye tyurki, antropologicheskiy ocherk* (The Altay-Sayan Turks, a physical anthropological sketch), Abakan, 1948.

40. S. I. Rudenko, *Bashkiry, Opyt etnograficheskoy monografii* (The Bashkirs, an experimental ethnographic monograph), part I, (Physical type of the Bashkirs, St. Petersburg, 1916.

41. T. A. Trofimova, Etnogenez tatar Srednego Povolzhya v svete dannykh antropologii (Ethnogenesis of the middle Volga Tatars in the light of anthropological evidence), *Sovetskaya etnografiya*, 1946, no. 3, pp. 51–74; *idem*, *Etnogenez tatar Povolzhya v svete dannykh antropologii.*

42. Trofimova, Antropologicheskiye materialy k voprosu o proiskhozdenii chuvashey.

43. N. N. Cheboksarov, Russkiye severa Yevropeyskoy chasti SSSR (Russians in the north of the European part of the U.S.S.R.), *Kratkiye soobshcheniya o rabote In-ta i Muzeya antropologii MGU*, 1941, pp. 65–66.

44. N. N. Cheboksarov, Iz istorii svetlykh rasovykh tipov Yevrazii (The history of light-colored racial types of Eurasia), *Antropol. zhurn.*, 1936, no. 2, pp. 193–227; Ilmenskiye poozery, pp. 247–258.

45. N. N. Cheboksarov, Osnovnye printsipy antropologicheskikh klassifikatsiy (Basic principles of physical anthropological classification), in the collection: *Proiskhozhdeniye cheloveka i drevneye rasseleniye chelovechestva* (Origin of man and the early distribution of mankind), Moscow, 1951, p. 316.

46. J. Aul, *Anthropologische Forschungen in Eesti*, Tartu, 1935.

47. J. Vilde, *Materiali par Libiesu anthropologiju*, Latvijas Univers, Raksti, 1924, vol. 2, pp. 93–181.

48. G. F. Debets, Vepsy (The Veps), *Uchenye zapiski Mosk. gos. un-ta*, no. 63, 1941, pp. 139–174.

49. D. A. Zolotarev, *Karely SSSR*; T. U. Roschier, Anthropologische Untersuchungen an Bewohner der Landschaft Karjala, *Acta Inst. Anat. Univers (Helsinki)*, no. 4, 1931.

50. Y. Kajava, Die anthropologischen Untersuchungen des finnischen Volkes, *Anthr. Anz.*, 1925, no. 2; A. O. Archo, Anthropologische Untersuchungen in den Landschaften Aland und Varsinais-Suomi, *Acta Inst. Anat. Univers (Helsinki)*, no. 6, 1936.

51. Cheboksarov, Etnogenez komi po dannym antropologii.

52. G. F. Debets, Antropologicheskiy ocherk byvsh. Lukoyanovskogo uyezda (An anthropological sketch of the former Lukoyanov uyezd), *Uchenye zapiski Mosk gos. un-ta*, no. 63, Antropologiya, Moscow, 1941.

53. M. Hesch, *Letten, Litauer, Weissrussen*, Wien, 1933; N. Jerums and T. M. Vittols, *Beiträge zur Anthropologie der Letten*, Latvijas Univers, Raksti, 1928, vol. 18, pp. 279–342.

54. For a survey of the basic data on these people, see my article "Ilmenskiye poozery"—Author.

55. *Ibidem*, pp. 258–264.

56. Cheboksarov, Osnovnye printsipy antropologicheskikh klassifikatsiy, p. 312.

57. T. A. Trofimova and N. N. Cheboksarov, Antropologicheskoye izucheniye mansi (A physical anthropological study of the Mansiets), *Kratkiye soobshcheniya IIMK,* no. 9, 1940, pp. 28–37.

58. M. A. Gremyatski, Antropologicheskiy tip invenskikh komi (permyakov) (The physical type of the Inva Komi—Permyaks), *Uchenye zapiski Mosk. gos. un-ta,* no. 63, 1941; Cheboksarov, Etnogenez komi po dannym antropologii, pp. 57–58.

59. P. I. Zenkevich, Kharakteristika vostochnykh finnov (Characteristics of the eastern Finns).

60. G. F. Debets, Tak nazyvaemy "vostochny velikoruss" (The so-called "eastern Great Russian"), *Antropol. zhurn.,* 1933, nos. 1–2, pp. 34–69.

61. T. A. Trofimova, *Etnogenez tatar Povolzhya v svete dannykh antropologii,* part iii, pp. 117–249.

62. J. Drontschilow, Beiträge zur Anthropologie der Bulgaren, *Arch. f. Anthropologie,* n.s., vol. 14, 1915.

63. V. I. Levin, Etno-geograficheskoye raspredeleniye nekotorykh rasovykh priznakov u naseleniya Severnogo Kavkaza (The ethnogeographic distribution of certain racial traits in the population of the northern Caucasus), *Antropolog. zhurn.,* 1932, no. 2, pp. 84–88.

64. L. Bartucz, Ein Abriss der Rassengeschichte in Ungarn, *Ztschr. f. Rassenkunde,* no. 1, 1935, pp. 225–239; N. N. Cheboksarov, Antropologicheskiy sostav sovremennykh nemtsev (The physical anthropological composition of the contemporary Germans), Uchenye zapiski Mosk. Gos. un-ta, no. 63, 1941, pp. 271–308.

65. See, for example, B. V. Gornung, V. D. Levin, and V. N. Sidorov, Problema obrazovaniya i razvitiya yazykovykh semey (Problems in the formation and growth of language families), Subjects of reports of the scientific associates of the Institute of Linguistics for the united session of the Institute of Ethnography, the Institute of the History of Material Culture, and the Institute of Linguistics, AN USSR, Moscow, 1951.

66. Bunak, Antropologicheskiy tip cheremis; also: V. Bunak, Neues Material zur Aussonderung anthropologischer Typen unter der Bevölkerung Osteuropas, *Ztschr. f. Morphol. u. Anthropol.,* vol. 30, 1932, pp. 441–503.

67. D. V. Bubrikh, Finnougorskiye yazyki Yevropy (The Finno-Ugrian languages of Europe), manuscript, 1949.

B. O. DOLGIKH

ON THE ORIGIN OF THE NGANASANS—
PRELIMINARY REMARKS*†

WE TERM AS Samoyed all those peoples who speak languages of the Samoyed (or Samodiysk, as G. N. Prokofyev proposes to call it) language group. Thus, by language, to the Samoyed group belong the Nenets (Samoyeds-Yuraks), Enets (the Yenisey Samoyeds), Nganasans (the Tavg[hi]-Samoyeds), and Selkups (Ostyak-Samoyeds). To the Samoyed group also belong the languages of some now-vanished Sayan tribes—the Kamasins, Motors, and Karagas. At present, descendants of these Sayan tribes speak either Turkic languages or Russian.

The term "Samoyeds" (anciently "Samoyad") is an old Russian name for the Nenets, Enets, and Nganasans. Only the Selkups were called Ostyaks by the Russians. The term "Samoyeds" had no derogatory meaning‡ and, as can be surmised, represents a modification of the expression *same-edne*, i.e., "Land of the Saams." This term was transferred from the Saam tribes, which evidently occupied at one time the entire north of European Russia, to the Nenets, who appeared there later, and thereafter to the Enets and Nganasans. These three peoples possess certain similar traits, even in their material culture—as, for instance, in the general character and in the technical details of reindeer breeding, in the basic type of dwelling, to some extent in clothing, in the type of sleds. They sharply differ from the Selkups, who are culturally closer to the Ostyaks—the Khants and Kets. Therefore, when we mention Samoyed culture, we have in mind just the northern reindeer-breeding Samoyed peoples—the Nenets, Enets, and Nganasans. The Selkups and Sayan Samoyeds (the Kamasins and Motors) are not included here.

The Nganasans were not distinguishable by their mode of life and material culture from their western neighbors—the Tundra Enets—and represented, together with the latter, a separate Samoyed group of a somewhat archaic character, differing from the Nenets in many respects.

At present, the Nganasans comprise a part of the population of the Taymyr National Okrug in the Avam and Khatanga regions. During the summer they nomadize to the tundra of the interior of the Taymyr peninsula, returning for the winter to the northern limits of the forest. Their main occupations were the hunting of wild deer, polar fox, and geese, reindeer-breeding, and fishing. Like the Olenek Tungus, the Anadyr and Lower Kolyma Yukagirs, the Caribou Eskimos, and others, the Nganasans formerly hunted for wild deer mainly in the fall, by hunting collectively at river crossings, slaughtering them with spears (*fonka*) from boats. Until recently they also used special leather nets into which the deer were driven by the hunters. Besides, during the summer and fall, the Nganasans hunted wild deer on foot, both alone and in small groups.

*Translated from *Trudy instituta etnografii*, n.s., vol. 18, 1952, pp. 5–87.

†[The five opening paragraphs of this article were omitted. They describe the former application of Marr's theories to ethnologic interpretations and the author's disapproval of this methodology.]

‡[Formerly the term was sometimes incorrectly interpreted as "self-eating," i.e., cannibalistic. —Editor.]

Polar fox was bagged with wooden snare jaws and bought traps. Geese were hunted mostly when molting. Fish were caught mainly with nets placed both in open water and under the ice. Fishhooks and bone points [spear heads] were of lesser importance.

Reindeer-husbandry in the form in which the author observed it during the period 1926–38 was typically Samoyed, using sleds. In the past, sometimes the carcasses of wild deer were brought to the tents on the backs of domesticated deer, but often such carcasses were brought home by the hunters themselves after they had cut them in two lengthwise.

Vetki (boats) were Yakut,[1] usually bought ones, with two-bladed oars. The Nganasans related that in olden times they also had skin boats. They did not have skis, these being mentioned only in folklore.

In the recent past, the only type of dwelling was a movable conic tent of reindeer hide of the Samoyed type, with the Samoyed lay-out in which the living space consists of two parts, on both sides of the hearth, to the right and left of the entrance. In the past the Nganasans, according to their traditions, had wooden conical yurts (*golomo*), covered with earth, and semisubterranean dwellings over which was erected a small tent or a roof built of driftwood, skins, sod, and other materials. According to the Nganasans there still are, along the Taymyr river, depressions of semisubterranean huts in which their ancestors lived. The construction of the Nganasan tent differs in a number of details from the construction of the Nenets tent, in the number of poles, the arrangement of the entrance, the cut of covering skins, and so on.

Generally, the clothing of the Nganasans does not differ from that of the Tundra Enets, but it differs sharply from that of the Nenets.[2] The Nganasans and Tundra Enets carry their knives like the Tungus do, i.e., on the lower belt, attached to the leg, and not on the belt worn over the fur parka* as the Nenets do. The Nganasans did not wear upper belts with their everyday clothing. Only the women wore hats; the men replaced them with parka and coat (*sokui*) hoods. Women's hats were of the fur-trimmed hood type, widespread in the north of Yakutia, among the Evenk and also the Chukchi, and worn both by men and women. Worn winter clothing usually served the Nganasans as summer clothing. The women's parka (*lakhariye*) should also be noted. It resembles the Tungus parka. The Nganasans think that their ancestors wore such parkas and hats like the ones now worn by the women.

Before collectivization, notwithstanding the large number of domesticated reindeer, the Nganasans usually led a life of near-starvation, particularly in the spring. Only in the fall, with the beginning of mass hunting of wild deer and fishing under the ice, was the supply of food plentiful. At this time supplies of food for the winter were put away. The meat and fat of wild deer were the favorite foods, this animal being regarded with almost a kind of reverence, while at the same time there was a comparative indifference to the meat of domesticated deer. Although, recently, domesticated deer, fishing, and polar fox hunting have given them in general a better means of subsistence than the hunting of wild deer, in the main all thoughts of the Nganasans have been concentrated on the latter.

Shamans were found among the Nganasans. With the majority of shamans the drum had an asymmetrical, oval form, similar to that of the Dolgans. The drumstick—a curved piece with a figured handle—was also of the Dolgan type.

Nganasan folklore is very varied and rich. One part of the folklore—*sitabi*—

*[*Malitsa* in the original.—Editor.]

deals with epic stories about heroes. Even the Nganasans consider these as Nenets, the names of the persons in them are Nenets, and all of the surroundings in which the heroes live represent a poetized Nenets way of life.[3] The very word *sitabi* is a Nenets one—cf., *syudbabi* (song about heroes)—in the Nenets language.

Another part of the folklore—*dyurume*, "messages"—to a considerable degree represents subjects similar to those of the Olenek Khosun [warrior] epos. We shall touch on these legends in more detail later. In some *dyurume*, oral chronicles of a kind, the Nganasans introduce the names of their heroes (*tonkaga* or *tonsaga*) such as *Timi-Khoti Toruda* ("Gap-toothed Toruda") [or] *Soymu-nyuo* ("son of Soymu"), *Sangudy*.

Generally, the Nganasans differ from the Nenets by their dialect, by the particular importance of wild-deer hunting in their economy, by their habits and traditions of hunting on foot, by their lack of a strong reindeer-breeding tradition, by their clothing, by their way of carrying the knife, in details of tent construction, type of sled used, and so on. Also by the non-Samoyed attributes of shamanism, and finally by a tradition according to which the Nganasans considered the Nenets as a completely strange people, not related to them.

Soviet ethnographers and linguists, interested in the question of the origin of northern Siberian peoples, agree at the present that these peoples came to the north of Siberia from the south. Also, all of the present population of northern Siberia is divided into two basic groups according to origin: peoples speaking the so-called Paleo-Asiatic languages and peoples speaking Uralic and Altay languages. To the first group belong the northeastern Paleo-Asiatics—the Chukchi, Koryaks, and Itelmens; the Nivkhs at the mouth of the Amur and in northern Sakhalin; and finally the Yukagirs who occupied in the 17th century, at the time of the arrival of the Russians in Siberia, the enormous territory from the mouth of the Lena in the west to Chaun bay and the shores of Bering sea in the east. At the time of the Russian arrival all these peoples still lived in the conditions of a stone age. Metals penetrated into their way of life irregularly, in small quantities, and with some people—the Chukchi and Itelmens—hardly at all. Thus the Indigirka Yukagirs were armed in the 1690's with stone hatchets and wore bone armor. These Paleo-Asiatics may be considered the most ancient population of the greater part of Siberia. The Yukagir tribes evidently populated the enormous interior areas of northern Siberia; the Chukchi, Koryaks, and Itelmens, and also Eskimos, the peninsulas and coasts of the extreme northeast of Siberia; the Nivkhs, the lower Amur, northern Sakhalin, and part of the coast adjoining the mouth of the Amur. All these peoples spread over Siberia and penetrated to the extreme north as early as the Neolithic era. In comparison with ethnic groups that arrived in northern Siberia later, these Paleo-Asiatics may be termed its aboriginal population.

The ethnic groups that arrived in northern Siberia later are: peoples speaking Uralic languages, Ugrian and Samoyed, to the west and east of the Yenisey; and peoples speaking Altayan Tungus languages, i.e., in the north, Evenks and Evens, and in the Amur region, the ancestors of the Nanayets tribes. In distinction from the Paleo-Asiatics who are concentrated in northern Siberia and at the mouth of the Amur (the Nivkhs), peoples speaking the Altay and Uralic languages have, or had comparatively recently, peoples related to them [and living] in the south of Siberia and even beyond its confines—to the west and farther to the south. Thus, the Magyars (Hungarians) are related by language to the Ob Ugrians. It may be supposed that in the more remote past the ancestors of the Bashkirs also spoke an Ugrian language. We have already mentioned the Sayan tribes, the Motors, Kamasins, and Karagas, who spoke Samoyed languages. Moreover,

FIGURE 2. Nganasan female *ledovka* (above-ground burial). *Ledovka* was made in 1927. The deceased lay on the front mound, had slipped sidewise, and had been disturbed by a bear. (Photograph of I. I. Baluyev, 1938.)

FIGURE 1. Hunter brings in a killed wild deer. Neighbors divide the meat. (After photograph of I. I. Baluyev, 1938.)

many peoples who speak the Finnic languages are also linguistically related to the Ugrians and Samoyeds and belong, as do the latter, to the Uralic language community.[4] The language of the Manchurians in T'ung-pei (northeastern China) is related to the Tungus and Nanayets languages of northern Siberia and the [Soviet] Far East. Not long ago, the numerous horse-breeding Evenks in the Trans-Baykal and in northern Mongolia spoke Tungus, and only recently have these acquired the Russian and Mongol languages respectively. Besides, all of the Tungus-Manchurian languages are related to the Mongolian and numerous Turkic languages and form, together with them, one Altayan language community. Together, the Uralic and Altayan language communities number many millions of people, although the total number of Paleo-Asiatics does not exceed 30,000. At that, only the languages of the northeastern Paleo-Asiatics are interrelated. The languages of the Yukagirs and Nivkhs are related neither to each other, nor to the languages of the northeastern Paleo-Asiatics (the Chukchis, Koryaks, and Itelmens).

Additionally, on the Yenisey, also from the south and also comparatively late, the languages of the Ket group, possibly related to Tibeto-Burman languages, began to spread. This spreading northward began even later than for the Samoyed languages.

In contrast to the Paleo-Asiatics, among whom even at the time of the arrival of the Russians Neolithic techniques predominated, the Uralic peoples (including the Samoyeds), the Altayans, and Ket-speaking peoples arrived in northern Siberia already acquainted with metals. It was from them that metals penetrated to the aboriginal Paleo-Asiatic population. Moreover, Samoyed-speaking peoples to the west of the Yenisey and the Tungus to the east of it brought with them and disseminated reindeer-breeding over northern Siberia. By the time the Russians arrived, reindeer-breeding had spread from the Tungus to the Yukagirs and also to some of the Koryaks and Chukchis.

As they spread over northern Siberia, the languages of Ugrian, Samoyed, Ket, and Tungus tribes intermixed with the languages of the aboriginal Paleo-Asiatics. Some of the Samoyed and Tungus tribes found by the Russians in northern Siberia represented just such Paleo-Asiatics who had been "Samoyedized" or "Tungusized." Stalin points out that

It would be completely wrong to consider that as a result of an intermixture of, let us say, two languages, a new, third language is obtained, which does not resemble either of the intermixed languages and which qualitatively differs from both. In reality, when languages are intermixed one of the languages usually dominates, retains its grammatical structure and its basic vocabulary and continues developing in accordance with its inner laws of development, while the other language gradually loses its quality and slowly dies out.[5]

The process of absorption of the ancient Paleo-Asiatic population of northern Siberia by the Uralic and Altayan tribes may be thought of as a basic process, which led to the ethnic composition of northern Siberia found there by the Russians. (The distribution of the Ket language was of a limited local character and was of less import.)

The formation of the Nganasan people appears to be one of the instances of this general process, a frequent ethnogenetic process, taking place in the northernmost part of Siberia, in the basins of the Pyasina, Taymyr, and Khatanga rivers.

Certainly, not everything is completely clear to us in these ethnogenetic processes. We do know, for instance, the ethnic sources of the aboriginal Paleo-Asiatic population of northern Siberia to the west of the Lena, but, concerning this, we can only point to more or less substantiated suppositions. We do not know yet the exact ways, the time, and the circumstances of the northward spread of the Samoyeds in western Siberia and that of the Tungus in eastern Siberia. All of these questions require separate investigations, and in all of them we are forced, at present, to limit ourselves to suppositions. However, the formation of the present-day Nganasan people from different (in origin) tribal groups took place also in historical times, under the eyes of the Russians, and we have at our disposal considerable documentary material on this problem; this material, with ethnographic data, forms the basis of the present article.

The problem of ethnogenesis is, first of all, a historical linguistic problem. Only linguistics can point to the origin of the language of an ethnic group. But the knowledge of the origin of a language does not mean knowledge of the origin of the people.

The origin of the Samoyed languages is evidently not connected with the origin of the Nganasans. The Samoyed languages, as we have already indicated, were formed somewhere in the south. This supposition is supported by their existence among the Sayans until the very beginning of the 20th century. The progeny of migrants from the south could be sought among the Nenets, Enets, and Selkups. Part of these peoples lived, and live now, far to the south of the tundra zone, in the direction of the Sayan mountains. But this cannot be said for the Nganasans, who live now, and already had lived at the time of the arrival of the Russians, far to the north. We have a basis for proposing that the ancestors of the Nganasans did not come from the Sayans as a Samoyed-speaking people and only acquired the Samoyed language and the elements of Samoyed culture when they were already in the extreme north. Consequently, for the solution of the problem of Nganasan origins, the clarification of the question of the origin of Samoyed languages is not as important as establishing which ethnic groups in their time acquired the Samoyed language and how, out of these "Samoyedized" elements, there formed the present-day Nganasan people.

Could it be supposed that, after acquiring a Samoyed language, the ancestors of the Nganasans were completely absorbed by some other ethnic group? This we cannot say. As we have seen and as we shall see below, the Nganasans sharply differentiate themselves from other Samoyed peoples, except for a part of the Enets. Also, the Russians in the 17th century distinguished their ancestors from other Samoyed groups. Therefore, this is a special ethnic group. True, we can not answer the question about the origin of the peculiarities of the present-day Nganasan dialect when compared with other Samoyed languages and dialects. This is the task of the linguists. But, properly, the historical part of the problem of Nganasan origins should be solved through a historical-ethnographic approach.

We have set for ourselves the task of answering the following questions: (1) What component parts (clans, tribes) make up the Nganasan people of our time, when they are subjected to ethnographic investigation? (2) What were the tribes and clans of the ancestors of the Nganasans and where were they found by the Russians in the 17th century? (3) In what manner were the Nganasan people formed out of these component elements? (4) What were the origins of the component parts of the Nganasan people whom the Russians encountered in the 17th century?

A detailed answer can be given to the first three questions. The last question can be answered only in a very general way, as this question is bound with the problem of the origin not only of the Nganasans but also of a number of other peoples. In this investigation we shall often meet with the concepts of "clan" and "tribe." We should therefore define our meaning of these terms.

When we regard the Nganasan, Enets, or Evenk tribes in the form in which they were found toward the beginning of the 20th century, we find that they were of considerable numbers (from 200–300 up to 1500 persons). Each tribe had a defined territory. Its members spoke one language, i.e., one dialect of a language. Ethnic groups, consisting of a large number of tribes (for instance, the Evenks), had a separate dialect for each tribe. Each tribe had its own name. Each tribe was a self-governing unit, with an elected "princeling" at its head and other elected officials. There was a well-expressed consciousness of belonging to a tribe and, to a certain extent, a tribal patriotism and setting off of one's own tribe against other tribes, even of the same ethnic group.

Each tribe was composed of clans. The number of clans varied from 3–4 to 12–14. Each clan had its name. Members of the same clan could not intermarry, i.e., the clan was exogamous. Members of the clan aided each other, collecting, for instance, for a member of the clan the necessary means for wife-purchase. In the past, members of the clan revenged their kinsmen and generally defended their interests in relations with members of other clans. Usually members of the clan were considered to be descended from a single male ancestor, i.e., descent was patrilineal; kinship on the mother's side usually was not taken into consideration.

In the 17th century the northern peoples were also divided into tribes and clans. The tribes numbered from 400 to 1000 persons, the clans 40 to 100. But, in addition to the clans comprising a tribe, there were special clans, sometimes large ones of 200 to 300 persons, which seemed to exist outside a tribal union, but which still were exogamous. Such clans were ancestral to the forest Enets —the Muggad, Bay, Uchi, Aseda, and Salerta; they were [also] found among the Evenks, Selkups, and Kets. Similar independent clans also formed a part of the ancestral Nganasans. As a rule, these large clans were, in turn, divided into small clans, usually of 50 to 80 members. In one case known to us, such a subdivision of a large clan was named in a document—a *stanitsa*.* Such a large clan with its subdivisions resembled a tribe but was distinguished from it by being an exogamous unit. Even more, it resembled a phratry divided into clans, but differed from it in not forming a tribe with another phratry. These independent, large "clan-phratries" without tribal affiliations were a rather characteristic phenomenon of the ancient tribal social order of the peoples of northern Siberia and require special investigation. We have also called them exogamous tribes. As will be seen further on, the indigenous population of northern Siberia had a special expression for them, differing from the words denoting "clan" and "tribe." These social formations were maintained longest among the Karasin Enets and, it seems, also among the forest Nenets. With the Nganasans, as will be seen below, they merged into one tribe, each forming a separate exogamous clan of the tribe.

A few words about terminology. We use in the text names like "Samoyeds," "Tungus," and others. The origin of the first name (Samoyed) was given above. We employ it as a general name for all peoples of this linguistic group or in conjunction with old names for tribes and administrative units. The name "Tungus" is also used in a broader sense than "Evenk" or "Even." Moreover, in the archival materials used by us, the term "Tungus" is always written. In employing the name "Evenk" in the author's text and "Tungus" in quotations from

*[*Stanitsa* normally implies a large cossack village.—Translator.]

archival materials, we risk introducing unnecessarily variegated terminology. In many cases we simply do not know the number of Tungus groups extant in the 17th century and whether they were Evenks or Evens. The use of "Tungus" as a more general term frees us from using "Evenk" or "Even" with the attendant risk of making a mistake. Therefore, we retain in this presentation the old names of some of the peoples.

Tribes and Clans of the Nganasans and Their Territorial Distribution

When formerly the Nganasans had to speak Russian, they called themselves Samoyeds (sg.: *samodín*; pl.: *sàmodi*). But more readily and specifically they used this name in referring to the Madu or Somatu Enets (the Khantayka Samoyeds), preferring sometimes to call themselves "Avam people," in comparison with the latter. Generally, the word "Samoyed" had a special meaning among the Nganasans. They never called the Nenets Samoyeds and seldom the Karasin Enets, preferring to call the latter by their clan-tribal names Muggadi and Bay. Aside from these, they called by the name Samoyed their supposed relatives to the east (*vide infra*).

The Russian name "Samoyed" corresponded with them to the expression *ngano-nganasana*—"real people." This expression covered not only themselves, but again the Madu Enets, or more exactly, all those who wore a white plume (*sungúku* in Nganasan or *nakà* in Enets) on the *sokui* [coat].

In their own language the Nganasans call themselves *nya-tansa*. *Tansa* means "people," "tribe" (cf. the Nenets *tenz*). The word *nya* is also Samoyed. The Nganasans translate it as "comrade."* In Nenets *nya* means "brother" (evidently in the classificatory sense), "neighbor," "comrade," "member of a clan or phratry."[6]

A male among the Nganasans is called *nya-nganasa*, a female *nya-ny* (*nya-ne*). Thus their autonym and words derived from it actually mean "related people," "related man," "related woman," and have no ethnic content whatever.

The Nganasans call the Nenets *yuraka-tansa*, *yuraka-nganasa*, *yuraka-ny* and the Madu Enets *somatu-tansa*, *somatu-nganasa*, *somatu-ny*, etc.

The Russians used to call the Nganasans *sàmodi* (plural), *samodín* (singular), and the Evenks *samail* (plural); the Yakuts and Dolgans they called *samay* (singular), *samaydar* (plural).

Other names for the Nganasans exist among their western neighbors. The Enets call them *maú*, the Nenets, *tavys*, *tavú* or *tavó*. The adjective "nganasan" in the Nenets language is [expressed with] *tavgy*.[7] As is known, the Russians also called the ancestors of the Nganasans in the 17th century (at first in part and afterwards all) "Tavgi" and "Tavgi Samoyad" [both plurals].

By 1926–7 the Nganasans consisted of two tribes, the Avam and Vadeyev Nganasans, and a separate clan Oko or Dolgan. The clan composition of the tribes and the number of clan members are shown in Table 1.

The large number of deer in the possession of the Nganasans was not distributed equably: the big reindeer-breeders, who comprised only about 10% of all households, owned more than 60%.

Today the Nganasans use the above-mentioned term *tansa* to designate their tribe; a clan is called *fonka* (*khonka*). The word *fonka* also means "spear" (used in drives, hunts).[8]

*[*Tovarishch* in the original.—Editor.]

TABLE 1*

| Names of clans | Number of families | Persons | | Number of reindeer owned |
		Total in clan	Per single family	
Avam Nganasans				
Chunanchera	20	103	5.1	4495
Linanchera (Turdagins)	29	139	4.8	4475
Ninonde or Falysyada (Porbins)	39	175	4.5	9254
Ngomde (rarely Ngomdichera)	14	76	5.4	4931
Ngamtuso (Kosterkins)	16	81	5.1	1316
Total	118	574	4.9	24471
Vadeyev Nganasans				
Asyandu (Tynta)	6	31	5.5	307
Kupchik (Nyayme?)	12	73	5.9	1904
Kokary (Asya?)	15	73	4.9	672
Lapsakha	5	24	4.8	642
Ngoybu	2	12	6.0	103
Nërkho	1	11	11.0	170
Total	41	224	5.0	3798
Dolgans-Nganasans				
Oko (Yarotskiy)	11	69	6.3	3625
Grand total	170	867	5.1	31894

*P. Ye. Ostrovskikh names the Ninonde clan of the Avam Nganasans Lyagi (*lahi*), and mentions in addition the Tonida clan (Botadin). Lyagi is the subdivision of the Ninonde clan taking its origin from an old man called Lagi. Concerning the Tonida clan, the Nganasans claim that this is a subdivision of the Chunanchera clan. Thus, the "prince" Nyarmadu-Boli was a Tonida but at the same time also a Chunanchera. P. Ye. Ostrovskikh names the clans Nyayme (Neyme) and Asya for the Vadeyev Nganasans but does not mention the clans Kokary and Kupchik. Insofar as Ostrovskikh notes that in 1900 a Terepte belonged to the Nyayme clan and that in 1926 the old shaman Tere (Chere) belonged to the Kupchik clan, it is probable that Nyayme is another name for the Kupchik clan. If this be the case, the clan Asya of Ostrovskikh probably corresponds to the Kokary clan. This becomes more plausible because *asya* means "Tungus" and Kokary's ancestor is supposed to have been a real Tungus.

In 1926–7 the Nganasans were clearly aware of their division into two tribes. At the same time, the Avam Nganasans were considered the "real" Nganasans, that is, the older, big "horde," while the Vadeyev were not so "real" and were a younger "horde."

Membership in a tribe was determined first of all by membership in a clan. All members of the clans Chunanchera, Linanchera, Ngomdichera (Ngomde), Ninonde, and Ngamtuso belonged to the Avam tribe of Nganasans, while members of the clans Asyandu, Kokary, Kupchik, Lapsakha, Ngoybu, and Nërkhu belonged to the Vadeyev tribe, regardless of their actual place of habitation.

A person who did not belong to any of the clans of the tribe was not considered a member of the tribe, even if all his life was spent with the Nganasans and he did not differ from them in any way. Thus, descendants of the Dolgan Oko were not included in either of the Nganasan tribes and were considered Dolgans; they rode to Dolgan meetings and were subordinate to a Dolgan "prince," although by language and culture they were true Nganasans, and lived with them since the first half of the 19th century. Only after the Taymyr administrative divisions were changed in Soviet times in accordance with territorial principles did they enter into the Nganasan nomadic councils. Only in the case of adoption did the descendants of the adopted son, entering the clan of the foster father, become members of the corresponding tribe.

Clan membership was reckoned in the male line. Clans of the Avam Nganasans sometimes had subdivisions whose ancestors were considered to be specific persons. In the Chunanchera clan there was a subdivision Faló; in the Ngomde (Ngomdichera) clan, a subdivision Syáde; in the Ninonde clan, Láteda, etc. But the clans proper of Avam Nganasans did not attach their origin to specific ancestors but considered themselves collective units existing from times immemorial. The clans of the Vadeyev Nganasans usually traced their origin to a specific ancestor.

In addition to the terms *tansa* and *fonka*, the Nganasans also use the term *chera* for clan designation. This form has become fixed in the names of the clans of the Avam Nganasans—Chunanchera, Linanchera, and, less often, Ngomdichera

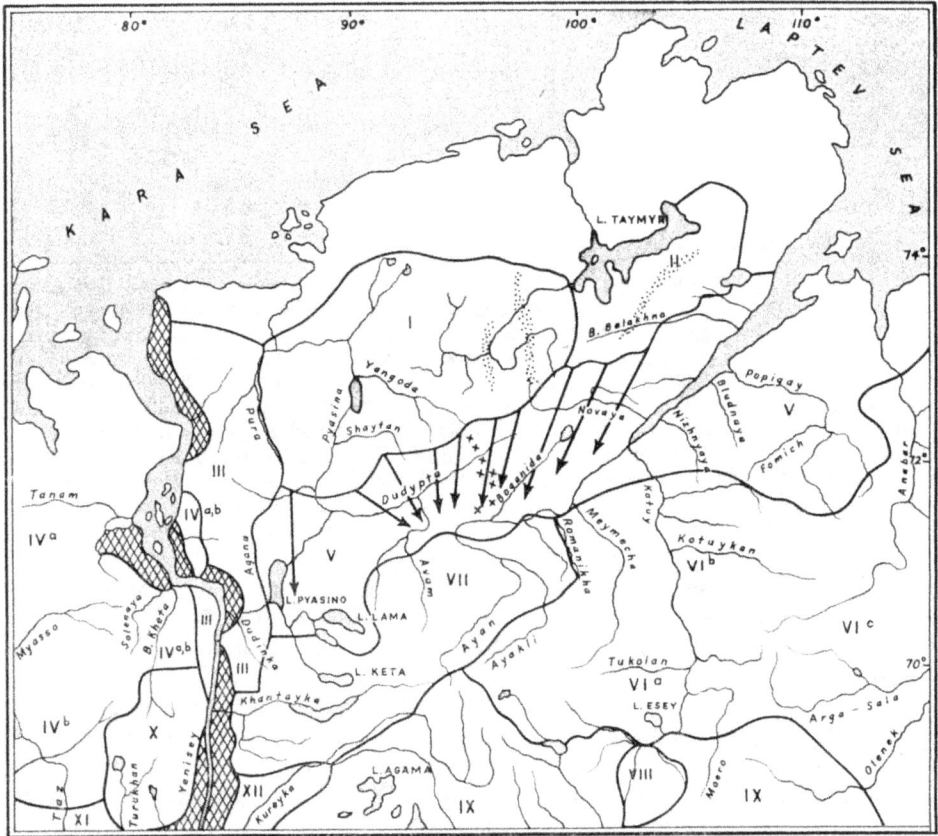

FIGURE 3.   Territory of the Nganasan tribes and of neighboring peoples and tribes in 1926–7. I. Avam Nganasans. II. Vadeyev Nganasans. III. Enets (Khantayka and Karasinsk Samoyeds). IV. Nenets (Yuraks): *a*, Obdorsk (Salyander); *b*, Tazov (Aseda). V. Mixed Yakut-speaking population: Dolgans (groups of Dolgans, Dongot, Edyan, Karanto), Lower Zatundrinsk Yakuts, "Tundra" peasants, and also individual migrants from various Tungus tribes, Yesey Yakuts, and Enets. VI. Yesey and Olenek Yakut reindeer-breeders and "Yakutized" Tungus from the camps of: *a*, Khatygyn (clans Osogostokh, Botulu, Yëspëkh, and others); *b*, Chordu; *c*, Beti and others. VII. Goragir Tungus (summer). VIII. Bayagir Tungus (Turyzhsk). IX. Nyurumnyal Tungus (Ilimpey). X. Pankagir Tungus (Chapogir) who migrated beyond the Yenisey, including the clan Tavinduk.   XI. Tazov Selkups. XII. Kets. Checkered areas represent Russian settlement; dots, territory of the Nganasan clan Oko; arrows, winter nomadizing of the Nganasans beyond their own tribal territory; crosses, locale of the Mayat clan who migrated to the Zatundra (to the "Lama").

and Ninondechera. It is met also in the self-designations *Dyangúra-mou-chera, Dyaruáma-mou-chera, Avama-mou-chera,* and *Ngili-chera,*[9] of which the first is translated "people of the tundra land"; the second, "people of the unknown land"; the third, "people of the Avam land." These designations refer mainly to the Avam Nganasans. The fourth is translated "lower people" and refers to the Vadeyev Nganasans, as living "down" from the Avam Nganasans.[9]

The word *chera,* which is used only by Avam clans (and not Vadeyev ones), probably corresponds to the Enets *tyde,* the Selkups *tadzhe* or *chadzh,* and the Kamasin *tël.* Among the Nganasans it probably indicated the originally exogamous unit, the phratry, larger than the clan (*fonka*), which apparently was only a subdivision of the *chera.* The difference between the Nganasan terms *chera* and *fonka* and the Enets *tydë* and *fogga,* they themselves explain thus: *chera* (*tydë*) is "breed," "species" (for instance, the breeds or species of animals are named so), while *fónka* (*fógga*) means "butt," "stem," "persons originating from one ancestor," from one "stem."

Nganasan clans are exogamous. Until 1948 there were no violations. Earlier it was also forbidden to take a wife from the mother's clan, and some Nganasans insisted on this rule even in 1940. Also among the Vadeyev Nganasans a tendency to avoid marriages within one's tribe was noted.

Both Nganasan tribes had their definite territories, as shown on the map (Fig. 3). For the winter, the Nganasans moved out of their tribal territories; their routes are indicated on the map by arrows.

The Nganasans moved from the forest to the tundra and back on parallel routes, in groups ("heaps," i.e., *malir* in Nganasan) of two or three, seldom four or five families, with two or three families staying in one tent. Their nomadic routes were permanent. When one knew the region of the winter family campings one could determine the rest of the route almost without error.

All the 40 or 50 routes of separate Nganasan "heaps" may be reduced to six basic ones, connecting a definite region of winter nomadizing, a definite region of summer nomadizing and hunting areas, and a belt of land over which was carried out the movement from the edge of the forest to the tundra and back. These six basic routes are indicated in Figure 4. Table 2 shows the composition of the clans and families using these routes.

Thus, while the tribes more or less retained their territorial unity, the clans of the Avam Nganasans greatly intermixed although there did remain some regularity in their disposition; this will be noted further. With the Vadeyev Nganasans, the clans were grouped more compactly, which, however, could have been due to their lesser numbers.

Within the framework of the present article, the custom of the Nganasans of giving names in honor of famous kinsmen should be noted at this point. Thus, the father or grandfather of the Kondyue and Jalopte Turdagin Nganasans was named Soyum, in honor of a hero who sprang from their clan, and so on.

We have seen that the Nganasans were composed of two tribes and one separate clan. In solving the question of their origin, it is necessary to examine separately the origin of each of the parts, beginning with those of most recent origin, in order to pass thereafter to the original elements of the constituent parts.

The Origin of the Separate Clan Oko

The solution of the origin of the Oko clan is simple. Oko was a real person, whom Middendorf met in 1843.[10] He reported that Oko and both of his sons,

TABLE 2

Route number[*]	Region of summer nomadizing	Region of winter nomadizing	Names of clans		Number of families in clan
I	Together with the Enets, between the Gulf of Yenisey and the Pura river, tributary of the Pyasina	With the Enets on the Dudinka and Ambarnaya rivers between Yenisey and Lake Pyasina	Linanchera Ngamtuso		9 4
				Total	13
II	In the basin of the Pura river, a tributary of the Pyasina	To the east of Lake Pyasina in the basin of the Yelovaya river	Ngamtuso Ninonde		10 5
				Total	15
III	At the bend of the Pyasina river, between it and the Pura; the middle reaches of the Pyasina	The mouth of the Avam, along the Dudypta river and the lower reaches of the Avam, to the west from there to the Medvezhiy Yar river (Kystyktakh)	Linanchera Ninonde Chunanchera Ngomde Ngamtuso		13 8 7 3 2
				Total	33
IV	In the basin of Yangoda river, a tributary of the Pyasina, in the basin of Dëgade river, a tributary of the Taymyr	Along the Dudypta river near the site of Staroye Letovye, at the Letovye trading station to the east of the Avam river	Chunanchera Ninonde Linanchera		8 4 3
				Total	15
V	In the basin of the Taymyr river and its tributaries, the Gordita and the Logata	In the basin of the Bagnida river, a tributary to the Kheta, at the sites Barkhatov, Mironovskaya, Payturma, and Rassokha	Ninonde Ngomde Chunanchera Linanchera Oko Vadeyevs of the Kokara clan		20 11 5 4 8 2
				Total	50
VI	To the south and east of Lake Taymyr, mainly in the basin of Dyamu-Tarida and Bolshaya Balakhna rivers	Between the Boganida and Kheta rivers at the sites of Belenkiy Gorelyy, Baykalovskiy Rassomazhiy, and Isayevskiy	Vadeyevs Oko Ninonde		39 3 2
				Total	44
				Grand total	170

[*]Route I passed over Enets territory; Routes II, III, IV, and V over the territory of the Avam Nganasans; Route VI is that of the Vadeyev Nganasans. The data are as of 1926–7 (see Fig. 4).

while considered Dolgans in origin, lived with the Nganasans, were married to Nganasan women, and spoke only Nganasan, although Oko himself knew also a few Dolgan words. Oko was very rich and Middendorf called him a "Samoyed Croesus."

All eleven families of the Oko clan were considered descendants of Oko's sons, Lonire[11] and Fei, who bore the family name Yarotskiy.

The son of Lonire, Murko, was still alive in the winter of 1926–7. The sons of Murko were Khunsaré, Ártya,[12] Fádopte, and Baykalé. In 1938 Artya gave

FIGURE 4. Groupings of Nganasans in 1926–7 on the basis of routes taken from the forest to the tundra and back. Route numbers are as indicated in Table 2; dotted line, northern limit of forest; arrows, directions of nomadizing of Yakuts and Dolgans over the Khatanga; this corresponds with the route by which the ancestors of the Tavg Nganasans probably penetrated to the Taymyr.

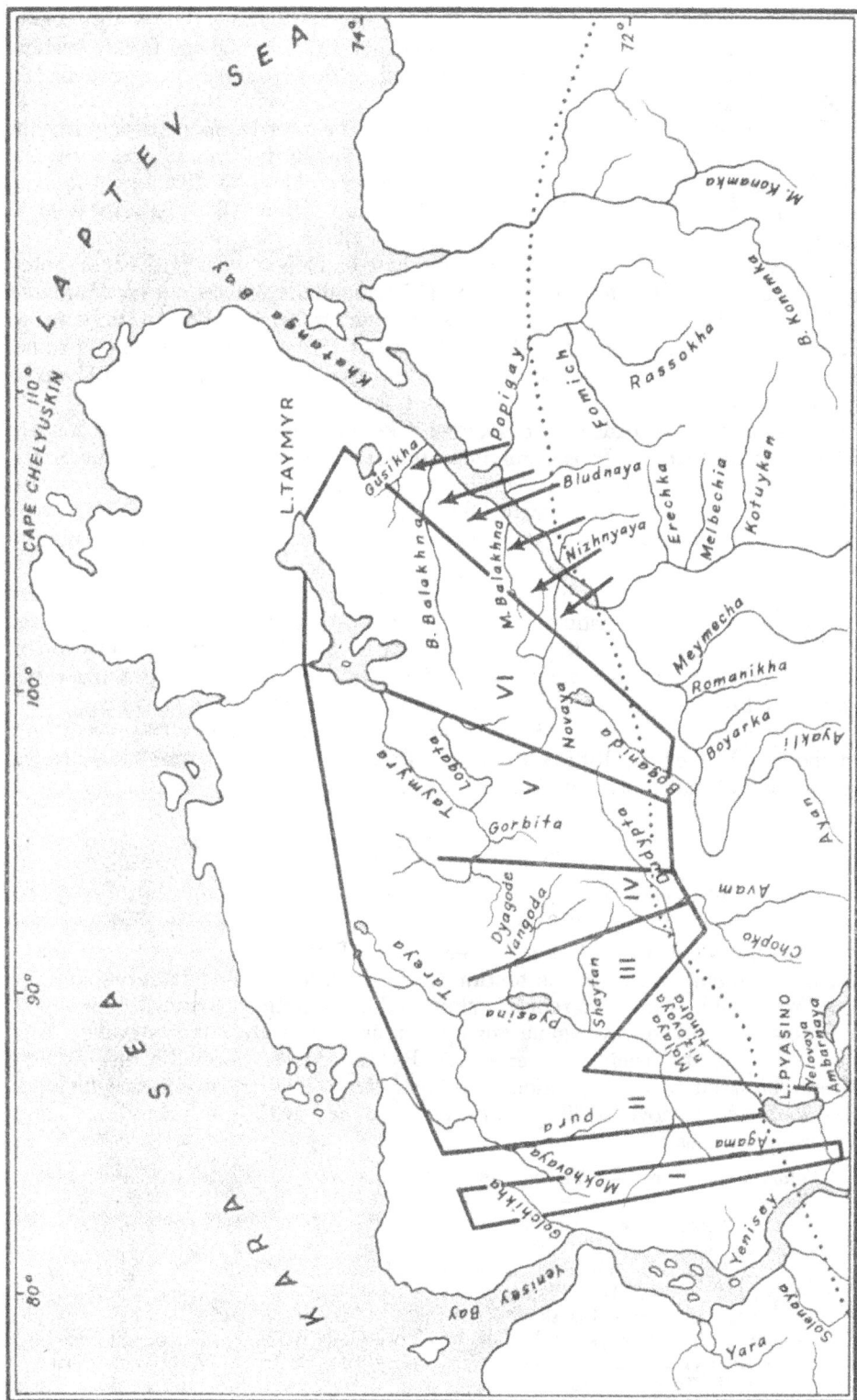

the author of this article a packet of documents, representing the family archive of Oko's descendants, and the robe* and sash with which Oko was rewarded in 1837 for donating 100 reindeer to the treasury.

The earliest document in Oko's archive was a receipt for the payment of fur-tribute for three people in 1818. The latest, bearing his name, was a receipt for the assignment of bread from the treasury [office] in 1853. In 1854 the accounting for bread was already made to Lonire. Thus, Oko probably died in 1853.

The census of 1897 noted that the number of Dolgans of the Dolgan-Yesey *uprava*, to whom the Samoyed language ("Tavgiy dialect") was native, amounted to 27 men and 18 women.[13] In the earliest documents Oko is called an "unbaptized Tungus of Dolgan origin from Esey *volost*," but in the documents related to his reward he is called a Samoyed. In the receipt of 1854 Lonire is called a "Dolgan of Dolgan-Yesey region."

The reasons that caused the Dolgan Oko to live with the Nganasans are difficult to determine. It is sometimes said that he married a rich Nganasan widow.[14] According to another version, Oko, an orphan, was brought up by the Nganasans. According to a third, Oko was a Nganasan to whom the Dolgans gave a girl in marriage so that he would join their tribe.[15] In this explanation a prevalent folklore motive comes to fore—the establishment of friendship between tribes by giving away a girl in marriage. In the light of the documents from Oko's archive and the testimony of Middendorf there is no doubt that Oko was a Dolgan by birth. According to a fourth version, a Nganasan girl, an orphan, was brought up by the Dolgans, and when she grew up a Dolgan married her and went to live with the Samoyeds. From him descended the Oko clan.

At any rate, the ancestor of the separate clan Oko became a Nganasan only in the first half of the 19th century, and the clan itself was formed only in the second half of that century and until our time was considered Dolgan.

The Vadeyev Samoyeds and the Vadeyev Tungus

As far as we know the Vadeyev Nganasans are mentioned as Samoyeds for the first time in 1818 or 1819 in a criminal case where a "Samoyed of Vadayev origin, Mikhaylo Portnyagin abandoned . . . the Turukhansk citizen Vasily Duboglazov in an empty area of the tundra, from which he got a cold, and in addition took from him by force two reindeer stags and five roubles of money."[16]

Officially the Vadeyev Nganasans appear as a separate administrative "clan" in 1824 when the Yenisey governor, A. P. Stepanov, divided the then-existing Yesey *volost* into six independent administrative "clans," of which one included the Vadeyev Samoyeds—20 persons of male sex with the princeling Kanta Kurlyshkin as head.[17]

*[*Kaftan* in the original.—Editor.]

FIGURE 5.   Approximate distribution of tribes over the Taymyr and territories adjoining it during the first half of the 17th century. I. Ancestors of the Avam Nganasans: a, "Pyasida Samoyad"; b, Kuraks; c, Tidiris; d, Kheta Tavgs of princeling Adamula; e, Anabar Tavgs of princelings Khal and Pud II. Ancestors of the Vadeyev Nganasans: a, Tungus of the Vanyadyr tribe; b, Malgachagir clan (Muansk). III. Ancestors of the Somatu Enets, i.e., Samoyeds who paid tribute in the Khantayka and Ledenkin Shar tribute quarters. IV. Yuraks (Nenets). V. Tungus tribe of Adyan (Edyan). VI. Tungus tribe of Sinigir. VII. Tungus tribe of Goragir.   VIII. Tungus tribes—a, Bayagir; and b, Dogochagir—who paid tribute in the Turyzhsk tribute quarters (the Dogochagir are apparently the ancestors of the Dongot Dolgans. IX. Ancestors of the Karasinsk Enets (Bay and Muggadi), and of the Tazov Nenets (Aseda).

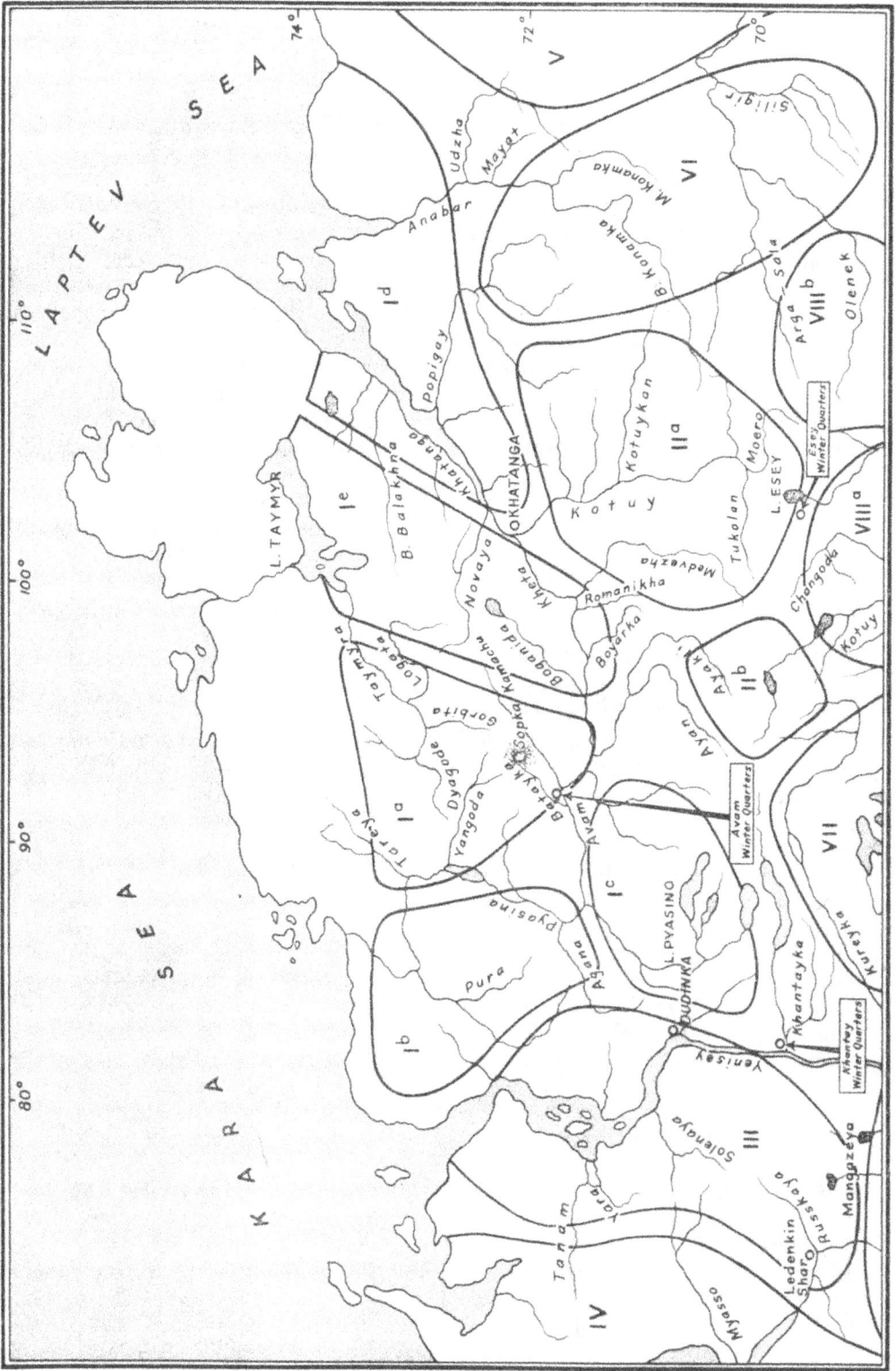

In 1832 there were already 44 male Vadeyev Nganasans, and there were 56 in 1859.[18] According to the 1897 census, there were 31 families of the "Vadeyev Samoyed clan"—93 males and 84 females.[19]

The fact that Stepanov was the first to separate the Vadeyev Nganasans from the Yesey volost does not mean that prior to 1824 they did not exist as a separate tribal group. Before 1824 the Yesey volost included six different clan, tribal, and even ethnic groups, mostly completely independent of each other. Their only connection was that they paid tribute at one point, in the Khatanga settlement, where the tribute winter quarters had been moved already at the end of the 17th century from Lake Yesey. Five of the six groups of the Yesey volost of 1844 were emigrants from Yakutia who migrated to the Khatanga basin mostly in the second half of the 18th century and in the beginning of the 19th. For tribute-paying purposes these immigrants were attached by the Turukhan authorities to the "Yesey" winter tribute-quarters closest to northwestern Yakutia, and thus, all in all, six independent clan, tribal, and ethnic groups were found in the Yesey volost. In 1824 Stepanov only brought the actual conditions into accord with official nomenclature.

The six groups who paid tribute at the beginning of the 19th century in Yesey volost were: the remnant of the Tungus tribe of Dolgans (from 1824 the Dolgan-Yesey uprava), the large Tungus clan Dongot (the Dolgan-Tungus uprava), the Edyan-Karanto clan of the Tungus tribe (the Boganido-Tungus uprava), another remnant of the same tribe, retaining its tribal name Edyan (the Zhigan-Tungus uprava), Yakuts who formed the Lower Zatundrinsk Yakut uprava, and the Nganasans of the Vadeyev-Samoyed uprava.

That the Vadeyev Nganasans represented "Samoyedized" Tungus from the upper reaches of the Kheta and Khatanga was mentioned already by Middendorf.[20] They are marked thus on the old maps too. In 1926–7 the old Vadeyev shaman Kupchik Tere (Chere) as well as the shaman Kheripte of the Oko clan still sang in Tungus while conducting their shaman rites. Also, in the lists of inhabited places of the Yenisey *guberniya* for 1859, the Vadeyev Nganasans were entered as Tungus.

Judging by the Tax Record of the First Tribute Commission of the Yenisey province in 1786,[21] the Yesey volost had the following composition. Under the heading "Yesey volost," there is a list of 16 "unbaptized Tungus" tribute payers (i.e., males of age 18 to 50), with the "princeling" Kelyunts as their head, and of 18 persons either younger or older than the tribute age, i.e., a total of 34 males.

Thereafter follows a rather vague subheading "Attached to above volost those who were not formerly taxed and are now attached to the tax lists, since according to the 1761 census they are shown as tribute-paying baptized Yakuts." This is followed by a list of 96 Yakuts (including 44 tribute payers) headed by the "princeling" Pyotr Semenov, among whom the names Tyuprin, Fedoseyev, Spiridonov, and others make it easy to recognize the ancestors of the Lower Zatundrin Yakuts.

Further on, there is again a subheading "Not included in the tax list and now attached to the above Yesey volost [the following] unbaptized Tungus." The roll contains 62 males (including 30 tribute payers) headed by the "princeling" Kholostoy. Included above the last 15 men of the princeling Kholostoy is another subheading, "Cherpovsk clan," but no other princeling is indicated. The names of the Tungus of princeling Kholostoy and the "Cherpovsk clan" are partly Russian names and nicknames (Byelogolovyy, Shitik, Proshka, Khudoy, Dimitrey), partly purely Tungus (Shaldyul, Nurgoul, Dishkoul, Unga, etc.).

Among the Dolgans of Dolgan-Yesey uprava, the clan Chorpok was preserved to our days.[22] In 1926–7 it contained only 18 persons of both sexes. Evidently, most of the descendants of this clan called themselves simply Dolgans, although by origin they were probably locally born Tungus and not the so-called Dolgans who are emigrants from Yakutia.

Thus, the Tungus of the princeling Kholostoy may be considered the ancestors of the Dolgans of the "future" Dolgan-Yesey uprava, who resettled in the Mangazeysk *uyezd* by the middle of the 18th century[23] and who were included in the Yesey volost in 1786. In 1832, among the Dolgans of the Dolgan-Yesey uprava, one of the elders bore the surname of Prokhorov, while in 1786 in the rolls of the Tungus of princeling Kholostoy, as noted above, there was counted a Proshka. Middendorf mentions a Dolgan elder whom he calls the "influential Artsya." In the 1786 roll of Dolgans there is Archa, aged 9, who was thus 84 years old in the year of Middendorf's travels (1843). The same name was also borne by a Nganasan, a descendant of Oko, who also came from the Dolgan-Yesey uprava —the above-mentioned Artya. Apparently this name was hereditary with the Dolgans who formed the Dolgan-Yesey uprava.

There were no other groups in the composition of Yesey volost in 1708. The ancestors of the Vadeyev Nganasans could thus be sought among the Tungus of the princeling Kelyuntsa. Indeed, in the roll of 1768 there is a Kurlyshka, 20 years old, son of Ultyga, and in 1824, as pointed out above, the princeling of the Vadeyev Nganasans was Kanta Kurlyshkin. At the sources of the river Bolshaya Balakhna in the territory of the Vadeyev Nganasans there is a lake Kurlyshka (in Yakut Kurluska). The Yakuts say that this lake received its name from the name of a Vadeyev Samoyed who was making his living there.

In 1768, part of the Tungus of the princeling Kelyuntsa, mainly the older generation, had characteristic Tungus names: Soleul, Ultyga, Doldyul, also Kelyuntsa, Khurkokon. Others, mainly the younger ones, had Nganasan names, such as: Forma, Kilirfuyu, Kadoku, Kurdirfuyu. Indeed, some of these names have meaning when translated into the Nganasan language: Toma (*tomu*)— mouse; Bolyu (*bolua*)—angry; Yaka—twin; Fuya (*fuaya*)—rear, etc.

Thus, the Tungus of the princeling Kelyuntsa are, without doubt, the ancestors of the Vadeyev Nganasans. Indeed, as the varied character of their names indicates, in 1768 the process of changing from a Tungus language to Samoyed (Nganasan) was still in full swing. From the tax records of 1768 it is clear that the ancestors of the Vadeyev Nganasans were the basic tribe of the Yesey volost; they were first to be registered and without any reservations, while the Dolgans and Yakuts were registered officially only in 1768, a fact which, as pointed out above, was specifically mentioned in the tax records.[24]

In the tax record of 1768 the word "Vadeyev" is not to be found, but in one document of 1771 there is an entry: "From unbaptized Tungus of the Vadeyev clan, two sables."[25]

The Legend about the Lake Yesey Mayats

In the upper reaches of the Khatanga river, in the region of Lake Yesey in the Olenek basin, in the folklore, combined under a generic name of the "Olenek Khosun epos," the Mayat people (*Mayattar* in Yakut, *Mayadol* in Evenk) are often mentioned.

Within these legends, there is the following episode: In the region of Lake Yesey there lives the numerous and reckless tribe of the Mayats. Twelve cossacks come to Yesey to subjugate them to the Russian tsar. But the Mayats "who acknowledge no laws" kill these cossacks; one of the cossacks runs around the lake three times before the Mayats succeed in killing him. Fearing punishment, the Mayats decide to go away and move over the ice of Lake Yesey. In the middle of the lake they find a tusk ("horn") of a mammoth protruding from the ice. They proceed to cut it. From the tusk blood begins to flow. An old woman shaman urges the Mayats to stop the cutting. But the ill-natured Mayats do no listen to her. Then the old woman takes her two sons and leaves. Just as she reaches the shore, the tusk falls, the lake ice breaks, and the Mayats perish. The other part of the Mayats, on the Olenek, faithful to their ill nature, trap wild deer, skin them alive, and blind them for amusement. Because of this, the wild deer leave the Olenek. The Mayats go to their stores of meat, but the stores move away from them and the Mayats die of hunger. According to a different version, the Mayats are destroyed by other inhabitants of the Olenek, apparently by some Tungus tribe.

A few of the families in the "Yakutized," but Tungus by origin, settlement of Beti[26] are considered to be the descendants of the surviving Mayats, the sons of the old woman shaman. In 1926–34 they lived in camp [*stanka*] Mironovskiy, in the Avam area of the Taymyr National Okrug, but only two families of these acknowledge themselves as descendants of the Mayats, while others denied this odious origin (see preceding passages). However, the surrounding population of the Second Mironovskiy camp called them Mayattar (i.e., Mayats). In the matriculations of the Khatanga church for 1868 are found marriage entries of the "Yesey Yakut Grigoriy Moyat and a Yesey, also Yakut [woman] . . . Ioday," and, in 1871, of the "Tungus from the Second Summer uprava . . . Neltanov" and "the Yakut daughter Moyat."[27]

But there are also other descendants of these Mayats. The descendants of Mayats living in the Mironovskiy camp, Ivan Khristoforovich Mayat and Ilya Nikolayevich Beti, claimed that the Vadeyev Samoyeds are their relatives. The Zatundrinsk peasants also confirmed that their old people, when speaking among themselves in Yakut, called the Vadeyev Samoyeds "Mayats." The Dolgans said that the name Mayat is the "old name of the Vadeyev Samoyeds." The Yakuts of the Betu settlement in Kirbey say that they call the Samoyeds (i.e., Nganasans) Mayats in general, and Vadeyev Samoyeds in particular. Many more such examples could be cited.

In 1902, P. Ye. Ostrovskikh also heard about the murder on Lake Yesey:

. . . 'we personally heard from an elderly blind man on the Lama (i.e., in the basin of the Kheta—Author) that on Lake Yesey there was previously a Russian town—there were many cabins—but all Russians were killed by the Vadeyev Samoyeds. . . . One Russian cossack they could not kill at once, they vainly ran after him three times around the lake and then decided to ambush him, and so he was killed. . . .' So goes the legend, but whatever the case, the fact remains that nobody denies the killing of the Russians.[28]

The legend about the mammoth in Lake Yesey and about the old woman shaman is told also by K. M. Rychkov, without, however, naming either the Mayats or the Vadeyev Nganasans.[29]

We see that the killing on Lake Yesey was quite clouded by legend. But at the same time this legend is known to every Yesey Yakut and to every Evenk in the neighborhood of Lake Yesey. There is also no doubt that oral traditions clearly connect the Mayats, who killed the cossacks on Lake Yesey, with the Vadeyev Nganasans.

The Vanyad Tribe

Beginning with 1636, the winter quarters on Lake Yesey were the place of tribute payment for a rather large number of Tungus groups.

At first, after the incorporation of Tungus territory east of the Yenisey into Russia, some Tungus tribes and clans had to pay the tribute rather far from their areas of habitation. Thus, the Yesey Tungus appear in the tribute registers for the first time in 1625,[30] when 19 "Vonodyrs" paid their tribute on the lower Tunguska.

In 1637–9 some Yesey Vanyadyrs still paid the tribute in the Ust-Titey winter quarters on the Lower Tunguska,[31] but in 1639 they were attached to Yesey winter quarters "because their previous earnings were on the Yesey lake and they should not be expected to pay tribute on the Tunguska at the mouth of the river Titey."[32]

The first available roll of the Yesey Tungus[33] is for 1634:

Khatansk winter quarters, and there paid the tsar's tribute anew the Katansk Samoyad:

The Vanyader Clan

Uldins:	4 sables taken	Gireul:	2 sables taken
Kandans:	3 sables taken	Bintoka:	1 sable taken
Tiksicha:	3 sables taken	Bayagirets Yalkiga:	1 sable taken

These Tungus were called Samoyeds either by mistake (since before them there are long entries of the ancestors of the Avam Nganasans, the Samoyeds of Pyasida), or because of the fact that between these Tungus and the "Pyasitsk Samoyeds"—ancestors of the Avam Nganasans—there was sensed a certain kinship. Inasmuch as the former were called Samoyeds, the name was transferred to the latter; though the names of the latter are purely Tungus and, later on, they are always called Tungus.[34]

The Bayagirs are a Tungus tribe living to the south of Lake Yesey, a tribe that paid tribute in the Turyzh winter quarters. In the list reproduced above, the "Bayagirets" was included probably as a neighbor of the Vanyadyrs.

The winter quarters, although called "Khatansk," were probably the Yesey ones, the ones that are always called "Khatansk-Yesey" afterwards; sometimes in the headings and in the text of the documents the form "on the Khatanga, on Yesey lake" or "from Pyasida of Khatanga of Yesey lake" is used.[35]

With the passage of time, the separate tribute-collecting winter quarters became places of payment for specific tribes only. The place where the tribe of Vanyads or Vanyadyrs paid tribute was the Yesey winter quarters.

The collection of tribute on the Yesey is shown in Table 3. Until 1661 there was no census of the Yesey Tungus and we have only data on the quantity of furs collected. By dividing the total number of tribute sables collected, and other furs equalized to sables, by three—the tribute rate on the Yesey amounted to three sables per man—we get the approximate number of tribute payers. For the years beginning with 1661 the number of tribute payers is stated. Variations in the quantity of tribute collected and in the number of tribute payers resulting from temporary payments of tribute on the Yesey by other tribes or parts of tribes, or as a result of some event, will be explained below.

In addition to the Vanyads, in 1636–8 tribute was paid on the Yesey by the Dogochagirs (ancestors of the Dongot group of Dolgans, *vide infra*); in 1644, tribute was paid by the Sinigirs and the "Mugalsk clan" (Malgachagirs). This

TABLE 3

COLLECTION OF TRIBUTE AND THE NUMBER OF TRIBUTE PAYERS IN THE
YESEY TRIBUTE WINTER QUARTERS

Year	Tribute collected adjusted in terms of sables*	Number of tribute payers (to 1661)	Sources
1634	16	6	TsGADA, Sib. prikaz, bk. 986, leaf 441
1636	ca. 310	104	bk. 95, leaf 295
1638	337	113	bk. 150, leaf 1027
1639	256	86 ⎫	p. 105, leaves 228, 239
1640	258	87 ⎬	
1641	297	99 ⎭	art. 111, s. 126
1645	475	159	bk. 285, leaves 159–161
1647	389	130	art. 308, s. 209
1648	423	141	art. 331, s. 406
1649	454	152	art. 375, s. 242
1651	457	153	art. 382, s. 142
1652	412	138 ⎫	bk. 320, leaves 24–26, 100
1653	508	170 ⎭	
1655	483	161	art. 442, s. 187
1656	477	159 ⎫	bk. 504, leaves 108, 132–133
1657	476	159 ⎭	
1658	480	160	art. 572, ss. 94, 95
1659	489	163	art. 567, ss. 201, 202
1661	476	162 ⎫	bk. 442, leaf 243
1662	478	162 ⎭	
1664	398	129 ⎫	bk. 478, leaves 58–59
1665	—	126 ⎭	
1667	383	123 ⎫	bk. 513, leaf 341
1668	381	122 ⎭	
1669	—	123 ⎫	bk. 537, leaves 190–191
1670	—	126 ⎭	
1671	384	133	bk. 548, leaves 271–284
1672	—	133 ⎫	bk. 563, leaves 268–282
1673	—	136 ⎭	
1674	—	144 ⎫	bk. 597, leaves 119–136
1675	—	144 ⎭	
1676	—	151	bk. 592
1677	—	152 ⎫	bk. 624
1678	—	154 ⎭	
1679	475	152 ⎫	art. 726, bk. 592
1680	451	151 ⎭	
1681	—	142	bk. 756
1682	—	145	bk. 732, leaf 176
1683	—	8	bk. 807, leaves 115–116
1684	—	11 ⎫	bk. 827, leaves 114–138
1685	—	21 ⎭	
1686	—	40 ⎫	bk. 855, leaves 95–115
1687	—	65 ⎭	
1688	—	97 ⎫	bk. 1030, leaf 74
1689	—	96 ⎭	
1690	—	101	bk. 986, leaves 123–147
1691	—	102	bk. 954, leaves 145–148
1692	—	99	bk. 1097, leaves 103–134
1693	—	112	bk. 1050, leaves 95–96
1696	—	152	bk. 1107, leaves 62–102
1697	—	142	bk. 1165, leaves 70–124
1699	—	123 ⎫	bk. 1220, leaves 117–118
1700	—	119 ⎭	
1701	—	120	bk. 1353, leaves 78–97
1702	—	105	bk. 1293, leaf 61
1703	—	106	bk. 1422, leaves 210–211
1704	—	107	
1728	15	5 ⎫	Arkhiv AN SSSR, sec. 21, op. 4, no. 27, leaves 73, 90
1730	15	5 ⎭	
1761	21	7 ⎫	TsGADA, Sib. prikaz, bk. 1648, leaves 4 et al.
1768	26 (foxes)	13 ⎭	

*Each sable pelt [*plastina*] was considered by us equal to one sable, while each sable coat was valued at 10 sables. The first evaluation is somewhat exaggerated, the second is an underestimation, but in the general quantity of tribute collected on the Yesey, the pelts and fur coats had a comparatively insignificant value.

increased the amount of tribute collected. In 1646, part of the Sinigirs were transferred to the jurisdiction of the Olenek winter quarters.

Beginning with 1653, still another group of Sinigirs began paying tribute on the Yesey. They were the so-called Anabar Tungus, and as a result of their payments the amount of tribute collected increased again. Between 1662 and 1664, the Sinigirs (with the exception of the Anabar ones) were finally excluded from among the tribute payers on the Yesey and, as a result, the number again decreased.

The tribal composition of the Yesey Tungus during the whole of this period can be determined by the number of hostages (*amanat*). In 1636–7 there were, in the "Khatansk winter quarters," two amanats of the "Vanyadyr clan" and one "Dogocharets"; in 1639, two amanats were of the "Vanyadir clan" and one of the Azyan; in 1640, both amanats were of the "Vanyadyr clan"; in 1644, there were five amanats of the "Vonyadyr clan," two of the Sinigir, and one of the "Azyan." All eight amanats taken in 1644 ran away in the same year, and in place of them new ones were taken: six persons of the "Vanyad clan," one of the "Sinigir clan," and one of the "Mugal clan." The Vanyad amanats were taken one person each from the six clans of this tribe—the Telegin, Kunedin, Tyrin, Dargidin, Sein, and Kuznetsov.[36]

For 1682 very detailed data are available, as in this year a census was taken on the Yesey. The census data are summarized in Table 4. The "Mugal clan" is apparently the clan Malgachagir, which lived to the west of Yesey, at the headwaters of the Kotuy. Later on, it became a part of the so-called "Summer" Tungus (the tribe Goragir). In the beginning of the 17th century, the Malgachagirs paid tribute in the Letneye and Turukhansk winter quarters. They did not become a part of the Vanyad tribe.

According to I. S. Gurvich, the Tungus who lived on the Anabar were known under the name of "Kokuyev children" in the 1640's. They comprised a clan numbering more than 30 adult men. The leader of this clan, Kokuy, was taken

TABLE 4*

Clan names	Tribute payers	Males under 16	Total
Telegin	22	8	30
Kunedin	22	16	38
Yulegin	19	19	38
Kunedekov	16	11	27
Munukov	26	15	41
Kuznetsov	18	8	26
Total of Vanyad tribe	123	77	200
Mugal	16	10	26
"Anabar Tungus who pay tribute on Lake Yesey"	6	2	8
"Tungus who live on Lake Yesey, but pay tribute at the Ust-Titeysk collection point, the Uyuryulets clan"	14'	12	26
Grand total	159	101	260

*This table was prepared in accordance with data of book 732 of "Sib. prikaz" (leaf 176 ff.). Incidentally, on the title page of this census, the Yesey tribute quarters are named "Vanyat," after the tribe that paid its tribute there.

as an amanat to the Olenek winter quarters in 1643 and two of his sons were taken as amanats to Anabar by the Mangazeysk officials in 1644. However, notwith-standing this, the "Kokuyev children" did not pay the tribute, freed their amanats by force from Anabar, and raided the Russians. In 1646 they were defeated by the Azyans of the Gaseyev clan, after which they started paying tribute on the Olenek. In 1653, the Mangazeysk *pyatidesyatnik** Ivan Sorokin with the help of the Vanyads led them from the Olenek back to the Anabar in the Mangazeysk uyezd. They paid 64 sables in 1653–4, 42 sables in 1655, 36 sables in 1656, 33 sables in 1657–9, i.e., in 1653–4 there were 20 to 25 tribute payers, while in 1657–9 there were 11. Thereafter they also were registered. There were 10 payers in 1661–2, seven in 1664, eight in 1665–78, seven in 1679, six in 1680–2. They probably belonged to the Sinigir clan. The "Yakutized" Tungus "Sidimi" (the Tyuprins) among the "Zatundrin" Yakuts may be considered their descendants. The greater part of the latter still live on the lower Anabar today.

The "Uyuryulets clan" is a part of the Nyuryumnyal tribe, the major part of whose members paid tribute in the Ilimpey winter quarters. To the present time, part of the Nyuryumnyals live near Yesey, some 60 to 70 kilometers to the south.

Thus, in 1645 and in 1681, there were six clans in the tribe of Vanyads. Three names are the same in 1645 and 1681, while the others changed. A change in the names of clans to conform to names of persons who were at their head is a rather frequent occurrence in the history of north Siberian peoples. In this manner, the Muchugir clan was called the Moykanov in the 17th century, the Khamerin in the beginning of the 18th century, the Nemirovshin in the second half of the 18th century, and the Cherochin in the 19th century. Among the Nganasans, the clan Asyandu was called Tynty after the princeling shaman, who stood at its head, and so on.

In all, the number of tribute payers in the Vanyad tribe, in 1682, amounted to 123 men, which corresponds to a minimum [tribal] population of 450 persons of both sexes. On the map (Fig. 5) the territory of the Vanyads is delineated in accordance with traditions and archival data.

The sharp reduction in the number of Vanyads in 1683 merits explanation at this point.

The Yesey Slaughter of 1683

In 1639–40 and in 1648–9 the Vanyads were subjected to raids by the Azyans and Sinigirs.[37] In 1653, with the help of Russian fusiliers under Ivan Sorokin, the Vanyads penetrated deep into Azyan territory and reached the Olenek winter tribute quarters.[38] In 1661 they again marched against the Azyans and Sinigirs. In 1683 they rebelled against the authorities of the Mangazeysk uyezd. The "Yesey bailiff . . . Timoshka Petukhov had their headman Mudirya of the Muyatsk (i.e., Mugalsk—Author) clan hanged. . . . The Yesey bailiff . . . Tomilko Panteleyev beat up . . . Dubgunya, the nephew of Kitanichkin, and that Tungus died as a result of the beating, and from the Tungus . . . Albuga, the cossack Pyatunko Sukholom forcibly took to himself his wife." Moreover, the authorities "took . . . their huts, furs of polar foxes, wolves, wolverines, lynx and deer parkas and forced their children to work for them." When the Yesey Tungus went to complain about this to the Mangazeysk "governor . . . he ordered them to be whipped for complaining."[39]

In 1683, the bailiff of the Yesey winter quarters, fusilier Ilya Ryabov, continued

*[Officer in command of 50 men.]

this policy of extortion, and in order to intimidate the Tungus, he ordered the young fusilier Terentiy Krylov to build a gallows. Krylov refused, but the gallows was built after all. The Tungus found out about the intention of Ryabov to hang their "best men" and on January 22 (old style), 1683, they massacred the entire Yesey garrison composed of 11 men, while the 12th, the above-mentioned Krylov, was taken prisoner. It seems that some tradesmen were also killed there. Later on Krylov testified that, in all, "about 100 Tungus participated in the massacre headed by Gigaleyko, Tokolachko, Tychaneyko, Dorkigachko, Yelzyaulko, Yumiulko, and Sintaneyko."[40]

Afterwards, on June 20, 1683, the Yesey Tungus of the "Vanandyr clan—Gigaleyko, Boldrygachko, and Tokochko" and Kitanichko of the "Muansk clan" appeared in Yakutsk and informed Governor Priklonskiy about the happenings. They named 11 important men of the "Vanandyr clan" who were present at the massacre—Gigaleyko, Kylmanichko, Charchygachko, Sintachko, Syuyagachko, Dyukachko, Dedgalyachko, Bolkigachko, Odechko, Albugachko, Nanbachko—and gave the total number of the rebels as 150.[41] Priklonskiy made three of those who came to him amanats,[42] and let Bolkigachko go, ordered the Yesey Tungus to pay their tribute in the Olenek winter quarters, and sent a report about the events to Moscow.

There ensued correspondence between Moscow, Mangazeysk, and Yakutsk. In the same year (1683) "to Yesey lake were sent for investigation . . . government officials."[43]

Naturally, the collection of tribute on the Yesey was unsuccessful and the number of tribute payers there reached its former size only in 1693 although the amanats of the "Vanyadir clan" had already been returned from Zhigansk to Yesey in 1691.[44] An edict of 1686 prohibited not only the tribute collectors, but even the governors, from carrying out death sentences without approval from Moscow. An inspection of Mangazeysk uyezd was ordered.[45]

These, then, were the actual events that represent the basis for the legend about the massacre of 12 cossacks by the Mayats or Vadeyev Nganasans on Lake Yesey.

Not all clans of the Vanyads took an equally active part in the rebellion. The Kuznetsov clan completely evaded participating in it and a part of the clan headed by Shilo moved the same year to Turyzhsk winter quarters, paid their tribute, and actively assisted in the search for other members of their clan who had scampered away.

Of the four Tungus who came to Yakutsk, Boldyga, 46 years of age[46] (cf. Boldrygachko *supra*), was entered first in the 1682 census of the Yulegin clan; Tokoda, 52 years of age (Tokochko), was first in the list of Kunedekov clan, and Tychaney ("Kitanichko"), first in the list of Mugal clan. Of the names given by T. I. Krylov, Belzyaul, 45 years of age (Yelzeulko), was first in the list of the Manukov clan and Dorkiga, 56 years of age, was the second entry of adult men of the Telegin clan (after Tarey, 61 years of age).

In the lists of Siberian tribute payers in the 17th century the elders of the clan were usually placed at the head. In the lists of the Yesey Tungus of 1682 the term "princeling" was not used but there is no doubt that the five Tungus named above were the heads of the five clans who participated in the rebellion. Evidently Dorkiga replaced aged Tarey, who is not mentioned even once in connection with the rebellion. Of the other three Tungus named by Krylov or who came [later] to Yakutsk, Yumiul, aged 30, was 13th in the roll of adult males of the Mugal clan and Gigaley, aged 31 (Gigaleyko), and Sintaltsa, aged 39

(Sintaneyko), were the second and the third adult males in the rolls of the Munukov clan.

The most interesting figure is Gigaley. Although in 1683 he was only 31 years of age and not the head of his clan (Belzyaul was), in all lists of the Tungus connected with the rebellion he was entered first. Sometimes the documents only mention the form "Gigaleyko with companions." Gigaley's name also appeared first among the Yesey Tungus who confirmed by oath the correctness of the 1682 census. Gigaley was probably the military leader of the Munukov clan as well as of the whole tribe of Vanyads.[47]

Judging by the above-mentioned names, the following clans participated in the rebellion: Telegin, Yulegin, Kunedekov, Mugal, and particularly the Munukov clan. In 1682 there were 99 adult men in these five clans, which corresponds with the statement of Krylov that "about a hundred Tungus were at the massacre." Gigaley and his companions, seemingly desiring to show general participation in the rebellion, somewhat overstated the number of its participants. The figure given by them, "a hundred and fifty and more," corresponds to the total number of tribute payers in Yesey (159 in 1682), including 14 Nyurumnyals, although probably the Kunedin clan with its leader Mikita and certainly the Kuznetsov clan (Tavinduk) did not participate in the rebellion.

There is another point of interest. Of the 11 names of the "best men" given by Gigaley and the clan elders in Yakutsk, 10 belong to the Munukov clan. They are: Gigaley himself, age 31; Kyrmaney, age 26; Charkyga, age 22; Sintaltea, age 39; Sizyuga, age 24; Yuga, age 28; Dolgoley, age 33; Bolkaga, age 42; Oldey, age 31; Nalboga, age 34.[48] Only Olbuga, age 34, belonged to the Kunedekov clan. If we really see, in the Tungus who came to Yakutsk and in the majority of those Tungus who were named by Krylov, the "best men" of the tribe—the heads of clans and the military leader—then here, excepting Gigaley, we have before us mainly ordinary members of the clan.

There is no doubt that in the list of "best men" who were present at the massacre, the "best men" should not be figured in the meaning this expression had in the 17th century, but as the most active participants in the rebellion, independent of their social standing. Further, as the number of cossacks killed amounts to 11 and here 11 names are also given, it can be suggested that we have here the names of persons who directly participated in the killings, of whom, according to Tungus beliefs, the Russians could demand an account according to the principle of "head for head." This proposition is the more probable because the list was presented by the Tungus themselves.

It follows from the above that the 1683 rebellion on Lake Yesey was carried out mainly by the Munukov clan and by the military leader of the clan and of the whole Vanyad tribe—Gigaley. The other clans only supported, more or less actively, this clan or took a neutral position (the Kunedin clan) or even clearly tried to evade participating in the rebellion (the Kuznetsov clan). Only one member of the Kunedekov clan, the injured husband Albuga (Olbuga), apparently played as active a role as the members of the Munukov clan.

Disappearance of the Vanyad Tribe

After 1683, as can be seen in Table 3, we have data on the number of tribute payers in the Yesey winter quarters up to and including 1704. In 1702, 18 of the tribute payers of the Yesey winter quarters died, which explains the decrease of tribute payers in 1703. Moreover, in the beginning of the 18th century there was apparently again some kind of disturbance among the Yesey Tungus, as in 1704, in addition to 107 men who paid their tribute, there were 45 payers who were counted as "not found," i.e., they were in flight.

After 1704 there is a gap in our information about the Yesey winter quarters until 1728, when only 5 tribute payers were to be found among the Yesey Tungus. In 1730 there were the same number, and thereafter there is again a gap until 1761, when there were only 7 "tribute-paying souls," 7 "old and crippled," and 19 men below the age of 18, i.e., altogether 33 males. It should be noted that in the tribute register of the Olenek winter quarters of the Yakutsk uyezd for 1721 there are numbered among the Tungus and Yakuts of the Olenek river basin 51 Tungus of the "Mayadyl clan" who paid tribute in the Olenek winter quarters.[49] Apparently, these are the same Vanyads who again escaped to Yakutsk uyezd.

Thus, between 1704 and 1728, the Vanyad tribe disintegrated. A small part of it survived as the Tungus of the "Vadeyev clan," a greater part moved to the Olenek where it began to merge with the Yakut. What exactly happened during this time we can only guess.

P. Tretyakov offers a story told by a Zatundrin peasant relating that "our great-grandfather, the cossack Laptukov, said that our ancestor was present at Yesey lake for the suppression of a Tungus rebellion."[50] Tretyakov heard this in the middle of the 19th century and, counting 25 years per generation, we can figure that the "rebellion" must have taken place in the 1720's.

Another report of Tretyakov reads:

Once a Tungus princeling Lumba, whose horde numbered about 50 tribute-payers, massacred all the cossacks on the river Kheta. . . . Sergeant Smirnov, with the help of neighboring natives, forced Lumba to come to him with his whole horde, approached him and said: 'Now Lumba, you did not hide yourself in the ground, nor did you fly to the skies,' and with these words Smirnov hit Lumba with an oaken club held in one hand, while piercing him with a dagger held in the other. Thereafter, the whole horde of this princeling was exterminated.[51]

The title of "Sergeant" points to the 18th century and, further, this event could have taken place only in the first half of the 18th century, as after 1761 not a single Tungus tribe of the Turukhansk kray shows a sharp decrease in its numbers.

Among Tungus, only the Vanyads could have killed the Russians on the Kheta river. They paid tribute on the Kheta already in 1702.[52]

Comparing both stories of Tretyakov with the fact of the sharp decrease in the number of Yesey Tungus permits the supposition that in the first quarter of the 18th century the Vanyads rebelled again, were subjected to cruel repressions as a result of which they were partly exterminated while a larger part of them moved to Yakutsk uyezd, and finally the tribe fell apart.

Part of the Vanyads, "the Vadeyev Tungus," who still kept the tribal name, moved to the Taymyr tundra and there, from the Avam Nganasans, adopted the Samoyed language. The other part merged with the population of the Olenek, and in particular, as we know, entered the Beti camp [*nasleg*] as the separate Mayat clan, and was "Yakutized." Part of the Vanyads also entered into some of the neighboring Tungus tribes and Yakut camps [*naslegi*].

The names "Vanyad" (Vanyadyr, Vanandyr, Vonyadyr, etc.), "Mayat" (Mayad, Mayadol), and—taking into account the interchange of consonants N and D— "Vadeyev" obviously represent variants of one and the same name. Already in the first half of the 17th century, in place of Vanyad, Vanyadyr, etc., "Mayad" was written. A "Moyad Samoyad" was sought in the basin of the Anabar in 1659.[53] In 1691, in the Yakutsk uyezd, a Vanyadyr named Denucha was called a Tungus of the "Mayadil clan."[54] Earlier we have shown that the name "Mayadyl clan" was used in describing the Vanyadirs, who had moved into Yakutsk uyezd as early as 1721. In present-day folklore the term "Mayat" represents the Yakut pronunciation of the earlier "Vanyad," "Mayad."

Thus, the Vadeyev Nganasans are undoubtedly descendants of the legendary Yesey Mayats, or Vanyad Tungus, who paid tribute in the Yesey winter quarters in the 17th century.

As we know, the main participants in the events of 1683 came from the Munukov clan. The name "Munukov" is clearly formed from the Tungus *munnukan*—hare. We know that the Vadeyev Nganasans avoided killing hares and the Avam Nganasans used to say that formerly the Vadeyev Nganasans neither killed nor ate hares. "The Vadeyev Nganasans, in distinction from the Avam and Taymyr ones, are deadly afraid of shooting hares. A wounded hare cries loudly—the cries are a malediction and the hunter who hears them is fated to die."[55] Neither the Avam Nganasans nor the Nenets or Enets have this attitude toward the hare. With the Vadeyev Nganasans this attitude is probably connected with their descent from the Hare (Munukov) clan: the hare was considered the ancestor of the clan and, certainly, the curse of an ancestor could bring death to a descendant who raised arms against him.

Thus, it is proposed that the Vadeyev Nganasans are descendants of the Vanyad or Vanyadyr tribe and, in particular, primarily of the Hare (Munukov) clan of that tribe.

During the first half of the 18th century, when the Vanyad tribe disintegrated, the Munukov clan settled to the east of the Avam Nganasans and, as we know, it was "Samoyedized" during the second half of the 18th century. In the 19th century, there took place a rapid increase in the numbers of this group of "Samoyedized" Tungus, possibly through the addition of new Tungus migrants who formed separate clans of the Vadeyev Nganasans; there are certain traditions about this.

In this way was formed the tribe of the Vadeyev Nganasans who are the successors of the vanished Tungus tribe of Vanyads (Vanyadyrs, Vanadyrs), or of the legendary Mayats of Lake Yesey.

Now we can pass to the history of the formation of the nucleus of the Nganasans—the tribe of Avam Nganasans.

Samoyeds of the "Pyasida-Kheta" or Avam Winter Quarters

The Russians began collecting tribute from the population in the region around the mouth of the Yenisey in 1614. The first verifiable information contained in the Russian sources about groups that entered later into the composition of the Avam Nganasans is a notation in the tribute register of Mangazeysk uyezd for 1618 to the effect that 27 "Pyasid Samoyeds paid their tribute at the rate of 1, 2, and 3 sables."[56]

In 1618 the Russians used the term "Pyasida" not only for the Pyasina river and its basin but also for the basin of the Kheta and sometimes also for the entire basin of the Khatanga.[57] The word *pyasida* means "forestless" [treeless] in Nenets.[58] In 1625, the Kuraks, still another group of Samoyeds that entered into the composition of the Avam Nganasans, started paying tribute,[59] and in

1627 for the first time the collection of tribute from the Tavgs—in the future to comprise the major part of the Avam Nganasans—is mentioned.[60] At the same time, the tax was imposed on another group that also entered later into the composition of the Avam Nganasans, namely the Tidiris. One "Tidiris" is registered among the tribute-paying Tungus already in 1615.[61] In 1627 tribute was paid by 12 Tidiris,[62] while the first roll of Tidiris names, together with those of the Somatu Enets, is available in the tribute register of the "Khantayka winter quarters" for 1629.[63] By 1634, with the exception of some clan groups, families, and individuals, the "taxing" of the ancestors of the Avam Nganasans was essentially completed.

The history of the tribe of the Avam Nganasans during the 17th, 18th, and 19th centuries is the history of Samoyeds who paid tribute first in the "Pyasida-Kheta" and later in the Avam winter quarters. The Avam winter quarters were located on the river Dudypta—a tributary to the Pyasina—at the mouth of the river Avam. At the end of the 17th century and during the 18th, a branch of the Avam winter quarters existed on the Yenisey, some 60 kilometers north of Dudinka. The location of the "Pyasida-Kheta" (sometimes simply Pyasida, sometimes Kheta) winter quarters is not clear. It was situated on the river Kheta, probably above the mouth of its tributary, the Medvezhya, but where exactly is unknown. As early as 1666, the collectors of tribute from the ancestors of the Nganasans were found "on the Avam."[64] According to folklore, the Avam was the center of the ancestors of the Avam Nganasans even before the tribute quarters were established there. In Table 5 are presented data on the numbers of tribute payers in the "Pyasida-Kheta" and later in the Avam winter quarters. In addition, data are also available on the number of males and, for some years of the 19th century, the number of females. We submit these also (Table 5a).

Let us comment briefly on these figures.

At first there was the custom of registering ancestors of the Avam Nganasans. Thus, in 1639, there arrived at the "Pyasita-Kheta" winter quarters "new people Samoyad, but they did not tell the tribute collectors to which clan they belonged, where they had nomadized before, or where they had paid tribute before, or how they made their living, but paid tribute for themselves again in 147" [1639].[65] Of such "new Samoyeds," 23 came in 1639. From 1639 to 1665 the number of tribute payers in the "Pyasid-Kheta" winter quarters was rather stable. Only the year 1654 is exceptional. Here, the difficulty of which the tribute collectors of the 1630's and 1640's complained became apparent, i.e., the complaint that the "Pyasid Samoyad always change their names every year during tribute collection time."[66] In 1636, for example, 218 men paid tribute. In 1637 the tribute was being collected in accordance with the registers for 1636, but only 153 men paid tribute under the "old names." In addition, 52 men who were not entered on the 1636 rolls paid tribute, while 65 payers who were listed in 1636 were not to be found in 1637. When the tribute collector Ivan Sorokin tried to clear this up, the Nganasans said "truly, according to their religion, that they have no more tribute payers in that year 145 (1637) than those whose names are entered in the register."[67] The tribute collectors could not find out whether the 52 payers appearing newly were among the 65 missing according to the 1636 register. Ivan Sorokin simply excluded the 65 men who were not found from the 1637 register. But in 1654, when a similar occurrence probably took place, 46 of the "lost" men were retained in the register and thus increased the number of Avam Nganasans for that year.

In the same year there were again "found" 21 adolescents who "reached the

TABLE 5
THE NUMBER OF TRIBUTE PAYERS IN THE AVAM ("PYASIDA-KHETA") TRIBUTE WINTER QUARTERS

Year	Number of tribute payers	Sources
1630	78	TsGADA, Sib. prikaz, bk. 22, leaves 48–51
1631	115	bk. 32, leaves 332–339
1632	149 ⎫	
1633	174 ⎪	
1634	181 ⎬	bk. 986, leaves 257–512 et al.
1635	185 ⎭	
1636	218 ⎫	
1637	205 ⎬	bk. 95, leaves 269–287
1638	213 ⎭	
1639	245	bk. 150, leaves 1019–1020
1640	244 ⎫	bk. 144, leaves 1060 et al.
1641	249 ⎭	
1644	238 ⎫	
1645	239 ⎬	bk. 285, leaves 50, 132–147
1653	227 ⎭	
1654	280 (234)	bk. 320, leaf 20
1661	227 ⎫	bk. 442, leaves 239 et al.
1662	227 ⎭	
1664	228 ⎫	bk. 478, leaves 54–55
1665	220 ⎭	
1667	188 ⎫	bk. 513, leaves 336–337
1668	159 ⎭	
1669	159	bk. 537, leaves 177–191
1670	144 ⎫	bk. 548, leaves 271–284
1671	146 ⎭	
1672	141 ⎫	bk. 536, leaves 268–282; bk. 561
1673	148 ⎭	
1674	148	bk. 597, leaves 119–136
1675	181 ⎫	bk. 592
1676	189 ⎭	
1677	185 ⎫	bk. 624
1678	180 ⎭	
1679	174 ⎫	art. 726
1680	167 ⎭	
1681	163; 171 ⎫	art. 756; bk. 708, leaves 60–90
1682	169 ⎭	
1683	169 ⎫	bk. 807, leaf 110
1684	188 ⎭	
1685	195; 202	bk. 827, leaves 113–138; bk. 855, leaves 95–115
1686	209 ⎫	bk. 855, leaves 95–115; bk. 827, leaves 114–138
1687	209 ⎭	
1688		
1689		bk. 1030, leaves 57–76
1690	216 ⎫	bk. 986, leaves 125–147; bk. 954, leaves 145–148; bk. 1047, leaves 103–134
1691	221 ⎭	
1692	229 ⎫	bk. 1050, leaves 82–99
1693	228 ⎭	
1695	239	bk. 1107, leaves 62–112
1697	239	bk. 1165, leaves 70–124
1699	244 ⎫	bk. 1220, leaves 88–126
1700	253 ⎭	
1701	247	bk. 1353, leaves 78–97
1702	242	bk. 1293, leaf 61
1703	257 ⎫	bk. 1422, leaves 211–212
1704	264 ⎭	
1728	212 ⎫	Arkhiv AN SSSR sec. 21, op. 4, no. 27, leaves 74, 93
1730	209 ⎭	
1761	155 ⎫	TsGADA, Sib. prikaz, bk. 1648, leaves 1, 14–26
1768	131 ⎭	
1832	105 ⎫	P. Tretyakov, Turukhanskiy kray, p. 373
1859	98 ⎭	

TABLE 5a

Year	Tribute payers	No. of males	No. of females	Source
1681	171	264	N.I.°	*TsGADA*, Sib. prikaz, bk. 708, leaves 60–90
1761	155	293	N.I.	
1768	131	293	N.I.	*TsGADA*, Sib. prikaz, bk. 1648, leaves 1, 14–26
1816	N.I.	246	N.I.	Irkutsk obl. arkhiv, sec. 2, Upravleniye Vostochnoy Sibiri, document 405
1832	105	198	105 (205?)	P. Tretyakov, *Turukhanskiy kray*, p. 373
1838	N.I.	202	214	A. V. Middendorf, *Sibirische Reise*, part 2, list 3, St. Petersburg, 1875, p. 1438
1859	98	242	213	P. Tretyakov, *Turukhanskiy kray*, p. 377.
1897	N.I.	336	318	S. Patkanov, *Statisticheskiye dannye*, p. 390
1926	—	310	264	Census of 1926–7

°N.I.—No information.

tribute age" and 39 lazy, unproductive ones. Probably these 39 men were included in the number of the 46 "lost" men, but took on new names, as happened in 1637. In each case we retained these "lost" men in the list of tribute payers until they were excluded officially, although in their number there was probably always a certain percentage of "dead souls." In any case, we consider the data for 1654 exaggerated and indicate in parentheses the probable number of tribute payers.

We have no data for 1666 but, starting with 1667, there begins a sharp dip in the number of the ancestors of the Avam Nganasans, which continues until 1672, when it reaches a minimum. Evidently something happened about 1666–70.

And, indeed, the "thieving Tavg Samoyad" in 1666 killed, in the mountains to the south of the Kheta, a detachment of fusiliers traveling with "tribute treasure" from Yesey, the tribute collectors, and an interpreter in Avam, and, moreover, trading people "on Kheta river." On the 17th century scale of Mangazeysk, this "thievery" was considerable. In the mountains south of the Kheta 12 soldiers headed by an officer Timofey Dementyev were killed; also 7 Avam tribute collectors including 2 interpreters, 12 trading people (both on the Kheta and the ones who traveled with the soldiers from Yesey), and finally 4 Tungus amanats from the Turyzhsk winter quarters who were traveling with Dementyev were killed. Altogether 35 men were killed "and others many wounded."[68] Among the latter were probably the soldiers "Larka Kalinin with companions who after this fight remained alive."

The Nganasans divided among themselves the sables, which were being carried from Yesey, fawns (*rorduga*) that were collected from them as tribute on the Avam, and also the property and the sables that belonged to the killed.

In 1667, Ivan Sorokin, who was ordered to collect the tribute and apprehend the "thieves," recovered 79 sables, the property of the killed Russians and Tungus,[69] but the fawns had "all died from hunger."[70] Ivan Sorokin succeeded in making about 100 Nganasans appear before him at the mouth of the river Dudinka (where, in 1667, he built winter quarters, which later on grew to become the village and now town of Dudinka, the capital of the Taymyr National Okrug). There the Nganasans "with great need" paid 358 fawns for 1667, and 70 fawns for the preceding year; also they delivered six "thieves" and three amanats. The same Nganasans said that 53 persons died (probably from hunger) in the spring of 1667 and 47 persons fled "between the Pyasida and Khatanga down to the sea."[71] The exactness of the numbers 53 and 47 is doubtful (their sum is exactly 100), but all these events do explain the decrease in the number of tribute payers attached to the Avam winter quarters in 1667.

The famine, probably the result of the change in migration routes of the wild deer, continued also in the following years. Thirty-two men died in 1668 and 71 did not come to the tribute quarters although they were registered. Some of the "thieves" probably died also, since in Turukhansk "they were tortured and were given 45 strokes each and burned by the fire."

In 1675 there were readily "found" 32 "adolescent" and one "lazy" [payers], but at the end of the 1670's there was an epidemic, which again reduced the number of tribute payers among both the Avam Nganasans and the Khantayka Enets.

For 1681 there are two figures: one from the tribute register of 163 men, and one from the special control census of 171 men. The census that was taken after the tribute collection apparently defined the number of tribute payers more exactly. Nineteen juveniles were "found" in 1684.

For 1685 there are also two figures: 195 men on the basis of an "estimate," and 202 men according to the "collection books." Similar discrepancies were found in that year at almost all tribute collection points of the Mangazeysk uyezd. But "why the aforementioned estimates and data of the collection books do not agree . . . and why this really cannot be questioned and the details investigated is due to the fact that the clerk who compiled and compared these estimates and tax collection books, and who officiated in the tax collection headquarters, is dead."[72]

However, after this [year] the fluctuation in the number of tribute payers is based on the data from the collection books, i.e., the larger figure. On the average, at the end of the 17th century seven or eight adolescents are [newly] entered yearly, and three or four adult tribute payers die.

In 1704 the number of Avam Nganasan tribute payers reaches a maximum. Then there follows a 24-year gap in the data until 1728–30, when the number of the Avam Nganasans is found to be considerably lower than in 1704. Again there is a 30-year gap in the data and again the number of tribute payers diminishes. This decrease continues into the 19th century. These reductions were apparently caused by epidemics and famines that occurred during the 18th and 19th centuries. However, they could also be caused by the differences in the methods of tribute collecting. In the 17th century the Nganasans paid tribute from age 16 until senility, i.e., for most, practically until the age of 60 to 65. In the 18th century, at any rate from 1761 to 1768, the Nganasans paid tribute only from age 18 to 50. Thus the contingent of the tribute payers was likely to become smaller, independent of numerical changes in the population. Moreover, in connection with the adjustment of the tribute-paying age, there arose a tendency to evade payment by increasing one's age and decreasing the age of one's sons.

To all appearances, the data for 1832–59 reflect this evasion, since while the number of tribute payers declines, the total population increases. To a certain extent this probably happens also in 1761–8, when with almost no change in the number of males, the number of tribute payers sharply declines. In the census of 1681 a certain number of young men were probably not accounted for, as well as a number of persons above the age of 60, who did not pay tribute.

The second half of the 19th century was comparatively fortunate, but the epidemic of smallpox of 1907–8 again reduced the number of Avam Nganasans.[73] Thus, their number was smaller in 1926 than in 1897.

A number of calculations brought us to the conclusion that in order to determine the total number of Avam Nganasans in the 17th century it is necessary to multiply the number of tribute payers by 3.7. Thus, in 1641 there were about 970 Avam Nganasans (without the part of the Tidiris who paid tribute in Khantayka), while in 1672 there were about 520, and at the end of the 17th century and the beginning of the 18th, about 960 persons; in the middle of the 18th century the count is 550, and in the beginning of the 19th about 500.

The history of the Avam Nganasans is closely connected to the history of the Khantayka Enets (the tribe of Madu). This tribe numbered about 650 persons in 1629 and about 400 in 1681; in 1761 there were 420, in 1897 their descendants numbered 205, and in 1926 there were just 219 persons.[74]

In the first half of the 17th century there were, among the tribute payers of the "Pyasida-Kheta" and "Khantaysk" winter quarters, groups with similar clan names. One of these was the Munzuyev clan and another the so-called "Tidiris." Concerning the Munzuyev clan, we have direct evidence that it was the "Pyasid Samoyad."[75] As far as the Tidiris are concerned, they usually were regarded as a clan, but there are frequent references that lead us to propose that they were also considered as a separate tribe. For example: "There passed by the Khantaysk tribute quarters, the tribute-paying Samoyad and Tidiris. . . ."[76]

The division of the Munzuyev clan and the Tidiris between the "Khantaysk" and "Pyasid-Kheta" winter tribute quarters is shown in Table 6. If we also take into account that, in 1681, there was a "Tidiris" clan among the Nganasans, we may conclude that between 1640 and 1645 the major part of the Tidiris moved from the "Khantaysk" tribute quarters to the "Pyasida-Kheta" (Avam) ones. The eight Tidiris who remained with the "Khantaysk" tribute quarters probably also moved to the Avam quarters. Already in 1645 four of them were mentioned as "lost." On the contrary, the Munzuyev clan, which figured among the ancestors of the Avam Nganasans, probably died out and among the Khantayka Enets its descendants formed the clan Sado (Pilko, Filkovy). Thus, we may consider the Tidiris a group that entered into the composition of the Avam Nganasans, even though in the beginning of the 17th century most of them paid tribute in Khantayka.

Now we shall examine the Samoyed "clans" of the Pyasida-Kheta" (Avam) winter tribute quarters that are mentioned in 17th century sources, taking into consideration also the Khantayka Tidiris.

TABLE 6*

NUMBERS OF TRIBUTE PAYERS

Year	"Khantaysk" tribute quarters		"Pyasida-Kheta" tribute quarters	
	Munzuyev clan	Tidiris	Munzuyev clan	Tidiris
1627	3	5	5	7
1628	3	12	3	10
1629	2	15	4	7
1630	—	16	2	3
1634	10	28	4	5
1637	7	25	3	—
1640	8	31	2	—
1645	7	8	1	20

*The data for this table were drawn from the books of TsGADA, Sib. prikaz: for 1629, book 19; 1630, book 22, leaves 2–6, 48–51; 1634, book 986, leaves 355–369; 1637, book 95, leaves 141–162, 268–287; 1640, book 150, leaves 1032–1052, 1010–1023; 1645, leaves 52–59, 132–147. For data for 1627 and 1628, see: *Arkhiv AN SSSR*, sec. 21, op. 4, no. 21, leaves 29, 30, 32–33, 36, and 39.

The "Pyasida Samoyad"

In the "extracts" for 1625-9 and in the tribute books for 1630-45, a prominent place was occupied by a group of Samoyeds containing the clans Kudesnikov[*] or (from 1634) Pyakov, Munzuyev, Tabachiyev, and Serokuyev. The rolls of the tribute payers in the "Pyasida-Kheta" tribute quarters begin with these clans. The membership of this group was very stable; in all tribute registers that came down to us, the same names are repeated in the same sequence in the same clans year after year from 1630 to 1645. Only occasionally, names of Samoyeds of other groups are added[77] to some of these clans or names of these clans are omitted.[78] In 1630, however, these clans are registered in two places—at the beginning and at the end of the rolls. Here, after the first group of members of the Kudesnikov clan, there is also entered an outsider (Kuratskiy) Tunuderin clan.

The general clan composition of the "Pyasida Samoyad" is as given in Table 7. Utilizing the coefficient of 3.7, we arrive at the membership of 130 for this group. The "Moyat" clan, which appears in the tribute rolls from 1639 on, represents, judging by the personal names, a part of the Kudesnikov clan registered separately. Here, we must take into consideration that the main part of the Munzuyev clan (30 to 40 people) was entered into the composition of the Khantayka Enets from 1634.

The list of the Pyasida Samoyeds, and later of all tribute payers of the "Pyasida-Kheta" tribute quarters, always begins with the name of a certain Pyak, who is called a "princeling" from 1632, and after whom the whole clan Kudesnikov is called from 1634 on. The princeling Pyak was apparently an influential person among the ancestors of the Avam Nganasans and, until 1666, enjoyed the trust of the Russians. In 1635 he was sent by the tribute collectors to search for those Samoyeds of the "Pyasida-Kheta" tribute quarters who did not appear for tribute payment and he traveled on this task "for about six weeks."[79] His son was the princeling Batayko, registered first in the census of 1681 of the Avam winter quarters,[80] and Batay's descendants ("Batayevy") also headed the 1768 rolls of the Avam Samoyeds, being registered immediately after the princeling.[81] Apparently the princeling Pyak stood at the head of the group of these four clans, as further on in the tribute registers groups headed by other princelings are given. Pyak was involved in the rebellion of 1666 and arrested, but was later released by Ivan Sorokin because of illness. In the summer of 1667, when he was sought again, [it was discovered] that he was already dead and, instead, his son Batay was brought to Turukhansk.

TABLE 7[*]

Clans	1625	1626	1627	1628	1629	1630	1631	1632	1633	1634	1637	1639	1645
Kudesnikov (since 1634, Pyakov)	19	14	17	15	14	14	13	13	14	15	12	14	11
Munzuyev	4	2	5	3	4	2	3	3	3	4	3	3	1
Tabachiyev	5	7	7	6	5	5	5	5	5	5	4	3	3
Serokuyev	4	5	7	6	4	2	3	3	3	2	1	1	1
Moyat	—	—	—	—	—	—	—	—	—	—	—	2	5
Total	32	29[?]	36	30	27	22[?]	24	24	25	26	20	23	21

[*]Contents of this table are drawn from "Sib. prikaz," books 22, 32, 986, 45, 150, 285, and from *Arkhiv AN SSSR*, sec. 21, op. 4, no. 21. The figures indicate the number of tribute payers.

[*][Some of the names of the clans were left in the original possessive case to more readily differentiate them from the person after whom they were named.—Editor.]

The names of clans belonging to the group of Samoyeds of the princeling Pyak originated from personal names. People with those names headed the corresponding clans. The clan of Pyak himself [the Kudesnikov clan] received its name seemingly from some shaman who headed the clan before Pyak, or else Pyak was a shaman ["kudesnik"—Editor] himself.[82]

The fact that Pyak's Samoyeds always head the lists, that they are very stable in their composition in contradistinction to other groups of Avam Nganasans, and that they are not supplemented by any repeatedly rediscovered groups during 1625–45 indicates that in these Samoyeds we have "old tribute payers, firmly established under the tsar's aegis and accustomed to payment of tribute."

As early as 1629, Tabachiy and Serokuy, complaining against Yerofey Khabarov, are contrasting themselves as old tribute payers to "other Samoyad" in the same region of the "Pyasida-Kheta" tribute quarters, i.e., to other component parts of the Avam Nganasans.[83]

As we already know, the first ancestors of the Avam Nganasans to be subjected to tribute (in 1618) were the "Pyasida Samoyad." Closer acquaintance with the tribute registers suggests that this appellation was not used as a general name for all Samoyeds who nomadized in the Pyasida, but had a more narrow, definitive meaning. For instance, in the Khantayka winter quarters the name "Pyasida Samoyad" included only Munzuy, who is known to us, and his clan, but not the Tidiris, although the latter were also inhabitants of the geographical Pyasida. The Kuraks, another tribe also nomadizing in the Pyasida, likewise were not included. In 1625 and 1627 the tribute was collected from the "Pyasida Samoyad and the Kuraks."[84] Also the Tavg are not called "Pyasida Samoyad."

In the tribute register of the "Pyasida-Kheta" winter quarters for 1630, the ethnic identity of the payers is specified as "Pyasida Samoyad." But following the list of the Tavg, when again begin the rolls of the group that interests us here (as already indicated, in this register this group of Samoyeds is registered in two places), there is a subheading "The Samoyad Kudesnikov clan."[85] This creates the impression that the Tavgs were not considered "Samoyad," particularly not "Pyasida Samoyad."

In all probability, in the four clans headed by the princeling Pyak, we have a separate tribe, which was originally and particularly considered "Pyasida Samoyad." It seems that only this tribe paid tribute as early as 1618, earlier than any other tribe of the geographical Pyasida.

The present-day Nganasan clan Ngomde (see Table 1) should be, above all, considered descendant from the "Pyasida Samoyad" of the 17th century and of the Kudesnikov clan in particular. In 1645, the Kudesnikov clan (together with the "Moyat" clan) comprised three-quarters of the "Pyasida Samoyeds." The other clans of the "Pyasida Samoyeds" (who numbered only a few as early as the middle of the 17th century) probably died out, and the Munzuyev clan moved to the area of the "Khantaysk" winter quarters, where it merged with the Madu Enets.

As was shown, there is a subdivision Syade in the Ngomde clan. Its ancestor was the "white-headed old man Seya" or Saya. Among the Samoyeds of the Kudesnikov (Pyak's) clan in the 17th century, there was a man whose name varies in the following manner: Sesya Ugegey (in 1630–1), Syusya Gagytov (1632), Sesya Gefytov (1633), Seya (1634), Sezya (1637), Sega (1639), and Sezya (1645). No doubt, this is one and the same person. This name is always inscribed in the same place, among other recurrent names, the order of which does not change. The interchange of the sounds *s*, *y*, and *d* is very characteristic of the Nganasan language (cf.: *asya, aya, adya*—"Tungus"; *basa, baya*—"iron").[86] Only Sega seems to be a slip of the pen. In Enets, *sey* means "eye." In 1768 there was a "clan" of "white-eyed" among the Avam Nganasans.[87] The present tradition about the "white-headed Seya" is a more exact transmittal of the name and the nickname of this person, who was probably called "Seya, the White."

The river Batayka is a right tributary of the Dudypta. The Zatundrinsk peasants told us that this river got its name from a rich Samoyed "prince" who used to winter there, and the Nganasans confirmed that the prince, Batay, was of the Ngomde clan. In the tribute register for 1645 after the name of the "princeling" Pyak is entered "his son Batay."[88] As mentioned above, Batay was arrested in 1667 and brought to Turukhansk, but he was still alive in 1681, for the "princeling Batayko" was the only Nganasan who paid five fawns yearly in that year.[89] The other princelings of the Avam winter quarters paid four, and ordinary Nganasans three. Also in 1926 the Ngomde clan was, comparatively speaking, the richest Nganasan clan (Table 1).[90] We have already pointed out that the Nganasan routes remain rather constant and that if the region of winter quarters is known it is easy to determine the summer quarters and vice versa. Since Batay and probably his father Pyak wintered on the Batayka, they must have used Route IV (Table 2).

In 1926–7, three families of the Ngomde clan moved along Route III and eleven families along Route IV, this indicating the western and the eastern limits of their ancestors, the "Pyasida Samoyeds," prior to the time the Tavgs began wandering over their territory (see below). The dying out of a number of "Pyasida Samoyed" clans, the emigration of the Munzuyev clan to the Enets, and the general diminution of their numbers, in the end caused the middle region of wanderings to be occupied by the descendants of the Tavgs and, in part, of the Tidiris. The rivers Taymyr and Logata within the territory of Route V represent the central region of the Taymyr peninsula, the best for hunting wild deer and rich in fish. Probably because of this the surviving descendants of the "Pyasida Samoyeds" retained just this area, leaving to the Tavgs and Tidiris who came to these regions later the area between the Pyasina and the Taymyr, which is comparatively poorer for deer hunting and particularly for fishing. Lately, the principal area of the Ngomde clan is considered to be the basin of the river Taymyr before it discharges into the lake and the basin of the above-mentioned tributary of the Taymyr, the Logata. But, since the toponymy of the Taymyr basin is Tungus in character, it is probably not the indigenous territory of the Ngomde.

There is no doubt that the ancestors of the Ngomde clan, the "Pyasida Samoyad," were a Samoyed group already in the 17th century. We have reasons to believe that they spoke a dialect close to the tundra dialect of the Somatu Enets. It is quite possible that in the "Pyasida Samoyad" we have the basic indigenous population of the Pyasina basin, which was subjected to "Samoyedization" just prior to the 17th century. The Samoyed language, reindeer-breeding, and Samoyed culture could penetrate to the Taymyr from the southwest, from the ancestors of the Enets, among whom it is even now possible to distinguish clans of local, aboriginal, and of immigrant, Samoyed, origin.

The clan Ngomde occupies a somewhat special position among the Nganasans. It is considered a clan of pure "Samoyed" origin. In other words, its members are "real people" (*vide supra*) from the Nganasan point of view. Even when it is supposed that some clans of the Avam Nganasans lived somewhere to the south, west, or east before, regarding the Ngomde clan, it is usually claimed that it "always" lived in the Taymyr tundra.

Having learned that the present-day Ngomde clan is descended from the Kudesnikov clan of the "Pyasida Samoyad," we suggest that the name Ngomde is derived from the word *ngo*, meaning shaman. But the Nganasans as a rule deny this etymology and either refuse to translate this name or present another explanation (from *ngoa*, door, etc.). However, the name seems to be an adjective derived from a noun.

The Ngomde clan also used to have another name—*Lenekhe* (*Lengfa*), "eagle." In Müller's abstract we find the following passage: "In 7127 (1619), August 14, the fusilier Nikifor Starodubets . . . with companions brought from the Pyasida a two years' parcel of 68 sables . . . on August 19, the fusilier Smirnoy Ivanov with companions brought a year's parcel from Pyasida, from 'Eagle' [*Orlova* in the original—Editor] village, seven sables."[91]

The tribute register for 1619 for Mangazeysk uyezd was preserved only in the form of an "abstract," made by the order of Müller. Obviously Müller's clerks made an error in copying, taking the expression "Eagle clan" [Orlovago rodu] for "Eagle village" [Orlova gorodu]. During the whole of the 17th century there is no single case in which villages are mentioned in the Mangazeysk uyezd for the aboriginal population. Müller annotated this comment as follows: "It is unknown where this village is located, as at the present there has been preserved no sign of its existence." Probably there was no "Eagle village." In 1619 only the "Pyasida Samoyeds" paid tribute in Pyasida, i.e., those Samoyeds we propose as the ancestors of the Ngomde or "Eagle" clan. Very probably both Nikifor Starodubets and Smirniy Ivanov collected tribute from the same people but called them by different names: one by the territorial, official name, the other by the clan, totemic name. Obviously Ivanov was sent "to secure new tribute payers." In this he did not succeed (we know that the other Pyasida tribes began paying tribute later) and he had to be satisfied by receiving a few additional sables from the same "Pyasida Samoyad" from whom Starodubets had already collected the usual yearly tribute.

The Kuraks

Sixteen Kuraks paid tribute in 1625, 22 in 1626, 21 in 1627, 38 in 1628, and 23 in 1629. In 1630 tribute was paid by the Kurak clan Tunuderin for 3 men and, in addition, 7 Kuraks were attached to the Tabachiyev clan of the "Pyasida Samoyad." In 1631, among the rolls of tribute payers of the "Pyasida-Kheta" winter quarters there is a list with the heading "the Kurak clan." It contains the names of 30 people and opposite 2 names there is a note that they are Tidiris.[92] At the head of the list there are the two princelings Turoa and Solyudu.

In 1632 the same list is repeated, with the same princelings, and in addition another "Kurak clan" with 10 names headed by a certain "Vaska" is given and, thereafter, still another clan Tunoderin of 4 men,[93] which may also be considered Kurak.

In the rolls of 1633 there are a "Kurak clan" of 21 persons, the clan Tunoderin headed by Tunodera, of 14 persons, and, additionally, to the Serokuyev clan of the "Pyasida Samoyad" there are attached 8 Kuraks[94] and 1 Tidiris, probably by error, when a clean copy was made.

In 1634, the rolls contain two Kurak clans (of 7 and of 30 men, respectively), headed by the princelings Seledo and Toroy, and the Tunutorin clan of 8 persons headed by Solido (namesake of Seledo?), among whose members there is also an "old man Tunutor."

In 1637, in the roll of the Tavgs, of the "clan Kudesnikov," there begins a list, headed by Padaku, of 56 names with a predominance of Kuraks[95] including

Solodu and Vaska, after which follows the Soloduyev clan in which the first 25 names are also mainly Kurak,[96] including Toroy. In 1639 we have the same persons, numbering 83 altogether, and in this number 4 were "not found."[97]

In 1645, the clan Tanadiravd (i.e., Tunoderin) of 49 persons is registered, including Solodu, Toroy, Vaska, and the Kurak clan of 7 persons, with Tomade among its members.

The above data permit the construction of Table 8.

TABLE 8

Year	1615	1626	1627	1628	1629	1630	1631	1632	1633	1634	1637	1639	1645
Kurak tribute payers	16	22	21	38	23	10	28	42	43	45	81(?)	83(?)	56

In 1637 and 1639 some Tavgs and perhaps Tidiris were apparently registered among the Kuraks. Therefore, it is safer to consider that their number amounted not to 81 and 83, but to about 60 tribute payers. In all, in the first half of the 17th century, there were probably about 220 Kuraks. According to Siberian scales of the times, this is a fairly large group.

The tribute collectors did not confuse the Kuraks with other Samoyed groups, for beginning with 1625 tribute was received "from the Pyasida Samoyad and from the new people, the Kuraks."[98] They were considered a separate group also by other Samoyed tribes. Speaking about an old Khantayka Samoyed Urito who did not come to the Khantayka winter quarters in 1635–6, his fellow tribesmen said that "he was fed during the years of his absence by the untaxed Kurak Samoyad."[99] In 1638, concerning 8 Khantayka Samoyeds it was found that "they, in the past years, went to earn their living to the Pyasida, to the untaxed Samoyad, the Kuraks, and these untaxed Samoyad, the Kurak people, killed those Khantayka tribute-paying Samoyad in Pyasida, while they were going about their business."[100] In the same year, 1638, another four Khantay Samoyeds "were killed in Pyasida on unoccupied rivers by untaxed Kurak Samoyads."[101]

We know that the Kuraks had their princelings Solyuda (Seledo, Soloduy) and Turoa (Toroy) and others—the old men Tonutora, Vaska, and Podoru—who probably headed separate clans or territorial groupings of Kuraks. In 1681, the name Tonuderin (Tonutorin) was preserved in the name of the Tueder clan of 8 tribute payers, headed by the 56-year-old princeling Tomuda (probably Tomade, who in 1645 was inscribed in the rolls of the Kurak clan).[102] Another clan in the 1681 census was also called "of the Kuraks."[103]

The [present-day] Ngamtuso ("generous") clan may be regarded as descendant from the 17th century Kuraks. Since the beginning of the 19th century, members of this clan bear the surname Kosterkin. The name "kurak" is derived from the Enets kure, kureke, which means "raven."[104] The Nganasans of the Ngamtuso clan told us that their other old name was kulá, which also means "raven" (in Nganasan).[105]

The raven and the eagle were perhaps the only birds in which the Nganasans were interested except those that they hunted. To kill a raven or an eagle was considered sinful. The Nganasans did not eat ravens or eagles. Judging by the name "Kurak" and the proper names, the ancestors of the Ngamtuso clan spoke an Enets dialect in the 17th century.

In 1926–7, the members of the Ngamtuso clan nomadized mainly along Route II (see Table 2). They did so in the beginning of the 19th century also. In 1829, the Zatundrin peasant Aleksey Laptukov complained that his and other peasants' [wooden] traps were being broken and used as fuel by the Samoyeds and that the worst robbers and the most uncouth ones were the Samoyeds of the "Kosterkin horde." The traps of Laptukov were situated in the area between the sources of the rivers Pyasita and Agapa, i.e., just along Route II of the Nganasans.

Nganasan tradition considers the basin of the river Pura as Ngamtuso territory, i.e., the summer quarters of Nganasans using Route II. Most probably Kurak territory in the 17th century included all of the tundra between the mouth of the Yenisey and the Yenisey gulf on the west and the river Pyasina on the east, including the basin of the river Pura. Later on, the Kuraks, much diminished in numbers, retained only the use of the Pura basin and even this not exclusively. The region between the Pura basin and Yenisey gulf was occupied by the Enets and the western bend of the Pyasina by the Nganasans, descendants of the Tavgs and Tidiris. However, in 1926–7, a small group of Kuraks was also found to the west of the Pura, nomadizing along Route I together with the Enets (Table 2). To the present the Enets still remember that these were Kureke people and identify them with Nganasans of the Ngamtuso clan (Kosterkins). They say that the route of these Kureke led from Yelovyy Kamen [Spruce Stone] through the Pyasina to the mouth of the Chernaya to the Pura [and] through three lakes to its source. This corresponds to Route II. They also said that at the place Bala on the Pura there always lived the *Kula* (Kureke) without reindeer who hunted geese found there in large numbers. The territory of the Kuraks delineated on the map is based on all of these data (Fig. 4). The Enets also call the descendants of the Kuraks *Orok-tau*, a name that we find difficult to explain.

The Kuraks, like the "Pyasida Samoyad," are called Samoyeds in 17th century sources. According to traditions preserved by the Nganasans, the ancestors of the Ngamtuso clan came to the Pura and generally into the Pyasina basin from the west, from beyond the Yenisey, from the "Tazov side." Some of the Nganasans, the descendants of the Tavgs (*quod vide*), also considered the Ngamtuso a clan of the Madu Enets. The Nenets have a tradition that they forced some Manto, i.e., Madu Enets, from the tundra between Tazov bay and Yenisey gulf to the east, beyond the Yenisey.

Probably the Kurak ancestors of the Ngamtuso clan, as well as the ancestors of a part of the Madu Enets, once formed the aboriginal population of the region of forests and tundra between the Yenisey and the Taz. Here they were assimilated by the Samoyeds, and from here, possibly not long before the arrival of the Russians, they moved beyond the Yenisey, into the Pyasida basin. In origin they may be considered a group related to the Madu Enets.

The Tidiris

In the "Pyasida-Kheta" tribute quarters in 1627 is registered a "Tigiris clan" of 7 persons.

In 1628 [it is] the "Tidiris clan" of 10 persons.

In 1629, the "Tigiritts clan" of 7 persons.

In 1630 the "Tidiris clan" of 3 persons is registered.[106]

In 1631 in the "Kurats clan" are registered the "Tidiris Khovebuya" and the "Tidiris Monako."[107]

In 1632 among the Kuraks are registered the same two Tidiris and in addition, also with the Kuraks, the "Tidiris Polyude."

In 1633, among the Kuraks listed with the Serokuyev clan of the "Pyasida Samoyad" is again listed the "Tidiris Polutu."

In 1634 [there is listed] the "Tidiris clan" of 5 persons including Korchey, Nokhoro, and Khabako.[108]

In 1637 and 1639 there are no Tidiris recorded in the "Pyasida-Kheta" tribute quarters, but in 1645 there appears a "Tidiris clan" of 20 persons.[109]

Besides, in 1631 and 1632 Korcheya (Khorcheya) and Nasaro (Namsoko), and in 1633 Kabaka, are listed among the Kuraks, i.e., the same persons who were registered under the heading of the "Tidiris clan" in 1634. There are other similar cases. The Tidiris were probably among payers of the "Pyasida-Kheta" tribute quarters also in 1637 and 1639, although there are no notations to this effect in the registers.

In the "Khantaysk tribute quarters" in 1627 on "Tidiris lake" the "Tidiris clan" of 5 persons paid [taxes] and in 1628 the "Tidiris clan" of 12 persons paid, and for 1629 there is a list of the "Tidiris clan" of 15 persons headed by Yumba.[110] In 1632 Yumba is replaced by his son Lobotey. The membership of this clan is very stable until 1640, but by 1645 only 5 persons remain (including Lobotey), of whom 3 are listed as "not found."[111]

In 1632, in the tribute registers of "Khantaysk" tribute quarters, there appears a new "Tidiris clan" of 13 persons, headed by Mygoko.[112] The membership of this clan is also very stable, but in 1637–9 its numbers are greatly reduced and in 1645 there remain only 3 persons including 1 "not found."[113]

The general picture of the changes in the numbers of Tidiris in relation to tribute quarters and to separate clans is presented in Table 9. The increase in

TABLE 9*

Year	Khantaysk winter quarters			Pyasida-Kheta winter quarters			Totals
	Yumba clan	Mygoko clan	No. of persons	Tidiris clan	Tidiris in other groups	No. of persons	
1627	5	—	5	7	N.I.†	7	12
1628	12	—	12	10	N.I.	10	22
1629	15	—	15	7	N.I.	7	22
1630	16	—	16	3	—	3	19
1631	N.I.	N.I.	N.I.	—	2	2	—
1632	15	13	28	—	3	3	31
1633	16	12	28	—	1	1	29
1634	16	12	28	5	—	5	33
1635	16	11	27	N.I.	N.I.	N.I.	—
1636	18	11	29	N.I.	N.I.	N.I.	—
1637	17	8	25	—	—	—	—
1638	20	6	26	N.I.	N.I.	N.I.	—
1639	24	6	30	—	—	—	—
1640	21	10	31	N.I.	N.I.	N.I.	—
1645	5	3	8	20	—	20	28

*This table is drawn from "Müllers Extracts" (*Arkhiv AN SSSR*) and from the tribute books of "Sib. prikaz" (*TsGADA*). For 1629, book 19 was used; for 1630, book 22, leaves 3–7, 51 ob.; for 1631, book 32, leaves 334–335; for 1632, 1633, 1634, 1635, and 1636, books 45, 47, and 986; for 1637, book 95, leaves 141–144; for 1638, book 117, leaves 435–450; for 1639 and 1640, book 150, leaves 1033–1040; for 1645, book 285, leaves 52, 59, 141, 144. On leaves 41–43 of this book‡ there is a list of Tidiris who were "not found" and, at that, "not found" for a long time as the tribute owed by them was for "past years." These Tidiris, including "Yunbin, younger brother of Taromed" and Mygoko, were not included in the table. They number 21 men of the Yumba clan and 9 of the Mygoko clan. They probably were, in part, included among the 20 Tidiris men of the "Pyasida-Kheta" winter tribute quarters who paid tribute there in 1645.

†N.I.—No information.

‡[Number of book not stated. Probably refers to book 19 for 1629.—Editor.]

the numbers of the Yumba clan is at times parallel to the decreases in the membership of the Mygoko clan. However, the names of the disappearing Mygoko clansmen do not coincide with those of the newly appearing Yumba clansmen. The latter are mainly sons and nephews of the older members of the clan and can not therefore be considered persons transferred from the Mygoko clan. Evidently, the Mygoko clan and, after 1640, both clans diminished at the expense of transfers to the "Tavgs" into the region assigned to the "Pyasida-Kheta" tribute quarters.

It seems that in the Yumba clan there were 16 to 24, and in the Mygoko clan 10 to 15, tribute payers. A few (3 to 5) of the Tidiris stayed in the region of the "Pyasida-Kheta" tribute quarters all the time. Thus, there were altogether 30 to 40 Tidiris tribute payers or about 130 men, women, and children.

The fact that the tribute collectors considered the Tidiris a separate tribe was already noted above. Sources of the first half of the 17th century do not indicate the Tidiris as Samoyeds in a single case. The tribute collectors made a special notation about them only when they found them among the tribute-paying Kuraks (*vide supra*). In the 1633 tribute register of "Khantaysk" tribute quarters it is specifically noted that tribute was collected from the "Samoyad and Tidiris."[114] As already pointed out above, "tribute-paying Samoyad and Tidiris" passed by the site of the Khantaysk tribute quarters in 1629. However, these Tidiris already spoke Samoyed.

As early as 1621, from the Bukansk tribute quarters there was brought to Mangazeysk "a captive girl of Tidiris origin," who spent two years in captivity of the Bulyash Tungus (Nyurumnyal). This "Tidiris girl" in Mangazeysk "began speaking the Samoyad language" but the "Bulyash language," i.e., Tungus, she learned only during the two years of captivity.[115]

The Linanchera clan of the Avam Nganasans may be considered descendant from the 17th century Tidiris. They had the surname Turdagin or, in the 18th and the beginning of 19th century, Turudakin. It may be surmised that the lands of this clan were once situated near Lake Pyasino. About this clan the Nganasans say that formerly it paid tribute with the Khantayka Madu Enets in Khantayka.

According to tradition, the Linanchera clan was foremost a warrior clan. The famous *tonsaga*, the "heroes" of the Nganasans—Soymu-nyuo (Soymu-son) and Timi-Khoti (Gap-toothed), or Toruda—were from this clan. Until recently, the name Soymu was, as indicated above, a hereditary one in the Linanchera clan. In particular, the well-known public servant and the first Nganasan communist Kondyue Turdagin has as his patronymic "Soymuvich."

Among the Tidiris of the Yumba clan in the 17th century there is a notable stable group of brothers headed by Netola. In 1629 and 1630, in the tribute register they are named as "Netola and Shcherbak with brothers, seven persons."[116] Moreover, in 1629-40 another, eighth brother Lazoryaku is mentioned and, from 1634 on, there is a "Khadamuy, son of Netola."[117] Among the Khantayka Enets in 1629 and also later are mentioned "Netola's son-in-law" and Netola's brother-in-law."[118] It is difficult to say whether Netola himself was "Shcherbatyy" [i.e., "the Gap-toothed"] or whether "Shcherbak" was one of his brothers. After 1630, the word "Shcherbak" disappears from the rolls of the Tidiris and there remains only "Netola with brothers." However, no doubt there was in this big, closely knit family (they even paid tribute together) a man with the nickname "Shcherbak."[119]

One of the heroes of Nganasan folklore, as mentioned earlier, was the "Gap-toothed" Timi-Khoti or Toruda, who according to traditions lived for some time among the Khantayka Samoyeds (Enets) and together with them fought against the Yuraks (Nenets). The legend very realistically pictures the person of Timi-Khoti "A small man with a dark face and a missing front tooth, in place of which he inserted a plate of mammoth's 'horn.'"

It is possible that the Tidiris of the Yumba clan and in particular Netola's family, being kin and neighbors of the Khantayka Enets, were personified in the legend of Timi-Khoti. The second name of Timi-Khoti, Toruda, is still kept as a surname of the Nganasan clan Linanchera [in the forms] Turdaginy, Torudakiny, Turudakiny.

In 1926, the main part of the Linachera clan used Route III (13 families) and Route I together with the Enets (9 families). The remaining 7 families of the clan used Route IV (3 families) and Route V (4 families). See Table 2.

According to the legends, the struggle of Soymu-son and Timi-Khoti (Toruda) against the Yuraks (Nenets) took place in the region of Lake Pyasina, mainly to the west of it, between the lake and the Yenisey, in the Dudinka river basin, and at Lake Sigovoy.

The habitat of the ancestors of the Linanchera was in particular the Paytyurma forest near Lake Pyasina, from which flow the rivers Bakunatu and Torisema. The legend points out that they lived there together with the Madu Enets.

We have shown earlier that the first tribute was given by the Tidiris on "Lake Tidiris." At that time tribute was given at the lake from the Tidiris, "from the Munduks and Sans and the tundra Samoyad of the Selyaka clan."[120] The "Munduks," "Sans," and the "tundra Samoyad of the Selyaka clan" all are the ancestors of Madu Enets, and of the Mundide clan in particular. According to legend, the chief of the Enets with whom Timi-Khoti fought against the Nenets was called Sali. In the Enets language, this would be pronounced Seli, and in its diminutive form, Seliku or Selyaku.

It is probable that in the beginning of the 17th century the region inhabited by the Tidiris was in the vicinity of Lake Pyasina. Apparently this lake was called "Tidiris" in the beginning of the 17th century. To the north and northeast of Lake Pyasina was Kurak land,[121] to the southeast Tungus, to the west the Khantayka Samoyeds, and farther to the west began the land of the Yuraks (Nenets). All this corresponds to what we know of the Tidiris and their relations with other ethnic groups.

Concerning the nomadizing along the Nganasan Route III the following is of interest. During [the movements of] summer nomadizing, this route intersects Route II. In the basin of the river Pura, Route III merges with Route I. Thus, from the region of their summer habitat, the Tidiris could either use Route I in the fall and spend the winter to the west of Lake Pyasino or move along Route III and then spend the winter at the mouth of the Avam, on the Dudypta. As we have learned, some families of the Linanchera clan did just this. This peculiarity in the movements of the Linanchera clan explains the circumstance that the Tidiris paid tribute sometimes in Khantayka (stopping evidently at Lake Pyasina) or sometimes in the "Pyasida" (stopping at the Avam) in the 17th century. In crossing Route II, they mixed with the Kuraks and consequently, in the 17th century, Tidiris were registered among the latter.

In the 17th century these movements along Route I evidently led to friendly relations between the Tidiris and the Khantayka Enets (Madu). Toward the end of the 19th century and the beginning of the 20th, crossing from Route III to Route I was motivated by the desire to be closer to the Yenisey from which the supply of Russian goods originated.

Additionally, it may be suggested that at the beginning of the 17th century the Tidiris were a comparatively new element in the region of Lake Pyasino and the Avam. Therefore, their route crossed the routes of other tribal groups (for example the Kuraks) or else the Tidiris moved from place to place with these groups in the territories of the latter (for instance, the mixing of the Tidiris with the Khantayka Enets near Lake Pyasina). Judging from the contents of the Soymu-son legend, the Tidiris sometimes also nomadized along Route IV.

Today neither the Nganasans nor the Enets know the name Tidiris. However, in the Enets language there is the word *tidero* which designates members of the mother's clan, her younger brothers and sons of her elder brothers. The stem of this word is *tide*, meaning consanguineous group, exogamous clan. We know that the Tidiris were bound with the Enets by marriage and actually were *tidero* to them. Possibly the Tidiris were *tidero* also to the "Pyasida Samoyeds" and the Kuraks.

The Nganasans and Enets cannot translate the name "Linanchera." The second part of this name, *chera*, is a Nganasan word for a "phratry" type of clan (*vide supra*), an equivalent of the Enets word *tide*. *Lina* cannot be explained on the basis of Nganasan and Enets linguistic sources. It is probably based on a proper name.

We have no direct indications about the ethnic origin of the Tidiris. As we know, they were not considered Samoyeds in the first half of the 17th century, although they apparently spoke an Enets dialect. Apart from Samoyeds we met only Tungus on the right bank of the lower Yenisey. According to legend, the son of Soymu spoke Tungus well. In one of these legends an old man, the ancestor of Linanchera, is directly called a Tungus. The very word "Tidiris" probably derived from the composite *tidero-osya*, i.e., "relatives through mother Tungus" (in Enets).

The region of Lake Pyasino, together with the entire group of the Norilsk lakes to the south, was a region to which there arrived from the south and south-east different groups of Tungus (Dongot, Edyan, Goragir, and others) during the 19th century. Probably the Tidiris were also such a Tungus group, which came from the south into the region of the Norilsk lakes and Lake Pyasina even before the beginning of the 17th century and nomadized there either with the ancestors of the Enets or with the Kuraks and "Pyasida Samoyeds," i.e., with groups who later entered into the composition of the Avam Nganasans. As we know, the Tidiris finally merged with the latter.

Thus, in the Tidiris we see the extreme northwestern group of Tungus, assimilated by the Samoyeds not long before the Russians arrived in the lower reaches of the Yenisey.

The Tavgs

Let us now consider the largest ancestral component of the Avam Nganasans, the Tavgs.

In 1627 there were 22 men of the Tavg clan who paid tribute, one of the Unyadets clan, four of the Mayabdin, and 13 of the Yakuts clan.

In 1628, tribute was paid by 13 Tavgs and 14 "Samoyad" of the Makgits clan.

In 1629, 11 men of Taygis clan paid tribute, 23 of the Yureli clan, 20 of the Yakuns clan, 5 of the Tagey, 3 of the Unyay, 11 of the Noyab, 2 of the Mangas, one of the Matgets, and 3 of the Yaguts clan.

These data are adopted from the Mangazeysk copies of Müller.[122] The names of clans had been very much distorted by the copyists. Most of the names were apparently formed from proper names. It is also possible that among these "clans" from Miller's copies there are separate "clans" of other groups ancestral to the Avam Nganasans, for instance, the Kuraks.

Later, from 1630 to 1645, we have the actual tribute registers with individual Tavgs named, although it should be remembered that these registers were also copied in the Mangazeysk office for dispatch to Moscow.

In 1630 there is registered a "Tavgits clan" of 43 payers, headed by princeling Khal. Among others, an Udamo was registered.[123]

In 1631 a "clan Taigids" of 48 men headed by Udamole Sonitsu is registered; there are 10 men, "also Tavgs," headed by the sorcerer Sokdoza and among them is Gamiga. There were, "also of the clan Tavgidts," 5 men headed by Varabde.[124]

In 1632 the "clan Tamgits" numbers 46 men headed by princeling Udamula Sonichu; there are 11 men "also of the Tavg clan" headed by the sorcerer Sokdozo, "also the Tavgits clan" of 5 men headed by Varede, a "Tavgits clan" of 9 men headed by princeling Pudu, and "the clan Mardi" of 9 men headed by Yemedaku.[125]

In 1633 the "clan Taigits" of 23 men headed by princeling Puda is registered. Among its members is Khal and "again newly found Senzika of the deer." Further on, the "clan Tavgits" of 33 men, headed by princeling Adamul, is entered, followed by 19 men "also Tavgits clan" headed by the sorcerer Sokdozo and, after a subheading "In year 141 again found," the "clan Solenya" of 12 men headed by Poe, the "also Tavg clan" of 4 men headed by Moderyu, and the "clan Madets" of 14 men headed by Khadyaku.[125]

In 1634 the "clan Tavgits" of 19 (16) men headed by Khal is entered, the "clan Inokdeye" of 17 (15) men headed by the sorcerer Bolery. Among its members is registered an "old Tavgits sorcerer Uredity." Further on there is the "Tavgits clan Udamuli" of 17 (15) men headed by princeling Udamula, the "clan of Tavgits sorcerers" of 16 (14) men headed by the sorcerer Sokdozo, the "Tavgits clan" of 12 (10) men headed by princeling Pudu and having among its members Poe and Soziko, and the "Tavgits clan Makidin" of 24 (18) men headed by Yegnoda and with Khodyaku among its members.[125]

In 1637, there is the Adamulev clan of 20 men headed by Adamyl, and among its members is the princeling Neyaptu. There follows the "Sorcerer's clan" in which we should distinguish the first 33 men headed by Khal and then, under the same heading, beginning with the name "old Tondi," an additional group of 23 men and, with the name "sorcerer," another 9 men. Further on, and to the end of the roll of the "Sorcerer's clan," the Kuraks are entered. In the "Soloduyev clan," starting with the name of Neloku and to the end of the roll, another 20 Tavgs can be distinguished.[126]

In 1639, the register included the Adamylev clan of 19 men headed by Adamyl and with princeling Neyaptu in the list. Thereafter, under the heading of "Sorcerer's clan," there is Khal's group of 31 men, the group of the old man Tondi of 17 men, and the group of the sorcerer Belyada comprising 9 men. In the "Soloduyev clan," the group of Neloko of 24 men is composed of Tavgs and closes the list. Further, under the heading "New Samoyad" there is a group of 23 men and 16 "juveniles newly found."[127] The "New-Samoyad" and the juveniles are mostly Tavgs as shown by comparison of their names with the names of Tavgs in the 1645 registers.

In 1645, there is the "Adamyl clan" of 18 men headed by Adamyl and containing the princeling Neyaptu. The "Sorcerer's clan" of 26 men is headed by Khal. Then there are the "Umchin clan" of 17 men headed by the old man Tondi, the "clan Ninichey" of 10 men headed by the sorcerer Belyary, the "Tavgits clan" of 34 men headed by Neloko. Also, in 1645, there were two clans which were completely "not found," namely the "clan Tavgits" of 16 men headed by Neroko, and the "Terey clan" of 21 men headed by Syuyka.[128]

The data just reviewed are presented in tabular form [Table 10] indicating the change in the numbers of Tavg tribute payers. It may be calculated that in the first half of the 17th century there were about 520 Tavgs altogether.

TABLE 10

Year	1627	1628	1629	1630	1631	1632	1633	1634	1637	1639	1645
Tribute payers	40	27	79	43	63	80	105	105	105	140	142

In 1631, as we have already seen, the list of Tavgs is headed by Udamole Sonitsu, later mentioned as Adamul, Udamul, Adamyl in all the lists of Tavgs up to and including 1645. Apparently he headed the Tavg tribe. The circumstances surrounding the subjection of the Tavgs by the Russians are given in the following petition of the Mangazeysk cossack lieutenant, Ivan Patrikeyev. In view of the significance this document has in the history of the Nganasans— the circumstances of their submission to the Russians, the estimate of their numbers, their territorial distribution, and relations with other tribes, and so on, we present it here in full.

To the Governors of the Sovereign Tsar and Grand Duke Mikhail Feodorovich of all Russia, to Vasiliy Alekseyevich and Dmitriy Fedorovich, lowly bows Ivashko Patrikeyev. In the past year, 139, Governor Andrey Palitsyn sent from the Yenisey portage to Pyasida for the collection of the Tsar's tribute an assistant clerk Petr Kuznetsov and a Mangazeysk fusilier Grigoriy Kisel. And in the current year, 140, it became known to me in the Turukhansk winter quarters that this Petr Kuznetsov with companions wanted to go to Pyasida by way of a wrong river, but lost his way and did not get to Pyasida. And now he wanted, this Petr, to move on from the Khantaysk winter quarters to Pyasida using an early winter road and having started it seems that he will not get to the tribute quarters (because) the way is long and hard and he does not have new guides. And, in the past year, 139, the Governors of Mangazeysk town, Grigoriy Kokorev and Andrey Palitsyn, sent me to Pyasida for the collection of the Tsar's tribute and I according to the Tsar's law took the Tsar's tribute from the old, taxed Samoyad—from 24 men on the Kheta. And [then] after finding him, I called on the princeling of Tavg land, Udamolu Sonitsu, and on the 65 Tavgs with him and the two Kurak princelings Torba and Solyuda and the 31 Kuraks with them. And this Tavg princeling, Udamul Sonitsa, said that his clan on the seashore at the mouth of river Anybura contains 80 persons and that hearing about the majesty and mercy of the Sovereign Tsar and Grand Duke Mikhail Fedorovich of all Russia, sent to them, his kin, his own brother Gamiga and ordered them to come to the Kheta, to the tribute quarters with the Tsar's tribute and to be with him, Adamul, together under the Tsar's high protection. And, having done this, he Udamula Sonitsu with all Tavgs submitted to the Sovereign Tsar and Grand Duke of all Russia in my presence, in the Kheta tribute quarters. And I, according to the Tsar's decree and the Governors' instructions, told them to rely on the Tsar's mercy and as concerns [the fact] that they, the Tavgs, were killed and robbed by the Yenisey Samoyad of the Parasey clan and the Syruye who took their wives and children captive, [they], the Tavgs, were rewarded by the Tsar who ordered that they be defended against the Parasey and Syruye. And then, Grigoriy Ivanovich Kokorev and Andrey Fedorovich Palitsyn according to the Tsar's order found those Parasey and their princeling Idybazi and kept him in Mangazeya town for investigation of mutual complaints. And the Tavgs were ordered to send two or three persons to Mangazeya town for confronting the princeling of the Parasey, Idybazi. And in the past year, 139, towards the end of winter that Tavg princeling Sonitsu left Pyasida with me for the Yenisey. And having heard from the Tiguris (Tidiris—Author) that the Parasey princeling, Idybazi, was not let go, he, Udamoliy, did not come with me to Mangazeya town and returned to Pyasida. And now this Petr Kuznetsov with companions will not reach by winter road the Kheta, the tribute quarters, and will begin (?)* that Davdyts

*[Author's question mark. Perhaps this could be translated as "will cause" rather than "will begin."—Editor.]

(Tavgiyets*—Author) princeling Udamul with all the Tavgs to move from the tribute quarters to his previous, customary wanderings, because he is a new and unrewarded man. And it may be expected that in the present year, 140, there will be no officials in the Kheta tribute quarters to collect the Tsar's tribute and the Tsar's tribute will be greatly in arrears.[129]

The apprehensions of Ivan Patrikeyev in regard to the collection of tribute from the Tavgs in 1632 did not materialize. In that year, 62 of Udamul's Tavgs again paid tribute and so did, in addition, 18 men headed by the "princeling" Puda who had not paid tribute in 1631. The latter probably were part of the Anabar Tavgs. According to information given by Udamul to Ivan Patrikeyev, there were altogether 145 Tavg adult men; of these, 65 (according to the tribute register, 63) nomadized with Udamul to the west of the Khatanga, and 80 to the east of the Khatanga, along the shore of the Laptev Sea at the lower reaches of the Anabar. This part of the Tavgs was apparently headed by Puda and Khal. According to the registers, after all Tavgs became tribute payers, there were 140 men in 1639, and 142 men in 1645. Thus, the data supplied by Ivan Patrikeyev are fully confirmed. Certainly, Patrikeyev unjustifiedly ascribed to himself the submission of the Tavgs to tribute paying. As we know, the Tavgs, including those of the Anabar (Khal), paid tribute before. He only brought about the formal submission to Russia of the western part of the Tavgs headed by Udamul.

Patrikeyev's reports about skirmishes of the Tavgs with the ancestors of the Khantayka Enets and about the attempt of the Russian authorities to reconcile the parties are confirmed by Nganasan traditions of wars with the Enets and by the role of mediation by the Russian authorities in cases of intertribal collisions in, for instance, the legends about Soymu-son and Munkhu-brother and others.[130]

In the documents of the 17th century the Tavgs appear as a fully independent territorial and ethnic unit. Such phrases as "lived for a long time wandering in the Pyasida among the Tavgs along the rivers and in the tundra,"[131] "left for the Pyasida rivers for the Tavgs," and so on, are often found attached to the names of payers in the Khantayka tribute quarters. Above, we also noted that the adjective "Tavgitskiy" [Tavg, of the Tavgs] has a wider meaning than simply a clan name, as the Tavgs consisted of a large number of small clans.

In the first half of the 17th century, the sources do not directly designate the Tavgs as Samoyeds. In the second half of the 17th century an appellation "Tavg Samoyad" appears, which covers not only the Tavgs, but also the "Pyasida Samoyad" and perhaps also the Kuraks. This is a sign of the start of the tribal consolidation that resulted in the present-day Avam Nganasans.

In 1634 the tribute register is a most satisfactorily composed one. Up to 1634, the tribute registers reflected not so much division by clans as the stages of submitting the Tavgs to tribute payment. As we have noted, in 1637 and 1639 the tribute registers have sometimes combined under one heading most diverse elements, which could be differentiated only by comparing these registers with that of 1645. But even in the latter list the heading "Tavg clan" probably represents not members of one clan, but a partial list of [all] Tavgs, without the clan divisions. The list headed "Sorcerer's clan" (also in the register of 1645) is apparently of similar nature.

Turning to the 1634 tribute register, we see that a Tavg clan numbers from 10 to 18 adult payers. The clans Solenya, Sokdozo, Madets (in 1633), Adamyl, Umchin, Ninichey (in 1645), and the clans corresponding to them in 1637 and 1639, and others, all are of approximately the same numbers. On the average about

*[Transliterated to show connection to "Davdyts."—Editor.]

15 male hunters composed a Tavg clan. This is approximately the number of hunters required for a successful collective hunt of wild northern deer with spears at a river ford (*pokolka*) or with the help of a leather net in the open tundra (*nevodba*).*

The Avam Nganasan clans Chunanchera and Ninonde may be considered the [linear] descendants of the 17th century Tavgs. We find the name Ninonde in 1634 as the Inokdey clan of the Anabar Tavgs headed by the sorcerer Bolery, and in 1645 as the clan Ninichey with the same sorcerer Bolyary at its head. Today, the Nganasans rarely use the name Ninonde in combination with the word *chera* (as in Linanchera, Chunanchera), but evidently in the 17th century this was usual practice. *Inokde* is the Enets pronunciation of this name. *Nino* (according to Castren, *nginua*) means "rich" in Nganasan, while in Enets "rich" is *ine*, from which the derivation should be *Inende*; the "k" in place of the "n" is probably a slip of the pen.

In 1637 and 1639 the Kudesnikov (Sorcerer's), Umchin, and Ninichey clans are enumerated on one list headed by Khal. As we know, the Ninonde clan has other names: Falysyada, Falyka (Khalysyada, Khalyka). A similar name, Falo (Khalo), has been used also for a part of the Chunachera clan that is supposed to be descended from an adopted Tungus. However, the Nganasans do distinguish Falo—a part of the Chunachera clan—and Falysyada—the other name for the Ninonde clan. Members of the Falo subdivision could not enter into marriage with other members of the Chunachera clan but could and often did marry members of the Ninonde (Falysyada) clan. The very well informed Nganasan Nomopte Porbin, in supporting his statement that Falo is a part of the Chunanchera, told a legend about a quarrel between the Chunanchera and Falysyada, about how a Chunanchera married a Falysyada girl, and that Falysyada is the old name of his clan Ninonde. The name Falysyada could have originated from the proper name of the princeling Khala (Fala),[132] who apparently headed the ancestors of the Ninonde clan in 1630–45. Now, according to the 1681 census, among the Avam Samoyeds there was a princeling Khalo.[133] This could not be the Khal of 1630–45, because in 1681 Khalo was only about 46 years old. According to the tax register of 1768 this Khalo is probably the ancestor of the Kamenev Avam Samoyeds, and of the present-day Khalo (Falo) subdivision of the Chunanchera clan.[134]

Into the river Yangoda, a tributary of the Pyasina, enters a left tributary, the river Sonite (same in Russian and Yakut) along which is one of the most favored regions for the summer camps of the Nganasans. About this river, and also about the Batayka river, the "tundra" peasants used to say that it received its name from a Samoyed prince who nomadized there. The Nganasans said that the prince was from the Chunanchera clan. We know that Adamul had the nickname Sonitsu or Sonichu. He probably gave the name to the river Sonite. This river is within the territory of Route IV used by the Nganasans, predominantly by the Chunanchera clan. (See Table 2.) The very name of the clan Chuna-n-chera also probably originated from the name Soni-Chu (cf. the Nganasan–Tungus agreement [in the transposition] of "ch" and "s" as in the words *satara* and *chatara*, "polar fox," *simka*, and *chimka*, "a special category of tent poles," etc.).

The Ninonde clan nomadizes mainly along Route V, i.e., considerably to the east. True, small groups of this, the most numerous clan, are met with everywhere, with the exception of Route I; however, the main body clearly holds to Route V. As pointed out earlier, in the beginning of the 17th century the ancestors

*[*Pokolka* thus may be translated as "spearing" and *nevodba* as "net hunting."—Editor.]

of the Ninonde clan lived to the east of the Khatanga. In addition to the rivers Anabar and Popigay (*Fa-bigay*, in Nganasan, "Forest river"), they probably nomadized along the river Suoleme (cf. the clan "Solenya"). The ancestors of the Chunanchera clan with Adamul at its head apparently wandered at first along the present-day Route VI, leading to the river Kheta, the region of their winter quarters. Both oral tradition and the documents concur in this. In 1631, the fusilier Semeyka Shekhtin took tribute from a group of Tavgs, ancestors of the Chunanchera, headed by Varrede, "meeting them on the road . . . to the mouth of the Kheta river." Another Tavg of Adamul, Marasida from the Sokdoza clan, paid tribute on the Khatanga in the same year. Farther to the south of the Kheta, in the upper reaches of the river Romanikha, there is a "Samoyed range," where according to tradition the ancestors of the Nganasans stayed in winter.

After accepting subjection to the Russians, the Kheta Tavgs of Adamul, ancestors to the Chunanchera, moved westward to the region of the Avam, to the territory of the "Pyasida Samoyad," and continued to nomadize, in the main, somewhat farther to the west (along Route IV) but the Anabar Tavgs of Khal and Puda, ancestors of the Ninonde clan, nomadized farther to the east (along Route V).

Before the "Pyasida Samoyeds" moved from the Pyasina to the Taymyr river, the ancestors of the Tavgs were apparently taking over the basin of the latter. Thus, the Tungus toponymy in the Taymyr basin, as we shall see later. But at that time they probably nomadized not along Route V, but moved from southeast to northwest, as did more recently the Yakuts and Dolgans from the lower reaches of the Kheta and Khatanga rivers when traveling to the Taymyr basin.

With the Avam Nganasans there existed a tradition of choosing the head of the tribe, the princeling or *barbu* (in Nganasan), mainly from the Chunanchera clan. No doubt this tradition goes back to the time of Adamul, the head of the Tavgs during the period of their submission to the Russians. In 1637 the aging Adamul was replaced by Neyaptu from the same clan. During 1637–45, besides Neyaptu, the title "princeling" was retained only by the head of the "Pyasida Samoyeds," Pyak. The "Tavg" and "Kurak" princelings are not distinguished so any more. Evidently it is at this time that there begins a consolidation of the tribe of Avam Nganasans out of all elements described above.

Not all Tavg clans can be distributed between the ancestors of Chunanchera and Ninonde. Thus, in 1633–4, the clans Adamulo and Sokdozo were probably Kheta Tavgs (Chunanchera), while the clans Pudu, Khal, Inokdey, and Solenya were Anabar Tavgs (Ninonde). But we have no data in this respect about the Madets or Makidin clans. Also, in 1645 the clan Adamyl appears to be ancestral to the Chunanchera and Kudesnikov (Sorcerers') clans, and the Unchin and Ninichey clans ancestral to the Ninonde. There are no data about where the clans headed by Neloko and Noroko and the clan Terey should be placed.

In the Evenk (Lamut) language *tavgich* is a word with the original meaning of "from the other side."[135] G. N. Prokofiyev points out that in the "Nganasan dialect there are found a number of words of Tungus (or Lamut) origin."[136] In the Nganasan traditions about their origin there is an ever-present episode about the crossing of some water boundary, after which they find themselves in the Taymyr.

At present, the Nganasans do not use the name "Tavg," but as pointed out, it was retained in the languages of their neighbors. In Lamut, the word *tavgach* may also mean "one who is on the other side."[137] Thus the ancestors of the Tavgs could have called themselves Tavgs both before their arrival from beyond the

Khatanga—or after they were already in the Taymyr—if they spoke the Lamut language. We shall return later to the question of the Tungus ethnic element in the composition of the Nganasans. In any case, as we have pointed out, the Tavgs were not entered as Samoyeds in the sources from the beginning of the 17th century, but the name Tavg is bound with the meaning of "arrived from beyond something" or "being beyond something" in the Tungus (Lamut) language. This "something" is most probably the Khatanga river and Khatanga gulf.

Judging by their proper names, the Tavgs spoke Samoyed already in the 17th century. It seems to have been a dialect close to the present-day Nganasan language.

Thus, it is very probable that the Tavgs were originally Tungus groups who lived in the lower reaches of the Kheta, Khatanga, Anabar, and Popigay rivers and who moved to the Taymyr and were probably "Samoyedized" not long before the arrival of the Russians there.

From all that has been presented above, it is possible to deduce that the Avam Nganasans were composed of two groups, which were called Samoyeds by the Russians in the 17th century, but which probably represented aboriginal Paleo-Asiatics assimilated by the Samoyeds, and three groups, Tungus by origin, which the Russians initially did not consider Samoyeds. Of these groups, one (the Tidiris) came to the Taymyr probably from the south and the two others (both of Tavg origin), from the east or southeast. There are a number of reasons for considering these, particularly the Tavgs, not simply Tungus, but also Paleo-Asiatic aboriginal groups assimilated by the Tungus. This question will be dealt with below.

Table 11 shows the composition of the Nganasans in the 17th century and compares their composite parts with the clans of the Avam Nganasans in 1926.

In addition to the general reduction in the number of Avam Nganasans caused by the difficult conditions of their existence in tsarist Russia and by disease and famines (*vide supra*), we should note the change in the proportion of the different elements of which they were composed. The main difference is in the reduction in the number of Kuraks and the increase of the Tidiris. Although the proportion of the Tavgs is somewhat decreased, this change is not great—from 52 per cent to 48.5 per cent. The proportion of the descendants of the "Pyasida Samoyeds" hardly changed at all.

During the second half of the 17th century and during the 18th century, an intensive process of merging of all these tribal groups into one tribe took place. We shall examine the major phases of this process below.

TABLE 11

First half of the 17th century			1926			
Names of ancestors of the Avam Nganasans	No. of persons male and female	%	Names of Avam Nganasan clans	No. of persons male and female	%	Percentage of 1926 population to that of the 17th century
Pyasida Samoyed	130	13.0	Ngomde	76	13.2	58.5
Kuraks	220	22.0	Ngamtuso	81	14.1	36.8
Tidiris	130	13.0	Linanchera	139	24.2	106.9
Kheta Tavgs	230	23.0	Chunanchera	103	18.0	44.3
Anabar Tavgs	290	29.0	Ninonde	175	30.5	60.4
Total	1000*	100.0		574	100.0	57.4

*Not counting 30 to 40 persons of the Munzuyev clan who joined the Khantayka Enets and counting all of the Tidiris.

The Avam Nganasans in the Censuses of 1681 and 1768

The results of the census taken in March of 1681 of Samoyeds who paid tribute in the Avam tribute quarters are compiled in Table 12.[138]

It is likely that a number of children, who did not pay tribute, as well as old people and disabled persons were not fully accounted for in this census. It contains very few people who paid tribute for more than 35 years and whose names could therefore be compared with the names of the ancestors of the Nganasans in the tribute registers of 1645. The tribute was paid for 40 years only by the princelings Batayko, Yegir, Ononta, Tomuda, Tentevoy, and by "rank and file" Nganasans Nazey, Montyya, Gadanya, and Mogoo (the last two of Minan clan, the first two not assigned to a particular clan). In addition, in the Kurak clan Kumasey, the old princeling Yumo (Vostroy) paid tribute for 35 years but died not long before the census was taken.

From these names it is possible to identify with assurance only Batay and Tomuda among the names in the 1645 registers. The first 19 tents evidently represent Nganasans who were in the immediate neighborhood of the mouth of the Avam, and perhaps assembled for the celebration of the "clean tent." The remaining 5 clans represent separate camps situated at some distance from the winter quarters. Judging by the latter, the camps still had a clan character and the average membership in these clans-camps approximated that of the clans in 1634.

The clans Tuyeder (Tunuderin) and Kuryets represent the Kuraks; the clan Tidiris, the Tidiris; the Mamnen, probably the Ngomde; and the Minan, the Ninonde. Among the first 19 tents there is the family of Batayko of the Ngomde clan, and [the family] Khalo of the Chunanchera, but as yet it is difficult to distribute the remainder by clans.

The census of 1681 draws our attention because the heads of 20 families are called "princelings." If the last 6 princelings named (Nina, Tomuda, Buinkogo, Lobkura, Tentevoy, and Poletey) are regarded as heads of clans (khonka), then for each of the 14 princelings named in the list of Nganasans and not attached to a clan, there would be only 5 or 6 adult men. Among the other Samoyeds of the Avam tribute quarters, the princelings are distinguished in the census of 1681 only in that they pay not three fawns each but four (Batay paid five). Apparently these were simply persons who were "better off," and the large category of princelings was probably established to differentiate the size of tribute in accordance with the property qualification of the tribute payer.

TABLE 12

Groupings	Names of princelings	No. of tents	No. of tribute payers	Total no. of males
Without clan division	Batayko, Khalo, and 12 other princelings	19	92	150
Mamnenskiy clan	Nina, Poletey	3	27	33
Tuyederskiy clan	Tomuda	2	11	24
Kuratskiy clan	Buinkogo	2	14	24
Tidirisskiy clan	Lobkura	2	11	15
Minanskiy clan	Tentevoy	2	16	19
Total of clan division		11	79	115
Grand total		30	171	265

Concerning the word "princeling," one should keep in mind that the Nganasan word *barba* has two meanings: (1) "Head of tribe," "prince," and (2) "master," "head of family." In the second meaning, a woman could also be called *barba* as the wife of the head of the family, the mistress of the tent. Certainly among the princelings of the 1681 census there probably was a real princeling, perhaps one of these four (Nosifey, Yumitin, Lasifey, and Khalo) who signed the census book and whom S. V. Bakhrushin calls the principal ones.[139]

In all, the 1681 census gives little material for [the elucidation of] our subject. The only thing that unquestionably follows from its data is the sufficiently advanced merging of the component elements of the Avam Nganasans into one tribe, in which we can suppose they lose their separateness and retain only the exogamous units present in them to our days.

For the 18th century we have available the materials of the First Tax Commission. Unlike all earlier lists of Avam Nganasans, the census made by the Commission is distinguished in that it contains a larger number and more detail about clans enumerated in it. The data of Table 13 were taken out of the tax book of 1768 compiled by the Commission of Yeniseysk province under the direction of Captain Norov.

Notwithstanding the fact that this list is separated from the census of 1681 by an interval of 87 years, it is very easy, in a number of cases, to establish the origin of "clans" enumerated in it. The Batayevs are the descendants of Batay, son of Pyak; the already known to us Lomovs, descendants of a certain Lomo of the 1681 census; the Kamenevs, of Khalo (*vide supra*); the Pirogovs, of Firogo; the Porvins, of Forbuyya of the Minan clan; the Bortsovs, of Barko of the Tuyeder clan; the Vostrovs, of Vostrogo (alias "Yumo"); the Yuntalins, of Yumtalonyu (alias "Talo"); the Lobovs, of Lobo (alias "Komiko"); the Yuyarins, of Yuyaga, brother of Khalo; the Kovrins, of Adamul's son Kobra (Khobyrada); the Belyarins, of the sorcerer Belyary; the Soloduyevs, manifestly the Kuraks of the Soloduyev clan, probably of Soloduy (Soledo) himself; and so on.

Inversely, the data of 1768 already connect directly with present-day data. In the Topudin clan there was Kursima Topudin, and in the beginning of the 20th

TABLE 13*

Names of "clans"	No. of families	No. of males	Names of "clans"	No. of families	No. of males	Names of "clans"	No. of families	No. of males
Sonfokin	1	3	Bartsov	2	4	Yermon	1	4
Batayev	2	4	Soloduyev	3	15	Bakunin	2	10
Yukagir Funsota	1	3	Vostrov	2	7	Strelenoy	1	6
Lomov	3	7	Kelmov	1	6	Shandurov	1	4
Kamenev	2	3	Turudakin	5	18	Yurakov	2	4
Topudin	4	27	Kovrin	4	20	Soltov	1	8
Beloglazov	4	18	Yuntalin	1	5	Kalimov	1	3
Yentifantyev	1	3	Lobov	3	17	Yazykov	1	7
Pirogov	4	10	Natalin	1	1	Momzin	1	3
Naroyev	5	13	Yefremov	2	3	Sedankov	1	4
Porvin	7	27	Studenye	3	12	Yuyarin	3	8
Belyarin	3	7						

In addition, a "newly baptized" Ivan Semenov, 1 family, 2 men

Grand total: 80 families, 296 males†

*TsGADA, Sib. prikaz, book 1648.
†The tax book for 1768 contains the total of 293 persons, which was indicated by us above (see Table 5 for changes in the numbers of Avam Nganasans according to tribute registers). However, our calculations gave us the total of 296, which is shown here.

century there was still a Kursimin family in the Chunanchera clan.[140] The Pirogovs are a part of the Ngomde, who carried this surname in the beginning of the 20th century. The Porvins are the present-day Porbins (Khorbins, Forbins) of the Ninonde. The Turudakins are the present-day Turdagins, i.e., Linancheras, descendants of Toruda (Timi-Khoti) or Netolada Shcherbak of the 17th century.

But while it is a connecting link between the materials of the 17th century and recent ones, the tax register of 1786 also poses questions: What do these many clans represent? How can it be explained that, with approximately equal populations in 1926 and 1768, there were only five clans in 1926 while there were over 30 in 1768?

The tax register of 1768 could not record clans of the type found in 1634 or even in 1681 as they did not persist to the second half of the 18th century. However, in the 18th century, in many groups of the indigenous population of Siberia there appeared [extended] families that were formed in the names of fathers, grandfathers, and great-grandfathers who headed the families.[141]

Thus, persons bearing the same surname were often actually people of the same origin. But in a number of cases the heads of families received different surnames after the names of their fathers, although they had common grandfathers and great-grandfathers. Rich families, which in the past were the nuclei of clans, evidently received surnames of rather remote ancestors, as for instance, the Turudakins, Batayevs, Belyarins, Kovrins, Soloduyevs, Beloglazovs, and Kamenevs, while the poor families of collateral lineage, of one origin with them, could receive other surnames after the names of their fathers. The surnames represent partly Russian nicknames (Strelenoy, Vostrov) or translations of the names of Nganasan ancestors into Russian (Beloglazovs, Kamenevs), etc. Consequently, the clans of the "tax book" for 1768 represent the Russianized nicknames of related, patrilineal groups, sometimes reflecting the clan groups into which, as we know, the "Pyasida Samoyeds," Kuraks, Tidiris, and Tavgs of the 17th century were divided. Together with these names, the tax registers contained ordinary surnames of separate families which could have constituted a part of this or that clan group.

Today, of the 34 families in the list of 1768, there remain only two, the Porbins (Porvins) and the Turdagins (Turudakins). At the turn of the 20th century the Nganasans also had the surnames Pirogov, Kursimin, and Botadin; neither of the last two surnames was mentioned in the list of 1768, nor the present-day surname Kosterkin.

The transition from the many surnames created for the Avam Nganasans in the 18th century, and in part kept in the 19th century, particularly during its first half, to the five (or six, if the Botadins be counted) surnames of the 20th century could have taken place for a variety of reasons.

First, the five basic exogamous units (the present-day clans) of the Avam Nganasans undoubtedly existed also during the whole period. Thus, the question concerns not so much the contraction of the number of exogamous units as the spread of some surnames to those exogamous units that had already become the exogamous clans of a single tribe in the 18th century.

Second, besides these five basic clans there were among the Avam Nganasans during the 18th and 19th centuries, and perhaps in the 17th century also, other clans that died out later on. We know of three such groups:

(1) In the 18th century a Nganasan woman was married to a Nenets (Yurak) of the Lambay clan. After the death of her husband she returned to the Nganasans. Her sons by the Nenets husband formed the clan "Yura-Fonka" (according

to the 1768 tax book, the "clan" Yurakov: *vide supra*). This clan died out in the beginning of the 20th century.

(2) In the beginning of the 20th century a small clan of the Avam Nganasans, Tonida (Botadin), died out; it originated, according to tradition, from an Enets or Nenets who joined the Nganasan clan of Chunanchera.

(3) The Nganasans remember that there had been a "family" Sonfokin, which also died out recently. They say that it was founded by the shaman Sonfoka. The Sonfokins were apparently Chunancheras by origin, as in 1768 Muduka Sonfokin was a "prince" of the Avam Nganasans.

Naturally with the dying out of these groups their surnames also disappeared.

In tracing the origin of separate groups of the northern Siberian population through documents and their genealogies, it is possible to establish that the origin of the present-day, sometimes rather large clans can be traced usually to a comparatively small number of males who lived some 150–200 years ago. At the time when these ancestors lived, there were naturally other men in their clans, but the further we go back, the smaller is the number of men from whom descended the present-day group now under investigation.

This process apparently took place also with the Nganasans and this naturally brought about the reduction of the number of surnames. Some of the surnames were simply forgotten and the descendants began using either the clan name (Chunanchera, Ngomde) or took the surname that began to predominate in a given clan. For instance, in the Chunanchera clan, all of whose members now use the surname Chunanchar, it is possible to distinguish the descendants of Khalo (the Kamenevs), and of Kursima Topudin; in the clan Linanchera, not all are descended from the Turudakins, although the entire clan bears the surname Turdagin. The present-day Nganasans of the Ngomde clan are descended probably and mainly from the Pirogovs and Beloglazovs of the 1768 tax book,[142] while the descendants of the Batayevs seemingly died out, and so on.

In 1768, the Avam Nganasans were headed by only one prince, the above-mentioned Muduka Sonfokin. Even the descendants of Pyak and Batay—the Batayevs—are already registered as "ordinary." The consolidation of the tribe was finished by this time, and at the head of a single tribe stood one "prince."

In the 1768 tax book there is a detail that deserves special attention. The list of "Avam unbaptized Samoyad" begins as follows:[143]

THE SONOFOKIN CLAN

	(age)
1. Princeling Muduka Sonfokin	45
and his children	
2. Monyuka	20
3. Lonfa	18
ordinary, registered in the preceding census	
4. Notida Batayev	65
and his son	
5. Chersuka	5
6. Dyutumu Batayev	30
and his son	
7. Lomida	4
8. Yukagir Funsota	33
and his children	
9. Basuka	9
born after census	
10. Somnovy	3

THE LOMOV CLAN
Children of Buturanta Lomov

11. Nivoka   35

etc.

Thus, after the princeling and his family and the rich "aristocratic" Batayev family, the list or really "ordinary" Nganasans is opened by the family of a certain Funsota, who is called a Yukagir.

This raises the question of how the word "Yukagir" can be explained in a document of the 18th century, relating to the Avam Nganasans. Possibly the members of the Tribute Commission of 1768 in the Yeniseysk province indicated interest in the origin of the Avam Samoyeds and the latter, who probably knew Russian in the 18th century, gave answers to this question using the name Yukagir for the people from which, in their own opinion, they originated. As we shall see later, the Avam Nganasans remembered about their origin in our times, but they forgot the name "Yukagir." However, it is possible that Funsota was a Yukagir, who somehow came to the Avam Nganasans. The point is, though, that the word *funsa* means "stranger" in Nganasan and the name Funsota may be translated as "outlander."

On the other hand, separate families of northern peoples, migrating here and there, often had in mind some kinship with the population of the region for which they were bound. Therefore, if Funsota was a Yukagir newcomer, the circumstance that he joined the Avam Nganasans and not the "Tundra" Yakuts or Dolgans proves that some Yukagirs were conscious of their kinship with the ancestors of the Nganasans.

With this we end the analysis of the formation of the Avam Nganasan tribe through historical documentary materials. Now let us see what information may be obtained about the origin of the Nganasans from ethnography and, in particular, folklore.

The Traditions of the Nganasans about Their Origin

The fundamental legend on this subject, known to almost every Nganasan, is the story of their arrival from the northeast, from "below."[144] Five written variations of this story are known. All give the common groundwork of the legend, differing only in length and in details. I present the content of this legend, taking into consideration all its variations.

The ancestors of the Avam Nganasans lived somewhere to the east of their present habitation, beyond a big river or beyond a large body of water. In hunting wild deer they went far beyond this water, in the direction of where they live now. Then they dressed differently and, in particular, wore the same short open parkas that are worn now by their women. They were wild, warlike people, good archers. They were not acquainted with nets and speared their fish. Once, they decided not to return "beyond the big water" and remained in the region of their summer hunts. Sometimes this decision is explained by the "big water" not freezing in time, and sometimes even by the unexpected appearance of the "big water" on their return trip.

From the region of their summer hunt they move toward the southwest ("up") and find the Khantayka Somatu Samoyeds of whom they ask for wives. The Somatu refuse and a fight ensues near the Kamagu hill (two to three kilometers from the Dudypta river, near the settlement of the Staryy Barkatovskiy). The ancestors of the Nganasans expel the Somatu beyond the Pyasina (or even beyond the Yenisey). Thereafter, they make peace and exchange women. It is often told that the fight at Kamagu was not only with the Somatu but also with the Yuraks (Nenets), and sometimes only with the Yuraks, and that afterwards the Yuraks came anew to the land of the Nganasans and were defeated again. From the Somatu women the Nganasans got their present clothing because they [the women] did not know how to make any other kind. Meanwhile the Yuraks attack the Somatu and the latter ask the Nganasans for help, particularly of Timi-Khoti.

Usually the Nganasans say that the ancestors of all five clans arrived from "below," from beyond the "big water," but sometimes the Ngamtuso clan is excluded and they speak of only four clans, from each of which the Somatu are given one girl. (In reference to the Ngomde clan, it is stated at the same time that it always lived on the Taymyr; *vide supra*.)

In conclusion, the arrival of the Russians is related and how, by raising the authority of the "prince," the Russians stopped internecine fighting among the Nganasans.

Sometimes the subject of the last war with the Yuraks is developed as an independent subject, with Timi-Khoti as the hero (*vide supra*), and the story of still another collision with the Yuraks is added, in which the hero is Sanguda Chunanchera. The legend of Soymu-son and his fights with the Nenets and Tungus usually stands separately.

In conclusion the episode of the killing of 30, or 12, or 7, cossacks is also introduced (recollection of the happenings of 1666).

The universal elements in all these legends with their variations are: the arrival from "below" in the course of going for a wild deer hunt beyond the "big water"; the meeting of the Somatu, the Kamaga fight, the driving away of the Somatu, marriage ties, and acquisition of the language and culture of the Somatu. The ethnic origin of the newcomers is not given in the legend. Very likely the Ngamtuso clan was included with the clans coming "from below" only later. As we have shown already, the better-informed Nganasans spoke without hesitation of the Ngamtuso coming from the "Tazov side," and the most conservative even considered them Somatu rather than Nganasan. The Yuraks (Nenets) were also included in the legend about the origin of the Nganasans later, probably under the influence of encounters with them on the Yenisey. As late as the 17th century there were no Yuraks on the Taymyr.

In 1927, A. P. Lekarenko recorded a legend, told by a Nganasan shaman of the Ngamtuso clan, Dyufade Kosterkin, about the origin of the Nganasans, of a totally different kind. It begins with a myth about the arrival of the first people and then tells about the arrival of the ancestors of the Nganasans, first at the Pyasina river, and about the consequent passage of a part of them to the Taymyr river. In this legend the Nganasans came from the southwest, i.e., they are shown arriving from the opposite direction [compared with the other legends]. Moreover, as we know, the usual story is that the Nganasans arrive at the Taymyr for the wild deer hunt, while in Dyufade's legend the ancestors of the Nganasans have deer, which they held tethered before coming to the Pyasina. But two of the deer ran away and thus came about the wild deer, i.e., it presents a concept of a totally different character. This legend probably reflects the appearance of the deer-breeding Samoyeds in the northern reaches of the Yenisey, who absorbed the aborigines and in particular the "raven" ancestors of Dyufade.

As far as the legend about the arrival of the ancestors of Nganasans from the east goes, it basically presents, in our opinion, the arrival at the Taymyr of the Tavgs from beyond the Khatanga, i.e., the arrival of the ancestors of the Chunanchera and Ninonde clans. The Linanchera and Ngomde were probably included in the legend later, when the different histories of the Avam Nganasan clans were forgotten. For this reason, the legend now includes the Ngamtuso clan also. The "Somatu Samoyeds," whom the ancestors of the Tavgs met, according to legend, after their arrival at the Taymyr, are probably ancestors of the Ngomde clan, that is, of the "Pyasida Samoyeds."

In this legend is reflected the early phase of Tavg history during which they, as a result of constant contact and marriage with the "Pyasida Samoyeds," acquired the Samoyed language, and those elements of material and spiritual culture that are now characteristic for both the Nganasans and Enets.

As pointed out by G. N. Prokofyev, words that are lacking in the [present-day] Nenets language and that represent the "heritage maintained in the Nganasan language from the Samoyed language of the Sayan highlands"[145] were most probably introduced into the Nganasan language by the Kuraks and "Pyasida Samoyad."

Legend about the Wars with the "Sewnfaces"

In addition to the basic legend about their origin presented above, the Nganasans have a special cycle of legends that they also tell in response to a request to tell something about their past. Over 30 texts of this cycle that have been recorded thus far are legends of the type that can be united under a common name of "Legends about the wars with the 'sewn faces.'"

These legends remind us of the folklore of the northern Yakuts and northwestern Tungus, among whom they are known as the "Olenek Khosun epos," and have a distribution from the Khatanga to the Yana.

Although the subjects of Nganasan legends about wars with the "Sewnfaces" are very diverse, particularly in their details, they may be divided into five basic groups.

(1) A "Tundra" Tungus is hunting wild deer near the mountains to the south of the tundra. From the mountains, from the south, there comes to him on foot a tattooed man, literally a *khoro-sochema* (*Fora-sochema*), i.e., a "Sewnface," a Forest Tungus, and remains to spend the night. The master of the reindeer tent guesses the intention of the guest to kill him and his family, takes measures, looks out for him outside the tent, and in the ensuing combat during the night, gains a victory. In the mountains not far from his tent the "Tundra" Tungus finds the sled of his guest, kettles with fat (sometimes human fat), a bow, a spear (*palma*), and a dog tethered to the sled. There are variants where the Forest Tungus come one after another and the third kills the master of the tent. However, the son of the latter flees to the tundra and assembles his kinsmen and goes to avenge his father. Sometimes the "Tundra" Tungus, after his victory over the Forest Tungus, finds Somatu Samoyeds in the tundra and joins them, or the opposite: a Somatu Samoyed comes to the Tundra Tungus and settles with him. In some versions either the Tundra Tungus himself or the Somatu Samoyed forgets a hatchet and returns to pick it up. In the abandoned camp there appears a "wild Tungus" from whom he saves himself only thanks to the fleetness of his riding deer. In this case the riding deer is given to the Somatu Samoyed by his friend, the Tundra Tungus.

(2) A Somatu Samoyed is hunting wild deer near the mountains to the south of the tundra. In his absence a *khoro-sochema,* a Forest Tungus named Chinchir,[146] arrives and abducts his wife. Then the Samoyed meets a "Tundra" Tungus, who undertakes to help him. They both go south, kill the abductor and his numerous men, and free the Samoyed's wife. Out of gratitude the Samoyed gives his metallic armor to the Tundra Tungus. Afterward either the Tungus joins the Samoyeds, or he is later killed by the Forest Tungus and the surviving members of his family join the Samoyeds.

(3) On the bank of a big river in the forested tundra in a semisubterranean hut (*golomo*) lives a poor old man, a Tundra Tungus (or Nganasan), with his sons. This old man is a shaman, and his name is Lakuna. His oldest sons, including one named "Red Skis," are killed by Forest Tungus during a hunt for wild deer. The old man dies. The continuation of the story has two versions: (*a*) The sons of Lakuna (usually the younger ones) go to the land of the "sewnface" Forest Tungus and live with them. The Tungus attempt to kill them. But the sons of Lakuna annihilate the Tungus, free their fellow tribesmen who are held captive by the Forest Tungus, and finally return to the tundra. (*b*) After the death of the father, the brothers settle on the same river, only lower along its flow, at a "spearing place" [i.e., ford] where they kill many wild deer. From up-river there comes to them a large horde of deer-riding Forest Tungus. For some time the brothers live with them but then they annihilate the Forest Tungus. After that the brothers find their tribesmen, go together with them to the land of the Forest Tungus, and free their sisters-in-law. On the way to the land of the Forest Tungus the brothers kill the soul of the Tungus shaman which sits on top of a tree in the form of a falcon.

(4) Tundra Tungus hunting wild deer in the forested tundra are attacked at night by tattooed Forest Tungus who have arrived on riding deer. Later, the Tundra Tungus, sometimes in alliance with the Samoyeds, go to take vengeance on the Forest Tungus and annihilate them, usually with the exception of one elusive Tungus in a white parka, made of polar fox skin.

In these legends there are almost always included such details as an old shaman-seer, the soul of the enemy shaman in the guise of a bird on a high tree, wild deer swimming across the river to reveal themselves as masked avengers, the leap of a pursued Tungus over a river, a wound in the heel tendon, and so on, details characteristic of the Olenek Khosun epos.

(5) Here we have several variants, united by the important role the bears play in them. (*a*) Bears steal fish from an old shaman, a Tundra Tungus (very similar to Lakuna). The old man dances with a bear and during the dance kills him. Then, tattooed Forest Tungus either attack the old man or intend to attack him. In the first version he kills them in a fight. In one such legend the old man is called Linanchera directly. In the second version the old man kills an elk with iron hair, thus killing the chief shaman of the Forest Tungus. (*b*) Bears kill a Tundra Tungus hunter. His sons settle with the Forest Tungus, but afterwards kill them, including a smith, move to the tundra, and there the surviving son of the hunter, a Tundra Tungus, settles among the Samoyeds and marries one of their girls. (*c*) The family of a Forest Tungus who is hunting wild deer, as well as he, are killed by other Forest Tungus. A surviving boy is brought up by bears, who live as people do. The boy grows up and, following the advice of an old bear, annihilates his enemies. Thereafter, the son of the bear's ward settles with the Tundra Tungus in the forested tundra region, from where he, together with the Samoyeds, makes another march against the Forest Tungus.

With these short accounts we have not covered even the basic content of the legends, not to speak about the details. These legends are so popular that they are known to every Nganasan, and each of the legends can be written down not in three or four or five or six versions, but literally in dozens of them.

In these legends the following is of interest to us at the present:

(1) Although these legends are considered genuinely Nganasan (this is often emphasized), the main actors in them are the Tundra Tungus.

(2) In these legends there are the Tundra Tungus, who have complete Nganasan sympathy; there are the enemies, *khoro-sochema*, Forest Tungus; and there are the Somatu Samoyeds. As a rule, the Nganasans themselves do not appear, or they appear in some of the later versions in place of the Somatu Samoyeds or the Tundra Tungus.

(3) The typical situation in these legends is the alliance between the Tundra Tungus and the Somatu Samoyeds against the Forest Tungus, attacking them from the south. The wild deer hunt is included in all Nganasan legends of this type.

In the Olenek Khosun epos we also have two conflicting parties. One, personified by Yungkebil and his brother Edzhen-khosun [warrior], lives in the tundra and forested tundra and is being attacked. The other, personified by Uren or Chempere and their men, attacks from the south.

In the Nganasan legends about the wars with the "Sewnfaces," the place of Yungkebil and his brothers is taken by the Tundra Tungus ("Dolgans" according to present-day explanations of the Nganasans), while the place of Uren, Chempere, and their men *khoro-sochema*, the "Sewnfaces," by the Forest Tungus headed by Chinchir.

The Olenek Khosun epos, in various regions of its circulation, was apparently connected to concrete local, historical events. Complete analysis of it does not fall within the framework of this study. But there is no doubt about its importance for the Nganasans. They or, more correctly, their ancestors—the Tavgs and Tidiris—conserved in it the intertribal wars experienced by them, their retreat to the tundra, and their uniting with the Samoyeds. Calling the heroes of the epos "Dolgans" is certainly a later addition, when the Tavgs and Tidiris themselves became Samoyeds and lost the knowledge that in their time they were Tungus. At the same time, and I note this specifically, the Nganasans never considered the present-day Dolgans their relatives. Regarding the Somatu Samoyeds, who play a role in these legends, they are, first of all, supposed to be the ancestors of the Ngomde clan, "Pyasida Samoyeds."

Thus, data from folklore confirm the existence of Tungus elements in the composition of the ancestors of the Avam Nganasans, i.e., confirm the conclusion at which we arrived by analyzing historical materials. Which of these legends are connected directly with the origin of the Tavgs, i.e., reflect their history, and which reflect that of the Tidiris, is difficult to say now. It may be only suggested that those legends that are close to the typical Olenek legends were introduced into Nganasan folklore by the Tavgs and, to the contrary, those legends with Tungus heroes that have no parallel on the Olenek probably formed the folklore of the Tidiris, the more westerly Tungus, whose culture, including folklore, was created under different conditions.

Toponymy and Lexicology

The toponymy in Nganasan territory is rather complex. At present, most rivers there have two, and sometimes three names: Russian, Nganasan, and Yakut.

However, there is a group of large rivers that have the same names in all these languages, which can be derived from existing data on the Tungus language or which exist in Tungus regions.

The river Taymyr, or Taymuramu, has a namesake in the river Taymur, a large left tributary to the Nizhnyaya Tunguska. The Nganasans are unable to translate the name Taymyr or Taymura, but say that the river got its name from the fact that there were many wild deer and fish taken from it and that it is a rich, abundant river. And, actually, Taymyr was the foremost region for hunting wild deer. From the mouth of the Gorbita to the discharge of the Taymyr into Lake Taymyr, ten "spearing places" [pokolka] were counted. There was no such high number on any other river, excepting perhaps the Olenek. In Tungus, *tamura* means "dear," "valuable."[147] The Tungus translated the name *Taymura* for us as "dear," "bountiful," "generous." In Nganasan the name of the river Taymyr is pronounced *Taymuramu; amo, amut* in Tungus is "lake." The word *amo* is often added to the names of lakes or rivers flowing through lakes. Thus the river and lake Khantayka are called *Putor-amo.* Consequently, the river Taymyr, which flows through Lake Taymyr, should be called *Taymur-amo* in Tungus, which corresponds completely to the Nganasan *Taymuramu.*

The river Lagota, a right tributary to the Taymyr, is the main region of summer nomadizing for the Nganasans of Route V. At its mouth is found the greatest "spearing place" and also the richest place for under-ice fishing. The Nganasans also cannot translate the word *Logata* in terms of their present-day Samoyed language, but they say that the river got its name because particularly large numbers of wild deer were hunted there, so that it "was all filled in with hooks for meat drying." In Nganasan the hook for drying meat is called *teder,* but in Tungus it is called *logan.* The suffix *ta* or *da* (*nda, ngda*) is usual in Tungus names for rivers and lakes—Changada, Chavida, Ingoda, Khuringda, Agata, Murukta, etc.

The river Gorbita (sometimes Gormida) is also one of the favorite regions for summer nomadizing of the Nganasans of Route V. Near its mouth, on the Taymyr river, there are two "spearing places." Today, the Nganasans are unable to translate the word *gorbita,* but say that the origin of the name is due to the fact that molting geese were hunted on this river. "The heads of geese out here came as thick as a forest." In Nganasan the place for geese hunting is *deptuluto.* In Tungus *gor* means "molting bird," *gorkit,* "place of bird molting," *gormimi,* "hunting during bird molting time," etc.[148]

The origin of the name of the river Yangoda, the principal region of summer nomadizing for the Nganasans of Route IV, was explained thus: "It flows among treeless mountain ranges." In Nganasan a mountain range without forest is called *koadya* (*khodya*).[149] In Tungus *yang* means "treeless plateau," "hill," "barren."

The name of one of the large right tributaries of the upper Taymyr where the Nganasans using Route IV go for wild deer hunting, the river Dëgadë (in Yakut, Luktakh), is explained by the Nganasans as follows. In the past there was an encounter between the ancestors of the Nganasans and the Somatu Samoyed. Retreating, the "Somatu crossed that river." At this, the Nganasans would explain that river is *yakha* (*dyakha*) in Enets. But in Tungus this name is explained very exactly: *dyaga-si-m* means simply "to cross the river."[150] The name of the river Avam means, in Tungus, "wide" (applied to fabrics, cloth),[151] i.e., in the sense of "wide strip."[152]

The name of the river Khatanga is also a Tungus one. It coincides with the names of rivers Nizhnyaya [Lower] and Podkamenaya [Stony] Tunguska (Katanga). The river Kheta, a tributary of the Khatanga, in addition to its Samoyed name (i.e., Enets—cf. the rivers Bolshaya [Great] and Malaya [Little] Kheta, tributaries of the Yenisey south of Dudinka), has also a Tungus one, Lama.

Thus, not only are the names of large rivers of the Taymyr found to be Tungus, but concerning a number of these rivers, the Nganasans remembered even the meaning of these names, although they do not speak the Tungus language any more.

But this situation prevails only in the territory of Routes IV and V and partially of Route III. All regions of Routes I and II are situated within the Samoyed zone or, in their more southern parts, in the zone of Russian-Yakut toponymy.[153]

The present-day Tungus appeared in the "Zatundra" only in the 18th century and occupied but its southern edge ("Kamen"*). They did not nomadize on the Logata, Gorbita, Dyagade, or Yangode. True, now they occupy the upper reaches of the Avam, but this name existed in the 17th century too, and then only the ancestors of the Nganasans lived there. No doubt, the ancestors of the Nganasans, the Tavgs, brought this Tungus toponymy to the Taymyr. G. N. Prokofyev quotes the Nganasan words *nyamy*, "doe," and *turku*, "sled," which have the same meaning in Tungus dialects.[154] To this could be added the word *satera*, "polar fox," which is *chatara* in Tungus, *seroko*, *sedoro* in Enets, and *nokho* in Nenets. But the most interesting point is that the name for wild deer, the main source in the economy of the ancestors of the Nganasans, is closer to the Tungus name and has nothing to do with the Samoyed expression. In Nganasan wild deer is *bakhi, bafi*; in Tungus, *bae-n, beyu-n*; in Lamut, *buyu-n*[155]; while in Enets it is *kere, kede* and in Nenets, *ilebts*.

The Nganasans sometimes liked to show off by using what they called "ancient" words. In telling a legend they would have the hero address the fleeing wounded deer with the word *boyëna*. They often called dried meat *ulikta*, etc. All these words were found to be Tungus. The name of the old shaman Lakuna, one of their ancestors, the Nganasans translated as "tubercular." He is represented as such in a legend. In Tungus *lekin* means "tuberculosis."[156] The name of Lakuna's son, "Red skis," is *Khula-tuta* or *Dyurama-tuta* in Nganasan; "red" in Nganasan is (according to Castren) *Yabakua*, and "skis," *tuta*; in Tungus "red" is *khula-ma*.

In the legend about the first Nganasan shaman (also not a Samoyed but a Tundra Tungus) there is the following episode. When the hero of the legend destroys the camp of the "Sewnfaces," the Forest Tungus, from the last small tent a worker of the Forest Tungus, Nyukhoy, comes out and wounds the hero with an arrow, so that the latter is compelled to flee. This Nyukhoy, it turns out, was a "Russian physician," a shaman. In the end the hero, bringing into play his shamanistic powers, conquers Nyukhoy but not without difficulty. According to the narrator's explanation, one Togo Ngomde, also a shaman, Nyukhoy used snuff, and from that comes his name. It is clear that in a legend about the first shaman the presence of a Russian physician and explanation of his name by a Russian verb "nyukhat" [to sniff] is more than doubtful.

In the Olenek Khosun epos, Uren and Chempere often have a worker, *Nyuchcha*, i.e., "Russian" (in Yakut). No doubt, the Russian workman, the physician Nyukhoy in the Nganasan legend, and the workman Nyuchcha of the Olenek Yakuts, all are one and the same person.

In Lamut, a Yakut is called *nëka*.[157] We recorded this word from the Tompon Lamuts as *nyukho* in 1945. Thus, both the physician Nyukhoy of the Nganasans and the worker Nyuchcha of the Olenek epos were probably Yakuts. But in the first case, the ancestors of the Nganasans, keeping the original form of the word

*["Stone," "stony."—Editor.]

and having already forgotten their former language, explained it by use of the Russian word *nyukhat,* and in the second case, the Yakut narrators, who also did not understand it, connected it with the word *nyuchcha* ("Russian")—and also arrived at [the explanation] "Russian workman."

It may be assumed, therefore, that both the legends of the Nganasans and the Olenek Khosun epos were originally told in a language close to Lamut and that the epos was composed at the time when the Yakuts had already appeared among the Tungus-speaking tribes of northern Siberia.[158]

The name of a 17th century Tavg princeling Udamula or Adamula (Adamylya) obviously has a Tungus character. Among the Tungus the suffix *vul* is very characteristic in forming proper male names.[159] The sound *v* is altogether lacking in the Nganasan language and usually *m* or *b* is used in place of it. In Tungus the name Adavul means "elusive."[160]

For indicating the Tungus and Dolgans, the Nganasans use the word *asya* (singular) and *adya-aya* (plural). Castren construed this word as "younger brother"[161] probably by consonance with *ngadya-ma, ngaya-ma,* "younger brother, sister." Castren, as we know, was dealing with the most western Nganasans, who have the Enets tendency to omit the initial letters *ng* and *n.* Among the eastern Nganasans, *adya* and *ngadya* would not be confused. K. M. Rychkov derives the Nganasan *asya, aya* from the Evenk *aya,* "good-hearted," "good."[162] This explanation is hardly acceptable.

The basin of the middle and lower reaches of the Olenek was occupied in the 17th century by a Tungus tribe called by the Russians Adyan-y, Azyan-y, or Ozyan-y.* The descendants of this tribe are the Dolgans of the Edyan and Karanto clans, 323 persons in 1926; a "Yakutized" Tungus "clan" in the region of Buluna, the Ezhanets, 70 persons in 1897; the Ezhen clan in the Kangalas camp [nasleg] of Bulunsk okrug, 69 persons in 1916; in all about 500 people. In 1645, in just three clans of the Adyan tribe—the Galaniyev (Shanyan), Gaziyev, and Karatun—there were 85 tribute payers, i.e., about 350 persons. Besides, it possibly contained also the Nemnin and Andrizin clans. According to I. S. Gurvich, the tribe contained up to 500 persons.

Castren spelled the name of the "Edyan" Dolgans who lived in his time at Lake Pyasina, "Adyan," i.e., as it was spelled in the 17th century by the Russians on the Olenek.[163] It seems natural to suggest that the ancestors of the Nganasans were neighbors of the Adyans and transferred their name to all of the Tungus.

To be neighbors of the Adyans, the ancestors of the Nganasans, the Tavgs, must have lived between the Khatanga and the mouth of the Olenek, in the basins of the rivers Anabar and Popigay. As we know, the Tavgs lived just in those places.

The present population of the lower reaches of the Popigay and of the tundra between it and the Anabar used to move to the Taymyr peninsula in the summer to hunt wild deer. To do this they went into the tundra towards the northwest, crossed the lower reaches of the Khatanga on the ice, and went on deep into the Taymyr to Portnyagin lake, into the basins of the rivers Bolshaya Balakhna and others. They returned by the same route. Apparently the ancestors of the Tavgs from beyond the Khatanga used the same route in going to the Taymyr for wild deer hunting (from which comes the Tungus hunting toponymy in the Taymyr, as mentioned above). When they ceased to return to beyond the Khatanga, i.e., "below," and moved from the tundra to the forests of the Boganida

*[These are plural forms in Russian in which the plural-forming suffix has been separated by the author in order to emphasize the stem.—Editor.]

and Kheta basins, i.e., "up," then Route VI was formed, over which probably the Tavgs of Adamul nomadized in the beginning of the 17th century.

By the time the Russians arrived beyond the Khatanga, the Tavgs had as neighbors, in addition to the Adyans, also the Chinagir Tungus (Sinigir). As we have already pointed out, the latter were apparently the subjects of the Olenek and Nganasan legends that mention Tungus headed by Chinchir (Chinkire). Apparently, the encroachment of the warlike Chinagirs (Sinigirs) forced the Tavgs to leave westward from the Khatanga. Nowadays, the lower reaches of the Anabar are occupied by the "Yakutized" Sidemi Tungus in whom, as in the "Yakutized" Tungus of the Beti camp area, may be seen the descendants of the Chinagirs (Sinagirs) of the 17th century.

Thus, in the Nganasans merged the extreme northeastern Samoyed or "Samoyedized" groups and the extreme northwestern Tungus or "Tungusized" groups. The prevalence in the crossing of these languages was achieved by the Samoyed language and, specifically, the Tavg dialect of the latter, which became the basis of the Nganasan language. The solution of the question of how the northeastern groups of Samoyeds, i.e., the Kuraks and the "Pyasida Samoyad," were formed is connected with the problem of the origin of the Enets. We intend to take up this subject in a special work. There remains only to say a few words about the formation of those Tungus groups of the extreme north, whose "Samoyedized" descendants compose not only the Vadeyev but also the majority of the Avam Nganasans.

The Uldycha Samoyeds and the Khuldicha Yukagirs

The Tungus and Yakut term *samail, samaydar* (doubtlessly borrowed from the Russians) reflects the present-day Samoyed ethnic affiliation of the Nganasans but it hardly could have been applied to them before the arrival of the Russians, when they were not, as yet, Samoyeds.

K. M. Rychkov relates that, according to Tungus tradition, in the past the Samoyeds (by context it is clear that this pertained to the Nganasans)

occupied the present-day territory of a northwestern group of Tungus clans (i.e., of the Goragir tribe, now actually inhabiting the territory which was in part occupied by the Tavgs and Tidiris in the 17th century—Author) which pushed out the Samoyeds into the depth of tundra, northward . . . judging by traditions, the Tungus had to fight the Samoyed tribesmen, the Uldyga, who customarily used tattooing . . . while the Samoyeds . . . had to push out the Chukchis. No trace remained of the Uldyga and Chukchis but the Samoyed clans are also rapidly dying out.[164]

On the Taymyr they often talk about the Chukchis.[165] In Nganasan legends the Chukchis are sometimes presented as possessing utterly unhuman features. In Lamut *chukcha* means "evil spirit." The Nganasans apparently retained some legends about these spirits and retained the very term from their Tungus-speaking (Lamut) past. On the other hand, though, some tales about the Chukchi could have penetrated to the Nganasans through the Tungus-Yukagir environment related to them. Regarding the legend, recorded by A. A. Popov, in which the Chukchis appear beyond the Khatanga, it is most probably related to the folklore of Russian old-timers in northern Siberia and was cast under the influence of Russian-Chukchi contact on the Kolyma.[166]

For us the name *Uldyga* in Rychkov's report is interesting. We think that here we have a misprint (there are many in this work of Rychkov), and that instead of *Uldyga* it should read *Uldycha*. The Uldycha Samoyeds in the given case could have been only the ancestors of the Tavg Nganasans (and Tidiris). As the late G. D. Verbov told me, the Enets and Nenets still have a notion that the Nganasans formerly used to tattoo themselves, The word *uldycha* is explained by the Tungus expression *khuldi-mi*, "to sew through with thread," *khuldicha* [therefore] "a sewn, tattooed face."[167] The initial *kh* in Tungus is often omitted. For instance, *khunat—unat*, "girl," *khuto—uto*, "son."[168] Thus, the Uldycha could have been the tattooed "Samoyeds."[169]

But the term *khuldicha* or *uldycha* has another, a more definite, and to us a more interesting meaning. According to V. G. Bogoraz, "Khuldicha is the Tundra Tungus-Yukagir (among the Indigirka Lamuts)."[170]

A name of an ethnic group in northern Siberia, formed because of some distinguishing but not necessarily exclusive peculiarity, may afterwards turn into a proper name. The Lamut term for the Yukagirs, *bulen, bolen,* has undoubtedly in its root the word *bule*, "bog," "swamp," "tundra." We have also the Lamut and Tungus *bulen*, "enemy," and the Tungus *bulen-mi*, "to wage war," "to be at war." Thus, the term for inhabitants of tundras, swamps, became a term to indicate enemies in general and the Yukagirs in particular.[171] The Khuldicha Tungus-Yukagirs of the "Great Tundra" between the Indigirka and Kolyma called themselves, according to Jochelson, Voduls, i.e., Yukagirs, and spoke a Yukagir dialect. At the end of the 19th century they comprised four tribes, each headed by a princeling, but forming a confederation with a common "head." The confederation consisted of: the *Alai* (the First Alazey "clan"), the aboriginal Yukagirs of the Great Tundra; the *Dudki* (the Second Alazey "clan"), the offspring of a "Lamutized" Yukagir tribe of the Indigirka basin; the *Khodeydzhil* (the Second Kamenno-Lamut "clan"), a part of the "Lamutized" Yukagirs, the "Khodynets" of the 17th century, immigrants from the eastern bank of the Kolyma; the *Vagaril* or *Bagaril* (a Betil Tungus "clan") which considered itself immigrant from the "Yakut side." Apparently, it was this clan that paid tribute in the Ust-Yansk winter quarters as Yukagirs of the Petay "clan" in the 17th century.

Data on the numerical strength of the composite parts of the Khuldicha confederation are given in Table 14.

In 1897, the 66 families of the Khuldicha had 1020 reindeer in all. Like the Nganasans, they also nomadized in a meridional direction. In summer, they met the Chukchi in the tundra; in winter, they met Yakuts and Russians[172] in the forested tundra. Ethnographically, in spiritual and material culture, the Khuldicha (according to Jochelson) were a complete unit, although according to the latest data of I. S. Gurvich they still preserve two languages—Tungus and Yukagir.

TABLE 14

Names of tribal groups	Number of males and females	
	1850	1859
Alai	99	86
Dudek	58	45
Khodeydzhil	151	141
Vagaril	287	264
Total	595	536

It is not difficult to see that approximately the same conditions existed for the Khuldicha in the 19th century as for the ancestors of the Nganasans in the 17th century. Separate groups of the ancestors of the Avam Nganasans also had separate princelings in the beginning of the 17th century, and only with the passage of time did they merge into one tribe. At that, to trace those composite parts from which the tribe of Avam Nganasans was formed represents a very difficult task, while with the Khuldicha they are clearly visible.

The Khuldicha Yukagirs remind us of the Uldycha Samoyeds not only in the history of the organization of their tribal self-government and the merging of the groups, which formed the confederation into one tribe. Both the Uldycha Samoyeds and the Khuldicha Yukagirs undoubtedly represent the remains of an aboriginal population that lived in the north of Siberia before the arrival there of the Samoyeds and Tungus. The Yukagirs appear to be such an aboriginal population. To the east of the Lena, the Khuldicha and the Upper Kolyma Yukagirs also preserved their language. To the west of the Lena, they were completely absorbed by the Tungus and, afterwards, partially by the Samoyeds. Therefore, in the west, only the Tungus can be discerned in the composition of the Uldycha Samoyeds.

The following should be noted. Although, judging by tradition and toponymy, the ancestors of the Nganasans were close to the Tungus (Lamut) tribes, it was impossible to find among them, as already indicated, even a hint of identification with the present-day Tungus or Dolgans. Further, even in 1926–7 there existed a certain estrangement between the Nganasans and the neighboring Tungus groups.

The same was true to the east of the Lena. Entire Yukagir tribes, the Khodeydzhil, Dudki, the greater part of the Omolon Yukagirs, were "Lamutized." Individual groups of Lamuts (the Second Kamenno-Delyan "clan") became Yukagirs. And still Yukagirs had no doubt about the difference between them and the Lamuts, and there existed a feeling of certain estrangement if not enmity between the two peoples.[173]

There is no doubt that the Tavgs who came from the east were not originally Samoyeds. But, although they spoke Tungus in the past, they were not Tungus (Lamut) in origin. It is proposed that the ancestors of the Nganasans were some other element, neighbors to the Tungus (Lamuts) who borrowed from them, at some time, the language, probably reindeer-breeding, etc., but who retained the cognizance of their differences from the native, rooted Tungus tribes.

The Nganasans were firmly convinced that somewhere to the east there live the people from whom their ancestors originated and separated. Almost every Nganasan with whom we talked about their origin asked us in his turn if there was information that somewhere in the east there live their relatives. In this situation they did not want to hear about the Western Samoyeds, the Nenets.

In particular the Avam Nganasans related that "once a Yakut went far beyond the Khatanga, to the east. Having crossed two big rivers, between which is situated the country of the "Wild," "Shaggy-haired" Tungus, he found near the Chukchis a people from whom once separated the ancestors of the "Nya" (i.e., the Avam Nganasans). The men of this people wear parkas . . . similar to those worn by the Tavg Samoyed women (i.e., buttoned in the front), with a collar of a polar fox's tail. Their hats are made of dog skin with a reindeer tail worn as a plume over the forehead (similar to the Sokuyev Tavgs). Returning home (the story is about a Yakut from the Khatanga basin), this Yakut became ill and before he died he said in addition that this people still had the names of all five Avam blood-related clans and that their "prince," when talking to him, confirmed that once a part of his tribe went to the west, and "from that time it is not known what happened to this part." In 1948, I recorded an analogous legend about relatives of Nganasans living near the Chukchis. In this case, however, the trip to the east is taken not by a Yakut, but by a "Yurak" (i.e., a Nenets).

Most probably, these legends of the Avam Nganasans are foggy notions about Yukagirs and an echo of the awareness of their kinship to them. The Nganasans know the Tungus, Dolgans, and Yakuts very well, and if they considered themselves originating from one of these peoples, it would not be difficult for them to show this. Possibly we have here a confusion of some information about the Khuldicha (in later times the Yukagirs nearest to the Nganasans who still retained their language) obtained by them from some worldly wise Yakut.[174]

As is known, the Khuldicha are neighbors of the Chukchi and the Bolshaya Chukochya river flows in the region of their nomadizing. This circumstance may also have helped, to a certain extent, to revitalize the legend about Chukchis on the Taymyr and the appearance of the Kolyma-oriented episode about Chukchis beyond the Khatanga, recorded by Popov.

Concerning the details about the clothing and hats of the eastern relatives of the Nganasans, here we may have something of a remembrance of the ancient clothing. But then, judging from Jochelson's photographs, the Khuldicha do wear loose parkas resembling those of Nganasan women and their hats do resemble those of the Nganasan women.

Comparative Ethnographic and Archaeological Data

At present, unfortunately we can not use with complete assurance the available data for a comparative analysis of the material and spiritual culture of the Ngnasans and Yukagirs for the solution of the problem at hand. A great amount of preparatory work is yet necessary for a comparative ethnographic description of the peoples of northern Siberia in order to establish the characteristics of individual peoples, to isolate that which is common in the culture of larger groupings of northern Siberian peoples, to determine what is borrowed and what the source is, to trace the spread of the elements of culture, their evolution, and so on.

In an attempt to solve the genesis of the present material and spiritual culture of the Nganasans, we are immediately confronted by a number of questions.

Thus, for instance, the Nganasans themselves consider their present-day clothing borrowed from the Enets. However, with this Nganasan-Enets clothing there is connected the Tungus way of carrying the knife. This detail is probably an ancient common possession of the Paleo-Asiatic hunters, Yukagirs, and from them, of the Tungus, Enets, Nganasans, and others, and it was not borrowed by the Nganasans from the Enets. In any case, it is not the way the Nenets carry their knives. It is very uncomfortable in sleigh riding and in getting into the sled from the left side, and the Nenets say that if one hurriedly gets into a sled with a knife on the leg, the way the Nganasans wear it, it is easy to break a leg.

The Enets-Nganasan parkas (*lu*) are themselves a rather puzzling item. This is a completely closed garment with a hood, but short and completely unlike the Nenets long parka, the *malitsa*. In particular, the hood of the Nganasan-Enets parka is cut out together with the back of the parka, while the Nenets hood is simply a cap sewn to the parka. In the north, parkas with hoods were not exclusive to the Nganasans. Jochelson suggests that the Yukagirs, before they started wearing their Lamut clothing (during the time we knew them), used a completely closed garment of the "Paleo-Asiatic type."[175]

Examination of the cut shows that the Nganasan parka has no connection with the Nenets parka (*malitsa*) and represents a more archaic type of a completely closed garment. While the *malitsa* is a garment of sled-using reindeer-breeders, the Nganasan-Enets parka is still a garment of foot hunters. When looking at a Nganasan parka from the front, an impression is gained that its trim resembles the Tungus-Lamut apron (which existed also among the Yukagirs in Jochelson's time) and that it represents a loose parka onto which the apron is sewn at both [side-]hems, thus forming the present-day closed parka. From the rear the trim and the cut of the *lu* very much resemble the ancient Tungus parka. On the other hand, the *lu* of the Nganasans also resembles Eskimo clothing.

The peculiar Enets-Nganasan footwear without an instep is probably the result of a comparatively recent evolution. Middendorf presents a sketch of a Nganasan *bakar* [footwear made from reindeer skin—Editor] with a clearly indicated instep. The women's *bakar*, white in color—like almost all Nganasan clothing—always has a dark strip on both side of the boot top and along the foot exactly like those on the white footwear of the Yakuts and Dolgans in the basin of the Khatanga and farther to the east to the Lena, and also common among the Yukagirs living in the tundra between the Indigirka and the Kolyma.

The undergarments of Nganasan women resemble overalls without sleeves. The front of this garment has sewn on it, in this sequence, the following: copper half-moons, up to seven in number, garlands of copper rings, pipes, a needlecase, a flint on a heavy chain, a pipe-case, a tobacco pouch, and even small bells. With each step the woman takes, this mass of metal clanks.

Among the Yukagir women in the tundra to the east of the Indigirka (i.e., among the Khuldicha mentioned earlier), the leather apron under a parka made of reindeer skin

is draped with large, hammered copper and steel rings. On its belt hangs a flint . . . a large tin or copper needlecase . . . a smoking pipe with an embroidered tobacco pouch . . . a large bell . . . to the apron are also fastened glittering rings, apparently representations of the sun or moon . . . small cymbals and all kinds of noise-makers. All this clanks with every step the woman takes.[176]

To complete the resemblance, it may be pointed out that the combination undergarment of the Nganasan woman has no back and actually resembles trousers on to which a [high] apron is sewn. A parka, which is usually not tied inside the tent, is worn over it and thus all ornaments on the apron remain visible, similar to the case of the Yukagir women described above.

A number of other details in the everyday life of the Yukagirs in the tundra east of the Indigirka also remind one of the Nganasans: such as the pose of the Yukagir women, resting on one knee, while the other is free, in distinction from the men who sit with crossed legs; or the black band on white footwear. The resemblance would be even greater if the Khuldicha had not been baptized and subjected to the influence of Russian and Chukchi culture, and if the Nganasans had not undergone "Samoyedization."

With the Nganasans, as with the Enets and Nenets, the tent plan is such that areas on both sides of the tent are used for living space, i.e., on both the left and the right of the entrance, while the space beyond the fireplace, opposite the entrance, is not so used. The Tungus tent plan is directly opposite to this: in it the living area is around the walls of the tent, and space by the fireplace, opposite the entrance, is the most favored and honored. Among the Khuldicha Yukagirs and the Lamuts we also find a division of the tent in two halves, with the non-living area situated beyond the fireplace, opposite the entrance. True, with the Khuldicha, in distinction from the Upper Kolyma Yukagirs, the tent is not conical but of the *yaranga* type.

An additional detail may be pointed out. During the summer, the Lamut-Yukagir tent of the yaranga type has two entrances, opposite each other, on two sides of the fire.[177] The same arrangement is found in the Nganasan reindeer tent, which also has usually two entrances during the summer, the principal one from the southeast and the additional one from the northwest.

To this should be added a number of linguistic connections, in the vocabulary, but mainly in the morphology, discovered recently between the Samoyed (in particular the Nenets) languages and Yukagir.

There is also an opinion that the autonym *madu* of the tundra Enets represents a variation of *Vodu-l* (the autonym of the Khuldicha Yukagirs corresponding to *Odu* of the upper Kolyma).

Seroshevskiy describes Yukagir snow goggles, seen by him in the Irkutsk museum, as a thin silver plate with two narrow appertures.[178] Exactly the same type of snow goggles (with other types as well) is found among the Nganasans.

The resemblance between the Nganasans and Yukagirs becomes greater when we compare the importance which the "spearing hunt" [pokolka] had for them in the past. On the Kolyma this "spearing hunt" is called *na plavyakh.** In one Nganasan legend it is directly stated that their ancestors, in contradistinction to the Tungus, did not know how to hunt with decoys.

The Yukagir custom of removing the flesh from the bones of a deceased shaman is reflected in a Nganasan legend, in which the angered spirit of the fire (more correctly "mother of fire") causes a shaman to die in such a way that all his flesh crawls from his bones "as if it were boiled." In their wanderings the Yukagirs formerly carried with them the image of a dead shaman with his skull placed in a special wooden box.[179] Among the Nganasans, the "mother of fire" carries around the shaman caught by her in a wooden box.

The Yukagir custom of calling the parents by the name of their eldest child is usual among the Yakuts and Dolgans of the Khatanga and Anabar basins and among the Nganasans.

The skinning alive of wild reindeer for sport and the punishment for this in the consequent disappearance of wild deer, as told in the legend about the Mayats (*vide supra*), is known to the Nganasans and also figures in the Yukagir legend when reasons for the disappearance of deer on the Kolyma are given.[180] This episode is generally particular to Tungus legends about aborigines who lived to the north of them.

Before moving to the tundra in the spring the Nganasans used to erect gates of flagstones. After a shamanistic ceremony, all present passed through the gate.[181] Jochelson describes a similar custom for the Yukagirs:

When in the spring the Yukagirs prepare to hunt the elk (. . . wild deer), they build an arch of two trees with a crosspiece beam. On this arch they hang the pelts of a squirrel, hare or fox, ornament it with multicolored rags, ribbons, dyed deer hair and other sacrificial objects and, dressed in traveling clothes, with skis and ski-poles, the Yukagirs pass through the arch. . . .[182]

*[*Na plavyakh* may be loosely translated "in the bogs," i.e., those bogs adjacent to rivers where the deer would cross.—Editor.]

The ties of Nganasan culture with those of northeastern Siberia are undoubted. Examining a mummified body of a Yakut woman from an ancient burial, in September of 1945 in the Yakutsk museum, we were amazed by the detailed resemblance of her garment to the burial clothing of the Dolgans and Nganasans. On the belt of the deceased woman in the Yakutsk museum were suspended stamped, round copper pieces, and on the hems of her garment were sewn strips of leather also with a number of stamped copper plates of three merging circles. This is completely analogous to the ornaments which are necessary in a Nganasan female burial garment, made by the Nganasans themselves. Parenthetically, it should be noted that the everyday Nganasan female garment does not have an upper [outer] belt, but there is one on the burial garment and it is ornamented with silver and copper plates of the same type found on ornamented Yakut belts. In reference to the beaded ornament on the garment of the woman in the Yakutsk museum, it had, in its individual elements, a Dolgan character.

The Lamut-Tungus character of ancient Yakut clothing was known to us, but the resemblance of it to Nganasan burial garments was completely unexpected.

Necessary parts of the Nganasan female burial clothing were the little copper bells sewn onto it. These bells were characteristic of the female clothing of the tundra Yukagirs even in the beginning of our century and were seen sometimes on the everyday clothing of Nganasan women (vide supra).

According to Jochelson, the Yukagirs wore on the neck a special amulet in the form of a copper disk which they called "the chest sun." The Nganasans wore a similar copper disk, which they called dyaly-koyka-kousey, i.e., "the sun eye of the luck devil." In 1949, a specimen of such a Nganasan amulet was given by us to the Museum of Anthropology and Ethnography of the U.S.S.R. Academy of Sciences. The Nganasans thought that having this amulet was ". . . like holding the sun."

There are a number of parallels in Nganasan and Yukagir folklore. In Yukagir "heart" and "bravery" are synonyms.[183] The same is true of Nganasan: "This man has a heart," i.e., he is a brave man.

In the Yukagir fairy tale about the old man "White Eye," the hero kills a Lamut woman-shaman, who threatens to expose him, during her magic performance by throwing her into a boiling cauldron.[184] Among the Nganasans, Dyayku kills an old she-wolf shaman in a similar way, throwing her into a fire.[185] In this fairy tale the number of coinciding details is striking.

Among the Yukagirs, a son of a rich Lamut is killed; among the Nganasans it is the son of a rich Yakut, Karakkan-toyon. In the Yukagir tale, the Lamut woman-shaman has five sons about whom the old man "White Eye" is apprehensive, while with the Nganasans the she-wolf shaman comes with six pups— sons about whom Dyayku is apprehensive. In describing the burial of a Yukagir shaman, Jochelson writes: "On the Korkodon, the reindeer skin tent where the meat and the killed dogs lie was covered with earth and wood in the form of a tripod (pyramid)."[186] In one of the legends about Lakuna, his sons leave him after death in a golomo, i.e., in a conic structure covered with earth, and weigh it down with logs. A similar episode is found in another Nganasan legend, where the old shaman gets the corpse of his daughter from the grave, which is described by the narrator as a conic structure of logs. Generally, according to the Nganasans and the Madu Enets, in times past they always erected over a dead person, if he was being buried in the forest region, a wooden structure, which in Nganasan was called motalir ma.

Dogs played a big role in the Yukagir cult. They were placed with dead shamans. The Nganasans had a special dogs' god, *bana-nguo* [to whom] dogs were sacrificed and, during the tribal ceremony of the "clean tent," the poles of the tent were smeared with the blood of a killed dog.[187]

The number of these examples could be multiplied. The question is, to what extent do these or other elements of cultural similarity between the Nganasans and Yukagirs represent proof of a direct connection between them, and to what extent does this similarity represent the common cultural equipment of the peoples of northern Siberia?

Certainly, a number of the above-noted features, similar to both Nganasans and Yukagirs, are widespread among the northern Yakuts, Evenks, Selkups, and others. Here an extensive comparative-ethnographic study is necessary, but all in all, the existence of direct Yukagir-Nganasan ethnographic ties is indubitable, and those ties that exist among the Yukagirs and Nganasans in common with cultures of other peoples of northern Siberia also go back, to a certain extent, to their Paleo-Asiatic Yukagir substratum.

Archaeological materials of the ancient population of the territory inhabited by the Nganasans are limited to those of A. P. Okladnikov, contained in his article "Ancient settlements in the Khatanga river valley."[188] In 1945, Okladnikov discovered in four places, near the settlement of Khatanga on the bank of the Khatanga river, ancient cultural remains of the Neolithic and Early Iron ages. He establishes that a fragment of a large lamellar knife of black slate from the findings is analogous to the large retouched knives from sites in Yakutia, including those "of an early Bronze Age burial on the Bukachan river below Zhigansk, of the early settlement in old Siktyakh in Bulunsk rayon, and also of a Neolithic settlement in the locality of Kestruryunkya."

After describing the contents of the site with two fire pits (scrapers, gravers, arrowheads and spearheads, knives, punches, knifelike blades, fragments of large polished implements, and fragments of clay vessels), Okladnikov states:

> When these enumerated findings are examined, it is easy to see that they differ strongly from anything that has been discovered up to the present time in the inventories of Neolithic sites to the west of the Yenisey and in the southern reaches of Yenisey kray, beginning from Krasnoyarsk, where in many respects they come close to the Neolithic [complex] of the eastern Urals. They [the Khatanga finds] differ also from the Neolithic finds of the lower Angara, which in turn have a considerable resemblance to the Cis-Baykal area finds as was pointed out by us already in 1937.
>
> The objects found at Khatanga disclose in all their principal traits a full analogy with the Neolithic artifacts of the middle Lena and, partly, the lower Lena regions.[189]

Later, describing a thin-walled clay vessel with large, appliquéd cylinders, resembling the ceramics of the Early Iron Age of Yakutia, and a find of a potsherd, a few pebbles chipped over-all, a number of evenly sized large rough chips, three copper plates of an elongated rectangular shape, and two knifelike blades of chalcedony, also datable to the Early Iron Age, Okladnikov comes to the conclusion that

> even in the era of metals, the [material] culture of the inhabitants of the Khatanga region was very close to that of the neighboring regions of Yakutia.
>
> It is from there, from the east, that man probably settled these raw regions, in the depth of the Arctic, to the north of the 70th parallel, i.e., considerably farther north than any other region of the Soviet Union, where relics of the Neolithic type are known.[190]

On the other hand, in the valley of the Kolyma river, the basin of which was settled in the 17th century by the Yukagirs, there were "discovered Neolithic sites and workshops indicating that the settling of this river was carried out from the west, from the lower Lena (the Uolba culture)."

Paleo-Asiatics—The Hunters of Northern Siberia

In the preceding sections of this work we referred several times to the Olenek Khosun epos. We have at our disposal texts of this epos recorded in 1923–4 in the lower reaches of the Lena, my notes of 1936–9 taken on lake Yesey, and the notes of I. S. Gurvich of 1943–5 taken in the basins of the Olenek and Anabar. The most interesting for the purpose of the present work are the notes of I. S. Gurvich, made by him in the very center of the territory where the Olenek Khosun epos is found. These contain a number of details lacking in other notes. We use them, therefore, as the basis for further exposition.

The basic theme of the Olenek Khosun legendary epos is as follows: A Khosun living on the Olenek river, usually [named] Uren, is attacked by enemies. If they come from the north, they are usually headed by Yungkebil and his brothers; if from the south, they are usually headed by Chempere. Sometimes the encounter takes place between Yungkebil and Chempere. The Khosun is killed but his son grows up and revenges him.

The usual details of this theme are as follows: The heroes are hunting wild deer and live near "spearing places." The killer of Uren abducts his wife. The infant son of Uren is brought up by his old grandfather. Often Uren has a workman, the Nyuchcha mentioned earlier, who helps his enemies. Uren is killed by a wound in his knee or in his heel tendon, while jumping over a river. The enemies of Uren have a shaman who assures for them the successful outcome of the attack. The enemies steal near, usually in the guise of deer, and so on.

As was mentioned, Uren is usually attacked by Yungkebil and his brothers from the north. In the notes of Gurvich the Yakut narrators call them Mayats or Mayats-Samoyeds (Mayaattar-Samaydar) or Mayats-foreigners (Mayaattar-omuktar). These Mayats are placed not on the Yesey, which is situated to the west of the basin of the Olenek and where tradition locates the Mayats-Vanyads, the ancestors of the Vadeyev Nganasans, but either in the tundra at the seashore (in this case of Laptev Sea) or in the basin of the Anabar and in the lower reaches of the Olenek.

One Nganasan legend about the origin of the Khalo subdivision in the Chunanchera clan recorded by me begins with the phrase: "The Nganasans were born from the skin hairs of the wild deer." In a number of passages in the notes of Gurvich (including one from the lower Lena), the Mayats are often described by the epithet "numerous as the hair on the skin of a white deer" (maagan taba tiiüte akhsaannaakh mayaat omuk). According to Gurvich's text, the Olenek Yakuts explained the origin of this epithet thus: Once two women were disputing as to which deer skin contained more hair. The Mayat woman who had a white deer skin won. Clearly, the Olenek epithet about the Mayats and the ideas of the Nganasans about their origin are connected. The ancestors of the Nganasans are personified in the image of wild deer, their main source of existence, in the same way in which they themselves personify the Tungus in the image of the elk.

In one Nganasan legend, mentioned earlier, one of their ancestors, a shaman, kills an iron elk with bow and arrow. As a result of this the chief shaman of the hostile Tungus, who was approaching in the guise of an elk, dies. Another

Nganasan legend is a variation of the Olenek one about an attack of the Mayats on Uren, but told not from the point of view of the descendants of the Uren's fellow tribesmen (as on the Olenek), but from the point of view of the descendants of the Mayats. In this variation, the Nganasan shaman approaches the camp of hostile Tungus in the guise of a wild deer, which is similar to the Olenek legend in which the Mayats steal to the camp of Uren in the guise of wild deer.

According to Gurvich's data, the Olenek narrators definitely identify the Mayats and Samoyeds, i.e., Nganasans. A 72-year-old narrator, M. G. Grigoryev, answered Gurvich's bidding to tell something about Uren and the Mayats by saying, "Don't get confused, the Mayats are Samoyeds, but Uren lived long ago."

The following detail is very interesting. While the Olenek Tungus wore their hair in braids, and the Yakuts cut theirs, the Nganasans were, until recently, the only people in that part of Siberia who wore their hair long, loose, and falling to their shoulders. In Olenek Khosun legends recorded by Gurvich, the arrival of the Mayats is described as follows: "In the evening came the Mayats. There were as many of them as there are mosquitoes. At the head was the leader of the Mayats, Magan-Mekhche ("White Parka"), and after him came his brother, Yungkebil-Khosun, with long hair, like a woman's. . . ." Later, the son of Uren kills Yungkebil-Khosun, who gets entangled in his hair. In one text, recorded by Gurvich, from a story told by a 70-year-old man, Spiridonov, Taymyr is indicated as the place inhabited by the Mayats. And, a storyteller Anna Nikolayeva replied, when questioned about Yungkebil: "In the opinion of some, Yungkebil was a Yukagir."[191]

The population of the Olenek, personified by Uren or Chempere (Chimkire), fighting with Mayats-Samoyeds who live near the sea, is considered to be Tungus and in the Olenek Khosun epos it is given typically Tungus features, such as the braids, tattooing, aprons, and Tungus spears (*palmas*).* According to Nganasan traditions these Tungus rode deer. They apparently used iron, since in the Olenek legends smiths are usually mentioned, who supply the son of Uren with arms before his march against the Mayats. The Tungus also had slaves—prisoners-of-war. The usual outcome of the encounter of Yungkebil's Mayats and Uren's Tungus is the mass annihilation of the Mayats and the flight of the survivors.

It is understandable why the Olenek legends regard the Mayats as Samoyeds: the descendants of the Mayats are now really Samoyeds.

In all probability, folklore in the basins of the Khatanga, Anabar, and Olenek, in referring to the Mayats, considered them the ancient Paleo-Asiatic population of this region, a population known to the east of the Lena as the Yukagirs.

Folklore, recorded by us in the Lake Yesey region, reveals that the Mayats lived by hunting wild deer, which they killed at river crossings or in organized roundups [battue]. The Mayats were armed with bows, arrows, and spears. The tips of the arrows and spears were made of stone, elk antler, [fossilized] mammoth ivory, or a loon's beak. They did not keep tame deer or had very few. In the spring the Mayats used skis, in summer and winter they moved on foot. In hunting, the wild deer were surrounded and, after the ring of hunters was narrowed, they were killed with arrows. They also built fences (*tomu*) between two parallel flowing streams and at the entrance to these they set up bows which automatically discharged arrows when triggered, or placed noose snares made of twisted tendons. They lived in groups of 20 to 30 male hunters with a

*[*Palma*, a long knife fastened to a wooden shaft.—Editor.]

corresponding number of women and children. Among them only the best hunters, khosuns, were distinguished. The Mayats liked to attack their neighbors and take their supplies from them. The Mayats lived in semisubterranean huts (golomo), which were built all over their territory, one day's foot-march apart. After a "roundup" or "spearing hunt" the meat of the deer was placed in storage places or hidden in pits covered with skins and stones, at the very place of the hunt. Close to these storage places the Mayats immediately built a golomo or a mud hut and during the winter, when the hunt ceased, they would move from one storage place to another, living in the dwellings they had built earlier. From the skins of deer, the Mayats made closed parkas. Fish were secured by building screens across rivers and scooping the fish out. The Mayats did not have nets. The fire pits were made of clay. Water was kept in holes made in the clay with a mammoth's tusk. They made boxes of birch bark. They had no kettles and ate their meat either raw or fried.

How far these folkloristic data reflect the actual conditions is still a question. The finds of Okladnikov on the Khatanga establish that ceramics were used there in Neolithic times. But much of this seems plausible and may relate to a primitive, hunting population of northern Siberia, similar to the Yukagirs as they were until the arrival of the Tungus.

To the west of the Lena these Yukagirs were absorbed even before the 17th century partly by Samoyeds and partly by Tungus, and in the memory of the populace there remained only a legendary people retaining, in the basins of the Khatanga, Anabar, and Olenek, the name of "Mayats," of Tungus-Yakut origin.

Judging by Taymyr toponymy and other data (*vide supra*) and also by the proper names of the Mayats of the Olenek epos, which names have a Tungus character (Yungkebil, Dëgdoti, Edzhan), the ancestors of the Nganasans, the Mayats, changed over to the Tungus language early. In the legends of the Olenek epos are depicted not only encounters of the Mayats with the Olenek Tungus. In one text of Gurvich, the son of Uren-Khosun goes to the lower reaches of the Anabar to seek the daughter of Yungkebil in marriage. In Nganasan legends there are also episodes of cohabitation of Nganasans and the hostile Tungus. Because of such neighboring contacts the Paleo-Asiatic Yukagirs (Mayats) no doubt lost their own language in the course of centuries.

The struggle of Mayats-Yukagirs with the Tungus, as reflected in the epos, was carried out mainly for the possession of hunting grounds, spearing places, and regions for the roundup of wild deer. In the Nganasan legends of the Olenek type it is told how, to the ancestors of the Nganasans, waiting at the spearing places, there come the Tungus from the upper reaches of the river looking for a place to hunt wild deer. The Tungus are not always the aggressors. In the texts of Gurvich and of others, the Mayats come to the Olenek with the obvious intention of taking the stores of meat from the Olenek Tungus. In Nganasan legends their ancestors also go raiding to the south to capture deer from the Tungus. But in the end the Tungus prevail and the Mayat survivors have to retreat to the seashore and afterwards to the Taymyr peninsula.

Echoes of the struggle endured by the ancestors of the Nganasans are reflected not only in the epos. In 1629 to "Pyasida," to the tribute collector Ivan Gorokhov,

came . . . to the tribute quarters from the Khatanga many strangers, not paying tribute, and pleaded and said . . . they, the best princelings and all of the Khatansk (Khatanga —Author) Samoyad, not paying tribute (i.e., the Tavgs—Author) . . . that they suffer crowding and great loss from [peoples of] other regions and other clans and asked that you, Great Tsar and Grand Duke of all Russia, Mikhail Fedorovich, favor them, non-taxed people, by ordering them defended against other hordes . . . and they, non-taxed people, desire to pay to you, Lord, tribute for themselves and their clans.[192]

The Tavgs, the principal element among the ancestors of the present-day Nganasans, in distinction from other tribes of Mangazeysk uyezd, applied for Russian protection themselves, as even in 1629 they felt some necessity for defence "from other hordes."

It appears, then, that the original designation "Mayats-Vanyads" was applied to the entire aboriginal "Tungusized" population of the lower reaches of the Olenek, Anabar, and Khatanga. Even before the arrival of the Russians part of these Mayats were "Samoyedized" and were known as the Tavgs. The name Mayat (Vanyad) was preserved in the 17th century only by that part of the Mayat living to the southwest, in the middle reaches of the Khatanga and near Lake Yesey. It became known to the Russians as "the Tungus of the "Vanyadir clan."

The Russians, when they arrived in Siberia, did not find the tribes in exactly that state of economic development that is reflected in the legends about Mayats in the context of the Olenek Khosun epos and in the Nganasan legends, i.e., foot hunters of northern wild reindeer (without tame reindeer). Excepting the Tungus, almost all Yukagirs in the northern reaches of east Siberia had tame reindeer by the time of Russian arrival, although they still kept their language and still used stone implements, since iron penetrated to them in very limited quantities from the south, through the Tungus. The lack of tame deer among the upper Kolyma Yukagirs, described by Jochelson, is the result of a decline in the Yukagir economy resulting from the exploitation of them by a feudalistic, serf-owning system, by mercantile capitalism, and also for various other reasons. The upper Kolyma Yukagirs themselves have no doubt that they formerly had deer. The Khuldicha Yukagirs were reindeer-breeders in the 17th century and even during the time of Jochelson. In order to look for [present-day] ethnographic parallels for the hypothetical economy of the ancestors of the Nganasans-Mayats, we shall have to search beyond the confines of Asia. In Asia, because of the cultural influences penetrating from the south, the economic and cultural development of even the inhabitants of its northern edges progressed with much greater speed than in some other parts of the world.

The closest ethnographic parallel to that stage of economic development that is reflected in the legends of the ancestors of the Yukagirs-Mayats is presented probably by the Caribou Eskimos of Canada as described by Birket-Smith.[193] They also nomadize on foot and are tundra hunters of wild deer, which they kill with a spear thrown from a canoe mainly at river crossings or by battue moving them in the direction of river crossings. Also, like the Nganasans, they were accustomed to hunting individually on foot. The conic tent of the Caribou, which very much resembles the light reindeer-skin tent of the Nganasans, is still used by them for light travel with overnight stops. The resemblance is not so much in the conic shape, which is common to all tents of Siberia except for the yarangas of the northeast, but in the tent plan, where the living area is on one side of the fireplace, sideways from the entrance. This tent plan is common to both the Caribou Eskimos and to the light tent of the Nganasans. Certainly, there are substantial differences between the Caribou Eskimos and the Nganasans. The Nganasans are not acquainted with sea hunting and the developed dog transport of the Eskimos. A number of other details of their material cultures is also different. But these are individual peculiarities of these two peoples, who are far removed from each other, that evolved as a consequence of their different histories, different ethnic affiliation, and different geographic conditions.

Aside from these details, the ancestors of the Nganasans and, generally, all of the ancient Yukagirs (before they became acquainted with reindeer-breeding) as well as the Caribou Eskimos, may be looked on as representatives of one economic-cultural type—as Neolithic, subarctic hunters of wild deer.

In northern Asia, before the spread of the Samoyed and Tungus deer-breeders, there existed at least two Paleo-Asiatic, Neolithic cultures representing two different economic-cultural types and bound with different ethnic elements. One of these economic-cultural types was the fishermen and sea hunters of the Okhotsk and Bering seas—the northeastern Paleo-Asiatics. As they spread north-ward, sea hunting began to predominate in their economy (the coastal Chukchi); their southern part retained a predominance of fishing (the Itelmens), while in the middle part there is a combination of fishing and sea hunting (Koryaks).[194]

The second economic-cultural type of northern Asia was represented by the hunters of the northern deer mentioned above and, partially, by the fishermen of the land area that begins with the Anadyr in the east and extends in the west along a zone of tundra and forested tundra, and at least to the lower reaches of the Taz and perhaps even farther. Ethnically, these were Yukagirs. Certainly, they should not be viewed as a single people spread within this area. If among the northeastern Paleo-Asiatics we now distinguish three peoples—the Chukchi, Koryaks, and Kamchadals (Itelmens)—doubtless the aborigines of Yukagir ethnic cast, spread over the enormous interior of northern Asia, also represented very different, numerous tribes. It is not by chance that the Yukagir tribes of the 17th century and even now are considered separate peoples (the Chuvanets, "Omok," Khodynets, Anauls, and others). Instead of the name Yukagir, in the meaning in which it is used in this study, it would be altogether fitting to say "Northern Paleo-Asiatics" or "Intracontinental North Siberian Paleo-Asiatics" as distinguished from "Northeastern Paleo-Asiatics" or "Northeastern Coastal Paleo-Asiatics" (the Chukchis, Koryaks, and Itelmens), although in regard to the latter, the term "coastal" is not exact. These continental Paleo-Asiatics were diffused and partly assimilated by the Samoyeds in the west and the Tungus in the east and, in the 17th century, the Russians found them only in the basins of the Yana, Indigirka, Kolyma, and Anadyr, although already as reindeer-breeders, as indicated earlier. Only separate groups of Yukagirs, among them the Anauls on the Anadyr, probably did not have tame deer at all.

Conclusion

On the basis of all the materials examined, the origin of the Nganasans may be reconstructed as follows: The Nganasans are basically descendants of the ancient Paleo-Asiatic population of northern Asia, Neolithic hunters of wild deer. Ethnically, these Paleo-Asiatics represent the western periphery of [the territory occupied by the] Yukagirs, who probably spread also to the west of the Lena and into the zone of forested tundra and tundra, possibly to the Taz and even farther.

The Paleo-Asiatics between the Taz and the Yenisey were assimilated by Samoyeds who came from the south and in this way, among others, there was formed a Samoyed group of "Ravens," the Kuraks. In the Pyasina basin, the Paleo-Asiatics assimilated by the Samoyeds formed a group of "Eagles," the "Pyasida Samoyeds," as they were called by the Russians at the beginning of the 17th century. Even before the Russians arrived, the "Samoyeds-Ravens" crossed the Yenisey and penetrated into the tundra between Yenisey gulf and the river Pyasina, where they were found by the Russians. By the time the Russians arrived, the "Samoyeds-Eagles" had spread to the east of the Pyasina into the basin of the Taymyr river, where they came into contact with a Tungus-speaking population, also aboriginal.

Even before the arrival of the Russians, a group of Tungus penetrated from the south into the region of Lake Pyasina and the Avam river and was assimilated there by the "Samoyeds-Ravens" and "Samoyeds-Eagles" and also by the ancestors of the present-day Enets of the Madu tribe (Somatu). Thus, from these Tungus there was formed a Samoyed-speaking group, the Tidiris.

The Paleo-Asiatics, who lived originally in the basins of the Khatanga and Anabar, were linguistically absorbed by the Tungus even before the arrival of the Russians in Siberia. They penetrated into the basin of the Taymyr river already as a Tungus-speaking ethnic group and subsequently came into contact with the "Psyasida Samoyeds." Later on, these "Tungusized" Paleo-Asiatics (the Tungus called them Vanyads or Mayads, and the Yakut legends, Mayats) formed the tribe of Tavgs on the Taymyr and the Kheta, and in the lower reaches of the Khatanga and Anabar, and the tribe of Vanyadyrs (Vanyads) in the middle reaches of the Khatanga (Kotuy). Through constant contact with the "Pyasida Samoyeds" and the Tidiris, the Tavgs, who, as we have reasons to believe, were originally a comparatively small group, acquired the Samoyed language. As a result of this there appeared a Samoyed Tavg dialect, which was distinguished from other Samoyed dialects, in particular, by rather considerable borrowings from the Tungus language and by the influence on it of Tungus phonetics. Even before the arrival of the Russians, the Tavgs became a comparatively large Samoyed-speaking tribe. But they suffered much from the attacks of the Tungus from the southeast and finally, even after the arrival of the Russians in the 17th century, they were pushed out, by the Tungus (mainly the Sinigirs), from the Anabar and from the right bank of the Khatanga to the left, that is, to the Taymyr peninsula.

During the second half of the 17th and the beginning of the 18th century, the "Pyasida Samoyeds," the Kuraks, the Tidiris, and the Tavgs, living in the tundra and forested tundra between the Yenisey and Khatanga, formed at first something like a confederation and then merged into one tribe of the Avam Nganasans, Samoyed by language and culture. Among the Samoyed dialects spoken by these elements of the tribe of Avam Nganasans, prevalence was achieved by the dialect of the Tavgs, the most numerous group of ancestors of the Avam Nganasans in the 17th century. This dialect formed the base of the present-day Nganasan language.

The other tribe mentioned earlier, also "Tungusized" but aboriginal Paleo-Asiatic in origin and occupying the middle reaches of the Khatanga, was known to the Russians as the Vanyad Tungus or Vanyadyrs. It disintegrated during the first half of the 18th century. Part of it, the Munukov "Hare" clan, also moved to the Taymyr, settled to the east of the Avam Nganasans, and, during the second half of the 18th century, became "Samoyedized." Speedily increasing in numbers, partly at the expense of various Tungus and perhaps Avam Nganasan emigrants, toward the end of the 18th century and the first half of the 19th century this group became the tribe of Vadeyev Nganasans, speaking the same language as the Avam Nganasans.

In the beginning of the 19th century, a Tungus of the Dolgan tribe, Oko by name, was assimilated by the Nganasans. By the end of the 19th century his descendants formed a separate Nganasan clan, Oko or Dolgan, which did not enter into either of the two tribes and which continued to be regarded as a part of the Dolgans, from whom the originator had come.

From a wider point of view, the formation of the Nganasan people came as a concluding stage of a movement to the extreme north of central Siberia of peoples of the Uralic and Altaic language groups—Samoyeds to the west of the Yenisey and Tungus to the east of it. Both the Tungus and the Samoyeds influenced the ancestors of the Nganasans, the Neolithic Paleo-Asiatic population of the Taymyr, the Khatanga, and the Anabar, but final dominance was achieved by the Samoyed language, which prevailed over the Paleo-Asiatic Yukagir as well as the Tungus languages. In the same way, the Samoyed economic system, Samoyed material culture, and social organization in general supplanted not only those of the Yukagir hunters but also those of the Tungus.

Nevertheless, the culture of the Neolithic Paleo-Asiatic hunters, the Yukagirs, survived in the Nganasans in the form of relics and ethnographic peculiarities to a greater degree than with other peoples to the west of the Lena with the exception of the Madu Enets.

Notes and References

1. For a description of such boats, see: V. Seroshevskiy, *Yakuty* (The Yakuts), St. Petersburg, 1896, p. 302. Seroshevskiy thinks these *vetki* were borrowed by the Yakuts from the Yukagirs.

2. For a description of Nganasan clothing, see: A. A. Popov, *Tavgiytsy* (The Tavgs), Moscow–Leningrad, 1936, pp. 16–21 and figures on pp. 22–30.

3. Because of this, P. Tretyakov in his *Turukhanskiy kray* (in *Zap. I.R.G.O.*, General Geography, vol. 2, St. Petersburg, 1869), p. 404, comes to the conclusion that Samoyed fairy tales were borrowed from the Yuraks (i.e., Nenets).

4. On the question as to whether the Samoyed languages belong to the same linguistic group as the Finnic and Ugrian languages, there are differences of opinion. It is possible that the Samoyed languages form an independent linguistic group.

5. I. Stalin, *Marxizm i voprosy yazykoznaniya* (Marxism and questions of linguistics),Gospolitizdat, 1950, pp. 29–30.

6. M. A. Castren, *Wörterverzeichnisse aus den Samojedishen Sprachen*, St. Petersburg, 1855, pp. 19, 57; G. D. Verbov, *Kratkiy Nenetsko-Russkiy i Russko-Nenetskiy slovar* (Concise Nenets–Russian and Russian–Nenets dictionary), Salekhard, 1937, p. 49.

7. Castren, *op. cit.*, pp. 24, 57.

8. Castren translates the word *tansa* as "clan" (Geschlecht), but generally he had a very hazy notion about clans and tribes (see cited work, pp. 61, 238). On the other hand, even the Nganasans are confused about both these terms nowadays. The word *fonka* Castren translates with the terms "schaft, stiel am beil, hammer," but still he did not exhaust all meanings of this word.

9. *Ngili* means "below," i.e., northeast. "Up" is southwest; "the forest side," southeast; the "tundra side," northwest. "Below" [includes the territory] beyond the Khatanga eastward to the shores of the Laptev sea, while "up" includes the territory beyond Dudinka and up to the Yenisey. (See: *Legendy i skazki Nganasanov*—Legends and fairy tales of the Nganasans—Krasnoyarsk, 1938, p. 15.)

10. Middendorf, *Puteshestviye na sever i vostok Sibiri* (Journey to the north and east of Siberia), part 2, sec. 6, St. Petersburg, 1878, pp. 622, 650, 653, 680, 683, 690, 692–694.

11. Lonire is mentioned by Tretyakov as the richest "Dolgan," who had about 1500 reindeer (P. Tretyakov, *Turukhanskiy kray*, p. 454).

12. Namesake of the Dolgan elder ("the influential Artsya") mentioned by Middendorf (*op. cit.*, p. 693). About this name, see below.

13. S. K. Patkanov, *Statisticheskiye dannye, pokazyvayushchiye plemennoy sostav naseleniya Sibiri, yazyk i rody inorodtsev* (Statistical data indicating the tribal composition of the Siberian population, the language and the clans of the natives), vol. 2, St. Petersburg, 1911, p. 393.

14. Personal communication of A. A. Popov.

15. Patkanov, *op. cit.*, p. 52.

16. S. Pruchenko, *Sibirskiye okrainy* (The edges of Siberia), St. Petersburg, 1899, p. 118.

17. Irkutskiy obl. arkhiv MVD, fond Glavnogo upravleniya Vostochnoy Sibiri, d. no. 405 (Irkutsk regional archive of the M.V.D., section of the main administration of eastern Siberia, document no. 405). Deals with the implementation of statutes for natives. See also: I. Ya Chibizov, Inorodtsy Yeniseyskoy gubernii v pervyye gody eye sushchestvovaniya (Natives of the Yeniseysk guberniya province during the first years of its existence), *Sibirskiy arkhiv*, 1914, no. 9.

18. Tretyakov, *op. cit.*, p. 373. The Eighth Audit was carried out in 1834–99[?] but did not affect the "tribute-paying natives" in the Yeniseysk province, as in 1832 the Second Tribute Commission did its work there, and it took the place of the Eighth Audit.

19. Patkanov, *op. cit.*, pp. 390–391, 393.

20. Middendorf, *op. cit.*, p. 1448.

21. *TsGADA*, Sib. prikaz, book 1648, leaves 4–14.

22. V. Ye. Vasilyev, Kratkiy ocherk inorodtsev Turukhanskogo kraya (A brief sketch of the natives of the Turukhansk kray), *Yezhegodn. Russk. antropolog. obshch.*, vol. 2, 1908, p. 8; B. Dolgikh, Naseleniye poluostrova Taymyr (Population of the Taymyr peninsula), *Severnaya Aziya*, 1929, no. 2, p. 63.

23. The Turukhansk kray of the 19th and beginning of the 20th century coincides generally with the Mangazeysk uyezd of the 17th and 18th centuries. We use, therefore, both names.

24. The Dongor, Edyan, and Karanto Dolgans were altogether absent in the composition of Yesey volost in 1768. But on the map of the Yeniseysk guberniya of 1828 they are already indicated in the same places where they are living now. Additionally there is a note on the map pertaining to the Edyan tribe: "A Zhigansk clan which migrated from Irkutsk guberniya." Since the Yakutsk *oblast* was separated from Irkutsk guberniya in 1805, the migration of the last Dolgan groups to the Taymyr must have taken place between 1768 and 1805.

25. *TsGADA*, Gos. arkhiv, no. 24, leaf 244 obverse.

26. In 1926 in this camping area (*nasleg*) there were 42 families of 220 persons who owned 1200 reindeer; of this number 8 families, or 37 persons with 400 reindeer, were descendants of the Mayats. In 1859 in the Beti nasleg there were 202 persons (*Pamyatnaya knizhka Yakutskoy oblasti za 1863 god.*, St. Petersburg, 1864, p. 68).

27. Migration of the "Yakutized" descendants of the Mayats from Yesey to Taymyr ended only recently. I met the last family moving from Yesey on the road in January, 1927. This family of I. Kh. Mayat and his uncle, who came a year earlier (I. N. Beti), are two of the "Yakutized" descendants of the Mayats who acknowledged their "Mayat" descent.

28. Poyezdka na ozero Yesey (Journey to Lake Yesey), *Izvestiya Krasnoyarskogo podotdela RGO*, vol. 1, 1904, no. 6, p. 28.

29. Yeniseyskiye Tungusy (The Yenisey Tungus), supplement to the journal *Zemlevedeniye*, 1922, p. 93.

30. *Arkhiv AN SSSR*, sec. 21, op. 4, no. 21, leaf 25.

31. *TsGADA*, Sib. prikaz, book 95, leaf 265 ob.; book 117.

32. *Ibidem*, book 127, leaves 692 ob., 683.

33. *Ibidem*, book 986, leaf 441 ob.

34. And even the Yesey Tungus were subjected to tribute by the Russians who

came from the northwest, from the Samoyeds, and perhaps even accompanied by them (as they tell about it nowadays on the Yesey). During almost the entire 17th century, the tribute collectors came to Yesey and carried the furs out through Pyasida. Only towards the end of the 17th century was there established a definite route to Yesey from the Nizhnyaya [Lower] Tunguska, as indicated in Remezov's *Atlas*.

35. *TsGADA*, Sib. prikaz, book 127, leaf 710

36. *TsGADA*, Sib. prikaz, book 285, leaves 159 ob., 160, 160 ob. Although amanats were taken from the Azyans, in the 1640's at least they did not pay tribute for their amanat at Yesey (*LOII*, index 6, article 5, leaf 3). True, from the entry for 1645 it may be supposed that in 1644 624 sables were collected, but we have no data to indicate that it was a real tribute collection and not a part of past tribute that had not been paid.

37. *TsGADA*, Sib. prikaz, book 144, leaf 913 ob.

38. *Kolonialnaya politika Moskovskogo Gosudarstva v Yakutii 17 v.* (Colonial policy of the Moscow Government in Yakutia in the 17th century), Leningrad 1936, pp. 53–54. They remembered this "war" for a long time. See, A. A. Tokarev, *Obshchestvenny stroy Yakutov 17–18 vv.* (The social order of the Yakuts in the 17th and 18th centuries), Yakutsk, 1945, p. 96.

39. *Dopolneniya k "Aktam istoricheskim"* (Addenda to "Historical Acts"), vol. 10, St. Petersburg, 1867, p. 345; vol. 11, St. Petersburg, 1869, p. 66. (Cited below as: *DAI*.)

40. *DAI*, vol. 11, p. 66; *Colonial policy . . .*, p. 245.

41. *DAI*, vol. 10, pp. 345–346.

42. All of these amanats died afterward in prison from "sickness" (*DAI*, vol. 10, p. 346).

43. *TsGADA*, Sib. prikaz, book 756, leaf 310. However, there are no data about punitive excesses. The unpleasantness resulted mainly because of the Mangazeysk administration, which was accused by Moscow of extorting tribute payers, etc.

44. *DAI*, vol. 11, pp. 68, 81. In this year the last 14 persons returned from the Olenek (*TsGADA*, Sib. prikaz, book 1050, leaves 74–114).

45. *TsGADA*, Sib. prikaz, book 756, leaves 310 ob., 311; *DAI*, vol. 11, p. 19.

46. The age was determined by the fact that, in the census of 1682, it was indicated how many years each tribute payer had paid tribute. Tribute paying started at the age of 16. (See: *TsGADA*, Sib. prikaz, books 708 and 732.) Certainly these determinations of age are far from being exact, but they still give the approximate position in this regard.

47. We cannot examine this question in detail, but the supposition that Gigaley was also a military leader is confirmed by ethnographic data about this institution among the Evenks and Nganasans. A young, able man was a military leader; as he grew older, he would become a civil head in his clan.

48. The names of Tungus, named in Yakutsk, were presented above according to *DAI*; here they are from the original. In *DAI*, we are convinced, the native names are badly distorted. They were written down on being heard, by different people, independently of each other, and in Yakutsk; in addition to that they were written in abbreviated form (in Russian). All of this was compounded in the transcription of names.

49. *TsGADA*, Sib. prikaz, book 980, leaves 138, 149, 147, 155, 179, 180.

50. Tretyakov, *Turukhanskiy kray*, p. 332.

51. *Ibidem*, p. 357.

52. *TsGADA*, Sib. prikaz, book 1293, leaf 61: "The Yesey tribute quarters from tribute-paying Tungus, which tribute payers pay all the time tribute in the Mangazeysk uyezd on the river Kheta."

53. *Arkhiv AN SSSR*, sec. 21, op. 4, no. 21, leaf 249.

54. *LOII, YaA*, index 44, art. 4, leaves 16–17.

55. As reported by A. A. Popov.

56. *Arkhiv AN SSSR*, sec. 21, op. 4, no. 21, leaf 19 ob.

57. Including sometimes also the region of Lake Yesey; cf. "in Pyasida, on lake Yesey" (*TsGADA*, Sib. prikaz, book 127, leaves 692 ob., 693).

58. See also: Müller, *Istoriya Sibiri* (The History of Siberia), part II, Moscow–Leningrad, 1941, p. 24.

59. *TsGADA*, Sib. prikaz, art. 11, p. 117; *Arkhiv AN SSSR*, sec. 21, op. 4, no. 21, leaf 25.

60. *Arkhiv AN SSSR*, sec. 21, op. 4, no. 21, leaf 32 ob.

61. *Ibidem*, leaf 19 ob.

62. *TsGADA*, Sib. prikaz, art. 20, leaf 155; *Arkhiv AN SSSR*, sec. 21, op. 4, no. 21, leaves 30 and 32 ob.

63. *TsGADA*, Sib. prikaz, book 19.

64. *Arkhiv AN SSSR*, sec. 21, op. 4, no. 21, leaf 277; *DAI*, vol. 5, St. Petersburg, 1855, p. 160.

65. *Ibidem*, book 150, leaf 1021 ob.

66. *Ibidem*, book 95, leaf 268.

67. *Ibidem*, book 95, leaf 285. It should be pointed out that sometimes the tribute collectors unnecessarily complained about the changing of names. For instance, in the same year, 1637, the tribute collectors note the absence of Syunzey, who had been registered in 1636, although a few lines lower they themselves entered Senzey (book 95, leaf 270). The confusion about names was seemingly due, to a considerable extent, not to the changing of names by the Samoyeds but to distortion during the copying of the draft tribute registers to the clean ones and then again into the collection books, and so on. For example, the names of the Samoyeds who complained against Yerofey Khabarov in 1629 are written in one place as Tobachiyke, Paravda, and Serokuy and in another as Paracheyko, Paradu, and Syarokuy (*TsGADA*, Prikaznyye dela starykh let —Departmental files of previous years—no. 28, leaf 892; no. 55, leaf 209, etc.).

68. *Arkhiv AN SSSR*, sec. 21, op. 4, leaves 274, 277.

69. *TsGADA*, Sib. prikaz, art. 864, leaves 157, 159, 169.

70. *DAI*, vol. 5, p. 160.

71. *Ibidem*. In folklore, the events of 1661 found their reflection in the legend about 12 cossacks (*Legendy i skazki Nganasanov*, p. 101). Sometimes this legend is an episode in the oral rendition. But, notwithstanding its great scope, the popularity of events of 1666 can not be compared with the reaction brought about by the events of 1683 on the Yesey. The following unusual detail is characteristic of the folklore. In 1666, together with the Russians, four Tungus were killed. In the legend, to the contrary, the Tungus, on orders from the Russian tsar, arranged for a massacre of the Nganasans, thus punishing them for the murder of the cossacks. In a different version of this legend recorded in 1948 it is pointed out that the officials who were attacked were leaving the territory of Vadeyev Nganasans, i.e., from Lake Yesey. In this version the number of Russians killed is 29 (actually 31), and the place where this event took place is exactly indicated—the "Stone" (*Kamen*) on the way from the land of the Vadeyevs at the source of the Pyasina.

72. *TsGADA*, Sib. prikaz, book 27, leaves 113–114.

73. A. Melnikov, Turukhanskiy kray (Turukhansk region), pp. 1, 4, 6, 20–21.

74. According to the same sources and calculations that were used in connection with the Avam Nganasans; for 1629, in accordance with book 19 of "Sib. prikaz."

75. *TsGADA*, Sib. prikaz, article 20, p. 154 ("In the same Khantaysk winter quarters to the Tsar a Pyasida Samoyad Munzuy brought a sable, value of 20 altyns"); book 19 ("Pyasida Samoyad Munzu, Nary"); book 986, leaves 183, 366–367.

76. *TsGADA*, Prikaznye dela starykh let, 1630, no. 55, pp. 131–132.

77. In 1633, there were 9 names attached to the Serokuyev clan, and, in 1630, there were 7 names attached to the Tabachiyev—although the bearers of these names had no connection with the clans (book 986; book 22, leaves 48 ob., 49).

78. In 1637 and 1639 the names of the Serokuyev and Tabachiyev clans were omitted and all members of these clans were entered in the Munzuyev clan (book 95, leaf 270 ob.; book 150, leaf 1011 ob.).

79. *TsGADA*, Sib. prikaz, book 986, leaf 542.

80. *Ibidem*, book 708, leaf 60.

81. *Ibidem,* book 1648, leaf 14.

82. By 1637, one of these Tavg clans begins to be called "Sorcerers" because it was led by a sorcerer (shaman) Sokdoza.

83. S. V. Bakhrushin, Yasak v Sibiri v XVII v. (Fur tribute in Siberia in the 17th century), *Sib. ogni,* 1927, no. 3, p. 118. Paravda or Paradu, the third Samoyed who complained against E. P. Khabarov, belonged to the Kudesnik clan of princeling Pyak.

84. *TsGADA,* Sib. prikaz, art. 11, ss. 108, 117; art. 20, leaf 147.

85. *Ibidem,* book 22, leaves 48, 50.

86. See: G. N. Prokofyev, *Nganasanskiy (Tavgiyskiy) dialekt: Yazyki i pismennost narodov severa* (The Nganasan (Tavg) dialect: Spoken and written languages of northern peoples), part 1, Leningrad, 1937, p. 58.

87. *TsGADA,* Sib. prikaz, book 1648, leaves 14–26.

88. *Ibidem,* book 285, leaf 132.

89. *Ibidem,* book 708, leaf 30.

90. The name *Ngomde,* particularly in the west, near Enets territory is often pronounced as *Uamde, Uamze.* In 1667 a Samoyed of the "Uamzin clan Syuma" is mentioned (*DAI,* vol. 5, p. 160).

91. *Arkhiv AN SSSR,* sec. 21, op. 4, no. 21, leaf 20 ob.; see also: Müller, *Istoriya Sibiri* (The history of Siberia), Moscow–Leningrad, 1941, part II, p. 25.

92. *TsGADA,* Sib. prikaz, book 32, leaf 334.—*Sotnik* [captain of 100 cossacks] Ivan Patrikeyev, who was collecting tribute that year in Khatanga, reports that he collected tribute from 31 Kuraks. But one name was apparently omitted during the copying of the list for delivery to Moscow. The petition of Patrikeyev is presented later (see the section "The Tavgs" of this article).

93. *Ibidem,* book 986, leaf 257 ff. In the Vaska clan 11 persons were [recorded] but one of them was a Tidiris.

94. One of them is certainly a Tavg. He is the last one in the list, and is called *taugeseryaet* Tepchelya, i.e., "my Tavg brother-in-law, Tepchelya."

95. *TsGADA,* Sib. prikaz, book 95, leaf 275 ob.

96. *Ibidem,* leaves 279–280 ob.

97. *Ibidem,* book 150, leaves 1015–1018a.

98. *TsGADA,* Sib. prikaz, art. 11, s. 117.

99. *Ibidem,* book 117, leaf 435.

100. *Ibidem,* leaf 443.

101. *Ibidem,* leaf 439.

102. *Ibidem,* book 285, leaf 138 ob.

103. *Ibidem,* book 708, leaves 60–90.

104. M. A. Castren, *Wörterverzeichnisse aus den Samojedischen Sprachen,* St. Petersburg, 1885, p. 260.

105. *Ibidem,* pp. 50, 260.

106. *TsGADA,* Sib. prikaz, book 22, leaf 51 ob.

107. *Ibidem,* book 32, leaves 332–340.

108. *TsGADA,* Sib. prikaz, book 986, leaf 257.

109. *Ibidem,* book 285, leaves 140, 143.

110. *Ibidem,* book 19.

111. *Ibidem,* book 285, leaf 55; see also leaves 41–42.

112. *Ibidem,* book 986, leaves 359 ob., 360.

113. *Ibidem,* book 285, leaf 55; see also leaves 42–43.

114. *TsGADA,* Sib. prikaz, art. 105, leaf 229.

115. A. L. Andreyev, Bulyashi (The Bulyash), *Sov. etnografiya,* 1937, nos. 2–3, p. 112; *TsGADA,* Sib. prikaz, book 6, leaves 454, 455, 456.—The Bukansk winter quarters were situated at the Bukan river not far from the Voyevoli lakes in the present-day Ilimpeysk rayon of the Evenk National Okrug.

116. *TsGADA,* Sib. prikaz, book 19; book 22, leaf 4 ob.

117. *Ibidem,* book 986, leaves 184, 359; book 22, leaf 5.

118. *Ibidem,* book 19; book 986, leaf 185 *et al.*

119. Butsinskiy read "Netola Dashcherbak" (in "Mangazeya and Mangazeysk uyezd," *Zap. Kharkovsk. univ.*, 1891, no. 1). This is the least probable reading. It could be "Netolada Shcherbak," as the syllable "da" is often met with at the end of Samoyed names in documents of the 17th century, but later it is always Netola and not Netolada. The nickname "Shcherbak" often occurs among the tribute payers of the 18th century.

120. *TsGADA*, Sib. prikaz, p. [?] 20, leaf 155.

121. In the legend of Soymu-son, he flees from the Tungus who attack his tent and comes to Ngamtuso Karutide (more correctly Kuratide, i.e., *Kurak*, an old man). (In *Legendy i skazki Nganasanov*, p. 25).

122. *Arkhiv AN SSSR*, sec. 21, op. 4, no. 21, leaves 32, 36, 39.

123. *TsGADA*, Sib. prikaz, book 22, leaves 49–50 ob.

124. *Ibidem*, book 32, leaves 335–338.

125. *Ibidem*, book 986. In brackets, for 1634, the number of tribute payers, excluding adolescents; i.e., only the adult men are given in brackets.

126. *Ibidem*, book 95, leaves 271–275 ob., 280–281 ob.

127. *Ibidem*, book 150, leaves 1012–1015 ob., 1018a–1019, 1021 ob.–1023.

128. *Ibidem*, book 285, leaves 133–147.

129. *Arkhiv AN SSSR*, sec. 21, op. 4, no. 21, leaves 148 ob.–149 ob.

130. *Legendy i skazki Nganasanov*.

131. *TsGADA*, Sib. prikaz, book 95, leaf 149.

132. Among the Nganasans, the shifting of the sounds "kh" and "f" is characteristic; here the northern Tungus "kh-sounding" speech of their Tungus-speaking ancestors is seemingly manifested.

133. *TsGADA*, Sib. prikaz, book 708.

134. The name of the Khalo subdivision was explained to us thus: The Khalo are descended from a Tungus, and since the Tungus were born from the "stone" (mountains) therefrom comes their name Khalo. In Nganasan *fala* (*khala*) means "stone."

135. V. Levin, *Kratkiy Eveno-Russkiy slovar* (A concise Evenk–Russian dictionary), Moscow–Leningrad, 1936, p. 92.

136. *Yazyki i pismennost narodov severa* (Spoken and written languages of northern peoples), Moscow–Leningrad, 1937, p. 55.

137. We form this word in analogy with *bargach*, "from beyond the river" (see: V. Levin, *op. cit.*, p. 19).

138. *TsGADA*, Sib. prikaz, book 708.

139. S. V. Bakhrushin, Samoyedy v 17 veke (The Samoyeds in the 17th century), *Sev. Aziya*, 1925, nos. 5–6, p. 88. The suffix *fey* is the Nganasan suffix *pte* with the help of which the Nganasans usually formed their proper names—Khelipte, Vosipte, Fadopte, and so on.

140. *Legendy i skazki Nganasanov*, p. 104.

141. Many groups of the indigenous population of Siberia received family names as early as the 17th century, but in the Mangazeysk uyezd this was done only in the 18th century.

142. Incidentally, the Avam Nganasans have no notion about an ancestral eponym of the clan, in contrast with the Vadeyev Nganasans, the Tungus, and other peoples of northern Siberia. What was said earlier about the origin of their clans from previously independent, large exogamous groups of the phratry type explains this peculiarity.

143. *TsGADA*, Sib. prikaz, book 1648, leaves 14 ob., 15.

144. Two were recorded by me (one of these is published; see: *Legendy i skazki Nganasanov*, pp. 21–22), two were recorded by A. P. Lekarenko, and one by A. A. Popov, who kindly placed them at my disposal.

145. *Yazyki i pismennost narodov Sibiri* (Spoken and written languages of Siberian peoples), part 1, Moscow–Leningrad, 1937, p. 55.

146. Compare Chempere, Chyngkhara, and Chimkere of the Olenek Khosun epos, and also the clan-tribal name Chinagir (Chinigir) or Sinigir, which in the 17th century was used by the Tungus who lived in the upper reaches of the Anabar and Olenek.

147. *Evenkiysko-Russkiy slovar* (Evenk–Russian dictionary), Moscow, 1940, p. 123.
148. *Ibidem*, pp. 61, 133.
149. The name of the highland Yukagirs, "Khodyntsy" (*khodeydzhil*), also probably originated from this word.
150. *Evenkiysko-Russkiy slovar*, p. 46.
151. *Ibidem*, p. 10.
152. Formerly the Nganasans called the river Dudypta, below the mouth of the Avam, the Avam. The Dudypta is really a very broad river in its lower reaches.
153. Incidentally, most of the latter also have Nganasan names. For example, the river Kystyktakh is called *Norka-diko-bigay*, i.e., "the river of the steep bear slope," and Samoyed river, *Nya-bigay*, etc.
154. Etnogoniya narodnostey Ob-Yeniseyskogo basseyna (Ethnogeny of the peoples of the Ob-Yenisey basin), Symposium *Sovetskaya etnografiya*, 1940, no. 3, p. 75, note 4.
155. Levin, *Kratkiy Evenko-Russkiy slovar*, p. 22.
156. *Evenkiysko-Russkiy slovar* (Evenk–Russian dictionary) Leningrad, 1934, p. 123. In Nganasan *laku* means "Tungus sword" (Castren, *op. cit.*, p. 55), i.e., probably "palma." As in his youth Lakuna was a "great warrior," this name is suitable also; whichever the case, both explanations of the name Lakuna are connected with the Tungus.
157. Levin, *op. cit.*, p. 82.
158. Before the Yakuts, this slave worker was probably a Yukagir. We shall return to this question again in another work.
159. *Evenkiysko-Russkiy slovar*, p. 194.
160. *Ada-ga-m, ada-va-m*, "to evade a blow."
161. *Evenkiysko-Russkiy slovar*, p. 44.
162. Yeniseyskiye Tungusy (The Yenesey Tungus), supplement to the journal *Zemlevedeniye*, 1917, pp. 30–31.
163. M. A. Castren, *Reiseberichte und Briefe*, St. Petersburg, 1856, p. 266 (Adjan).
164. *The Yenisey Tungus*, part 1, Moscow, 1917, p. 10.
165. A. A. Popov, Materialy po rodovomu stroyu Dolgan (Contributions to the clan structure of the Dolgans), *Sovetskaya etnografiya*, 1934, nos. 3–4, pp. 120–121; *Legendy i skazki Nganasanov*, p. 22; B. Dolgikh, Naseleniye Taymyr (The population of the Taymyr), *Severnaya Aziya*, 1929, no. 2, p. 54.
166. This is so much a Kolyma legend by its content that A. P. Okladnikov relates it directly to the Kolyma (*Ocherki istorii zapadnykh Buryat-Mongolov*—Historical sketches of the western Buryat-Mongols, Leningrad, 1937, p. 326). Of course, it is possible that Chukchis from the region to the west of the Kolyma did wander even farther west and were annihilated by the ancestors of the Nganasans.
167. *Evenkiysko-Russkiy slovar*, p. 87.
168. *Ibidem*, Introduction, p. 25.
169. True, a Tungus tribe Chemdal formerly had a similar name—Khuladal, Khu-ladygir. In 1640, the Tungus of the Nep winter quarters, the Muchugirs, moved "to Khulidygiry on the river Lena." In Tungus, *khuli-di-gir* means "riverside." The Chemdal tribe was officially called, until 1824, the Tetersk riverside volost.
170. V. G. Bogoraz, Materialy po lamutskomu yazyku (Materials on Lamut language), in *Tungusskiy sbornik*, Leningrad, 1931, p. 91.
171. A name similar to *Bulën* or *Bolën*, namely, *Bulyashi* or *Bolyashi* (manifestly from the Evenk *bulesel*, "roaming over the marsh"), was applied in the 17th century to the Tungus tribe to the west of the Lena, the Nyurumnyal. This tribe came from the region of Nyurba and probably represented the aborigines of the Vilyuy. The name Bulyash may be an indication that the Yukagirs also lived to the west of the Lena and even on the Vilyuy.
172. This characterization of the "Khuldicha" was drawn from the following works: V. I. Jochelson, Brodyachiye rody tundry mezhdu Indigirkoy i Kolymoy (Wandering clans of the tundra between the Indigirka and Kolyma), *Zhivaya starina*, St. Petersburg, 1900, nos. I–II, pp. 151–193; V. I. Jochelson, *Materialy po izucheniyu Yukagirskogo*

yazyka i folklora (Contributions to the study of the Yukagir language and folklore), St. Petersburg, 1900, pp. 198–225; W. Jochelson, *The Yukaghir*, New York, 1926, pp. 48–50; S. K. Patkanov, *Statisticheskiye dannye* . . . (Statistical data . . .), vol. 3, St. Petersburg, 1912, p. 789; *Pamyatnaya knizhka Yakutskoy oblasti za 1863* (Commemorative book of the Yakutsk region for 1863), St. Petersburg, 1864, p. 120.

173. V. I. Jochelson, Brodyachiye rody tundry . . ., p. 159; *Materialy po . . .,* Introduction, pp. 97–98, 134–137, 209–210.

174. It is possible that the same legend was told by the Nganasans to the members of the First Tribute Commission in 1768; at that time they may have called their eastern kin Yukagirs directly (see above, p. 270).

175. V. I. Jochelson, *op. cit.*, p. 126.

176. V. gostyakh u Yukagirov (A guest of the Yukagirs), *Etnograf. obozreniye*, 1914, nos. 1–2, p. 118.

177. Oral report of M. G. Levin.

178. V. Seroshevskiy, *Yakuty* (The Yakuts), St. Petersburg, 1896, p. 328.

179. V. I. Jochelson, *op. cit.*, p. 145.

180. V. I. Jochelson, *Ocherk zveropromyshlennosti i torgovli mekhami v Kolymskom okruge* (An outline of fur-production and fur-trade in the Kolyma region), St. Petersburg, 1898, footnote p. 141.

181. This Nganasan ceremony was described by me in a separate work (see: *Kratkiye soobshcheniya Instituta etnografii*, no. 13, 1951).

182. V. I. Jochelson, *Materialy po . . .,* p. 123

183. V. I. Jochelson, *op. cit.*, p. 124.

184. W. Jochelson, *The Yukaghirs*, p. 292.

185. *Legendy i skazki Nganasanov*, pp. 118–119

186. W. Jochelson, *op. cit.*, p. 164.

187. P. Tretyakov, *Turukhanskiy kray* (The Turukhansk kray), St. Petersburg, 1869, p. 435.

188. *Kratkiye soobshcheniya Instituta istorii materialnoy kultury*, 1947, no. 18, pp. 38–45.

189. *Ibidem*, p. 43.

190. *Ibidem*, p. 45.

191. As is known, the Yakuts call the *aurora borealis* the "Yukagir fire," i.e., *Yukagir uota*. In this connection it is worth noting that the Dolgans on the Taymyr call the *aurora borealis*, *Yungkebil-uota*, i.e., "The fire of Yungkebil."

192. *TsGADA*, Prikaznye dela starykh let, 1630, no. 55, pp. 169–170. There it is also indicated that the Tavgs beat up about 50 tribute-paying Khantayka Samoyeds so that the latter had to go "beyond the Taz" (leaf 117).

193. Kai Birket-Smith, *The Caribou Eskimos*, Kopenhagen, 1929.

194. Meanwhile, let us digress to the question of outside influences, for instance, the influence of the Eskimos on the Chukchis, and from the question of the development of reindeer-breeding among the Chukchis and Koryaks. The Nivkhs represent a separate Paleo-Asiatic ethnic group. But neither they nor the Kets are people of northern Siberia, the latter having hardly appeared in the region of the middle Yenisey before the migration of the Samoyeds from the Sayan mountains northward. Generally, the Kets cannot be considered northern Paleo-Asiatics. Their culture contains traits of southern origin and their linguistic connections lead to the south or to the southwest. I take this opportunity to state that I consider completely erroneous my suppositions about the existence of connections between the languages and the names of the Kets and Kmers, the Athabaskans, Chaldeans, Khetts, Sumers, Iberians, and Basques, as well as my position in regard to the "Japhetic" languages and peoples. See my: *Kety* (The Kets), Irkutsk, 1934, pp. 43–45.

These errors were due to the uncritical utilization, in this case, of the methodology and propositions of Marr and of some statements by Bogoraz.

B. O. DOLGIKH and M. G. LEVIN

TRANSITION FROM KINSHIP TO TERRITORIAL RELATIONSHIPS IN THE HISTORY OF THE PEOPLES OF NORTHERN SIBERIA*

EXTENSIVE LITERATURE is devoted to problems of the social organization of the peoples of northern Siberia. The overwhelming majority of these works touch only upon specific forms of social organization of this or that people, and we can point to only a few research papers in which these problems were examined from general theoretical positions. Moreover, these few studies, as a rule, focus their attention on archaic institutions and survivals, reflecting the general trend of ethnographic research in the recent past. Prerevolutionary investigations distinguished only the clan and various archaic forms of the family in the social organization of the peoples of the North, thus reducing social organization to a false system, which divided the peoples of northern Siberia into clans, and clans into families, but was baffled by all cases where the concrete data would not fit. Thus, the vagueness with respect to problems of the social organization of the Chukchi, the Koryaks, and the Eskimo, whose clan organization did not follow the forms to which the investigators were accustomed. This system evolved from ill-devised general aims, under which the clan and the family were static and separated from the concrete historical conditions of their development, and in which all other forms of social organization were disregarded.

A few slight attempts to go beyond the bounds of this system were statements of the necessity to distinguish between the strictly genealogical clans and administrative "clans," arbitrarily set up among the people of Siberia by the Russian administration (Patkanov, Shternberg, Rykhov, and others). However, this changed the general system but little.

Only Soviet investigators, taking as a starting point the classical works of Marxism, broke away from this traditional system and first raised the question of the past existence of tribes and phratries among the people of the North. Here should be mentioned the works of S. V. Bakhrushin, S. A. Tokarev, A. M. Zolotarev, V. N. Chernetsov, A. F. Anisimov, N. N. Stepanov, and others. The analysis of new historical and ethnographic data permitted the establishment of valid ancient forms of social organization for the peoples of the North: the presence of tribes, phratries (undeniably present among several peoples), and clans ascribable to phratries and tribes. The study of the history of the so-called administrative "clans" indicated that, in most cases, they correspond to tribes which, at the time, served the Russian administration as a base for the organization of administrative units (the *volost*, the *uprava*, administrations for "clans"). However, at the same time not enough attention was paid in our Soviet literature to forms of deterioration in the mentioned ancient social institutions among the peoples of the North and to those actual social forms which had already long existed among the peoples of the North, displacing and changing the old tribal, phratral, and clan structures.

*Translated from *Trudy instituta etnografii im. N.N. Miklukho-Maklaya*, n.s., vol. 14, 1951, pp. 95–108.

There is little doubt that the mentioned forms of clan-tribal organization among the peoples of northern Siberia are of a vestigial nature not only in the 20th century, but were so even much earlier. The earlier tribal structure may be reconstructed from fragments in historical sources of the 17th and 18th centuries, folklore data, and also the peculiarities of the prerevolutionary administrative organization with the help of which the tsarist government conserved a clan-tribal structure that had outlived itself. Tribal dialects were also preserved, simplifying the task of reconstructing former tribes.

The structure of phratries is revealed to us only in terms of exogamic rules and a series of religious-social traditions. The clan, while it had preserved its outward formal characteristics more distinctly, nevertheless had almost completely lost its economic meaning—a fact about which various field workers have written repeatedly.

About the time of the October socialist revolution, among all the peoples of northern Siberia the clan had become so diffused that it could be distinguished only by separate, vestigial characteristics which conserved only some secondary functions of a socio-religious aspect, mainly exogamy. Among all peoples the clan had lost its territorial character, and, as a rule, clans were not organized as territorial units, the families of one clan being scattered in various regions, living together with members of other clans, tribes, and even nations. Camps and villages in which members of only one clan lived were more the exception than the rule. This applied not only to groups of nomadic reindeer-herders but also to settled hunting and fishing groups; among the latter, however, the process by which the clan lost its territorial unity had not always gone as far. Thus, Shternberg has written about the Nivkhs:

In spite of a natural tendency for kinsmen to stick together, the *principle of territoriality does not, in fact, exist.* In a large majority of Gilyak villages the composition of the population is mixed. . . . There are clans whose branches are to be found in the most varied and remote places in Gilyak territory. This existing diffusion, proceeding, as it were, counter to clan principles, is nevertheless inevitable under the existing economic and social conditions.[1]

Shternberg's statements, pertaining to the 1890's, are particularly significant for us since Shternberg, as is known, was not at all inclined to modernize the social structure of the Nivkhs, but rather he emphasized its archaic characteristics. The lack of territorial unity among the Evenk clans has been demonstrated by various authors. Even Shirokogorov, in his work on the social organization of the northern Tungus—a work distinguished on the whole by its artificial construction and interpretations obviously warped to favor archaisms in the social structure of the Tungus—had to point out the factual loss of territorial unity to the Tungus clans.[2]

We shall not refer to statements of other authors which support the loss of territorial unity by the clan among the various peoples of northern Siberia. The number of such examples could be significantly increased, and we shall return later to this question.

The lack of territorial unity for the phratries among the peoples of Siberia dates as far back as it is possible to trace with the available ethnographic sources. As we have shown already, the administrative system of the tsarist government fostered an artificial conservation of tribal divisions as administrative-taxation units. Nevertheless, with few exceptions this did not halt the loss by tribes of their territorial unity and the mixing of members of various tribes in one territory (or in individual camps and villages). The loss of territorial unity was also fostered by processes of assimilation which changed the ethnographic affiliations of various groups, often affecting part of a tribe so that members, originally of one tribe, began to affiliate with various peoples. Examples of this may be read from the ethnographies of the Nganasans and Dolgans, the Yakuts and Evenks, the Yukagirs and Lamuts, the Kets and Selkups, the Nenets and Enets, and of others.

Thus, it was not the tribe, the phratry, or the clan that decided the social organization and territorial distribution of the peoples of northern Siberia in the period to which the majority of our ethnographic data pertain. What were those forms of real, living, economic and social units that replaced the ancient clan-tribal organization? This is the subject of the present article.

In a draft of his letter to Vera Zasulich, Marx points out that "not all primitive communities are based on one and the same model. To the contrary, they represent a series of social formations differing one from the other both typologically as well as by the antiquity of their existence and represent phases of consecutive evolution." Marx then adds that ancient communities ". . . rest upon the blood-kinship relationships among their members. To them are admitted only blood or adopted relatives. Their structure is the structure of the genealogical tree. The 'agricultural community' was the first social union of free people not linked by blood ties."[3] Engels also notes the imperceptible transition from clan structure to territorial organization for the nations of western Europe.[4] These tenets of Marx and Engels form the basis of the present work. We aim to show that the peoples of northern Siberia, in spite of conserving many vestiges of a clan system, in spite of preserving elements of an earlier clan structure, in the main evolved into territorially organized units quite a long time ago.

Naturally, territorial units of the peoples of northern Siberia differed in many ways from neighboring communities of agricultural peoples. But in the North, too, as we shall see further on, there appeared those same general natural laws that govern the disintegration of clan ties and their replacement with territorial ties, there existed that same dualism characteristic, in its different forms, of neighborly communities. This dualism was expressed in the coexistence of ancient principles of collectivism (collective ownership of territory, elements of collectivism in production, and so on) and of private property (ownership of deer, individual possession of furs—the basic object of trade—and so on).

Although the peoples of the Far North, in distinction from the larger, economically and culturally more developed peoples of southern Siberia, had to a significant degree preserved many archaic forms of economy and mode of life up to the revolution, it would be entirely wrong to look upon them as out of touch with peoples of more southerly regions. Archaeological materials reveal in more and more detail the ties of the population of the North with the southern regions of Siberia and, through them, with the ancient centers of civilization of the East and West. Since ancient times, the costly pelts of the North had appeared in the markets of China, Central Asia, and other countries from whence, in turn, separate elements of culture penetrated far to the North. These ties could not but influence the social organization of the peoples of the North who, long before the arrival of the Russians, were producing pelts of great trading value. The rise of reindeer-herding as one of the types of animal-husbandry fostered the development of private property in the form of reindeer herds under the ownership of separate families. This alone damaged the economic bases of clan organization among the nomadic reindeer-herders.

The entry of the peoples of the North into the sphere of economic influence of Russian trading capital further hastened the process of the breaking up of the relations of private ownership within the clan society.

In Soviet ethnological and economic literature on the peoples of northern Siberia, along with a description of vestiges of the clan-tribal organization, one runs across statements alluding to the existence among these peoples of territorial units composed, as a rule, of mixed clans. We find descriptions of the composition of individual camps which note that the inhabitants belong to different clans. We find information on production groups given not on a clan but on a territorial basis. And finally, we find data on more extended territorial groupings which incorporate economic pursuits with a membership varied not only with respect to clan membership but also with respect to its tribal and even ethnic composition. These materials were of special interest in connection with the implementation of Soviet construction in the Far North, where the creation of local Soviet authorities faced practical workers and investigators with the necessity of studying the concrete forms of social units among the small peoples of the North. During the first stage, organs of power were founded once again on the "clan" principle with clan soviets (councils) taking the place of former "clan" administrations. This form of organization was brought into being not because of real clan-tribal bonds existing in the units of the peoples of the North, but by the necessity, during the first stages, of using the old administrative units to which they were accustomed.[5]

However, the lack of agreement between the "clan" principle in the administrative organization of the peoples of the North and the actual economic and territorial ties quickly became obvious. Even at the very beginning of "sovietization," as M. A. Sergeyev points out, among several groups of the population of the North, councils [soviets] were organized on a territorial basis and, during the first years, the transition from the "clan" to the territorial system was universally undertaken. In 1929, according to Sergeyev, there were about 100 councils in the North organized on the basis of the territorial principle. In 1931, this transition to the new territorial system of organization of councils among the small peoples of the North was completed by the formation of village and nomadic councils. This brought to an end the "clan" principle, which reached back as far as the 17th century and which subsequently outlived itself. Thus, the question of territorial groupings of the peoples of the Far North was raised by the practical application of socialist construction. But it must be specified that the character of these territorial units was not sufficiently clarified in the scientific literature.

One should distinguish two different forms of ties between neighboring peoples in northern Siberia. One, of broader territorial scope, conformed to those groupings which, in 1931, were used as a basis for organizing the nomadic and village councils. The second, narrower in scope, and existing within the boundaries of the first, was the production union of a relatively small group of households. First, we shall examine these latter units.

Many authors have written about production unions among various peoples of the North which existed before collectivization, largely in connection with the role of primitive-communal traditions under the conditions of formation of a collective economy. A. P. Kurilovich and N. P. Naumov,[6] A. F. Anisimov,[7] and N. N. Kovyazin[8] wrote about these production unions among the Evenks and N. P. Nikulshin, who dedicated a special monograph to this problem,[9] wrote about them particularly minutely. With respect to the Nenets, this problem engendered a polemic between P. Maslov and P. E. Terletskiy,[10] who differ in their evaluations of the characteristics of the Nenets *parma* (production union of reindeer-herders) and *edoma* (production union of fishermen). But today it is important for us to note that both authors found that these production unions really existed among the Nenets—among both the reindeer-herders and the fishermen. In a special ethnographic project these territorial production unions were described repeatedly. One may point, for instance, to the detailed description of such groups among the Dolgans in the works of A. A. Popov.[11]

What are these frequently described territorial production unions?

N. P. Nikulshin described in detail temporary unions among the Evenks (usually independent of family ties) for collective fishing, hunting, and mainly for the organization of the joint pasturing of reindeer. He correctly emphasizes the peculiarities of the complex economy of the Evenks resulting in the necessity of the formation of temporary unions of separate households to enable, for instance, the combination of seasonal summer fishing with the organization of the pasturing of reindeer—during this time some of the members of the union catch fish and the others go off with the herds to the summer pastures. Nikulshin's concrete data on the composition of these unions convincingly demonstrate that clan ties play no role in them. He wrote:

The primitive production unions of the Evenks arose spontaneously during the hunting season, for fishing and pasturing of reindeer, including in their composition from 2 to 15 households and being operative for the time of the seasonal undertaking. . . . They united not only kinsmen and blood relations but also individuals not linked by bonds of kinship. They united not the members of the single collective economy of a clan or a large family, but separate, economically detached households of smaller producers and were not permanent but temporary production unions.[12]

A. A. Popov also gives a detailed description of production unions of just such a character among the Dolgans. The complex economy of the Dolgans, combining reindeer-herding with fishing and various forms of collective and individual hunting, also gave rise to these unions. In the summer "several households gather their reindeer into a common herd, this resulting in a summer territorial unit of several families. The groups of small numbers thus formed are based not on kinship but on unions of people brought together by economic interest only. . . ."[13] "In such unions," A. A. Popov continues, "ethnographic traits even become completely obliterated: thus, in the composition of nomadic groups except for the Dolgans and peasants who have taken to the tundra (who in essence do not differ from the former), one can also find tundra Yakuts and Tungus."[13]

Such production unions among the Evens (Lamuts) of the Okhotsk coast were studied by M. G. Levin, in 1930–2. Both among the semisettled and especially among the nomadic population there existed, even before the introduction of collectivization, unions composed of households for joint pasturing in the winter and for joint fishing in the summer. Since fishing in this region was tied to the appearance, at the mouths of rivers near the sea, of the Siberian and hump-backed salmon, which were caught and prepared for winter consumption, the individual households were faced with the necessity of grouping together their herds of reindeer for summer pasturing and detaching for this work from the production unions shepherds who would then receive their share from the stock of fish caught. Households not belonging to such unions were forced to let the reindeer run loose during the summer, a practice ruinous to reindeer-herding. The reindeer remained totally uncared for, wandered through the taiga, and, in the fall and winter months, after the roundup, they fell to various owners. The number of households in these unions varied, ranging on the average from 5 to 10. The blood-ties in the formation of these groups were not traced. The study of the composition of these groups over many years (by inquiries) revealed that, in general, while their composition did change, the nucleus of the union remained more or less constant, attracting to it, over the years, different neighboring households. We shall come back to the social characterization of these unions later on.

Among the Nganasans, according to observations of B. O. Dolgikh, in the period 1926–35 there also existed groups of households that nomadized together. These groups were made up of two to four households in the winter and enlarged to 5 to 10 households in the summer when the Nganasans were distributed in fishing sites or places for wild reindeer "spearings." Even here these groups were of mixed composition with respect to clan and tribe affiliation. In one camp lived not only the families of various clans, to offer one example, of the Avam Nganasans, but some of the Avam Nganasans together with some of the Vadeyev Nganasans, although these latter cases were rare and occurred mainly in the border areas between the Avam and the Vadeyev Nganasans. The same was observed among the Enets, where, into the composition of households migrating together, there entered not only representatives of various Enets clans but also those of the Nganasans and Nenets. Both among the Nganasans as well as among the Enets it was the practice to join the herds of the members of the group in the summer and to select shepherds to pasture them. Moreover, in the autumn the Nganasan household unions migrating together selected still other special hunting parties who set out to hunt wild reindeer further to the north. Like the shepherds, these hunters were usually members of various clans. These unions had special names: the local Russian population called them *kucha* [heap, lump] and in the Nganasan language the word for one was *malir*. Usually the base of the *malir* was a household or two but others were of more variable composition.

Small territorial unions were not restricted to reindeer-herders. Thus, the Kets along the lower reaches of the Podkamennaya Tunguska river who were not reindeer-herders (according to data of Dolgikh) dispersed in the autumn into earthen huts holding separate groups of four to six households. In the summer they united into larger camps at fishing sites. The underlying economic principle in these unions does not stand out as clearly as among the Evenks and the Evens (Lamuts) with their complex economies, but even among the Kets these unions can, with sufficient grounds, be called territorial production unions. Each such group was united by the use of predetermined hunting territories or fishing sites, by mutual aid among neighbors, and so on. One can establish no clan beginnings in the organization of such unions among the Kets, although the composition of the group was more or less constant over the course of many years.

The problem of the social composition of territorial production unions requires special examination. We have already referred to the discussion between P. Maslov and P. E. Terletskiy in the pages of the journal *Sovetskiy sever* on the question of the social nature of the Nenets *parma*. While Maslov saw the *parma* as a union of households grouped basically around a *kulak* household, Terletskiy showed that the basic type of organization of the *parma* was a union of independent *srednyak* and *bednyak* households. According to Terletskiy's data, in 1927 only 11 out of 60 parmas investigated were united around a kulak household. A. A. Popov, without specially examining the problem of the social composition of the nomadic groups of Dolgans, nevertheless shows that "each of them attempts to include in its composition a few more-prosperous people." Unfortunately, this formulation suffers from its extreme vagueness. N. P. Nikulshin arrived at the conclusion that the social composition of the "primitive production unions" among the Evenks was varied. He made a special study of this question in connection with the problem of the role of primitive communal survivals in the socialist reconstruction of the economy of the peoples of the North. Together with production unions that included households owning few reindeer and of similar property status, there existed unions which included, along with such households, owners of large herds as well. Data available to us, pertaining to the years previous to collectivization among the peoples of the North, support the points of view set forth by Nikulshin and Terletskiy. Field data on the Lamuts of the Okhotsk coast (M. G. Levin), the Nganasans, the Enets, and the Dolgans (B. O. Dolgikh) are similar.

In connection with the problem of the composition and social structure of territorial production unions, the problem of the *varat* among the Chukchi merits special examination. The most detailed data on the *varat* are attributed, as is known, to V. G. Bogoraz. Examining the social organization of the Chukchi, Bogoraz incorrectly adjudged it the "first embryo of clan organization,"[14] and saw the beginnings of the clan in this very Chukchi *varat*. Naturally, any examination of the social organization of the Chukchi in its entirety goes beyond the bounds of the present article. We are interested here only in the social aspect of the *varat*. Bogoraz shows that the term *varat* literally means "a collection of those who are together."[15] Defining the *varat* as a group of related families and even calling it "the family group," Bogoraz at the same time notes that the *varat* is "extremely unstable" and the number of families that "live together" changes almost every year.[16] Bogoraz's descriptions in this section are so inconsistent and confused that it is particularly difficult to clarify even the relation between the *varat* and the camp, which latter Bogoraz describes separately, noting in reference to it that "the organization of the camp of the reindeer-herding Chukchi is connected with relationships of the family group."[15] In the *varat*, Bogoraz saw the embryo of the clan and considered that the "family group" is defined by a common fire-pit, "blood-smearing" marks, and *tamgi* [property mark], but here he also notes that all these elements of unification do not lead to durability in the family group: "family groups are always breaking up and overflowing into new confines." Reconstructing the older form of the *varat*, Bogoraz writes: "This social unit included 10 to 15 families who always camped near each other. During the summer, when reindeer-herders go to the seashore, all families generally merged into one big camp. Some of the young men remained with the herd, which at that time was not large. The others were occupied with fishing and hunting of sea mammals."[16] It is likely that here we have unions based upon territorial and economic ties. But since, within these unions, there were families linked by kin and property relationships, Bogaraz, apparently careless in differentiating the exact clan and blood relationships among separate families, baselessly transferred these indications of kinship into a characterization of the *varat* as a whole.

In connection with what has been presented, Bogoraz's data on the maritime Chukchi and Eskimo become clearer. Bogoraz writes:

Among them the family and the village are the units of social life. Many villages are inhabited by relatives, especially among the Eskimos who are less inclined than the

Chukchi to wander from village to village. However, there are other villages composed of elements of distinct ethnic extraction: for instance, the village of Cecin is inhabited by Eskimos, maritime Chukchi and by a large admixture of reindeer Chukchi who have lost their herds and have settled on the shore . . . on the whole, the settlement is a territorial unit.[19]

Concerning the reindeer-herding Chukchi, the camp, as Bogoraz's data clearly show, also was not always composed of families linked by bonds of kinship and its composition also changed. The camp sometimes coincided with the *varat*, sometimes contained its subdivisions, as is understandable in the conditions of a nomadic economy. Bogoraz demonstrates well that the social compositions of the camp and the *varat* were entirely different: sometimes the *varat* was a union of independent households and at others a group of households economically dependent on an owner of a large reindeer herd. Similar relationships obtained, too, in the villages of the settled Chukchi but here the second type of union— around a wealthy household—occurred less frequently and was less distinct, since the processes of differentiation by property among the maritime hunters of sea mammals had not developed as highly as among the reindeer-herding Chukchi.

In the comprehensive ethnographic literature on the peoples of northern Siberia, starting with the works of the 17th century and ending with present-day studies, we find a great wealth of data testifying to the presence of primitive community relationships among these peoples in the past. Elements of collective production and distribution, mutual aid, collective ownership of territory and natural resources—all are phenomena known in the past of all the peoples of northern Siberia. The custom of the *nimat* among the Evenks, the *bakhid* among the Nganasans, and similar usages among other peoples are described with notable ethnographic completeness. However, a good deal less clear is the character of the groups within the society in which these primitive social customs were practiced. As a rule, in the literature, all these customs were defined as clan-based and were linked with the clan. To be sure, the opinion that they led back to the institutions of clan structure is not challenged. But, when concrete ethnographic descriptions are analyzed, one usually becomes convinced that very often writers archaize phenomena that they have observed and also attribute to the clan structure relationships that have, in fact, lost their original clan charac- ter. They also fail to note that customs and institutions that actually fit into the clan structure change their content as the clan organization decays and disintegrates.

In a special monograph devoted to the clan structure of the Evenks, A. F. Anisimov refers to a large number of very interesting data on survivals of various forms of primitive communal organization, collective customs in the organization of hunting and fishing, mutual aid, and hospitality. But he does not always define clearly the collectives in which these norms exist. Of course, Anisimov is right when he links their origin to the clan structure, but unfor- tunately he does not disclose the more important tenet that all the above- enumerated economic ties of a primitive communal character are, in fact, not part of the clan but of unions of a different kind. Depending on older writers (M. F. Krivoshapkin, V. Arefev, P. I. Tretyakov, V. N. Vasilev), on I. M. Suslov's data and his own materials, Anisimov correctly shows the collective, *artel*[*] nature of the industries, but from this demonstration it does not at all follow that the

[*] ["Association for common work."]

unions had a clan character. To the contrary, Anisimov himself described those economic-territorial unions which also are the bearers of these traditions of collectivism. He wrote:

We find that the following two basic forms of the collective process of work are still in existence: (a) the migration together of srednyak [middle-peasant] and bednyak [poor-peasant] families; (b) hunting artels, these being temporary artels based on cooperation in the hunt. A group of families, migrating together, usually makes up the Evenk camp. The custom of *umundu inbawat*—"migrating together"—is characterized, from the economic point of view, by the following two attributes: (a) common ownership of hunting and fishing grounds and of reindeer-pasturing areas, usually along two or three or four rivers (depending on the number of families); these rivers are considered their family-clan sites and are the common property of all members of the camp; (b) known forms of collective activity, for instance, the pasturing of reindeer together, the collective fencing of corrals for reindeer in the spring, fishing expeditions (generally on rivers having the most fish), and a number of other types of mutual work.[18]

Anisimov attempts to find a clan principle in these unions and cites specifically a case of a camp made up of four families from one clan, but if one remembers what has already been said about the mixed composition (with respect to their clan relationships) of Evenk camps, then one must admit that the "group of families migrating together" is, in final analysis, a territorial production union that has lost its clan character.[19]

We have already mentioned such traditions of collective distribution as, for instance, the *nimat*, which was known not only to the Evenks but to all the peoples of the North under various names. Available materials bear witness to the fact that the circle of individuals linked by *nimat* relationships corresponded, as a rule, to a group of neighbors. It is known that the rules of the *nimat* prescribed a division of the spoils with any neighbor or any persons chancing to be on the move together, independent of their clan-tribal or even their ethnic affiliation. Here one could refer to a wealth of data cited in the literature, starting perhaps with Middendorf and ending with any field ethnographer of recent times. The economic aspect of the *nimat* was analyzed in detail by M. K. Rastsvetayev.[20] Not being an ethnographer, this writer left without sufficient attention the question of the clan-tribal structure of the Myamyal Tungus, a people he had studied. But he shows quite definitely that the *nimat* "pertains only to persons (families) located in one and the same camp in the immediate neighborhood."[21]

In the economic area, as we have shown, collective traditions were brought out in hunting, fishing, and the pasturing of reindeer undertaken together. What has been said above about the character of territorial production unions is sufficient to indicate that here we have a principle of unification based on neighborhood rather than clan relationships.

We come to the conclusion that among the peoples of northern Siberia, in the period to which the great majority of ethnographic data pertain, the ancient rules of clan organization for production and consumption were not designed on clan-based unions of blood relationship but on unions of a different kind, that is, those organized for production on a territorial-neighborhood basis, and these unions came into being as a result of the disintegration of real clan bonds. This conclusion, with respect to the Evenks, had already been reached by N. P. Nikulshin, who wrote about primitive production unions as well as about unions that could be characterized as a community of neighbors.[22]

It was shown earlier that Soviet construction efforts came into contact with existing territorial groupings of the peoples of the North, which, during the first stages of the transition from "clan" to nomadic and village soviets [councils], to a significant degree formed the basis for the organization of these latter. Such groupings were characterized primarily by having sufficiently well defined boundaries and specific centers of economic gravitation. The territory of such a group generally encompassed a river basin or part of a river basin, a group of lakes with their basins, a defined stretch of seacoast including rivers discharging into the sea, a defined mountainous area, and so on.

In the past the centers of economic gravitation of such territorial groupings were market sites or trading points, and more recently trading posts. During certain periods these economic centers served also as assemblage points for households in one territorial group, centers where conferences were held, communal affairs settled, and so on. In a nomadic economy the members of such a territorial grouping dispersed over certain routes, forming smaller units brought together by interests of production and economy, to return again at a given time to their center. The composition of these smaller units was not always constant but, as a rule, did not go beyond the bounds of a given grouping. These smaller units were characterized above as territorial production unions. Among the settled population the territorial grouping included several settlements, again united by the single center of economic gravitation and by a number of ties between neighbors.

An analysis of the census data of 1926–7 and of a great many ethnographic descriptions of the end of the 19th and the first third of the 20th centuries reveals with sufficient clarity the appearance in the recent past of territorial groupings among the whole indigenous population of northern Siberia. Such generally accepted names in the ethnographic literature as the Sym, the Tokma, the Uchur, and the Komov Evenks, the Podkamennaya Tunguska, the Eloguy and the Kureyka Kets, the Norilsk and the Popigay Dolgans, the Taymyr Nganasans, the Upper Kolyma Yukagirs, the Vilyuney, Telpek, Anyuy, and Anguem Chukchi, the Viligin and Varkhalam Lamuts of the Okhotsk coast, and so on— all are an expression of the existence of such territorial groupings.

The numerical composition of these territorial groupings varied, but with rare exceptions, generally did not surpass 100 to 120 households, and more often it fluctuated within the range of several tens of households. These figures are very relative since the numerical composition of a group is linked to the type of households, environmental conditions, the history and economy of the region as a whole, and so on.

Along with a defined territory and defined economic centers, the territorial groupings possessed still other vital socio-economic ties among their members. The members were aware of their union and contrasted themselves to the members of other territorial groupings. The names of territorial groupings presented above as examples are not theoretically conceived by the ethnographic literature but are a reflection of the real unity recognized by the population itself. Often, the boundaries of such groupings coincided with the boundaries of dialects and subdialects[23]; in any case, the boundaries of existing dialects did not transact the boundaries of the groupings although the area of distribution for a given dialect might include not a single but several groupings. In this distribution we can already see a demonstration of the connection between the appearance of territorial groupings and the disintegration of ancient tribal unions. The territorial groupings of the recent past were heterogeneous with respect to their clan-tribal composition. Sometimes even households of various ethnic stocks were united in one grouping.

Let us present a few examples from data of the Subarctic census of 1926–7 in the Evenk and Taymyr national okrugs. In the territory of the present-day Taymyr National Okrug, the existence of 23 territorial groupings could be established for 1926–7. The specific history of these groupings varies. Several of them could be traced to the old tribal divisions. Such is the case, for example, for a territorial grouping containing 41 households (242 persons of both sexes), roaming in the basins of the Balakhna river and Lake Taymyr, and generally coinciding with the tribe of the Vadeyev Nganasans. Only 5 of the 41 households were not Vadeyev Nganasan in origin. A grouping delimited by the lower reaches of the Yenisey and Yenisey gulf on the west and the Pura river (a branch of the Pyasina) and Pyasina lake on the east can serve as an example of a territorial grouping mixed not only with respect to its clan-tribal but also its ethnic composition. In it there were about 100 households (about 500 persons of both sexes) of which Enets households of various clan and tribal origins numbered up to 60, Nenets households about 30, and Nganasan ones about 10 or 11. Tracing the history of the formation of this grouping discloses that the ancestors of those very households who were mentioned in the 1926–7 data were traveling together toward the end of the 19th century and that part of the Nenets people only moved to the area later on, at the beginning of the 20th century. The same kind of distribution can be seen in the territory of the present-day Evenk okrug. Of 19 territorial groupings present in this area in 1926–7, the majority were of mixed clan-tribal composition. Thus, in the territorial grouping which gravitated to the trading post of Vanovar there were 32 households (159 persons). Of these, 17 households were of the Chemdal tribe, 9 were Kukogir, 5 Pankagir, and 1 family was from the Chilchagir clan. The specific history and age of separate territorial groupings varies considerably. In some cases we may establish a mixed clan-tribal composition for the population of a given territory as early as the end of the 17th century; in others the formation of territorial groupings took place in relatively recent times.

On the one hand, the inclusion of the peoples of northern Siberia into the structure of the Russian state conserved, by its administrative system, the formal existence of tribes as administrative "clans" and, on the other, undeniably hastened the processes of disintegration of the clan-tribal links and the formation of territorial groupings unconnected to the clan and the tribe.

Along with such processes as the penetration of new trade relations, the strengthening of a prosperous elite, which took upon itself the role of an intermediary between the mass of its fellow tribesmen and the Russian administrators and tradesmen, the replacement of old clan-tribal links with new territorial links also favored the appearance of new economic centers founded by Russians.

In tracing the history of a number of 17th century winter posts for the collection of fur tributes, one discovers that the choice of the location for them was usually not haphazard and took into account the real centers of gravitation of this or that group of the indigenous population. It often happened that an originally unsuccessfully chosen site for the development of a fur tribute collection point was subsequently changed with the recognition of the actual centers of gravitation for the population. In its turn, the founding of such Russian collection points established not only a gravitation center for the tribes for whose tribute they were built, but also for neighboring clans from tribes registered at other collection points. Naturally, this led to the mixing of the members of various tribes in one territory.

Unfortunately, the study of these territorial groupings as units actually existing did not attract the proper attention of ethnographers. True, the practice of research led to the study and description of separate territorial groupings among various peoples, but the lack of a clear presentation of the character of these groupings and the faulty practice of archaizing existing phenomena—the search for only outlived clan-tribal formations—resulted in a lack, in the literature, of sufficiently distinct definitions of the essence of these territorial groupings (communities of neighbors), their boundaries, their history, and those relationships which make up their internal bond.

The practice of Soviet construction, for the first time attacking through detailed study the problem of the location of the indigenous population of the North by territories, thus outstripped ethnographic theory.

The task of studying these neighboring communities is the more essential because in them we may find those processes that create an ethnographic community through its various elements, differing in origin. This will allow us to clarify also the problems of ethnogenesis of separate peoples of northern Siberia. More important, of course, is the study of these groups for the applications of Soviet socialist construction to the peoples of the North.

It remains for us to say a few words about the paths of development of production unions and territorial groupings under the conditions of socialism.

We have already remarked on the production unions in connection with their role in the social reconstruction of the economy and mode of life of the peoples of northern Siberia. We pointed to the varied social nature of these units. One part was made up of independent households cooperating with each other; within these was preserved a tradition of collectivism that developed from a primitive-communal structure. The other part of these economically linked units was represented by groups of households dependent on households of a kulak type where, under the cover of primitive-communal tradition, there were practiced various types of exploitation and economic coercion. Concerning this, we refer to the literature mentioned earlier.

The development of socialist construction, the formation of kolkhozes [collectives], and the liquidation of exploitative elements led to a fundamental change in the whole socio-economic life of the peoples of the North. The kolkhoz became the basic economic unit among all the peoples of the North. The main economic units of the northern kolkhoz became the brigades and, to a lesser extent, the *zveno* [literally "link"]. The predominating type of camps today are those based on the brigade and *zveno*. In connection with the process of settling the nomadic population there appeared a new type of settlement—kolkhoz centers—kolkhoz settlements to which are linked groups of households that continue, in response to the demands of their economic activities, to live a mobile way of life.

All these new forms of economic-territorial unions that replaced the unions of the past are qualitatively a new type of social union. If during the first stages of collectivization the old economic unions to some degree affected the formation of simpler unions, subsequent organizational and economic consolidation of the collectives and their adherence to the regulations of an agricultural artel caused the disappearance of the old traditional unions and their replacement with completely new ones. These were determined by the tasks falling to the kolkhoz economic sphere of activity and formed by kolkhoz management, which developed from a production plan and economic expediency.

A slightly different route was taken by the larger units, the territorial groupings, under the conditions of socialist construction. As we indicated above, many of these were the basis for the nomadic and village soviets organized on the territorial principle. In the organization of kolkhozes many of them coincided (in composition of the households and territories which were attached them) with the earlier territorial groupings. In other cases, several kolkhozes formed within the boundaries of large territorial groupings. And, inversely, with the consolidation of nomadic and village soviets and kolkhozes, in certain cases one nomadic soviet and one kolkhoz united several formerly small territorial groupings.

But even those territorial groupings that formed the base of many nomadic and village soviets and kolkhozes also changed fundamentally with respect to their content and the character of links among their members. In a number of cases, significant shifts of the population from one former territorial grouping to another occurred. In some instances these shifts completely altered the ethnic composition of the nomadic and village soviets and kolkhozes. The introduction of kolkhoz economy and way of life led to changes in the territorial shifts of population. The construction of new settlements, supply points, stores, schools, and the more complete and more rational use of natural resources, not only altered fundamentally shifts in the population but also, in many cases, led to a re-examination of the earlier boundaries of kolkhozes and village soviets, which no longer served the conditions of the socialist construction.

Thus, the old communities of neighbors (the territorial groupings), which at one time had entered into the history of the peoples of the North as a result of the disintegration of the clan-tribal structure, in their turn gave up their place to new forms of socialist territorial unions constructed under new conditions of socialism. An exact analysis and exposition of this process must be the object of special investigation.

Notes and References

1. L. Ya Shternberg, *Gilyaki, Orochi, Goldy, Negidaltsy, Ayny* (The Gilyaks, the Orochs, the Golds, the Negidalets, the Ainus), Khabarovsk, 1933, p. 110.

2. S. M. Shirokogorov, *Social organization of the northern Tungus*, Shanghai, 1929, p. 195 *et al.*

3. K. Marx and F. Engels, *Sochineniya* (Works), vol. 27, pp. 693, 694.

4. See: F. Engels, *Proiskhozhdenie semi, chastnoy sobstvennosti i gosudarstva* (Origin of the family, private property, and the state), 1948 edition.

5. A review of the basic stages of Soviet construction in the North is given in the pithy article by M. R. Sergeyev: Malye narody Severa v epokhu sotsializma (The small peoples of the North during the era) of socialism), *Sovetskaya etnografiya*, 1947, no. 4, pp. 126–158. However, we can not agree with one particular observation of the author that "the only possible basis for the organization of the population was recognized by themselves as the clan bond" (p. 129). Obviously what is being discussed is not clan bonds but the affiliation with specific "clan" administrations, i.e., to the old administrative-taxation units.

6. A. P. Kurilovich and N. P. Naumov, *Sovetskaya Tungusiya*, Moscow, 1934. p. 152.

7. A. F. Anismov, *Rodovoe obshchestvo evenkov (tungusov)*—Social structure of the Evenks (Tungus), Leningrad, 1936, pp. 68–70, 159, 160.

8. In the collection *Ocherki po promyslovomu khozyaystvu i olenevodstvu Kraynego Severa* (Essays on the productive economy and reindeer herding in the Far North), Moscow, 1933, p. 33.

9. N. P. Nikulshin, *Pervobytnye proizvodstvennye obedineniya i sotsialisticheskoe stroitelstvo u evenkov* (Primitive economic units and socialist construction among the Evenks), Leningrad, 1939.

10. P. Maslov, Kochevoye obedineniye edinolichnykh khozyaystv v tundre Severnogo Kraya (Nomadic units of individual economies in the tundra of the northern regions),

Sovetskiy Sever, 1934, no. 5; P. E. Terletskiy, K voprosu o parmakh v nenetskom okruge (The problem of the *parma* in the Nenets okrug), *Sovetskiy Sever*, 1934, no. 5.

11. N. P. Nikulshin (*op. cit.*) calls them "primitive economic units"; they are also called "everyday economic units"; A. A. Popov, in describing such units among the Dolgans, names them "nomadic groups"—see his: Materialy po rodovomu stroyu dolgan. (Materials on the social structure of the Dolgans), *Sovetskaya etnografiya*, 1934, no. 6, pp. 124–126; Okhota i rybolovstvo u dolgan, *Sbornik pamyati V. C. Bogoraza* (Hunting and fishing among the Dolgans, Collection in memory of V. C. Bogoraz), 1937, p. 90 *et al.*

12. Nikulshin, *op. cit.*, pp. 135–136.

13. A. A. Popov, Materialy po rodovomu stroyu dolgan, p. 124.

14. V. G. Bogoraz, *Chukchi* (The Chukchi), part I, p. 94, Introduction, chap. 18.

15. *Op. cit.*, p. 94.

16. Bogoraz, *op. cit.*, p. 95.

17. Bogoraz, *op. cit.*, p. 96.

18. Anisimov, *op. cit.*, pp. 68–69.

19. When A. F. Anisimov writes on the family-clan sites and on the distribution by the clan council of hunting sites, he evidently does not differentiate sufficiently between the genuine paternal clan and the administrative "clan" (*vide supra*). The latter, indeed, had administrative functions and regulated the use of sites by individual families and groups of households nomadizing together.

20. M. K. Rastsvetayev, Tungusy Myamyal'skogo roda (The Tungus of the Myamyal clan), *Trudy SOPS AN SSSR*, no. 8, Leningrad, 1933 (seriya yakutskaya).

21. Rastsvetayev, *op. cit.*, p. 43.

22. Nikulshin, *op cit.*, p. 136.

23. G. M. Vasilevich's data on the dialects of various Evenk groups in comparison with the boundaries of territorial groupings disclose significant coincidence in a number of cases.

THE ARCTIC INSTITUTE OF NORTH AMERICA

The Arctic Institute of North America was founded to further the scientific study and exploration of the Arctic. The Institute provides information on the Arctic through its three offices, awards research grants, and publishes scientific papers and other contributions in its journal *Arctic*. Those interested in this work are invited to become Members. Members receive all numbers of the journal. The Library and Map Collection at the Montreal office are principally for their use, and they are welcome there and at the other Institute offices.